YEARBOOK OF AMERICAN & CANADIAN CHURCHES 2000

Previous Issues

Sixty-Eighth Issue   Annual

YEARBOOK OF AMERICAN & CANADIAN CHURCHES 2000

Edited by Eileen W. Lindner

Prepared and edited for the
National Council of the Churches of Christ in the U.S.A.
475 Riverside Drive, New York, NY 10115-0050

Published and Distributed
by Abingdon Press
Nashville

YEARBOOK OF AMERICAN & CANADIAN CHURCHES
2000

Telephone: (212) 870-2031

Fax: (212) 870-2817

E-mail: yearbook@ncccusa.org

Printed in the United States of America
ISBN 0-687-09094-6
ISSN 0195-9034
Library of Congress catalog card number
16-5726

Preparation of this *Yearbook* is an annual project of the National Council of the Churches of Christ in the United States of America.

This is the sixty-eighth edition of a yearbook that was first published in 1916. Previous editions have been entitled: *Federal Council Yearbook* (1916-1917), *Yearbook of the Churches* (1918-1925), The *Handbook of the Churches* (1927), *The New* *Handbook of the Churches* (1928), *Yearbook of American Churches* (1933-1972), and *Yearbook of American & Canadian Churches* (1973-1999).

Eileen W. Lindner	*Editor*
Marcel A. Welty	*Redevelopment & Technical Director*
Derek J. Lander	*Assistant Editor*

Editor's Preface

A Word of Thanks

The year 2000 *Yearbook of American & Canadian Churches*, like its predecessors, is the result of the labors of hundreds of individuals who gather, review, and transmit data of all types to our offices. From statistical data related to benevolence giving and church membership to corrected copy for directories and the chapter on the electronic church, the *Yearbook* would not be possible without the careful labors of those who furnish us with information. As in recent years, Sylvia and John Ronsville of the *empty tomb, inc.* gave generously of their time and considerable knowledge as we secured and analyzed giving trends. Nancy Merrill of the Association of Theological Schools; Mark Duffey, Episcopal Church Archivist; Rev. Will Krieger of Ecumenical Books in San Antonio, Texas; and Ric Justice of Wylie, Texas, have each contributed to specific sections of the *Yearbook* and deserve the thanks of both ourselves and our readers.

Features of the 2000 Yearbook

- At the dawn of a new millennium, we have chosen to focus on the growing religious pluralism in North America. Few persons today offer keener insight into the challenges and possibilities implicit in such growing pluralism than does Professor Diana L. Eck of Harvard University. Her guest editorial provides the backdrop for several treatments of this year's theme.
- Owing both to a generous redevelopment grant awarded to the *Yearbook* by the Lilly Endowment and to an advance in computer technology, this edition of the *Yearbook* has returned to the use of graphics to interpret the demographic patterns of seminary enrollments.
- The maps printed inside the front and back covers are drawn from the forthcoming *The New Historical Atlas of Religion in America* (Oxford University Press), by Edwin Scott Gaustad and Philip L. Barlow. These illustrations graphically demonstrate the growing religious pluralism of the United States.
- For the first time the *Yearbook* includes an annotated listing of contacts for non-Christian religious groups within the United States in keeping with our theme of religious pluralism. These much-sought-after contacts will be updated regularly and published within our religious research sources section in subsequent years.
- The Lilly grant has also enabled the expansion of the "Sources of Religion-related Research" chapter, which should prove invaluable to scholars and religious newswriters alike.
- The chapter "The Emerging Electronic Church" has been consolidated in response to the emergence of more effective search engines and more current church websites. Extensive links to additional sites can be accessed from our electronic church website at www.electronicchurch.org.

At millennium's close, it is not only a shift in religious pluralism that can be observed. The very processes for preparing a manuscript and the extent of the data reported in this *Yearbook* are appreciably altered by the technological resources now available to us and to the church agencies from which we collect data. The reader is urged to visit the *Yearbook* website at www.ncccusa.org, where more information can be found. In the months to come we plan to enlarge the website and move toward the production of an electronic as well as a hardcopy edition of the *Yearbook*.

To our many colleagues who share with us data and updated information, we extend our thanks. To our readers we pledge our continued diligence in providing the most accurate, timely, and comprehensive data available at the date of publication.

Eileen W. Lindner
Editor

Contents

I
PERSPECTIVES ON AMERICA'S RELIGIOUS LANDSCAPE

Trends & Developments, 2000

A Special Theme Chapter

The *Yearbook of American & Canadian Churches*, now in its 68th edition, has long sought to contribute to a discerning analysis of the American religious landscape. Once each year this publication has the opportunity to render a snapshot of churches in the United States and Canada; a review of a host of ecumenical and interfaith organizations; and some statistical analysis related to church finances, membership, demographic patterns in theological education, and the like. In recent years the *Yearbook* has featured a theme chapter designed to provide a more detailed inquiry into an issue of currency regarding the ever-changing American religious landscape.

While much of the world marks the opening of the third millenium—as measured from the date of Jesus' birth—the religious composition of North America is becoming ever more pluralistic. We wanted to take the occasion of millenium's end to reflect upon this increasing, strong, and persistent trend in the religious life of this continent. To effectively address the issue of pluralism we have:

- invited Dr. Diana Eck of Harvard University and Director for the Pluralism Project to provide an overview essay that outlines the scope and nature of our growing religious pluralism.
- printed two sample maps that are illustrative of the geographic patterns of the growth of religious pluralism. The first map plots the location of mosques and Islamic centers in the U.S. The second shows the number of Buddhist temples and churches per county in America. Both maps are drawn from Edwin Scott Gaustad and Philip L. Barlow, *New Historical Atlas of Religion in America* (New York: Oxford University Press, 2000).
- furnished the reader with a directory of selected faith traditions in America, with assistance from the Interfaith Relations Office of the National Council of Churches of Christ in the U.S.A. We will incorporate and regularly update this resource as an on-going feature of the *Yearbook*.

The evidence of the persistence of religious pluralism can be measured in part by the increasing numbers of ecumenical agencies that are engaged in active programs of interfaith dialogue and relationships. Within the "Index of Select Programs for U.S. Regional and Local Ecumenical Bodies" in chapter II, one may find a list of such agencies that programmatically address issues of interfaith relations.

Introduction to Church Trends 2000

Even with the special emphasis upon religious pluralism, the central focus of the *Yearbook of American & Canadian Churches* remains the churches of America. The Christian component of the religious landscape is hardly more static than the experience of other faith traditions.

For more than a decade the once reliable hegemony of "mainline" Protestant churches has been recognized as an artifact belonging to an earlier age of American religious life. Many correctives and great refinements have been added within church demographic literature to more precisely describe the various growth and decline cycles of specific religious

Table 1
INCLUSIVE MEMBERSHIP 1890–1998

Year	Membership	Source	Year	Membership	Source
1890	41,699,342	CRB	1964	123,307,499	YBAC
1906	35,068,058	CRB	1965	124,682,422	YBAC
1916	41,926,852	CRB	1966	125,778,656	YBAC
1926	54,576,346	CRB	1967	126,556,110	YBAC
1931	59,268,764	CH	1968	128,469,636	YBAC
1932	60,157,392	CH	1969	128,505,084	YBAC
1933	60,812,624	CH	1970	131,045,053	YBAC
1934	62,007,376	CH	1971	131,389,642	YBAC
1935	62,678,177	CH	1972	131,424,564	YBAC
1936	55,807,366	CRB	1973	131,245,139	YBAC
1936	63,221,996	CH	1974	131,871,743	YBACC
1937	63,848,094	CH	1975	131,012,953	YBACC
1938	64,156,895	YBAC	1976	131,897,539	YBACC
1940	64,501,594	YBAC	1977	131,812,470	YBACC
1942	68,501,186	YBAC	1978	133,388,776	YBACC
1944	72,492,699	YBAC	1979	133,469,690	YBACC
1945	71,700,142	CH	1980	134,816,943	YBACC
1946	73,673,182	CH	1981	138,452,614	YBACC
1947	77,386,188	CH	1982	139,603,059	YBACC
1948	79,435,605	CH	1983	140,816,385	YBACC
1949	81,862,328	CH	1984	142,132,178	YBACC
1950	86,830,490	YBAC	1985	142,926,363	YBACC
1951	88,673,005	YBAC	1986	142,799,662	YBACC
1952	92,277,129	YBAC	1987	143,830,806	YBACC
1953	94,842,845	YBAC	1988	145,383,739	YBACC
1954	97,482,611	YBAC	1989	147,607,394	YBACC
1955	100,162,529	YBAC	1990	156,331,704	YBACC
1956	103,224,954	YBAC	1991	156,629,918	YBACC
1957	104,189,678	YBAC	1992	156,557,746	YBACC
1958	109,557,741	YBAC	1993	153,127,045	YBACC
1959	112,226,905	YBAC	1994	158,218,427	YBACC
1960	114,449,217	YBAC	1995	157,984,194	YBACC
1961	116,109,929	YBAC	1996	159,471,758	YBACC
1962	117,946,002	YBAC	1997	157,503,033	YBACC
1963	120,965,238	YBAC	1998	158,294,022	YBACC

CRB—Census of Religious Bodies, Bureau of the Census, Washington   CH—*The Christian Herald,* New York
YBAC—*Yearbook of American Churches,* New York
YBACC—*Yearbook of American & Canadian Churches,* New York

traditions during the last quarter of the twentieth century. The early, easy assertion that liberal progressive churches are declining while conservative churches are growing has been increasingly amended to provide a more nuanced interpretation. Only a very dynamic view that takes account of multiple factors will provide a sufficient hypothesis by which to examine and understand the co-variant trends in American religious life at the close of the millenium. *The Yearbook of American & Canadian Churches* is privy to data from a large but not nearly complete portion of the religious community and, with care and many caveats, can contribute insight to that complex picture of American religious life.

Church Membership Trends

Table 1 offers a longitudinal view of church membership within the United States. This membership total as reported in the *Yearbook* rose steadily from its inception in 1890 to 1993 when a decline in membership was first reported. From 1993 to the present the total church membership has alternated between modest increases and modest declines. It must be noted that church membership reported here refers to the total of the churches reported within the *Yearbook of American & Canadian Churches.* These churches, taken as a whole, over time serve as the point of religious identity for a substantial, but declining, percentage

Table 2
US MEMBERSHIP CHANGES

Denomination	1997 Edition Membership Change	Percentage Change	1998 Edition Membership Change	Percentage Change	1999 Edition Membership Change	Percentage Change	2000 Edition Membership Change	Percentage Change
The Roman Catholic Church	89,849	0.15	927,460	1.54	355,855	0.58	810,522	1.30
Southern Baptist Convention	49,236	0.32	28,668	0.18	199,550	1.25	-162,158	-1.03
The United Methodist Church	-45,463	-0.53	-43,284	-0.51	*	*	-38,477	-0.45
Evangelical Lutheran Church in America	-4,629	-0.12	-9,579	-0.18	4,145	0.08	-6,830	-0.13
The Church of Jesus Christ of Latter-Day Saints	98,400	2.39	88,500	1.88	123,100	2.50	-35,794	*
Presbyterian Church (U.S.A.)	-32,986	-1.22	-32,114	-0.88	-26,622	-0.74	-8,632	-0.99
The Lutheran Church—Missouri Synod	-1,624	-0.08	6,589	0.25	1,892	0.07		-0.33
Assemblies of God	22,983	1.70	79,606	3.33	26,986	1.08	31,238	1.25
American Baptist Churches in the U.S.A.	9,466	0.63	-14,133	-0.93	2,066	.14	2,067	0.14

Table 3
US FINANCIAL SUMMARIES 1992–1998

Edition Year	Number Reporting	Full or Confirmed Members	Per Capita Inclusive Members	Inclusive Members	Total Contributions	Per Capita Full or Confirmed Members	Per Capita Inclusive Members	Total Congregational Contributions
1992	44	39,521,497	$314.09	43,191,444	$16,647,464,955	$421.23	$385.43	$13,565,854,125
1993	52	41,842,642	$346.11	46,667,687	$19,631,560,798	$469.18	$420.67	$16,152,245,431
1994	47	40,997,058	$341.05	44,886,207	$15,308,625,032	$373.41	$341.05	$15,308,625,032
1995	55	43,104,555	$368.77	48,115,704	$21,433,517,908	$497.24	$445.46	$17,743,597,668
1996	55	43,321,039	$408.06	50,047,599	$24,970,133,464	$576.40	$498.93	$20,422,403,297
1997	58	44,804,383	$424.79	49,936,836	$25,181,416,276	$562.03	$504.27	$21,212,711,615
1998	62	44,574,101	$446.91	49,679,497	$26,242,626,313	$588.74	$528.24	$22,202,379,038

Edition Year	Per Capita Full or Confirmed Members	Per Capita Inclusive Members	Total Benevolences	Per Capita Full or Confirmed Members	Per Capita Inclusive Members	Benevolences as a Percentage of Total Contributions
1992	$343.25	$314.09	$3,081,610,830	$77.97	$71.35	19%
1993	$386.02	$346.11	$3,481,455,047	$83.20	$74.60	18%
1994	$373.41	$341.05	$3,259,090,326	$79.50	$72.61	21%
1995	$411.64	$368.77	$3,689,920,239	$85.60	$76.69	17%
1996	$473.42	$408.06	$3,739,584,874	$86.32	$74.72	15%
1997	$473.45	$424.79	$3,968,704,661	$88.58	$79.47	16%
1998	$498.10	$446.91	$4,040,247,275	$90.64	$81.33	15%

of the U.S. population. Even though the figure for 1998 reported a slight membership increase, this increase does not keep pace with the growth in population. This may be due more to religious pluralism than to a decline in overall religious affiliation rates. Research by others, such as Gallup, Roper, *et al.*, continues to report extremely high religious affiliation rates among Americans. Even as the number of those who name Christianity as their religious preference declines (as expressed as a percentage of the population), the affiliation remains high when all religions are taken into account.

Within the larger picture of church membership patterns, the *Yearbook* has for three years focused upon some "bellwether" communions to isolate both the direction and rate of change in membership. **Table 2** offers comparative data that may suggest broader currents in affiliation patterns. The Roman Catholic Church reported an increase in membership that nearly doubles the rate of growth observable a year ago and returns it to a rate comparable to that reported in 1998. This change, while reflecting greater birth rates and higher retention rates, likely corrects a reporting error of a year ago. For the first time the Southern Baptist Convention reports a loss rather than a gain in membership. The percentage of membership loss for the Convention is virtually identical to that of the Presbyterian Church (U.S.A.), raising increasing doubts about the adequacy of a conservative church growth as opposed to a progressive church decline scenario. On the other hand, a solid and consistent growth pattern continues to be reported by the Assemblies of God, a Pentecostal denomination often identified as a growing conservative communion.

Church Finance Trends

The identification of trends in church financial giving should be done only preliminarily, and even then, only with a heightened sense of caution. Utilizing the figures reported for 1998, an upward trend in giving now appears to be emerging among the sixty-two churches that reported financial statistics to the *Yearbook*. As **Table 3** indicates, both local and benevolence giving continue what is now a four-year upward trend, with congregational figures topping $22 billion and benevolences breaking the $4 billion mark. Over the four-year period, benevolent giving (that is, funds spent for the well-being of others—whether around the world or across the street) has been increasing a bit more slowly than has congregational giving. Moreover, this year benevolences account for a slightly lower percentage of the total contributions than they did last year. This observation bears careful watching over the next several years to see if a trend can be identified.

If the sixty-two churches reporting are suggestive of the whole of the religious community, such faith groups remain an important feature of the American economy and of American philanthropy, with receipts of more than $26 billion. "According to *Giving USA,* an annual report by the American Association of Fund-Raising Counsel Trust for Philanthropy...in 1998...44 percent of all gifts—from foundations, corporations, and individuals (both during their lifetimes and in bequests)—went to religious groups" (Debra E. Blum and Grant Williams, "Tax Watch," *The Chronicle of Philanthropy*, Vol. XII, No. 3, Nov. 18, 1999, p. 43).

As the century closes with unprecedented growth in the stock markets, the lowest unemployment rate in thirty years, and a prolonged period of economic expansion, the whole question of church finances has to be viewed in a broader frame. For example, another dimension to this complex picture would be an assessment of the growth and/or decline in church endowment funds. However, no data are available at present to enable such an assessment.

Trends in Theological Education

A decade ago the new trend in theological education was the sharp upturn in enrollment figures for women. In the last third of the century, women, emboldened by the women's movement, encouraged by a new willingness among some denominations to offer ordination, and enabled by an increasing number of seminary programs offered on a part-time basis, enrolled in seminaries and divinity schools. As **Table 4** indicates, that figure has

12

now reached an all-time high of 34%, as reported by The Association of Theological Schools in the United States and Canada.

Growing diversity in theological education is not limited to gender. The pastors, priests, and Christian educators of the future will comprise a more diverse group than their predecessors if seminary enrollment figures offer a basis for forecast. **Table 5** shows that nearly a third of all persons enrolled in theological schools today identify themselves as "African American," "Hispanic," "Pacific/Asian" or some other category. A decade ago, 80% of all students identified themselves as "White." For both theological and practical reasons, the increasing diversity of those drawn to theological education and presumably on to professional church leadership, is a trend that will be celebrated for both its direction and its promise to the church.

TABLE 4

TABLE 5

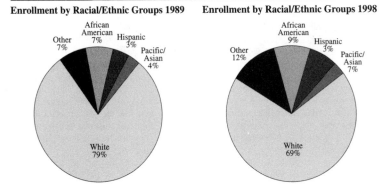

Religious Pluralism:
America in the Year 2000

Dr. Diana L. Eck
Professor of Comparative Religion and Indian Studies
at Harvard University

As we begin a new century and a new millennium, we in America are on new religious terrain. America has truly become a multireligious nation. Of course, the United States has always been a place of religious diversity, for the proliferation of religious groups comes with our common Constitutional commitment to the "non-establishment" and "free-exercise" of religion. For those who framed the Constitution and the Bill of Rights, this meant the diversity of Christian and theist religious communities, especially the inherent diversity of Protestant churches that took root in the colonies. In the nineteenth century significant numbers of Roman Catholic and Jewish immigrants tested and extended the embrace of religious freedom, as did nineteenth- and early twentieth-century immigrants who practiced Chinese religion, Islam, and Sikhism. It was not, however, until America's immigration policy changed in 1965 that significant communities of Muslims, Hindus, Buddhists, Sikhs, and Jains settled in the United States. Today at century's end, "we the people" of the United States are more religiously diverse than ever before.

In the last three decades all of us have become increasingly aware of our new cultural and racial diversity, but many of us are still unaware of the religious diversity that has come with the new immigration. We are surprised to find that there are more than twice as many Muslim Americans today as Episcopalians, that there are more Muslims than members of the Presbyterian Church (U.S.A.), and about as many Muslims as Jews—some five or six million in all. Most of us are surprised to see the range of who "we the people" have become. Today there are large new mosques in cities like Toledo, Cleveland, and Houston. There are beautiful new Hindu temples in Atlanta, Louisville, and Nashville; and Jain and Zoroastrian temples in the suburbs of Chicago. Many people are astonished to learn that Los Angeles is the most complex Buddhist city in the world, with a Buddhist population spanning the whole range of the Asian Buddhist world from Sri Lanka to Korea, and with a multitude of native-born American Buddhists as well. In some places in America one can see it all in a single neighborhood. On New Hampshire Avenue in Silver Spring, Maryland, for example, we find a Cambodian Buddhist monastery, a Ukrainian Orthodox Church, a Muslim Community Center, and the Mangal Mandir Hindu Temple, all virtually next-door neighbors.

As citizens, America's "we" today includes Buddhist Americans, like the Hawaiian born Jodo Shinshu Buddhist astronaut who died on the Challenger. We include Muslim Americans, like the Muslim major in the Oklahoma City Fire Department who spent two weeks working in the rubble of the Murrah Federal Building. We are Jains, like the Cincinnati businessman who is past president of the Jain Association of North America; and Hindus, like the engineer from Boston Edison who was the first president of the Hindu temple in Ashland, Massachusetts. We also are Sikhs, like the research scientist in Fairfax, Virginia; and Zoroastrians, like the computer engineer in San Jose, California, who also serves as the *mobed,* or priest, of the Zoroastrian Temple.

Our public awareness, our community life, and our public policy are just beginning to catch up with these changes in our demography. For example, in 1997 the governor of Kansas concluded his first official proclamation on the Muslim observance of Ramadan with these words: "Now, therefore, I, Bill Graves, Governor of the State of Kansas, do hereby proclaim the month January 10 to February 9, 1997, a month of special assistance to the needy, in the spirit of Ramadan, and call upon citizens of the State of Kansas to recognize the dedication and service of Muslims as an important part of the fabric of religious pluralism which enriches us all." In the same spirit, President Clinton issued official greetings to the Sikh community of the United States in November of 1998 on the occasion of the 529th birthday of the teacher who launched the Sikh movement in the 16th century, Guru Nanak. The President wrote, "We are grateful for the teachings of Guru Nanak, which celebrate the equality of all in the eyes of God, a message that strengthens our efforts to build one America. Religious pluralism in our nation is bringing us together in new and powerful ways."

There are many Americans, however, for whom religious pluralism is not a vision that enriches us all and brings us together, but one that is threatening, or perhaps tears us apart. At the same time as our religious diversity becomes more complex, many are concerned about a growing climate of intolerance for religious and cultural difference. The shadow of vandalism and violence perpetrated against religious groups, particularly minority or ethnic communities, has fallen markedly on the last years of this century. Hate crimes are registered on a regular basis: the firebombings of three Jewish synagogues in Sacramento; a Hindu temple in Atlanta vandalized five times in a nine month period; the arson of a Minneapolis mosque; and the strewing of nails across the parking lot of the Islamic Center in Flint, Michigan. Unfortunately, these incidents are not isolated: Arson has damaged mosques in South Carolina, Massachusetts, California, and Illinois. The story of the Atlanta temple, the Greater Atlanta Vedic Center in Lilburn, is one shared by numerous Hindu temples in America as well as many Sikh gurdwaras, mosques, synagogues, and minority Christian churches.

There are also many other controversies that engage our new religious differences around complex issues. Can a turbaned Sikh work on a hard-hat job or wear his turban in the U.S. Army? Can a Sikh high school student carry the symbolic dagger of Sikh religious initiation to school? Will the Whirlpool Corporation in Nashville find a way for Muslim employees to meet their obligations for prayer? Will a Dulles Airport security firm be allowed to fire Muslim women wearing the head scarf? Does a Hindu temple have to look more "Spanish" to meet the planning board standards of Norwalk, California? Should states post the Ten Commandments in public schools? Zoning boards, school boards, city and state judicial bodies have become the sites of interreligious encounter as new questions like these are posed; and in many cases they need the assistance of religious communities and interfaith councils to sort out the issues.

When they wrote the sixteen words of the First Amendment, "Congress shall make no law respecting an establishment of religion or prohibiting the free exercise thereof," the founders unquestionably did not have Buddhism or the Santeria tradition in mind. But the principles they articulated have provided a sturdy rudder through the past two centuries as our religious diversity has expanded. Step by step, we are beginning to claim and affirm what the framers of the Constitution did not imagine, but equipped us to embrace.

In the constitutional arena, all of us are clear about the fact that our own rights are secure only if the rights of our neighbors are secure. Whether we are Sikh, Muslim, or Roman Catholic, where the rights of one are threatened, all are threatened. Here our challenge is that of awareness. As vigilant as we are about the threat to our own rights, we often don't know how are neighbors are faring, even in this age of the worldwide web. But the Constitution is only one of the arenas in which we struggle with the issues of religious difference in America.

Beyond the constitutional arena are the moral and social questions of the civic arena. Not all of us share religious or theological ideas to be sure. But we do share a concern for the quality of our common life as communities. There are many forms of threat, belligerence, and discrimination that are not legally actionable, but have severe consequences for our lives together as neighbors. They are insensitive, provocative, and ugly, but not illegal. The negative stereotypes we hold of one another, the benign ignorance and willful misrepresentation of each other—these are matters of great importance, for we know that our society is shaped by the quality of our relationships and by forces for good or ill that governments simply cannot legislate.

So, what might "pluralism" mean in this new multireligious context? Religious traditions are irreducible, and they tend to resist syncretistic amalgamation; for this reason,

15

religious pluralism is an essential and preliminary focus for probing America's new challenge of pluralism. Religions don't "melt" in the so-called melting pot of America. However, pluralism is not just difference, but engagement with our differences. It means involvement and participation in common life, despite our differences. It means traffic, exchange, dialogue, and debate. Pluralism is not simply a "given" with our new diversity, but must be created. The makings of pluralism are surely there on New Hampshire Avenue; but without any real engagement with one another, without being attuned to the life and energies of one another, this might prove to be just a colorful example of diversity —interesting, but inconsequential and maybe divisive for American society.

In the late 1950s the Roman Catholic thinker John Courtney Murray described pluralism as the vigorous engagement of people of different religious beliefs around the "common table" of discussion and debate. He wrote, "By pluralism here I mean the coexistence within the one political community of groups who hold divergent and incompatible views with regard to religious questions. . . . Pluralism therefore implies disagreement and dissension within a community. There is no small political problem here. If society is to be at all a rational process, some set of principles must motivate the general participation of all religious groups, despite their dissension, in the oneness of the community. On the other hand, these common principles must not hinder the maintenance by each group of its own different identity."

The engagement of difference in a pluralistic society is not modeled on the structure of competition, but on the structure of dialogue. Vigorous engagement, even argument, around the common table is vital to the very heart of a democratic society. One might also contend that it is also vital to the health of religious faith, which must be appropriated not by habit or heritage alone, but within the context of dialogue with the commitments of those of other faiths. Such dialogue is not aimed at achieving agreement, but achieving something far more important: relationship, based on real give and take. Even still, we must remember that there are pluralities within faith groups themselves that wrestle with each other over this particular issue. Many faithful find themselves unfamiliar or uncomfortable with the discourse of interfaith religious dialogue and find themselves scrutinizing the cogency of these suppositions about the value of dialogue. Rather than strengthening and reaffirming faith, many fear that such relationships are risky, that they may weaken their community by eroding the traditions that bind it. Hence the real challenge of religious pluralism in the new millenium is to demonstrate for these more hesitant voices that such engagement is indeed worth the risk, that true, egalitarian dialogue cannot destroy the purity of faith, that it can only strengthen it, and thus communities must take steps toward establishing relationships with other communities. Whether in the public square or interfaith council, commitments are not left at the door. Indeed, the "naked public square" so repudiated by Richard Neuhaus two decades ago, will soon become the multireligious public square in which many new voices are heard.

Finally, the process of pluralism is never completed and settled, but is the ongoing work of each generation. In America we might go further to say that part of the engagement of pluralism is participation in the "idea of America." After all, America is a nation formed not by a race or a single people, but by the ideals articulated in the succession of founding documents, beginning with the Declaration of Independence. To say, "We hold these truths. . ." is not to hold them in the safe deposit box of the past, but to keep them alive through argument and dialogue in the present. This will be our task as we enter a new century and a new millennium.

Directory of Selected Faith Traditions in America

Compiling a directory of faith groups is an arduous, but rewarding, task in religiously plural America, in part because the very self-understanding and definition of community varies so greatly from faith group to faith group. In order to present a reasonably parallel and well balanced listing of organizations for each faith, care must be taken not to impose categories or terms from one's own universe of understanding upon other contexts. The very terms, "church," "membership," "denomination," "hierarchy," which are essential constructs of certain Christian universes of understanding, are rendered meaningless when applied to other faith groups.

Further, it is important to remember that many religious traditions lack a centralized organization that speaks for the whole of the community. Often, this lack of centralization speaks to the existence of several distinct forms or branches of the religion. In some instances, different ethnic groups immigrating to the U.S. bring with them a distinctive form of their religion, which is particular to their culture of origin. In other cases, plural forms of a faith exist, resulting from theological, political, or economic differences. Still other faith groups may be more tightly organized, but the religious center that provides guidance in matters of faith and, perhaps, even organizational discipline may not be in the United States. Hence the organizations before us are not necessarily religious hierarchical organizations, but are often groups assembled for other purposes that are associated with a particular faith group or subdivision of that faith group. Caution is advised in regarding these entries as one might regard a church headquarters.

The compilation of any directory relies upon the existence of some common organizational structures within all the entities listed. Yet, when compiling a directory of faith groups, it cannot be assumed that such organizational parallels exist. Oblique ways must be found to adequately represent individual faith groups. The many religious communities in the United States are associated with myriad organizations of all different types. Some of these are primarily places of worship; others are organizations seeking to represent either the religious community as a whole or some particular constituency within it. Others are community centers; some are educational groups; some are organizations particularly for women or youth; and some are political action groups. Still others are peace organizations or relief organizations. That said, a directory of this sort cannot include an exhaustive list of organizations for each faith group nationwide. The omission of any particular organization or branch of any of the major faith groups listed does not reflect a deliberate attempt to homogenize the rich pluralities that exist within faith groups. Instead, the listings that follow are intended to provided the interested reader with a few initial contacts within each religious community.

Despite the above cautions, this directory provides a rich resource for readers and researchers who wish to learn more about other faith groups. The bodies listed here consist of organizations of importance within the communities they represent and serve as excellent introductory points of contact with those communities.

In some cases, these religious communities are in a state of flux; those with access to the Internet will often find it an excellent way to keep contact with changing religious organizations. There is a plethora of information available about nearly all religious traditions on the Internet with varying degrees of accuracy. Some sites provide extensive links to information and to organizations on the web. For an extensive listing of religious search engines, please see Directory 5, "The Electronic Church."

For directory information about national interfaith organizations in the United States, please see Directory 1, "U.S. Cooperative Organizations." For directory information on local interfaith organizations, please see Directory 7, "U.S. Regional and Local Ecumenical Bodies."

Baha'ism

Baha'ism was founded in Persia during the late 19th century by Mirza Hussein Ali Nuri, also known as Baha'ullah, which means "Glory of God" in Arabic. Baha'i is an outgrowth of an earlier Persian religious movement called Babism, which was initiated by Mirza Ali Muhammad, who was referred to as the "Bab." In 1844, the Bab prophesied that in nineteen years, a divine manifestation of God would appear. Shortly afterward, the Babis endured a massive period of persecution in which the Bab was martyred. In 1863, Baha'ullah, a close follower of the Bab, claimed that he himself was this divine manifestation of God. Further, he claimed that he was the last in a line of such divine figures, which included Zoroaster, the Buddha, Christ, and Muhammad. Along these lines, Baha'ullah's teachings called for a religious universalism in which moral truths could be gleaned from all faiths. His son, Abd al-Baha, spread his father's teachings to the Western world, insisting on certain social principles such as universal equality of the sexes, or races, and of religious adherence.

The Baha'i National Center of the U.S.A.
536 Sheridan Road
Wilmette, IL 60091
Tel: (708) 869-9039
Website: www.bahai.org

 This center can provide information about the Baha'i faith and provide contacts with Baha'i organizations throughout the country and the world. There are over 1,400 Baha'i local spiritual assemblies in the United States. The community is very concerned about issues involving peace, justice, racial unity, economic development, and education (among others) and has available resources on a number of these issues as well as on Baha'i scriptures and theology. The website listed above is the official Baha'i website on the Internet.

Buddhism

 Buddhism began in northern India between the 6th and 5th centuries BCE with the teachings of Siddhartha Gautama, who is called the Buddha, which means "The One Who is Enlightened."

 Buddhism grew out of the Hindu tradition of the time, but it rejected certain fundamental philosophical, cosmological, social, hierarchical, and scriptural aspects of that tradition, which set the two deeply apart from each other. Most Buddhists believe that suffering is the central predicament of life, and that desires are the source of this suffering. One need only remove desires and it follows that suffering disappears as well. Buddhism has grown in different directions over the centuries among many different cultures, and its traditions have varied widely. All are usually characterized by an emphasis on meditation and compassion. Buddhism is divided into three major branches: *Theravada*, "the way of the Elders," *Mahayana* "the Great Vehicle," and *Vajrayana*, "the indestructible vehicle" or path of devotion. Buddhism spread through parts of South Asia, the Himalayan region, all over China, Japan, and Korea, and deeply into South East Asia. Although its origins are Indian, today Buddhism is almost entirely absent from that country. In the past hundred and fifty years, Buddhism has spread to the Western world. In this religious tradition, with few national bodies and great variation among particular branches and cultural expressions, organization is more localized than in some other faith groups.

American Buddhist Congress
4267 West Third Street
Los Angeles, CA 20020
Tel: 213-386-8139

 An association of leaders from a variety of Buddhist traditions in the U.S.

Buddhist Churches of America
1710 Octavia Street
San Francisco, CA 94109
Tel: 415-776-5600
FAX: 415-771-6293
Bishop, Ven. Hakubun Watanabe

 The national body of Japanese Shin tradition was founded in 1899. It provides programmatic resources for local temples around the U.S.

Buddhist Council of the Midwest
2400 Prairie
Evanston, IL 60201
Tel: 847-869-4975

 A regional organization active in coordinating activities among the Buddhist communities in the mid-west.

Buddhist Sangha Council of Southern California
933 South New Hampshire Ave.
Los Angeles, CA 90006
Tel: 213-739-1270
FAX: 213-386-6643

 The umbrella organization of Buddhist communities in Southern California.

Texas Buddhist Council
8727 Radio Road
Houston, TX 77075
Tel: 713-744-1334

 The regional coordinating body for Buddhists in Texas.

The Buddhist Peace Fellowship
P. O. Box 4650
Berkeley, CA 94704
Tel: 510-655-6169
FAX: 510-655-1369
Email: bpf@bpf.org
Director, Alan Senauke
   A national organization through which Buddhists of many traditions work for peace and justice.

Insight Meditation Society
1230 Pleasant Street
Barre, MA 01005
Tel: 508-355-4378
FAX 508-355-6398
Guiding Teachers, Joseph Goldstein, Sharon Salzberg
   This is a nonsectarian Theravada center established in 1975.

Shambhala International
1084 Tower Road
Halifax, Nova Scotia B3H 2Y5
Tel: 902-425-4257
FAX 902-423-2750
Email: shambint@ra.isisnet.com
Spiritual Head, Sakyong Mipham Rinpoche
Exec. Dir., John Rockwell
   This network of over 100 organizations of the Tibetan Kagyu-Nyingma lineage was founded in 1970.

Zen Mountain Monastery
P.O. Box 197, South Plank Road
Mt. Tremper, NY 12457
Tel: 914-688-2228
FAX 914-688-2415
Email: dharmacom@mhv.net
Resident Teacher, John Daido Loori, Roshi
   This monastery, established in 1980, is the headquarters of the Mountains and River Order, Japanese Soto-Rinzai lineage.

Hinduism

   Hinduism has been evolving since roughly 1500 BCE and has its origins in India. Most of the inhabitants of India are still Hindus, but many have emigrated to the Europe, North America, East Africa, South and South East Asia. The beliefs and practices of Hinduism vary so deeply and widely throughout India, and are so diffused throughout every aspect of life, that one may describe Hinduism not so much as a tradition, but more accurately as the collection of many traditions, encompassed by the great history and geography of India. Throughout its history, Hinduism has had an enormous propensity for the absorption of new elements into its practices and its understanding of deity. There is no central authority or priestly hierarchy that regulates the evolution of Hinduism; very few traditions are shared by all Hindus. Adaptations and evolutions can and do occur, but usually at the regional level. Simultaneously, ancient practices and beliefs persist in some places, where elsewhere, they have been long since replaced or never occurred. Nevertheless, all Hindus believe in the authority of the *Vedas*, the ancient scriptural tradition of India. All accept the *dharma*, or "way," of the four *varnas*, or social classes, which constitute the complex caste system, which is interwoven in the practice of the religion. Further, most Hindus worship Shiva or Vishnu or Devi, in addition to individual devotions to other deities or divine manifestations. Most Hindus are vegetarians.

The International Society for Krishna Consciousness
North American Communications
10310 Oaklyn Drive
Potomac, MD 20854
Tel: 301-299-9707
FAX: 301-299-5025
Email: anuttama.acbsp@com.bbt.se
Communications Director, Anuttama Dasa

19

Council of Hindu Temples of North America
45-57 Bowne Street
Flushing, NY 11355
Tel: 1-800-99HINDU
> One of a number of Hindu organizations, which connect Hindus in certain regions of the U.S.

American Hindus Against Defamation
8914 Rotherdam Avenue
San Diego, CA 92129
Tel: 619-484-4564
Email: ajay@hindunet.org
Director, Mr. Ajay Shah
> A new organization devoted to defending Hindus from stereotyping and discriminatory or defamatory acts/speech.

Islam
Islam began in 7th century Arabia under the leadership of the Prophet Muhammad, to whom God (*Allah* in Arabic) revealed a collection of verses known as the *Holy Qur'an*. The word *islam* means "making peace through submission" and in the context of religion, it means "submission to the will of God." A person who practices Islam is a Muslim, meaning, "one who is submitting to the will of God." A Muslim follows the teachings of the *Holy Qur'an*, which was presented to human kind by Muhammad, but which is the very word of the one and only God, and is therefore perfect and complete. Integral to the Muslim Tradition are the "Five Pillars of Islam," which are the five obligations each Muslim must uphold. The first of these is the *shahadah*, or profession of faith, which states, "There is no God but God, and Muhammad is his prophet." The second obligation is that a Muslim prays five times each day at prescribed times. Third, a Muslim must pay the *zakat*, which is a form of mandatory almsgiving. Fourth, a Muslim is required to fast from dawn until sunset during the month of *Ramadan*, the ninth month of the Muslim year. And finally, if able, once in his/her lifetime, every Muslim is required to make a pilgrimage called the *Hajj* to the holy city of Mekkah, where the *ka'bah* is housed, a stone structure, built by Abraham and Ishmael. Early in the history of the Islam, the religion split into two distinct branches, known as the Sunni and the Shiah, both of which contain subbranches. Muslims worldwide constitute an enormous community which is rapidly spreading throughout North America as a result of recent immigration as well as conversion.

The Islamic Society of North America (ISNA)
P.O. Box 38
Plainfield, IN 46168
Tel: (317) 839-8157
Website: www.isna.net
Dr. Sayyid M. Syeed, General Secretary
> The Islamic Society of North America grew out of the Muslim Students Association and is one of the oldest national Muslim organizations in the United States. It has a varied program primarily serving the Muslim community, but also seeks to promote friendly relations between Muslims and non-Muslims. It has a speakers' bureau, film loans, library assistance program, and several other services. It has also has a number of publications. Since ISNA is well represented throughout much of the United States, it is a good initial contact. It has been very active in the area of interfaith relations.

The Islamic Circle of North America (ICNA)
166-22 89th Ave.
Jamaica, NY 11432
Tel: (718) 658-1199
Web site: www.icna.org
> The Islamic Circle of North America is a smaller national organization than ISNA, but is involved in many of the same activities. They also have a presence in many different parts of the country and provide a number of resources both to Muslims and non-Muslims. ICNA also has been very active in the world of interfaith relations.

The Muslim American Society
The Ministry of W. Deen Mohammed
P.O. Box 1944
Calumet City, IL 60409
> This is the community of Imam W. Deen Mohammed and represents the largest single grouping of orthodox African-American Muslims in the United States. It is important to distinguish this group

from the Nation of Islam (Black Muslims). African Americans constitute probably the largest single group of Muslims in the United States. Given the loose structure of the organization, it is often both possible and helpful to make contact with a local mosque in your area.

The American Muslim Council
1212 New York Ave., NW
Washington, DC 20005
Tel: (202) 789-22 62
Web sight: www.amermuslim.org
Dr. Aly R. Abuzaakouk, Executive Director
   An organization which exists, in part, to represent the political and social interests of American Muslims and to defend their rights. It often has information about Muslim reaction to national and international events and also publishes informative booklets and brochures which include basic information on Islam and a journalistic style sheet.

Jainism

   Jainism was founded in the 6th century BCE in India by Vardhamana Jnatiputra (also known as Natapputta Mahavira), whom the Jains call Jina, which means "Spiritual Conqueror." Mahavira was a contemporary of the Buddha, and to some extent, Buddhism was an important rival to Jainism at the time. Both grew out of the Hindu tradition but rejected certain of its aspects. Jains honor a number of saints, or prophets from remote history called *tirthankaras,* who had liberated themselves from the bondage of *karma,* and hence from the cycle of reincarnation. Mahavira is the 24th of these *tirthankaras.* Emulating these saints, one may free the soul from the shackles of *karma* and rebirth, by observing the "three jewels" of "right faith," "right knowledge," "and right conduct." There is a strong emphasis in Jainism on peacefulness, moderation, and the refusal to injure animals in any way. There are religious orders, called *yatis,* which observe strict vows. The laity hold a pious respect for the *yatis.* There are two main branches of Jainism, the *Digambara* (sky-clad or naked) and the *Svetambara* (white-clad). Despite the fact the Jains constitute a relatively small proportion of the Indian population, they have a great influence on the Hindu community. The essential philosophy of non-violence had a great effect on the teachings of Gandhi in this century.

Federation of Jain Associations in North America
66 Viscount
Williamsville, NY 14221
Tel: 716-688-3030

Siddhachalam/International Mahavira Jain Mission
65 Mud Pond Road
Blairstown, NJ 07285
Tel: 908-362-9793
   A residential center for the teaching of the Jain way of life in the United States.

Judaism

   Judaism is one of the world's oldest religions, encompassing a rich and complex tradition that has evolved over centuries and has given rise to, or influenced, other major world traditions. Numerous expressions of Judaism have always coexisted with one another, as they do today. The central concern shared by all is to live in relation to God and to follow God's will. Jews understand themselves to be in covenant with God, who is the one transcendent God, Creator of the Universe. God revealed the Torah to the people of Israel as his way of life. History brought the Jewish people into contact with many cultures and civilizations, contacts that continuously transformed the nature of their worship, the understanding of God's law, and even their conceptualization of peoplehood. At the time of the second Diaspora, or great migration of Jews throughout the Middle East, North Africa, and Europe at the beginning of the common era, was the rise of the Rabbinical Tradition, with its emphasis on the study of scripture. Today's Judaism has grown out of these roots. In the 19th century, Reform Judaism arose in Europe and the United States as one Jewish response to modernity. Conservative Judaism and Reconstructionism are branches of Jewish practice that first developed in America. Orthodox Judaism also has a number of modern forms.

American Jewish Committee
165 East 56th Street,
New York, NY 10022
Tel: 212-751-4000

FAX: 212-750-0326
Executive Director, David A. Harris
> Founded in 1906, The AJC protects the rights and freedoms of Jews world-wide; combats bigotry and anti-Semitism and promotes democracy and human rights for all. It is an independent community-relations organization, with strong interest in interreligious relations and public-policy advocacy. The AJC publishes the *American Jewish Yearbook*, and *Commentary magazine*.

The Anti-Defamation League of B'nai B'rith
823 United Nations Plaza
New York, NY 10017
Tel: 212-885-7700
FAX: 212-867-0779
Website: www.adl.org
Director, Abraham H. Foxman
> Since 1913, the Anti-Defamation League has been involved in combating and documenting anti-Semitism. It also works to secure fair treatment for all citizens through law, education and community relations.

Jewish Council for Public Affairs
443 Park Avenue South, 11th Floor
New York, NY 10016
Tel: 212-684-6950
FAX: 212-686-1353
Website: www.thejcpa.org
Executive Vice Chairman, Lawrence Rubin
> This national coordinating body for the field of Jewish community relations comprises 13 national and 122 local Jewish communal agencies. Through the Council's work, and in its collaboration with other religious groups, its constituent agencies work on public policy issues, both international and domestic.

Jewish Reconstructionist Federation
7804 Montgomery Ave., Suite 9
Elkins Park, PA 19027
Tel: 212-782-8500
Email: jfrnatl@aol.com
Executive Director, Rabbi Mordechai Liebling
> Fosters the establishment and ongoing life of Reconstructionist congregations and fellowship groups. Publishes *The Reconstructionist* and other materials. Rabbis who relate to this branch of Judaism are often members of the Reconstructionist Rabbinical Association.

Union of American Hebrew Congregations
633 Third Avenue
New York, NY 10017
Tel: 212-650-4000
FAX: 212-650-4169
Website: www.uahc.org
President: Rabbi Eric H. Yoffie
> The central congregational body of Reform Judaism, founded in 1873. It serves approx. 875 affiliated temples and its members through religious, educational, cultural and administrative programs. Women's Men's and Youth organizations. *Reform Judaism* is one of its publications. The Central Conference of American Rabbis is the affiliated rabbinical body.

The Union of Orthodox Jewish Congregations of America
333 Seventh Avenue
New York, NY 10001
Tel: 212-563-4000
FAX: 212-564-9058
Website: www.ou.org
Executive Vice-President, Rabbi Raphael Butler
> The national central body of Orthodox synagogues since 1898, providing kashrut supervision, women's and youth organizations, and a variety of educational, religious and public policy programs and activities. Publishers of *Jewish Action* magazine and other materials. The Rabbinical Council of America is the related organization for Orthodox Rabbis.

The United Synagogue of Conservative Judaism
155 Fifth Avenue
New York, NY 10010-6802
Tel: 212-533-7800
FAX: 212-353-9439
Executive Vice-President, Rabbi Jerome M. Epstein

The International organization of 800 congregations, founded in 1913. Provides religious, educational, youth, community and administrative programming. Publishes *United Synagogue Review* and other materials. The Rabbinical Assembly is the association of Conservative Rabbis.

Native American Traditional Spirituality

Native American spirituality is difficult to define or categorize because it varies so greatly across the continent. Further, it is deeply entwined with elements of nature which are associated with different geographical regions. For example, while Plains Indians possess a spiritual relationship with the buffalo, Indigenous Peoples from the Northwest share a similar relationship with salmon. Hence, the character of Native American spirituality is dependent, to some extent, on the surrounding geography and its incumbent ecosystems. Despite this great variety, there are some similarities which allow us to consider the many Native American forms of spirituality together: Contrary to popular belief, Native American peoples are monotheistic; they do not worship the sun or buffalo or salmon, but rather understand that these elements of nature are gifts from the "Great Mystery," and are parts of it. Today, while still working toward religious freedom in the United States, Native Americans are also struggling to protect sacred sites, which they consider to be comparable to churches. But since these sites are actually part of the land, not man-made structures, many are constantly under attack for the natural resources they contain. Such exploitation of these resources is an offense to the Native American sense of spirituality, which views resources like timber, oil, and gold, as gifts from the Great Mystery. The struggle to protect and respect these sacred sites is a universal and essential part of Native American spirituality.

National Congress of American Indians (NCAI)
1301 Connecticut Ave., NW
Suite 200
Washington, DC 20036
Tel: (202) 466-7767
Fax: (202) 466-7797
Email: jdossett@erols.com
Website: www.ncai.org
Exec. Dir., JoAnn K. Chase

The National Congress of American Indians (NCAI), founded in 1944, is the oldest, largest and most representative national Indian organization serving the needs of a broad membership of American Indian and Alaska Native governments. NCAI stresses the need for unity and cooperation among tribal governments and people for the security and protection of treaty and sovereign rights. As the preeminent national Indian organization, NCAI is organized as a representative congress aiming for consensus on national priority issues.

The NCAI website contains links for a directory of Indian nations in the continental U.S. and Alaska as well as a directory of tribal governments. There are also links to other Native American websites.

Native American Rights Fund (NARF)
1506 Broadway
Boulder, CO 80302
Tel: (303) 447-8760
Fax: (303) 433-7776
Email: pereira@narf.org
Website: www.narf.org
Exec. Dir., Walter Echohawk

The Native American Rights Fund is the non-profit legal organization devoted to defending and promoting the legal rights of the Indian people. NARF attorneys, most of whom are Native Americans, defend tribes who otherwise cannot bear the financial burden of obtaining justice in the courts of the United States. The NARF mission statement outlines five areas of concentration: 1) Preservation of tribal existence; 2) Protection of tribal natural resources; 3) Promotion of human rights; 4) Accountability of government; 5) Development of Indian law.

Sikhism

Sikhism was founded by Guru Nanak during the 15th and 16th centuries CE in the state of Punjab in northwestern India. Nanak was greatly influenced by the teachings of Kabir, a Muslim who became deeply inspired by Hindu philosophies. Kabir's poems called for a synthesis between Islam and Hinduism. In the footsteps of Kabir's wisdom, Nanak drew upon elements of Bhakti Hinduism and Sufi Islam: He stressed the existence of a universal, single God, who transcends religious distinctions. Union with God is accomplished through meditation and surrender to the divine will. Nanak also called for the belief in reincarnation, karma, and also the cyclical destruction and recreation of the universe. However, he rejected the caste system, the devotion to divine incarnations, priesthood, idol worship, all of which were elements of the Hindu tradition. Nanak was the first of ten *gurus*, or teachers. The fourth guru, built the Golden Temple in Amritsar, the Sikh religious center. The fifth guru compiled the *Adi Granth*, a sort of hymn book of spiritual authority. All male sikhs are initiated into the religious brotherhood called the *Khalsa*. Members of this order vow never to cut their beard or hair, to wear special pants, to wear an iron bangle as an amulet against evil, to carry a steel dagger and a comb.

The Sikh Center of Orange County

2514 West Warner Ave.
Santa Ana, CA 92704
Tel: (714) 979-9328
Website: www.sikhcenter.org

The Sikh Center of Orange County describes itself as follows: "Our mission, in following the tradition and teaching of our honorable Guru Nanak, is to provide accurate, reliable and complete religious, social and cultural teachings and understanding of Sikhism and the people who practice it."

II

DIRECTORIES

1. United States Cooperative Organizations, National

The organizations listed in this section are cooperative religious organizations that are national in scope. Regional cooperative organizations in the United States are listed in Directory 7, "United States Regional and Local Ecumenical Bodies."

The Alban Institute, Inc.

Founded in 1974, the Alban Institute, Inc. is a non-profit, non-denominational membership organization. Its mission is to work to encourage local congregations to be vigorous and faithful so that they may equip the people of God to minister within their faith communities and in the world. Through its publications, education programs, consulting and training services and research, the Alban Institute provides resources and services to congregations and judicatories of all denominations and their lay and ordained leaders.

The Institute has long been a pioneer in identifying, researching and publishing information about key issues in the religious world such as conflict management, clergy transition, and involuntary termination of clergy and lay leadership. The Institute's resources include over 100 book titles, over 40 courses offered nationally each year, and a staff of senior consultants located across the country ready to assist local congregations. Individuals, congregations, and institutions may support Alban's work as well as maintain their cutting-edge skills for ministry through membership in the Institute.

Headquarters

7315 Wisconsin Ave., Ste. 1250 W., Bethesda, MD 20814-3211 Tel. (800)486-1318
Email: pwalker@alban.org
Website: http://www. alban.org
Media Contact, Marketing and Communications Director, Holly Hemphill

Officers

Pres., The Rev. James P. Wind, Ph.D.
Exec. Vice-Pres., Leslie L. Buhler

American Bible Society

In 1816, pastors and laymen representing a variety of Christian denominations gathered in New York City to establish an organization "to disseminate the Gospel of Christ throughout the habitable world." Since that time the American Bible Society (ABS) has continued to provide God's Word, without doctrinal note or comment, wherever it is needed and in the language and format the reader can most easily use and understand. The ABS is the servant of the denominations and local churches. It provides Scriptures at exceptionally low costs in various attractive formats for their use in outreach ministries here in the United States and all across the world.

Today the ABS serves more than 100 denominations and agencies, and its board of trustees is composed of distinguished laity and clergy drawn from these Christian groups.

Fifty years ago the American Bible Society played a leading role in the founding of the United Bible Societies, a federation of 138 national Bible Societies around the world that enables global cooperation in Scripture translation, publication and distribution in more than 200 countries and territories. The ABS contributes approximately 45 percent of the support provided by the UBS to those national Bible Societies which request support to meet the total Scripture needs of people in their countries.

The work of the ABS is supported through gifts from individuals, local churches, denominations and cooperating agencies. Their generosity helped make the distribution of 287.2 million copies of the Scriptures during 1994, out of a total of 608 millon copies of the Scriptures distributed by all member societies of the UBS.

Headquarters

National Service Center, 1865 Broadway, New York, NY 10023 Tel. (212)408-1200
Media Contact, Dir. Communications, Mike Maus, Tel. (212)408-1419 Fax (212)408-1456
Email: mmaus@americanbible.org
Website: http://www.americanbible.org

Officers

Chpsn., Sally Shoemaker Robinson
Vice-Chpsn., Harold Bennett
Pres., Dr. Eugene B. Habecker
Exec. Vice-Pres., Peter Bradley
Vice-Pres. for Scripture Publications, Maria I. Martinez

Vice-Pres. for Development and Communications, Arthur Caccese

Vice-Pres. for Finance and Administration, Patrick English

Acting Vice-Pres. for Marketing, John Cruz

Department Heads: Church Relations, Rev. Fred A. Allen; Scripture Publications, Assoc. Vice-Pres., Rev. Dr. David G. Burke; Volunteer Activities & Field Services, Dir., Frank Gomez; Catholic Ministries, Dir., Jeanette Russo; Human Resources, Dir., Steven King; Communications, Dir., Mike Maus; Scripture Production Services, Dir., Alain Sasson; Publications, Dir., David Singer; Development and Communications, Assoc. Vice-Pres., Jeffrey Towers; Finance and Administration, Assoc. Vice-Pres. and Controller, Donald Cavanaugh

American Council of Christian Churches

The American Council of Christian Churches is a Fundamentalist multidenominational organization whose purposes are to provide information, encouragement, and assistance to Bible-believing churches, fellowships, and individuals; to preserve our Christian heritage through exposure of, opposition to, and separation from doctrinal impurity and compromise in current religious trends and movements; to protect churches from religious and political restrictions, subtle or obvious, that would hinder their ministries for Christ; and to promote obedience to the inerrant Word of God.

Founded in 1941, The American Council of Christian Churches (ACCC) is a multi-denominational agency for fellowship and cooperation among Bible-believing churches in various denominations/ fellowships: Bible Presbyterian Church, Evangelical Methodist Church, Fellowship of Fundamental Bible Churches (formerly Bible Protestant), Free Presbyterian Church of North America, Fundamental Methodist Church, General Association of Regular Baptist Churches, Independent Baptist Fellowship of North America, Independent Churches Affiliated, along with hundreds of independent churches. The total membership nears 2 million. Each denomination retains its identity and full autonomy, but cannot be associated with the World Council of Churches, National Council of Churches or National Association of Evangelicals.

Headquarters

P.O. Box 5455, Bethlehem, PA 18015 Tel. (610)865-3009 Fax (610)865-3033

Email: accc@juno.com

Website: http://www.amcouncilc.org

Media Contact, Exec. Dir., Dr. Ralph Colas

Officers

Pres., Dr. Richard A. Harris

Vice-Pres., Rev. Mark Franklin

Exec. Sec., Dr. Ralph Colas

Sec., Dr. John McKnight

Treas., William H. Worrilow, Jr.

Commissions: Chaplaincy; Education; Laymen; Literature; Missions; Radio & Audio Visual; Relief; Youth

American Friends Service Committee

Founded: 1917, Regional Groups: 9. Founded by and related to the Religious Society of Friends (Quakers) but supported and staffed by individuals sharing basic values regardless of religious affiliation. Attempts to relieve human suffering and find new approaches to world peace and social justice through nonviolence. Work in 22 countries includes development and refugee relief, peace education, and community organizing. Sponsors off-the-record seminars around the world to build better international understanding. Conducts programs with U.S. communities on the problems of minority groups such as housing, employment, and denial of legal rights. Maintains Washington, D.C. office to present AFSC experience and perspectives to policymakers. Seeks to build informed public resistance to militarism and the military-industrial complex. A co-recipient of the Noble Peace Prize. Programs are multiracial, non-denominational, and international.

Divisions: Community Relations, International, Peace Education.

Headquarters

1501 Cherry St., Philadelphia, PA 19102 Tel. (215)241-7000 Fax (215)864-0104

Email: afscinfo@afsc.org

Website: http://www.afsc.org

Dir. of Media Relations, Carl Mangeri

Officers

Chpsn., Donald Gann

Treas., Kate Nicklin

Exec. Dir., Kara Newell

The American Theological Library Association, Inc.

The American Theological Library Association, Inc. (ATLA) is a library association that works to improve theological and religious libraries and librarianship by providing continuing education, developing standards, promoting research and experimental projects, encouraging cooperative programs and publishing and disseminating research tools and aids. Founded in 1946, ATLA currently has a membership of over 245 institutions and 550 individuals.

Headquarters

820 Church St., Ste. 400, Evanston, IL 60201 Tel. (847)869-7788 Fax (847)869-8513

Email: Alta@alta.com

Website: www.atla.com

Media Contact, Dir. of Member Services

Officers

Pres., Milton J. (Joe) Coalter, Louisville Presbyterian Theological Seminary, 1646 Cowling Ave., Louisville, KY 40205-1370

Vice-Pres., William Hook, Vanderbilt Divinity School, 419 21st Avene S., Nashville, TN 37240-0007

Sec., Eileen Saner, Associated Mennonite Biblical Seminary, 3003 Benham Ave., Elkhart, IN 46517-1999

Exec. Dir. & CEO, Dennis A. Norlin, 820 Church St., Ste. 400, Evanston, IL 60201

American Tract Society

The American Tract Society is a nonprofit, interdenominational organization, instituted in 1825 through the merger of most of the then-existing tract societies. As one of the earliest religious publishing bodies in the United States, ATS has pioneered in the publishing of Christian books, booklets and leaflets. The volume of distribution has risen to 25-30 million pieces of literature annually. For free samples or a free catalog contact 1-800-54-TRACT.

Headquarters

P.O. Box 462008, Garland, TX 75046 Tel. (972)276-9408 Fax (972)272-9642

Media Contact, Vice-Pres. Marketing, Tom Friday

Officers

Chpsn., John A. Mawhinney

The American Waldensian Society

The American Waldensian Society (AWS) promotes ministry linkages, broadly ecumenical, between U.S. churches and Waldensian (Reformed)-Methodist constituencies in Italy and Waldensian constituencies in Argentina-Uruguay. Founded in 1906, AWS aims to enlarge mission discovery and partnership among overseas Waldensian-Methodist forces and denominational forces in the U.S.

AWS is governed by a national ecumenical board, although it consults and collaborates closely with the three overseas Waldensian-Methodist boards.

The Waldensian experience is the earliest continuing Protestant experience

Headquarters

475 Riverside Dr., Rm. 1850, New York, NY 10115 Tel. (212)870-2671 Fax (212)870-2499

Media Contact, Exec. Dir., Rev. Frank G. Gibson, Jr.

Officers

Pres., Rev. Laura R. Jervis

Vice-Pres., Rev. James O'Dell

Sec., Rev. Kent Jackson

Treas., Lon Haines

Exec. Dir., Rev. Frank G. Gibson, Jr.

Appalachian Ministries Educational Resource Center (AMERC)

The Appalachian Ministries Educational Resource Center (AMERC) is the largest ecumenical consortial effort in the history of theological education in the U.S. Forty-nine seminaries comprise the consortium with 39 other theological institutions sending their students for AMERC training programs. Forty-nine denominations are represented in its students.

The goal of AMERC is to train persons for the Christian ministry in small towns and rural communities in Appalachia and beyond. In order to fulfill this goal, AMERC has the following objectives: (1) to provide participants with the highest quality of training in relating to Christian Theology and ministry to the people, cultures and political economies of Appalachia; (2) to provide direct experiences of Appalachian life both religious and secular and to help participants reflect theologically these experiences; (3) to recruit, support and encourage persons considering ministry in Appalachia and similar settings; (4) to provide and promote research of Appalachia and its churches; (5) to cooperate with religious bodies in the region in planning and implementing educational programs; (6) to provide training for theological faculty and denominational leaders; and (7) to seek and find spiritual, personal, financial, and administrative resources to suppport AMERC programs.

Headquarters

300 Harrison Rd., Berea, KY 40403 Tel. (606) 986-8789 Fax (606)986-2576

Media Contact, Devel. Coord., Kathy Williams

Officers

Co-Exec. Dir., Rev. Dr. Mary Lee Daugherty

Co-Exec. Dir., Rev. Dr. J. Stephen Rhodes

Chpsn. of Board, Dr. Douglass Lewis

The Associated Church Press

The Associated Church Press was organized in 1916. Its member publications include major Protestant, Catholic, and Orthodox groups in the U.S. and Canada. Some major ecumenical journals are also members. It is a professional Christian journalistic association seeking to promote excellence among editors and writers, recognize achievements, and represent the interests of the religious press. It sponsors seminars, conventions, awards programs, and workshops for editors, staff people, and business managers. It is active in postal rates and regulations on behalf of the religious press.

Headquarters

Media Contact, Exec. Dir., Dr. John Stapert, P.O. Box 30215, Phoenix, AZ 85046-0215 Tel. (602)569-6371 Fax (602)569-6180

Email: john_stapert@ecunet.org

US COOPERATIVE ORGANIZATIONS

27

Pres.,Roger Kahle, 8765 West Higgins Rd., Chicago , Il. 60631

Exec. Dir., Dr. John Stapert, P.O. Box 30215, Phoenix, AZ 85046-0215 Tel. (602)569-6371

Treas., Nena Asquith, P.O. Box 1245, Bethlehem, PA 18016-1245

The Associated Gospel Churches

Organized in 1939, The Associated Gospel Churches (AGC) endorses chaplains primarily for Fundamental Independent Baptist and Bible Churches to the U.S. Armed Forces. The AGC has been recognized by the U.S. Department of Defense for 57 years as an Endorsing Agency, and it supports a strong national defense. The AGC also endorses VA chaplains, police, correctional system and civil air patrol chaplains.

The AGC provides support for its associated constituent churches, (Fundamental Independent Churches), seminaries, Bible colleges and missionaries.

The AGC believes in the sovereignty of the local church, the historic doctrines of the Christian faith and the infallibility of the Bible.

The AGC is a member of the National Conference on Ministry to the Armed Forces (NCMAF).

Headquarters

Media Contact, Pres., George W. Baugham, D.D., National Hdqt., P.O. Box 733, Taylors, SC 29687 Tel. (864)268-9617 Fax (864)268-0166

Officers

Commission on Chaplains, Pres. and Chmn., Billy Baugham, D.D.

Vice-Pres., Rev. Chuck Flesher

Sec.-Treas., Eva Baugham

Natl. Field Sec., -vacant-

ADRIS/Association for the Development of Religious Information Services

The Association for the Development of Religious Information Services was established in 1971 to facilitate coordination and cooperation among information services that pertain to religion. Its goal is a worldwide network that is interdisciplinary, inter-faith and interdenominational to serve both administrative and research applications. ADRIS publishes a newsletter and provides internet consulting services toward these goals.

Headquarters

ADRIS Newsletter Office, P.O. Box 210735, Nashville, TN 37221-0735 Tel. (615)429-8744 Fax (508)632-0370

Email: dodds@home.com

Website: http://members.home.com/dodds

Media Contact, Newsletter Ed., Edward W. Dodds, P.O. Box 210735, Nashville, TN 37221-0735 Tel. (615)429-8744Fax (508)632-0370

Association of Catholic Diocesan Archivists

The Association of Catholic Diocesan Archivists, which began in 1979, has been committed to the active promotion of professionalism in the management of diocesan archives. The Association meets annually: in the even years it has its own summer conference, in the odd years it meets in conjunction with the Society of American Archivists. Publications include Standards for Diocesan Archives, Access Policy for Diocesan Archives and the quarterly Bulletin.

Headquarters

Archives & Records Center, 711 West Monroe, Chicago, IL 60661 Tel. (312)831-0711 Fax (312)736-0488

Media Contact, Ms. Nancy Sandlebac

Officers

Episcopal Mod., ⸺

Pres., Msgr. Francis J. Weber, 15151 San Fernando Mission Blvd., Mission Hills, CA 91345 Tel. (818)365-1501

Vice-Pres., Dr. Charles Nolan, 1100 Chartres St., New Orleans, LA 70116 Tel. (504)529-2651 Fax (504)529-2001

Sec.-Treas., Sr. Catherine Louise LaCoste, C.S.J., 10291/2 Hayes Ave., San Diego, CA 92103 Tel. (619)298-6608

Bd. Members: Kinga Perzynska, P.O. Box 13124, Capital Station, Austin, TX 78711 Tel. (512)476-6296 Fax (512)476-3715; Timothy Cary, P.O. Box 07912, Milwaukee, WI 19807 Tel. (414)769-3407 Fax (414)769-3408; Lisa May, P.O. Box 907, 1700 San Jacinto, Houston, TX 77001 Tel. (713)659-5461 Fax (713)759-9151; John J. Treanor, 711 W. Monroe, Chicago, IL 60661 Tel. (312)736-5150 Fax (312)736-0488; Bernice Mooney, 27 C St., Salt Lake City, UT 84103-2397 Tel. (801)328-8641 Fax (801)328-9680

Newsletter Editor, Nancy Sandleback

Association of Statisticians of American Religious Bodies

This Association was organized in 1934 and grew out of personal consultations held by representatives from The Yearbook of American Churches, The National (now Official) Catholic Directory, the Jewish Statistical Bureau, The Methodist (now The United Methodist), the Lutheran and the Presbyterian churches.

ASARB has a variety of purposes: to bring together those officially and professionally responsible for gathering, compiling, and publishing denominational statistics; to provide a forum for the exchange of ideas and sharing of problems in statistical methods and procedure; and to seek such standardization as may be possible in religious statistical data.

Headquarters

c/o John P. Marcum, Presbyterian Church (U.S.A.), 100 Witherspoon St., Rm. 2623, Louisville, KY 40202-1396 Tel. (502)569-5161 Fax (502)569-5501
Email: jackm@ctr.pcusa.org
Media Contact, Sec./Treas., John P. Marcum

Officers

Pres., Richard H. Taylor, United Church of Christ, 300 Weybosset Street, Providence, RI 02903 Tel. (401) 331-9844 Fax (401) 331-0023
1st Vice-Pres., Cliff Tharp, Southern Baptist Convention, 127 Ninth Ave. N., Nashville, TN 37220 Tel. (615)251-2517 Fax (615)251-5636
2nd Vice-Pres., Rich Houseal, Church of the Nazarene, 6401 The Paseo, Kansas City, MO 64131 Tel. (816)333-7000 Fax (816)361-5202
Sec./Treas., ohn P. Marcum, Presbyterian Church (U.S.A.), 100 Witherspoon St., Rm. 2623, Louisville, KY 40202-1396 Tel. (502)569-5161 Fax (502)569-5501

Members-at-Large

Clifford Grammich, 3166 South Bentley Ave., Los Angeles, CA 90034-3008 Tel. (310) 444-1826
James Schwartz, UJA Federations of N.A., 111 Eighth Ave., Suite 11E, New York, NY 10011-5201 Tel. (212)284-6729 Fax (212)284-6805

The Association of Theological Schools in the United States and Canada

The Association of Theological Schools is the accrediting and program agency for graduate theological education in North America. Its member schools offer graduate professional and academic degrees for church-related professions. For information about enrollment in member schools see "Trends in Seminary Enrollment" in the statistical section of this book beginning on page 326.

Headquarters

10 Summit Park Drive, Pittsburgh, PA 15275-1103 Tel. (412)788-6505 Fax (412)788-6510
Email: ats@ats.edu
Website: http://www.ats.edu
Media Contact, Dir. Of Comm., Nancy Merrill, Tel. (412)788-6505

Officers

Pres., Luder G. Whitlock, Jr., Reformed Theological Seminary, Jackson, MS
Vice-Pres., Martha J. Horne, Protestant Episcopal Theological Seminary in Virginia, Alexandria, VA
Secretary, M. William Howard, New York Theological Seminary, New York, NY
Treasurer, Thomas E. Fahey, Ernst & Young, New York, NY

Staff

Executive Director, Daniel O. Aleshire

Blanton-Peale Institute

Blanton-Peale Institute is dedicated to helping people overcome emotional obstacles by joining mental health expertise with religious faith and values. The Blanton-Peale Graduate Institute provides advanced training in marriage and family therapy, psychotherapy and pastoral care for ministers, rabbis, sisters, priests and other counselors. The Blanton-Peale Counseling Centers provide counseling for individuals, couples, families and groups. Blanton-Peale also offers a nationwide telephone support service for clergy, social service agencies, and other employers and promotes interdisciplinary communication among theology, medicine and the behavioral sciences. Blanton-Peale was founded in 1937 by Dr. Norman Vincent Peale and psychiatrist Smiley Blanton, M.D.

Headquarters

3 W. 29th St., New York, NY 10001 Tel. (212)725-7850 Fax (212)689-3212
Media Contact, ——

Officers

Chpsn., John Allen
Vice-Chpsn., Arthur Caliandro
Sec., Janet E. Hunt
Treas., Mary McNamara
Pres. & CEO, Dr. Holly Johnson

Bread For The World

Bread for the World is a non-profit, nondenominational Christian citizen's movement of 45,000 members that advocates specific hunger policy changes and seeks justice for hungry people at home and abroad. Founded in 1974, Bread for the World is supported by more than 45 Protestant, Catholic and Evangelical denominations and church agencies. Rooted in the gospel of God's love in Jesus Christ, its 45,000 members write, call and visit their members of Congress to win specific legislative changes that help hungry people, and place the issue of hunger on the nation's policy agenda.

Bread for the World works closely with Bread for the World Institute. The Institute seeks to inform, educate, nurture and motivate concerned citizens for action on policies that affect hungry people.

Headquarters

1100 Wayne Ave., Suite 1000, Silver Spring, MD 20910 Tel. (301)608-2400 Fax (301)608-2401
Email: bread@bread.org
Website: http://www.bread.org
Media Contact, Andrea Jeyaveeran, 1100 Wayne Ave., Suite 1000, Silver Spring, MD 20910 Tel. (301)608-2400 Fax (301)608-2401

Officers

Pres., Rev. David Beckmann
Bd. Chpsn., Patricia Ayers
Bd. Vice-Chpsn., Fr. Clarence Williams, CPPS

29

Campus Crusade for Christ International

Campus Crusade for Christ International is an interdenominational, evangelistic and discipleship ministry dedicated to helping fulfill the Great Commission through the multiplication strategy of "win-build-send." Formed in 1951 on the campus of UCLA, the organization now includes 68 plus separate ministries and special projects reaching out to almost every segment of society. There are more than 20,500 staff members and 663,000 trained volunteers in 181 countries. The NewLife 2000 strategy helps to give every person on earth an opportunity to say "yes" to Jesus Christ by the end of the year 2000.

Headquarters

100 Lake Hart Dr., Orlando, FL 32832 Tel. (407) 826-2000 Fax (407)826-2120
Email: ofcom@ccci.org
Website: http://www.ccci.org
Media Contact, Sid Wright

Officers

Pres., William R. Bright
Exec. Vice-Pres., Stephen B. Douglass
Vice-Pres. of Admn. & Chief Fin. Officer, Kenneth P. Heckman
Vice-Pres. of Intl. Ministries, Bailey E. Marks

CARA-Center for Applied Research in the Apostolate

CARA-the Center for Applied Research in the Apostolate is a not-for-profit research organization of the Roman Catholic Church. It operates on the premise that not only theological principles but also findings of the social sciences must be the basis for pastoral care.

CARA's mission since its founding in 1964 has been "To discover, promote, and apply modern techniques and scientific informational resources for practical use in a coordinated and effective approach to the Church's social and religious mission in the modern world, at home and overseas."

CARA performs a wide range of research studies and consulting services. Since its roots are Roman Catholic, many of its studies are done for dioceses, religious orders, parishes, and the National Conference of Catholic Bishops. Interdenominational studies are also performed. Publishes The CARA Report, a research newsletter on Catholic Church related topics, four times a year and The Catholic Ministry Formation Directory, a guide and statistical compilation of enrollments for Catholic seminaries, diaconate formation programs, and lay ministry formation programs.

Headquarters

Georgetown University, Washington, DC 20057-1203 Tel. (202)687-8080 Fax (202)687-8083
Email: cara@gunet.georgetown.edu
Website: http://www.georgetown.edu/research/cara/index.html

Media Contact, Executive Director, Dr. Bryan Froehle

Officers

Bishop William B. Friend, Chair, CARA Board of Directors

Periodical

The CARA Report

Center for Parish Development

The Center for Parish Development is an ecumenical, non-profit research and development agency whose mission is to help church bodies learn to become faithful expressions of God's mission in today's post-modern, post-Christendom world. Founded in 1968, the Center brings to its client-partners a strong theological orientation, a missional ecclesial paradigm with a focus on faithful Christian communities as the locus of mission, research-based theory and practice of major change, a systems approach, and years of experience working with national, regional, and local church bodies.

The Center staff provides research, consulting and training support for church organizations engaging in major change. The Center is governed by a 12-member Board of Directors.

Headquarters

5407 S. University Ave., Chicago, IL 60615 Tel. (773)752-1596
Media Contact, Exec. Dir., Paul M. Dietterich

Officers

Chpsn., Eugene L. Delves, 9142 S. Winchester Ave., Chicago, IL 60620
Vice-Chpsn., Pastor Gordon Nusz, United Methodist Church, 111 E. Ridge St., Marquette, MI 49855
Sec., Delton Krueger, 10616 Penn Ave. South, Bloomington, MN 55431
Exec. Dir., Paul M. Dietterich

Chaplaincy of Full Gospel Churches

The Chaplaincy of Full Gospel Churches (CFGC) is a unique coalition of 129 nondenominational churches and networks of churches united for the purpose of being represented in military and civilian chaplaincies. Since its inception in 1984, CFGC has grown rapidly-recently representing over 7.5 million American Christians.

Churches, fellowships and networks of churches which affirm the CFGC statement of faith that "Jesus is Savior, Lord and Baptizer in the Holy Spirit today, with signs, wonders and gifts following" may join the endorsing agency. CFGC represents its 129 member-networks of churches (consisting of over 60,000 churches nation wide) before the Pentagon's Armed Forces Chaplains Board, the National Conference of Ministry to the Armed Forces, Endorsers Conference for Veterans Affairs

Chaplaincy, Federal Bureau of Prisons, Association of Professional Chaplains, and other groups requiring professional chaplaincy endorsement. The organization also ecclesiastically credentials professional counselors.

Headquarters
2715 Whitewood Dr., Dallas, TX 75233 Tel. (214)331-4373 Fax (214)333-4401
Email: cfgc@fastlane.net
Media Contact, Rev. Dr. E. H. Jim Ammerman

Officers
Pres. & Dir., Rev. Dr. E. H. Jim Ammerman
Deputy Dir., Rev. Dr. Charlene Ammerman
Vice-Pres., Ed Leach

Christian Endeavor International
Christian Endeavor International is a Christ-centered, youth-oriented ministry which assists local churches in reaching young people with the gospel of Jesus Christ, discipling them in the Christian faith, and equipping them for Christian ministry and service in their local church, community and world.It trains youth leasers for effective ministry and provides opportunities for Christian inspiration, spiritual growth, fellowship, and service. Christian Endevor International reaches across denominational, cultural, racial and geographical boundaries.

Headquarters
1221 East Broad St., P.O. Box 2106, Columbus, OH 43216-2106 Tel. (614)258-3947 Fax (614)258-4950
Media Contact, Exec. Dir., Rev. David G. Jackson

Officers
Pres., Dr. Kent D. Maxwell
Exec. Dir., Rev. David G. Jackson

Christian Management Association
Christian Management Association provides management training and leadership resources for Christian organizations and larger churches. It's membership represents CEOs/executive directors, pastors, church administrators, finance officers and other managers from more than 1,600 organizations in the United States. CMA publishes a bi-monthly magazine, *Christian Management Report*, a monthly newsletter, an annual *Who's Who in Christian Management Membership* directory, and other resources. CMA also provide comprehensive training and strategic networking opportunities through CMA's annual leadership and management conference for Christian organizations (the next conference is CMA Colorado Springs 99, Feb. 15-18, 1999), CEO Dialogues one-day roundtables, the all new, School of Management (multiple sites), local chapter meetings, management books and audiotapes. Annual membership is open to Christian Organizations and individuals. Companies that provide products or services to Christian organizations and churches may apply for Business Membership. Contact CMA for a FREE membership information packet and sample publications.

Headquarters
P.O. Box 4638, Diamond Bar, CA 91765 Tel. (909)861-8861 Fax (909)860-8247
John Pearson, CEO
Media Contact, Director of Membership Development, Jackie Tsujimoto
Email: CMA@CMAonline.org
Website: http://www. CMAonline.org

Officers
Chairman, Mark G. Holbrook, President/CEO, Evangelical Christian Credit Union
Vice-Chairman, Frank Sommerville, Attorney, Weycer, Kaplan, Pulaski & Zuber, P.C.
Secretary, Robert Peterson, Retired Chief Financial Officer, Evangelical Free Church of America
Treas., James A. Canning, Vice-President Finance & Administration, World Vision International
CEO, John Pearson

A Christian Ministry in the National Parks
This ministry is recognized by over 40 Christian denominations and extends the ministry of Christ to the millions of people who live, work and vacation in our National Parks. Ministry Staff Members conduct services of worship in the parks on Sundays. The staff is employed by park concessionaires and have a full-time job in which their actions, attitudes, and commitment to Christ serve as witness. Room and board are provided at a minimal cost; minimum commitment of 90 days needed.

Headquarters
45 School Street, Boston, MA 02108 Tel. (617)720-5655 Fax (617)720-7899
Email: acmnp@juno.com
Website: www.coolworks.com/acmnp/
Media Contact, The Rev. Richard P. Camp, Jr.

Officers
Dir., The Rev. Richard P. Camp, Jr.

Church Growth Center
The Church Growth Center is an interfaith, nonprofit, professional organization which exists to bring transformational change of the Christian church toward the effective implementation of the Lord's Great Commission, to make disciples of all people. This effort is done through consultations, resources, and educational events.
Founded in 1978 by Kent R. Hunter, president and chairman of the board, the Church Growth Center offers several services including church consultations by experienced consultants under the Creative Consultation Services arm, cutting edge

resources through our bookstore, The Church Doctor™ Resource Center, and by providing educational events at churches and organizations in the way of providing speakers and resources at seminars, workshops, and conferences.

Other ministries under the arm of the Church Growth Center include Mission Teams International (taking teams overseas to train pastors to be more effective in their churches), The Church Doctor"! daily radio program (which is practical direction and helps for the lay person in the church), Nehemiah Guest Missionary House (where short-term missionaries may stay while learning church growth and working at the Center), and *Strategies for Todays Leader* (a quarterly magazine with timely thematic issues geared for pastors and leaders).

Headquarters

1230 U. S. Highway Six, P.O. Box 145, Corunna, IN 46730 Tel. (219)281-2452 Fax (219)281-2167

Email: churchgrowth@juno.com

Media Contact, Assistant to Pres., Cheryl A. Kroemer

Officers

Pres., Dr. Kent R. Hunter, D.min, Ph.D.

Vice-Pres., Rev. Paul Griebel, 312 S. Oak St., Kendallville, IN 46755

Sec.-Treas., Roger Miller, 1060 Park Dr., Turkey Lake, LaGrange, IN 46761

Church Women United in the U.S.A.

Church Women United in the U.S.A. is a grassroots ecumenical movement of one-half million Protestant, Orthodox, Roman Catholic and other Christian women, organized into more than 1,300 local and state units throughout the United States and Puerto Rico. Founded in 1941, CWU works in coalition with religious and secular groups on issues of peace and justice. A major program emphasis in the 1996–2000 Quadrenium is Making the World Safer for Women and Children.

NATIONAL OFFICE

475 Riverside Dr., Ste. 500, New York, NY 10115 Tel. (800) CWU-5551 OR (212)870-2347 Fax (212)870-2338

Email: cwu@churchwomen.org

Website: http://www.churchwomen.org

Media Contact,Rev. Martha M. Cruz, Tel. (212) 870-2344, Email: mmcruz@churchwomen.org

LEGISLATIVE OFFICE

CWU Washington Ofc., 110 Maryland Ave. NE, Rm. 108, Washington, DC 20002 Tel. (202)544-8747, Fax (202)544-9133

Dir., Wash. Ofc., Ann Delorey, Email: adelorey@churchwomen.org

Legislative Asst., Wash. Ofc., Tiffany L. Heath, Email: tlheath@churchwomen.org

UNITED NATIONS OFFICE

475 Riverside Dr., Ste. 500, New York, NY 10115 Tel. (212)661-3856

UN Ofc., Staff Liaison, Jeannie H. Lee, Email: jhlee@churchwomen.org

ADMINISTRATION

General Director, Dr. Kathleen S. Hurty, Email: khurty@churchwomen.org

Deputy Gen. Dir. for Admin. and Comm., Rev. Martha M. Cruz, Tel. (212)870-2344 , Email: mmcruz@churchwomen.org

Controller, Roberto Vazquez, rvazquez@church-women.org

Officers

Pres., Susan Shank Mix, Lynchburg, VA

1st Vice-Pres., Dr. Thelma Adair, New York, NY

2nd Vice-Pres., Rev. Jerrye Champion, Scottsdale, AZ

Sec.-Treas., Joan Regal, Maplewood, MN

PROGRAM DIRECTORS

Ecumenical Celebrations, Interim Dir., Jeanette Zaragoza De Leon

Ecumenical Development, Dir., Jeannie H. Lee

Leadership Development, Ascension Day

Regional Coordinators: Central, Ednabelle Madushaw, Pewaukee, WI; East Central, Gladys Kapenga, Wyoming, MI; Mid-Atlantic, Judith Hill, Harrisburg, PA; Northeast, Debbie B. Kaynor, West Hartford, CT; Northwest, Edna Best, Billings, MT; South Central, Mickey Simpson, Tulsa, OK; Southeast, Morene Williams, Athens, GA; Southwest, Winifred Hardy, Bailey, CO

Consultation on Church Union

Officially constituted in 1962, the Consultation on Church Union is a venture in reconciliation of nine American communions. It has been authorized to explore the formation of a uniting church, truly catholic, truly evangelical and truly reformed. In 1992 the participating bodies were African Methodist Episcopal Church, African Methodist Episcopal Zion Church, Christian Church (Disciples of Christ), Christian Methodist Episcopal Church, The Episcopal Church, International Council of Community Churches, Presbyterian Church (U.S.A.), United Church of Christ and The United Methodist Church. These churches are at present, deciding whether to enter a relationship of covenanted communion, to be called "Churches Uniting in Christ" and is scheduled for inauguration in January 2000. At the January, 1999 Plenary, at St. Louis, Missouri, the Assembly affirmed the Visible Marks of Churches Uniting in Christ and the marks of the fuller unity sought by "entering into a new level of visible commitment" by openly inviting participating churches to enter into this new relationship in 2002 or "to be partners in continuing relationship to realize fully that unity for which Christ prayed." This 18th Plenary dared to hope that other American Christian bodies may enter this dialogue, commending "to the churches the actions recommended in 'A call to Christian

Commitment and Action to Combat Racism' approved by the 18th Plenary."

The Plenary Assembly is composed of 10 delegates and 10 associate delegates from each of the participating churches. Included also are observer-consultants from more than 20 other churches, other union negotiations and conciliar bodies. The Executive Committee is composed of the president, two representatives from each of the particiipating communions and the secretariat. The secretariat consists of the executive staff of the Consultation. In the fall of 1999, the National Office was moved from Princeton, New Jersey to Lowell, Massachusetts.

In addition to publishing documents commissioned by the Consultation, a Newsletter is distributed periodically to keep its constituency abreast of current ecumenical concerns facing the Consultation and to share examples of local initiatives in ecclesial cooperation. An Editorial Board prepares an annual Lenten Booklet of devotional meditations entitled: *Liberation and Unity*.

Headquarters
260 Gorham Street, Lowell, MA
Mailing Address: Highland Station, P.O. Box 2143, Lowell, MA 01851
Tel. & Fax, (978)453-2842
Media Contact, Associate General Secretary, The Rev. K. Gordon White

Officers
General Sec., The Rev. Dr. Michael Kinnamon
Pres., Dr. Vivian U. Robinson, 1256 Hernlen st., Augusta, GA 30901
Vice Pres., Bishop Vinton R. Anderson, 1134 11th St., NW, W 3rd Floor Suite, Washington, DC 20001
Sec., Abraham Wright, 1912-3 Rosemary Hills Drive, Silver Springs, MD 20910

Rep. from Participating Churches
African Methodist Episcopal Church: Bishop Vinton R. Anderson, 4144 Lindell Blvd., Ste. 222, St. Louis, MO 63108; Bishop McKinley Young, 1656 Adams Dr., Atlanta, GA 30311
African Methodist Episcopal Zion Church: Bishop Marshall H. Strickland, 2000 Cedar Circle Dr., Baltimore, MD 21228; Bishop Cecil Bishop, 2663 Oakmeade Dr., Charlotte, NC 28270
Christian Church (Disciples of Christ): Rev. Dr. Robert., P.O. Box 1986, Indianapolis, IN 46206; Rev. Dr. Suzanne Webb, 7018 Putney Road, Arcadia, MI 49613-9600
Christian Methodist Episcopal Church: Bishop Charles Helton, 6524 16th St, NW, Washington, DC 20012; Dr. Vivian U. Robinson, 8th Episcopal Dist. Hdqt., 1256 Hernlen St., Augusta, GA 30901
The Episcopal Church: Rev. Lucinda Laird, 330 N. Hubbards Lane, Louisville, KY 40207; Rt. Rev. Edwin F. Culick, Jr., 425 S. Second Street, Louisville, KY 40202

Intl. Council of Community Churches: Rev. Dr. Jeffrey R. Newhall, 19715 S. LaGrange Rd. Ste. C, Mokena., IL 60448; Abraham Wright, 1612-3 Rosemary Hills Dr., Silver Springs, MD 20910
Presbyterian Church (U.S.A.): Dorothy G. Barnard, 2410 Fairoyal Dr., St. Louis, MO 63131
United Church of Christ: Rev. Dr. Thomas E. Dipko, Exec. V.P. 1st. Christian Church, 700 Prospect Ave., Cleveland, OH 44115; Rev. Diane C. Kessler, Mass. Council of Churches, 14 Beacon St., Boston, MA 02108
The United Methodist Church: Bishop William B. Grove, 109 McDavid Lane, Charleston, W. Virginia 25311; Rev. Kathy Bannister, 204 W. First Street, P.O. Box 327, Bison, Kansas 67520

Evangelical Council for Financial Accountability
Founded in 1979, the Evangelical Council for Financial Accountability has the purpose of helping Christ-centered, evangelical, nonprofit organizations earn the publics trust through their ethical practices and financial accountability. ECFA assists its over 900 member organizations in making appropriate public disclosure of their financial practices and accomplishments, thus materially enhancing their credibility and support potential among present and prospective donors.

Headquarters
P.O. Box 17456, Washington, DC 20041-7456
Tel. (540)535-0103 Fax (540)535-0533
Email: webmaster@ecfa.org
Website: www.ecfa.org
Media Contact, Pres., Paul D. Nelson

Officers
Pres., Paul D. Nelson
Vice-Pres., Donor & Member Services, Daniel D. Busby
Dir. of Member Review & Compliance, Lucinda Repass
V.P. Member Review & Compliance, Bill Altman

Evangelical Press Association
The Evangelical Press Association is an organization of editors and publishers of Christian periodicals which seeks to promote the cause of Evangelical Christianity and enhance the influence of Christian journalism.

Headquarters
314 Dover Rd., Charlottesville, VA 22901 Tel. (804)973-5941 Fax (804)973-2710
Email: 74463,272@compuserve.com
Website: http://www. epassoc.org
Media Contact, Exec. Dir., Ronald Wilson

Officers
Pres., David Neff, Christianity Today, 465 Gundersen Dr., Carol Stream, IL, 60188

33

Pres-Elect, Terry White, Inside Journal, PO Box 17429, Washington, DC 20041-0429

Treas., Lamar Keener, Christian Times, PO Box 2606, El Cajon, CA 92021

Sec., Jeanette Thomason, Aspire, 107 Kenner Ave., Nashville, TN 37205

Advisor, Dean Ridings, Christian Camp & Conference Journal, PO Box 62189, Colorado Springs, CO 80962-2189

Advisor, Brian Peterson, New Man, 600 Rinehart Rd., Lake Mary, FL 32746

Exec. Dir., Ronald Wilson

Friends World Committee for Consultation (Section of the Americas)

The Friends World Committee for Consultation (FWCC) was formed in 1937. There has been an American Section as well as a European Section from the early days and an African Section was organized in 1971. In 1974 the name, Section of the Americas, was adopted by that part of the FWCC with constituency in North, Central, and South America and in the Caribbean area. In 1985 the Asia-West Pacific Section was organized. The purposes of FWCC are summarized as follows: To facilitate loving understanding of diversities among Friends while discovering together, with Gods help, a common spiritual ground; and to facilitate full expression of Friends testimonies in the world.

Headquarters

Section of the Americas Headquarters
1506 Race St., Philadelphia, PA 19102 Tel. (215)241-7250 Fax (215)241-7285
Email: Americas@FWCC.Quaker.org
Media Contact, Exec. Sec., Cilde Grover
Latin American Office, Guerrero 223 Pte., Zona Centro, Cd. Mante, TAM 89800 Mexico

Glenmary Research Center

The Research Center is a department of the Glenmary Home Missioners, a Catholic society of priests and brothers. The Center was established in 1966 to serve the rural research needs of the Catholic Church in the United States. Its research has led it to serve ecumenically a wide variety of church bodies. Local case studies as well as quantitative research is done to understand better the diversity of contexts in the rural sections of the country. The Centers statistical profiles of the nations counties cover both urban and rural counties.

Headquarters

1312 Fifth Ave. North, Nashville, TN 37208 Tel. (615)256-1905 Fax (615)256-1902
Email: GHMGRC@aol.com
Media Contact,

Officers

Pres., Rev. Gerald Dorn, P.O. Box 465618, Cincinnati, OH 45246-5618

1st Vice-Pres., Rev.Daniel Dorsey, P.O. Box 465618, Cincinnati, OH 45246-5618

2nd Vice-Pres., Bro. Jack Henn, P.O. Box 465618, Cincinnati, OH 45246-5618

Treas., Robert Knueven, P.O. Box 465618, Cincinnati, OH 45246-5618

Dir., Kenneth M. Sanchagrin, Ph.D.
Email: ksanchagrin@mhc.edu

Graymoor Ecumenical & Interreligious Institute (GEII)

Graymoor Ecumenical & Interreligious Institute has its roots in the Graymoor Ecumenical Institute which was founded in 1967 by the Franciscan Friars of the Atonement, to respond to the Friars historical concern for Christian Unity in light of the theological and ecumenical developments arising from the Second Vatican Council.

In 1991, in response to developments in both the Institute and the wider ecumenical scene, the Graymoor Ecumenical Institute was expanded into an information and service organization with a mission of Christian Unity and interreligious dialogue. Today, the Graymoor Ecumenical & Interreligious Institute employs several means to acomplish this goal. Among these are specialization desks for African-American Churches; Evangelical and Free Churches; Lutheran, Anglican, Roman Catholic Affairs; Interreligious Dialogue; and Social Ecumenism. Another is the annual Week of Prayer of Christian Unity a world-wide observance initiated in 1908 by the Rev. Paul Wattson, co-founder of the Society of the Atonement the theme and text of which are now chosen and prepared by the Pontifical Council for Promoting Christian Unity and representatives of the World Council of Churches. The Institute publishes the monthly journal Ecumenical Trends to keep clergy and laity abrest of developments in the ecumenical and interreligious movements; provides membership in, and collaboration with, national and local ecumenical and interreligious organizations and agencies; and cooperates with individuals engaged in ecumenical and interreligious work.

Over the years, the Graymoor Ecumenical & Interreligious Institute has sponsored and co-sponsored meetings, colloquia, and workshops in areas of ecumenical and interreligious dialogue. These have been as diverse as colloquia between African-American and Hispanic Pentecostal scholars; Christians, Muslims, and Jews; state Councils of Churches; and interfaith training workshops for Christian leaders.

Headquarters

475 Riverside Dr., Rm. 1960, New York, NY 10115-1999 Tel. (212)870-2330 Fax (212)870-2001
Email: lmnygeii@aol.com
Media Contact: Walter Gagne, SA, Graymoor, Route 9, PO Box 300, Garrison, NY 10524-0300 Tel. (914)424-3671 x. 3421 Fax (914)424-2160

Interreligious Affairs Desk, Dir., Elias D. Mallon, SA, Ph.D.

Lutheran, Anglican, Roman Catholic Affairs Research Desk, Assoc. Dir., Lorelei F. Fuchs, SA, MA, STL, Katholieke Universiteit Leuven, Groot Begijnhof 12/2, 3000 Leuven, Belgium Tel./Fax 011(3216)20.78.05
Email: 100772,372@compuserv.com

African American Churches, Assoc. Dir., Paul Teresa Hennessee, SA, MA

Evangelical & Free Churches, Assoc. Dir., Elizabeth H. Mellen, M.Div.

Ecumenical Trends, Editor, Assoc. Dir., Keven McMorrow, SA, STD, Graymoor, Route 9, PO Box 300, Garrison, NY 10524-0300 Tel. (914)424-3671 ext. 3120

Social Ecumenism/National Public Policy Ministries, Paul Ojibway, SA, MA, GEII/ Washington Office: 516 G Street NE-B, Washington, DC 20002 Tel. (202)543-2800 Fax (202)547-8107
Email: briefing@voicesforjustice.org
Website: http://www.voicesforjustice.org

Business Manager, Betty Fedro, Graymoor, Route 9, PO Box 300, Garrison, NY 10524-0300 Tel. (914)424-2109 Fax (914)424-2163

Inter-Varsity Christian Fellowship of the U.S.A.

Inter-Varsity Christian Fellowship is a nonprofit, interdenominational student movement that ministers to college and university students and faculty in the United States. Inter-Varsity began in the United States when students at the University of Michigan invited C. Stacey Woods, then General Secretary of the Canadian movement, to help establish an Inter-Varsity chapter on their campus. Inter-Varsity Christian Fellowship-USA was incorporated two years later, in 1941.

Inter-Varsitys uniqueness as a campus ministry lies in the fact that it is student-initiated and student-led. Inter-Varsity strives to build collegiate fellowships that engage their campus with the gospel of Jesus Christ and develop disciples who live out biblical values. Inter-Varsity students and faculty are encouraged in evangelism, spiritual discipleship, serving the church, human relationships, righteousness, vocational stewardship and world evangelization. A triennial missions conference held in Urbana, Illinois, jointly sponsored with Inter-Varsity-Canada, has long been a launching point for missionary service.

Headquarters
6400 Schroeder Rd., P.O. Box 7895, Madison, WI 53707 Tel. (608)274-9001 Fax (608)274-7882

Media Contact, Dir. of Development Services, Carole Sharkey, P.O. Box 7895, Madison, WI 53707 Tel. (608)274-9001 Fax (608)274-7882

Officers
Pres. & CEO, Stephen A. Hayner
Vice-Pres.: C. Barney Ford; Robert A. Fryling; Samuel Barkat; Ralph Thomas; Jim Malliet
Bd. Chpsn., Virginia Viola
Bd. Vice-Chpsn., E. Kenneth Nielson

Interfaith Impact for Justice and Peace

Interfaith Impact for Justice and Peace is the religious communitys united voice in Washington. It helps Protestant, Jewish, Muslim and Catholic national organizations have clout on Capitol Hill and brings grassroots groups and individual and congregational members to Washington and shows them how to turn their values into votes for justice and peace.

Interfaith Impact for Justice and Peace has established the following Advocacy Networks to advance the cause of justice and peace: Justice for Women; Health Care; Hunger and Poverty; International Justice and Peace; Civil and Human Rights. The Interfaith Impact Foundation provides an annual Legislative Briefing for their members.

Members receive the periodic Action alerts on initiatives, voting records, etc., and a free subscription to the Advocacy Networks of their choice.

Headquarters
100 Maryland Ave. N.E., Ste. 200, Washington, DC 20002 Tel. (202)543-2800 Fax (202)547-8107

Media Contact, Jane Hull Harvey

Officers
Chpsn. of Bd., Jane Hull Harvey, United Methodist Church

MEMBERS
African Methodist Episcopal Church
African Methodist Episcopal Zion Church
Alliance of Baptists
American Baptist Churches, USA: Washington Office; World Relief Office
American Ethical Union
American Muslim Council
Center of Concern
Christian Methodist Episcopal (CME) Church
Christian Church (Disciples of Christ)
Church of the Brethren
Church Women United
Commission on Religion in Appalachia
Episcopal Church
Episcopal Urban Caucus
Evangelical Lutheran Church in America
Federation of Southern Cooperatives/LAF
Federation for Rural Empowerment
Graymoor Ecumenical and Interreligious Institute
Jesuit Social Ministries
Maryknoll Fathers and Brothers
Moravian Church in America
National Council of Churches of Christ: Church World Service; Washington Office
National Council of Jewish Women

NETWORK

Peoria Citizens Committee
Presbyterian Church (USA)
Progressive National Baptist Convention
Presbyterian Hunger Fund
Reformed Church in America
Rural Advancement Fund
Society of African Missions
Southwest Organizing Project
Southwest Voter Registration/Education Project
Toledo Metropolitan Ministries
Union of American Hebrew Congregations
Unitarian Universalist Association
Unitarian Universalist Service Committee
United Church of Christ: Bd. for Homeland Ministries; Bd. for World Ministries; Hunger Action Ofc.; Ofc. of Church in Society
United Methodist Church: Gen. Bd. of Church & Society; Gen. Bd. of Global Ministries Natl. Div.; Gen. Bd. of Global Ministries Womens Div.; Gen. Bd. of Global Ministries World Div.
Virginia Council of Churches
Western Organization of Resource Councils

International Union of Gospel Missions

The International Union of Gospel Missions (IUGM) is an association of 275 rescue missions and other ministries that serve more than 7 million homeless and needy people in the inner cities of the U.S., Canada and overseas each year. Since 1913, IUGM member ministries have offered emergency food and shelter, evangelical outreach, Christian counsel, youth and family services, prison and jail outreach, rehabilitation and specialized programs for the mentally ill, the elderly, the urban poor and street youth. The IUGM operates RESCUE College, an Internet-based distance education program to prepare and train rescue mission workers. The IUGM sponsors Alcoholics Victorious, a network of Christian support groups.

Headquarters

1045 Swift, N. Kansas City, MO 64116-4127 Tel. (816)471-8020 Fax (816)471-3718
Email: iugm@igum.org
Website: http://www.iugm.org
Media Contact, Exec. Dir., Rev. Stephen E. Burger or Phil Rydman

Officers

Exec. Dir., Rev. Stephen E. Burger
Pres., Dr. Malcolm C. Lee, P.O. Box 1112, Richmond, CA 94802 Tel. (510)215-4888 Fax (510)215-0178
Vice-pres., Mr. Rick Alvis, 222 E. Ohio St. # 519, Indianapolis, IN 46204 Tel. (317)635-3575
Sec.-Treas., Lorraine Minor, 5409 W. 79th St.,Prairie Village, KS 66208 Tel. (816)474-9380 Fax (816)231-7597

NATIONAL PROGRAM UNITS AND STAFF

Education, Rev. Michael Liimatta
Membership Services, Debbie McClendon
Newsletter and Magazine: Stephen E. Burger; Philip Rydman
Convention, Stephen E. Burger
Business Admn., Len Conner
Historian, Delores Burger
Exec. Sec., Madeleine Wooley
Communications & Development, Phillip Rydman
Expansion, Philip Tisdale
Educational Associate, Dru Gray

Interreligious Foundation for Community Organization (IFCO)

IFCO is a national ecumenical agency created in 1966 by several Protestant, Roman Catholic and Jewish organizations, to be an interreligious, interracial agency for support of community organization and education in pursuit of social justice. Through IFCO, national and regional religious bodies collaborate in development of social justice strategies and provide financial support and technical assistance to local, national and international social-justice projects.

IFCO serves as a bridge between the churches and communities and acts as a resource for ministers and congregations wishing to better understand and do more to advance the struggles of the poor and oppressed. IFCO conducts workshops for community organizers and uses its national and international network of organizers, clergy and other professionals to act in the interest of justice.

Churches, foundations and individual donors use IFCO services as a fiscal agent to make donations to community organizing projects.

IFCO's global outreach includes humanitarian aid shipments through its Pastors for Peace program to Cuba, Haiti, Nicaragua, Honduras, and Chiapas, Mexico.

Headquarters

402 W. 145th St., New York, NY 10031 Tel. (212)926-5757 Fax (212)926-5842
Email: IFCO@igc.org
Website: www. IFCOnews.org
Media Contact, Dir. of Communications, Gail Walker

Officers

Pres., Rev. Schuyler Rhodes
Vice President & Treasurer, Marilyn Clement

The Liturgical Conference

Founded in 1940 by a group of Benedictines, the Liturgical Conference is an independent, ecumenical, international association of persons concerned about liturgical renewal and meaningful worship. The Liturgical Conference is known chiefly for its periodicals, books, materials and sponsorship of regional and local workshops on worship-related concerns in cooperation with various church groups.

Headquarters

8750 Georgia Ave., Ste. 123, Silver Spring, MD 20910-3621 Tel. (301)495-0885
Email: litconf@aol.com
Media Contact, Exec. Dir., Robert Brancatelli

Officers

Pres., Eleanor Bernstein
Vice-Pres., Samuel Torvend
Sec., Robert Rimbo
Treas., Victor Cinson

The Lord's Day Alliance of the United States

The Lord's Day Alliance of the United States, founded in 1888 in Washington, D.C., is the only national organization whose sole purpose is the preservation and cultivation of Sunday, the Lord's Day, as a day of rest and worship. The Alliance also seeks to safeguard a Day of Common Rest for all people regardless of their faith. Its Board of Managers is composed of representatives from 25 denominations.

It serves as an information bureau, publishes a magazine, *Sunday*, and furnishes speakers and a variety of materials such as pamphlets, a book, *The Lord's Day*, videos, posters, radio spot announcements, decals, cassettes, news releases, articles for magazines and television programs.

Headquarters

2930 Flowers Rd. S., Ste. 16, Atlanta, GA 30341 Tel. (770)936-5376 Fax (770)452-6582
Media Contact, Exec. Dir. & Ed., Dr. Jack P. Lowndes
Email: dlowndes@georgiabaptist.org
Website: http://www.gabaptist.org

Officers

Exec. Dir. & Ed., Dr. Jack P. Lowndes
Pres., Dr. Paul Craven, Jr.
Vice-Pres.: Charles Holland; Roger A. Kvam; Timothy E. Bird; John H. Schaal; William B. Shea; W. David Sapp
Sec., Rev. Donald Pepper
Treas., E. Larry Eidson

Lutheran World Relief

Lutheran World Relief (LWR) is an overseas development and relief agency based in New York City which responds quickly to natural and man-made disasters and supports more than 160 long-range development projects in countries throughout Africa, Asia, the Middle East and Latin America.

Founded in 1945 to act on behalf of Lutherans in the United States, LWR has as its mission to support the poor and oppressed overseas in their efforts to meet basic human needs and participate with dignity and equity in the life of their communities; and to alleviate human suffering resulting from natural disaster, war, social conflict or poverty.

Headquarters

700 Light Street, Baltimore, MD 21230-3850, Tel. 410-230-2700
Email: lwr@lwr.org
Website: www.lwr.org/
Media Contact, Jonathan C. Frerichs

Officers

Pres., Kathryn F. Wolford

The Mennonite Central Committee

The Mennonite Central Committee is the relief and service agency of North American Mennonite and Brethren in Christ Churches. Representatives from Mennonite and Brethren in Christ groups make up the MCC, which meets annually in February to review its program and to approve policies and budget. Founded in 1920, MCC administers and participates in programs of agricultural and economic development, education, health, self-help, relief, peace and disaster service. MCC has about 875 workers serving in 50 countries in Africa, Asia, Europe, Middle East and South, Central and North America.

MCC has service programs in North America that focus both on urban and rural poverty areas. There are also North American programs focusing on such diverse matters as community conciliation, employment creation and criminal justice issues. These programs are administered by two national bodies-MCC U.S. and MCC Canada.

Contributions from North American Mennonite and Brethren in Christ churches provide the largest part of MCCs support. Other sources of financial support include the contributed earnings of volunteers, grants from private and government agencies and contributions from Mennonite churches abroad. The total income in 1997, including material aid contributions, amounted to $48.9 million.

MCC tries to strengthen local communities by working in cooperation with local churches or other community groups. Many personnel are placed with other agencies, including missions. Programs are planned with sensitivity to locally felt needs.

Headquarters

21 S. 12th St., P.O. Box 500, Akron, PA 17501-0500 Tel. (717)859-1151 Fax (717)859-2171
Canadian Office, 134 Plaza Dr., Winnipeg, MB R3T 5K9 Tel. (204)261-6381 Fax (204)269-9875
Email: mailbox@mcc.org
Website: http://www. mennonitecc.ca/mcc/
Media Contact, Exec. Dir., Ronald J.R. Mathies, P.O. Box 500, Akron, PA 17501 Tel. (717)859-1151 Fax (717)859-2171

Officers

Exec. Directors.: Intl., Ronald J.R. Mathies; Canada, Marv Frey; U.S.A., Jose Orfiz

37

National Association of Ecumenical and Interreligious Staff

This is the successor organization to the Association of Council Secretaries which was founded in 1940. The name change was made in 1971.

NAES is an association of professional staff in ecumenical and interreligious work. It was established to provide creative relationships among them and to encourage mutual support and personal and professional growth. This is accomplished through training programs, through exchange and discussion of common concerns at conferences, and through the publication of the Corletter, in collaboration with NCCC Ecumenical Networks.

Headquarters

c/o National Council of Churches, 475 Riverside Dr., New York, NY 10115-0050 Tel. (212)870-2155 Fax (212)870-2690

Media Contact, Barbara George, Dir., Ecumenical Networks Office, NCCC USA

Officers

Pres., Dr. Jay T. Rock, Interfaith Relations Commission, NCCC USA, 475 Riverside Dr., New York, NY 10115 Tel. (212)870-2560 Fax (212)870-2158

Past-Pres., Arthur Lee, Emergency Feeding Program, Church Council of Greater Seattle, PO Box 18145, Seattle, WA 98118-0145 Tel. (206)723-0647

Sec. & Treas., Dr. Paul Teresa Hennessee, Greymoor Ecumenical and Interreligious Institute, 475 Riverside Dr., New York, NY 10115, Tel. (212) 870-2968 Fax (212) 870-2001

Membership Development, Janet E Leng, Associated Ministries of Tacoma, 1224 South I street Tacoma, WA 98405 Tel. (253) 383-3056 Fax (253) 383-2672

The National Association of Evangelicals

The National Association of Evangelicals (NAE) is a voluntary fellowship of evangelical denominations, churches, organizations and individuals demonstrating unity in the body of Christ by standing for biblical truth, speaking with a representative voice, and serving the evangelical community through united action, cooperative ministry and strategic planning.

The association is comprised of approximately 43,000 congregations nationwide from 50 member denominations and fellowships, as well as several hundred independent churches. The membership of the association includes over 250 parachurch ministries and educational institutions. Through the cooperative ministry of these members, NAE directly and indirectly benefits over 27 million people. These ministries represent a broad range of theological traditions, but all subscribe to the distinctly evangelical NAE

Statement of Faith. The association is a nationally recognized entity by the public sector with a reputation for integrity and effective service.

The cooperative ministries of the National Association of Evangelicals demonstrate the associations intentional desire to promote cooperation without compromise.

Headquarters

P.O. Box 1325, Azusa, CA 91702 Tel. (626)963-5966

NAE-Washington, 1001 Connecticut Ave., Suite 522, Washington, DC 20036 Tel. (202)789-1011 Fax (202)842-0392

Email: NAE@nae.net

Website: http://www. nae.net

Media Contact, Dr. Kevin W. Mannoia, P.O. Box 28, Wheaton, IL 60189 Tel. (630)665-0500 Fax (630)665-8575

Staff

President, Dr. Kevin Mannoia

Interim Director, NAE-Washington, Rev. Richard Cizik

Counsel, Forest Montgomery

MEMBER DENOMINATIONS

Advent Christian General Conference
Assemblies of God
Baptist General Conference
Brethren Church, The (Ashland, Ohio)
Brethren in Christ Church
Christian & Missionary Alliance
Christian Catholic Church(Evan. Protestant)
Christian Church of North America
Christian Reformed Church in Noth America
Christian Union
Church of God, Cleveland, TN
Church of God, Mountain Assembly
Church of the Nazarene
Church of the United Brethren in Christ
Churches of Christ in Christian Union
Congregational Holiness Church
Conservative Baptist Assoc. of America
Conservative Congregational Christian Conf.
Conservative Lutheran Association
Elim Fellowship
Evangelical Church of North America
Evangelical Congregational Church
Evangelical Free Church of America
Evangelical Friends Intl./North America
Evangelical Mennonite Church
Evangelical Methodist Church
Evangelical Presbyterian Church
Evangelistic Missionary Fellowship
Fellowship of Evangelical Bible Churches
Fire-Baptized Holiness Church of God of the Americas
Free Methodist Church of North America
General Association of General Baptists
Intl. Church of the Foursquare Gospel
Intl. Pentecostal Church of Christ
Intl. Pentecostal Holiness Church
Mennonite Brethren Churches, USA

Midwest Congregational Christian Fellowship
Missionary Church
Open Bible Standard Churches
Pentecostal Church of God
Pentecostal Free Will Baptist Church
Presbyterian Church in America
Primitive Methodist Church, USA
Reformed Episcopal Church
Reformed Presbyterian Church of N.A.
Salvation Army
Synod of Evangelical Fellowship Chapels of the Fellowship Deaconry, Inc.
Synod of Mid-America (Reformed Church in America)
Wesleyan Church
Worldwide Church of God

National Bible Association

The National Bible Association is an autonomous, interfaith organization of lay people who advocate regular Bible reading and sponsors National Bible Week (Thanksgiving week) each November. Program activities include public service advertising, distribution of nonsectarian literature and thousands of local Bible Week observances by secular and religious organizations. The Association also urges constitutionally acceptable use of the Bible in public school classrooms, i.e.the study of the Bible in literature. All support comes from individuals, corporations and foundations.

Founded in 1940 by a group of business and professional people, the Association offers daily Bible readings in several English and Spanish translations on its website and has the IRS non-profit status of a 501(c)(3) educational association.

Headquarters
1865 Broadway, New York, NY 10023 Tel. (212)408-1390 Fax (212)408-1448
Email: info@nationalbible.org
Website: www.nationalbible.org
Media Contact, Pres., Thomas R. May

Officers
Cpsn., Stewart S. Furlong
Vice-Cpsn., Robert Cavalero
Pres., Thomas R. May
Treas., Philip Clements
Sec., Max Chopnick, Esq.

The National Conference for Community and Justice

The National Conference for Community and Justice, founded in 1927 as the National Conference of Christians and Jews, is a human relations organization dedicated to fighting bias, bigotry and racism in America. The NCCJ promotes understanding and respect among all races, religions and cultures through advocacy, conflict resolution and education.

Programmatic strategies include interfaith and interracial dialogue, youth leadership workshops, workplace training, human relations research, and the building of community coalitions. NCCJ has 65 regional offices staffed by approximately 350 people. Nearly 200 members comprise the National Board of Advisors and members from that group form the 27-member National Board of Directors. Each regional office has its own Regional Board of Directors with a total of about 2,800. The National Board of Advisors meets once annually, the National Board of Directors at least three times annually.

Headquarters
475 Park Ave. South, New York, NY 10016 Tel. (212)545-1300 Fax (212)545-8053
Media Contact, Dir. of Communications, Joyce Dubensky

Officers
Pres. & CEO, Sanford Cloud, Jr.

National Conference on Ministry to the Armed Forces

The Conference is an incorporated civilian agency. Representation in the Conference with all privileges of the same is open to all endorsing or certifying agencies or groups authorized to provide chaplains for any branch of the Armed Forces.

The purpose of this organization is to provide a means of dialogue to discuss concerns and objectives and, when agreed upon, to take action with the appropriate authority to support the spiritual ministry to and the moral welfare of Armed Forces personnel.

Headquarters
4141 N. Henderson Rd., Ste. 13, Arlington, VA 22203 Tel. (703)276-7905 Fax (703)276-7906
Email: jackw@erols.com & maureen.francis@tcs.wap.org
Media Contact, Jack Williamson

Staff
Coord., Jack Williamson
Admn. Asst., Maureen Francis

Officers
Chpsn., Rodger Venzke
Chpsn.-elect, Robert Vickers
Sec., J. Paul Jenson
Treas., Jacob Heerema
Committee Members: Catholic Rep., John J. Glynn; Protestant Rep., Jeannette Flynn; Jewish Rep., David Lapp; Orthodox Rep., Ted Boback; Member-at-Large, McKinley Young; Past Chair, Richard O. Stenbakken

National Council of the Churches of Christ in the U.S.A.

The National Council of the Churches of Christ in the U.S.A. is the preeminent expression in the United States of the movement toward Christian unity. The NCCs 35 member communions, including Protestant, Orthodox and

39

Anglican church bodies, work together on a wide range of activities that further Christian unity, that witness to the faith, that promote peace and justice and that serve people throughout the world. Approximately 52 million U.S. Christians belong to churches that hold Council membership. The Council was formed in 1950 in Cleveland, Ohio, by the action of representatives of the member churches and by the merger of 12 previously existing ecumenical agencies, each of which had a different program focus. The roots of some of these agencies go back to the 19th century.

Headquarters

475 Riverside Dr., New York, NY 10115. Tel. (212)870-2141

Media Contact, Dir. of News Services, Carol J. Fouke, 475 Riverside Dr., Rm. 850, New York, NY 10115, Tel. (212)870-2252, Fax (212)870-2030

Website: http://www.ncccusa.org

General Officers

Pres., The Hon. Andrew J. Young
Gen. Sec., Rev. Dr. Robert W. Edgar
Pres.-elect, Ms. Elenie K. Huszagh, Esq.
Immediate Past Pres., Rt. Rev. Craig B. Anderson
Sec., Rev. Roberto Delgado
Treas., Mr. Philip Young
Vice-Pres., Church World Service and Witness, Rev. Patrick Mauney
Vice-Pres., National Ministries, Dr. Audrey Miller
Vice-Pres. at large: Bishop Jon S. Enslin, Rev. Dr. Bertrice Wood, Ms. Barbara Ricks Thompson
THE GENERAL SECRETARY
Tel. (212)870-2141 Fax (212)870-2817
Gen. Sec., Rev. Robert W. Edgar
Deputy Gen. Sec., ———
WASHINGTON OFFICE
110 Maryland Ave. NE, Washington, D.C. 20002 Tel. (202)544-2350 Fax (202)543-1297
Interim Dir., Rev. Jay Lintner
Assoc. Dir., Rev. Archie LeMone
COMMUNICATIONS COMMISSION
Tel. (212)870-2574 Fax (212)870-2030
Assoc. Gen. Sec. for Communication and Interpretation, Rev. Randy Naylor
Dir., News Services, Carol J. Fouke
Dir., Electronic Media, Rev. David W. Pomeroy
Dir., Interpretation Resources, Sarah Vilankulu
Assoc. Dir., Electronic Media, Rev. Roy T. Lloyd
Design and Print Services, Manager, Sean Grandits
UNITY, EDUCATION, AND JUSTICE PROGRAM
Unity Cluster:
Program Coordinator, Rev. Dr. William G. Rusch Tel. (212)870-2569
Faith and Order, Rev. Dr. William G. Rusch
Interfaith Relations, Rev. Dr. Bert Breiner Tel. (212)870-2156 and Dr. Jay T. Rock Tel. (212)870-2560
Black Church Liaison, Ms. Carolyn Scavella

Orthodox Liaison, Mr. Gabriel Habib
Yearbook of American & Canadian Churches Editor, Rev. Dr. Eileen W. Lindner Tel. (212)870-2333
Redevelopment and Technical Dir., Rev. Marcel A. Welty Tel. (212)870-2379
Assistant Editor, Mr. Derek J. Lander Tel. (212)870-2031 Fax (212)870-2817
Education Cluster:
Program Coordinator, Rev. Patrice Rosner
Ministries in Christian Education, Dr. Joe Leonard Tel. (212)870-2673
Justice Cluster:
Program Coordinator, Ms. Nell Gibson Tel. (212)870-2916
Inclusiveness and Justice, Ms. Nell Gibson
Environmental Justice, Rev. Richard Killmer Tel. (212)870-2385
Economic Justice, Rev. Richard Killmer
EPRUS/AmeriCorps
Managing Dir., EPRUS/AmeriCorps, Rev. George Beukema
Director, Black Church EPRUS/AmeriCorps, Ms. Gloria White
Director, Hispanic Church EPRUS/AmeriCorps, Rev. Eddie Lopez
CRVA EPRUS/AmeriCorps, Fred Gilbert
Healthcare, Dr. Robb Burlage
Related Movements:
Interfaith Center for Corporate Responsibility, Timothy Smith Tel. (212)870-2293
Natl. Farm Worker Ministry, Executive Director, Rev. David Crump, Tel. (312)829-6436
CHURCH WORLD SERVICE AND WITNESS
Tel. (212)870-2061 Fax (212)870-3523
Unit Dir./Deputy Gen. Sec., Rev. Dr. Rodney I. Page
Dir. of Programs and Operations, Linda Hartke
Dir., Agricultural Missions, Rev. Eva Jensen
Interim Dir., International Relations and Human Rights, Kathy Todd
Dir. on Development Policy CWS/LWR, Lisa Wright, 110 Maryland Ave., NE, Suite 108, Washington, DC 20002 Tel. (202)543-6336 Fax (202)543-1297
Dir., Emergency Response, Rick Augsburger
Interim Dir., Immigration and Refugee Program, William Sage
Dir., Leadership Development, John W. Backer
Manager, Overseas Program Administration, David Herrell
Dir., Intl. Congregations, Rev. Arthur O. Bauer
Dir., Africa, Willis H. Logan
Dir., Latin America and Caribbean, Rev. Oscar Bolioli, Fax (212)870-3220
Dir., East Asia and the Pacific, Rev. Victor W. C. Hsu
Dir., Japan North America Commission (JNAC), Patricia Patterson
Dir., Europe, Rev. Paul Wilson
Dir., Middle East, David Weaver
Elkhart, IN 46515 Tel. (219)264-3102 Fax (219) 262-0966

ADMINISTRATION AND FINANCE
Tel. (212)870-2088 Fax (212)870-3112
Chief Financial Officer and Interim General
  Manager, Dr. Barbara Ellen Black
Deputy for Research and Development, Rev. Dr.
  Eileen W. Lindner
Financial Services:
Controller, Ms. Valerie Fields
Dept. of Business Services:
Dir., Melrose B. Corley
Dept. of Information Technology:
Dir., Rev. Nelson R. Murphy
Office of Human Resources:
Director, Ms. Denise Dalton

CONSTITUENT BODIES OF THE NATIONAL
COUNCIL (with membership dates)
African Methodist Episcopal Church (1950)
African Methodist Episcopal Zion Church (1950)
American Baptist Churches in the U.S.A. (1950)
The Antiochian Orthodox Christian Archdiocese
  of North America (1966)
Armenian Apostolic Church of America, Diocese
  of the (1957)
Christian Church (Disciples of Christ) (1950)
Christian Methodist Episcopal Church (1950)
Church of the Brethren (1950)
Coptic Orthodox Church (1978)
The Episcopal Church (1950)
Evangelical Lutheran Church in America (1950)
Friends United Meeting (1950)
Greek Orthodox Archdiocese of America (1952)
Hungarian Reformed Church in America (1957)
Intl. Council of Community Churches (1977)
Korean Presbyterian Church in America, Gen.
  Assembly of the (1986)
Malankara Orthodox Syrian Church, Diocese of
  America (1998)
Mar Thoma Church (1997)
Moravian Church in America, Northern
  Province, Southern Province (1950)
National Baptist Convention of America, Inc.
  (1950)
National Baptist Convention, U.S.A., Inc. (1950)
National Missionary Baptist Convention of
  America (1995)
Orthodox Church in America (1950)
Philadelphia Yearly Meeting of the Religious
  Society of Friends (1950)
Polish Natl. Catholic Church of America (1957)
Presbyterian Church (U.S.A.) (1950)
Progressive Natl. Baptist Convention, Inc. (1966)
Reformed Church in America (1950)
Russian Orthodox Church in the U.S.A.,
  Patriarchal Parishes of the (1966)
Serbian Orthodox Church in the U.S.A. &
  Canada (1957)
The Swedenborgian Church (1966)
Syrian Orthodox Church of Antioch(Archdiocese
  of the U.S. and Canada) (1960)
Ukrainian Orthodox Church in America (1950)
United Church of Christ (1950)
The United Methodist Church (1950)

National Institute of Business and Industrial Chaplains

NIBIC is the professional organization for
industrial chaplains, that includes members from
a wide variety of denominations and work settings, including corporations, manufacturing
plants, air and sea ports, labor unions and pastoral counseling centers. NIBIC has six membership categories, including Clinical, Professional,
Affiliates and Organizational.

NIBIC works to establish professional standards for education and practice; promotes and
conducts training programs; provides mentoring, networking and chaplaincy information;
encourages research and public information dissemination; communicates with business leaders
and conducts professional meetings. NIBIC
publishes a quarterly newsletter and co-sponsors
The Journal of Pastoral Care. A public membership meeting and training conference is held
annually.

Headquarters
7100 Regency Square Blvd., Ste. 210, Houston,
  TX 77036-3202 Tel. (713)266-2456 Fax
  (713)266-0845
Email: info@nibic.com
Website: http://www. nibic.com
Media Contact, Rev. Diana C. Dale, 7100 Regency
  Square Blvd., Ste. 210, Houston, TX 77036-
  3202 Tel. (713)266-2456 Fax (713)266-0845

Officers
Executive Dir., Rev. Diana C. Dale, D.Min.
Vice-Pres., Rev. Stephen Holden
President, Rev. Timothy Bancroft, D.Min.
Sec., Rev. Gregory Edwards

National Interfaith Cable Coalition, Inc.

The National Interfaith Cable Coalition, Inc.
(NICC) was formed as a not-for-profit 501 (c)(3)
corporation, in December 1987 and is currently
comprised of nearly 70 Protestant, Catholic,
Jewish and Eastern Orthodox faith groups.
NICCs mission is to make faith visible on television.

NICC is the parent organization of Odyssey, a
cable channel presenting a mix of faith-based
and family-oriented programming.

Odyssey was launched in September 1988 as
VISN (Vision Interfaith Satellite Network). The
channels name was changed in October 1992 to
VISN/ACTS, in 1994 to the Faith & Values
Channel, and in 1996 to Odyssey.

In November 1998, NICC entered into a new
partnership with Hallmark Entertainment, The
Jim Henson Company and Liberty Media Corp.
as owners of Odyssey. NICC provides Odyssey
with a minimum of 30 hours of programming per
week and co-produces an additional 10 hours per

41

week of faith-and-values programming with Hallmark and Henson companies.

Headquarters
74 Trinity Place, Ste. 1550, New York, NY 10006 Tel. (212)406-4121 Fax (212)406-4105
Media Contact, Beverly Judge
Email: bjudge@mail.nicc-usa.org

Officers
Chair, Dr. Daniel Paul Matthews
Vice Chair, Ralph Hardy Jr., Esq.
Secretary, Rabbi Paul J. Menitoff
Treasurer, Betty Elam

Staff
President and CEO, Edward J. Murray
Vice President, Beverly Judge

National Interfaith Coalition on Aging

The National Interfaith Coalition on Aging (NICA), a constituent unit of the National Council on Aging, is composed of Protestant, Roman Catholic, Jewish and Orthodox national and regional organizations and individuals concerned about the needs of older people and the religious communitys response to problems facing the aging population in the United States. NICA was organized in 1972 to address spiritual concerns of older adults through religious sector action.

Mission Statement: The National Interfaith Coalition on Aging (NICA), affiliated with the National Council on the Aging (NCOA), is a diverse network of religious and other related organizations and individual members which promotes the spiritual well being of older adults and the preparation of persons of all ages for the spiritual tasks of aging. NICA serves as a catalyst for new and effective research, networking opportunities, resource development, service provision, and dissemination of information.

Headquarters
c/o NCOA, 409 Third St., SW, 2nd Floor, Washington, DC 20024 Tel. (202)479-6655 Fax (202)479-0735
Media Contact, NCOA Dir. of Communications, Michael Reinemer

Officers
Chpsn., Rev. Dr. Richard H. Gentzler, Jr.
Chpsn.-Elect, Rev. Dr. Robert W. Carlson
Past Chpsn., Josselyn Bennett
Sec., Rev. Dr. James W. Ellor
Vol. Dir., Dr. Rita K. Chow

National Interfaith Committee for Worker Justice

The National Interfaith Committee for Worker Justice (NICWJ) is a network of forty-five interfaith groups and people of faith who educate and mobilize the U.S. religious community on issues and campaigns to improve wages, benefits and working conditions for workers, especially low-wage workers. The organization rebuilds relationships between the religious community and organized labor.

The organization supports and organizes local interfaith worker justice groups around the country, publishes *Faith Works* six times a year providing congregations resources and updates on religion-labor work, coordinates the Poultry Justice project to improve conditions for poultry workers, and promotes healthy dialogue between management and unions in religious owned or sponsored health care facilities.

Headquarters
1020 West Bryn Mawr, 4th floor, Chicago, IL 60660-4627. Tel. (773)728-8400 Fax (773) 728-8409
Email: nicwj@igc.org
Website: http://www.igc.org/nicwj
Media Contact: Mr. Toure Muhammed

Officers
President, Bishop Jesse DeWitt (retired United Methodist Bishop)
Vice President, Bishop Howard Hubbard (Bishop of the Catholic Diocese of Albany)
Secretary-Treasurer, Rev. Jim Sessions (Highland Research and Education Center)
Chair of Action & Issues Committee, Rev. Michael Rouse (Pastor, St. Catherine African Methodist Episcopal Zion Church)
Chair of Education Committee, Rabbi Robert Marx (Congregation Hakafa)
Chair of Board Development Committee, Ms. Evely Laser Shlensky (Committee on Social Action of Reform Judaism)

Staff
Executive Director, Ms. Kim Bobo
Education & Outreach Coordinator, Ms. Regina Botterill
Poultry Justice Coordinator, Ms. Miltoria Bey
North Carolina Poultry Justice Coordinator, Ms. Deborah Young
Religious Employers Project Coordinator, Sr. Barbara Pfarr
Communications Coordinator, Mr. Toure Muhammed
Office Manager, Ms. Bridget Harris

NETWORK AFFILIATES
ARIZONA
Phoenix Interfaith Committee for Worker Justice, 4302 N. 87th Pl., Scottsdale, AZ 85251; Tel. (602)946-5843; Contact: Mrs. Margaret Grannis
ARKANSAS
Western Arkansas Labor Coalition, P.O. Box 1122, Alma, AK 7921; Tel. (501)783-1149; Matt Joyce

Little Rock Religion and Labor Committee of Jobs with Justice, PO Box 477, Hampton, AK 71744; Tel. (840)783-1149; Fax (840)783-0512; Contact Rev. Steve Copley

CALIFORNIA

Los Angeles Clergy and Laity United for Economic Justice, 548 S. Spring St., Suite 630, Los Angeles, CA 90013-2313; Tel. (213)486-9880 x103; Fax (213)486-9886; Contact Ms. Linda Lotz

San Jose Interfaith Council on Race, Religion, Economic & Social Justice, 2102 Almaden Rd., #107, Santa Clara, CA 95125; Tel. (408)269-7872; Email: tic@atwork.org Coordinator: Poncho Guevara

DELAWARE

Delmarva Poultry Justice Alliance, c/o La Esperanza, 319 Race St., Georgetown, DE 19947; Tel. (302)854-9264; Fax (302)854-9277 Contact: Ms. Andrea Lukowsky

FLORIDA

Immokalee Religious Leaders Concerned, 3619 Woodlake Drive, Bonita Springs, FL 34134; Tel. (941)495-1679; Fax (941)495-6595; Contact: Rhea Gray.

South Florida Interfaith Committee for Worker Justice, 6801 NW 15th Ave., Miami, FL 33147; Tel. (305)835-9808; Fax (305)835-7227; Contact: Rev. Richard Bennett

ILLINOIS

Chicago Interfaith Committee on Worker Issues, 1020 West Bryn Mawr, Chicago, IL 60660-4627; Tel. (773)728-8400; Fax (773)728-8409; Contact: Rev. Richard Bundy or Ms. Kristi Sanford

INDIANA

Northwest Indiana Calumet Project, 7128 Arizona Ave., Hammond, IN 46323-2223; Tel. (219)845-5008; Fax (219)845-5032; Contact: Mr. Steven Ashby

Central Indiana St. Joseph Valley Project, 2015 W. Western, #209, South Bend, IN 46629; Tel. (219)287-3834; Fax (219)233-5543; Coordinator: Mr. Dan Lane

Indianapolis Interfaith Committee for Worker Justice, c/o East Tenth United Methodist Church, 2327 East 10th St., Indianapolis, IN 46220-0530; Tel. (317)636-9017; Fax (317)633-8368; Contact: Rev. Darren Cushman-Wood

KENTUCKY

Worker Rights Outreach & Kentucky Jobs with Justice, 1815 Fernwood Avenue, Louisville, KY 40205; Tel. (502)568-5600; Fax (502)581-1437; Contact: Mr. Chris Sanders

MASSACHUSETTS

Massachusetts Interfaith Committee for Worker Justice, 33 Harrison Ave., 4th floor, Boston, MA 02111; Tel. (617)574-9296; Fax (617) 426-7684; Email: inalliance@aol.com; Contact: Dr. Jonathan Fine

Religion & Labor Committee, c/o Labor Guild of Boston, 883 Hancock St., Quincy, MA 02170;

Tel. (617)786-1822; Fax (617)472-2486; Contact: Father Edward Boyle

Holy Cross Student Labor Action Committee, PO Box 840, College of the Holy Cross, Worcester, MA 01610; Email: mldorosa@holycross.edu

MICHIGAN

Detroit Interfaith Committee on Worker Issues, 1641 Webb, Detroit, MI 48206; Tel. (313)869-1632; Fax (313)869-8266; Contact: Ms. Barbara Hunt

MISSOURI

Kansas City Religion and Labor Coalition, PO Box 240595, Kansas City, MO 64124; Tel. (816)861-0073; Fax (816)861-0071; Contact: Mr. Jerry Meszaros

Labor & Religion Committee of the Human Rights Commission, 3519 N. 14th St., St. Louis, MO 63107; Tel. (314)241-9165; Fax (314)436-9291; Contact Rev. Rich Creason

NEVADA

Las Vegas Interfaith Council for Worker Justice, 1630 S. Commerce St., Las Vegas, NV 89102; Tel. (702)386-5258; Fax (702)384-0845; Contact: Ms. Paula Tusiani

NEW HAMPSHIRE

Interfaith Committee for Worker Justice, PO Box 292, Goffstown, NH 03045; Tel. (603)497-5167; Contact: Fred Robinson

NEW YORK

Albany Capitol District Labor Religion Coalition, 159 Wolf Road, Albany, NY 12205; Tel. (518)459-5400; Fax (518)454-6411; Contact: Ms. Margaret Shirk

Buffalo Coalition for Economic Justice, 2123 Bailey Ave., Buffalo, NY 14211; Tel. (716) 894-2013; Contact: Ms. Joan Malone

New York City Labor-Religion Coalition, 40 Fulton St., 22nd Floor, New York, NY 10038; Tel. (212)406-2156, ext. 237; Fax (212)406-2296; Contact: Rabbi Michael Feinberg

New York City Staten Island Religion Labor Coalition, 32D Franklin Lane, Staten Island, NY 10306; Tel. (212)406-2156; Fax (212)406-2296; Contact: Ms. Lilly Gioia

New York State Labor-Religion Coalition, 159 Wolf Road, Albany, NY 12205; Tel. (518)459-5400; Contact: Mr. Brian OShaughnessy

Syracuse Central New York Labor Religion Coalition, 614 James St., Syracuse, NY 13201; Tel. (315)445-1690; Fax (315)445-1690; Contact: Ms. Mary Hannick

NORTH CAROLINA

North Carolina Poultry Justice Alliance, 417 Arlington St., Greensboro, NC 27406; Tel. (336)271-4070; Email: jtaylor54@juno.com; Contact: Dr. Jerry Taylor

Pulpit Forum, 1310 MLK Dr., Greensboro, NC 27406; Tel. (336)272-8441; Fax (336)378-1165; Contact: Rev. W.F. Wright

OHIO

Central Ohio Religion-Labor Network, Office of Social Action, Diocese of Columbus, Columbus,

43

OH 42315; Tel. (614)241-2541; Contact: Mr. Mark Huddy

Cincinnati Interfaith Committee on Worker Justice, c/o Social Action Office, 100 E. 8th St., Cincinnati, OH 45212; Tel. (513)421-3131; Fax (513)421-1582; Contact: Mr. Thomas Choquette

Cleveland Jobs with Justice, 20525 Center Ridge Rd., Rocky River, OH 44116; Tel. (440)333-6363; Fax (440)333-1491; Contact: Mr. Steve Cagan

OKLAHOMA

Labor-Religion Council of Oklahoma, PO Box 2009, Tulsa, OK 74101-2009; Tel. (918)587-3115; Fax (918)587-6692; Contact: Rev. Donald Brooks

OREGON

Eugene-Springfield Solidarity Network, 4355 Pinecrest Dr., Eugene, OR 97405; Tel. (541)345-3253; Fax (541)346-2790; Contact: Mr. Charles Spencer

PENNSYVANIA

Area Religious Task Force on the Economy, 5125 Tenn. Ave., Pittsburgh, PA 15224; Tel. (412)361-3022; Contact: Rev. Ted Erickson

TENNESSEE

Nashville Middle Tennessee Jobs with Justice, 516 Riverwood Circle, Nashville, TN 37216; Tel. (615)226-9420; Fax (615)227-3185; Contact: Ms. Laurie Bullock

Knoxville Religious Outreach Committee, Jobs with Justice, 1959 Highlander Way, New Market, TN 37820; Tel. (423)933-3443; Fax (423)933-3424; Contact: Rev. Jim Sessions

TEXAS

Brazor Valley Interfaith Alliance for Worker Justice, St. Marys Catholic Church, 603 Church St., College Station, TX 77840; Tel. (409)846-5717; Contact: Ms. Maureen Murray

Dallas Jobs with Justice, c/o Camp Wisdom UMC, 1300 W. Camp Wisdom Rd., Dallas, TX 75232; Tel. (972)224-4556; Fax (972)228-9434; Contact: Rev Charles Stovall

Houston Interfaith Committee for Worker Justice, c/o Worklife Ministries, 7100 Regency Sq., Suite 210, Houston, TX 77036; Tel. (713)266-2456; Fax (713)266-0845; Contact: Rev. Diana Dale

WASHINGTON

Washington Religious Labor Partnership, c/o Wash. Association of Churches, 419 Occidental Ave., South, #201, Seattle, WA 98104; Tel. (206)625-9790 Fax (206)625-9791; Contact: Rev. John Boonstra

WISCONSIN

Faith Community for Worker Justice, 2128 N. 73rd St., Wauwatosa, WI 53213; Tel. (414)771-7250; Fax (414)771-0509; Contact: Mr. Bill Lange

National Interreligious Service Board for Conscientious Objectors

NISBCO, formed in 1940, is a nonprofit service organization supported by individual contributions and relating to more than thirty religious organizations. Its purpose is to defend and extend the rights of conscientious objectors to war and organized violence. NISBCO provides information on how to register for the draft and to document ones convictions and qualify as a conscientious objector, how to cope with penalties if one does not cooperate, and how to qualify as a conscientious objector while in the Armed Forces. It also provides more general information for counselors and the public about conscientious objection, military service and the operation of the draft and possible programs for national service. It provides resources concerning conscientious objector status in other countries.

As a national resource center it assists research in its area of interest including the peace witness of religious bodies. Its staff provides referral to local counselors and attorneys and professional support for them. Through publications and speaking, NISBCO encourages people to decide for themselves what they believe about participation in war and to act on the basis of the dictates of their own informed consciences.

Headquarters

1830 Connecticut Ave. NW, Washington, DC 20009-5732 Tel. (202)483-2220 Fax (202) 483-1246
Email: nisbco@igc.apc.org
Website: http://www. nisbco.org
Media Contact, Exec. Dir., Shazia N. Anwar

Officers

Exec. Dir., J.E. McNeil
Chpsn., Jonathan Ogle
Vice-Chpsn., Clayton Ramey
Sec., William Galvin
Treas., John Michael Sophos

National Religious Broadcasters

National Religious Broadcasters is an association of more than 1,000 organizations which produce religious programs for radio and television and other forms of electronic mass media or operate stations carrying predominately religious programs. NRB member organizations are responsible for more than 75 percent of all religious radio and television in the United States, reaching an average weekly audience of millions by radio, television, and other broadcast media.

Dedicated to the communication of the Gospel, NRB was founded in 1944 to safeguard free and complete access to the broadcast media. By encouraging the development of Christian programs and stations, NRB helps make it possible for millions to hear the good news of Jesus Christ through the electronic media.

Headquarters

7839 Ashton Ave., Manassas, VA 20109 Tel. (703)330-7000 Fax (703)330-7100
Email: info@nrb.org
Website: http://www.nrb.org

Media Contact, Pres., Brandt Gustavson; Vice-Pres., Michael Glenn

Officers
Chmn., David W. Clark, Family Net, Ft. Worth, TX
1st Vice Chmn., Thomas Rogeberg, In Touch Min., Atlanta, GA.
2nd Vice Chmn., Glenn Plummer, Christian Television Network, Detroit, MI
Sec., Wayne Pederson, Skylight Network, Minneapolis, MN
Treas., John Corts, Billy Graham Evan. Assoc., Minneapolis, MN

National Woman's Christian Temperance Union

The National WCTU is a not-for-profit, non-partisan, interdenominational organization dedicated to the education of our nations citizens, especially children and teens, on the harmful effects of alcoholic beverages, other drugs and tobacco on the human body and the society in which we live. The WCTU believes in a strong family unit and, through legislation, education and prayer, works to strengthen the home and family.

WCTU, which began in 1874 with the motto, For God and Home and Every Land, is organized in 58 countries.

Headquarters
1730 Chicago Ave., Evanston, IL 60201 Tel. (708)864-1396
Website: http://www.wctu.org
Media Contact, Sarah F. Ward, Tel. 765-345-7600

Officers
Pres., Sarah F. Ward, 33 N. Franklin, Knightstown, IN 46148
Email: sarah@wctu.org
Vice-Pres., Rita Wert, 2250 Creek Hill Rd., Lancaster, PA 17601
Promotion Dir., Nancy Zabel, 1730 Chicago Ave., Evanston, IL 60201-4585
Treas., Faye Pohl, P.O. Box 739, Meade, KS 67864
Rec. Sec., Dorothy Russell, 18900 Nestueca Dr., Cloverdale, OR 97112

MEMBER ORGANIZATIONS
Loyal Temperance Legion (LTL), for boys and girls ages 6-12
Youth Temperance Council (YTC), for teens through college age

North American Baptist Fellowship

Organized in 1964, the North American Baptist Fellowship is a voluntary organization of Baptist Conventions in Canada and the United States, functioning as a regional body within the Baptist World Alliance. Its objectives are: (a) to promote fellowship and cooperation among Baptists in North America and (b) to further the aims and objectives of the Baptist World Alliance so far as these affect the life of the Baptist churches in North America. Its membership, however, is not identical with the North American membership of the Baptist World Alliance.

Church membership of the Fellowship bodies is more than 28 million.

The NABF assembles representatives of the member bodies once a year for exchange of information and views in such fields as evangelism and education, missions, stewardship promotion, lay activities and theological education. It conducts occasional consultations for denominational leaders on such subjects as church extension. It encourages cooperation at the city and county level where churches of more than one member group are located.

Headquarters
Baptist World Alliance Bldg., 6733 Curran St., McLean, VA 22101
Email: nabf@bwanet.org
Website: http://www. bwanet.org
Media Contact, Dr. Denton Lotz

Officers
Pres., Dr. Morris M. Chapman, 901 Commerce St., Nashville, TN 37203
Vice-Pres., Dr. Robert Ricker, 2002 S. Arlington Heights Rd., Arlington Heights, IL 60005
Vice-Pres., Dr. Tyronne Pitts, 601 50th St., NE, Washington, DC 20019
Vice-Pres., Dr. Robert Wilkins, 7185 Millcreek Dr. Mississauga, ON 15N 5R4, Canada

MEMBER BODIES
American Baptist Churches in the USA
Baptist General Conference
Canadian Baptist Federation
General Association of General Baptists
National Baptist Convention of America
National Baptist Convention, USA, Inc.
Progressive National Baptist Convention, Inc.
Seventh Day Baptist General Conference
North American Baptist Conference
Southern Baptist Convention

Oikocredit: Ecumenical Development Cooperative Society

Based in the Netherlands, EDCS is often called the churches bank for the poor. EDCS borrows funds from churches, religious communities and concerned individuals and re-lends the funds to enterprises operated by low-income communities. Launched in 1975 through an initiative of the World Council of Churches, EDCS is organized as a cooperative of religious institutions and is governed by annual membership meetings and an elected board of religious leaders and development and financial professionals.

An international network of 15 EDCS Regional Managers is responsible for lending funds to cooperative enterprises and microcredit institutions. At the present time over $50 million is at work in coffee shops, fishing enterprises, handicraft production, truck farming, and many other commercial ventures owned and operated by poor people.

EDCS is represented in the United States by the Ecumenical Development Corporation- USA (EDC-USA), a 501(c)3 non-profit corporation. American individuals and congregations can invest in EDCS by purchasing one, three, and five year notes paying 0-2% interest that are issued by EDC-USA.

U.S. Headquarters
475 Riverside Dr., 16th Floor, New York, NY 10115 Tel. (212)870-2725 Fax (212)870-2722
Email: edcusa@erols.com
Media Contact, Regional Manager for North America, The Rev. Louis L. Knowles

Officers, EDC-USA
Chpsn., The Rev. Dr. DarEll Weist
Vice-Chpsn., Thomas Dowdell
Treas., Bruce Foresman
Sec., Suzanne Sattler, IHM

Parish Resource Center, Inc.

Parish Resource Center, Inc. promotes, establishes, nurtures and accredits local Affiliate Parish Resource Centers. Affiliate centers educate, equip and strengthen subscribing congregations of all faiths by providing professional consultants, resource materials and workshops. The Parish Resource Center was founded in 1976. In 1999, there were six free-standing affiliates located in Lancaster, PA; Long Island, NY; South Bend, IN.; Denver, CO.; Dayton, OH and New York City. These centers serve congregations from 49 faith traditions.

Headquarters
633 Community Way, Lancaster, PA 17603 Tel. (717)299-2223 Fax (717)299-7229
Email: prcinc@redrose.net
Media Contact, Pres., Dr. D. Douglas Whiting

Officers
Chair, Richard J. Ashby, Jr.
Vice-Chair, Margaret M. Obrecht
Sec., Dr. Robert Webber
Treas., Stephen C. Eyre
Pres., Dr. D. Douglas Whiting

Pentecostal/Charismatic Churches of North America

The Pentecostal/Charismatic Churches of North America (PCCNA) was organized October 19, 1994, in Memphis TN. This organizational meeting came the day after the Pentecostal Fellowship of North America (PFNA) voted itself out of existence in order to make way for the new fellowship.

The PFNA had been formed in October 1948 in Des Moines, IA. It was composed of white-led Pentecostal denominations. The move to develop a multiracial fellowship began when the PFNA Board of Administration initiated a series of discussions with African-American Pentecostal leaders. The first meeting was held July 10-11, 1992, in Dallas, TX. A second meeting convened in Phoenix, AZ, January 4-5, 1993. On January 10-11, 1994, 20 representatives from each of the two groups met in Memphis to make final plans for a Dialogue which was held in Memphis, October 1994.

This racial reconciliation meeting has been called The Memphis Miracle. During this meeting the PFNA was disbanded, and the PCCNA was organized. The new organization quickly adopted the Racial Reconciliation Manifesto. Subsequent meetings were held in Memphis, TN (1996), Washington, DC (1997), Tulsa, OK (1998), and Hampton, VA (1999)

Forty thousand copies of the PCCNA- sponsored magazines inaugural issue of *Reconciliation* were published in June, 1998 and distributed to pastors in PCCNA- member churches. Dr. Harold D. Hunter and Dr. Cecil M. Robeck, Jr., are co-editors of this publication.

Headquarters
1910 W. Sunset Blvd. Ste. 200, Los Angeles, CA 90026-0176 Tel. (213)484-2400, ext. 309 Fax (213)413-3824
Email: comm@foursquare.org
Website: http://www. iphc.org/pccna/index.html
Media Contact, Dr. Ronald Williams

Executive Committee
Co-Chpsn., Bishop Gilbert E. Patterson, 240 E. Raines Rd., Memphis, TN 38109
Co-Chpsn., Rev. Thomas Trask, 1445 Boonville Ave., Springfield, MO 65802
1st. Vice-Chpsn., Bishop Barbara Amos, 1010 East 26th St., Norfolk, VA 23504
2nd Vice-Chpsn., Rev. Rev. Billy Joe Daugherty, 7700 S. Lewis, Tulsa, OK 74136-6600
Sec., Rev. Oswill Williams, 3720 N Keith Street, Cleveland, TN 37320
Treas., Dr. Ronald Williams, P.O. Box 26902, Los Angeles, CA 90026
Co-Editors of Reconciliation: Dr. Harold D. Hunter, PO Box 12609, Oklahoma City, OK 73157; Dr. Cecil M. Robeck, Jr., 135 North Oakland Ave., Pasadena, CA 91182
Members: Bishop Ithiel Clemmons, 221 Kingston Ave., Brooklyn, NY 11213; Rev. Bishop Rodderick Ceasar, 110-25 Buy Brewer Blvd., Jamaica Queens, NY 11433; Bishop George D. McKinney, 5825 Imperial Ave., San Diego, CA 92114; Bishop James Leggett, P.O. Box 12609, Oklahoma City, OK 73157; Dr. Paul Walker, 2055 Mount Paran Rd., NW, Atlanta, GA 30327; Rev. Ann Gimenez, 640 Kempsville Rd., Virginia Beach, VA 23464
Advisors: Bishop B.E. Underwood, 172 Tanglewood South, Royston, GA 30662; Rev. Perry Gillum, 3720 N. Keith St., Cleveland, TN 37320; Dr. Vinson Synan, Regent University, P.O.Box 1056, Chesapeake, VA 23327; Dr. Ray Hughes, P.O.Box 2430, Cleveland, TN 37320

Project Equality, Inc.

Project Equality is a non-profit national interfaith program for affirmative action and equal employment opportunity.

Project Equality serves as a central agency to receive and validate the equal employment commitment of suppliers of goods and services to sponsoring organizations and participating institutions, congregations and individuals. Employers filing an accepted Annual Participation Report are included in the Project Equality Buyers Guide.

Workshops, training events and consultant services in affirmative action, diversity, and equal employment practices in recruitment, selection, placement, transfer, promotion, discipline and discharge are also available to sponsors and participants.

Headquarters

Pres., 7132 Main St., Kansas City, MO 64114-1406 Tel. (816)361-9222 or toll free 1877-PE-IS-EEO Fax (816)361-8997
Email: KirkP@projectequality.org
Website: http://www.projectequality.org
Media Contact, Pres., Rev. Kirk P. Perucca

Officers

Chpsn., Donald Hayashi
Vice-Chpsn., Cheryl Hammond-Hopewell
Sec., Barbara George
Treas., Joan Green
Pres., Rev. Kirk P. Perucca

SPONSORS/ENDORSING ORGANIZATIONS

American Baptist Churches in the U.S.A.
American Friends Service Committee
American Jewish Committee
Assoc. Of Junior Leagues, Intl.
Central Conference of American Rabbis
Church of the Brethren
Church Women United
Consultation on Church Union
The Episcopal Church
Evangelical Lutheran Church in America
Nat. Assoc.of Church Personnel Administrators
National Council of Churches of Christ in the U.S.A.
National Education Association
Presbyterian Church (USA)
Reformed Church in America
Reorganized Church of Jesus Christ of Latter-Day Saints
Roman Catholic Dioceses & Religious Orders
The United Methodist Church
Unitarian Universalist Association
Union of American Hebrew Congregations
United Church of Christ
United Methodist Assoc. of Health & Welfare Ministries
YWCA of the USA

Protestant Radio and Television Center, Inc.

The Protestant Radio and Television Center, Inc. (PRTVC) is an interdenominational organization dedicated to the purpose of creating, producing, marketing and distributing audio-visual products for the non-profit sector. Its primary constituency is religious, educational and service-oriented groups. The Flagship production is the weekly radio show The Protestant Hour.

Chartered in 1949, PRTVC provides a state-of-the-art studio facility, professional staff and a talent pool for radio, TV, cassettes and other forms of media production.

Affiliate members include the Episcopal Radio & TV Foundation, Evangelical Lutheran Church in America, Presbyterian Church (U.S.A.), United Methodist Communications, Agnes Scott College, Candler School of Theology, Emory University and Columbia Theological Seminary.

Headquarters

1727 Clifton Rd., NE, Atlanta, GA 30329 Tel. (404)634-3324 Fax (404)634-3326
Media Contact, Sandra Rogers

Officers

Bd. Chpsn., Dr. Gerald Troutman
Vice-Chpsn., Dale VanCantfort
Pres., J. Paul Howard
Treas., William W. Horlock
Sec., Betty Chilton

The Religion Communicators Council, Inc.

RCC is an international, interfaith, interdisciplinary association of professional communicators who work for religious groups and causes. It was founded in 1929 and is the oldest non-profit professional public relations organization in the world. RCCs 600 members include those who work in communications and related fields for church-related institutions, denominational agencies, non-and interdenominational organizations and communications firms who primarily serve religious organizations.

Members represent a wide range of faiths, including Presbyterian, Baptist, Methodist, Lutheran, Episcopalian, Mennonite, Roman Catholic, Seventh-day Adventist, Jewish, Salvation Army, Brethren, Bahá'í, Disciples, Latter-Day Saints and others.

On the national level, RCC sponsors an annual three-day convention, and has published five editions of a *Religious Public Relations Handbook* for churches and church organizations (6th Edition to be published in 1999), and a videostrip, The Church at Jackrabbit Junction. Members receive a quarterly newsletter (*Counselor*). RCC also co-sponsors an annual national satellite teleconference. There are 11 regional chapters.

RCC administers the annual Wilbur Awards competition to recognize high quality coverage of religious values and issues in the public media. Wilbur winners include producers, reporters, editors and broadcasters nationwide. To recognize communications excellence within church communities, RCC also sponsors the annual DeRose-Hinkhouse Awards for its own members.

In 1970, 1980 and 1990, RCC initiated a global Religious Communications Congress bringing together thousands of persons from western, eastern and third-world nations who are involved in communicating religious faith. Another Congress is planned for 2000 in Chicago, IL. March 29-April 1, 2000, Chicago Marriott Downtown Hotel.

Headquarters

475 Riverside Dr., Rm. 1948A, New York, NY 10115-1948 Tel. (212)870-2985 Fax (212) 870-3578

Website: http://www.rprc.org

Officers

Pres., Thomas R. May, National Bible Association, 1865 Broadway, New York, NY 10023 Tel. (212)408-1432

Vice-Pres., Richard Duerksen, Director, Spiritual Devlopment, Florida Hospital, 601 East Rollins St., Orlando, FL 32803 Tel. (407)895-7782

Religion In American Life, Inc.

Religion In American Life (RIAL) is a unique cooperative program of some 50 major national religious groups (Catholic, Eastern Orthodox, Jewish, Protestant, Muslim, etc.). It provides services for denominationally-supported, congregation-based outreach and growth projects such as the current Invite a Friend program. These projects are promoted through national advertising campaigns reaching the American public by the use of all media. The ad campaigns are produced by a volunteer agency with production/distribution and administration costs funded by denominations and business groups, as well as by individuals.

Since 1949, RIAL ad campaign projects have been among the much coveted major campaigns of The Advertising Council. This results in as much as $30 million worth of time and space in a single year, contributed by media as a public service. Through RIAL, religious groups demonstrate respect for other traditions and the value of religious freedom. The RIAL program also includes seminars and symposia, research and leadership awards.

Headquarters

2 Queenston Pl., Rm. 200, Princeton, NJ 08540 Tel. (609)921-3639 Fax (609)921-0551

Media Contact, Manager, Sharon E. Lloyd, Tel. (609)921-3639

Executive Committee

Natl. Chpsn., Thomas S. Johnson, Chairman & CEO, Greenpoint Bank, NY

Chpsn. of Bd., Robert A. Wilson

Vice-Chpsns.: Bishop Khajag Barsamian, Primate (Armenian Church of America);The Rev. Dr. M. William Howard, (President, New York Theological Seminary); Most Rev. William Cardinal Keeler, (Archbishop of Baltimore); Rabbi Ronald B. Sobel, (Cong. Emanu-El of the City of N.Y.)

Sec.,Sonia Francis, (The Episcopal Church)

Treas., Robertson H. Bennett

Staff

Pres., -vacant-

Manager, Sharon E. Lloyd

Religion News Service

Religion News Service (RNS) has provided news and information to the media for more than 60 years. Owned by the Newhouse News Service, it is staffed by veteran jounalists who cover stories on all of the world religions as well as trends in ethics, morality and spirituality.

RNS provides a daily news service, a weekly news report, and photo and graphic services. The daily service is available via the AP Data Features wire, fax, Ecunet, or e-mail. The weekly report is available electronically or by mail. Photos and graphics are supplied electronically.

Headquarters

1101 Connecticut Ave. NW, Ste. 350, Washington, DC 20036 Tel. (202)463-8777 Fax (202) 463-0033

Email: info@religionnews.com

Website: http://www. religionnews.com

Media Contact, Dale Hanson Bourke

Officers

Publisher, Dale Hanson Bourke

Editor, David Anderson

Religion Newswriters Association

Founded in 1949, the RNA is a professional association of religion news editors and reporters on secular daily and weekly newspapers, news services, news magazines, radio and television stations. It sponsors five annual contests for excellence in religion news coverage in the secular press. Annual meetings are held anytimefrom late spring to early fall.

Headquarters

P.O. Box 2037, Westerville, OH 43086 Tel. (614)891-9001 Fax (614) 891-9774

Email: rnastuff@aol.com

Website: http://www.rna.org

Media Contact, Exec. Dir., Debra Mason

Officers

Pres., Gayle White, Journal Constitution, Atlanta, GA

1st Vice-Pres., David Briggs, Cleveland Plein Dealer

2nd Vice-Pres., Sandy Dolbee, San Diego Union Tribune, San Diego, CA

Treas., Jeff Sheler, U.S. News and World Report
Sec.,

Presbyterian Church (U.S.A.)
United Church of Christ

Religious Conference Management Association, Inc.

The Religious Conference Management Association, Inc. (RCMA) is an interfaith, non-profit, professional organization of men and women who have responsibility for planning and/or managing meetings, seminars, conferences, conventions, assemblies or other gatherings for religious organizations.

Founded in 1972, RCMA is dedicated to promoting the highest professional performance by its members and associate members through the mutual exchange of ideas, techniques and methods.

Today RCMA has more than 3,000 members and associate members.

The association conducts an annual conference and exposition which provides a forum for its membership to gain increased knowledge in the arts and sciences of religious meeting planning and management.

Headquarters

One RCA Dome, Ste. 120, Indianapolis, IN 46225 Tel. (317)632-1888 Fax (317)632-7909
Website: http://www.aip.com
Media Contact, Exec. Dir., Dr. DeWayne S. Woodring

Officers

Pres., Dr. Jack Stone, Church of the Nazarene, 6401 The Paswo, Kansas City, MO 64131-1213
Vice-Pres., Ms. Lola Conrad, General Council on Ministries, The United Methodist Church, 60 W. Riverview Avenue, Dayton, OH 45406
Sec.-Treas., Dr. Melvin Worthington, Natl. Assoc. of Free Will Baptists, P.O. Box 5002, Antioch, TN 37011-5002
Exec. Dir., Dr. DeWayne S. Woodring

United Ministries in Higher Education

United Ministries in Higher Education is a cooperative effort to provide religious programs and services to those engaged in higher education ministries.

Headquarters

7407 Steele Creek Rd., Charlotte, NC 28217 Tel. (704)588-2182 Fax (704)588-3652
Media Contact, Res. Sec., Linda Danby Freeman
Email: linda_freeman@ecunet.org

Officers

Treas., Linda Danby Freeman
Personnel Service, Kathy Carson, 11720 Borman Dr., Ste. 240, St.Louis, MO 63146 Tel. (314)991-3000 Fax (314)991-2957
Resource Center, Linda Danby Freeman

PARTICIPATING DENOMINATIONS
Christian Church (Disciples of Christ)

United Religions Initiative

The purpose of the United Religions Initiative is to create the United Religions a permanent public forum where people of many faiths gather in mutual respect to pursue justice, healing and peace, with reverence for all life. The United Religions will have global visibility and stature, and will be a vital presence in local communities all over the world. The goal of the United Religions Initiative is to give birth to the United Religions in June 2000.

In 1993, the Rt. Rev. William Swing, Bishop of the Episcopal Diocese of California, was asked by the United Nations to host an interfaith service to commemorate 50 years of political leaders working together daily for peace. As he thought of religions role in armed conflicts all over the world, he wondered why there was no permanent forum where the worlds religions leaders worked together daily for peace. If a United Nations, why not a United Religions?

During the next three years, Bishop Swing and a small interfaith group consulted with many leaders in interfaith dialogue and hosted an international youth conference. In 1996, Bishop Swing undertook a three-month pilgrimage around the world. The vision of a United Religions became part of a worldwide conversation rooted in over 100 years of international interfaith work.

Launched at its first global summit in San Francisco in June 1996, the United Religions Initiative has rapidly become one of the most ambitious and hopeful interreligious initiatives in the world. In the past two years, over 1,000 participants at six regional conferences on four continents, and three global summits have developed the vision of a United Religions. These grassroots and global leaders from over 40 spiritual traditions have begun many pilot projects models of a United Religions in action. In two years, world of the United Religions Initiative has reached more than a million people throughout the world. The United Religions Initiative has an active presence on every continent. Its global headquarters and interfaith Board of Directors are in San Francisco.

Headquarters

P.O. Box 29242, San Francisco, CA 94129-0242 Tel. (415)561-2300 Fax (415)562-2313
Email: office@united-religions.org
Website: www.united-religions.org
Media Contact: Barbara H. Hartford, Operations Manager

Staff

Exec Dir., The Rev. Cn. Charles Gibbs
Vice-Pres., The Rev. William Rankin
Operations Mgr., Ms. Barbara Hartford
Project Mgr., Ms. Sally Mahe Ackerly
Project Mgr., Mr. Paul Andrews
Latin American Coord., Fr. Luis Dolan

49

European Coord., Mr. Josef Boehle
SIGMA/ African Coord., Mr. Godwin Hlatshwayo
SIGMA, Mr. David Cooperrider
SIGMA, Mr. Gurudev Khalsa
The Chaordic Alliance, Mr. Dee Hock
D.B. Robbins Consulting, Ms. Diane Robbins
Corporation for Positive Change, Ms. Diana Whitney
Youth Projects, Ms. Jennifer Peace

Board Members
Pres., Bishop William Swing
Chair, Ms. Rita Semel
Vice-Chair, Rev. Dr. Jack Lundin
Treas., Mr. Rick Murray
Sec., Rev. Paul Chaffee

Vellore Christian Medical College Board (USA), Inc.

The Vellore Christian Medical College Board has been linked since 1900 to the vision of the young

American medical doctor, Ida S. Scudder. Dr. Idas dream initially was to ensure quality health care for women and children in India.

American women and men representing several church denominations wanted to be a part of Dr. Idas dream and in 1916 recommended Vellore as the site for the proposed Missionary Medical College for Women. Since 1947 the Christian Medical College has admitted women and men. The hospital has a commitment to serve all regardless of ability to pay. The partnership between Vellore India and Vellore USA has continued uninterrupted to the present time.

Headquarters
475 Riverside Dr., Rm. 243, New York, NY 10115 Tel. (212)870-2640 Fax (212)870-2173
Email: usaboard@vellorecmc.org
Website: http://www.vellorecmc.org
Media Contact, President, Rev. William Salmond
Email: wsalmond@vellorecmc.org

Officers
Chair., Alfred E. Berthold, 2452 Club Rd., Columbus, OH 43221
Vice-Chair., Miriam Ballert, 7104 Olde Oak Ct., Prospect, KY 40059
Sec., Michael Holt, P.O. Box 509, Franklin Lakes, NJ 07417
Treas., Anish Mathai, 235 W. 56th St., Apt. 25M, New York, NY 10119

The World Conference on Religion and Peace (WCRP/USA)

The World Conference on Religion and Peace in the United States (WCRP/USA) provides a forum for the nations religious bodies based upon respect for religious differences. In todays world cooperation among religions offers an important opportunity to mobilize and coordinate the great moral and sociological capacities for constructive action inherent in religious communities.

WCRP/USA provides American religious bodies with opportunities for the following: to clarify their respective orientation to both national and international social concerns; to coordinate their efforts with other religious groups on behalf of widely-shared concerns; to design, undertake and evaluate joint action projects; and to communicate and collaborate with similar national religious forums organized by WCRP, and with other organizations as well, around the world.

Headquarters
WCRP/USA OFFICE, 777 United Nations Plaza, New York, NY 10017 Tel. (212)687-2163 Fax (212)983-0566
Email: wcrp_usa@wcrp.org
Media Contact, Ms. Ann Borroughs

Officers
Sec. Gen., Mr. Antonios Kireopoulos
Moderator, V. Rev. Leonid Kishkovsky

World Council of Churches, United States Office

The United States Conference of the World Council of Churches was formed in 1938 when the WCC itself was still in the Process of Formation. Henry Smith Leiper, an American with many national and international connections, was given the title of Associate General Secretary of the WCC and asked to carry out WCC work in the U.S. After the World Council of Churches was officially born in 1948 in Amsterdam, Netherlands, Leiper raised millions of dollars for WCC programs.

Today the U.S. Conference of the WCC is composed of representatives of U.S. member churches of the worldwide body. The U.S. Office of the WCC works to develop relationships among the churches, advance the work of WCC and interpret the council in the United States.

Headquarters
475 Riverside Dr., Rm. 915, New York, NY 10115 Tel. (212)870-2533 Fax (212)870-2528
Email: worldcoun@mail.wcc-coe.org
Website: http://www.wcc-coe.org
Media Contact, Philip E. Jenks

Officers
WCC President from North America, Rev. Kathryn Bannister, United Methodist Church
Moderator, Bishop Vinton R. Anderson, African Methodist Episcopal Church
Vice-Moderator, The Rev. Leonid Kishkovsky, Orthodox Church in America
Secretary, Kristine Thompson, Presbyterian Church (USA)

Staff
Exec. Dir., Jean S. Stromberg, Tel. (212)870-2522
Comm. & Publ. Officer, Philip E. Jenks, Tel. (212)870-3193
Office Admn., Sonia P. Omulepu, (212)870-2470

World Day of Prayer

World Day of Prayer is an ecumenical movement initiated and carried out by Christian women in 170 countries who conduct a common day of prayer on the first Friday of March to which all people are welcome. There is an annual theme for the worship service that has been prepared by women in a different country each year. For 2000 the women of Indonesia have prepared a worship service on the theme, "Talitha Kumi-Young Woman Stand Up". The WDP motto is informed prayer and prayerful action. The offering at this service is gathered by each WDP National/Regional Committee and given to help people who are in need.

Headquarters

World Day of Prayer International Comm., 475 Riverside Dr., Rm. 560, New York, NY 10115 Tel. (212)870-3049 Fax (212)870-3587 Email: WDPIC@aol.com
Media Contact, Exec. Dir., Eileen King

Officers

Chairperson, Yvonne Harrison
Treasurer, Karen Prudente
North America, Susan Shank Mix (USA); Sylvia Lisk Vanhaverbeke (Canada)
Africa, Sarie Jansen; Karen Ngigi
Asia, Shunila Ruth; Jong Ok Lee
Caribbean, Waveney Benjamin; Neva Edwards
Europe, Inge Lise Lollike; Alena Naimanova
Latin America, Renee Carter; Inez Proverbs
Middle East, Aida Haddad; Nadia Menes
Pacific, Margaret Kenna; Gwen Tulo
Member at Large, Maria Gabriela Trimbitas

World Methodist Council-North American Section

The World Methodist Council, one of the 30 or so Christian World Communions, shares a general tradition which is common to all Christians.

The world organization of Methodists and related United Churches is comprised of 73 churches with roots in the Methodist tradition. These churches found in 108 countries have a membership of more than 33 million.

The Councils North American Section, comprised of nine Methodist and United Church denominations, provides a regional focus for the Council in Canada, the United States and Mexico. The North American Section meets at the time of the quinquennial World Conference and Council, and separately as Section between world meetings. The Section met in Rio de Janeiro, Brazil in August 1996 during the 17th World Methodist Conference to elect its officers for the 1997-2001 quinquennium.

North American Churches related to the World Methodist Council have a membership of approximately 15 million and a church community of more than 29 million.

Headquarters

P.O. Box 518, Lake Junaluska, NC 28745 Tel. (828)456-9432 Fax (828)456-9433
Email: wmc6@juno.com
Website: worldmethodistcouncil.org
Media Contact, Gen. Sec., Joe Hale

Officers

Section Pres., Bishop Neil L. Irons, 900 S. Arlington Ave., Rm. 214, Harrisburg, PA 17109-5086 Tel. (717)652-6705 Fax (717)652-5109
First Vice-Pres., Bishop Thomas L. Hoyt, CME Church
Vice-Pres.: Bishop John R. Bryant, AME Church; Bishop Cecil Bishop, AMEZ Church; Bishop Richard D. Snyder, Free Methodist Church; Bishop Gracela Alverez, Methodist Church in Mexico; Bishop Keith Elford, Free Methodist Church of Canada; Dr. Brian D. Thorpe, United Church of Canada; Dr. Earle L. Wilson, The Wesleyan Church; Chairman, Finance Committee, Dr. Donald V. Fites
Treas., Dr. James W. Holsinger, Jr.
Asst. Treas., Edna Alsdurf
General Sec., Dr. Joe Hale
World Officers from North America: Dr. Frances M. Alguire; Dr. Maxie D. Dunnam; Bishop Donald Ming

YMCA of the USA

The YMCA is one of the largest private voluntary organizations in the world, serving about 30 million people in more than 100 countries. In the United States, more than 2,000 local branches, units, camps and centers annually serve more than 14 million people of all ages, races and abilities. About half of those served are female. No one is turned away because of an inability to pay.

The Y teaches youngsters to swim, organizes youth basketball games and offers adult aerobics. But the Y represents more than fitness it works to strengthen families and help people develop values and behavior that are consistent with Christian principles.

The Y offers hundreds of programs including day camp for children, child care, exercise for people with disabilities, teen clubs, environmental programs, substance abuse prevention, family nights, job training and many more programs from infant mortality prevention to overnight camping for seniors.

The kind of programs offered at a YMCA will vary; each is controlled by volunteer board members who make their own program, policy, and financial decisions based on the special needs of their community. In its own way, every Y works to build strong kids, strong families, and strong communities.

The YMCA was founded in London, England, in 1844 by George Williams and friends who lived and worked together as clerks. Their goal was to save other live-in clerks from the wicked

51

life of the London streets. The first members were evangelical Protestants who prayed and studied the Bible as an alternative to vice. The Y has always been nonsectarian and today accepts those of all faiths at all levels of the organization.

Headquarters
101 N. Wacker Dr., Chicago, IL 60606 Tel. (312)977-0031 Fax (312)977-9063
Website: http://www.ymca.net
Media Contact, Media Relations Manager, Arnie Collins

Officers
Board Chpsn., Daniel E. Emerson
Exec. Dir., David R. Mercer
(Int.) Public Relations Assoc., Mary Pyke Gover

Young Womens Christian Association of the United States
The YWCA of the U.S.A. is comprised of 364 affiliates in communities and on college campuses across the United States. It serves one million members and program participants. It seeks to empower women and girls to enable them, coming together across lines of age, race, religious belief, economic and occupational status to make a significant contribution to the elimination of racism and the achievement of peace, justice, freedom and dignity for all people. Its leadership is vested in a National Board, whose functions are to unite into an effective continuing organization the autonomous member Associations for furthering the purposes of the National Association and to participate in the work of the World YWCA.

Headquarters
Empire State Building,350 fifth Ave., Ste. 301 New York, NY 10118 Tel. (212)273-7800 Fax (212)465-2281
Email: HN2062@handsnet.org
Website: http://www.ywca.org
Media Contact, Chief of Staff, Cynthia Sutliff

Officers
National Pres., Alexine Clement Jackson
Sec., Tina Maree Herrera
Cheif Exec. Officer, Prema Mathai-Davis

Youth for Christ/USA
Founded in 1944, as part of the body of Christ, our vision is to see every young person in every people group in every nation have the opportunity to make an informed decision to be a follower of Jesus Christ and become a part of a local church.

There are 237 locally controlled YFC programs serving in cities and metropolitan areas of the United States.

YFCs Campus Life Club program involves teens who attend approximately 1,557 high schools in the United States. YFCs staff now numbers approximately 1,000. In addition, near-

ly 21,000 part-time and volunteer staff supplement the full-time staff. Youth Guidance, a ministry for nonschool-oriented youth includes group homes, court referrals, institutional services and neighborhood ministries. The year-round conference and camping program involves approximately 200,000 young people each year. Other ministries include DC Ministries, World Outreach, Project Serve, and Teen Moms. Independent, indigenous YFC organizations also work in 127 countries overseas.

Headquarters
U.S. Headquarters, P.O. Box 228822, Denver, CO 80222 Te. (303)843-9000 Fax (303)843-9002
Canadian Organization, 1212-31 Avenue NE< #540, Calgary, AB T2E7S8
Website: http://www.yfc.org
Media Contact, Pres., Roger Cross

Officers
United States, president, Roger Cross
Canada, Pres., Randy L. Steinwand
Intl. Organization: Acting Pres., Jean-Jacques Weiler

2. Canadian Cooperative Organizations, National

In most cases the organizations listed here work on a national level and cooperate across denominational lines. Regional cooperative organizations in Canada are listed in Directory 8, "Canadian Regional and Local Ecumenical Bodies."

Aboriginal Rights Coalition (Project North)

ARC works towards the transformation of the relationship between Canadian society and Aboriginal peoples. Through education, research, advocacy and action, this coalition of national churches, other faith bodies, and regional groups works in solidarity with Aboriginal peoples. ARC seeks to embody true partnership by building authentic allinces in the global struggle for Aboriginal justice.

Headquarters
153 Laurier Ave. East, 2nd Floor, Ottawa, ON K1N 6N8 Tel. (613)235-9956 Fax (613)235-1302
Email: arc@istar.ca
Media Contact, Natl. Coord., Ed Bianchi

Officers
Chpsn.: Joe Gunn
Natl. Coord., Ed Bianchi

MEMBER ORGANIZATIONS
Anglican Church of Canada
Canadian Conference of Catholic Bishops
Canadian Religious Conference
Council of Christian Reformed Churches in Canada
Evangelical Lutheran Church in Canada
Mennonite Central Committee
Oblate Conference in Canada
Presbyterian Church of Canada
Religious Society of Friends (Quakers)
Society of Jesus (Jesuits)
Canadian Unitarian Council
United Church of Canada

Alliance For Life-Alliance Pour La Vie

Alliance For Life was incorporated in 1972 to promote the right to life from conception to natural death. A registered charity for the purpose of education, Alliance conducts research on all life issues: abortion, infanticide, euthanasia and more. Alliance publishes materials to disseminate the information gained through that research. Alliance has prepared a one-hour documentary on untimely pregnancy and maintains a toll-free line to counsel women with inconveniently timed pregnancies and to help others suffering from post-abortion syndrome.

Alliance is the umbrella organization for 245 pro-life organizations in Canada. Governed by a Board of Directors composed of representatives from all provinces, it holds annual conferences in alternating provinces. Conferences are open to the public.

In 1992, Alliance For Life was split to permit the establishment of Alliance Action, Inc., a non-profit, non-charitable entity which is mandated to do advocacy work which Alliance For Life cannot do as a charity. It is located at the same address and publishes Pro Life News magazine 10 times annually.

Headquarters
B1-90 Garry St., Winnipeg, MB R3C 4H1 Tel. (204)942-4772 Fax (204)943-9283
Media Contact, Exec. Dir., Anna M. Desilets

Officers
Pres., Chuck Smith
1st Vice-Pres., Rachel Murray
Treas., Jim Arsenault
Sec., Keith McCormick

Alliance Action Officers
Pres., Rachel Murray
Media Contact, Exec. Dir., Ingrid Krueger, Tel. (204)943-5273 Fax (204)943-9283
1st Vice-Pres., Chuck Smith
Treas., Jim Arsenault
Sec., Keith McCormick
Medical Advisor, Dr. J. L. Reynolds

Association of Canadian Bible Colleges

The Association brings into cooperative association Bible colleges in Canada that are evangelical in doctrine and whose objectives are similar. Services are provided to improve the quality of Bible college education in Canada and to further the interests of the Association by means of conferences, seminars, cooperative undertakings, information services, research, publications and other projects.

Headquarters
Box 4000, Three Hills, AB T0M 2N0 Tel. (403) 443-3051 Fax (403)443-5540
Media Contact, Sec./Treas., Peter Doell, Email: peter.doell@pbi.ab.ca

Officers
Pres., Larry J. McKinney, Tel. (204)433-7488 Fax (204)433-7158
Vice-Pres., James Cianca, Tel. (519)434-6801 Fax (519)434-4998

Sec./Treas., Peter Doell, Tel. (403)443-3051 Fax (403)443-5540

Members-at-Large: Virginia Sherman, Tel. (403)284-5100 Fax (403)220-9567; David Boyd, Tel. (705)748-9111 Fax (705)748-3931; Walter Unger, Tel. (604)853-3358 Fax (604) 853-3063

Canadian Bible Society

As early as 1804, the British and Foreign Bible Society was at work in Canada. The oldest Bible Society branch is at Truro, Nova Scotia, and has been functioning continually since 1810. In 1904, the various auxiliaries of the British and Foreign Bible Society joined to form the Canadian Bible Society.

The Canadian Bible Society has 16 district offices across Canada, each managed by a District Secretary. The Society holds an annual meeting consisting of one representative from each district, plus an Executive Committee whose members are appointed by the General Board.

Each year contributions, bequests and annuity income of $11 million come from Canadian supporters. Through the Canadian Bible Society's membership in the United Bible Societies' fellowship, over 74 million Bibles, Testaments and Portions were distributed globally in 1994. At least one book of the Bible is now available in over 2090 languages.

The Canadian Bible Society is nondenominational. Its mandate is to translate, publish and distribute the Scriptures, without doctrinal note or comment, in languages that can be easily read and understood.

Headquarters

10 Carnforth Rd., Toronto, ON M4A 2S4 Tel. (416)757-4171 Fax (416)757-3376

Media Contact, Dir., Ministry Funding, Barbara Walkden

Officers

Gen. Sec., Dr. Floyd C. Babcock

Canadian Centre for Ecumenism

The Centre has facilitated understanding and cooperation among believers of various Christian traditions and world religions since 1963. An active interdenominational Board of Directors meets annually.

Outreach:

ECUMENISM, a quarterly publication, develops central themes such as Rites of Passage, Sacred Space, Interfaith Marriages, Care of the Earth, etc. through contributions from writers of various churches and religions in addition to its regular ecumenical news summaries, book reviews and resources.

A specialized LIBRARY is open to the public for consultation in the areas of religion, dialogue, evangelism, ethics, spirituality, etc.

CONFERENCES and SESSIONS are offered on themes such as Ecumenism and Pastoral Work, Pluralism, World Religions, Prayer and Unity.

Headquarters

2065 Sherbrooke St. W. Montreal, QC H3H 1G6 Tel. (514)937-9176 Fax (514)937-2684

Email: cco.cce@sympatico.ca

Officers

Media Contact, Bernice Baranowski

Directors: Emmanuel Lapierre, O.F.; Diane Willey, N.D.S.

Canadian Evangelical Theological Association

In May 1990, about 60 scholars, pastors and other interested persons met together in Toronto to form a new theological society. Arising out of the Canadian chapter of the Evangelical Theological Society, the new association established itself as a distinctly Canadian group with a new name. It sponsored its first conference as CETA in Kingston, Ontario, in May 1991.

CETA provides a forum for scholarly contributions to the renewal of theology and church in Canada. CETA seeks to promote theological work which is loyal to Christ and his Gospel, faithful to the primacy and authority of Scripture and responsive to the guiding force of the historic creeds and Protestant confessions of the Christian Church. In its newsletters and conferences, CETA seeks presentations that will speak to a general theologically-educated audience, rather than to specialists.

CETA has special interest in evangelical points of view upon and contributions to the wider conversations regarding religious studies and church life. Members therefore include pastors, students and other interested persons as well as professional academicians. CETA currently includes about 100 members, many of whom attend its annual conference in the early summer. It publishes the Canadian Evangelical Review and supports an active internet discussion group, which may be accessed through listserv@listserv.uottawa.ca.

Headquarters

Dr. Gordon T. Smith, c/o Regent College, 5800 University Blvd., Vancouver, BC V6T 2E4

Media Contact, Dr. Gordon Smith

Officers

Pres., Dr. Gordon Smith

Sec./Treas., Dr. David Priestley

Publications Coord., Dr. John G. Stackhouse, Jr.

CETA-List Coord., Alan Bulley

Executive Members: Dr. Edith Humphrey; Dr. Stanley Grenz

Canadian Tract Society

The Canadian Tract Society was organized in 1970 as an independent distributor of Gospel leaflets to provide Canadian churches and individual Christians with quality materials proclaiming the Gospel through the printed page. It is affiliated with the American Tract Society, which encouraged its formation and assisted in its founding, and for whom it serves as an exclusive Canadian distributor. The CTS is a nonprofit international service ministry.

Headquarters
26 Hale Rd., P.O. Box 2156, Brampton, ON L6T 3S4 Tel. (905)457-4559 Fax (905)457-40529
Media Contact, Mgr., Donna Croft

Officers
Director/Sec., Robert J. Burns
Director, John Neufeld

The Canadian Council of Churches
The Canadian Council of Churches was organized in 1944. Its basic purpose is to provide the churches with an agency for conference and consultation and for such common planning and common action as they desire to undertake. It encourages ecumenical understanding and action throughout Canada through local councils of churches. It also relates to the World Council of Churches and other agencies serving the world-wide ecumenical movement.

The Council has a Governing Board which meets semiannually and an Executive Committee. Program is administered through two commissions-Faith and Witness, Justice and Peace.

Headquarters
3250 Bloor St. West, 2nd Floor, Toronto, ON M8X 2Y4 Tel. (416)232-6070 Fax (416)236-4532
Media Contact, General Secretary
Email: ccchurch@web.net
Website: http://www.web.net/~ccchurch

Officers
Pres., Archbishop J. Barry Curtis
Vice-Presidents.: Dr. Dorcas Gordon; Rev. Robert Hankinson; Most Rev. Brendan O'Brien
Treas., Mr. Jack Hart
Gen. Secretary., Ms. Janet Somerville

MEMBER CHURCHES:
The Anglican Church of Canada
The Armenian Orthodox Church-Diocese of Canada
Baptist Convention of Ontario and Quebec
British Methodist Episcopal Church*
Canadian Conference of Catholic Bishops
Christian Church (Disciples of Christ)
Coptic Orthodox Church of Canada
Christian Reformed Church in North America-Canadian Ministries
Ethiopian Orthodox Church in Canada
Evangelical Lutheran Church in Canada
Greek Orthodox Metropolis of Toronto, Canada
Orthodox Church in America, Diocese of Canada

Polish National Catholic Church
Presbyterian Church in Canada
Reformed Church in Canada
Religious Society of Friends-Canada Yearly Meeting
Salvation Army-Canada and Bermuda
The Ukrainian Orthodox Church
The United Church of Canada
*Associate Member

Canadian Society of Biblical Studies/Société Canadienne des Études Bibliques
The object of the Society shall be to stimulate the critical investigation of the classical biblical literatures, together with other related literature, by the exchange of scholarly research both in published form and in public forum.

Headquarters
Dept. of Religion and Culture, Wilfrid Laurier University, Waterloo, ON N2L 3C5 Tel. (519)884-0710, ext.3323 Fax (519)884-9387
Email: mdesjard@wlu.ca
Media Contact, Exec. Sec., Dr. Michel Desjardins

Officers
President ('98-'99), Daniel Fraikin, Queen's Theological College, Kingston, ON K7L 3N6 Tel. (613)545-2110, Email: fraikind@post.queensu.ca
Vice-Pres. ('98-'99), John Van Seters, Department of Religious Studies, University of North Carolina, 101 Saunders Hall, CB3225, Chapel Hill, NC 27599 Tel. (919)962-3929, Email: jvanset@email.unc.edu
Exec. Secretary. ('97-'02), Dr. Michel Desjardins, Dept. of Religion and Culture, Wilfrid Laurier University, Waterloo, ON N2L 3C5 Tel. (519)884-0710, ext.3323, Email: mdesjard@mach1.wlu.ca
Treas. ('97-'02), William Morrow, Queen's Theological College, Kingston, ON K7L 3N6 Tel. (613)545-2110, Email: morroww@post.queensu.ca
Publications Officer ('96-'99), Steven N. Mason,York University, 219 Vanier College, North York, ON M3J 1P3 Tel. (416)736-2110, ext.66987, Email: smason@yorku.ca
Programme Coord. ('98-'01), Edith Humphrey, 42 Belmont, Aylmer, QC J9H 2M7 Tel. (819)682-9257, Email: ehumphre@ccs.carleton.ca
Student Member-at-Large ('98-'99), Jane Webster, 233 Lock St. West, Dunnville, ON N1A 1V3 Tel. (905)774-4489, Email: webster@linetap.com

The Church Army in Canada
The Church Army in Canada has been involved in evangelism and Christian social service since 1929.

Headquarters
397 Brunswick Ave., Toronto, ON M5R 2Z2 Tel. (416)924-9279 Fax (416)924-2931
Media Contact, National Dir., Capt. Walter W. Marshall

Officers
National Dir., Capt. R. Bruce Smith
Dir. of Training, Capt. Roy E. Dickson
Field Sec., Capt. Reed S. Fleming
Bd. Chmn., Ivor S. Joshua, C.A.

The Churches' Council on Theological Education in Canada: An Ecumenical Foundation

The Churches' Council (CCTE:EF) maintains an overview of theological education in Canada on behalf of its constituent churches and functions as a bridge between the schools of theology and the churches which they serve.

Founded in 1970 with a national and ecumenical mandate, the CCTE:EF provides resources for research into matters pertaining to theological education, opportunities for consultation and cooperation and a limited amount of funding in the form of grants for the furtherance of ecumenical theological education.

Headquarters
60 St. Clair Avenue E, Ste. 302, Toronto, ON M4T 1N5 Tel. (416)928-3223 Fax (416)928-3563
Media Contact, Exec. Dir., Dr. Stewart Gillan
Email: ccte@web.net
Website: www.web.net/~ccte

Officers
Bd. of Dir., Chpsn., Dr. Richard C. Crossman, Waterloo Lutheran Seminary, 75 University Ave. W., Waterloo, ON N2L 3C5
Bd. of Dir., Vice-Chpsn., Sr. Ellen Leonard, CSJ, Univ. of St. Michaels's College, 81 St. Mary St., Toronto, ON M5S 1J4
Interim Treas., John Wevers, 60 Southport St. Ut.# 6, Toronto, ON M6S 3N4
Exec. Dir., Dr. Stewart Gillan

MEMBER ORGANIZATIONS
The General Synod of the Anglican Church of Canada
Canadian Baptist Ministries
The Evangelical Lutheran Church in Canada
The Presbyterian Church in Canada
The Canadian Conference of Catholic Bishops
The United Church of Canada

Concerns, Canada: a corporate division of Alcohol & Drug Concerns, Inc.

Concerns, Canada is a registered, non-profit, charitable organization that has been closely associated with the Christian Church throughout its long history. The organization's mandate is "to promote and encourage a positive lifestyle free from dependence upon alcohol, tobacco and other drugs."

The organization was granted a national charter in 1987, moving from an Ontario charter dating back to 1934. Among its services are: Toc Alpha (its youth wing for 14 to 24 year olds; PLUS (Positive Life-Using Skills), a teacher curriculum for grades 4 to 8; two Institutes on Addiction Studies; courses for clients of the Ontario Ministry of Corrections; and educational materials for target groups.

Headquarters
4500 Sheppard Ave. E, Ste. 112H, Agincourt, ON M1S 3R6 Tel. (416)293-3400
Media Contact, CEO, Rev. Karl N. Burden

Officers
Pres., Rev. Larry Gillians, 11 Dundas St. West, Napanee, ON K7R 1Z3
Vice-Pres.: Scot Lougheed, 97 Dean Ave., Guelph, ON N1G 1L7
Treas., Jean Desgagne, Union Bank of Switzerland, 154 Univeristy Ave., Toronto, ON M5H 3Z4
CEO, Rev. Karl N. Burden

Ecumenical Coalition for Economic Justice (ECEJ)

The Ecumenical Coalition for Economic Justice (ECEJ) enables member churches to have a more effective public voice in advocating for a just, moral and sustainable economy. ECEJ undertakes research, education and advocacy to promote economic policy alternatives that are grounded in a Christian perspective. Sponsoring denominations include: the Anglican Church of Canada, the Canadian Catholic Bishops Conference, the Evangelical Lutheran Church in Canada, the Presbyterian Church in Canada and the United Church of Canada. ECEJ also acts as a link to social movements and coalitions to bring a collective church presence to them and to inform our own analysis.

The program focus of the next three years will be to advance alternative economic policies which support our vision of an "economy of hope". This includes proposing different ways to assess economic prosperity, challenging the growth model, envisioning a new model for social programs in global economy, and presenting alternative fiscal and monetary policies.

ECEJ publishes a quarterly briefing paper on current issues, the Economic Justice Report, as well as education and action resources.

An Administrative Committee oversees ECEJ and is made up of representatives from the sponsoring denominations as well as participating members which currently include: the School Sisters of Notre Dame, the Scarboro Foreign Mission, and the Religious Society of Friends (Quaker).

Headquarters
77 Charles St. W, Ste. 402, Toronto, ON M5S 1K5 Tel. (416)921-4615 Fax (416)922-1419

Media Contact, Educ. & Communications, Jennifer Henry
Email:gattfly@web.net

Officers
Co-Chpsn., Doryne Kirby
Co-Chpsn., Jim Marshall

Staff
Research, John Dillon
Women & Economic Justice Programme, Kathryn Robertson
Education/Communication, Jennifer Henry
Administration/Finance, Diana Gibbs

Evangelical Fellowship of Canada

The Fellowship was formed in 1964. There are 31 denominations, 124 organizations, 1,200 local churches and 11,000 individual members.

Its purposes are: "Fellowship in the gospel" (Phil. 1:5), "the defence and confirmation of the gospel" (Phil. 1:7) and "the furtherance of the gospel" (Phil. 1:12). The Fellowship believes the Holy Scriptures, as originally given, are infallible and that salvation through the Lord Jesus Christ is by faith apart from works.

In national and regional conventions the Fellowship urges Christians to live exemplary lives and to openly challenge the evils and injustices of society. It encourages cooperation with various agencies in Canada and overseas that are sensitive to social and spiritual needs.

Headquarters
Office: 600 Alden Rd. Ste. 300, Markham, ON L3R 0E7 Tel. (905)479-5885 Fax (905)479-4742
Mailing Address: M.I.P. Box 3745, Markham, ON L3R 0Y4
Media Contact, Pres., Dr. Gary Walsh, 600 Alden Rd., Ste. 300, Markham, ON L3R 0E7 Tel. (905)479-5885 Fax (905)479-4742
Email: efc@efc-canada.com

Officers
Pres., Dr. Gary Walsh
Chair, Rev. Ken Birch
Vice-Chair, Dr. Rick Penner
Sec., Marjorie Osborne
Treas., Lt. Col. Ralph Stanley
Past Pres., Dr. Donald Jost

EXECUTIVE COMMITTEE
Rev. Scott Campbell; Rev. Carson Pue; Ms. Ruth Andrews; Rev. Stewart Hunter; Ms. Jacqueline Dugas; Dr. Rick Penner; Lt. Col. David Luginbuhl; Dr. Ralph Richardson; Rev. Abe Funk; Rev. Gillis Killam; Dr. Paul Magnus; Rev. Winston Thurton
Task Force on Evangelism-(Vision Canada), Chpsns., Mr. Ross Rains, Dr. John Hull, Rev. T.V. Thomas
Social Action Commission, Chpsn., Dr. James Read
Education Commission, Chpsn., Dr. Glenn Smith
Women in Ministry Task Force, Chpsn., Rev. Eileen Stewart-Rhude

Aboriginal Task Force, Co-Chairs, Ray Aldred; Wendy Peterson
Religious Liberties Commission, Chpsn., Dr. Paul Marshall
Task Force on Global Mission, Chpsn., Dr. Geoff Tunnicliffe

Inter-Varsity Christian Fellowship of Canada

Inter-Varsity Christian Fellowship is a non-profit, interdenominational student movement centering on the witness to Jesus Christ in campus communities, universities, colleges and high schools and through a Canada-wide Pioneer Camping program. It also ministers to professionals and teachers through Nurses and Teacher Christian Fellowship.

IVCF was officially formed in 1928-29 by the late Dr. Howard Guinness, whose arrival from Britain challenged students to follow the example of the British Inter-Varsity Fellowship by organizing themselves into prayer and Bible study fellowship groups. Inter-Varsity has always been a student-initiated movement emphasizing and developing leadership in the campus to call Christians to outreach, challenging other students to a personal faith in Jesus Christ and studying the Bible as God's revealed truth within a fellowship of believers. A strong stress has been placed on missionary activity, and the triennial conference held at Urbana, IL. (jointly sponsored by U.S. and Canadian IVCF) has been a means of challenging many young people to service in Christian vocations. Inter-Varsity works closely with and is a strong believer in the work of local and national churches.

Headquarters
Unit 17, 40 Vogell Rd., Richmond Hill, ON L4B 3N6 Tel. (905)884-6880 Fax (905)884-6550
Media Contact, Gen. Dir., Rob Regier

Officers
Gen. Dir., Rob Regier

Interchurch Communications

Interchurch Communications is made up of the communication units of the Anglican Church of Canada, the Evangelical Lutheran Church in Canada, the Presbyterian Church in Canada, the Canadian Conference of Catholic Bishops (English Sector), and the United Church of Canada. ICC members collaborate on occasional video or print coproductions and on addressing public policy issues affecting religious communications.

Headquarters
3250 Bloor St. W., Etobicoke, ON M8X 2Y4
Media Contact, Chpsn., Douglas Tindal, Anglican Church of Canada, 600 Jarvis St., Toronto, ON M4Y 2J6 Tel. (416)924-9199 Fax (416)968-7983
Email: doug.tindal@national.anglican.ca

MEMBERS

Ms. Helga Dyck, Evangelical Lutheran Church in Canada, 302-393 Portage Ave., Winnipeg, MB R3B 3H6 Tel. (204)984-9166 Fax (204)984-9185

Rev. Glenn Cooper, Presbyterian Church in Canada, 50 Wynford Dr., Don Mills, ON M3C 1J7 Tel. (902)485-1561 Fax (902)485-1562, Email: gcooper@atcon.com

Rev. Rod Booth, Religious Television Associates, 3250 Bloor St. W., Etobicoke, ON M8X 2Y4 Tel. (416)231-7680 Fax (416)232-6004, Email: rbooth@uccon.org

Mr. Douglas Tindal, Anglican Church of Canada, 600 Jarvis St., Toronto, ON M4Y 2J6 Tel. (416)924-9199 ext.286 Fax (416)968-7983, Email: doug.tindal@ecunet.org

Ms. Linda E. Slough, United Church of Canada, 3250 Bloor St. W., Etobicoke, ON M8X 2Y4 Tel. (416)231-7680 ext.4011 Fax (416)232-6004, Email: lslough@uccon.org

Mr. William Kokesch, Canadian Conference of Catholic Bishops, 90 Parent Ave., Ottawa, ON K1N 7B1 Tel. (613)241-9461 Fax (613)241-8117, Email: kokesch@cccb.ca

John Howard Society of Ontario

The John Howard Society of Ontario is a registered non-profit charitable organization providing services to individuals, families and groups at all stages in the youth and criminal justice system. The Society also provides community education on critical issues in the justice system and advocacy for reform of the justice system. The mandate of the Society is the prevention of crime through service, community education, advocacy and reform.

Founded in 1929, the Society has grown from a one-office service in Toronto to 17 local branches providing direct services in the major cities of Ontario and a provincial office providing justice policy analysis, advocacy for reform and support to branches.

Headquarters

6 Jackson Pl., Toronto, ON M6P 1T6 Tel. (416) 604-8412 Fax (416)604-8948

Media Contact, Exec. Dir., William Sparks

Officers

Pres., Susan Reid-MacNevin, Dept. of Sociology, Univ. Of Guelph, Guelph, ON N1G 2W1

Vice-Pres., Richard Beaupe, 4165 Fernand St., Hamner, ON B3A 1X4

Treas., Jack Battler, Waterloo, ON

Sec., Peter Angeline, OISE, 252 Bloor St. W., Toronto, ON

Exec. Dir., William Sparks

LOCAL SOCIETIES

Collins Bay; Hamilton; Kingston; Lindsay; London; Niagara; Oshawa; Ottawa; Peel; Peterborough; Sarnia; Sault Ste. Marie; Sudbury; Thunder Bay; Toronto; Waterloo; Windsor

John Milton Society for the Blind in Canada

The John Milton Society for the Blind in Canada is an interdenominational Christian charity whose mandate is producing Christian publications for Canadian adults or young people who are visually impaired or blind. As such, it produces Insight, a large-print magazine, Insound, a cassette magazine and In Touch, a braille magazine. The John Milton Society also features an audio cassette library called the Library in Sound, which contains Christian music, sermons, seasonal materials and workshops.

Founded in 1970, the Society is committed to seeing that visually-impaired people receive accessible Christian materials by mail.

Headquarters

40 St. Clair Ave. E., Ste. 202, Toronto, ON M4T 1M9 Tel. (416)960-3953

Media Contact, Ex. Dir., The Rev. Barry R. Brown

Officers

Exec. Dir., The Rev. Barry R. Brown
Pres., The Rev. Ian Nichols

Lutheran Council in Canada

The Lutheran Council in Canada was organized in 1967 and is a cooperative agency of the Evangelical Lutheran Church in Canada and Lutheran Church-Canada.

The Council's activities include communications, coordinative service and national liaison in social ministry, chaplaincy and scout activity.

Headquarters

3074 Portage Ave., Winnipeg, MB R3K 0Y2 Tel. (204)895-3433 Fax (204)897-4319

Media Contact, Pres., Bishop Rev. Ralph Mayan Email: icc@mts.net

Officers

Pres.,Rev. Ralph Mayan
Treas., Stephen Klinck

Mennonite Central Committee Canada (MCCC)

Mennonite Central Committee Canada was organized in 1964 to continue the work which several regional Canadian inter-Mennonite agencies had been doing in relief, service, immigration and peace. All but a few of the smaller Mennonite groups in Canada belong to MCC Canada.

MCCC is part of the bi-national Mennonite Central Committee (MCC) which has its headquarters in Akron, Pa. from where most of the overseas development and relief projects are administered. In 1996-97 MCCC's income was $22 million, about 36 percent of the total MCC income. There were 347 Canadians out of a total of 867 MCC workers serving in North America and abroad during the same time period.

The MCC office in Winnipeg administers projects located in Canada. Domestic programs of Voluntary Service, Native Concerns, Peace and Social Concerns, Food Program, Employment Concerns, Ottawa Office, Victim/Offender Ministries, Mental Health and immigration are all part of MCC's Canadian ministry. Whenever it undertakes a project, MCCC attempts to relate to the church or churches in the area.

Headquarters
134 Plaza Dr., Winnipeg, MB R3T 5K9 Tel. (204)261-6381 Fax (204)269-9875
Communications, Rick Fast, 134 Plaza Dr., Winnipeg, MT R3T 5K9 Tel. (204)261-6381 Fax (204)269-9875

Officers
Exec. Dir., Marvin Frey

Project Ploughshares
The founding of Project Ploughshares in 1976 was premised on the biblical vision of transforming the material and human wealth consumed by military preparations into resources for human development. An internationally recognized Canadian peace and justice organization, the Project undertakes research, education, and advocacy programs on common security, demilitarization, security alternatives, arms transfer controls, demobilization and peace building. Project Ploughshares is a project of the Canadian Council of Churches and is supported by national churches, civic agencies, affiliated community groups and more than 10,000 individuals.

Publications: the Ploughshares Monitor (quarterly), the Armed Conflicts Report(annual), Briefings and Working Papers(occasional).

Headquarters
Institute of Peace and Conflict Studies, Conrad Grebel College, Waterloo, ON N2L 3G6 Tel. (519)888-6541 Fax (519)885-0806
Media Contact, Director, Ernie Regehr
Email:plough@ploughshares.ca
Website: www.ploughshares.ca

Officers
Chair, Walter Pitman
Treasurer, Philip Creighton

SPONSORING ORGANIZATIONS
Anglican Church of Canada
Canadian Catholic Organization for Development & Peace
Canadian Friends Service Committee
Canadian Voice of Women for Peace
Conrad Grebel College
Evangelical Lutheran Church in Canada
Mennonite Central Committee Canada
Presbyterian Church in Canada
United Church of Canada

Religious Television Associates
Religious Television Associates was formed in the early 1960s for the production units of the Anglican, Baptist, Presbyterian, Roman Catholic Churches and the United Church of Canada. In the intervening years, the Baptists have withdrawn and the Lutherans have come in. RTA provides an ecumenical umbrella for joint productions in broadcasting and development education. The directors are the heads of the Communications Departments participating in Interchurch Communications.

Headquarters
3250 Bloor St. W., Etobicoke, ON M8X 2Y4 Tel. (416)231-7680 ext. 4051 Fax (416)232-6004
Media Contact, Exec. Dir., Rod Booth
Email:rbooth@uccan.org

MEMBER ORGANIZATIONS
The Anglican Church of Canada
Canadian Conference of Catholic Bishops
The Canadian Council of Churches
The Evangelical Lutheran Church in Canada
The Presbyterian Church in Canada
The United Church of Canada

Scripture Union
Scripture Union is an international interdenominational missionary movement working in 120 countries.

Scripture Union aims to work with the churches to make God's Good News known to children, young people and families and to encourage people of all ages to meet God daily through the Bible and prayer.

In Canada, a range of daily Bible guides are offered to individuals, churches, and bookstores from age four through adult. Sunday School curriculum and various evangelism and discipling materials are also offered for sale.

A program of youth and family evangelism, including beach missions and community-based evangelistic holiday clubs, is also undertaken.

Headquarters
1885 Clements Rd., Unit 226, Pickering, ON L1W 3V4 Tel. (905)427-4947 Fax (905)427-0334
Email: sucan@istar.ca
Website: http://home.istar.ca/~sucan
Media Contact, Gen. Dir., John Irwin

DIRECTORS
Harold Murray, 216 McKinnon Pl. NE, Calgary, AB T2E 7B9

Student Christian Movement of Canada
The Student Christian Movement of Canada was formed in 1921 from the student arm of the YMCA. It has its roots in the Social Gospel movements of the late 19th and early 20th centuries. Throughout its intellectual history, the

SCM in Canada has sought to relate the Christian faith to the living realities of the social and political context of each student generation.

The present priorities are built around the need to form more and stronger critical Christian communities on Canadian campuses within which individuals may develop their social and political analyses, experience spiritual growth and fellowship and bring Christian ecumenical witness to the university.

The Student Christian Movement of Canada is affiliated with the World Student Christian Federation.

Headquarters
310 Danforth Ave., Ste. C3, Toronto, ON M4K 1N6 Tel. (416)463-4312 Fax (416)466-6854
Email: scmcan@web.net
Website: http://www.web.net/~scmcan/
Media Contact, Natl. Coord., Rick Garland

Officers
Natl. Coord., Rick Garland

Taskforce on the Churches and Corporate Responsibility

The Taskforce on the Churches and Corporate Responsibility is a national ecumenical coalition of the major churches in Canada. Official representatives from the General Synod of the Anglican Church of Canada, the Canadian Conference of Catholic Bishops, the Evangelical Lutheran Church in Canada, the Presbyterian Church in Canada, the Religious Society of Friends (Quakers), the United Church of Canada, CUSO, the YWCA, and a number of religious orders of women and men, serve as links between the Taskforce and the decision-making structures of the members. The Taskforce assists the members in implementing policies adopted by the churches in the areas of corporate responsibility. Among the policies and issues placed on the agenda of the Taskforce by the participating churches are: principles for global corporate responsibility and bench marks for measuring business performance; corporate operating practices and codes of operation conduct; environmental reporting; human rights and Aboriginal land rights in relation to corporate conduct; social and environmental issues relative to corporate global citizenship; corporate governance issues; responsible investing issues.

Headquarters
129 St. Clair Ave., W., Toronto, ON M4V 1N5 Tel. (416)923-1758 Fax (416)927-7554
Email: tccr@web.net
Website: web.net/~tccr
Media Contact, Coord., Daniel Gennarelli, Tel. (416)923-1758 Fax (416)927-7554

Officers
Coord., Daniel Gennarelli
Bd. Co-Chpsns.: Norah Murphy; Tim Ryan
Treas., Doug Peter

Chpsn., Corp. Governance Comm., Richard Soo
Chpsn. Inter-Church Comm. on Ecology, Joy Kennedy

MEMBERS
Anglican Church of Canada
Basilians
Baptist Convention Ontario/Quebec
Canadian Conference of Catholic Bishops
Canadian University Service Overseas
Christian Reformed Church in Canada
Congregation of Notre Dame
Evangelical Lutheran Church in Canada
Grey Sisters of the Immaculate Conception
Jesuit Fathers of Upper Canada
Les Soeurs de Sainte-Anne
Oblate Conference of Canada
Presbyterian Church in Canada
Redemptorist Fathers
Religious Hospitallers of St. Joseph
School Sisters of Notre Dame
Scarboro Foreign Mission Society
Sisterhood of St. John the Divine
Sisters of Charity-Mount St. Vincent
Sisters of Charity of the Immaculate Conception
Sisters of Mercy Generalate
Sisters of St. Joseph-Diocese of London
Sisters of Service of Canada
Sisters of St. Joseph-Sault Ste. Marie
Sisters of St. Joseph-Toronto
Sisters of the Holy Names of Jesus & Mary Windsor, ON
Sisters of Holy Names of Jesus and Mary, Longueil, P.Q.
Sisters of Providence of St. Vincent dePaul
Sisters of St. Martha
United Church of Canada
Ursulines of Chatham Union
Young Women's Christian Association

Ten Days for Global Justice

Supported by five of Canada's major Christian denominations. Ten Days is dedicated to helping people discover, examine and reflect on the ways global and domestic structures and policies promote and perpetuate poverty and injustice for the majority of the world's people. Ten Days is an education and action program that attempts to influence the policies and practice of Canadian churches, government, business, labour, education and the media.

Headquarters
77 Charles St. W. Ste. 401, Toronto, ON M5S 1K5 Tel. (416)922-0591 Fax (416)922-1419
Email: tendays@web.net
Website: http://www.web.net/~tendays
Media Contact, Natl. Coord., Dennis Howlett

Staff
Natl. Coord., Dennis Howlett
Coord. for Leadership Dev. & Regional Communication, David Reid
Resource Coord., Julie Graham
Admn. Asst., Ramya Hemachandra

Anglican Church of Canada
Canadian Cath. Orgn. for Dev. & Peace
Evangelical Lutheran Church in Canada
Presbyterian Church in Canada
United Church of Canada

Women's Interchurch Council of Canada

Women's Inter-Church Council of Canada is a national Christian women's council that encourages women to grow in ecumenism, to strengthen ecumenical community, to share their spirituality and prayer, to engage in dialogue about women's concerns and to stand in solidarity with one another. The Council calls women to respond to national and international issues affecting women and to take action together for justice. WICC sponsors the World Day of Prayer and Fellowship of the Least Coin in Canada. Human rights projects for women are supported and a quarterly newsletter distributed.

Headquarters
Suite 201, 394 Bloor St. W, Toronto, ON M5S 1X4 Tel. (416)929-5184 Fax (416)929-4064
Website: www.wicc.org
Media Contact, Exec. Dir., Karen Hincke

Officers
Pres., Ann Austin Cardwell
Exec. Dir., Karen Hincke

CHURCH MEMBER BODIES
African Methodist Episcopal, Anglican Church of Canada, Baptist Convention of Ontario & Quebec, Christian Church (Disciples of Christ), Evangelical Lutheran Church in Canada, Mennonite Central Committee, Presbyterian Church in Canada, Religious Society of Friends, Roman Catholic Church, Salvation Army in Canada, United Church of Canada

World Vision Canada

World Vision Canada is a Christian humanitarian relief and development organization. Although its main international commitment is to translate child sponsorship into holistic, sustainable community development, World Vision also allocates resources to help Canada's poor and complement the mission of the church.
World Vision's Reception Centre assists government-sponsored refugees entering Canada. The NeighbourLink program mobilizes church volunteers to respond locally to people's needs. A quarterly publication, Context, provides data on the Canadian family to help churches effectively reach their communities. The development education program provides resources on development issues. During the annual 30-Hour Famine, people fast for 30 hours while discussing poverty and raising funds to support aid programs.

Headquarters
6630 Turner Valley Rd., Mississauga, ON L5N 2S4 Tel. (905)821-3030 Fax (905)821-1356
Email:info@worldvision.ca
Website: www.worldvision.ca
Media Contact, Philip Maher, Tel. (905)567-2726

Officers
Pres., Dave Toycen
Vice-Pres.: Intl. & Govt. Relations, Linda Tripp; Natl. Programs, Don Posterski; Fin. & Admin., Charlie Fluit; Donor Development Group, Brian Tizzard

Young Men's Christian Association in Canada

The YMCA began as a Christian association to help young men find healthy recreation and meditation, as well as opportunities for education, in the industrial slums of 19th century England. It came to Canada in 1851 with the same mission in mind for young men working in camps and on the railways.
Today, the YMCA maintains its original mission, helping individuals to grow and develop in spirit, mind and body, but attends to those needs for men and women of all ages and religious beliefs. The YMCA registers almost 1 million participants and 300,000 annual members in 64 autonomous associations representative of their communities.
The program of each association differs according to the needs of the community, but most offer one or more programs in each of the following categories: community support, housing and shelters, guidance and counselling, camping and outdoor education, leadership development, refugee and immigrant services, international development and education.
The YMCA encourages people of all ages, races, abilities, income and beliefs to mix in an environment which promotes balance in life, breaking down barriers and helping to create healthier communities.

Headquarters
42 Charles St. E., 6th Floor., Toronto, ON M4Y 1T4 Tel. (416)967-9622 Fax (416)967-9618
Media Contact, Dir., Communications, Pat Thompson

Officers
Chpsn., E. G. (Ted) Robinson
CEO, Sol Kasimer

Young Women's Christian Association of/du Canada

The YWCA of/du Canada is a national voluntary organization serving 44 YWCAs and YM-YWCAs across Canada. Dedicated to the development and improved status of women and their families, the YWCA is committed to service delivery and to being a source of public education on women's issues and an advocate of social change. Services provided by YWCAs and YM-YWCAs include adult education programs, residences and shelters, child care, fitness activities, wellness programs and international development education. As a member of the World YWCA, the YWCA of/du Canada is part of the largest women's organization in the world.

Headquarters
80 Gerrard St. E., Toronto, ON M5B 1G6 Tel.
(416)593-9886 Fax (416)971-8084
Media Contact, Int. CEO, Margaret MacKenzie

Officers
Pres., Ann Mowatt

Youth for Christ/Canada

Youth For Christ is an interdenominational organization founded in 1944 by Torrey Johnson. Under the leadership of YFC's 11 national board of directors, Youth For Christ/Canada cooperates with churches and serves as a mission agency reaching out to young people and their families through a variety of ministries.

YFC seeks to have maximum influence in a world of youth through high-interest activities and personal involvement. Individual attention is given to each teenager through small group involvement and counselling. These activities and relationships become vehicles for communicating the message of the Gospel.

Headquarters
822-167 Lombard Ave., Winnipeg, MB R3B 0V3
Tel. (204)989-0056 Fax (204)989-0067

Officers
Natl. Dir., Randy L. Steinwand

3. Religious Bodies in the United States

The United States, with its staunch constitutional stance on religious freedom and successive waves of immigrants over the last three centuries, has proved to be a fertile soil for the development of varied Christian traditions. In the directory that follows, some 215 distinct church traditions are represented. Many of these groups represent the processes of dividing and reuniting that are a hallmark of the American religious contexts. Churches listed here represent those with a long tradition in Europe, Africa, or Asia predating their American tenure. Others are American-born churches. The researcher may be helped by consulting the churches grouped by tradition at the end of this directory in the section entitled, "Religious Bodies in the United States Arranged by Families." In this section all the Baptists bodies are listed together, all the Lutheran bodies, Methodists, etc.

The following directory information is supplied by the national headquarters of each church. Each listing contains a brief description of the church, followed by the national headquarters contact information, which includes a mailing address, telephone and fax numbers, email and website addresses (when available), and the name of the media contact. After the headquarters there are data regarding the church officers or leaders, including names, titles, and contact information (when contact information differs from the headquarters). There is a staggering array of churches, each with its own form of organization; not all of them refer to their leaders as "officers." In some places the reader will find the term "Bishops," "Board Members," or "Executives" in place of "Officers." Finally, when applicable, each entry contains a list of the names of church publications.

The churches are printed in alphabetical order by the official name of the organization. There are a few instances in which certain churches are more commonly known by another name. In such cases, the reader is referred incidentally within the text to the appropriate official name.

Other useful information about the churches listed here can be found in other chapters or directories within the book: Statistical information for these churches can be found in the tables toward the end of this book in chapter III. Further, more extensive information about the publications listed in this directory can be found in Directory 11, "Religious Periodicals in the United States." For a list of church websites, see Directory 5, "The Emerging Electronic Church."

The organizations listed here represent the denominations to which the vast majority of church members in the United States belong. It does not include all religious bodies functioning in the United States. The Encyclopedia of American Religions (Gale Research Inc., P.O. Box 33477, Detroit MI 48232-5477) contains names and addresses of additional religious bodies.

Advent Christian Church

The Advent Christian Church is a conservative, evangelical denomination which grew out of the Millerite movement of the 1830s and 1840s. The members stress the authority of Scripture, justification by faith in Jesus Christ alone, the importance of evangelism and world missions and the soon visible return of Jesus Christ.

Organized in 1860, the Advent Christian Church maintains headquarters in Charlotte, N.C., with regional offices in Rochester, N. H., Princeton, N.C., Ellisville, MO., Lewiston, Idaho, and Lenoir, N.C. Missions are maintained in India, Nigeria, Ghana, Japan, Liberia, Croatia, New Zealand, Malaysia, the Philippines, Mexico, South Africa, Honduras and Memphis, Tenn.

The Advent Christian Church maintains doctrinal distinctives in three areas: conditional immortality, the sleep of the dead until the return of Christ and belief that the kingdom of God will be established on earth made new by Jesus Christ.

Headquarters

P.O. Box 23152, Charlotte, NC 28227 Tel. (704) 545-6161 Fax (704)573-0712

Media Contact, Exec. Director, David E. Ross Email: acpub@adventchristian.org

Officers

Pres., Rev. James Crouse, 326 9th St., Baraboo, WI 53913

Exec. Dir., David E. Ross

Sec., Rev. Thomas S. Warren II, 8912 Snow Hill Ln., Jacksonville, FL 32221

Appalachian Vice-Pres., Rev. James Lee, 1338 Delwood Dr. SW, Lenoir, NC 28645

Central Vice-Pres., Rev. Glenn Fell, 1525 Plainfield Rd., LaGrange, IL 60525

Eastern Vice-Pres., Rev. Glenn Rice, 130 Leighton St., Bangor, ME 04401

Southern Vice-Pres., Rev. Brent Ross, 3635 Andrea Lee Ct., Snellville, GA 30278-4941

Western Vice-Pres., Brad Neil, 4035 S. 275th Pl., Auburn, WA 98001

The Woman's Home & Foreign Mission Soc., Pres., Hazel Blackstone, 2141 Broadway, Bangor, ME 04901

Periodicals

Advent Christian News; The Advent Christian Witness; Insight; Maranatha; "Henceforth"; *Coast to Coast on Campus; Leadership Letter*

African Methodist Episcopal Church

This church began in 1787 in Philadelphia when persons in St. George's Methodist

Episcopal Church withdrew as a protest against color segregation. In 1816 the denomination was started, led by Rev. Richard Allen who had been ordained deacon by Bishop Francis Asbury and was subsequently ordained elder and elected and consecrated bishop.

Headquarters
1134 11th St., NW, Washington, DC 20001 Tel. (202)371-8700

Officers
Senior Bishop, Bishop John Hurst Adams, Presiding Bishop, Seventh Episcopal District, African Methodist Episcopal Church, 110 Pisgah Church Rd., Columbia, SC 29203 Tel. (803)935-0500, Fax (803)935-0830

Chief Ecumenical & Urban Affairs Officer, Bishop McKinley Young, AME, 700 Martin Luther King, Jr. Dr., SW, Atlanta, GA 30314-4143 Tel. 404-522-0800 Fax 404-522-6600

President, General Board, Bishop Donald George K. Ming, Sixth Episcopal District, African Methodist Episcopal Church, 208 Auburn Ave., NW, Atlanta, GA 30303, Tel. 404-524-8279 Fax 404-524-0778

President, Council of Bishops 1999-2000, Bishop C. Garnett Henning, Sr. Nineteenth Episcopal District, African Methodist Episcopal Church, 9301 S. 11th Ave., Inglewood, CA 90305, 310-677-4779

President, Council of Bishops 2000-2001, Bishop William P. DeVeaux, Eighteenth Episcopal District, African Methodist Episcopal Church, 88660 Woodland Dr., Silver Springs, MD 20910 Tel. 301-585-8288 Fax 301-585-3192

General Secretary, Dr. Cecil W. Howard, 4144 Lindell Blvd., Suite 122, St. Louis, MO 63108, Tel. 314-534-5118, Fax 314-534-7419

Treasurer, Mr. Richard A. Lewis, 1134 11th St., NW, Washington, DC 20001, Tel. 202-371-8700, Fax 202-371-8735

President, Lay Organization, Mr. J. L. Williams, 1840 Francis St., Jacksonville, FL 32209, Tel. 904-765-9150, Fax 904-765-9156

Publisher, Dr. A. Lee Henderson, 500 8th Avenue, S., Suite 200, Nashville, TN 37203, Tel. 615-256-5882, Fax 613-244-7604

President, Women's Missionary Society, Dr. Dorothy Adams Peck, 1134 11th St., NW, Washington, DC 20001, Tel. 202-371-8886, Fax 202-371-8820

Director, Young People's Division, Ms. Adrienne A. Morris, Women's Missionary Society, 327 Washington Av., Wyoming, OH 45115, Tel. 513-821-1481 Fax 513-821-3073

Periodicals
The Christian Recorder; A.M.E. Church Review; Journal of Christian Education; Secret Chamber; Women's Missionary Magazine, Voice of Mission, YPD Newsletter

African Methodist Episcopal Zion Church
The A.M.E. Zion Church is an independent body, having withdrawn from the John Street Methodist Church of New York City in 1796. The first bishop was James Varick.

Headquarters
Dept. of Records & Research, P.O. Box 32843, Charlotte, NC 28232 Tel. (704)332-3851 Fax (704)333-1769

Media Contact, Gen. Sec.-Aud., Dr. W. Robert Johnson, III

BOARD OF BISHOPS
Officers
*President, Bishop George W.C. Walker, Sr., 137 Talcott Notch Rd., Farmington, CT 06032 Tel. (860) 676-8414 Fax (860)676-8424

Fax (773)684-0810

Secretary., Bishop Marshall H. Strickland I, 2000 Cedar Circle Dr., Baltimore, MD 21215 Tel. (410)744-7330

Fax (410)728-5510

Asst. Sec., Bishop Clarence Carr, 2600 Normandy Dr., Greendale, MO 63121, Tel. (314)727-2931 Fax (314)727-0663

Treas., Bishop George Washington Carver Walker, Sr., 137 Talcott Notch Rd., Farmington, CT 06032 Tel. (860)676-8414 Fax (860)676-8424

*Note: Presidency rotates every six months according to seniority.

MEMBERS
ACTIVE
Battle, Jr. George Edward, 8403 Dembridge Ln., Davidson, NC 28036 Tel. (704)895-2236 Office Tel. (704)332-7600 Fax (704)343-3745

Bishop, Cecil, 2663 Oakmeade Dr., Charlotte, NC 28270 Tel. (704)846-9370 Fax (704)846-9371

Brown, Warren Matthew, 22 Crowley Dr., Randolph, MA 02368 Tel. (781)961-2434 Fax (781)961-2939

Carr, Clarence, 2600 Normandy Dr., Greendale, MO 63121, Tel. (314)727-2931 Fax (314)727-0663

Ekeman, Sr., Samuel Chuka, 98 Okigwe Rd., PO Box 1149, Owerri, Nigeria West Africa Tel. (011)234-83-232271

Jarrett, Jr., Nathaniel, 7322 South Clyde Ave., Chicago, IL 60649 Tel. (773)684-8098 Fax (773)684-0810

Johnson, Joseph, 320 Walnut Point Dr., PO Box 608 Matthews, NC 28106 Tel. (704)849-0521 Fax (704)849-0571

Rochester, Enoch Benjamin, Office: Hwy. 130 South, Suite 2A, Cinnaminson, NJ 08077 Tel. (609)786-2555 Fax (609) 786-8568; Home: 129 Sagebush Dr., Belleville, IL 62221 Tel. (618)257-8481

Strickland I, Marshall Hayward, 2000 Cedar

Circle Dr., Baltimore, MD 21215 Tel. (410)744-7330
Fax (410)788-5510
Thompson, Richard Keith, 1420 Missouri Ave., N.W., Washington, DC 20011, Mailing Address: PO Box 55458, Washington, DC, 20040 Tel. (202)723-8993 Fax (202)722-1840
Walker, Sr., George Washington Carver, 137 Talcott Notch Rd., Farmington, CT 06032 Tel. (860)676-8414 Fax (860)676-8424
Williams, Milton Alexander, 12904 Canoe Court, Fort Washington, MD 20744 Tel. (301)292-0002 Fax (301)292-6655; Office: 2001 Ninth St., N.W., Suite 306, Box 322, Washington, DC 20001 Tel. (202)265-9590 Fax (202)265-9593

RETIRED
Foggie, Charles H., 1200 Windermere Dr., Pittsburgh, PA 15218 Tel. (412)242-5842
Hilliard , William Alexander, 690 Chicago Blvd., Detroit, MI 48202
Hoggard, James Clinton, 4515 Willard Ave., Apt, 2203, South Chevy Chase, MD 20815 Tel. (301)652-9010; Office: Howard University School of Divinity, 1400 Shepherd St., N.E., Suite 189/191, Washington, DC 20017 Tel. (202)635-6201
Miller, Sr., John Henry, Springdale Estates, 8605 Caswell Ct., Raleigh, NC 27612 Tel. (919)848-6915
Speaks, Ruben Lee, P.O. Box 986, Salisbury, NC 28145 Tel. (704)637-6018 Fax (704) 639-0059

EPISCOPAL ASSIGNMENTS
Piedmont Episcopal District: Blue Ridge, West Central North Carolina, Western North Carolina, and Jamaica Conferences: Bishop Cecil Bishop
North Eastern Episcopal District: New England, New York, Western New York, and Bahamas Islands Conferences: Bishop George W. Walker, Sr.
Mid-Atlantic II Episcopal District: East Tennessee-Virginia, India, London-Birmingham, Manchester- Midland, Philadelphia-Baltimore, and Virginia Conferences: Bishop Milton A. Williams
Eastern West Africa Episcopal District: Central Nigeria, Lagos- West Nigeria, Nigeria, Northern Nigeria, and Rivers Conferences: Bishop S. Chuka Ekemam, Sr.
Eastern North Carolina Episcopal District: Albemarle, Cape Fear, Central North Carolina, North Carolina, and Virgin Islands Conferences: Bishop George E. Battle, Jr.
South Atlantic Episcopal District: Georgia, Palmetto, Pee Dee, South Carolina, and South Georgia Conferences: Bishop Joseph Johnson
Alabama-Florida Episcopal District: Alabama, Cahaba, Central Alabama, North Alabama, South Alabama, West Alabama, Florida, and South Florida Conferences: Bishop Richard K. Thompson
Mid-West Episcopal District: Indiana, Kentucky,

Michigan, Missouri, Tennessee, and South Africa Conferences: Bishop Enoch B. Rochester
Mid-Atlantic I Episcopal District: Allegheny, New Jersey, Ohio, Guyana, Trinidad-Tobago, and Barbados Conferences: Bishop Marshall Haywood Strickland I
Western Episcopal District: Alaska, Arizona, California, Oregon-Washington, Southwest Rocky Mountain, and Colorado Conferences: Bishop Clarence Carr
Southwestern Delta: Arkansas, Louisiana, Oklahoma, South Mississippi, West Tennessee-Mississippi, and Texas Conferences: Bishop Nathaniel Jarrett
Western West Africa: Cote D'Ivore, East Ghana, Liberia, Mid-Ghana, and West Ghana Conferences: Bishop Warren Matthew Brown

General Officers and Departments
Dept. of Records & Research, Gen. Sec.-Aud., Dr. W. Robert Johnson, III, 401 E. Second St., Ste. 108, Charlotte, NC 28202 Tel. (704)332-3851 Fax (704)333-1769; Mailing Address: P.O. Box 32843, Charlotte, NC 28232
Dept. of Finance, Chief Financial Officer, Dr. Madie Simpson, 401 E. Second St., Ste. 101, Charlotte, NC 28202 Tel. (704)333-4847 Fax (704)333-6517; Mailing Address: P.O. Box 31005, Charlotte, NC 28231
Star of Zion, Morgan W. Tann, Editor, 401 E. Second St., Suite 106, Charlotte, NC 28202 Tel. (704)377-4329 Fax (704)377-4329 Fax (704)377-2809; Email: starozion@juno.com Mailing Address: PO Box 31005, Charlotte, NC 28231
A.M.E. Zion Quarterly Review and Historical Society: James D. Armstong, Sec.-Ed., 401 E. Second St., Suite 103, Charlotte, NC 28202 Tel. (704)334-0728 Fax (704)333-1769 Mailing Address: PO Box 33247, Charlotte, NC 28231
Dept. of Overseas Missions and Missionary Seer: Sec.-Ed., Dr. Kermit J. DeGraffenreidt, 475 Riverside Dr., Rm. 1935, New York, NY 10115 Tel. (212)870-2952 Fax (212)870-2808
Dept. Brotherhood Pensions & Min. Relief: Sec.-Treas., Dr. David Miller, 401 E. Second St., Suite 209, Charlotte, NC 28202 Tel. (704)333-3779 or 1-800-762-5106 Fax (704)333-3867P.O. Box 34454, Charlotte, NC 28234-4454
Christian Education Dept.: Gen. Sec., Rev. Raymon Hunt, 401 E. Second St., Suite 207, Charlotte, NC 28202 Tel. (704)332-9323 Fax (704)332-9332 Email: ced1amez@juno.com Mailing Address: P.O. Box 32305, Charlotte, NC 28232-2305
Dept. of Church School Literature: Ed., Dr. Mary A. Love, 401 E. Second St., Suite 208, Charlotte, NC 28202 Tel. (704)332-1034 Fax (704)333-1769 Mailing Address: P.O. Box 31005, Charlotte, NC 28231
Dept. of Church Extension & Home Mission:

Sec-Treas., Dr. Lem Long, Jr., 401 E. Second St., Suite 104, Charlotte, NC 28202 Tel. (704)334-2519 Fax (704)334-3806 Mailing Address: P.O. Box 31005, Charlotte, NC 28231

Bureau of Evangelism: Dir., Rev. Darryl B. Starnes, Sr., 401 E. Second St., Suite 111, Charlotte, NC 28202 Tel. (704)342-3070 Fax (704)342-2389 Mailing Address: P.O. Box 33623, Charlotte, NC 28233-3623

Public Affairs and Convention Manager: Dir., Rev. George E. McKain, II, 943 West 1st North St., Summerville, SC 29483 Tel. (803)873-2475

Dept. of Health & Social Concerns: Dir., Dr. Bernard H. Sullivan, P.O. Box 972, Gastonia, NC 28053 Tel. (704)866-0325 or (704)864-1791 Fax (704)864-7641

A.M.E. Zion Publishing House: Int. Gen. Mgr., Dr. David Miller, 401 E. Second St., Suite 106, Charlotte, NC 28202 Tel. (704)334-9596 Fax (704)334-9592; 1-800-343-9835 Mailing Address: PO Box 30714, Charlotte, NC 28230

JUDICIAL COUNCIL

Pres., Judge Adele M. Riley, 625 Ellsworth Dr., Dayton, OH 45426

Vice-Pres., Robert E. Richardson, Esq., 1511 K St. NW, Ste. 438, Washington, DC 20005

Clk., Dr. Mozella G. Mitchell, P.O. Box 1855, Brandon, FL 33509

MEMBERS

Rev. Monica H. Royce, Esq., 1330 Kingston Ave., Alexandria, VA 22302

Alean Rush, 22 Parkview Dr., Rochester, NY 14625

Dr. E. Alex Brower, Esq., 604 Second St., Mamaroneck, NY 10543

Rev. Medis Cheek, 4072 Sloop Trail, Chesapeake, VA 23323

Dr. George L. Blackwell, 220 N. Elm St., Williamston, NC 27892

Neville Tucker, Esq., 865 S. Figueroa, Ste. 2640, Los Angeles, CA 90017

CONNECTIONAL LAY COUNCIL

Pres., Mrs. Lula K. Howard, 4009 Landside Dr., Louisville, KY 40220-3080 Tel. (502) 499-7842

1st. Vice-Pres., Mr. Jasper McCormick, 9510 Ave "N", Brooklyn, NY 11236 Tel. (718) 531-1436

2nd Vice-Pres., Linda F. Starnes, 505 Starnes Ct., Gastonia, NC 28052 Tel. (704)865-1763

Sec., Frances J. Glenn, 221 Emmett St., Rock Hill, SC 29730 Tel. (803)329-2271

Treas., Ervin D. Reid, 5309 Dayan Dr., Charlotte, NC 28216-2156 Tel. (704)596-7330

Chaplain, Mrs. Annie M. Williams, 2416 Heyward Brockington Rd., Columbia, SC 29203-9681 Tel. (803) 754-8561

Editor, "The laity Speaks", Theodore Shaw, 7529 South Rhodes Ave., Chicago, IL 60619 Tel. (312)488-0057

Pres. Emeritus, Arthur Brooks, 778 Hobart Pl. N.W., Washington, DC 20001 Tel. (202)462-3159

General Officers of the Womans Home and Overseas Missionary Society

Pres., Dr. Adlise Ivey Porter, 1991 Thornhill Pl., Detroit, MI 48207 Tel. (313)393-0601 Fax (313)393-0590 Email: aporter@edcen.ehhs.cmich.edu

1st Vice-Pres., Margie J. Bonner, 12 Eldridge St., Waterbury, CT 06704 (203)756-1829

2nd Vice-Pres., Dr. Sandra L. Gadson, 1808 Heather Hill Court, Flossmoor, IL 60422 (708)957-0114 Fax (708)957-9087

Exec. Sec., Alice Steele-Robinson, 3510 Rock Hill Church Rd., Concord, NC 28027 Tel. (704)795-1506 Fax (704)795-3925; Office: 401 E. Second St., Suite 113, Charlotte, NC 28202 Tel. (704)344-9085

Recording Sec., Vivian Brown, 3130 Greenvale Way, Decatur, GA 30034 Tel. (770)593-1566

General Treas., Elease W. Johnson, P.O. Box 25582, Charlotte, NC 28229 Tel. (704)535-3193 Office: 401 E. Second St., Suite 113, Charlotte, NC 28202 Tel. (704)344-9085

Gen. Coord. of YAMS, Sandra B. Crowder, 960 Autumn Harvest Dr., Virginia Beach, VA 23464 Tel. (757)495-8728

Sec. of Young Women, Millicent D. Thomas, 1312 North 55th St., Philadelphia, PA 19131 Tel. (215) 477-3226

Supt. of Buds of Promise, Vicki L. Lewis, 20 Crestwood Ln., New Britain, CT 06053 Tel. (860) 225-1167

Sec., Bureau of Supplies, Annette E. Whitted, P.O. Box 994, Salisbury, NC 28145 Tel. (704)633-0278 Fax (704)639-1433

Chmn., Life Members Council, Juletha French, 500 State St., Mobile, AL 36603 (334)438-4096

Editor, Woman's Section, Missionary Seer, Ruth Jenkins Stevens, 1080 Lincoln Place, Brooklyn, NY 11213 (718)604-3681

Periodicals

Star of Zion; Quarterly Review; Church School Herald, Missionary Seer, and Vision Focus

Albanian Orthodox Archdiocese in America

The Albanian Orthodox Church in America traces its origins to the groups of Albanian immigrants which first arrived in the United States in 1886, seeking religious, cultural and economic freedoms denied them in the homeland.

In 1908 in Boston, the Rev. Fan Stylian Noli (later Archbishop) served the first liturgy in the Albanian language in 500 years, to which Orthodox Albanians rallied, forming their own diocese in 1919. Parishes began to spring up throughout New England and the Mid-Atlantic and Great Lakes states. In 1922, clergy from the United States traveled to Albania to proclaim the self-governance of the Orthodox Church in the homeland at the Congress of Berat.

In 1971 the Albanian Archdiocese sought and gained union with the Orthodox Church in America, expressing the desire to expand the Orthodox witness to America at large, giving it an indigenous character. The Albanian Archdiocese remains vigilant for its brothers and sisters in the homeland and serves as an important resource for human rights issues and Albanian affairs, in addition to its programs for youth, theological education, vocational interest programs and retreats for young adults and women.

Headquarters
523 E. Broadway, S. Boston, MA 02127
Media Contact, Sec., Dorothy Adams, Tel. (617) 268-1275 Fax (617)268-3184

Officers
Metropolitan Theodosius, Tel. (617)268-1275
Chancellor, V. Rev. Arthur E. Liolin, 60 Antwerp St., East Milton, MA 02186 Tel. (617)698-3366
Lay Chpsn., Gregory Costa, 727 Righters Mill Rd., Narberth, PA 19103 Tel. (610)664-8550
Treas., Ronald Nasson, 26 Enfield St., Jamaica Plains, MA 02130 Tel. (617)522-7715

Albanian Orthodox Diocese of America
This Diocese was organized in 1950 as a canonical body administering to the Albanian faithful. It is under the ecclesiastical jurisdiction of the Ecumenical Patriarchate of Constantinople (Istanbul).

Headquarters
6455 Silver Dawn Lane, Las Vegas, NV 89118 Tel. (702)221-8245 Fax (702)221-9167
Media Contact, Rev. Ik. Ilia Katre

Officers
Vicar General, Rev. Ik. Ilia Katre

Allegheny Wesleyan Methodist Connection (Original Allegheny Conference)
This body was formed in 1968 by members of the Allegheny Conference (located in eastern Ohio and western Pennsylvania) of the Wesleyan Methodist Church, which merged in 1966 with the Pilgrim Holiness Church to form The Wesleyan Church.

The Allegheny Wesleyan Methodist Connection is composed of persons "having the form and seeking the power of godliness, united in order to pray together, to receive the word of exhortation, and to watch over one another in love, that they may help each other to work out their salvation." There is a strong commitment to congregational government and to holiness of heart and life. There is a strong thrust in church extension within the United States and in missions worldwide.

Headquarters
P.O. Box 357, Salem, OH 44460 Tel. (330)337-9376
Media Contact, Pres., Rev. Michael Marshall
Email: awmc@juno.com

Officers
Pres., Rev. Michael Marshall, P.O. Box 357, Salem, OH 44460
Vice-Pres., Rev. William Cope, 1827 Allen Drive, Salem, OH 44460
Sec., Rev. Ray Satterfield, Rt. 4, Box 300, Salem, WV 26426
Treas., James Kunselman, 2161 Woodsdale Rd., Salem, OH 44460

Periodicals
The Allegheny Wesleyan Methodist

The American Association of Lutheran Churches
This church body was constituted on November 7, 1987. The AALC was formed by laity and pastors of the former American Lutheran Church in America who held to a high view of Scripture (inerrancy and infallibility). This church body also emphasizes the primacy of evangelism and world missions and the authority and autonomy of the local congregation.

Congregations of the AALC are distributed throughout the continental United States from Long Island, N.Y., to Los Angeles. The primary decision-making body is the General Convention, to which each congregation has proportionate representation.

Headquarters
The AALC National Office, 10800 Lyndale Ave. S., Ste. 210, Minneapolis, MN 55420-5614 Tel. (612)884-7784 Fax (612)884-7894, Website: www.taalc.org
The AALC Regional Office, 2211 Maynard St., Waterloo, IA 50701 Tel. (319)232-3971 Fax (319)232-1523
Media Contact, Admn. Coord., Rev. Charles D. Eidum, 10800 Lyndale Ave. So., # 210 Minneapolis, MN 55420-5614, Tel. (612) 884-7784 FAX (612) 884-7894, Email: chuckAALC @aol.com

Officers
Presiding Pastor, Rev. Thomas V. Addland, 10800, Lyndale Ave., So., #210, Minneapolis, MN 55420-5614, Tel. (612)884-7784 Fax (612)884-7894, Email: aadland@aol.com
Asst. Presiding Pastor, Rev. John A. Anderson, 310 Seventh St., Ames, IA 50010 Tel. (515)232-3815
Sec., Rev. Dick Hueter, N9945 Highway 180, Wausaukee, WI 54177 Tel. (715)732-0327
Treas., Rev. Dale Zastrow, 700 Second Ave. NE, Minot, ND 58703 Tel. (701)839-7474

Periodicals
The Evangel

67

The American Baptist Association

The American Baptist Association (ABA) is an international fellowship of independent Baptist churches voluntarily cooperating in missionary, evangelistic, benevolent and Christian education activities throughout the world. Its beginnings can be traced to the landmark movement of the 1850s. Led by James R. Graves and J.M. Pendleton, a significant number of Baptist churches in the South, claiming a New Testament heritage, rejected as extrascriptural the policies of the newly formed Southern Baptist Convention (SBC). Because they strongly advocated church equality, many of these churches continued doing mission and benevolent work apart from the SBC, electing to work through local associations. Meeting in Texarkana, TX, in 1924, messengers from the various churches effectively merged two of these major associations, the Baptist Missionary Association of Texas and the General Association, forming the American Baptist Association.

Since 1924, mission efforts have been supported in Australia, Africa, Asia, Canada, Central America, Europe, India, Israel, Japan, Korea, Mexico, New Zealand, South America and the South Pacific. An even more successful domestic mission effort has changed the ABA from a predominantly rural southern organization to one with churches in 48 states.

Through its publishing arm in Texarkana, the ABA publishes literature and books numbering into the thousands. Major seminaries include the Missionary Baptist Seminary, founded by Dr. Ben M. Bogard in Little Rock, AR; Texas Baptist Seminary, Henderson, TX; Oxford Baptist Institute, Oxford, MS; and Florida Baptist Schools in Lakeland, FL.

While no person may speak for the churches of the ABA, all accept the Bible as the inerrant Word of God. They believe Christ was the virgin-born Son of God, that God is a triune God, that the only church is the local congregation of scripturally baptized believers and that the work of the church is to spread the gospel.

Headquarters

4605 N State Line Ave. Texarkana, TX 75503
Tel. (903) 792-2783
Media Contact: Jim Jones, Public Relations Director
Email: bssc@abaptist.org

Officers

President: David Robinson, 15716 Marlene, Little Rock, AR 72206
Vice Presidents: Neal Clark, Rt. 1, Box 48A, Daingerfield, TX 75638; John Owen, P.O. Box 142, Bryant, AR 72089; George Raley, 9890 Hwy 15, Rison, AR 71665
Recording Clerks: Larry Clements, 270 Tracy Dr., Monticello, AR 71655; Gene Smith, 5602 Deer Creek Dr., Texarkana, TX 75503
Publications: Editor in Chief, Bill Johnson; Bus.

Mgr., Wayne Sewell, 4605 N. State Line Ave., Texarkana, TX 75503
Meeting Arrangements Director: Edgar N. Sutton, P.O. Box 240, Alexander, AR 72002
Sec.-Treas. of Missions: Randy Cloud, P.O. Box 1050 Texarkana, TX 75504

American Baptist Churches in the U.S.A.

Originally known as the Northern Baptist Convention, this body of Baptist churches changed the name to American Baptist Convention in 1950 with a commitment to "hold the name in trust for all Christians of like faith and mind who desire to bear witness to the historical Baptist convictions in a framework of cooperative Protestantism."

In 1972 American Baptist Churches in the U.S.A. was adopted as the new name. Although national missionary organizational developments began in 1814 with the establishment of the American Baptist Foreign Mission Society and continued with the organization of the American Baptist Publication Society in 1824 and the American Baptist Home Mission Society in 1832, the general denominational body was not formed until 1907. American Baptist work at the local level dates back to the organization by Roger Williams of the First Baptist Church in Providence, R. I. in 1638.

Headquarters

American Baptist Churches Mission Center
P.O. Box 851, Valley Forge, PA 19482-0851 Tel. (610)768-2000 Fax (610)768-2320
Media Contact, Dir., Office of Comm., Richard W. Schramm, Tel. (610)768-2077 Fax (610) 768-2320
Email: richard.schramm@abc-usa.org
Website: http://www.abc-usa.org

Officers

Pres., Trinette V. McCray
Vice-Pres., David Hunt
Budget Review Officer, Kenneth Hines
Gen. Sec., Daniel E. Weiss
Assoc. Gen. Sec.-Treas., Cheryl H. Wade

REGIONAL ORGANIZATIONS

Central Region, ABC of, Fred A. Ansell, 5833 SW 29th St., Topeka, KS 66614-2499
Chicago, ABC of Metro, Millie A. Myren, 28 E. Jackson Blvd., Ste. 210, Chicago, IL 60604-2207
Cleveland Baptist Assoc., Dennis E. Norris, 1836 Euclid Ave., Ste. 603, Cleveland, OH 44115-2234
Connecticut, ABC of, Lowell H. Fewster, 100 Bloomfield Ave., Hartford, CT 06105-1097
Dakotas, ABC of, Ronald E. Cowles, 1524 S. Summit Ave., Sioux Falls, SD 57105-1697
District of Columbia Bapt. Conv., W. Jere Allen, 1628 16th St., NW, Washington, DC 20009-3099

ABC of the Great Rivers Region, J. Dwight Stinnett, P.O. Box 3786, Springfield, IL 62708-3786

Indiana, ABC of, Larry Mason, 1350 N. Delaware St., Indianapolis, IN 46202-2493

Indianapolis, ABC of Greater, Larry D. Sayre, 1350 N. Delaware St., Indianapolis, IN 46202-2493

Los Angeles, ABC of, Samuel S. Chetti, 605 W. Olympia Blvd., Ste. 700, Los Angeles, CA 90015

Maine, ABC of, Foster Williams (Interim), 107 Winthrop St., P.O. Box 667, Augusta, ME 04332-0667

Massachusetts, ABC of, Linda C. Spoolstra, 20 Milton St., Dedham, MA 02026-2967

Metropolitan New York, ABC of, James D. Stallings, 475 Riverside Dr., Rm. 432, New York, NY 10115-0432

Michigan, ABC of, Michael A. Williams, 4578 S. Hagadorn Rd., East Lansing, MI 48823-5396

Mid-American Baptist Churches, Gary L. Grogan, Ste. 15, 2400 86th St., Des Moines, IA 50322-4380

Nebraska, ABC of, J. David Mallgren, 6404 Maple St., Omaha, NE 68104-4079

New Jersey, ABC of, A. Roy Medley, 3752 Nottingham Way, Ste. 101, Trenton, NJ 08690-3802

New York State, ABC of, William A. Carlson, 5842 Heritage Landing Dr., East Syracuse, NY 13057-9359

Northwest, ABC of, Paul D. Aita, 409 Third Ave. South, Suite A, Kent, WA 98032-5843

Ohio, ABC of, C. Jeff Woods, P.O. Box 376, Granville, OH 43023-0376

Oregon, ABC of, W. Wayne Brown, 0245 SW Bancroft St., Ste. G, Portland, OR 97201-4270

Pacific Southwest, ABC of the, Dale V. Salico, 970 Village Oaks Dr., Covina, CA 91724-3679

Pennsylvania & Delaware, ABC of, Clayton R. Woodbury, 106 Revere Lane, Coatesville, PA 19320

Philadelphia Baptist Assoc., Larry K. Waltz, 100 N. 17th St., Philadelphia, PA 19103-2736

Pittsburgh Baptist Assoc., Larry Swain, 429 Forbes Ave., #1620, Pittsburgh, PA 15219-1627

Puerto Rico, Baptist Churches of, E. Yamina, Mayaguez #21, Hato Rey, PR 00917

Rhode Island, ABC of, Donald R. Rasmussen, 734 Hope St., Providence, RI 02906-3549

Rochester-Genesee Region, ABC of, W. Kenneth Williams, 151 Brooks Ave., Rochester, NY 14619-2454

Rocky Mountains, ABC of, Louise B. Barger, 3900 Wadsworth Blvd. Suite 365, Lakewood, CO 80235

South, ABC of the, Walter L. Parrish, II, 5124 Greenwich Ave., Baltimore, MD 21229-2393

Vermont/New Hampshire, ABC of, Louis A. George, Wheeler Professional Park, One Oak Ridge Rd., Bldg. 3, Suite 4A, West Lebanon, NH 03784-3121

West, ABC of the, Conrad Lowe, P.O. Box 23204, Oakland, CA 94623-0204

West Virginia Baptist Convention, Lloyd D. Hamblin, Jr., P.O. Box 1019, Parkersburg, WV 26102-1019

Wisconsin, ABC of, George E. Daniels, 15330 W. Watertown Plank Rd., Elm Grove, WI 53122-2391

BOARDS

Bd. of Educational Ministries: Exec. Dir., Jean B. Kim; Pres., Kevin Rose

American Baptist Assembly: Green Lake, WI 54941; Pres., Kenneth P. Giacoletto; Chpsn., Patricia Kern

American Baptist Historical Society: 1106 S. Goodman St., Rochester, NY 14620; or P.O. Box 851, Valley Forge, PA 19482-0851; Admn./Archivist, Deborah B. VanBroekhoven; Pres., Loyd M. Starrett

American Baptist Men: Exec. Dir., Z. Allen Abbott, Jr.; Pres., David Gnirk

American Baptist Women's Ministries: Exec. Dir., Carol Franklin Sutton; Pres., Thelma Schaller

Ministerial Leadership Commission: Exec. Dir., Ivan George

Bd. of Intl. Ministries: Exec. Dir., John A. Sundquist; Pres., Stephen Hasper

Bd. of Natl. Ministries: Exec. Dir., Aidsand F. Wright-Riggins; Pres., Thomas Litwiler

Ministers & Missionaries Benefit Bd.: Exec. Dir., Sumner M. Grant; Pres., Mary H. Purcell, 475 Riverside Dr., New York, NY 10115

Minister Council: Dir., Carole (Kate) H. Harvey; Pres., G. Daniel Jones

Periodicals

Tomorrow Magazine; Baptist Leader; The Secret Place; American Baptist Quarterly; American Baptists In Mission

The American Carpatho-Russian Orthodox Greek Catholic Church

The American Carpatho-Russian Orthodox Greek Catholic Church is a self-governing diocese that is in communion with the Ecumenical Patriarchate of Constantinople. The late Patriarch Benjamin I, in an official Patriarchal Document dated Sept. 19, 1938, canonized the Diocese in the name of the Orthodox Church of Christ.

Headquarters

312 Garfield St., Johnstown, PA 15906 Tel. (814)539-4207

Media Contact, Chancellor, V. Rev. Protopresbyter Frank P. Miloro, Tel. (814)539-8086 Fax (814)536-4699

Officers

Bishop, Metropolitan Nicholas Smisko

Chancellor, V. Rev. Protopresbyter Frank P. Miloro, 127 Chandler Ave., Johnstown, PA 15906

Treas., V. Rev. Protopresbyter Ronald A. Hazuda, 115 East Ave., Erie, PA 16503

American Catholic Church

The American Catholic Church was founded in 1988, and incorporated in 1989, as an alternative to the structures and strictures of the Roman Catholic Church, yet without denying basic catholic beliefs of faith and love, spirituality and community, prayer and sacramentality. The American Catholic Church is a federation of independent churches offering a progressive alternative in the Catholic tradition. It is a newly formed rite, as in the tradition of the Orthodox churches of the Catholic tradition and the Old Catholic Church of Utrecht. It remains a Catholic Church, and its priets are considered Catholic priests.

Headquarters

Good Shepherd Rectory, P.O. Box 725, Hampton Bays, NY 11946 Tel. (516)723-2012, Fax (516)723-0348

Media Contact, Archbishop, Most Rev. Robert J. Allmen, D.D.

Officers

Archbishop, Most Rev. Robert J. Allmen, D.D.

American Evangelical Christian Churches

Founded in 1944, the AECC is composed of individual ministers and churches who are united in accepting "Seven Articles of Faith." These seven articles are: the Bible as the written word of God; the Virgin birth; the deity of Jesus Christ; Salvation through the atonement; guidance of our life through prayer; the return of the Saviour; the establishment of the Millennial Kingdom.

The American Evangelical Christian Churches offers the following credentials: Certified Christian Worker, Commission to Preach, Licensed Minister and Ordained Minister to those who accept the Seven Articles of Faith, who put unity in Christ first and are approved by AECC.

A.E.C.C. seeks to promote the gospel through its ministers, churches and missionary activities.

Churches operate independently with all decisions concerning local government left to the individual churches.

The organization also has ministers in Canada, England, Bolivia, Philippines Thailand, Brazil and South America.

Headquarters

P.O. Box 47312, Indianapolis, IN 46227 Tel. (941)314-9370 Fax (941)314-9570

Email: alpha@strato.net

Media Contact, International Mod., Dr. Otis O. Osborne, 1421 Roseland Ave., Sebring, FL 33870 Tel. (941)314-9370

INTERNATIONAL OFFICERS

Mod., Dr. Otis O. Osborne, 1421 Roseland Ave., Sebring, FL 33870 Tel. (941)314-9370

Sec., Dr. Charles Wasielewski, Box 51, Barton, NY 13734 Tel. (607)565-4074

Treas., Dr. S. Omar Overly, 2481 Red Rock Blvd., Grove City, OH 43123-1154 Tel. (614) 871-0710

REGIONAL MODERATORS

Northwest Region: Rev. Alvin House, PO Box 393, Darby MT 59829 Tel. (406)821-3141

Central-West Region: Rev. Charles Clark, Box 314, Rockport, IL 62370 Tel. (217)437-2507

Central Region: Dr. S. Omar Overly, 2481 Red Rock Blvd., Grove City, OH 43123-1154 Tel. (614)871-0710

Northeast Region: Rev. John Merrill, PO Box 183, East Smithfield, PA 18817 Tel. (717)596-4598

East Region: Rev. Larry Walker, PO Box 1165, Lillington, NC 27546 Tel. (919)893-9529

Southeast Region: Rev. James Fullwood, 207 5th Avenue, N.E., Lutz, FL 33549

STATE MODERATORS

Rev. James Brown:	Maryland
Rev. John W. Coats:	Delaware
Rev. Linda Felice:	New York
Dr. Berton G. Heleine:	Illinois
Rev. R. Eugene Hill:	New Jersey
Rev. Emma W. Layton:	West Virginia
Rev. Kenneth Pope:	Washington
Rev. Art Mirek:	Michigan
Rev. Charles Jennings:	Pennsylvania
Rev. Jerry Myers:	Indiana

FOREIGN OUTREACH MINISTRIES

American Evangelical Christian Churches- Canada

Regional Moderator, Dr. Stephen K. Massey, 730 Ontario street, Suite 709, Toronto, Ontario M4X 1N3, Canada (416) 323-9076

Philippine Evangelical Christian Churches

Director, Rev. Alan A. Olubalang, PO Box 540, Cotabato City, Philippines 9600

American Evangelical Christian Churches-Philippines

Regional Moderator, Rev. Oseas Andres, PO Box 2695, Central Post Office, 1166 Q.C. Metro Manila, Philippines 430-6549

Periodicals

The American Evangelical Christian Churches Newsletter- Monthly

American Rescue Workers

Major Thomas E. Moore was National Commander of Booth's Salvation Army when a dispute flared between Booth and Moore. Moore resigned from Booth's Army and due to the fact that Booth's Army was not incorporated at the time, Moore was able to incorporate under said name. The name was changed in 1890 to American Salvation Army. In 1913 the current name American Rescue Workers was adopted.

It is a national religious social service agency which operates on a quasimilitary basis. Membership includes officers (clergy), sol-diers/adherents (laity), members of various activity groups and volunteers who serve as advisors, associates and committed participants in ARW service functions.

The motivation of the organization is the love of God. Its message is based on the Bible. This is expressed by its spiritual Ministry, the purposes of which are to preach the gospel of Jesus Christ and to meet human needs in his name without discrimination. It is a branch of the Christian Church... A Church with a Mission.

Headquarters

Operational Headquarters: 25 Ross Street, Williamsport, PA 17701 Tel. (570)323-8693 Fax (570)323-8694

National Field Office, 1209 Hamilton Blvd., Hagerstown, MD 21742 Tel. (301)797-0061

Media Contact, Natl. Communication Sec., Col. Robert N. Coles, Rev., Natl. Field Ofc., Fax (301) 797-1480

Officers

Commander-In-Chief & Pres. Of Corp., General Claude S. Astin, Jr. Rev

Chief of Staff, Col. Larry D. Martin

Natl. Bd. Pres., Col. George B. Gossett, Rev.

Ordination Committee, Chpsn., Gen. Paul E. Martin, (Emeritus) Rev.

Natl. Chief Sec., Major Dawn R. Astin, NQ-643 Elmira St., Williamsport, PA 17701

Periodicals

The Rescue Herald

Amish—please see Old Order Amish Church

The Anglican Orthodox Church

This body, formed in 1963, is composed of clergy and parishes that are traditionally Anglican in practice and historically orthodox in doctrine. Congregations include both traditional Anglican parishes and Orthodox parishes using a Western liturgy. The church is a member of the worldwide Orthodox Anglican Communion, other branches being located in South Africa, Kenya, Liberia, Congo, Central African Republic, Madagascar, Pakistan, South India, the Philippines, Fiji, Japan, and Columbia.

In 1998, the Missionary Diocese of the United States was formed specifically to foster new parish formation and to encourage an expanded ministry of worker-priests throughout the country. The Mission Statement of the new Diocese seeks to identify the unique role this body plays in the greater Church. It is "to incarnate Christ specifically to those who understand the Bible as the Word of God and who sense their need for sacramental worship and ministy, as well as to those who seek a spiritual experience of God." The Rt. Rev. Scott McLaughlin was installed as Bishop of the Diocese on 1 May 1999.

The church operates the School of Divinity of the Orthodox Anglican communionl, a distance-learning educational consortium composed of Cranmer Seminary, in North Carolina, and the Theological College of Southern Africa, located in Johnnesburg, South Africa.

In the fall of 1999, the church announced an agreement of inter-communion— and began talks which may lead to eventual merger— with the Anglican Rite Synod in the Americas, the western hemisphere Anglican-rite jurisdiction established by the Philippine Independent Catholic Church in 1989.

Headquarters

The Chancery of the Archdiocese

2558 Hickory Tree Road, Winston-Salem, NC 27127-9145 Tel. (336)775-9866 Fax (336)775-9867

Media Contact, The Rev. Scott McLaughlin Email: aocbishop@aol.com Website: www.divinityschool.org

Officers

Presiding Bishop, Most Rev. Dr. Robert J. Godfrey and the Rt. Revd. Scott McLaughlin, The Chancery of the Archdiocese, 2558 Hickory Tree Road, Winston-Salem, NC 27127-9145 Tel. (336)775-9866 Fax (336)775-9867

Periodicals

The AOC Encounter

The Antiochian Orthodox Christian Archdiocese of North America

The spiritual needs of Antiochian faithful in North America were first served through the Syro-Arabian Mission of the Russian Orthodox Church in 1895. In 1895, the Syrian Orthodox Benevolent Society was organized by Antiochian immigrants in New York City. Raphael Hawaweeny, a young Damascene clergyman serving as professor of Arabic language at the Orthodox theological academy in Kazan, Russia, came to New York to organize the first Arabic-language parish in North America in 1895, after being canonically received under the omophorion of the head of the Russian Church in North America. Saint Nicholas Cathedral, now located at 355 State St. in Brooklyn, is considered the "mother parish" of the Archdiocese.

On March 12, 1904, Hawaweeny became the first Orthodox bishop to be consecrated in North America. He traveled throughout the continent and established new parishes. The unity of Orthodoxy in the New World, including the Syrian Greek Orthodox community, was ruptured after the death of Bishop Raphael in 1915 and by the Bolshevik revolution in Russia and the First World War. Unity returned in 1975 when Metropolitan Philip Saliba, of the Antiochian Archdiocese of New York, and Metropolitan Michael Shaheen of the Antiochian Archdiocese of Toledo, Ohio, signed the Articles of Reunification, ratified by the Holy Synod of the Patriarchate. Saliba was recognized as the Metropolitan Primate and Shaheen as Auxiliary Archbishop. A second auxiliary to the Metro-politan, Bishop Antoun Khouri, was consecrated at Brooklyn's Saint Nicholas Cathedral, in 1983. A third auxiliary, Bishop Basil Essey was consecrated at Wichita's St. George Cathedral in 1992. Two additional bishops were added in 1994: Bishop Joseph Zehlaoui and Bishop Demetri Khouri.

The Archdiocesan Board of Trustees (consisting of 60 elected and appointed clergy and lay members) and the Metropolitan's Advisory Council (consisting of clergy and lay representatives from each parish and mission) meet regularly to assist the Primate in the administration of the Archdiocese. Currently, there are 225 parishes and missions in the Archdiocese.

Headquarters
358 Mountain Rd., Englewood, NJ 07631 Tel. (201)871-1355 Fax (201)871-7954

Media Contact, Father Thomas Zain, 52 78th St., Brooklyn, NY 11209 Tel. (718)748-7940 Fax (718)855-3608

Officers
Primate, Metropolitan Philip Saliba
Auxiliary, Bishop Antoun Khouri
Auxiliary, Bishop Joseph Zehlaoui
Auxiliary, Bishop Basil Essey
Auxiliary, Bishop Demetri Khoury

Periodicals
The Word; Credo; Again Magazine

Apostolic Catholic Assyrian Church of the East, North American Dioceses

The Holy Apostolic Catholic Assyrian Church of the East is the ancient Christian church that developed within the Persian Empire from the day of Pentecost. The Apostolic traditions testify that the Church of the East was established by Sts. Peter, Thomas, Thaddaeus and Bartholomew from among the Twelve and by the labors of Mar Mari and Aggai of the Seventy. The Church grew and developed carrying the Christian gospel into the whole of Asia and islands of the Pacific. Prior to the Great Persecution at the hands of Tamer'leng the Mongol, it is said to have been the largest Christian church in the world.

The doctrinal identity of the church is that of the Apostles. The church stresses two natures and two Qnume in the One person, Perfect God-Perfect man. The church gives witness to the original Nicene Creed, the Ecumenical Councils of Nicea and Constantinople and the church fathers of that era. Since God is revealed as Trinity, the appellation "Mother of God" is rejected for the "Ever Virgin Blessed Mary Mother of Christ," we declare that she is Mother of Emmanuel, God with us!

The church has maintained a line of Catholicos Patriarchs from the time of the Holy Apostles until this present time. Today the present occupant of the Apostolic Throne is His Holiness Mar Dinkha IV, 120th successor to the See of Selucia Ctestiphon.

Headquarters
Catholicos Patriarch, His Holiness Mar Dinkha, IV, Metropolitanate Residence, The Assyrian Church of the East, Baghdad, Iraq

Media Contact, Rev. Chancellor C. H. Klutz, 7201 N. Ashland, Chicago, IL 60626 Tel. (773)465-4777 Fax (773)465-0776

BISHOPS—NORTH AMERICA
Diocese Eastern USA: His Grace Bishop Mar Aprim Khamis, 8908 Birch Ave., Morton Grove, IL 60053 Tel. (847)966-0617 Fax (847) 966-0012; Chancellor to the Bishop, Rev. Chancellor C. H. Klutz, 7201 N. Ashland, Chicago, IL 60626 Tel. (773)465-4777 Fax (773)465-0776

Diocese Western USA: ———, St. Joseph Cathedral, 680 Minnesota Ave., San Jose, CA 95125 Tel. (408)286-7377 Fax (408)286-1236

Diocese of Canada: His Grace Bishop Mar Emmanuel Joseph, St. Mary Cathedral, 57 Apted Ave., Weston, ON M9L 2P2 Tel. (416)744-9311

Comm. on Inter-Church & Religious Ed.: His Grace Bishop Mar Bawai, Diocese of Seattle in WA, 165 NW 65th, Seattle, WA 98117 Tel. (206)789-1843

Periodicals
Qala min M'Dinkha (Voice from the East)

Apostolic Christian Church (Nazarene)

This body was formed in America by an immigration from various European nations, from a movement begun by Rev. S. H. Froehlich, a Swiss pastor, whose followers are still found in Switzerland and Central Europe.

Headquarters
Apostolic Christian Church Foundation, 1135 Sholey Rd., Richmond, VA 23231 Tel. (804) 222-1943 Fax (804)236-0642

Media Contact, Exec. Dir., James Hodges

Officers
Exec. Dir., James Hodges

Apostolic Christian Churches of America

The Apostolic Christian Church of America was founded in the early 1830s in Switzerland by Samuel Froehlich, a young divinity student who had experienced a religious conversion based on the pattern found in the New Testament. The church, known then as Evangelical Baptist, spread to surrounding countries. A Froehlich associate, Elder Benedict Weyeneth, established the church's first American congregation in 1847 in upstate New York. In America, where the highest concentration today is in the Midwest farm belt, the church became known as Apostolic Christian.

Church doctrine is based on a literal interpretation of the Bible, the infallible Word of God. The church believes that a true faith in Christ's redemptive work at Calvary is manifested by a sincere repentance and conversion. Members strive for sanctification and separation from worldliness as a consequence of salvation, not as a means to obtain it. Security in Christ is believed to be conditional based on faithfulness. Uniform observance of scriptural standards of holiness are stressed. Holy Communion is confined to members of the church. Male members are willing to serve in the military, but do not bear arms. The holy kiss is practiced and women wear head coverings during prayer and worship.

Doctrinal authority rests with a council of elders, each of whom serves as a local elder (bishop). Both elders and ministers are chosen from local congregations, do not attend seminary and serve without compensation. Sermons are delivered extemporaneously as led by the Holy Spirit, using the Bible as a text.

Headquarters
3420 N. Sheridan Rd., Peoria, IL 61604
Media Contact, secretary., William R. Schlatter, 14834 Campbell Rd., Defiance, OH 43512 Tel. (419) 393-2621

Officers
Sec., Elder (Bishop) William R. Schlatter, 14834 Campbell Rd., Defiance, OH 43512 Tel. (419) 393-2621

Periodicals
The Silver Lining

Apostolic Episcopal Church
Apostolic Episcopal Church was founded in 1925 by a former priest of the Episcopal Church in USA, Rev. Arthur W. Brooks. The orientation of the new church was definitely New Age and New Thought with an emphasis on healing and charismatic teachings. When Bishop Brooks passed to his eternal reward, his successor as Bishop of the Province of the East was Dr. Harold Jarvis, Mar Haroldus, who established the visiting Church Missions. The purpose of the visiting Church Missions was to visit daily in homes, hospitals, prisons, and places of business. The sick, shut-ins, discouraged, imprisoned and those in need of pastoral counseling. Free of charge each person received prayer or healing or consolation or literature as required. This is still the Church's main goal and work, along with its sacramental ministry.

In 1978 upon the retirement of Dr. Jarvis, the Rev. Francis C. Spataro, Founder & President of the Vilatte Guild, became both Priest-in-Charge and Administrator of the Province of the East. Fr. Francis had been ordained priest on December 26,

1976 by Archbishop Uladyslau at the American College & Seminary. After 14 years as Administrator, Fr. Francis was elected & consecrated the Bishop on October 31, 1992 in London at Christ the King Cathedral by Archbishop Bertil Persson assisted by Bishops George Boyer and Eric Eades. On Setember 13, 1995, Bishop Spataro also succeeded the deceased Dr. Paul Schultz as Rector Pro Provincial of the U.S. Council of the Order of Corporate Re-union.

The Order of Corporate Re-union, founded in 1874, is dedicated to the restoration of unity in the Holy Catholic Church, Eastern & Western. In the U.S.A. it publishes the *Tover of St. Cassian* and hosts ecumenical gatherings in various churches; it works closely with the Temple of Understanding, a global interfaith forum as well as with the World Peace Prayer Society. On June 12, 1994, it donated a Peace Pole to the Church of St. Joseph of Arimathea, Preston Hollow, N.Y. Present for the dedication ceremoney in front of the Church were: Archbishop Bertil Persson, Mother Lucia L. Grosch, Bishop Francis C. Spataro and all the parishioners.

On August 21, 1993, Bishop Spataro assisted His Eminence Macario Ga, Obispo Maximo of the Iglesia Filipina Independiente to consecrate the new presiding archbishop of the continuing Anglican Church in the USA, M. Rev. H. Edwin Caudill in New York City at Holy Cross PNC Church in the East Village. Present were the heads of several independent Catholic & Orthodox Churches in New York City.

Headquarters
Tover Order of Corporate Reunion, 80-46 234 Street, Queens, NY 11427-2116 Tel. (718)740-4134; Holy Cross House 286 Union Ave., Brooklyn, NY 11211 (718) 387-2024
Media contact, Rt. Rev. Francis Spataro, Box 192B-1, Preston Hollow, NY 12469 (518) 239-5940
Office of The Tover of St. Cassian, 80-46 234 St., Queens, NY 11427-2116

Officers
Rt. Rev. Francis C. Spataro, President; Rt. Rev. Paget Maek, Coadjtor; Rt. Rev. Bertil Persson, Emeritus; Rt. Rev. Walter Walgraeve, E.U. Representative

Periodicals
The Tover of St. Cassian

Apostolic Faith Mission of Portland, Oregon
The Apostolic Faith Mission of Portland, Oregon, was founded in 1907. It had its beginning in the Latter Rain outpouring on Azusa Street in Los Angeles in 1906.

Some of the main doctrines are justification by faith which is a spiritual new birth, as Jesus told Nicodemus and as Martin Luther proclaimed in the Great Reformation; sanctification, a second definite work of grace; the Wesleyan teaching of holiness; the baptism of the Holy Ghost as experienced on the Day of Pentecost and again poured out at the beginning of the Latter Rain revival in Los Angeles.

Mrs. Florence L. Crawford, who had received the baptism of the Holy Ghost in Los Angeles, brought this Latter Rain message to Portland on Christmas Day 1906. It has spread to the world by means of literature which is still published and mailed everywhere without a subscription price. Collections are never taken in the meetings and the public is not asked for money.

Camp meetings have been held annually in Portland, Oregon since 1907, with delegations coming from around the world.

Missionaries from the Portland headquarters have established churches in Korea, Japan, the Philippines and many countries in Africa.

Headquarters
6615 SE 52nd Ave., Portland, OR 97206 Tel. (503)777-1741 Fax (503)777-1743
Media Contact, Superintendent General, Dwight L. Baltzell
Website:http:// www.apostolicfaith.org

Officers
President, Rev. Dwight L. Baltzell

Periodicals
Higher Way

Apostolic Faith Mission Church of God

The Apostolic Faith Mission Church of God was founded and organized July 10, 1906, by Bishop F. W. Williams in Mobile, Alabama.

Bishop Williams was saved and filled with the Holy Ghost at a revival in Los Angeles under Elder W. J. Seymour of The Divine Apostolic Faith Movement. After being called into the ministry, Bishop Williams went out to preach the gospel in Mississippi, then moved on to Mobile.

On Oct. 9, 1915, the Apostolic Faith Mission Church of God was incorporated in Mobile under Bishop Williams, who was also the general overseer of this church.

Headquarters
Ward's Temple, 806 Muscogee Rd., Cantonment, FL 32533
Media Contact, Natl. Sunday School Supt., Elder Thomas Brooks, 3298 Toney Dr., Decatur, GA 30032 Tel. (404)284-7596

BOARD OF BISHOPS
Presiding Bishop, Donice Brown, 2265 Welcome Cir., Cantonement, FL 32535 Tel. (904)968-5225
Bishop T.C. Talbert Sr., 226 Elston Ave., Anniston, AL, 36201; Bishop John Crum, 4236 Jackson St., Birmingham, AL, 35217; Bishop Samuel Darden, 25 Taunton Ave., Hyde Park, MA 02136; Bishop James Truss, P.O. Box 495, Lincoln, AL, 35096; Bishop T.C. Talbert, Jr., 768 Grayton Rd., Ohatchee, AL 36271; Bishop T. L. Frye, 223 Carver, Atmore, AL 36502

NATIONAL DEPARTMENTS
Missionary Dept., Pres., Sarah Ward, Cantonment, FL
Youth Dept., Pres., Johnny Kennedy, Birmingham, AL
Sunday School Dept., Supt., Thomas Brooks, Decatur, GA
Mother Dept., Pres., Mother Bessie Davis, 1003 Northeast St., Pensacola, FL 32501

INTERNATIONAL DEPARTMENTS
Morobia, Liberia, Bishop Beter T. Nelson, Box 3646, Bush Rhode Islane, Morobia, Liberia

Apostolic Lutheran Church of America

Organized in 1872 as the Solomon Korteniemi Lutheran Society, this Finnish body was incorporated in 1929 as the Finnish Apostolic Lutheran Church in America and changed its name to Apostolic Lutheran Church of America in 1962.

This body stresses preaching the Word of God. There is an absence of liturgy and formalism in worship. A seminary education is not required of pastors. Being called by God to preach the Word is the chief requirement for clergy and laity. The church stresses personal absolution and forgiveness of sins, as practiced by Martin Luther, and the importance of bringing converts into God's kingdom.

OFFICE OF THE SECRETARY
332 Mt. Washington Way, Clayton, CA 94517-1546 Tel. (925)672-3320 Fax (925)673-0965
Media Contact, Secretary, Ivan M. Seppala

Officers
Chairman, Richard C. Juuti, 119 Penny Way, Marquette, MI 49855
Treas., Ben Johnson, Rt. 2, Box 566, Astoria, OR 97103

Periodicals
Christian Monthly

Apostolic Orthodox Catholic Church

The Christian Church was established by the Lord Jesus Christ and His Holy Apostles in Jerusalem in 29 A.D. From Jerusalem, the Church spread to other centers of the known world, including Constantinople, founded in 37 A.D. by St. Andrew the First-Called Holy Apostle. In 864, the Church of Constantinople introduced the Orthodox Christian Faith to present-day Russia. In 988, Rus' Prince Vladimir converted and declared Orthodoxy the State religion, while hundreds of thousands were baptized at Kiev. The resulting Russian Orthodox Church became the greatest safe-guard and body of Orthodox Christians in the world.

The history of American Orthodox Catholic Christianity began in 1794 when Russian Orthodox Church missionaries established the first Orthodox mission on North American soil at present-day Alaska. Their missionary efforts continued down the Pacific coast in 1824, then across the whole continent. Being the canonical founder of Orthodox Christianity in North America, the Russian Orthodox Church maintained and presided over all Orthodox missions, churches, and Christians throughout North America without question or challenge for over 100 years. However, the 1917 Bolshevik Revolution which resulted in severe persecution and imprisonment of the Russian Orthodox Mother Church also resulted in the unrestrained rise of old-country nationalism and great ethnic turbulence between Orthodox Catholic Christians and their churches in North America. They seperated and divided, often violently, along ethnic and nationalist lines with each creating their own old-world ethnic administrations. The once long-held unity and single Orthodox Church canonical administration in North America was destroyed.

The Apostolic Orthodox Catholic Church (AOCC) is canonically indigenous to North America and comprised of bishops, clergy and faithful possessing unbroken Apostolic Succession since the time of Jesus Christ's appointment of His Twelve Holy Apostles to the present day through American Orthodoxy's Luminary and Defender, Russian Orthodox Prelate-Archbishop Aftimios Ofiesh of Blessed Memory.

The AOCC has unquestionable Apostolic Succession passed on to its bishops through the Russian Orthodox Church by Archbishop Aftimious Ofiesh, his succeeding Bishops Sophronios Beshara and Christopher Contogeorge, and through consecrating support of such memorable Orthodox leaders as Albanian Orthodox Church Metropolitan Theophan Noli. The Apostolic Succession and Canonicity of these bishops and their successors was declared valid, authentic and independent by the Orthodox Church Ecumenical Patriarchate of Constantinople in 1945, and re-affirmed in 1951. English-speaking and non-ethnic restrictive, the AOCC's further validity is evidenced by its life, mind, discourse and teaching all being governed and directed in accordance with the Sacred Canons of the Most Ancient Holy Orthodox Catholic Church. The AOCC embraces the ideals and theology of Orthodoxy and freedom which Archbishop Aftimios Ofiesh stood for, taught and passed on by selfless devotion and love for Christ and His Church, and by his personal example.

Headquarters

AOCC Chancery, P.O. Box 1834, Glendora, CA 91740-1834 Tel. (626)335-7369

Media Contact, Rt. Rev. Fr. Bartimaeus, Archpriest, Ecumenical Relations Officer, 1206 East Third Street, Anaconda, MT 59711-2704 Tel/Fax (406) 563-5426 AOCC Office of Communications & Policy, P.O. Box 1834, Glendora, CA 91740

Officers

Presiding Archbishop, Most Rev. Gorazd, Bishop of the Diocese of Los Angeles & Greater Pacific, P.O. Box 1834, Glendora, CA 91740-1834 Tel. (626)335-7369

Second-Presiding Archbishop, Most Rev. Aftimios II, Bishop of the Diocese of the Rocky Mountains & Midwest, 3512 South Hillcrest Dr., Denver, CO 80237 Tel. (303)753-1945, Email: BaftimII@aol.com,

Secretary Archbishop, Most Rev. Angelo, Bishop of the Diocese of the Eastern States, 37 Shippee School House Rd., Foster, RI 02825 Tel. (401)647-2867

Archbishop, Most Rev., Richard, Bishop of the Diocese of Indiana, 3615 Arizona Street # C, Lake Station, IN 46405

SEMINARY

Holy Trinity Apostolic Orthodox Catholic Seminary, PO Box 1834, Glendora, CA 91740-1834

Apostolic Overcoming Holy Church of God, Inc.

The Right Reverend William Thomas Phillips (1893-1973) was thoroughly convinced in 1912 that Holiness was a system through which God wanted him to serve. In 1916 he was led to Mobile, Alabama, where he organized the Ethiopian Overcoming Holy Church of God. In April 1941 the church was incorporated in Alabama under its present title.

Each congregation manages its own affairs, united under districts governed by overseers and diocesan bishops and assisted by an executive board comprised of bishops, ministers, laymen and the National Secretary. The General Assembly convenes annually.

The church's chief objective is to enlighten people of God's holy Word and to be a blessing to every nation. The main purpose of this church is to ordain elders, appoint pastors and send out divinely called missionaries and teachers. This church enforces all ordinances enacted by Jesus Christ. The church believes in water baptism (Acts 2:38, 8:12, and 10:47), administers the Lord's Supper, observes the washing of feet (John 13:4-7), believes that Jesus Christ shed his blood to sanctify the people and cleanse them from all sin and believes in the resurrection of the dead and the second coming of Christ.

Headquarters

1120 N. 24th St., Birmingham, AL 35234
Media Contact, People's Mouthpiece, The Office of the Senior Bishop (address above)

75

Officers

Senior Bishop & Exec. Head, Rt. Rev. Jasper Roby

National Treas., Elder W. T. Parker

Exec. Sec., Juanita R. Arrington (Retiring as of August 5th, 1999)

Periodicals

The People's Mouthpiece

Armenian Apostolic Church of America

Widespread movement of the Armenian people over the centuries caused the development of two seats of religious jurisdiction of the Armenian Apostolic Church in the World: the See of Etchmiadzin, in Armenia, and the See of Cilicia, in Lebanon.

In America, the Armenian Church functioned under the jurisdiction of the Etchmiadzin See from 1887 to 1933, when a division occurred within the American diocese over the condition of the church in Soviet Armenia. One group chose to remain independent until 1957, when the Holy See of Cilicia agreed to accept them under its jurisdiction.

Despite the existence of two dioceses in North America, the Armenian Church has always functioned as one church in dogma and liturgy.

Headquarters

Eastern Prelacy, 138 E. 39th St., New York, NY 10016 Tel. (212)689-7810 Fax (212)689-7168

Western Prelacy, 4401 Russel Ave., Los Angeles, CA 90027 Tel. (213)663-8273 Fax (213)663-0438

Media Contact, Vasken Ghougassian

Officers

Eastern Prelacy, Prelate, Archbishop Oshagan Choloyan

Eastern Prelacy, Chpsn., Jack Mardoian, Esq.

Western Prelacy, Prelate, Bishop Moushegh Mardirossian

Western Prelacy, Chpsn., Vatche Madenlian

DEPARTMENTS

Eastern Prelacy Offices, Executive Director, Vasken Ghougasian

AREC, Armenian Religious Educ. Council, Exec. Coord., Deacon Shant Kazanjian

ANEC, Armenian Natl. Educ. Council, Exec. Coord., Gilda Kupelian

Periodicals

Outreach

Armenian Apostolic Church, Diocese of America

The Armenian Apostolic Church was founded at the foot of the biblical mountain of Ararat in the ancient land of Armenia, where two of Christ's Holy Apostles, Saints Thaddeus and Bartholomew, preached Christianity. In A.D. 303 the historic Mother Church of Etchmiadzin was founded by Saint Gregory the Illuminator, the first Catholicos of All Armenians. This cathedral

still stands and serves as the center of the Armenian Church. A branch of this Church was established in North America in 1889. The first church building was consecrated in 1891 in Worcester, MA. The first Armenian Diocese was set up in 1898 by the then-Catholicos of All Armenians, Mgrditch Khrimian (Hairig). Armenian immigrants built the first Armenian church in the new world in Worcester, MA, under the jurisdiction of Holy Etchmiadzin.

In 1927, the churches and the parishes in California were formed into a Western Diocese and the parishes in Canada formed their own diocese in 1984. Other centers of major significance of the Armenian Apostolic Church are the Catholicate of Cilicia, now located in Lebanon, the Armenian Patriarchate of Jerusalem and the Armenian Patriarchate of Constantinople.

Headquarters

Eastern Diocese: 630 Second Ave., New York, NY 10016-4885 Tel. (212)686-0710 Fax (212) 779-3558

Western Diocese: 3325 North Glenoaks Blvd., Burbank, CA 91504 Tel. (818) 558-7474 FAX (818) 558-6333

Canadian Diocese: 615 Stuart Ave., Outremont, QC H2V 3H2 Tel. (514)276-9479 Fax (514)276-9960

Media Contact, Dir., Zohrab Information Ctr., V. Rev. Fr. Krikor Maksoudian, Eastern Diocese

Officers

Eastern Diocese

Primate, Archbishop Khajag Barsamian, Eastern Diocese Ofc.

Chancellor, Rev. Fr. Garabed Kochakian

Diocesan Council, Chpsn., Haig Dadourian, 415 Madison Ave., 7th Fl., New York, NY 10017

Western Diocese

Primate, His Em. Archbishop Vatche Hovsepian, Western Diocese Ofc.

Diocesan Council, Chpsn., Dn. Dr. Varouj Altebarmakian, 7290 North San Pedro, Fresno, CA 93011

Diocesan Council, Sec., Mr. John Yaldezian, 23221 Aetna St., Woodland Hills, CA 91367 Tel. (B) (818) 346-6163

Canadian Diocese

Primate, His Em. Archbishop Hovnan Derderian

Diocesan Council Chpsn, Mr. Takvor Hopyan, 20 Pineway,Blvd., Willowdale, ON M2H 1A1, Canada Tel. (B) (416) 222-2639

Diocesan Council secretary., Mr. Vahe Ketli, 750 Montpellier, # 909, St. Laurens, QC H4L 5A7, Canada Tel. (R) (514) 7i47-1347

Periodicals

The Armenian Church; The Mother Church

Assemblies of God

From a few hundred delegates at its founding convention in 1914 at Hot Springs, Ark., the Assemblies of God has become one of the largest church groups in the modern Pentecostal movement worldwide. Throughout its existence it has emphasized the power of the Holy Spirit to change lives and the participation of all members in the work of the church.

The revival that led to the formation of the Assemblies of God and numerous other church groups early in the 20th century began during times of intense prayer and Bible study. Believers in the United States and around the world received spiritual experiences like those described in the Book of Acts. Accompanied by baptism in the Holy Spirit and its initial physical evidence of "speaking in tongues," or a language unknown to the person, their experiences were associated with the coming of the Holy Spirit at Pentecost (Acts 2), so participants were called Pentecostals.

The church also believes that the Bible is God's infallible Word to man, that salvation is available only through Jesus Christ, that divine healing is made possible through Christ's suffering and that Christ will return again for those who love him. In recent years, this Pentecostal revival has spilled over into almost every denomination in a new wave of revival sometimes called the charismatic renewal.

Assemblies of God leaders credit their church's rapid and continuing growth to its acceptance of the New Testament as a model for the present-day church. Aggressive evangelism and missionary zeal at home and abroad characterize the denomination.

Assemblies of God believers observe two ordinances-water baptism by immersion and the Lord's Supper, or Holy Communion. The church is trinitarian, holding that God exists in three persons: Father, Son and Holy Spirit.

Headquarters

1445 Boonville Ave., Springfield, MO 65802
Tel. (417)862-2781 Fax (417)862-8558
Media Contact, Dir. of Public Relations, Juleen Turnage, Fax (417)862-5554

EXECUTIVE PRESBYTERY

Gen. Supt., Thomas E. Trask
Asst. Supt., Charles T. Crabtree
Gen. Sec., George O. Wood
Gen. Treas., James E. Bridges
Foreign Missions, Exec. Dir., John Bueno
Home Missions, Exec. Dir., Charles Hackett
Great Lakes, M. Wayne Benson, 2100 44th St. SW, Grand Rapids, MI 49509
Gulf, Gene Jackson, PO Box 307, Hendersonville, TN 37077
North Central, David Argue, 1111 Old Cheney Rd., Lincoln, NE 68512
Northeast, Almon Bartholomew, 13 Cedarwood Dr., Queensbury, NY 12804
Northwest, R. L. Brandt, 1601 Judd Circle, Billings, MT 59102
South Central, Armon Newburn, P.O. Box 13179, Oklahoma City, OK 73113

Southeast, Dan Betzer, 4701 Summerlin Rd., Ft. Myers, FL 33919
Southwest, Richard Dresselhaus, 8404 Phyllis Pl., San Diego, CA 92123
Language Area Spanish, Jesse Miranda, 3527 Thaxton, Hacienda Heights, CA 91745
Language Area Other, Nam Soo Kim, 130-30 31st Ave., 4th Fl, Whitestone, NY 11357
Ethnic Fellowship, Spencer Jones, 7724 S. Racine Ave., Chicago, IL 60620

International Headquarters

Division of the Treasury, Gen. Treas., James E. Bridges
Division of Christian Education, Natl. Dir., LeRoy Bartel
Division of Church Ministries, Natl. Dir.,———
Division of Foreign Missions, Exec Dir., John Bueno
Division of Home Missions, Exec. Dir., Charles Hackett
Div. of Publication, Gospel Publishing House, Natl. Dir., Arlyn Pember

Periodicals

Enrichment: A Journal for Pentecostal Ministry; At Ease; Caring; High Adventure; Club Connection; Pentecostal Evangel; Christian Education Counselor; Woman's Touch; Heritage; On Course

Assemblies of God International Fellowship (Independent/Not affiliated)

April 9, 1906 is the date commonly accepted by Pentecostals as the 20th-century outpouring of God's spirit in America, which began in a humble gospel mission at 312 Azusa Street in Los Angeles. This spirit movement spread across the United States and gave birth to the Independent Assemblies of God (Scandinavian). Early pioneers instrumental in guiding and shaping the fellowship of ministers and churches into a nucleus of independent churches included Pastor B. M. Johnson, founder of Lakeview Gospel Church in 1911; Rev. A. A. Holmgren, a Baptist minister who received his baptism of the Holy Spirit in the early Chicago outpourings, was publisher of Sanningens Vittne, a voice of the Scandinavian Independent Assemblies of God and also served as secretary of the fellowship for many years; Gunnar Wingren, missionary pioneer in Brazil; and Arthur F. Johnson, who served for many years as chairman of the Scandinavian Assemblies.

In 1935, the Scandinavian group dissolved its incorporation and united with the Independent Assemblies of God of the U.S. and Canada which by majority vote of members formed a new corporation in 1986, Assemblies of God International Fellowship (Independent/Not Affiliated).

Headquarters

5284 Eastgate Mall, San Diego, CA 92121 Tel. (619)677-9701 Fax (619)677-0038

77

Media Contact, Exec. Dir. & Ed., Rev. T. A.
Lanes
E-mial: agifellowship.org

Officers
Exec. Dir., Rev. T. A. Lanes
Sec., Rev. George E. Ekeroth
Treas., Dr. Joseph Bohac
Canada, Sec., Harry Nunn, Sr., 15 White Crest
Ct., St. Catherines, ON 62N 6Y1

Periodicals
The Fellowship Magazine

Associate Reformed Presbyterian Church (General Synod)

The Associate Reformed Presbyterian Church (General Synod) stems from the 1782 merger of Associate Presbyterians and Reformed Presbyterians. In 1822, the Synod of the Carolinas broke with the Associate Reformed Church (which eventually became part of the United Presbyterian Church of North America).

The story of the Synod of the Carolinas began with the Seceder Church, formed in Scotland in 1733 and representing a break from the established Church of Scotland. Seceders, in America called Associate Presbyterians, settled in South Carolina following the Revolutionary War. They were joined by a few Covenanter congregations which, along with the Seceders, had protested Scotland's established church. The Covenanters took their name from the Solemn League and Covenant of 1643, the guiding document of Scotch Presbyterians. In 1790, some Seceders and Covenanters formed the Presbytery of the Carolinas and Georgia at Long Cane, S.C. Thomas Clark and John Boyse led in the formation of this presbytery, a unit within the Associate Reformed Presbyterian Church. The presbytery represented the southern segment of that church.

In 1822 the southern church became independent of the northern Associate Reformed Presbyterian Church and formed the Associate Reformed Presbyterian Church of the South. "Of the South" was dropped in 1858 when the northern group joined the United Presbyterian Church and "General Synod" was added in 1935. The General Synod is the denomination's highest court; it is composed of all the teaching elders and at least one ruling elder from each congregation.

Doctrinally, the church holds to the Westminster Confession of Faith. Liturgically, the synod has been distinguished by its exclusive use of psalmody; in 1946 this practice became optional.

Headquarters
Associate Reformed Presbyterian Center, One Cleveland St., Greenville, SC 29601-3696 Tel. (864)232-8297 Fax (864)271-3729
Media Contact, Principal Clk., Rev. C. Ronald Beard, D.D., 3132 Grace Hill Rd., Columbia,

SC 29204 Tel. (803)787-6370. Email: dragondraw@aol.com
Moderatort: Rev. Dwight L. Pearson, D.D., PO Box 174, Chester, SC 29706-0174 Tel. (803)385-2228

AGENCIES AND INSTITUTIONS (IN THE A.R. PRESBYTERIAN CENTER IN GREENVILLE)
Admn. Ser. Dir., Ed Hogan
Christian Education, Dir., Dr. David Vickery
Church Extension, Dir., Rev. James T. Corbitt, D.D.
Publications, Editor, E. Benton Johnston
Treasurer, Guy H. Smith, III
World Witness, Bd. of Foreign Missions, Exec. Sec., John E. Mariner

OTHER INSTITUTIONS
Bonclarken Assembly, Dir., James T. Brice, 500 Pine St., Flat Rock, NC 28731 Tel. (704)692-2223
Erskine College, Pres., Rev. John L. Carson, Ph.D., Due West, SC 29639 Tel. (864)379-8759
Erskine Theological Seminary, Dean, Ralph J. Gore, Jr., Ph.D., Due West, SC 26939 Tel. (864) 379-8885

Periodicals
The Associate Reformed Presbyterian; The Adult Quarterly

The Association of Free Lutheran Congregations

The Association of Free Lutheran Congregations, rooted in the Scandinavian revival movements, was organized in 1962 by a Lutheran Free Church remnant which rejected merger with The American Lutheran Church. The original 42 congregations were joined by other like-minded conservative Lutherans, especially from the former Evangelical Lutheran Church and the Suomi Synod. There has been more than a fivefold increase in the number of congregations. Members subscribe to the Apostles*, Nicene and Athanasian creeds; Luther's Small Catechism; and the Unaltered Augsburg Confession. The Fundamental Principles and Rules for Work (1897) declare that the local congregation is the right form of the kingdom of God on earth, subject to no authority but the Word and the Spirit of God.

Distinctive emphases are: (1) the infallibility and inerrancy of Holy Scriptures as the Word of God; (2) congregational polity; (3) the spiritual unity of all believers, resulting in fellowship and cooperation transcending denominational lines; (4) evangelical outreach, calling all to enter a personal relationship with Jesus Christ; (5) a wholesome Lutheran pietism that proclaims the Lordship of Jesus Christ in all areas of life and results in believers becoming the salt and light in their communities; (6) a conservative stance on current social issues.

A two-year Bible school and a theological seminary are in suburban Minneapolis. Mission support is channeled to churches in Brazil, Mexico, Canada, India, and Portugal.

Headquarters
3110 E. Medicine Lake Blvd., Minneapolis, MN 55441 Tel. (612)545-5631 Fax (612)545-0079
Media Contact, Pres., Rev. Robert L. Lee
Website: www.aflc.org

Officers
Pres., Rev. Robert L. Lee
Vice-Pres., Rev. Elden K. Nelson, 1633 Co. Rd. 8 SE, Kandiyohi, MN 56251
Sec., Rev. Brian Davidson, 3110 E. Medicine Lake Blvd., Minneapolis, MN 55441

Periodicals
The Lutheran Ambassador

Baptist Bible Fellowship International

Organized on May 24, 1950 in Fort Worth, Tex., the Baptist Bible Fellowship was founded by about 100 pastors and lay people who had grown disenchanted with the policies and leadership of the World Fundamental Baptist Missionary Fellowship, an outgrowth of the Baptist Bible Union formed in Kansas City in 1923 by fundamentalist leaders from the Southern Baptist, Northern Baptist and Canadian Baptist Conventions. The BBF elected W. E. Dowell as its first president and established offices and a three-year (now four-year with a graduate school) Baptist Bible College.

The BBF statement of faith was essentially that of the Baptist Bible Union, adopted in 1923, a variation of the New Hampshire Confession of Faith. It presents an infallible Bible, belief in the substitutionary death of Christ, his physical resurrection and his premillennial return to earth. It advocates local church autonomy and strong pastoral leadership and maintains that the fundamental basis of fellowship is a missionary outreach. The BBF vigorously stresses evangelism and the international missions office reports 858 adult missionaries working on 107 fields throughout the world.

There are BBF-related churches in every state of the United States, with special strength in the upper South, the Great Lakes region, southern states west of the Mississippi, Kansas and California. There are six related colleges and one graduate school or seminary.

A Committee of Forty-Five, elected by pastors and churches within the states, sits as a representative body, meeting in three subcommittees, each chaired by one of the principal officers: an administration committee chaired by the president, a missions committee chaired by a vice-president and an education committee chaired by a vice-president.

Headquarters
Baptist Bible Fellowship Missions Bldg., 720 E. Kearney St., Springfield, MO 65803 Tel. (417)862-5001 Fax (417)865-0794
Mailing Address, P.O. Box 191, Springfield, MO 65801
Media Contact, Mission Dir., Dr. Bob Baird, P.O. Box 191, Springfield, MO 65801

Officers
Pres., Ken Gillming Sr., Cherry Street Baptist Church, 1201 S. Oak Grove Ave., Springfield, MO 65804
First Vice-Pres., Rev. Bill Monroe, Florence Baptist Temple, 2308 S. Irby Street, Florence, SC 29505-0809
Second Vice-Pres., Bill Dougherty, First Coast Baptist Church, 7587 Blanding Blvd., Jacksonville, FL 32244-5155
Sec., K. B. Murray, Millington Street Baptist Church, 1304 Millington St., Winfield, KS 67156
Treas., Wayne Guinn, Bethany Baptist Church, 1100 Dorchester Ave., Melborne, FL
Mission Dir., Dr. Bob Baird, P.O. Box 191, Springfield, MO 65801

Periodicals
The Baptist Bible Tribune; The Preacher; Global Partners

Baptist General Conference

The Baptist General Conference, rooted in the pietistic movement of Sweden during the 19th century, traces its history to Aug. 13, 1852. On that day a small group of believers at Rock Island, Illinois, under the leadership of Gustaf Palmquist, organized the first Swedish Baptist Church in America. Swedish Baptist churches flourished in the upper Midwest and Northeast, and by 1879, when the first annual meeting was held in Village Creek, Iowa, 65 churches had been organized, stretching from Maine to the Dakotas and south to Kansas and Missouri.

By 1871, John Alexis Edgren, an immigrant sea captain and pastor in Chicago, had begun the first publication and a theological seminary. The Conference grew to 324 churches and nearly 26,000 members by 1902. There were 40,000 members in 1945 and 135,000 in 1993.

Many churches began as Sunday schools. The seminary evolved into Bethel, a four-year liberal arts college with 1,800 students, and theological seminaries in Arden Hills, Minnesota. and San Diego, California. Missions and the planting of churches have been main objectives both in America and overseas. Today churches have been established in the United States, Canada and Mexico, as well as twenty countries overseas. In 1985 the churches of Canada founded an autonomous denomination, The Baptist General Conference of Canada.

The Baptist General Conference is a member of the Baptist World Alliance, the Baptist Joint

Committee on Public Affairs and the National Association of Evangelicals. It is characterized by the balancing of a conservative doctrine with an irenic and cooperative spirit. Its basic objective is to seek the fulfillment of the Great Commission and the Great Commandment.

Headquarters

2002 S. Arlington Heights Rd., Arlington Heights, IL 60005 Tel. (847)228-0200 Fax (847)228-5376

Media Contact, Pres., Dr. Robert S. Ricker

Email: gmbgcstd@aol.com

Website: http://www.bgc.bethel.edu

Officers

Pres. & Chief Exec. Officer, Dr. Robert Ricker

Exec, Vice-Pres., Ray Swatkowski

Vice-Pres. Of Ministry Partner Services, Dr. Lou Petrie

Vice-Pres. of Finance, Stephen R. Schultz

Vice Pres. of Church Enrichment, Dr. Richard Massey (Int.)

Vice-Pres. of Church Planting, Dr. Ronald Larson

OTHER ORGANIZATIONS

Bd. of Trustees: Bethel College & Seminary, Pres., Dr. George K. Brushaber, 3900 Bethel Dr., St. Paul, MN 55112

Periodicals

The Standard

Baptist Missionary Association of America

A group of regular Baptist churches organized in associational capacity in May, 1950, in Little Rock, Ark., as the North American Baptist Association. The name changed in 1969 to Baptist Missionary Association of America. There are several state and numerous local associations of cooperating churches. In theology, these churches are evangelical, missionary, fundamental and for the most part premillennial.

Headquarters

9219 Sibly Hole Rd., Little Rock, AR Tel. (501) 455-4977 Fax (501)455-3636

Mailing Address, P.O. Box 193920, Little Rock, AR 72219-3920

Media Contact, Dir. of Baptist News Service, Kenneth W. Vanderslice, P.O. Box 97, Jacksonville, TX 75766 Tel. (903)586-2501 Fax (903)586-0378

Officers

Pres., Ronald Morgan, 208 N. Arkansas St., Springhill, LA 71075-2704

Vice-Pres.: Leon J. Carmical, 85 Midway Church Rd., Sumrall, MS 39428; David T. Watkins, 1 Pineridge St., Magnolia, AR 71753

Rec. Sec.: Rev. Ralph Cottrell, P.O. Box 1203, Van, TX 75790; Don J. Brown, P.O. Box 8181, Laruel, MS 39441; James Ray Raines, 5609 N. Locust, N. Little Rock, AR 72116

DEPARTMENTS

Missions: Gen. Sec., Rev. F. Donald Collins, P.O. Box 193920, Little Rock, AR 72219-3920

Publications: Ed.-in-Chief, Rev. James L. Silvey, 311 Main St., P.O. Box 7270, Texarkana, TX 75505

Christian Education: Bapt. Missionary Assoc. Theological Sem., Pres., Dr. Charley Holmes, Seminary Heights, 1530 E. Pine St., Jacksonville, TX 75766

Baptist News Service: Dir., Rev. Kenneth W. Vanderslice, P.O. Box 97, Jacksonville, TX 75766

Life Word Broadcast Ministries: Dir., Rev. George Reddin, P.O. Box 6, Conway, AR 72032

Armed Forces Chaplaincy: Exec. Dir., Bobby C. Thornton, P.O. Box 240, Flint, TX 75762

BMAA Dept. of Church Ministries: Donny Parish, P.O. Box 10356, Conway, AR 72033

Daniel Springs Encampment: James Speer, P.O. Box 310, Gary, TX 75643

Ministers Resource Services: Craig Branham, 4001 Jefferson St., Texarkana, AR 75501

OTHER ORGANIZATIONS

Baptist Missionary Assoc. Brotherhood: Pres., Bill Looney, 107 Bearskin Dr., Sherwood, AR 72120

National Women's Missionary Auxiliary: Pres., Mrs. Bill Skinner, RR1 Box 213 B, Mineola, TX 75773-9742 Tel. 903-365-2465

Periodicals

The Gleaner

Beachy Amish Mennonite Churches

The Beachy Amish Mennonite Church was established in 1927 in Somerset County, Pa. following a division in the Amish Mennonite Church in that area. As congregations in other locations joined the movement, they were identified by the same name. There are currently 97 churches in the United States, 9 in Canada and 34 in other countries. Membership in the United States is 7,059, according to the 1996 Mennonite Yearbook.

Beachy Churches believe in one God eternally existent in three persons (Father, Son and Holy Spirit); that Jesus Christ is the one and only way to salvation; that the Bible is God's infallible Word to us, by which all will be judged; that heaven is the eternal abode of the redeemed in Christ; and that the wicked and unbelieving will endure hell eternally.

Evangelical mission boards sponsor missions in Central and South America, Belgium, Ireland, and in Kenya, Africa.

The Mission Interests Committee, founded in 1953 for evangelism and other Christian services, sponsors homes for handicapped youth and elderly people, mission outreaches among the North American Indians in Canada and a mission outreach in Europe.

Headquarters

Media Contact, David L. Miller, P.O. Box 73, Partridge, KS 67566 Te. (316)567-2376

Officers

Amish Mennonite Aid: Sec.-Treas., Vernon Miller, 2675 U.S. 42 NE, London, OH 43140 Tel. (614)879-8616

Mission Interests Committee: Sec.-Treas., Melvin Gingerich, 42555 900W, Topeka, IN 46571 Tel. (219)593-9090

Choice Books of Northern Virginia: Supervisor, Simon Schrock, 4614 Holly Ave., Fairfax, VA 22030 Tel. (703)830-2800

Calvary Bible School: HC 61, Box 202, Calico Rock, AR 72519 Tel. (501)297-8658; Sec.-Treas., Elmer Gingerich, HC 74, Box 282, Mountain View, AR 72560 Tel. (501)296-8764

Penn Valley Christian Retreat, Bd. Chmn., Wayne Schrock, RR 2, Box 165, McVeytown, PA 17015 Tel. (717)529-2935

Periodicals

The Calvary Messenger

Berean Fundamental Church

Founded 1932 in North Platte, Nebraska, this body emphasizes conservative Protestant doctrines.

Headquarters

Box 6103, Lincoln, NE 68506 Tel. (402)489-8056 Fax (402)489-8056

Media Contact, Pres., Pastor Doug Shada

Officers

Pres., Doug Shada

Vice-Pres., Richard Crocker, 419 Lafayette Blvd., Cheyenne, WY 82009 Tel. (307)635-5914

Sec., Roger Daum, 1510 O Street, Cozad, NE 69130 Tel. (308)784-3675

Treas., Virgil Wiebe, P.O. Box 6103, Lincoln, NE 68506

Exec. Advisor, Curt Lehman, Tel. (402)483-4840

Exec. Advisor, Carl M. Goltz, P.O. Box 397, North Platte, NE 69103 Tel. (308)532-6723

The Bible Church of Christ, Inc.

The Bible Church of Christ was founded on March 1, 1961 by Bishop Roy Bryant, Sr. Since that time, the Church has grown to include congregations in the United States, Africa and India. The church is trinitarian and accepts the Bible as the divinely inspired Word of God. Its doctrine includes miracles of healing, deliverance and the baptism of the Holy Ghost.

Headquarters

1358 Morris Ave., Bronx, NY 10456 Tel. (718) 588-2284 FAX (718) 992-5597

Media Contact, Pres., Bishop Roy Bryant, Sr

Officers

Pres., Bishop Roy Bryant, Sr.

V. Pres., Asst. Bishop Derek G. Owens

Sec., Sissieretta Bryant, Treas., Elder Artie Burney

Exec. Admn., Sr. Autholene Smith

EXECUTIVE TRUSTEE BOARD

Chpsns.: Elder Alberto L. Hope, 1358 Morris Ave., Bronx, NY 10456, Tel. (718)588-2284; Bishop Derek G. Owens, 100 W. 2nd St., Mount Vernon, NY 10550 Tel. (914)664-4602

OTHER ORGANIZATIONS

Bookstore: Mgr., Evangelist Beryl C. Foster, Tel. (718)293-1928

Evangelism: Intl. Pres., Evangelist Gloria Gray

Foreign Missions: Pres., Sr. Autholene Smith

Food Pantry: Dir., Evangelist Susie Jones

Home Missions: Pres., Evangelist Mary Jackson

Minister of Music: Ray Brown

Prison Ministry Team: Pres., Evangelist Marvin Lowe

Public Relations: Deacon Abraham Jones

Publications: Dir., Deaconess Betty Hamilton

Sunday Schools: Gen. Supt., Elder A. M. Jones

Theological Institute: Pres., Dr. Roy Bryant, Sr.; Dean, Elder A. M. Jones

Women's Committee: Natl. Chpsn., Sissieretta Bryant

Youth: Pres., Deacon Tommy Robinson, Presiding Elders: Delaware, Elder Edward Cannon, R R Box 70-B5, Diamond Acre, Dagsboro, DE 19939 Tel. (302)732-3351; Virginia, Elder Jesse Alston, 221 Keith Rd., Newport News, VA 23606 Tel. (804)930-2445; Monticello, 104 Waverly Ave., Monticello, NY 12701; Mount Vernon, Elder Artie Burney, 100 W. 2nd St., Mount Vernon, NY 10550; Bronx, Elder Anita Robinson, 1358 Morris Ave., Bronx, NY 10456, Tel. (718)588-2284; Annex, Elder Reginald Gullette, 1069 Morris Ave., Bronx, NY 10456 Tel. (718)992-4653; Bishop Derek Owens, Pasto, Minister Monica Hope, Assistant, 1140 Congress St., Schenectady, NY 12303; India, Dr. B. Veeraswamy, 46-7-34, Danavaya Peta, Rajahmunry, India, 533103; Haiti, Antoine Polycarpe, P.O. Box 197, Port-au-Prince, Haiti; St. Croix, Elder Floyd Thomas, 1-J Diamond Ruby, P.O. Box 5183, Sunny Isles, Christiansted, St. Croix Tel. (809)778-1002

Periodicals

The Voice; The Gospel Light; The Challenge

Bible Fellowship Church

The Bible Fellowship Church grew out of divisions in the Mennonite community in Pennsylvania in the 1850s. Traditional church leadership resisted the freedom of expression and prayer meetings initiated by several preachers and church leaders. These evangelical Mennonites formed the Evangelical Mennonite Society. Over the next two decades various like minded groups in Canada, Ohio and Pennsylvania joined the Society.

In 1959 the Conference became the Bible Fellowship Church and new articles of faith were ratified. They now hold a unique combination of Reformed doctrines with insistence on "Believer Baptism" and Premillennialism.

Headquarters
Bible Fellowship Church, 3000 Fellowship Dr., Whitehall, PA 18052
Media Contact, David J. Watkins, Greater Bible Fellowship Church, 693 Church Rd., Graterford, PA 19426 Tel. (610)489-9389

Officers
Chmn., Randall A. Grossman
Vice-Chmn., William G. Schlonecker
Sec., David A. Thomann
Asst. Sec., Robert W. Smock

BOARDS AND COMMITTEES
Bd. of Dir., Bible Fellowship Church
Bd. of Christian Education
Board of Extension
Bible Fellowship Church Homes, Inc.
Board of Pensions
Board of Pinebrook Bible Conference
Board of Missions
Board of Publication and Printing
Bd. of Victory Valley Camp
Board of Higher Education

Periodicals
Fellowship News

Bible Holiness Church
This church came into being about 1890 as the result of definite preaching on the doctrine of holiness in some Methodist churches in southeastern Kansas. It became known as The Southeast Kansas Fire Baptized Holiness Association. The name was changed in 1945 to The Fire Baptized Holiness Church and in 1995 to Bible Holiness Church. It is entirely Wesleyan in doctrine, episcopal in church organization and intensive in evangelistic zeal.

Headquarters
600 College Ave., Independence, KS 67301 Tel. (316)331-3049
Media Contact, Gen. Supt., Leroy Newport

Officers
Gen. Supt., Leroy Newport
Gen. Sec., Wayne Knipmeyer, Box 457, South Pekin, IL 61564
Gen. Treas., Robert Davolt, 1323 Laura, Wichita, KS 67211

Periodicals
The Flaming Sword; John Three Sixteen

Bible Way Church of Our Lord Jesus Christ World Wide, Inc.
This body was organized in 1957 in the Pentecostal tradition for the purpose of accelerating evangelistic and foreign missionary commitment and to effect a greater degree of collective leadership than leaders found in the body in which they had previously participated.

The doctrine is the same as that of the Church of Our Lord Jesus Christ of the Apostolic Faith, Inc., of which some of the churches and clergy were formerly members.

This organization has churches and missions in Africa, England, Guyana, Trinidad and Jamaica, and churches in 25 states in America. The Bible Way Church is involved in humanitarian as well as evangelical outreach with concerns for urban housing, education and economic development.

Headquarters
4949 Two-Notch Rd., Columbia, SC 29204 Tel. (800)432-5612 Fax (803)691-0583
Media Contact, Chief Apostle, Presiding Bishop Huie Rogers

Officers
Presiding Bishop, Bishop Huie Rogers, 4949 Two Notch Rd., Columbia, SC 29204 Tel. (800)432-5612 Fax (803)691-0583
Gen. Sec., Bishop Edward Williams, 5118 Clarendon Rd., Brooklyn, NY 11226 Tel. (718)451-1238

Brethren in Christ Church
The Brethren in Christ Church was founded in Lancaster County, Pa. in about the year 1778 and was an outgrowth of the religious awakening which occurred in that area during the latter part of the 18th century. This group became known as "River Brethren" because of their original location near the Susquehanna River. The name "Brethren in Christ" was officially adopted in 1863. In theology they have accents of the Pietist, Anabaptist, Wesleyan and Evangelical movements.

Headquarters
General Church Office, P.O. Box A, Grantham, PA 17027 Tel. (717)697-2634 Fax (717) 697-7714
Media Contact, Mod., Dr. Warren L. Hoffman, Tel. (717)697-2634 Fax (717)697-7714

Officers
Mod., Dr. Warren L. Hoffman, P.O. Box A, Grantham, PA 17027 Tel. (717)697-2634 Fax (717)697-7714
Gen. Sec., Rev. Kenneth O. Hoke
Tresurer, Allen Carr

OTHER ORGANIZATIONS
General Conference Board: Chpsn., Mark Garis, 504 Swartley Rd., Hatfield, PA 19440
Bd. for Media Ministries: Chpsn., Harold Chubb, P.O. Box 189, Nappanee, IN 46550
Bd. for World Missions: Chpsn., David Hall, 996 East Hight St., Elizabethtown, PA 17022 Fax 1; Exec. Dir., Rev. John Brubaker, P.O. Box 390, Grantham, PA 17027-0390
Jacob Engle Foundation Bd. of Dir.: CEO, Julie Stout, CPA
Pension Fund Trustees: Chpsn., Donald R. Zook
Bd. for Stewardship Services: Chpsn., Donald J. Winters, 2404 Willow Glen Dr., Lancaster, PA

17602; Exec. Dir., Rev. Phil Keefer, Box A, Grantham, PA 17027

Publishing House: Exec. Dir., Roger Williams, Evangel Press, P.O. Box 189, Nappanee, IN 46550

Periodicals
Evangelical Visitor; Yes!

Brethren Church (Ashland, Ohio)

The Brethren Church (Ashland, Ohio) was organized by progressive-minded German Baptist Brethren in 1883. They reaffirmed the teaching of the original founder of the Brethren movement, Alexander Mack, and returned to congregational government.

Headquarters
524 College Ave., Ashland, OH 44805 Tel. (419) 289-1708 Fax (419)281-0450

Media Contact, Editor of Publications, Richard C. Winfield

Email: brethren@bright.net

Website:http:// www.apollotrust.com/~brethren

Officers
Executive Dir., Dr. Emanuel W. Sandberg

Dir. of Missionary Ministries, Rev. Reilly Smith

Dir. of Congregational Ministries, Dr. Dan Lawson

Dir. of Pastoral Ministries, Rev. David Cooksey

Dir. of Administrative Services, Mr. Stanley Gentle

Director of Publications, Rev. Richard C. Winfield

Periodicals
The Brethren Evangelist

The Roman Catholic Church is listed under "R".

Christ Catholic Church

The church is a catholic communion established in 1968 to minister to the growing number of people who seek an experiential relationship with God and who desire to make a total commitment of their lives to God. The church is catholic in faith and tradition. Participating cathedrals, churches and missions are located in several states.

Headquarters
405 Kentling Rd., Highlandville, MO 65669 Tel. (417)443-3951

Media Contact, Archbishop, Most Rev. Karl Pruter

Officers
Archbishop, Most Rev. Karl Pruter, P.O. Box 98, Highlandville, MO 65669 Tel. (417)443-3951

Periodicals
St. Willibrord Journal

Christ Community Church (Evangelical-Protestant)

This church was founded by the Rev. John Alexander Dowie on Feb. 22, 1896 at Chicago, Ill. In 1901 the church founded the city of Zion, IL and moved their headquarters there. Theologically, the church is rooted in evangelical orthodoxy. The Scriptures are accepted as the rule of faith and practice. Other doctrines call for belief in the necessity of repentance for sin and personal trust in Christ for salvation. The church is Calvinistic in its approach to the scriptures and pre-millennial in its approach to prophecy.

The Christ Community Church is a denominational member of The National Association of Evangelicals. It has work in six other nations in addition to the United States. Branch ministries are found in Tonalea, Arizona and Lindenhurst, Illinois.

Headquarters
2500 Dowie Memorial Dr., Zion, IL 60099 Tel. (847)746-1411 Fax (847)746-1452

Officers
Senior Pastor, Ken Langley

Christadelphians

The Christadelphians are a body of people who believe the Bible to be the divinely inspired word of God, written by "Holy men who spoke as they were moved by the Holy Spirit" (2 Peter 1:21). They believe that the Old Testament presents God's plan to establish His Kingdom on earth in accord with the promises He made to Abraham and David; and that the New Testament declares how that plan works out in Jesus Christ, who died a sacrificial death to redeem sinners. They believe in the personal return of Jesus Christ as King, to establish "all that God spoke by the mouth of his holy prophets from of old" (Acts 3:21). They believe that at Christ's return many of the dead will be raised by the power of God to be judged. Those whom God deems worthy will be welcomed into eternal life in the Kingdom on earth. Christadelphians believe in the mortality of man; in spiritual rebirth requiring belief and immersion in the name of Jesus; and in a godly walk in this life. They have no ordained clergy, and are organized in a loose confederation of autonomous congregations (ecclesias) in approximately 100 countries. They are conscientiously apposed to participation in war. They endeavor to be enthusiastic in work, loyal in marriage, generous in giving, dedicated in preaching, and cheerful in living.

The denomination was organized in 1844 by a medical doctor, John Thomas, who came to the United States from England in 132, having survived a near shipwreck in a violent storm. This experience affected him profoundly, and he vowed to devote his life to a search for the truth of God and a future hope from the Bible.

Headquarters
Media Contact, Trustee, Norman D. Zilmer, Christadelphian Action Society, 1000 Mohawk Dr., Elgin, IL 60120-3148 Tel. (847)741-5253 Fax (847)888-3334

Email: Nzilmer@aol.com or nfadelle@juno.com

Website: www.tidings.org

Leaders

(Co-Ministers) Norman Fadelle, 815 Chippewa Dr., Elgin, IL 60120; Norman D. Zilmer, 1000 Mohawk Dr., Elgin, IL 60120

Periodicals

Christadelphian Tidings; Christadelphian Advocate

Christian Brethren (also known as Plymouth Brethren)

The Christian Brethren began in the 1820s as an orthodox and evangelical movement in the British Isles and is now worldwide. The name Plymouth Brethren was given by others because the group in Plymouth, England, was a large and influential congregation. In recent years the term Christian Brethren has replaced Plymouth Brethren for the "open" branch of the movement in Canada and British Commonwealth countries and to some extent in the United States.

The unwillingness to establish a denominational structure makes the autonomy of local congregations an important feature of the movement. Other features are weekly observance of the Lord's Supper and adherence to the doctrinal position of conservative, evangelical Christianity.

In the 1840s the movement divided. The "exclusive" branch, led by John Nelson Darby, stressed the interdependency of congregations. Since disciplinary decisions were held to be binding on all assemblies, exclusives had subdivided into seven or eight main groups by the end of the century. Since 1925 a trend toward reunification has reduced that number to three or four.

The "open" branch of the movement was led by George MÅller of orphanage fame. It stressed evangelism and foreign missions. Now the larger of the two branches, it has never experienced world-wide division.

CORRESPONDENT

James A. Stahr, 327 W. Prairie Ave., Wheaton, Il 60187-3408 Tel. (630)665-3757

RELATED ORGANIZATIONS

Interest Ministries, P.O. Box 940, Prospect Heights, IL 60070

Christian Missions in Many Lands, Box 13, Spring Lake, NJ 07762

Stewards Foundation, 14275 Midway Rd., Ste. 285, Addison, TX 75001

International Teams, 411 W. River Rd., Elgin, IL 60123

Emmaus Bible College, 2570 Asbury Rd., Dubuque, IA 52001

Stewards Ministries, 18-3 E. Dundee Rd., Ste. 100, Barrington, IL 60010

Christian Church (Disciples of Christ)

Born on the American frontier in the early 1800s as a movement to unify Christians, this body drew its major inspiration from Thomas and Alexander Campbell in western Pennsylvania and Barton W. Stone in Kentucky. Developing separately, the "Disciples, under Alexander Campbell, and the "Christians," led by Stone, united in 1832 in Lexington, Ky.

The Christian Church (Disciples of Christ) is marked by informality, openness, individualism and diversity. The Disciples claim no official doctrine or dogma. Membership is granted after a simple statement of belief in Jesus Christ and baptism by immersion-although most congregations accept transfers baptized by other forms in other denominations. The Lord's Supper-generally called Communion-is open to Christians of all persuasions. The practice is weekly Communion, although no church law insists upon it.

Thoroughly ecumenical, the Disciples helped organize the National and World Councils of Churches. The church is a member of the Consultation on Church Union. The Disciples and the United Church of Christ have declared themselves to be in "full communion" through the General Assembly and General Synod of the two churches. Official theological conversations have been going on since 1967 directly with the Roman Catholic Church, and since 1987 with the Russian Orthodox Church.

Disciples have vigorously supported world and national programs of education, agricultural assistance, urban reconciliation, care of persons with retardation, family planning and aid to victims of war and calamity. Operating ecumenically, Disciples" personnel or funds work in more than 100 countries outside North America.

Three manifestations or expressions of the church (general, regional and congregational) operate as equals, with strong but voluntary covenantal ties to one another. Entities in each manifestation manage their own finances, own their own property, and conduct their own programs. A General Assembly meets every two years and has voting representation from each congregation.

Headquarters

130 E. Washington St., P.O. Box 1986, Indianapolis, IN 46206-1986 Tel. (317)635-3100 Fax (317)635-3700

Media Contact, Dir. of News & Information, Cliff Willis

Email: cmiller@oc.disciples.org OR cwillis@oc.disciples.org

Website: http://www.disciples.org

Officers

Gen. Minister & Pres., Richard L. Hamm

Mod., Michael W. Mooty, Central Christian Church, 205 E. Short St., Lexingotn, KY 40591-1459

1st Vice-Mod., Zola M. Walker, Jarvis Christian College, PO Box 1470, Hawkins, TX 75765

General Officers

Gen. Minister & Pres., Richard L. Hamm

Assoc. Gen. Min. for Admn., Donald B. Manworren

84

ADMINISTRATIVE UNITS

Bd. of Church Extension: Pres., James L. Powell, 130 E. Washington St., P.O. Box 7030, Indianapolis, IN 46207-7030 Tel. (317)635-6500 Fax (317)635-6534

Christian Bd. of Publ. (Chalice Press): Pres., Cyrus N. White, 1316 Convention Plaza Dr., P.O. Box 179, St. Louis, MO 63166-0179 Tel. (314)231-8500 Fax (314)231-8524

Christian Church Foundation, Inc.: Pres., James P. Johnson, Fax (317)635-1991

Church Finance Council, Inc.: Pres., ""

Council on Christian Unity, Inc.: Pres., Robert K. Welsh

Disciples of Christ Historical Society: Pres., Peter M. Morgan, 1101 19th Ave. S., Nashville, TN 37212-2196 Tel. (615)327-1444 Fax (615)327-1445

Division of Higher Education: Int. Pres., Dennis L. Landon, 11780 Borman Dr., Ste. 100, St. Louis, MO 63146-4159 Tel. (314)991-3000 Fax (314)991-2957

Division of Homeland Ministries: Pres., Ann Updegraff Spleth, Fax (317)635-4426

Division of Overseas Ministries: Pres., Patricia Tucker Spier, Fax (317)635-4323

National Benevolent Association: Pres., Cindy Dougherty, 11780 Borman Dr., Ste. 200, St. Louis, MO 63146-4157 Tel. (314)993-9000 Fax (314)993-9018

Pension Fund: Pres., Arthur A. Hanna, 130 E. Washington St., Indianapolis, IN 46204-3645 Tel. (317)634-4504 Fax (317)634-4071

REGIONAL UNITS OF THE CHURCH

Alabama-Northwest Florida: Regional Minister, John P. Mobley, 1336 Montgomery Hwy. S., Birmingham, AL 35216-2799 Tel. (205)823-5647 Fax (205)823-5673

Arizona: Regional Minister, Gail F. Davis, 4423 N. 24th St., Ste 700, Phoenix, AZ 85016-5544 Tel. (602)468-3815 Fax (602)468-3816

Arkansas: Regional Min./Pres., Barbara E. Jones, 6100 Queensboro Dr., P.O. Box 191057, Little Rock, AR 72219-1057 Tel. (501)562-6053 Fax (501)562-7089

California North-Nevada: Int. Regional Min./Pres., Charles R. Blaisdell, 9260 Alcosta Blvd., C-18, San Ramon, CA 94583-4143 Tel. (510)556-9900 Fax (510)556-9904

Canada: Exec. Director, Stan Litke, 128 Woolwich St., Ste. 202, P.O. Box 64, Guelph, ON N1H 6J6 Tel. (519)823-5190 Fax (519)823-5766

Capital Area: Regional Minister, Wm. Chris Hobgood, 8901 Connecticut Ave., Chevy Chase, MD 20815-6700 Tel. (301)654-7794 Fax (301)654-8372

Central Rocky Mountain Region: Exec. Regional Minister, William E. Crowl, 4325 W. 29th Ave., P.O. Box 12186, Denver, CO 80212 Tel. (303)561-1790 Fax (303)561-1795

Florida: Regional Minister, Jimmie L. Gentle, 924 N. Magnolia, Ste. 200, Orlando, FL 32803 Tel. (407)843-4652 Fax (407)246-0019

Georgia: Regional Minister, David L. Alexander, 2370 Vineville Ave., Macon, GA 31204-3163 Tel. (912)743-8649 Fax (912)741-1508

Idaho-South: Regional Minister, Larry Crist, 4900 N. Five Mile Rd., Boise, ID 83713-1826 Tel. (208)322-0538 Fax (208)375-5442

Illinois-Wisconsin: Regional Minister/Pres., Nathan S. Smith, 1011 N. Main St., Bloomington, IL 61701-1797 Tel. (309)828-6293 Fax (309)829-4612

Indiana: Regional Minister, C. Edward Weisheimer, 1100 W. 42nd St., Indianapolis, IN 46208-3375 Tel. (317)926-6051 Fax (317) 931-2034

Kansas: Regional Minister/Pres., Patsie Sweeden, 2914 S.W. MacVicar Ave., Topeka, KS 66611-1787 Tel. (913)266-2914 Fax (913) 266-0174

Kansas City,Greater: Int. Regional Min./Pres., Paul J. Diehl, Jr., 5700 Broadmoor, Ste. 205, Mission, KS 66202-2405 Tel. (913)432-1414 Fax (913)432-3598

Kentucky: Gen. Minister, A. Guy Waldrop, 1125 Red Mile Rd., Lexington, KY 40504-2660 Tel. (606)233-1391 Fax (606)233-2079

Louisiana: Regional Minister, Bill R. Boswell, 3524 Holloway Prairie Rd., Pineville, LA 71360-5816 Tel. (318)443-0304 Fax (318) 449-1367

Michigan: Regional Minister, Morris Finch, Jr., 2820 Covington Ct., Lansing, MI 48912-4830 Tel. (517)372-3220 Fax (517)372-2705

Mid-America Region: Regional Minister, Stephen V. Cranford, Hwy. 54 W., P. O. Box 104298, Jefferson City, MO 65110-4298 Tel. (573)636-8149 Fax (573)636-2889

Mississippi: Regional Minister, William E. McKnight, 1619 N. West St., P.O. Box 4832, Jackson, MS 39296-4832 Tel. (601)352-6774 Fax (601)355-1221

Montana: Regional Minister, Karen Frank-Plumlee, 1019 Central Ave., Great Falls, MT 59401-3784 Tel. (406)452-7404

Nebraska: Interim Regional Ministers, John and Dawn Stemple, 1268 S. 20th St., Lincoln, NE 68502-1699 Tel. (402)476-0359 Fax (402) 476-0350

North Carolina: Regional Minister, Rexford L. Horne, 509 N.E. Lee St., P.O. Box 1568, Wilson, NC 27894 Tel. (919)291-4047 Fax (919)291-3338

Northeastern Region: Regional Minister, Charles F. Lamb, 1272 Delaware Ave., Buffalo, NY 14209-1531 Tel. (716)882-3735 Fax (716) 882-7671

Northwest Region: Regional Minister/Pres., Jack Sullivan, Jr., 6558-35th Ave. SW, Seattle, WA 98126-2899 Tel. (206)938-1008 Fax (206) 933-1163

Ohio: Regional Pastor/Pres., Howard M. Ratcliff, 38007 Butternut Ridge Rd., P.O. Box

299, Elyria, OH 44036-0299 Tel. (216)458-5112 Fax (216)458-5114

Oklahoma: Regional Pastor, Thomas R. Jewell, 301 N.W. 36th St., Oklahoma City, OK 73118-8661 Tel. (405)528-3577 Fax (405)528-3584

Oregon: Regional Minister, Mark K. Reid, 0245 S.W. Bancroft St., Ste. F, Portland, OR 97201-4267 Tel. (503)226-7648 Fax (503)228-6983

Pacific Southwest Region: Regional Minister/Pres., Don W. Shelton, 2401 N. Lake Ave., Altadena, CA 91001-2418 Tel. (818) 296-0385 Fax (818)296-1280

Pennsylvania: Regional Minister, W. Darwin Collins, 670 Rodi Rd., Pittsburgh, PA 15235-4524 Tel. (412)731-7000 Fax (412)731-4515

South Carolina: Interim Regional Minister, Carl R. Flock, 1098 E. Montague Ave., North Charleston, SC 29405-4837 Tel. (803)554-6886 Fax (803)554-6886

Southwest Region: Regional Minister, Ralph Glenn, 3209 S. University Dr., Fort Worth, TX 76109-2239 Tel. (817)926-4687 Fax (817) 926-5121

Tennessee: Regional Minister/Pres., Glen J. Stewart, 3700 Richland Ave., Nashville, TN 37205-2499 Tel. (615)269-3409 Fax (615) 269-3400

Upper Midwest Region: Regional Minister/Pres., Richard L. Guentert, 3300 University Ave., P.O. Box 1024, Des Moines, IA 50311-1024 Tel. (515)255-3168 Fax (515)255-2625

Virginia: Regional Minister, Lee Parker, 518 Brevard St., Lynchburg, VA 24501 Tel. (804)846-3400 Fax (804)528-4919

West Virginia: Regional Minister, William B. Allen, Rt. 5, Box 167, Parkersburg, WV 26101-9576 Tel. (304)428-1681 Fax (304) 428-1684

Periodicals

The Disciple; Vanguard; Mid-Stream: An Ecumenical Journal

Christian Church of North America, General Council

Originally known as the Italian Christian Church, its first General Council was held in 1927 at Niagara Falls, N.Y. This body was incorporated in 1948 at Pittsburgh, Pa., and is described as Pentecostal but does not engage in the "the excesses tolerated or practiced among some churches using the same name."

The movement recognizes two ordinances-baptism and the Lord's Supper. Its moral code is conservative and its teaching is orthodox. Members are exhorted to pursue a life of personal holiness, setting an example to others. A conservative position is held in regard to marriage and divorce. The governmental form is, by and large, congregational. District and National officiaries, however, are referred to as Presbyteries led by Overseers.

The group functions in cooperative fellowship with the Italian Pentecostal Church of Canada and the Evangelical Christian Churches-Assemblies of God in Italy. It is an affiliate member of the Pentecostal Fellowship of North America and of the National Association of Evangelicals.

Headquarters

1294 Rutledge Rd., Transfer, PA 16154-2299 Tel. (724)962-3501 Fax (724)962-1766

Exec. Sec., Terri Metcalfe

Officers

Executive Bd., Gen. Overseer, Rev. John DelTurco, P.O. Box 1198, Hermitage, PA 16148

Exec. Vice-Pres., Rev. Charles Gay, 26 Delafield Dr., Albany, NY 12205

Asst. Gen. Overseers: Rev. James Demola, P.O. Box 157, Mullica Hill, NJ 08062; Rev. Vincent Prestigiacomo, 21 Tyler Hill Rd., Jaffrey, NH 03452; Rev. Charles Gay, 26 Delafield Dr., Albany, NY 12205; Rev. Michael Trotta, 224 W. Winter Ave., New Castle, PA 16101; Rev. Douglas Bedgood, Sr., 442 Trinidad Ln., Teadkwood Village, Largo, FL 33770

DEPARTMENTS

Benevolence, Rev. John Del Turco, P.O. Box 1198, Hermitage, PA 16148

Home Missions, Rev. John Ferguson

Faith, Order & Credentials, Rev. Rev. Charles Gay, 26 Delafield Dr., Albany, NY 12205

Missions, Rev. David Verzilli, 4875 Shadow Oak, Youngstown, OH 44515

Publications Relations, Rev. John Tedesco, 1188 Heron Rd., Cherry Hill, NJ 08003

Lay Ministries: Rev, Eugene De Marco, 155 Scott St., New Brighton, PA 15066

Education: Rev. Lucian Gandolfo, 1030 Fairfield Circle, Clarks Summit, PA 18411

Periodicals

Vista

Christian Churches and Churches of Christ

The fellowship, whose churches were always strictly congregational in polity, has its origin in the American movement to "restore the New Testament church in doctrine, ordinances and life" initiated by Thomas and Alexander Campbell, Walter Scott and Barton W. Stone in the early 19th century.

Headquarters

Media Contact, No. American Christian Convention Dir., Rod Huron, 4210 Bridgetown Rd., Box 11326, Cincinnati, OH 45211 Tel. (513) 598-6222 Fax (513)598-6471

CONVENTIONS

North American Christian Convention: Dir., Rod Huron, 4210 Bridgetown Rd., Box 11326, Cincinnati, OH 45211 Tel. (513)598-6222; NACC Mailing Address, Box 39456, Cincinnati, OH 45239

National Missionary Convention, Coord., Walter Birney, Box 11, Copeland, KS 67837 Tel. (316)668-5250

Eastern Christian Convention, Kenneth Meade, 5300 Norbeck Rd., Rockville, MD 20853 Tel. (301)460-3550

Periodicals
Christian Standard; Restoration Herald; Horizons; The Lookout

The Christian Congregation, Inc.

The Christian Congregation is a denominational evangelistic association that originated in 1787 and was active on the frontier in areas adjacent to the Ohio River. The church was an unincorporated organization until 1887. At that time a group of ministers who desired closer cooperation formally constituted the church. The charter was revised in 1898 and again in 1970.

Governmental polity basically is congregational. Local units are semi-autonomous. Doctrinal positions, strongly biblical, are essentially universalist in the sense that ethical principles, which motivate us to creative activism, transcend national boundaries and racial barriers. A central tenet, John 13:34-35, translates to such respect for sanctity of life that abortions on demand, capital punishment and all warfare are vigorously opposed. All wars are considered unjust and obsolete as a means of resolving disputes.

Early leaders were John Chapman, John L. Puckett and Isaac V. Smith. Bishop O. J. Read was chief administrative and ecclesiastic officer for 40 years until 1961. Rev. Dr. Ora Wilbert Eads has been general Superintendent since 1961. Ministerial affiliation for independent clergymen is provided.

Headquarters
804 W. Hemlock St., LaFollette, TN 37766
Media Contact, Gen. Supt., Rev. Ora W. Eads, D.D., Tel. (423)562-6330

Officers
Gen. Supt., Rev. Ora W. Eads, D.D.

Christian Methodist Episcopal Church

In 1870 the General Conference of the Methodist Episcopal Church, South, approved the request of its colored membership for the formation of their conferences into a separate ecclesiastical body, which became the Colored Methodist Episcopal Church.

At its General Conference in Memphis, Tenn., May 1954, it was overwhelmingly voted to change the name of the Colored Methodist Episcopal Church to the Christian Methodist Episcopal Church. This became the official name on Jan. 3, 1956.

Headquarters
First Memphis Plaza, 4466 Elvis Presley Blvd., Memphis, TN 38116
Media Contact, Exec. Sec., Dr. W. Clyde Williams, 201 Ashby St., N.W., Ste. 212, Atlanta, GA 30314 Tel. (404)522-2736 Fax (404)522-2736

Officers
Exec. Sec., Dr. W. Clyde Williams, 201 Ashby St., NW, Suite 212, Atlanta, GA 30314 Tel. (404)522-2736
Sec. Gen. Conf., Rev. John Gilmore, Mt. Olive CME Church, 538 Linden Ave., Memphis, TN 38126

OTHER ORGANIZATIONS
Christian Education: Gen. Sec., Dr. Ronald M. Cunningham, 4466 Elvis Presley Blvd., Ste. 214, Box 193, Memphis, TN 38116-7100 Tel. (901)345-0580
Lay Ministry: Gen. Sec., Dr. I. Carlton Faulk, 1222 Rose St., Berkeley, CA 94702 Tel. (415) 655-4106
Evangelism, Missions & Human Concerns: Gen. Sec., Rev. Raymond F. Williams, 14244 Avenida Munoz, Riverside, CA 92508 Tel. (909)656-9716
Finance: Sec., Joseph C. Neal, Jr., P.O. Box 75085, Los Angeles, CA 90075 Tel. (213)233-5050
Publications: Gen. Sec., Rev. William George, 4466 Elvis Presley Blvd., Memphis, TN 38116 Tel. (901)345-0580
Personnel Services: Gen. Sec., Dr. N. Charles Thomas, P.O. Box 9, Memphis, TN 38101 Tel. (901)345-0580
Women's Missionary Council: Pres., Judith E. Grant, 723 E. Upsal St., Philadelphia, PA 19119 Tel. (215)843-7742

BISHOPS
First District: Bishop William H. Graves, 4466 Elvis Presley Blvd., Ste. 222, Memphis, TN 38116 Tel. (901)345-0580
Second District: Bishop Nathaniel L. Linsey, 6322 Elwynne Dr., Cincinnati, OH 45236 Tel. (513) 861-0655
Third District: Bishop Dotcy I. Isom, Jr., 5925 W. Florissant Ave., St. Louis, MO 63136 Tel. (314)381-3111
Fourth District: Bishop Thomas L. Hoyt, Jr., 109 Holcomb Dr., Shreveport, LA 71103 Tel. (318) 222-6284
Fifth District: Bishop Richard O. Bass, 310 18th St. N., Ste. 400, Birmingham, AL 35203 Tel. (205)252-2587
Sixth District: Bishop Othal H. Lakey, 2001 M.L. King, Jr. Dr. SW, Ste. 423, Atlanta, GA 30310 Tel. (404)752-7800
Seventh District: Bishop Oree Broomfield, Sr., 6524 16th St., N.W., Washington, DC 20012 Tel. (202)829-8070
Eighth District: Bishop Marshall Gilmore, Sr., 1616 E. Illinois, Dallas, TX 75216 Tel. (214) 372-9073
Ninth District: Bishop E. Lynn Brown, 3844 W. Slauson Ave., Ste. 1, Los Angeles, CA 90043 Tel. (213)294-3830
Tenth District: Bishop Charles Helton, 5937 Ruth Dr., Charlotte, NC 28215 Tel. (704)567-6092
Retired: Bishop Henry C. Bunton, 853 East

87

Dempster Ave., Memphis, TN 38106; Bishop Chester A. Kirkendoll, 10 Hurtland, Jackson, TN 38305; Bishop C. D. Coleman, Sr., 1000 Longmeadow Ln., DeSoto, TX 75115; Bishop Joseph C. Coles, Jr., P.O. Box 172, South Boston, VA 24592

Periodicals
The Christian Index; The Missionary Messenger

The Christian and Missionary Alliance

The Christian and Missionary Alliance was formed in 1897 by the merger of two organizations begun in 1887 by Dr. Albert B. Simpson, The Christian Alliance and the Evangelical Missionary Alliance. The Christian and Missionary Alliance is an evangelical church which stresses the sufficiency of Jesus as Savior, Sanctifier, Healer, and Coming King and has earned a worldwide reputation for its missionary accomplishments. The Canadian districts became autonomous in 1981 and formed The Christian and Missionary Alliance in Canada.

NATIONAL OFFICE
P.O. Box 35000, Colorado Springs, CO 80935-3500 Tel. (719)599-5999 Fax (719)593-8692
Media Contact, Rev. Robert L. Niklaus

Officers
Pres., Rev. Peter N. Nanfelt, D.D.
Corp. Vice Pres., Rev. Donald A. Wiggins, D.Min.
Sec., Rev. David L. Goodin
Vice Pres. for Operations/Treas., Mr. Duane A. Wheeland, CPA
Vice Pres. for National Church Ministries, Rev. P. David Klinsing
Vice Pres. for International Ministries, Rev. Robert L. Fetherlin, D.Min.
Vice Pres. for Advancement, Rev. Francis W. Grubbs, Ph.D.

Board of Managers
Chpsn., Rev. Richard W. Bailey, DD
Vice-Chpsn., Rev. Robert L. Thune

DISTRICTS
Cambodian: Rev. Nareth May, 1616 S. Palmetto Ave., Ontario, Ca 91762, Tel. 909-988-9434
Central: Dr. Gordon F. Meier, 1218 High St., Wadsworth, OH 44281, Tel. 303-336-2911
Central Pacific: Rev. Edward (Ted) A. Cline, 601 Court St., Woodland, CA 95695 Tel. 530-662-2500
E. Pennsylvania: Dr. Randall B. Corbin, 1200 Spring Garden Dr., Middletown, PA 17057, Tel. 717-985-9240
Great Lakes: Dr. Donald A Wiggins, 2250 Huron Parkway, Ann Arbor, MI 48104 Tel734-677-8555
Haitian North: Rev. Sainvilus Point Du Jour, P.O. Box 791, Nyack, NY 10960, Tel. 914-578-1804

Haitian South: Rev. Brave L. Laverdure, 2922 OakVista Way SW, Lawrenceville, GA 30044, Tel. 770-931-0456
Hmong: Re. Chong-Neng Thao, P.O. Box 219, Brighton, CO 80601, Tel. 303-659-1538
Korean: Rev. P. Gil Kim, 713 W. Commonwealth Ave., Ste. C, Fullerton, CA 92832, Tel. 714-879-5201
Laotian: Rev. Bouathong Vangsoulatda, 725 South Ave., Sacramento, CA 95838, Tel. 916-929-9397
Metropolitan: Rev. John F. Soper, 349 Watchung Ave., North Plainfield, NJ 07060, Tel. 908-668-8421
MidAmerica: Rev. Douglas L. Grogan, 1301 S. 119th St., Omaha, NE 68144, Tel. 402-330-1888
Mid-Atlantic: Rev. John E. Zuch, Jr., P.O. Box 1217, Frederick, MD 21702, Tel. 301-620-9934
Midwest: Dr. M. Fred Polding, 260 Glen Ellyn Road, Bloomingdale, IL 60108, Tel. 630-893-1355
Native American: Rev. Craig S. Smith, 19019 N. 74th Dr., Glendale, AZ 85308, Tel. 623-561-8134
New England: Dr. Richard E. Bush, P.O. Box 288, South Easton, MA 02375 Tel. 508-238-3820
Northeastern: Rev. David J. Phillips, 6275 Pillmore Dr., Rome, NY 13440 Tel. 315-336-4720
NorthWestern: Rev. Craig L. Strawser, 1813 Lexington Ave., N., Roseville, MN 55113 Tel. 651-489-1391
Ohio Valley, Dr. David F. Presher, 4050 Executive Park Dr., #402, Cincinnati, OH 45241, Tel. 513-733-4833
Pacific NW, Rev. Kelvin J. Gardiner, P.O. Box 1030, Canby, OR 97013 Tel. 503-266-2238
Puerto Rico: Rev. Julio A. Aponte, P.O. box 191794, San Juan, PR 00919-1794, Tel. 787-281-0101
Rocky Mountain: Rev. Delbert McKenzie, 2545 St. Johns Ave., Billings, MT 59012 Tel. 406-656-4233
South Atlantic: Rev. L. Ferrell Towns, 10801 Johnston Rd., Ste. 125, Charlotte, NC 28226, Tel. 704-543-0470
South Pacific: Rev. Bill J. Vaughn, 4130 Adams St., Ste. A, Riverside, CA 92504 Tel. 909-351-0111
Southeastern: Dr. Mark T. O' Farrell, P.O. Box 720430, Orlando, FL 32872-0430 Tel. 407-823-9662
Southern: Rev. A. Eugene Hall, 5998 Deerfoot Parkway, Russville, AL 35173 Tel. 205-661-9585
Southwestern: Rev. Daniel R. Wetzel, 5600 E. Loop 820 South Ste. 100, Fort Worth, TX 76119 Tel. 817-561-0879
Spanish Central: Rev. Jose Bruno, 260 Glen Ellyn Rd., Bloomingdale, IL 60108 Tel. 630-924-7171

Spanish Eastern: Rev. Marcelo Realpe, 3133 Central Ave. Suite 202, Union City, NJ 07087, Tel. 201-866-6676

Spanish Western: Rev. Douglas M. Domier, P.O. Box 3805, Dana Point, CA 92629 Tel. 949-489-3816

Vietnamese: Rev. Quang B. Nguyen, 2275 W. Lincoln Ave., Anaheim, CA 92801 Tel. 714-491-8007

W. Great Lakes: Rev John W. Fogal, W6107 Aerotech Dr., Appleton, WI 54915, Tel. 920-734-1123

W. Pennsyylvania, Rev. Palmer L. Zerbe, P.O. Box 429, Punxsutawney, PA 15767, Tel. 814-938-6920

NATIONAL ETHNIC ASSOCIATIONS

African-American: President, Rev. Gus H. Brown, 688 Diagonal Rd., Akron, OH 44320 Tel. 330-376-4654

Chinese: Exec. Sec., Rev. Peter Chu, 14209 Secluded Ln., N. Potomac, MD 20878 Tel. 301-294-8067

Filipino: President, Rev. Angelino B. Apelar, 20922 Longworth Ave., Lakewood, CA 90715 Tel. 562-924-6537

ETHNIC/CULTURAL MINISTRIES

Arab & South Asian: Rev. Joseph S. Kong, P.O. Box 35000, Colorado Springs, CO 80935 Tel. 719-599-5999 x. 2052

Dega: Mr. Glik Rahlan, 713 Highgate Pl., Raleigh, NC 27610 Tel. 919-821-2351

Alliance Jewish Ministries Association: Rev. Abraham Sandler, 9820 Woodfern Rd., Philadelphia, PA 19115 Tel. 215-676-5122

Periodicals

Alliance Life

Christian Reformed Church in North America

The Christian Reformed Church represents the historic faith of Protestantism. Founded in the United States in 1857 and active in Canada since 1908, it asserts its belief in the Bible as the inspired Word of God, and is creedally united in the Belgic Confession (1561), the Heidelberg Catechism (1563), and the Canons of Dort (1618-19).

Headquarters

2850 Kalamazoo Ave., SE, Grand Rapids, MI 49560 Tel. (616)224-0744 Fax (616)224-5895

Media Contact, Gen. Sec., Dr. David H. Engelhard; website: http://www.crcna.org

Officers

Gen. Sec., Dr. David H. Engelhard

Exec. Dir. of Ministries, Dr. Peter Borgdorff

Canadian Ministries Director, Raymond Elgersma, 3475 Mainway, PO Box 5070 STN LCR 1, Burlington, ON L7R 3Y8

Director of Finance and Administration, Kenneth Horjus

OTHER ORGANIZATIONS

The Back to God Hour: Dir. of Ministries, Dr. Calvin L. Bremer, International Headquarters, 6555 W. College Dr., Palos Heights, IL 60463

Christian Reformed Home Missions: Dir., Rev. John A. Rozeboom

Christian Reformed World Missions, US: Dir., Rev. Merle Den Bleyker

Christian Ref. World Missions, Canada: Dir., Albert Karsten, 3475 Mainway, P.O. Box 5070 STN LCR 1, Burlington, ON L7R 3Y8

Christian Reformed World Relief, US: Dir., Andrew Ryskamp

Christian Reformed World Relief, Canada: Dir., H. Wayne deJong, 3475 Mainway, P.O. Box 5070 STN LCR 1, Burlington, ON L7R 3Y8

CRC Publications: Dir., Gary Mulder

Ministers' Pension Fund: Admn., Kenneth Horjus

Periodicals

The Banner

Christian Union

Organized in 1864 in Columbus, Ohio, the Christian Union stresses the oneness of the Church with Christ as its only head. The Bible is the only rule of faith and practice and good fruits the only condition of fellowship. Each local church governs itself.

Headquarters

c/o Christian Union Bible College, P.O. Box 27, Greenfield, OH 45123 Tel. (513)981-2897

Media Contact, Pres., Dr. Joseph Harr, 3025 Converse-Roselm Rd., Grover Hill, OH 45849 Tel. (419)587-3226

Officers

Pres., Dr. Joseph Harr

Vice-Pres., Rev. Harold McElwee, P.O. Box 132, Milo, IA 50166 Tel. (419)822-4261

Sec., Rev. Joseph Cunningham, 1005 N. 5th St., Greenfield, OH 45123 Tel. (513)981-3476

Asst. Sec., Rev. Earl Mitchell, 17500 Hidden Valley Rd., Independence, MO 64057 Tel. (816)373-3416

Treas., Rev. Lawrence Rhoads, 902 N.E. Main St., West Union, OH 45693 Tel. (513)544-2950

Church of the United Brethren in Christ

The Church of the United Brethren in Christ had its beginning with Philip William Otterbein and Martin Boehm, who were leaders in the revival movement in Pennsylvania and Maryland from the late 1760s into the early 1800s.

On Sept. 25, 1800, they and others associated with them formed a society under the name of United Brethren in Christ. Subsequent conferences adopted a Confession of Faith in 1815 and a constitution in 1841. The Church of the United Brethren in Christ adheres to the original constitution as amended in 1957, 1961 and 1977.

89

Headquarters
302 Lake St., Huntington, IN 46750 Tel. (219) 356-2312 Fax (219)356-4730

Media Contact, Communications Dir., Steve Dennie

Email: sdennie@ub.org

Website: http:// www.ub.org

Officers
Bishop, Dr. Ray A. Seilhamer

Gen. Treas./Office Mgr., Marda J. Hoffman

Dept. of Education, Dir., Dr. G. Blair Dowden

Dept. of Church Services, Dir., Rev. Paul Hirschy

Dept. of Missions, Dir., Rev. Kyle McQuillen

Church of the Brethren
German pietists-anabaptists founded the Church of the Brethren in 1708 under Alexander Mack in Schwarzenau, Germany. They entered the colonies in 1719 and settled at Germantown, Pa. They have no other creed than the New Testament, hold to principles of nonviolence, temperance and volunteerism and emphasize religion in daily life.

Headquarters
Church of the Brethren General Offices, 1451 Dundee Ave., Elgin, IL 60120 Tel. (847)742-5100 Fax (847)742-6103

New Windsor Service Center, 500 Main Street, P.O. Box 188, New Windsor, MD 21776-0188 Tel. (410)635-6464 Fax (410)635-8789

Washington Office, 337 N. Carolina Ave. SE, Washington, DC 20003 Tel. (202)546-3202 Fax (202)544-5852

Media Contact, Staff for Interpretation, Howard Royer, Elgin Ofc.

Officers
Mod., Lowell A. Flory

Mod.-Elect, Emily M. Mumma

Sec., Cathy Huffman

GENERAL BOARD STAFF
Ofc. of Ex. Dir.: Ex. Dir., Judy Mills Reimer; Assistant to Ex. Dir., Sue Snyder; Coordinator of Human; Resources, Elsie Holderread

LEADERSHIP TEAM

Exec. Director, Judy Mills Reimer

Treas. & Director of Centralized Resources, Judy E. Keyser

Director & Publisher of Brethren Press, Wendy McFadden

Director of Brethren Witness, David Radcliff

Director of Congregational Life Ministries, Glenn F. Timmons

Director of Funding, Kenneth E. Neher

Director of Global Mission Partnerships, Mervin Keeney

Director of Ministry, Allen T. Hansell

Director of Volunteer Service Ministries, Dan McFadden

Periodicals
Messenger

Church of Christ
Joseph Smith and five others organized the Church of Christ on April 6, 1830 at Fayette, New York. In 1864 this body was directed by revelation through Granville Hedrick to return in 1867 to Independence, Missouri to the "consecrated land" dedicated by Joseph Smith. They did so and purchased the temple lot dedicated in 1831.

Headquarters
Temple Lot, 200 S. River St., P.O. Box 472, Independence, MO 64051 Tel. (816)833-3995

Media Contact, Gen. Church Rep., William A. Sheldon, P.O. Box 472, Independence, MO 64051 Tel. (816)833-3995

Officers
Council of Apostles, Secy., Apostle Smith N. Brickhouse, P.O. Box 472, Independence, MO 64051

Gen. Bus. Mgr., Bishop Alvin Harris, P.O. Box 472, Independence, MO 64051

Periodicals
Zion's Advocate

The Church of Christ (Holiness) U.S.A.
The Church of Christ (Holiness) U.S.A. has a Divine commission to propagate the gospel throughout the world, to seek the conversion of sinners, to reclaim backsliders, to encourage the sanctification of believers, to support divine healing, and to advance the truth for the return of our Lord and Savior Jesus Christ. This must be done through proper organization.

The fundamental principles of Christ's Church have remained the same. The laws founded upon these principles are to remain unchanged. The Church of Christ (Holiness) U.S.A. is representative in form of government; therefore, the final authority in defining the organizational responsibilities rests with the national convention. The bishops of the church are delegated special powers to act in behalf of or speak for the church. The pastors are ordained ministers, who under the call of God and His people, have divine oversight of local churches. However, the representative form of government gives ministry and laity equal authority in all deliberate bodies. With the leadership of the Holy Spirit, Respect, Loyalty and Love will greatly increase.

Headquarters
329 East Monument Street, P.O. Box 3622, Jackson, MS 39207 Tel. (601)353-0222 Fax (601)353-4002

Media Contact, Maurice D. Bingham, Ed. D., Senior Bishop

BOARD OF BISHOPS
Senior Bishop, Maurice D. Bingham, Ed. D.

Eastern Diocese, Bishop Lindsay E. Jones

North Central Diocese, Elder Bennett Wolfe

Northern Diocese, Bishop Emery Lindsay

Pacific Northwest Diocese, Bishop Robert Winn
South Central Diocese, Bishop Joseph Campbell
Southeastern Diocese, Bishop Victor P. Smith
Southwestern Diocese, Bishop Vernon Kennebrew
Western Diocese, Bishop Robert Winn
Board Member, Bishop James K. Mitchell

Church of Christ, Scientist

The Church of Christ, Scientist, was founded in 1879 by Mary Baker Eddy "to commemorate the word and works of our Master [Christ Jesus], which should reinstate primitive Christianity and its lost element of healing" (Church Manual, p. 17). Central to the Church's mission is responding to humanity's search for spiritual answers through its publications, especially Mrs. Eddy's definitive work on health and Bible-based Christian healing, Science and Health with Key to the Scriptures.

The Church also maintains and international speakers' bureau to introduce the public to Christian Science and Mrs. Eddy. Christian Science practitioners, living in hundreds of communities worldwide, are available full-time, to pray with anyone seeking comfort and healing. And Christian Science teachers hold yearly classes for those interested in a more specific understanding of how to practice the Christian Science system of healing.

The worldwide activities and business of the Church are transacted by a five-member Board of Directors in Boston. About 2200 congregations, each democratically organized and governed, are located in 74 countries. Since the church has no clergy, worship services are conducted by lay persons elected to serve as Readers. Each church maintains a Reading Room, a bookstore open to the community for spiritual inquiry and research, and a Sunday School where young people discuss the contemporary relevance of ideas from the Bible and Science and Health.

Headquarters

The First Church of Christ, Scientist, 175 Huntington Ave., Boston, MA 02115
Media Contact, Mgr., Comm. on Publication, Gary A. Jones, Tel. (617)450-3301 Fax (617) 450-3325
Website: www.tfccs.com

Officers

Bd. of Directors: Virginia S. Harris; Walter D. Jones; Olga M. Chaffee, John Lewis Selover; Paul D. Grimes
President, Jean Stark Hebenstreit
Treas., Walter D. Jones
Clk., Olga M. Chaffee
First Reader, J. Thomas Black
Second Reader, Patricia Tupper Hyatt

Periodicals

The Christian Science Monitor (website: www. csmonitor.com); *The Christian Science Journal; Christian Science Sentinel; The*
Herald of Christian Science (13 languages); Christian Science Quarterly Bible Lessons in 16 languages and English Braille

Church of God of Prophecy

The Church of God of Prophecy is one of the churches that grew out of the work of A. J. Tomlinson in the first half of the twentieth century. Historically it shares a common heritage with the Church of God (Cleveland Tennessee) and is in the mainstream of the classical Pentecostal-holiness tradition.

At the death of A. J. Tomlinson in 1943, M. A. Tomlinson was named General Overseer and served until retirement in 1990. He emphasized unity and fellowship unlimited by racial, social or political differences. The present general overseer, Billy D. Murray, Sr., is committed to promoting Christian unity world evangelization.

From its beginnings, the Church has based its beliefs on "the whole Bible, rightly divided," and has accepted the Bible as God's Holy Word, inspired, inerrant and infallible. The church is firm in its commitment to orthodox Christian belief. The Church affirms that there is one God, eternally existing in three persons: Father, Son and Holy Spirit. It believes in the deity of Christ, His virgin birth, His sinless life, the physical miracles He performed, His atoning death on the cross, His bodily resurrection, His ascension to the right hand of the Father and his Second coming. The church professes that salvation results from grace alone through faith in Christ, that regeneration by the Holy Spirit is essential for the salvation of sinful men, and that sanctification by the blood of Christ makes possible personal holiness. It affirms the present ministry of the Holy Spirit by Whose indwelling believers are able to live godly lives and have power for service. The church believes in, and promotes, the ultimate unity of believers as prayed for by Christ in John 17. The church stresses the sanctity of human life and is committed to the sanctity of the marriage bond and the importance of strong, loving Christian families.

Other official teachings include Holy Spirit baptism with tongues as initial evidence; manifestation of the spiritual gifts; divine healing; premillenial second-coming of Christ; total abstinence from the use of tobacco, alcohol and narcotics; water baptism by immersion; the Lord's supper and washing of the saints' feet; and a concern for moderation and holiness in all dimensions of lifestyle.

The Church is racially integrated on all levels, including top leadership. Women play a prominent role in church affairs, serving in pastoral roles and other leadership positions. The church presbytery has recently adopted plurality of leadership in the selection of a General Oversight Group. This group consists of three bishops who, along with the General Overseer, are responsible for inspirational leadership and vision casting for the church body. This group is presently composed of General Overseer Murray and Bishops Perry Gillum, José Reyes, and Larry Wilson.

The Church has local congregations in all 50 states and more than 100 nations worldwide. Organizationally there is a strong emphasis on international missions, evangelism, youth and children's ministries, women's and men's ministries, stewardship, communications, publishing, leadership development and discipleship.

INTERNATIONAL OFFICES

P.O. Box 2910, Cleveland, TN 37320-2910
Media Contact, Larry Wilson, Tel. (423)559-5125 Fax (423)559-5108
Email: wilson@wingnet.net
Website: http://www.cogop.org

Officers

General Oversight Group: Gen. Overseer, Bishop Billy D. Murray, Sr.; General Presbyters: Perry Gillum, José Reyes, and Larry Wilson
International Offices Ministries Dirs.: Admin. Services, Vernon Van Deventer; Communications/Publishing, John Pace; Global Outreach, Randy Howard; Leadership Development, Oswill Williams; Specialized Ministries, Larry Wilson

Periodicals

White Wing Messenger; Victory (Youth Magazine/Sunday School Curriculum); The Happy Harvester; Sunday School Info

Church of God (Anderson, Indiana)

The Church of God (Anderson, Indiana) began in 1881 when Daniel S. Warner and several associates felt constrained to forsake all denominational hierarchies and formal creeds, trusting solely in the Holy Spirit as their overseer and the Bible as their statement of belief. These people saw themselves at the forefront of a movement to restore unity and holiness to the church, not to establish another denomination, but to promote primary allegiance to Jesus Christ so as to transcend denominational loyalties.

Deeply influenced by Wesleyan theology and Pietism, the Church of God has emphasized conversion, holiness and attention to the Bible. Worship services tend to be informal, accentuating expository preaching and robust singing.

There is no formal membership. Persons are assumed to be members on the basis of witness to a conversion experience and evidence that supports such witness. The absence of formal membership is also consistent with the church's understanding of how Christian unity is to be achieved" that is, by preferring the label Christian before all others.

The Church of God is congregational in its government. Each local congregation is autonomous and may call any recognized Church of God minister to be its pastor and may retain him or her as long as is mutually pleasing. Ministers are ordained and disciplined by state or provincial

assemblies made up predominantly of ministers. National program boards serve the church through coordinated ministries and resource materials.

There are Church of God congregations in 89 foreign countries, most of which are resourced by one or more missionaries. There are slightly more Church of God adherents overseas than in North America. The heaviest concentration is in the nation of Kenya.

General Offices

Box 2420, Anderson, IN 46018-2420 Tel. (765) 648-2125 Fax (765) 648-2180
Media Contact, Gen. Director, Church of God Ministries, Robert W. Pearson
Email: bp46012@aol.com
Website: http://www. chog.org

CHURCH OF MINISTRIES

Gen. Dir., Robert W. Pearson, Box 2420, Anderson, IN 46018-2420 Tel. (765) 648-2125 Fax (765) 648-2180
Includes Congregational Ministries, Resource & Linking Ministries and Outreach Ministries

OTHER ORGANIZATIONS

Bd. of Church Extension, Pres., J. Perry Grubbs, Box 2069, Anderson, IN 46018
Women of the Church of God, Natl. Coord., Linda J. Mason, Box 2328, Anderson, IN 46018
Bd. of Pensions, Exec. Sec.-Treas., Jeffrey A. Jenness, Box 2299, Anderson, IN 46018

Periodicals

Inform; Church of God Missions; The Shining Light; Metro Voice

Church of God (Cleveland, Tennessee)

It is one of America's oldest Pentecostal churches founded in 1886 as an outgrowth of the holiness revival under the name Christian Union. In 1907 the church adopted the organizational name Church of God. It has its foundation upon the principles of Christ as revealed in the Bible. The Church of God is Christian, Protestant, foundational in its doctrine, evangelical in practice and distinctively Pentecostal. It maintains a centralized form of government and a commitment to world evangelization.

Headquarters

P.O. Box 2430, Cleveland, TN 37320 Tel. (423) 472-3361 Fax (423)478-7066
Media Contact, Dir. of Communications, Michael L. Baker, Tel. (423)478-7112 Fax (423)478-7066

EXECUTIVES

Gen. Overseer, Paul L. Walker
Asst. Gen. Overseers: R. Lamar Vest; G. Dennis McGuire; T. L. Lowery
Gen. Sec.-Treas., Bill F. Sheeks

DEPARTMENTS

Benefits Board, CEO, Arthur Rhodes

Benevolence, Dir., John D. Nichols

Black Ministries, Dir., Asbury R. Sellers

Business & Records, Dir., Julian B. Robinson

Chaplains Commission, Dir., Robert D. Crick

Communications/Media Ministries: Director, Michael L. Baker

Cross-Cultural Min., Dir., Billy J. Rayburn

European Bible Seminary, Dir., John Sims

Evangelism & Home Missions, Dir., Orville Hagan

Hispanic Institute of Ministry, Dir., Isaias Robles

Hispanic Ministry, Dir., Esdras Betancourt

International Bible College, Pres., Alex Allan

Lay Ministries, Dir., Leonard Albert

Lee University, Pres., C. Paul Conn

Legal Services, Dir., Dennis W. Watkins

Men/Women of Action, Dir., Robert D. Pace

Ministerial Development, Dir., Larry G. Hess

Ministry to Israel, Dir., J. Michael Utterback

Ministry to the Military, Dir.,Robert A. Moore

Music Ministries, Dir., Delton Alford

Native American Ministries, Dir., Douglas M. Cline

Patten College, Chancellor, Bebe Patten

Pentecostal Resource Center, Director, Frances Arrington

Publications, Dir., Daniel F. Boling

Communications, Dir., Michael L. Baker

Puerto Rico Bible School, Pres., Ildefonso Caraballo

School of Ministry, Chancellor, Paul L. Walker

Stewardship, Dir., Al Taylor

Theological Seminary, President, Donald M. Walker

Women's Ministries, Director, Rebecca J. Jenkins

World Missions, Dir., Gene D. Rice

Youth & Christian Education, Dir., David M. Griffis

Periodicals
Church of God Evangel; Save Our World; Ministry Now Profiles

The Church of God (Seventh Day), Denver, Colorado

The Church of God (Seventh Day) began in southwestern Michigan in 1858, when a group of Sabbath-keepers led by Gilbert Cranmer refused to give endorsement to the visions and writings of Ellen G. White, a principal in the formation of the Seventh-Day Adventist Church. Another branch of Sabbath-keepers, which developed near Cedar Rapids, Iowa, in 1860, joined the Michigan church in 1863 to publish a paper called *The Hope of Israel*, the predecessor to the *Bible Advocate*, the church's present publication. As membership grew and spread into Missouri and Nebraska, it organized the General Conference of the Church of God in 1884. The words "Seventh Day" were added to its name in 1923. The headquarters of the church was in Stanberry, Missouri, from 1888 until 1950, when it moved to Denver.

The church observes the seventh day as the Sabbath. It believes in the imminent, personal and visible return of Jesus; that the dead are in an unconscious state awaiting to be resurrected, the righteous to immortality and the wicked to extinction by fire; and that the earth will be the eternal abode of the righteous. It observes two ordinances: baptism by immersion and an annual Communion service accompanied by foot washing.

Headquarters
330 W. 152nd Ave., P.O. Box 33677, Denver, CO 80233 Tel. (303)452-7973 Fax (303)452-0657

Media Contact, Pres., Whaid Rose

Email: cofgsd@denver.net

http://www.denver.net/~cofgsd

Officers
Board Chpsn., Loren Stacy

Conference Pres., Whaid Rose

Dir. of Admin., John Crisp

Spring Vale Academy, Dir., John Tivald

Youth Agency, Dir., Kurt Lang

Bible Advocate Press, Dir., John Crisp

Women's Assoc., Pres., Emogene Coulter

Missions Abroad, Dir., Victor Burford

Summit School of Theology, Dir., Jerry Griffin

Periodicals
The Bible Advocate

Church of God by Faith, Inc.

Founded 1914, in Jacksonville Heights, Florida., by Elder John Bright, this church believes the word of God as interpreted by Jesus Christ to be the only hope of salvation and Jesus Christ the only mediator for people.

Headquarters
3220 Haines St., P.O. Box 3746, Jacksonville, FL 32206 Tel. (904)353-5111 Fax (904)355-8582

Media Contact, Ofc. Mgr., Sarah E. Lundy

Officers
Presiding Bishop, James E. McKnight, P.O. Box 121, Gainesville, FL 32601

Treas., Elder Theodore Brown, 93 Girard Pl., Newark, NJ 07108

Ruling Elders: Elder John Robinson, 300 Essex Dr., Ft. Pierce, FL 33450; Elder D. C. Rourk, 207 Chestnut Hill Dr., Rochester, NY 14617

Exec. Sec., Elder George Matthews, 8834 Camphor Dr., Jacksonville, FL 32208

Church of God General Conference (Oregon, IL and Morrow, GA)

This church is the outgrowth of several independent local groups of similar faith. Some were in existence as early as 1800, and others date their beginnings to the arrival of British immigrants around 1847. Many local churches carried the name Church of God of the Abrahamic Faith.

State and district conferences of these groups were formed as an expression of mutual cooperation. A national organization was instituted at Philadelphia in 1888. Because of strong convictions on the questions of congregational rights and authority, however, it ceased to function until 1921, when the present General Conference was formed at Waterloo, Iowa.

The Bible is accepted as the supreme standard of faith. Adventist in viewpoint, the second (pre-millenial) coming of Christ is strongly emphasized. The church teaches that the kingdom of God will be literal, beginning in Jerusalem at the time of the return of Christ and extending to all nations. Emphasis is placed on the oneness of God and the Sonship of Christ, that Jesus did not pre-exist prior to his birth in Bethlehem and that the Holy Spirit is the power and influence of God. Membership is dependent on faith, repentance and baptism by immersion.

The work of the General Conference is carried on under the direction of the board of directors. With a congregational church government, the General Conference exists primarily as a means of mutual cooperation and for the development of yearly projects and enterprises. The headquarters and Bible College were moved to Morrow, Ga. in 1991.

Headquarters
P.O. Box 100,000, Morrow, GA 30260 Tel. (404)362-0052 Fax (404)362-9307
Media Contact, Pres., David Krogh
Email: info@abc-coggc.org
Website: http://www.abc-coggc.org

Officers
Chpsn., Joe E. James, 100 Buck Dr., Piedmont, SC 29673
Vice-Chpsn., Charles Bottolfs, 43137 Happywoods Rd., Hammond, LA 70403
Pres., David Krogh, Georgia Ofc.
Sec., Pastor Greg Demmitt, 825 E. Drake Dr., Tempe, AZ 85283
Treas., Robert Huddlestun, 16440 Fairfield Ln., Granger, IN 46530

OTHER ORGANIZATIONS
Bus. Admn., Controller, Gary Burnham, Georgia Ofc.
Atlanta Bible College, Pres., David Krogh, Georgia Ofc.

Periodicals
The Restitution Herald; A Journal From the Radical Reformation; Church of God Progress Journal

Church of God in Christ, International

The Church of God in Christ, International was organized in 1969 in Kansas City, Mo., by 14 bishops of the Church of God in Christ of Memphis, Tenn. The doctrine is the same, but the separation came because of disagreement over polity and governmental authority. The Church is Wesleyan in theology (two works of grace) but

stresses the experience of full baptism of the Holy Ghost with the initial evidence of speaking with other tongues as the Spirit gives utterance.

Headquarters
170 Adelphi St., Brooklyn, NY 11205 Tel. (718) 625-9175
Media Contact, Natl. Sec., Rev. Sis. Sharon R. Dunn

Officers
Presiding Bishop, Most Rev. Carl E. Williams, Sr.
Vice-Presiding Bishop, Rt. Rev. J. P. Lucas, 90 Holland St., Newark, NJ 07103
Sec.-Gen., Deacon Dennis Duke, 360 Colorado Ave., Bridgeport, CT 06605
Exec. Admn., Horace K. Williams, Word of God Center, Newark, NJ
Women's Dept., Natl. Supervisor, Evangelist Elvonia Williams
Youth Dept., Pres., Dr. Joyce Taylor, 137-17 135th Ave., S., Ozone Park, NY 11420
Music Dept., Pres., Isaiah Heyward
Bd. of Bishops, Chpsn., Bishop J. C. White, 360 Colorado Ave., Bridgeport, CT 06605

Church of God in Christ, Mennonite

The Church of God in Christ, Mennonite was organized in Ohio in 1859 by the evangelist-reformer John Holdeman. The church unites with the faith of the Waldenses, Anabaptists and other such groups. Emphasis is placed on obedience to the teachings of the Bible, including the doctrine of the new birth and spiritual life, noninvolvement in government or the military, head-coverings for the women, beards for the men and separation from the world shown by simplicity in clothing, homes, possessions and life-style. The church has a worldwide membership of about 17,800, most of them in the United States and Canada.

Headquarters
P.O. Box 313, 420 N. Wedel Ave., Moundridge, KS 67107 Tel. (316)345-2532 Fax (316)345-2582
Media Contact, Dale Koehn, P.O. Box 230, Moundridge, KS 67107 Tel. (316)345-2532 Fax (316)345-2582

Periodicals
Messenger of Truth

The Church Of God In Christ

The Church of God in Christ was founded in 1907 in Memphis, Tennessee, and was organized by Bishop Charles Harrison Mason, a former Baptist minister who pioneered the embryonic stages of the Holiness movement beginning in 1895 in Mississippi.

Its founder organized four major departments between 1910-1916: the Women's Department,

94

the Sunday School, Young Peoples Willing Workers and Home and Foreign Mission.

The Church is trinitarian and teaches the infallibility of scripture, the need for regeneration and subsequent baptism of the Holy Ghost. It emphasizes holiness as God's standard for Christian conduct. It recognizes as ordinances Holy Communion, Water Baptism and Feet Washing. Its governmental structure is basically episcopal with the General Assembly being the Legislative body.

Headquarters

Mason Temple, 939 Mason St., Memphis, TN 38126

World Headquarters, 272 S. Main St., Memphis, TN 38103 Tel. (901)578-3800

Mailing Address, P.O. Box 320, Memphis, TN 38101

Temple Church Of God In Christ, 672 S. Lauderdale St., Memphis, TN 38126 Tel. (901)527-9202

GENERAL OFFICES

Office of the Presiding Bishop: Presiding Bishop, Bishop Chandler D. Owens, Tel. (901)578-3838; Exec. Sec., Elder A. Z. Hall, Jr.

Office of the General Secretary: Gen. Sec., Bishop W. W. Hamilton, (901)578-3858

Office of the Financial Secretary: Sec., Bishop Frank O. White, Tel. (901)578-3810

Office of the Board of Trustees: Chmn., Elder Dwight Green

Office of the Clergy Bureau: Dir., Bishop W. W. Hamilton, Tel. (901)578-3855

Office of Supt. of National Properties: Supt., Bishop W. L. Porter, Tel. (901)774-0710

Board of Publications: Chmn., Bishop Norman Quick, Tel. (901)578-3841

Publishing House: Mgr., Mr. Hughea Terry, Tel. (901)578-3842

Dept. of Missions: Pres., Bishop Carlis L. Moody, Tel. (901)578-3876; Exec. Sec., Elder Jesse W. Denny

Dept. of Women: Pres.-Gen. Supervisor, Mother Emma Crouch, Tel. (901)578-3834; Exec. Sec., Elizabeth C. Moore

Dept. of Evangelism: Pres., Dr. Edward L. Battles, 4310 Steeplechase Trail, Arlington, TX 76016 Tel. (817)429-7166

Dept. of Music: Pres., Lavonia Whitty, Chicago, IL

Dept. of Youth (Youth Congress): Pres., Bishop C. H. Brewer, 260 Roydon Rd., New Haven, CT 06511

Dept. of Sunday Schools: Gen. Supt., Elder Jerry Macklin, 1027 W. Tennyson Rd., Hayward, CA 94544

World Headquarters, C.O.O., Bishop G. E. Pattersen, 438 Mason, Memphis, TN 38126

Church of God in Christ Book Store: Mgr., Geraldine Miller, 272 S. Main St., Memphis, TN 38103 Tel. (901)578-3803

Charles Harrison Mason Foundation: Exec. Dir., 272 S. Main St., Memphis, TN 38103 Tel. (901)578-3803; Bd. of Dir., Chmn., Bishop P. A. Brooks

Dept. of Finance: Chief Financial Officer, Sylvia H. Law

Fine Arts Dept.: Dir., Sara J. Powell

BISHOPS IN THE U.S.A.

Alabama: First, Chester A. Ashworth, 2901 Snavely Ave., Birmingham, AL 35211; Second, W. S. Harris, 3005 Melrose Pl., N.W., Huntsville, AL 35810

Alaska: Charles D. Williams, 2212 Vanderbilt Cir., Anchorage, AK 99504

Arizona: Felton King, P.O. Box 3791, Phoenix, AZ 84030

Arkansas: First, L. T. Walker, 2315 Chester St., Little Rock, AR 72206; Second, D. L. Lindsey, 401 W. 23rd St., North Little Rock, AR 72114

California: North-Central, 815 Calmar Ave., Oakland, CA 94610; Northern, B. R. Stewart, 734 12th Ave., San Francisco, CA 94118; Northeast, L. B. Johnson, 3121 Patridge Ave., Oakland, CA 94605; Evangel, 31313 Braeburn Ct., Haywood, CA 96045; Northwest, Bishop W. W. Hamilton, 14145 Mountain Quail Rd., Salinas, CA 93906; Southern #1, C. E. Blake, 1731 Wellington Rd., Los Angeles, CA 90019; Southern #2, George McKinney, 5848 Arboles, San Diego, CA 92120; Southern Metropolitan, 12418 Gain St., Pacoima, CA 91331; Southwest, B. R. Benbow, 504 Rexford Dr., Beverly Hills, CA 90210; Valley, Warren S. Wilson, 1435 Modoc St., Fresno, CA 93706

Colorado: Colorado, Frank Johnson, 12231 E. Arkansas Pl., Aurora, CO 80014

Connecticut: First, Charles H. Brewer, Jr., 180 Osborne St., New Haven, CT 06515; Second, H. Bordeaux, 135 Westwood Rd., New Haven, CT 06511

Delaware: Lieutenant T. Blackshear, Sr., 17 S. Booth Dr., Penn Acres, New Castle, DE 19720

District of Columbia: Bishop W. Crudup, 5101 Martin Dr., Oxon Hill, MD 20745

Florida: Central, Calvin D. Kensey, 9462 August Dr., Jacksonville, FL 32208; Eastern, Jacob Cohen, 3120 N. W. 48th Terr., Miami, FL 33142; Southwestern, W. E. Davis, 2008 33rd Ave., Tampa, FL 33610; Western, P.O. Box 5472, Orlando, FL 32805

Georgia: Central & Southeast, P.O. Box 824, Atlanta, GA 30301; Southeast, Andrew Hunter, Rt. 4, Box 328, St. Simons Island, GA 31502; Northern, 1717 Havilon Dr., S.W., Atlanta, GA 30311; Southern, C. J. Hicks, 1894 Madden Ave., Macon, GA 31204

Hawaii: First, 1223 W. 80th St., Los Angeles, CA 90044

Idaho: Nathaniel Jones, 630 Chateau, Barstow, CA 92311

Illinois: Sixth, W. Haven Bonner, 1039 Bonner Ave., Aurora, IL 60505; Central, T. T. Rose,

1000 Dr. Taylor Rose Sq., Springfield, IL 62703; Northern, Cody Marshall, 8836 Blackstone, Chicago, IL 60637; Southeast, L. E. Moore, 7840 Contour Dr., St. Louis, MO 63121; Southern, J. Cobb, 323-30th St., Cairo, IL 62914

Indiana: First, Milton L. Hall, 1404 Delphos, Kokomo, IN 46901; Indiana Northern, J. T. Dupree, 1231 Hayden St., Fort Wayne, IN 40806

Iowa: Hurley Bassett, 1730 4th Ave., S.E., Cedar Rapids, IA 52403

Kansas: Central, I. B. Brown, 1635 Hudson Blvd., Topeka, KS 66607; East, William H. McDonald, 1627 N. 78th St., Kansas City, KS 66112; Southwest, J. L. Gilkey, 2403 Shadybrook, Wichita, KS 67214

Kentucky: First, Bishop M. Sykes, P.O. Box 682, Union City, TN 38621

Louisiana: Eastern, #1, Bishop J. E. Gordon, 6610 Chenault Dr., Marrero, LA 70072; Eastern #2, Bishop J. A. Thompson, 2180 Holiday, New Orleans, LA 70114; Eastern #3, Bishop H. E. Quillen, 1913 Lasley St., Bogalusa, LA 70427; Western, Roy L. H. Winbush, 235 Diamond Dr., Lafayette, LA 70501

Maine: Bishop D. W. Grayson, 1237 Eastern Pkwy., Brooklyn, NY 11213

Maryland: Central, S. L. Butts, P.O. Box 4504, Upper Marboro, MD 20775; Eastern Shore, James L. Eure, 635 West Main St., Salisbury, MD 21801; Greater, David Spann, 5023 Gwynn Oak Ave., Baltimore, MD 21207

Massachusetts: First, L. C. Young, 19 Almont St., Mattanpan, MA 02126; Second & New Hampshire, C. W. Williams, 270 Division St., Derby, CT 06418; West, Bryant Robinson, Sr., 1424 Plumtree Rd., Springfield, MA 01119

Michigan: Great Lakes, C. L. Anderson, 20485 Mendota, Detroit, MI 48221; North Central, Herbert J. Williams, 1600 Cedar St., Saginaw, MI 48601; Northeast, P. A. Brooks, II, 30945 Wendbrook Lane, Birmingham, MI 48010; Southwest, First, W. L. Harris, 1834 Outer Dr., Detroit, MI 48234; Second, Earl J. Wright, 18655 Autumn La., Southfield, MI 48076; Third, Rodger L. Jones, 1118 River Forest, Flint, MI 48594; Fourth, N. W. Wells, 530 Sue Lane, Muskegon, MI 49442

Minnesota: Bishop S. N. Frazier, 4309 Park Ave. So., Minneapolis, MN 55409

Mississippi: Northern, T. T. Scott, 1066 Barnes Ave., Clarksdale, MS 38614; Southern #1, Theodore Roosevelt Davis, 1704 Topp Ave., Jackson, MS 39204; Southern #2, Bishop R. Nance, 803 Fayard St., Biloxi, MS 39503

Missouri: Eastern #1, R. J. Ward, 4724 Palm Ave., St. Louis, MO 63115; Eastern #2, W. W. Sanders, 8167 Garner La., Berkeley, MO 63134; Western, E. Harris Moore, 405 E. 64th Terr., Kansas City, MO 64131

Montana: Bishop Carlis L. Moody, 2413 Lee St., Evanston, IL 60202

Nebraska: Eastern, Monte J. Bradford, 3901 Ramelle Dr., Council Bluff, IA 51501; Northeastern, B. T. McDaniels, 1106 N. 31st St., Omaha, NE 68103

Nevada: E. N. Webb, 1941 Goldhill, Las Vegas, NV 89106

New Jersey: First, Esau Courtney, 12 Clover Hill Cir., Trenton, NJ 08538; Third, Bishop William Cahoon, 14 Van Velsor Pl., Newark, NJ 07112

New Mexico: W. C. Griffin, 3322 Montclaire, Albuquerque, NM 87110

New York: Eastern #1, Bishop Ithiel Clemmons, 190-08 104th Ave., Hollis, NY 11412; Eastern #2, Bishop Frank O. White, 67 The Boulevard, Amityville, NY 11701; Eastern #3, Bishop D. W. Grayson, 1233 Eastern Pkwy., Brooklyn, NY 11213; Eastern #4, Bishop C. L. Sexton, 153 McDougal St., Brooklyn, NY 11233; Western #1, LeRoy R. Anderson, 265 Ranch Trail, W., Amherst, NY 14221; Western #2, Charles H. McCoy, 168 Brunswick Blvd., Buffalo, NY 14208

North Carolina: Greater, L. B. Davenport, P.O. Box 156, Plymouth, NC 28803; Second, J. Howard Sherman, Sr., P.O. Box 329, Charlotte, NC 28201

North Dakota: Mission Dept., Bishop Carlis L. Moody, 272 S. Main St., Memphis, TN 38103

Ohio: Northern, Bishop William James, 3758 Chippendale Ct., Toledo, OH 44320; Robert S. Fields, 419 Crandell Ave., Youngstown, OH 44504; Northwest, Robert L. Chapman, 3194 E. 18th St., Cleveland, OH 44120; Northern, Bishop Warren Miller, 3618 Beacon Dr., Cleveland, OH 44122; Southern, Floyde E. Perry, Jr., 3716 Rolliston Rd., Shaker Hts., OH 44120

Oklahoma: Northwest, J. A. Young, P.O. Box 844, Lawton, OK 73501; Southeast, Bishop F. D. Lawson, P.O. Box 581, Stillwater, OK 74076

Oregon: First, Bishop A. R. Hopkins, 1705 N.E. Dekum, Portland, OR 97211; Second, J. C. Foster, 2716 N.E. 9th Ave., Portland, OR 97212

Pennsylvania: Commonwealth, O. T. Jones, Jr., 363 N. 60th St., Philadelphia, PA 19139; Eastern, DeWitt A. Burton, 1400 Wistar Dr., Wyncote, PA 19095; Western, Gordon E. Vaughn, 6437 Stanton Ave., Pittsburgh, PA 15206

Rhode Island: Norman Quick, 1031 E. 215th St., Brooklyn, NY 11221

South Carolina: Johnnie Johnson, 679 Liberty Hall Rd., Goose Creek, SC 29445

South Dakota: Bishop Carlis L. Moody, 2413 Lee St., Evanston, IL 60202

Tennessee: Headquarters, Bishop J. O. Paterson, Jr., 229 Danny Thomas Blvd., Memphis, TN 38126; Second, H. Jenkins Bell, P.O. Box 6118, Knoxville, TN 37914; Central, W. L. Porter, 1235 East Parkway, S., Memphis, TN 38114

Texas: Eastern, J. E. Lee, 742 Calcutta Dr., Dallas, TX 75241; Northeast, J. Neauell Haynes, Watson, W. H, 15622 Rockhouse Rd., Houston, TX 77060; Southeast #1, Robert E. Woodard, Sr., 2614 Wichita, Houston, TX 77004; Southeast #2, A. LaDell Thomas, 4401 McArthur Dr., Waco, TX 76708; Southeast, R. E. Ranger, 325 Terrell Rd., San Antonio, TX 78209

Utah: Nathaniel Jones, c/o Mission Dept., 630 Chateau Rd., Barstow, CA 92311

Vermont:Virginia: First, Sr., 4145 Sunkist Rd., Chesapeake, VA 23321; Second, Samuel L. Green, Jr., 2416 Orcutt Ave., Newport News, VA 23607; Third, Levi E. Willis, Levi E., 5110 Nichal Ct., Norfolk, VA 23508

Washington: T. L. Westbrook, 1256 176th St., Spanaway, WA 98402

West Virginia: Northern, Bishop G. F. Walker, P.O. Box 1467, Princeton, VA 24740; Southern, St. Claire Y. Burnett, P.O. Box 245, Altamonte Springs, FL 32715

Wisconsin: First, Dennis Flakes, 3420 N. 1st St., Milwaukee, WI 53212; Third, J. C. Williams, 4232 N. 24th Pl., Milwaukee, WI 53209

Wyoming: A. W. Martin, 2453 N. Fountain St., Wichita, KS 67220

Periodicals

Whole Truth

The (Original) Church of God, Inc.

This body was organized in 1886 as the first church in the United States to take the name "The Church of God." In 1917 a difference of opinion led this particular group to include the word (Original) in its name. It is a holiness body and believes in the whole Bible, rightly divided, using the New Testament as its rule and government.

Headquarters

P.O. Box 592, Wytheville, VA 24382

Media Contact, Gen. Overseer, Rev. William Dale, Tel. (800)827-9234

Officers

Gen. Overseer, Rev. William Dale

Asst. Gen. Overseer, Rev. Alton Evans

Periodicals

The Messenger

Church of God, Mountain Assembly, Inc.

The church was formed in 1895 and organized in 1906 by J. H. Parks, S. N. Bryant, Tom Moses and William Douglas.

Headquarters

164 N. Florence Ave., P.O. Box 157, Jellico, TN 37762 Tel. (423)784-8260 Fax (423)784-3258

Media Contact, Gen. Sec.-Treas., Rev. Alfred Newton, Jr.

Email: cgmahdq@jellico.com

Website: www.cgmahdq.org

Officers

Gen. Overseer, Rev. Cecil Johnson

Asst. Gen. Overseer/World Missions Dir., Rev. Lonnie Lyke

Gen. Sec.-Treas., Rev. Alfred Newton, Jr.

Youth Ministries & Camp Dir., Rev. Ken Ellis

Periodicals

The Gospel Herald

The Church of Illumination

The Church of Illumination was organized in 1908 for the express purpose of establishing congregations at large, offering a spiritual, esoteric, philosophical interpretation of the vital biblical teachings, thereby satisfying the inner spiritual needs of those seeking spiritual truth, yet permitting them to remain in, or return to, their former church membership.

Headquarters

Beverly Hall, 5966 Clymer Rd., Quakertown, PA 18951 Tel. (800)779-3796

Media Contact, Dir. General, Gerald E. Poesnecker, P.O. Box 220, Quakertown, PA 18951 Tel. (215)536-7048 Fax (215) 536-7058

Email: bevhall@comcat.com

Website: http://www.soul.org

Officers

Dir.-General, Gerald E. Poesnecker, P.O. Box 220, Quakertown, PA 18951

The Church of Jesus Christ of Latter-day Saints

This church was organized April 6, 1830, at Fayette, N.Y., by Joseph Smith. Members believe Joseph Smith was divinely directed to restore the gospel to the earth, and that through him the keys to the Aaronic and Melchizedek priesthoods and temple work also were restored. Members believe that both the Bible and the Book of Mormon (a record of the Lord's dealings with His people on the American continent 600 B.C. - 421 A.D.) are scripture. Membership is over ten million.

In addition to the First Presidency, the governing bodies of the church include the Quorum of the Twelve Apostles, the Presidency of the Seventy, the Quorums of the Seventy and the Presiding Bishopric.

Headquarters

47 East South Temple St., Salt Lake City, UT 84150 Tel. (801)240-1000 Fax (801)240-1167

Media Contact, Dir., Media Relations, Michael Otterson, Tel. (801)240-4378 Fax (801)240-1167

Website: http://www.lds.org

Officers

Pres., Gordon B. Hinckley

1st Counselor, Thomas S. Monson

2nd Counselor, James E. Faust

Council of the Twelve Apostles: Pres., Boyd K. Packer; L. Tom Perry; David B. Haight; Neal

A. Maxwell; Russell M. Nelson; Dallin H. Oaks; M. Russell Ballard; Joseph B. Wirthlin; Richard G. Scott; Robert D. Hales; Jeffrey R. Holland; Henry B. Eyring

AUXILIARY ORGANIZATIONS

Sunday Schools, Gen. Pres., Harold G. Hillam
Relief Society, Gen. Pres., Mary Ellen Smoot
Young Women, Gen. Pres.,Margaret Nadauld
Young Men, Gen. Pres., Jack H. Goaslind
Primary, Gen. Pres., Patricia P. Pinegar

Periodicals

The Ensign; Liahona; The New Era; Friend Magazine

The Church of Jesus Christ of Latter-Day Saints (Reorganized)—Please see Reorganized Church of Jesus Christ of Latter-Day Saints.

The Church of Jesus Christ (Bickertonites)

This church was organized in 1862 at Green Oak, Pa., by William Bickerton, who obeyed the Restored Gospel under Sidney Rigdon's following in 1845.

Headquarters

Sixth & Lincoln Sts., Monongahela, PA 15063 Tel. (412)258-3066
Media Contact, Exec. Sec., John Manes, 2007 Cutter Dr., McKees Rocks, PA 15136 Tel. (412)771-4513

Officers

Pres., Dominic Thomas, 6010 Barrie, Dearborn, MI 48126
First Counselor, Paul Palmieri, 319 Pine Dr., Aliquippa, PA 15001 Tel. (412)378-4264
Second Counselor, Robert Watson, Star Rt. 5, Box 36, Gallup, NM 87301
Exec. Sec., John Manes, 2007 Cutter Dr., McKees Rocks, PA 15136 Tel. (412)771-4513

Periodicals

The Gospel News

Church of the Living God (Motto: Christian Workers for Fellowship)

The Church of the Living God was founded by William Christian in April 1889 at Caine Creek, Ark. It was the first black church in America without Anglo-Saxon roots and not begun by white missionaries.

Christian was born a slave in Mississippi on Nov. 10, 1856 and grew up uneducated. In 1875 he united with the Missionary Baptist Church and began to preach. In 1888 he left the Baptist Church and began what was known as Christian Friendship Work. Believing himself to have been inspired by the Spirit of God through divine revelation and close study of the Scriptures, he was led to the truth that the Bible refers to the church as The Church of the Living God (I Tim. 3:15).

The church believes in the infallibility of the Scriptures, is Trinitarian and believes there are three sacraments ordained by Christ: baptism (by immersion), the Lord's Supper (unleavened bread and water) and foot washing.

The Church of the Living God, C.W.F.F., believes in holiness as a gift of God subsequent to the New Birth and manifested only by a changed life acceptable to the Lord.

Headquarters

430 Forest Ave., Cincinnati, OH 45229 Tel. (513)569-5660
Media Contact, Chief Bishop, W. E. Crumes

EXECUTIVE BOARD

Chief Bishop, W. E. Crumes
Vice-Chief Bishop, Robert D. Tyler, 3802 Bedford, Omaha, NE 68110
Exec. Sec., Bishop C. A. Lewis, 1360 N. Boston, Tulsa, OK 73111
Gen. Sec., Gwendolyn Robinson, 8611 S. University, Chicago, IL 60619
Gen. Treas., Elder Harry Hendricks, 11935 Cimarron Ave., Hawthorne, CA 90250
Bishop E. L. Bowie, 2037 N.E. 18th St., Oklahoma City, OK 73111
Chaplain, Bishop E. A. Morgan, 735 S. Oakland Dr., Decatur, IL 65525;
Bishop Alonza Ponder, 5609 N. Terry, Oklahoma City, OK 73111
Bishop Luke C. Nichols, Louisville, KY
Bishop Jeff Ruffin, Phoenix, AZ
Bishop R. S. Morgan, 12100 Greystone,Terr., Oklahoma City, OK 73120
Bishop S. E. Shannon, 1034 S. King Hwy., St. Louis, MO 63110
Bishop J. C. Hawkins, 3804 N. Temple, Indianapolis, IN 46205
Overseer, Elbert Jones, 4522 Melwood, Memphis, TN 38109

NATIONAL DEPARTMENTS

Convention Planning Committee
Young People's Progressive Union
Christian Education Dept.
Sunday School Dept.
Natl. Evangelist Bd.
Natl. Nurses Guild
Natl. Women's Work Dept.
Natl. Music Dept.
Gen. Sec. Ofc.

Periodicals

The Gospel Truth

Church of the Lutheran Brethren of America

The Church of the Lutheran Brethren of America was organized in December 1900. Five independent Lutheran congregations met together in Milwaukee, Wisconsin, and adopted a constitution patterned very closely on that of the Lutheran Free Church of Norway.

The spiritual awakening in the Midwest during the 1890s crystallized into convictions that led to the formation of a new church body. Chief among the concerns were church membership practices, observance of Holy Communion, confirmation practices and local church government.

The Church of the Lutheran Brethren practices a simple order of worship with the sermon as the primary part of the worship service. It believes that personal profession of faith is the primary criterion for membership in the congregation. The Communion service is reserved for those who profess faith in Christ as savior. Each congregation is autonomous and the synod serves the congregations in advisory and cooperative capacities.

The synod supports a world mission program in Cameroon, Chad, Japan and Taiwan. Approximately 40 percent of the synodical budget is earmarked for world missions. A growing home mission ministry is planting new congregations in the United States and Canada. Affiliate organizations operate several retirement/nursing homes, conference and retreat centers.

Headquarters
1020 Alcott Ave., W., Box 655, Fergus Falls, MN 56538 Tel. (218)739-3336 Fax (218)739-5514
Media Contact, Pres., Rev. Robert M. Overgaard

Officers
Pres., Rev. Robert M. Overgaard, Sr.
Vice-Pres., Rev. David Rinden
Sec., Rev. Richard Vettrus, 707 Crestview Dr., West Union, IA 52175
Exec. Dir. of Finance, Bradley Martinson
Lutheran Brethren Schools, Pres., Rev. Joel Egge, Lutheran Brethren Schools, Box 317, Fergus Falls, MN 56538
World Missions, Exec. Dir., Rev. Matthew Rogness
Home Missions, Exec. Dir., Rev. Armin Jahr
Church Services, Exec. Dir., Rev. David Rinden
Youth Ministries, Exec. Dir., Nathan Lee

Periodicals
Faith & Fellowship

Church of the Lutheran Confession
The Church of the Lutheran Confession held its constituting convention in Watertown, S.D., in August of 1960. The Church of the Lutheran Confession was begun by people and congregations who withdrew from church bodies that made up what was then known as the Synodical Conference over the issue of unionism. Following such passages as I Corinthians 1:10 and Romans 16:17-18, the Church of the Lutheran Confession holds the conviction that mutual agreement with the doctrines of Scripture is essential and necessary before exercise of church fellowship is appropriate.

Members of the Church of the Lutheran Confession uncompromisingly believe the Holy Scriptures to be divinely inspired and therefore inerrant. They subscribe to the historic Lutheran Confessions as found in the Book of Concord of 1580 because they are a correct exposition of Scripture.

The Church of the Lutheran Confession exists to proclaim, preserve and spread the saving truth of the gospel of Jesus Christ, so that the redeemed of God may learn to know Jesus Christ as their Lord and Savior and follow him through this life to the life to come.

Headquarters
501 Grover Rd., Eau Claire, WI 54701 Tel. (715)836-6622
Media Contact, Pres., Daniel Fleischer Tel. (512)241-5147
Email: JohnHLau@juno.com
Website: http://www.primenet.com/~mpkelly/clc/clc.html

Officers
Pres., Rev. Daniel Fleischer, 201 Princess Dr., Corpus Christi, TX 78410-1615
Vice-Pres., Rev. Elton Hallauer, 608 1st St., Hancock, MN 56244
Mod., Prof. Ronald Roehl, 515 Ingram Dr. W., Eau Claire, WI 54701
Sec., Rev. James Albrecht, 102 Market St., P.O. Box 98 Okebena, MN 55432-2408
Treas., Lowell Moen, 3455 Jill Ave., Eau Claire, WI 54701
Archivist-Historian, David Lau
Statistician, Dr. James Sydow, 7863 Alden Way, Fridley, MN 55432-2408

Periodicals
The Lutheran Spokesman; Journal of Theology

Church of the Nazarene
The Church of the Nazarene resulted from the merger of three independent holiness groups. The Association of Pentecostal Churches in America, located principally in New York and New England, joined at Chicago in 1907 with a largely West Coast body called the Church of the Nazarene and formed the Pentecostal Church of the Nazarene. A southern group, the Holiness Church of Christ, united with the Pentecostal Church of the Nazarene at Pilot Point, Texas, in 1908. In 1919 the word "Pentecostal" was dropped from the name. Principal leaders in the organization were Phineas Bresee, William Howard Hoople, H. F. Reynolds and C. B. Jernigan. The first congregation in Canada was organized in November 1902 by Dr. H. F. Reynolds in Oxford, Nova Scotia.

The Church of the Nazarene emphasizes the doctrine of entire sanctification or Christian Holiness. It stresses the importance of a devout and holy life and a positive witness before the world by the power of the Holy Spirit. Nazarenes express their faith through evangelism, compassionate ministries, and education.

Nazarene government is representative, a

studied compromise between episcopacy and congregationalism. Quadrennially, the various districts elect delegates to a general assembly at which six general superintendents are elected.

The international denomination has 9 liberal arts colleges, two graduate seminaries, 43 Bible colleges, two schools of nursing, and a junior college. The church maintains over 600 missionaries in 119 world areas. World services include medical, educational and religious ministries. Books, periodicals and other Christian literature are published at the Nazarene Publishing House.

The church is a member of the Christian Holiness Partnership and the National Association of Evangelicals.

Headquarters

6401 The Paseo, Kansas City, MO 64131 Tel. (816)333-7000 Fax (816)822-9071

Media Contact, Gen. Sec./Headquarters Operations Officer (HOO), Dr. Jack Stone, Tel. (816)333-7000, Ext. 2517

Officers

Gen. Supts.: John A. Knight; William J. Prince; James H. Diehl; Paul G. Cunningham; Jerry D. Porter; Jim L. Bond

Gen. Sec. (HOO), Jack Stone

Gen. Treas. (HFO), Robert Foster

OTHER ORGANIZATIONS

General Bd.: Sec., Jack Stone; Treas., Robert Foster

Evangelism & Church Growth Div., Dir., Bill Sullivan

Chaplaincy Min., Dir., Curt Bowers

Pastoral Min., Dir., Wilbur Brannon

Communications Div., Dir., Michael Estep

NCN Productions, Dir., David Anderson

World Literature Ministries, Dir., Ray Hendrix

Int. Bd. of Educ., Ed. Commissioner, Jerry Lambert

Pensions & Benefits Services USA & Intl., Don Walter

Stewardship Development, Dir., Steve Weber

Sunday School Min. Div., Dir., Talmadge Johnson

Adult Min., Dir., David Felter

Children's Min., Dir., Lynda Boardman

Cirriculum Dir., Randy Cloud

NYI Min., Dir., Fred Fullerton

World Mission Div., Dir., Louie Bustle

Nazarene World Mission Soc., Dir., Nina Gunter

Mission Strategy, Dir., Tom Nees

Periodicals

Holiness Today; Preacher's Magazine; Cross Walk; Grow Magazine

Church of Our Lord Jesus Christ of the Apostolic Faith, Inc.

This church body was founded by Bishop R.C. Lawson in Columbus, Ohio, and moved to New York City in 1919. It is founded upon the teachings of the apostles and prophets, Jesus Christ being its chief cornerstone.

Headquarters

2081 Adam Clayton Powell Jr. Blvd., New York, NY 10027 Tel. (212)866-1700

Media Contact, Exec. Sec., Bishop T. E. Woolfolk, P.O. Box 119, Oxford, NC 27565 Tel. (919)693-9449 Fax (919)693-6115

Officers

Board of Apostles: Chief Apostle, Bishop William L. Bonner;

Presiding Apostle, Bishop Gentle L. Groover; Bishop Frank S. Solomon;

Vice-Presider, Bishop Matthew A. Norwood; Bishop James I. Clark, Jr.; Bishop Wilbur L. Jones; Bishop J. P. Steadman

Bd. of Bishops, Chmn., Bishop Henry A. Moultrie II

Bd. of Presbyters, Pres., Elder Michael A. Dixon

Exec. Sec., Bishop T. E. Woolfolk

Natl. Rec. Sec., Bishop Fred Rubin, Sr.

Natl. Fin. Sec., Bishop Clarence Groover

Natl. Corr. Sec., Bishop Raymond J. Keith, Jr.

Natl Treas., Elder Richard D. Williams

Periodicals

Contender for the Faith

Churches of Christ

Churches of Christ are autonomous congregations whose members appeal to the Bible alone to determine matters of faith and practice. There are no central offices or officers. Publications and institutions related to the churches are either under local congregational control or independent of any one congregation.

Churches of Christ shared a common fellowship in the 19th century with the Christian Churches/Churches of Christ and the Christian Church (Disciples of Christ). Fellowship was gradually estranged following the Civil War due to theistic evolution, higher critical theories, centralization of church-wide activities through a missionary society and addition of musical instruments.

Members of Churches of Christ believe in one God, one Lord and Savior, Jesus Christ, one Holy Spirit, one body or church of God, one baptism by immersion into Christ, one faith revealed in the Holy, inspired, inerrant scriptures and one hope of eternal life based on the grace of God in Christ and a response by each individual of faith and obedience to God's gracious instructions in scripture. The New Testament pattern is followed for salvation and church membership, church organization and standards of Christian living.

Headquarters

Media Contact, Ed., Gospel Advocate, Dr. F. Furman Kearley, 1404 Mockingbird Ln., Corsicana, TX 75110

Periodicals

Action; Christian Woman; Christian Bible Teacher; The Christian Chronicle; Firm Foundation; Gospel Advocate; Guardian of Truth; Restoration Quarterly; 21st Century

Christian; Upreach; Rocky Mountain Christian; The Spiritual Sword; Word and Work

Churches of Christ in Christian Union

Organized in 1909 at Washington Court House, Ohio, as the Churches of Christ in Christian Union, this body believes in the new birth and the baptism of the Holy Spirit for believers. It is Wesleyan, with an evangelistic and missionary emphasis.

The Reformed Methodist Church merged with the Churches of Christ in Christian Union in 1952.

Headquarters

1426 Lancaster Pike, Box 30, Circleville, OH 43113 Tel. (614)474-8856 Fax (614)477-7766
Media Contact, Dir. of Comm., Rev. Ralph Hux

Officers

Gen. Supt., Dr. Daniel Tipton
Asst. Gen. Supt., Rev. Ron Reese
Gen. Treas., Beverly R. Salley
Gen. Bd. of Trustees: Chpsn., Dr. Daniel Tipton; Vice-Chpsn., Rev. Ron Reese
District Superintendents: West Central District, Rev. Ron Reese; South Central District, Rev. Jack Norman; Northeast District, Rev. Don Seymour

Periodicals

The Evangelical Advocate

Churches of God, General Conference

The Churches of God, General Conference (CGGC) had its beginnings in Harrisburg, Pa., in 1825.

John Winebrenner, recognized founder of the Church of God movement, was an ordained minister of the German Reformed Church. His experience-centered form of Christianity, particularly the "new measures" he used to promote it, his close connection with the local Methodists, his "experience and conference meetings" in the church and his "social prayer meetings" in parishioners' homes resulted in differences of opinion and the establishment of new congregations. Extensive revivals, camp meetings and mission endeavors led to the organization of additional congregations across central Pennsylvania and westward through Ohio, Indiana, Illinois and Iowa.

In 1830 the first system of cooperation between local churches was initiated as an "eldership" in eastern Pennsylvania. The organization of other elderships followed. General Eldership was organized in 1845, and in 1974 the official name of the denomination was changed from General Eldership of the Churches of God in North America to its present name.

The Churches of God, General Conference, is composed of 16 conferences in the United States and 1 conference in Haiti. The polity of the church is presbyterial in form. The church has mission ministries in the southwest among native Americans and is extensively involved in church planting and whole life ministries in Bangladesh, Brazil, Haiti and India.

The General Conference convenes in business session triennially. An Administrative Council composed of 16 regional representatives is responsible for the administration and ministries of the church between sessions of the General Conference.

Headquarters

Legal Headquarters, United Church Center, Rm. 213, 900 S. Arlington Ave., Harrisburg, PA 17109 Tel. (717)652-0255
Administrative Offices, General Conf. Dir., Pastor Wayne W. Boyer, 700 E. Melrose Ave., P.O. Box 926, Findlay, OH 45839 Tel. (419)424-1961 Fax (419)424-3343
Media Contact, Editor, Martin A. Cordell, P.O. Box 926, Findlay, OH 45839 Tel. (419) 424-1961 Fax (419)424-3343
Email: cggc@bright.net
Website: http://www.cggc.org

Officers

Pres., Glenn E. Beatty, 1114 Circle Dr., Latrobe, PA 15650 Tel. (412)539-9400
Journaling Sec., Dr. C. Darrell Prichard, 2412 Sweetwater Dr., Findlay, OH 45840 Tel. (419)424-9777
Treas., Robert E. Stephenson, 700 E. Melrose Ave., P.O. Box 926, Findlay, OH 45839 Tel. (419)424-1961

DEPARTMENTS

Cross-Cultural Ministries, Pastor Don Dennison
Pensions, Mr. James P. Thomas
Denominational Comm., Martin A. Cordell
Church Renewal, Pastor Keith L. Raderstorf
Church Planting, -vacant-
Youth & Family Life Ministries, Susan L. Callaway

Periodicals

The Church Advocate; The Gem; The Missionary Signal

Congregational Holiness Church

This body was organized in 1921 and embraces the doctrine of Holiness and Pentecost. It carries on mission work in Mexico, Honduras, Costa Rica, Cuba, Brazil, Guatemala, India, Nicaragua, El Salvador, Belize, Venezuela and Panama.

Headquarters

3888 Fayetteville Hwy., Griffin, GA 30223 Tel. (404)228-4833 Fax (404)228-1177
Media Contact, Gen. Supt., Bishop Chet Smith
Website: www.ch.church.com

EXECUTIVE BOARD

Gen. Supt., Bishop Chet Smith

1st Asst. Gen. Supt., Rev. William L. Lewis
2nd Asst. Gen. Supt., Rev. Wayne Hicks
Gen. Sec., Rev. Leslee Bailey
Gen. Treas., Rev. Ronald Wilson

Periodicals
The Gospel Messenger

Conservative Baptist Association of America

The Conservative Baptist Association of America (now known as CBAmerica) was organized May 17, 1947 at Atlantic City, N.J. The Old and New Testaments are regarded as the divinely inspired Word of God and are therefore infallible and of supreme authority. Each local church is independent, autonomous and free from ecclesiastical or political authority.

CBAmerica provides wide-ranging support to its affiliate churches and individuals through nine regional associations. CBA offers personnel to assist churches in areas such as growth and health conflict resolution and financial analysis. The association supports its clergy with retirement planning, referrals for new places of ministry and spiritual counseling. The Conservative Baptist Women's Ministries assists women in the church to be effective in their personal growth and leadership.

Each June or July there is a National Conference giving members an opportunity for fellowship, inspiration and motivation.

Headquarters
1501 W. Mineral Ave., Suite B, Littleton, CO 80120-5612, Tel. (888)627-1995 or (720)283-3030 Fax (720)28-3333
Media Contact, Executive Administrator, Rev. Ed Mitchell
Email: cbamerica@aol.com
Website: http://www.cbamerica.org

OTHER ORGANIZATIONS
CBInternational, Exec. Dir., Dr. Hans Finzel, 1501 W. Mineral Ave., Littleton, CO 80120-5612
Mission to the Americas, Exec. Dir., Rev. Rick Miller, Box 828, Wheaton, IL 60189
Conservative Baptist Higher Ed. Council, Dr. Brent Garrison, Southwestern College, 2625 E. Cactus Rd., Phoenix, AZ 85032

Periodicals
Spectrum; Front Line

Conservative Congregational Christian Conference

In the 1930s, evangelicals within the Congregational Christian Churches felt a definite need for fellowship and service. By 1945, this loose association crystallized into the Conservative Congregational Christian Fellowship, committed to maintaining a faithful, biblical witness.

In 1948 in Chicago, the Conservative Congregational Christian Conference was established to provide a continuing fellowship for evangelical churches and ministers on the national level. In recent years, many churches have joined the Conference from backgrounds other than Congregational. These churches include Community or Bible Churches and churches from the Evangelical and Reformed background that are truly congregational in polity and thoroughly evangelical in conviction. The CCCC welcomes all evangelical churches that are, in fact, congregational. The CCCC believes in the necessity of a regenerate membership, the authority of the Holy Scriptures, the Lordship of Jesus Christ, the autonomy of the local church and the universal fellowship of all Christians.

The Conservative Congregational Christian Conference is a member of the World Evangelical Congregational Fellowship (formed in 1986 in London, England) and the National Association of Evangelicals.

Headquarters
7582 Currell Blvd., Ste. #108, St. Paul, MN 55125 Tel. (651)739-1474 Fax (651)739-0750
Media Contact, Conf. Min., Rev. Clifford R. Christensen

Officers
Vice-Pres., Rev. Larry Scovil, 317 W. 40th Street, Scottsbluff, NE 69361
Conf. Min., Rev. Clifford R. Christensen, 457 S. Mary St., Maplewood, MN 55119
Controller, Mr. Leslie Pierce, 5220 E. 105th St. S., Tulsa, OK 74137
Treas., Rev. Tay Kersey, 8450 Eastwood Rd., Moundsview, MN 55112
Rec. Sec., Peter Murdy, 4 Plympton St., Middleboro, MA 02346
Editor, Rev. Walter Smith, 10964 St. Hwy 37, Lisbon, NY 13658
Historian, Rev. Milton Reimer, 507 Central Ave., New Rockford, ND 58356

Periodicals
Foresee

Conservative Lutheran Association

The Conservative Lutheran Association (CLA) was originally named Lutheran's Alert National (LAN) when it was founded in 1965 by 10 conservative Lutheran pastors and laymen meeting in Cedar Rapids, Iowa. Its purpose was to help preserve from erosion the basic doctrines of Christian theology, including the inerrancy of Holy Scripture. The group grew to a worldwide constituency, similarly concerned with maintaining the doctrinal integrity of the Bible and the Lutheran Confessions.

Headquarters
Trinity Lutheran Church, 4101 E. Nohl Ranch Rd., Anaheim, CA 92807 Tel. (714)637-8370
Media Contact, Pres., Rev. P. J. Moore
Email: PastorPJ@ix.netcom.com

Officers
Pres., Rev. P. J. Moore, 420 Fernhill La., Anaheim, CA 92807 Tel. (714)637-8370
Vice-Pres., Rev. Dr. R. H. Redal, 409 Tacoma Ave. N., Tacoma, WA 98403 Tel. (206)383-5528
Faith Seminary, Dean, Rev. Dr. Michael J. Adams, 3504 N. Pearl St., P.O. Box 7186, Tacoma, WA 98407 Tel. (888)777-7675 Fax (206)759-1790

Coptic Orthodox Church

This body is part of the ancient Coptic Orthodox Church of Egypt which is currently headed by His Holiness Pope Shenouda III, 116th Successor to St. Mark the Apostle. Egyptian immigrants have organized many parishes in the United States. Copts exist outside Egypt in Ethiopia, Europe, Asia, Australia, Canada and the United States. The total world Coptic community is estimated at 27 million. The church is in full communion with the other members of The Oriental Orthodox Church Family, The Syrian Orthodox Church, Armenian Orthodox Church, Ethiopian Orthodox Church, the Syrian Orthodox Church in India and the Eritrean Orthodox Church.

Headquarters
427 West Side Ave., Jersey City, NJ 07304 Tel. (201)333-0004 Fax (201)333-0502
Media Contact, Fr. Abraam D. Sleman

CORRESPONDENT
Fr. Abraam D. Sleman

Cumberland Presbyterian Church

The Cumberland Presbyterian Church was organized in Dickson County, Tennessee, on Feb. 4, 1810. It was an outgrowth of the Great Revival of 1800 on the Kentucky and Tennessee frontier. The founders were Finis Ewing, Samuel King and Samuel McAdow, ministers in the Presbyterian Church who rejected the doctrine of election and reprobation as taught in the Westminster Confession of Faith.

By 1813, the Cumberland Presbytery had grown to encompass three presbyteries, which constituted a synod. This synod met at the Beech Church in Sumner County, Tenn., and formulated a "Brief Statement" which set forth the points in which Cumberland Presbyterians dissented from the Westminster Confession. These points are:
1. That there are no eternal reprobates;
2. That Christ died not for some, but for all people;
3. That all those dying in infancy are saved through Christ and the sanctification of the Spirit;
4. That the Spirit of God operates on the world, or as coextensively as Christ has made atonement, in such a manner as to leave everyone inexcusable.

From its birth in 1810, the Cumberland Presbyterian Church grew to a membership of 200,000 at the turn of the century. In 1906 the church voted to merge with the then-Presbyterian Church. Those who dissented from the merger became the nucleus of the continuing Cumberland Presbyterian Church.

Headquarters
1978 Union Ave., Memphis, TN 38104 Tel. (901)276-4572 Fax (901)272-3913
Media Contact, Stated Clk., Rev. Robert D. Rush, Fax (901)276-4578
Email: assembly@cumberland.org
Website: http://www.webmaster@cumberland.org

Officers
Mod., Gwendolyn G. Roddye, 3728 Wittenham Dr., Knoxville, TN 37921-1080 Tel. 423-938-2415, Email: RODDYE1@Juno.com
Stated Clk., Rev. Robert D. Rush, Tel. (901)276-4572 Fax (901) 276-4578
General Assembly Council, Exec. Dir., Davis Gray, Tel. (901)276-4572 x. 3316 Fax (901)272-3913

INSTITUTIONS
Cumberland Presbyterian Children's Home, Exec. Dir., Rev. Stan E. Rush, Drawer G, Denton, TX 76202 Tel. (940)382-5112 Fax (940)387-0821; Email: cpch@gte.net
Cumberland Presbyterian Center, Tel. (901)276-4572 Fax (901)272-3913
Memphis Theological Seminary, Pres., Dr. Larry Blakeburn, 168 E. Parkway S., Memphis, TN 38104 Tel. (901)458-8232 Fax (901)452-4051; Email: wa4mff@aol.com
Bethel College, Pres., Robert Prosser, 325 Cherry St., McKenzie, TN 38201 Tel. (901) 352-4004 Fax (901)352-4069; Email: walker mc@bethel-college.edu
Historical Foundation, Archivist, Susan K. Gore, 1978 Union Avenue, Memphis, TN 38104, Tel. 901-276-8602 Fax 901-272-3913

BOARDS
Bd. of Christian Education, Exec. Dir., Claudette Pickle
Bd. of Missions, Exec. Dir., Rev. Michael Sharpe
Bd. of Stewardship, Exec. Sec., Rev. Richard Magrill
Bd. Of the Cumberland Presbyterian, Editor, Rev. Dr. M. Jacqueline Warren

Periodicals
The Cumberland Presbyterian; The Missionary Messenger

Cumberland Presbyterian Church in America

This church, originally known as the Colored Cumberland Presbyterian Church, was formed in May 1874. In May 1869, at the General Assembly meeting in Murfreesboro, Tennessee, Moses Weir of the Black delegation sucessfully appealed for help in organizing a separate African church so that: Blacks could learn self-reliance and independence; they could have more financial assistance; they could minister more effectively among Blacks; and they could worship close to the altar, not in the balconies. He requested that the Cumberland Presbyterian Church organize Blacks into presbyteries and synods, develop schools to train black clergy, grant loans to assist Blacks to secure hymnbooks, Bibles and church buildings and establish a separate General Assembly.

In 1874 the first General Assembly of the Colored Cumberland Presbyterian Church met in Nashville. The moderator was Rev. P. Price and the stated clerk was Elder John Humphrey.

The denomination's General Assembly, the national governing body, is organized around its three program boards and agencies: Finance, Publication and Christian Education, and Missions and Evangelism. Other agencies of the General Assembly are under these three program boards.

The church has four synods (Alabama, Kentucky, Tennessee and Texas), 15 presbyteries and 153 congregations. The CPC extends as far north as Cleveland, Ohio, and Chicago, as far west as Marshalltown, Iowa, and Dallas, Tex., and as far south as Selma, Ala.

Headquarters
Media Contact, Stated Clk., Rev. Dr. Robert. Stanley Wood, 226 Church St., Huntsville, AL 35801 Tel. (205)536-7481 Fax (205)536-7482

Officers
Mod., Rev. Endia Scruggs, 1627 Carroll Rd., Harvest, AL 35749

Stated Clk., Rev. Dr. Rorbert. Stanley Wood, 226 Church St., Huntsville, AL 35801 Tel. (205) 536-7481

SYNODS
Alabama, Stated Clk., Arthur Hinton, 511 10th Ave. N.W., Aliceville, AL 35442

Kentucky, Stated Clk., Mary Martha Daniels, 8548 Rhodes Ave., Chicago, IL 60619

Tennessee, Stated Clk., Elder Clarence Norman, 145 Jones St., Huntington, TN 38334

Texas, Stated Clk., Arthur King, 2435 Kristen, Dallas, TX 75216

Periodicals
The Cumberland Flag

Disciples of Christ—please see **Christian Church (Disciples of Christ)**

Elim Fellowship
The Elim Fellowship, a Pentecostal Body established in 1947, is an outgrowth of the Elim Missionary Assemblies formed in 1933.

It is an association of churches, ministers and missionaries seeking to serve the whole Body of Christ. It is of Pentecostal conviction and charismatic orientation, providing ministerial credentials and counsel and encouraging fellowship among local churches. Elim Fellowship sponsors leadership seminars at home and abroad and serves as a transdenominational agency sending long-term, short-term and tent-making missionaries to work with national movements.

Headquarters
1703 Dalton Rd., Lima, NY 14485 Tel. (716)582-2790 Fax (716)624-1229

Media Contact, Gen. Sec., Paul Anderson

Officers
Gen. Chairman, Bernard J. Evans

Asst. Gen. Chairman, George Veach

Gen. Treas., Michael McDonald

Periodicals
Elim Herald

Episcopal Church
The Episcopal Church entered the colonies with the earliest settlers at Jamestown, Va., in 1607 as the Church of England. After the American Revolution, it became autonomous in 1789 as The Protestant Episcopal Church in the United States of America. (The Episcopal Church became the official alternate name in 1967.) Samuel Seabury of Connecticut was elected the first bishop and consecrated in Aberdeen by bishops of the Scottish Episcopal Church in 1784.

In organizing as an independent body, the Episcopal Church created a bicameral legislature, the General Convention, modeled after the new U.S. Congress. It comprises a House of Bishops and a House of Deputies and meets every three years. A 38-member Executive Council, which meets three times a year, is the interim governing body. An elected presiding bishop serves as Primate and Chief Pastor.

After severe setbacks in the years immediately following the Revolution because of its association with the British Crown and the fact that a number of its clergy and members were Loyalists, the church soon established its own identity and sense of mission. It sent missionaries into the newly settled territories of the United States, establishing dioceses from coast to coast, and also undertook substantial missionary work in Africa, Latin America and the Far East. Today, the overseas dioceses are developing into independent provinces of the Anglican Communion, the worldwide fellowship of 36 churches in communion with the Church of England and the Archbishop of Canterbury.

The beliefs and practices of The Episcopal Church, like those of other Anglican churches, are both Catholic and Reformed, with bishops in the apostolic succession and the historic creeds of Christendom regarded as essential elements of faith and order, along with the primary authority of Holy Scripture and the two chief sacraments of Baptism and Eucharist.

EPISCOPAL CHURCH CENTER
815 Second Ave., New York, NY 10017 Tel. (212)716-6240 or (800)334-7626 Fax (212) 867-0395 or (212)490-3298

Media Contact, Dir. of News & Info., James Solheim, (212)922-5385

Website: www.ecusa.anglican.org

Officers

Presiding Bishop & Primate, Most Rev. Frank Tracy Griswold III

Vice Pres & Assist. to the Presiding Bishop for Administration, Patricia C. Mordecai

Assistant to the Presiding Bishop for Communication, Barbara L. Braver

Assistant to the Presiding Bishop for Program, Ms. Sonia Francis

Treas., Stephen C. Duggan

Canon to the Primate and Presiding Bishop, The Rev. Canon Carlson Gerdau

House of Deputies: Pres., Pamela P. Chinnis

Exec. Officer of the General Convention, Sec. Of the House of Deputies, Sec. Of the Domestic and Foreign Missionary Society, and Sec. Of the Executive Council, The Rev. Rosemari Sullivan

OFFICE OF THE PRESIDING BISHOP

Presiding Bishop, Most Rev. Frank Tracy Griswold III, 212-9229-5322

Vice Pres. Assistant to the Presiding Bishop for Administration, Patricia Mordecai, 212-922-5313

Canon to the Presiding Bishop, Rev. Canon Carl Gerdau, 212-922-5282

Exec. Dir., Church Deployment Office, The Rev. James G. Wilson, 212-922-5251

Coordinator for Ministry Development, The Rev. Dr. Melford E. Holland, Jr., 212-922-5246

Exec. Dir., Office of Pastoral Dev., Rt. Rev. F. Clayton Mathews, 212-716-6163

Exec. Sec., General Board of Examining Chaplains, The Rev. Locke E. Bowman Jr., 919-489-1422

Suffragan Bishop for the Armed Forces, Rt. Rev. Charles L. Keyser, 212-922-5240

Suffragan Bishop for American Churches in Europe, Rt. Rev. Jeffery Rowthorn, 011-33-1-472-01792

Dir., Ecumenical and Interfaith Relations, The Rev. Canon David W. Perry, 212-716-6220

ADMINISTRATION AND FINANCE

Treasurer of the Domestic and Foreign Missionary Society and of the General Convention, Stephen C. Duggan, 212-922-5296

Controller, Thomas Hershkowitz, 212-922-5366

Archivist, Mark Duffy, 800-525-9329

Human Resources, John Colon, 212-922-5158

SERVICE, EDUCATION AND WITNESS

Asst. to the Presiding Bishop for Program, Sonia Francis, 212-922-5198

Dir., Anglican and Global Relations, The Rev. Canon Patrick Mauney, 212-716-6223

Dir., Congregational Ministries, Rev. Winston Ching, 212-922-5344

Editor, Episcopal Life, Jerry Hames, 212-716-6009

Interim Dir., Media Services, The Rev. Clement Lee, 212-922-5386

Dir., News & Information, James Solheim, 212-922-5385

Dir., Migration Ministries, Richard Parkins, 212-716-6252

Dir., Peace & Justice Ministries, The Rev. Brian Grieves, 212-922-5207

Dir., Ministries to the Young & Young Adult Ministries Staff Officer, Thomas Chu, 212-922-5267

Exec. Dir., Presiding Bishop's Fund for World Relief, Sandra Swan, 212-716-6020

BISHOPS IN THE U.S.A.

(C) = Coadjutor; (S) = Suffragan; (A) = Assistant

Address: Right Reverend

Presiding Bishop & Primate, Most Rev. Frank Tracy Griswold III; Pastoral Dev., Rt. Rev. Harold Hopkins; S. Bishop for Chaplaincies to Military\Prisons\Hosp., Rt. Rev. Charles L. Keyser 212-922-5240

Alabama: Henry N. Parsley, Jr., 521 N. 20th St., Birmingham, AL 35203, 205-715-2066

Alaska: Mark MacDonald, David Elsensohn, 1205 Denali Way, Fairbanks, AK 99701-4137, 907-452-3040

Albany: Daniel W. Herzog, 68 S. Swan St., Albany, NY 12210-2301, 518-465-4737

Arizona: Robert Shahan, 114 W.Roosevelt, Phoenix, AZ 85003-1406, 602-254-0976

Arkansas: Larry E. Maze, P.O. Box 162668, Little Rock, AR 72216-4668, 501-372-2168

Atlanta: Frank Kellog Allan, 2744 Peachtree Rd. N.W., Atlanta, GA 30363, 404-365-1010

Bethlehem: Paul Marshall, 333 Wyandotte St., Bethlehem, PA 18015, 610-691-5655

California: William E. Swing, 1055 Taylor St., San Francisco, CA 94115, 415-288-9712

Central Florida: John H. Howe, 1017 E. Robinson St., Orlando, FL 32801, 407-423-3567

Central Gulf Coast: Charles F. Duvall, P.O. Box 13330, Pensacola, FL 32591-3330, 904-434-7337

Central New York: David B. Joslin, 310 Montgomery St., Ste. 200, Syracuse, NY 13202,315-474-6596

Central Pennsylvania: Michael Creighton, P.O. Box 11937, Harrisburg, PA 17108, 717-236-5959

Chicago: William D. Persell, 65 E. Huron St., Chicago, IL 60611, 312-751-4200

Colorado: William J. Winterrowd, 1300 Washington St., Denver, CO 80203, 303-837-1173

Connecticut: Clarence N. Coleridge, 1335 Asylum Ave., Hartford, CT 06105, 203-233-4481

Dallas: James M. Stanton, 1630 Garrett St., Dallas, TX 75206, 214-826-8310

Delaware: Wayne P. Wright, 2020 Tatnall St., Wilmington, DE 19802, 302-656-5441

East Carolina: Clifton Daniel III, P.O. Box 1336, Kinston, NC 28501, 919-522-0885

105

East Tennessee: Charles Von Rosenberg, 401 Cumberland Ave., Knoxville, TN 37902-2302, 615-521-2900

Eastern Michigan: Edward Leidel, 4611 Swede Ave., Midland, MI 48642, 517-752-6020

Eastern Oregon: Rustin R. Kimsey, P.O. Box 620, The Dalles, OR 97058, 541-298-4477

Easton: Martin G. Townsend, P.O. Box 1027, Easton, MD 21601, 410-822-1919

Eau Claire: Keith B. Whitmore, 510 S. Farwell St., Eau Claire, WI 54701, 715-835-3331

El Camino Real: Richard Shimpfky, P.O. Box 1903, Monterey, CA 93940, 408-394-4465

Florida: Stephen H. Jecko, 325 Market St., Jacksonville, FL 32202, 904-356-1328

Fond du Lac: Russell E. Jacobus, P.O. Box 149, Fond du Lac, WI 54936, 414-921-8866

Fort Worth: Jack Iker, 6300 Ridgelea Pl., Ste. 1100, Fort Worth, TX 76116, 817-738-9952

Georgia: Henry Louttit, Jr., 611 East Bay St., Savannah, GA 31401, 912-236-4279

Hawaii: Richard Chang, 229 Queen Emma Square, Honolulu, HI 96813, 808-536-7776

Idaho: Harry B. Bainbridge, P.O. Box 936, Boise, ID 83701, 208-345-4440

Indianapolis: Catherine M. Waynick,1100 W. 42nd St., Indianapolis, IN 46208, 317-926-5454

Iowa: C. Christopher Epting, 225 37th St., Des Moines, IA 50312, 515-277-6165

Kansas: William E. Smalley, 833-35 Polk St., Topeka, KS 66612, 913-235-9255

Kentucky: Edwin F. Gulick, 600 E. Maine, Louisville, KY 40202, 502-584-7148

Lexington: Don A. Wimberly, P.O. Box 610, Lexington, KY 40586, 606-252-6527

Long Island: Orris G. Walker, 36 Cathedral Ave., Garden City, NY 11530, 516-248-4800

Los Angeles: Frederick H. Borsch; Chester Talton, (S), P.O. Box 2164, Los Angeles, CA 90051, 213-482-2040

Louisiana: Charles E. Jenkins, 1623 7th St., New Orleans, LA 70115-4411, 504-895-6634

Maine: Chilton Knudsen, 143 State St., Portland, ME 04101, 207-772-1953

Maryland: Bob Ihloff, 4 East University Pkwy., Baltimore, MD 21218-2437, 410-467-1399

Massachusetts: M. Thomas Shaw, SSJE; Barbara Harris, (S), 138 Tremont St., Boston, MA 02111, 617-482-5800

Michigan: R. Stewart Wood, Jr., 4800 Woodward Ave., Detroit, MI 48201, 313-832-4400

Milwaukee: Roger J. White, 804 E. Juneau Ave., Milwaukee, WI 53202, 414-272-3028

Minnesota: James L. Jelinek; 430 Oak Grove St., #306, Minneapolis, MN 55403, 612-871-5311

Mississippi: Alfred C. Marble, P.O. Box 23107, Jackson, MS 39225-3107, 601-948-5954

Missouri: Hays Rockwell, 1210 Locust St., St. Louis, MO 63103, 314-231-1220

Montana: Charles I. Jones, 515 North Park Ave., Helena, MT 59601, 406-442-2230

Nebraska: James E. Krotz, 200 N. 62nd St., Omaha, NE 68132, 402-341-5373

Nevada: Stewart C. Zabriskie, P.O. Box 6357, Reno, NV 89513, 702-737-9190

New Hampshire: Douglas E. Theuner, 63 Green St., Concord, NH 03301, 603-224-1914

New Jersey: Joe M. Doss, 808 W. State St., Trenton, NJ 08618

New York: Richard F. Grein, 1047 Amsterdam Ave., New York, NY 10025, 212-316-7413

Newark: John Shelby Spong; Jack McKelvey, (S), 24 Rector St., Newark, NJ 07102, 201-622-4306

North Carolina: Robert C. Johnson, Jr., 201 St. Albans Dr., Raleigh, NC 27619, 919-787-6313

North Dakota: Andrew H. Fairfield, P.O. Box 10337, Fargo, ND 58106-0337, 701-235-6688

Northern California: Jerry A. Lamb, P.O. Box 161268, Sacramento, CA 95816, 916-442-6918

Northern Indiana: Michael P. Basden, 117 N. Lafayette Blvd., South Bend, IN 46601, 219-233-6489

Northern Michigan: James Kelsey, 131 E. Ridge St., Marquette, MI 49855, 906-228-7160

Northwest Texas: C. Wallis Ohl, Jr., P.O. Box 1067, Lubbock, TX 79408, 806-763-1370

Northwestern Pennsylvania: Robert D. Rowley, 145 W. 6th St., Erie, PA 16501, 814-456-4203

Ohio: J. Clark Grew; Arthur B. Williams, (S), 2230 Euclid Ave., Cleveland, OH 44115, 216-771-4815

Oklahoma: Robert M. Moody; William J. Cox, (A), 924 N. Robinson, Oklahoma City, OK 73102, 405-232-4820

Olympia: Vincent W. Warner, P.O. Box 12126, Seattle, WA 98102, 206-325-4200

Oregon: Robert Louis Ladehoff, P.O. Box 467, Portland, OR 97034, 503-636-5613

Pennsylvania: Charles Bennison (Coady), 240 S. 4th St., Philadelphia, PA 19106, 215-627-6434

Pittsburgh: Robert W. Duncan, Jr., 325 Oliver Ave., Pittsburgh, PA 15222, 412-281-6131

Quincy: Keith L. Ackerman, 3601 N. North St., Peoria, IL 61604, 309-688-8221

Rhode Island: Geralyn Wolf, 275 N. Main St., Providence, RI 02903, 401-274-4500

Rio Grande: Terence Kelshaw, 4304 Carlisle St. NE, Albuquerque, NM 87107, 505-881-0636

Rochester: William G. Burrill, 935 East Ave., Rochester, NY 14607, 716-473-2977

San Diego: Gethin B. Hughes, St. Paul's Church, 2728 6th Ave., San Diego, CA 92103, 619-291-5947

San Joaquin: John-David Schofield, 4159 East Dakota Ave., Fresno, CA 93726, 209-244-4828

South Carolina: Edward L. Salmon, P.O. Box 20127, Charleston, SC 29413-0127, 843-722-4075

South Dakota: Creighton Robertson, 500 S. Main St., Sioux Falls, SD 57102-0914, 605-338-9751

Southeast Florida: Calvin O. Schofield, Jr., 525 NE 15th St., Miami, FL 33132, 305-373-0881

Southern Ohio: Herbert Thompson, Jr.; Kenneth

Price, (S), 412 Sycamore St., Cincinnati, OH 45202, 513-421-0311

Southern Virginia: David C. Bane, Jr., 600 Talbot Hall Rd., Norfolk, VA 23505, 804-423-8287

Southwest Florida: Rogers S. Harris, P.O. Box 491, St. Petersburg, FL 33731, 941-776-1018

Southwestern Virginia: John B. Lipscomb, P.O. Box 2279, Roanoke, VA 24009, 703-342-6797

Spokane: Frank J. Terry, 245 E. 13th Ave., Spokane, WA 99202, 509-624-3191

Springfield: Peter H. Beckwith, 821 S. 2nd St., Springfield, IL 62704, 217-525-1876

Tennessee: Bertram M. Herlong, One LaFleur Bldg., Ste. 100, 50 Vantage Way, Nashville, TN 37228, 615-251-3322

Texas: Claude E. Payne, 3203 W. Alabama St., Houston, TX 77098, 713-520-6444

Upper South Carolina: Dorsey F. Henderson, Jr., P.O. Box 1789, Columbia, SC 29202, 803-771-7800

Utah: Carolyn Irish, 231 E. First St. S., Salt Lake City, UT 84111, 801-322-4131

Vermont: Mary Adelia McLeod, Rock Point, Burlington, VT 05401, 802-863-3431

Virginia: Peter J. Lee; Clayton Matthews, (S), 110 W. Franklin St., Richmond, VA 23220, 804-643-8451

Washington: Ronald Haines; Jane H. Dixon, (S), Episc. Church House, Mt. St. Alban, Washington, DC 20016, 202-537-6555

West Missouri: John Buchanan, P.O. Box 413216, Kansas City, MO 64141, 816-471-6161

West Tennessee: James M. Coleman, 692 Poplar Ave., Memphis, TN 38105, 901-526-0023

West Texas: James E. Folts; Earl N. MacArthur, (S), P.O. Box 6885, San Antonio, TX 78209, 210-824-5387

West Virginia: John H. Smith, P.O. Box 5400, Charleston, WV 25361-0400, 304-344-3597

Western Kansas: Vernon Strickland, P.O. Box 2507, Salina, KS 67402, 913-825-1626

Western Louisiana: Robert J. Hargrove, Jr., P.O. Box 2031, Alexandria, LA 71309-2031, 318-442-1304

Western Massachusetts: Gordon P. Scruton, 37 Chestnut St., Springfield, MA 01103, 413-737-4786

Western Michigan: Edward L. Lee, 2600 Vincent Ave., Kalamazoo, MI 49008, 616-381-2710

Western New York: J. Michael Garrison, 1114 Delaware Ave., Buffalo, NY 14209, 716-881-0660

Western North Carolina: Robert H. Johnson, P.O. Box 369, Black Mountain, NC 28711, 704-669-2921

Wyoming: Bruce H. Johnson, 104 S. 4th St., Laramie, WY 82070, 307-742-6606

Am. Churches in Europe-Jurisdiction: Jeffery Rowthorn, The American Cathedral, 23 Avenue Georges V, 75008, Paris, France

Navajoland Area Mission: Steven Plummer, P.O. Box 40, Bluff, UT 84512, 505-327-7549

Periodicals

Episcopal Life

The Estonian Evangelical Lutheran Church

For information on the Estonian Evangelical Lutheran Church (EELC), please see the listing in Chapter 4, "Religious Bodies in Canada."

Headquarters

383 Jarvis St., Toronto, ON M5B 2C7

The Evangelical Church Alliance

What is known today as the Evangelical Church Alliance began in 1887 under the name "World's Faith Missionary Association." Years later, on March 28, 1928, a nonprofit organization was incorporated in the state of Missouri under the same name. In October, 1931, the name "Fundamental Ministerial Association" was chosen to reflect the organization's basis of unity.

On July 21, 1958, during the annual convention at Trinity Seminary and Bible College in Chicago, Illinois, a more comprehensive constitution was created and the name was changed to "The Evangelical Church Alliance."

The ECA licenses and ordains ministers who are qualified providing them with credentials from a recognized ecclesiastical body; provides training courses through the Bible Extension Institute for those who have not had the opportunity to attend Seminary or Bible School; provides Associate Membership for churches and Christian organizations giving opportunity for fellowship and networking with other evangelical ministers and organizations who share the same goals and mission, while remaining autonomous; provides Regional Conventions and an Annual International Convention where members can find fellowship, encouragement and training; cooperates with churches in finding new pastors when they have openings.

ECA is an international, nonsectarian, Evangelical organization. There are currently 2,264 ordained and licensed members not including churches and Christian Organizations.

Headquarters

205 W. Broadway St., P.O. Box 9, Bradley, IL 60915 Tel. (815)937-0720 Fax (815)937-0001
Media Contact, Pres./CEO, Dr. George L. Miller

Officers

Pres./CEO, Dr. George L. Miller

Chairman of the Board, Dr. Sterling L. Cauble, Sunman Bible Church, P.O. Box 216, Sunman, IN 47041

1st Vice-Chairman, Dr. Allen Hammond, 1921 Ohio St., Bluefield, WV 24701

2nd Vice-Chairman, Rev. Richard G. Sydnes, P.O. Box 355 Des Moines, IA 50302

Periodicals

The Evangel

107

The Evangelical Church

The Evangelical Church was born June 4, 1968 in Portland, Oregon, when 46 congregations and about 80 ministers, under the leadership of V. A. Ballantyne and George Millen, met in an organizing session. Within two weeks a group of about 20 churches and 30 ministers from the Evangelical United Brethren and Methodist churches in Montana and North Dakota became a part of the new church. Richard Kienitz and Robert Strutz were the superintendents.

Under the leadership of Superintendent Robert Trosen, the former Holiness Methodist Church became a part of the Evangelical Church in 1969, bringing its membership and a flourishing mission field in Bolivia. The Wesleyan Covenant Church joined in 1977, with its missionary work in Mexico, in Brownsville, Texas and among the Navajos in New Mexico.

The Evangelical Church in Canada, where T. J. Jesske was superintendent, became an autonomous organization on June 5, 1970. In 1982, after years of discussions with the Evangelical Church of North America, a founding General Convention was held at Billings, Montana, where the two churches united. In 1993 the Canadian conference merged with the Canadian portion of the Missionary Church to form the Evangelical Missionary Church. The new group maintains close ties with their American counterparts. Currently there are nearly 150 U.S. congregations of the Evangelical Church. The headquarters is located in Minneapolis, Minnisota.

The following guide the life, program and devotion of this church: faithful, biblical and sensible preaching and teaching of those truths proclaimed by scholars of the Wesleyan-Arminian viewpoint; an itinerant system which reckons with the rights of individuals and the desires of the congregation; local ownership of all church properties and assets.

The church is officially affiliated with the Christian Holiness Partnership, the National Association of Evangelicals, Wycliffe Bible Translators, World Gospel Mission and OMS International. The denomination has nearly 150 missionaries.

Headquarters

7733 West River Rd., Minneapolis, MN 55444 Tel. (612)561-0886 Fax (612)561-0774
Media Contact, Gen. Supt., John F. Sills

Officers

Gen. Supt., Dr. John F. Sills
Dir. of Missions, Rev. Duane Erickson

Periodicals

HeartBeat; The Evangelical Challenge

The Evangelical Congregational Church

This denomination had its beginning in the movement known as the Evangelical Associa-

tion, organized by Jacob Albright in 1800. A division which occurred in 1891 in the Evangelical Association resulted in the organization of the United Evangelical Church in 1894. An attempt to heal this division was made in 1922, but a portion of the United Evangelical Church was not satisfied with the plan of merger and remained apart, taking the above name in 1928. This denomination is Wesleyan-Arminian in doctrine, evangelistic in spirit and Methodist in church government, with congregational ownership of local church property.

Congregations are located from New Jersey to Illinois. A denominational center, a retirement village and a seminary are located in Myerstown, Pennsylvania. Three summer youth camps and four camp meetings continue evangelistic outreach. A worldwide missions movement includes conferences in North East India, Liberia, Mexico, Costa Rica, and Japan. The denomination is a member of National Association of Evangelicals.

Headquarters

Evangelical Congregational Church Center, 100 W. Park Ave., Myerstown, PA 17067 Tel. (800)866-7581 Fax (717)866-7383
Media Contact, Bishop, Rev. Michael W. Sigman, Tel. (717)866-7581
Email: eccenter@eccenter.com
Website: http://www.eccenter.com/church/

Officers

Presiding Bishop, Rev. Richard W. Kohl
1st Vice-Chpsn., Rev. Jack Ward, 452 Jarvis Rd., Akron, OH 44319
Sec., Rev. Robert J. Stahl, RD 2, Box 1468, Schuylkill Haven, PA 17972
Asst. Sec.: Rev. Gregory Dimick, Hatfield, PA; Rev. Bruce Ray, Chicago, IL
Treas., Norma Minnich, Reedsville, PA
E.C.C. Retirement Village, Supt., Rev. Bruce Hill, Fax (717)866-6448
Evangelical School of Theology, Pres., Dr. Kirby N. Keller, Fax (717)866-4667

OTHER ORGANIZATIONS

Administrative Council: Chpsn., Bishop Michael W. Sigman; Vice-Chpsn., Rev. Keith R. Miller; Treas., Norma Minnich
Div. of Evangelism & Spiritual Care, Chpsn., Bishop Michael W. Sigman
Div. of Church Ministries & Services, Chpsn., Rev. Keith R. Miller
Div. of Missions, Chpsn., Rev. John Ragsdale
Bd. of Pensions: Pres., William Kautz, New Cumberland, PA; Business Mgr., Rev. Keith R. Miller, Myerstown, PA 17067

Periodicals

Doors and Windows, Window on the World (EC Missions)

The Evangelical Covenant Church

The Evangelical Covenant Church has its roots in historic Christianity as it emerged during the Protestant Reformation, in the biblical instruction of the Lutheran State Church of Sweden and in the great spiritual awakenings of the 19th century.

The Covenant Church adheres to the affirmations of the Protestant Reformation regarding the Holy Scriptures, believing that the Old and the New Testament are the Word of God and the only perfect rule for faith, doctrine and conduct. It has traditionally valued the historic confessions of the Christian church, particularly the Apostles" Creed, while at the same time emphasizing the sovereignty of the Word over all creedal interpretations. It has especially cherished the pietistic restatement of the doctrine of justification by faith as basic to its dual task of evangelism and Christian nurture. It recognizes the New Testament emphasis upon personal faith in Jesus Christ as Savior and Lord, the reality of a fellowship of believers which acknowledges but transcends theological differences and the belief in baptism and the Lord's Supper as divinely ordained sacraments of the church.

While the denomination has traditionally practiced the baptism of infants, in conformity with its principle of freedom it has also recognized the practice of believer baptism. The principle of personal freedom, so highly esteemed by the Covenant, is to be distinguished from the individualism that disregards the centrality of the Word of God and the mutual responsibilities and disciplines of the spiritual community.

Headquarters

5101 N. Francisco Ave., Chicago, IL 60625 Tel. (773)784-3000 Fax (773)784-4366

Media Contact, Pres., Dr. Glenn R. Palmberg

Officers

Pres., Dr. Glenn R. Palmberg
Vice-Pres., Dr. Timothy C. Ek
Sec., Rev. Mary C. Miller
Treas., Dean A. Lundgren

ADMINISTRATIVE BOARDS

Bd. of Christian Educ. & Discipleship: Exec. Dir., Rev. Doreen L. Olson

Bd. of Church Growth & Evangelism: Exec. Dir., Rev. Gary B. Walter

Bd. of Covenant Women Ministries: Exec. Dir., Rev. Ruth Y. Hill

Bd. of Human Resources: Advisory Member, Rev. Mary C. Miller

Bd. of the Ministry: Exec. Dir., Rev. Donn N. Engebretson

Bd. of Pensions: Dir. of Pensions, Rev. Mary C. Miller

Bd. of Communication: Exec. Dir., Donald L. Meyer

Bd. of World Mission: Exec. Dir., Rev. James W. Gustafson

Bd. of Benevolence: Pres. of Covenant Ministries of Benevolence, Paul V. Peterson, 5145 N. California Ave., Chicago, IL 60625

North Park University & Theological Sem.:

Pres., Dr. David G. Horner, 3225 W. Foster Ave., Chicago, IL 60625

SERVICE ORGANIZATIONS

National Covenant Properties: Pres., David W. Johnson, 5101 N. Francisco, Chicago, IL 60625 Tel. (773)784-3000

Covenant Trust Company: Pres., Gilman G. Robinson, 5101 N. Francisco, Chicago, IL 60625 Tel. (773)784-9911

REGIONAL CONFERENCES OF THE E.C.C.

Central Conference: Supt., Herbert M. Freedholm, 3319 W. Foster Ave., Chicago, IL 60625 Tel. (773)267-3060

East Coast Conference: Supt., Robert C. Dvorak, Missionary Rd., Cromwell, CT 06416 Tel. (860)635-2691

Great Lakes Conference: Supt., David S. Dahlberg, 70 W. Streetsboro St., P.O. Box 728, Hudson, OH 44236 Tel. (330)655-9345

Midwest Conference: Supt., Kenneth P. Carlson, 13504 W. Center Rd. #229, Omaha, NE 68144 Tel. (402)334-3060

North Pacific Conference: Supt., Mark A. Novak, 925 116th Ave. NE, # 221, Bellevue, WA 98004 Tel. (425)451-7434

Northwest Conference: Supt., Paul Erickson, 4721 E. 31st St., Minneapolis, MN 55406 Tel. (612)721-4893

Pacific Southwest Conference: Supt., John D. Notehelfer, 2120 Foothill Blvd., #215, La-Verne, CA 91750 Tel. (909)596-6790

Southeast Conference: Supt., Kurt A. Miericke, 1759 W. Broadway St., #7, Oviedo, FL 32765 Tel. (407)977-8009

E.C.C. of Canada: Supt., Jeffrey Anderson, 2791 Pembina Hwy., Winnipeg, MN R3T 2H5 Tel. (204) 269-3437

Midsouth Region: Dir. MidSouth Ministries, Rick Larson, 11811 Misty Valley Dr., Houston, TX 77066 Tel. (281) 583-4673

E.C.C. of Alaska: Field Dir., Paul W. Wilson, P.O. Box 190729, Anchorage, AK 99519 Tel. (907)562-8623

Periodicals

Covenant Companion; Covenant Quarterly; Covenant Home Altar

The Evangelical Free Church of America

In October 1884, 27 representatives from Swedish churches met in Boone, Iowa, to establish the Swedish Evangelical Free Church. In the fall of that same year, two Norwegian-Danish groups began worship and fellowship (in Boston and in Tacoma) and by 1912 had established the Norwegian-Danish Evangelical Free Church Association. These two denominations, representing 275 congregations, came together at a merger conference in 1950.

The Evangelical Free Church of America is an association of local, autonomous churches across the United States and Canada, blended together by common principles, policies and practices. A 12-point statement addresses the major doctrines but also provides for differences of understanding on minor issues of faith and practice.

Overseas outreach includes 500 missionaries serving in 31 countries.

Headquarters

901 East 78th St., Minneapolis, MN 55420-1300 Tel. (612)854-1300 Fax (612)853-8488

Media Contact, Exec. Dir. of Ministry Advancement, Timothy Addington

Officers

Acting Pres./Exec. Vice-Pres., Rev. William Hamel

Moderator, Ronald Aucutt, 3417 Silver Maple Pl., Falls Church, VA 22042

Vice-Moderator, Rev. Mark J. Wold, 41827 Higgins Way, Fremont, CA 94539

Sec., Dr. Roland Peterson, 235 Craigbrook Way, NE, Fridley, MN 55432

Vice-Sec., Rev. William S. Wick, 92 South Main, Northfield, VT 05663

Chief Fin. Ofc., Robert Peterson

Exec. Dir., Evangelical Free Church Mission, Dr. Ben Swatsky

Assoc. Dir. of Mission USA, Rev. Steve Hudson

Periodicals

Evangelical Beacon; Pursuit

Evangelical Friends International— North American Region

The organization restructured from Evangelical Friends Alliance in 1990 to become internationalized for the benefit of its world-wide contacts. The North America Region continues to function within the United States as EFA formerly did. The organization represents one corporate step of denominational unity, brought about as a result of several movements of spiritual renewal within the Society of Friends. These movements are: (1) the general evangelical renewal within Christianity, (2) the new scholarly recognition of the evangelical nature of 17th-century Quakerism, and (3) EFA, which was formed in 1965.

The EFA is conservative in theology and makes use of local pastors. Sunday morning worship includes singing, Scripture reading, a period of open worship and a sermon by the pastor.

Headquarters

5350 Broadmoor Cir. NW, Canton, OH 44709 Tel. (330)493-1660 Fax (330)493-0852

Media Contact, Gen. Supt., Dr. John P. Williams, Jr.

YEARLY MEETINGS

Evangelical Friends Church, Eastern Region, Wayne Ickes, 5350 Broadmoor Cir., N.W., Canton, OH 44709 Tel. (330)493-1660 Fax (330)493-0852

Rocky Mountain YM, John Brawner, 3350 Reed St., Wheat Ridge, CO 80033 Tel. (303)238-5200 Fax (303)238-5200

Mid-America YM, Duane Hansen, 2018 Maple, Wichita, KS 67213 Tel. (316)267-0391 Fax (316)267-0681

Northwest YM, Mark Ankeny, 200 N. Meridian St., Newberg, OR 97132 Tel. (503)538-9419 Fax (503)538-9410

Alaska YM, Sam Williams, P.O. Box 687, Kotzebue, AK 99752 Tel. (907)442-3906

Periodicals

The Friends Voice

Evangelical Lutheran Church in America

The Evangelical Lutheran Church in America (ELCA) was organized April 30-May 3, 1987, in Columbus, Ohio, bringing together the 2.25 million-member American Lutheran Church, the 2.85 million-member Lutheran Church in America, and the 100,000-member Association of Evangelical Lutheran Churches.

The ELCA is, through its predecessors, the oldest of the major U.S. Lutheran churches. In the mid-17th century, a Dutch Lutheran congregation was formed in New Amsterdam (now New York). Other early congregations were begun by German and Scandinavian immigrants to Delaware, Pennsylvania, New York and the Carolinas.

The first Lutheran association of congregations, the Pennsylvania Ministerium, was organized in 1748 under Henry Melchior Muhlenberg. Numerous Lutheran organizations were formed as immigration continued and the United States grew.

In 1960, the American Lutheran Church (ALC) was created through a merger of an earlier American Lutheran Church, formed in 1930, the Evangelical Lutheran Church, begun in 1917, and the United Evangelical Lutheran Church in America started in 1896. In 1963 the Lutheran Free Church, formed in 1897, merged with the ALC.

In 1962, the Lutheran Church in America (LCA) was formed by a merger of the United Lutheran Church, formed in 1918, with the Augustana Lutheran Church, begun in 1860, the American Evangelical Lutheran Church, founded in 1872, and the Finnish Lutheran Church or Suomi Synod, founded in 1891.

The Association of Evangelical Lutheran Churches arose in 1976 from a doctrinal split with the Lutheran Church-Missouri Synod.

The ELCA, through its predecessor church bodies, was a founding member of the Lutheran World Federation, the World Council of Churches, and the National Council of the Churches of Christ in the USA.

The church is divided into 65 geographical areas or synods. These 65 synods are grouped into nine regions for mission, joint programs and service.

Headquarters
8765 W. Higgins Rd., Chicago, IL 60631 Tel. (773)380-2700 Fax (773)380-1465
Media Contact, Dir. for News, John Brooks, Tel. (773)380-2958 Fax (773)380-2406
Email: info@elca.org
Website: http://www.elca.org

Officers
Presiding Bishop, Rev. Dr. H. George Anderson
Sec., Rev. Dr. Lowell G. Almen
Treas., Richard L. McAuliffe
Vice-Pres., Dr. Addie J. Butler
Exec. for Admn., Rev. Dr. Robert N. Bacher
Office of the Bishop: Exec. Assts. for Federal Chaplaincies, Rev. Lloyd W. Lyngdal; Exec. Asst., Rev. Michael L. Cooper-White, Ms. Myrna J. Sheie

DIVISIONS
Div. for Congregational Min.: Co-Exec. Dir., Rev. Mark R. Moller-Gunderson; Co-Exec. Dir., Rev. M. Wyvetta Bullock; Bd. Chpsn., Rev. Nancy I. Amacher; Lutheran Youth Organization, Pres., Rebecca Lawrence
Div. for Higher Educ. & Schools: Exec. Dir., Rev. Dr. W. Robert Sorensen; Bd. Chpsn., Rev. John G. Andreasen
Div. for Global Mission: Exec. Dir., Rev. Bonnie L. Jensen; Bd. Chpsn., Dr. Winston D. Persaud
Div. for Ministry: Exec. Dir., Rev. Dr. Joseph M. Wagner; Bd. Chpsn., Dr. Nelvin Vos
Div. for Outreach: Exec. Dir., Rev. Dr. Richard A. Magnus, Jr.; Bd. Chpsn., Rev. Julius Carroll, IV
Div. for Church in Society: Exec. Dir., Rev. Charles S. Miller, Jr.; Chpsn., Rev. James M. Childs, Jr.

COMMISSIONS
Comm. for Multicultural Ministries: Exec. Dir., Rev. Frederick E.N. Rajan; Chpsn., Rev. W. Arthur Lewis
Comm. for Women: Exec. Dir., Joanne Chadwick; Chpsn., Rev. Ann M. Tiemeyer

CHURCHWIDE UNITS
Conference of Bishops: Asst. to the Bishop, Rev. Michael L. Cooper-White; Chpsn., Rev. Charles H. Maahs
ELCA Foundation: Exec. Dir., The Rev. Donald M. Hallberg, Chpsn., Mr. David D. Swartling
ELCA Publishing House: Exec. Dir., Rev. Marvin L. Roloff; Bd. Chpsn.,Mr. Richard E. Lodmill
ELCA Bd. of Pensions: Exec. Dir., John G. Kapanke; Bd. Chpsn., Emma Graeber Porter
Women of the ELCA: Exec. Dir., Catherine I. H. Braasch; Bd. Chpsn., Linda Chinnia

DEPARTMENTS
Dept. for Communication, Dir., Rev. Eric C. Shafer

Dept. for Ecumenical Affairs, Dir., Rev. Daniel F. Martensen; Committee Chpsn., Rev. Duane H. Larson
Dept. for Human Resources, Dir., Ms. Else Thompson
Dept. for Research & Evaluation, Dir., Dr. Kenneth W. Inskeep
Dept. for Synodical Relations, Dir., Rev. Michael L. Cooper-White

SYNODICAL BISHOPS
Region 1
Alaska, Rev. Larry J. Jorgenson (Interim), 1847 W. Northern Lights Blvd., #2, Anchorage, AK 99517-3343 Tel. (907)272-8899 Fax(907)274-3141
Northwest Washington, Rev. Donald H. Maier, 5519 Pinney Ave. N, Seattle, WA 98103-5899 Tel. (206)783-9292 Fax (206)783-9833
Southwestern Washington, Rev. David C. Wold, 420 121st St., S., Tacoma, WA 98444-5218 Tel. (253)535-8300 Fax(253)535-8315
Eastern Washington-Idaho, Rev. Martin D. Wells, 314 South Spruce St., Ste. A, Spokane, WA 99204-1098 Tel. (509)838-9871 Fax (509) 838-0941
Oregon, Rev. Paul R. Swanson, 2800 N. Vancouver Ave., Ste. 101, Portland, OR 97227-1643 Tel. (503) 413-4191 Fax (503) 413-2407
Montana, Rev. Dr. Mark R. Ramseth, 2415 13th Ave. S., Great Falls, MT 59405-5199 Tel. (406)453-1461 Fax (406)761-4632
Int. Regional Coord., Steven H. Lansing, Region 1, 766-B John St., Seattle, WA 98109-5186 Tel. (206)624-0093 Fax (206)626-0987

Region 2
Sierra Pacific, Rev. Robert W. Mattheis, 401 Roland Way, #215, Oakland, CA 94621-2011 Tel. (510)430-0500 Fax (510)430-8730
Southern California (West), Bishop, Rev. Paul W. Egertson, 1300 E. Colorado St., Glendale, CA 91205-1498 Tel. (818)507-9591 Fax (818) 507-9627
Pacifica, Rev. Murray D. Finck, 23655 Via Del Rio, Ste. B, Yorba Linda, CA 92887-2738 Tel. (714)692-2791 Fax (714)692-9317
Grand Canyon, Rev. Dr. Howard E. Wennes, INTERCHURCH CENTER 4423 N. 24th St., Ste. 400, Phoenix, AZ 85016-5544 Tel. (602)957-3223 Fax (602)956-8104
Rocky Mountain, Rev. Allan C. Bjornberg, 455 Sherman St., Ste. 160, Denver, CO 80203 Tel. (303)777-6700 Fax(303)733-0750
Region 2, Admn. ELCA, Margaret Schmitt Ajer, 3755 Avocado Blvd., Suite 411, La Mesa, CA 91941 Tel. (619)460-9312 Fax (619) 460-9314

Region 3
Western North Dakota, Rev. Duane C. Danielson, 1614 Capitol Way, P.O. Box 370, Bismarck, ND 58502-0370 Tel. (701)223-5312 Fax (701)223-1435
Eastern North Dakota, Rev. Richard J. Foss,

1703 32nd Ave., S., Fargo, ND 58103-5936 Tel. (701)232-3381 Fax (701)232-3180

South Dakota, Rev. Andrea F. DeGroot-Nesdahl, Augustana College, 29th & S. Summit, Sioux Falls, SD 57197-0001 Tel. (605)336-4011 Fax (605)336-4028

Northwestern Minnesota, Rev. Arlen D. Hermodson, Concordia College, 901 8th St. S., Moorhead, MN 56562-0001 Tel. (218)299-3019 Fax(218)299-3363

Northeastern Minnesota, Rev. E. Peter Strommen, 3900 London Rd., Duluth, MN 55804-2241 Tel. (218)525-1947 Fax (218) 525-7672

Southwestern Minnesota, Rev. Stanley N. Olson, 175 E. Bridge St., P.O. Box 499, Redwood Falls, MN 56283-0499 Tel. (507)637-3904 Fax (507)637-2809

Minneapolis Area, Rev. David W. Olson, 122 W. Franklin Ave., Ste. 600, Minneapolis, MN 55404-2474 Tel. (612)870-3610 Fax (612) 870-0170

Saint Paul Area, Rev. Mark S. Hanson, 105 W. University Ave., St. Paul, MN 55103-2094 Tel. (651)224-4313 Fax (651)224-5646

Southeastern Minnesota, Rev. Glenn W. Nycklemoe, Assisi Heights, 1001-14 St. NW, Ste. 300, Rochester, MN 55901-2511 Tel. (507)280-9457 Fax (507)280-8824

Regional Coord., Rev. Craig A. Boehlke, Region 3, Luther Seminary, 2481 Como Ave., St. Paul, MN 55108-1445 Tel. (651)649-0454 Fax(651)641-3425

Region 4

Nebraska, Rev. Dr. Richard N. Jessen, 4980 S. 118th St., Ste. D, Omaha, NE 68137-2220 Tel. (402)896-5311 Fax (402)896-5354

Central States, Rev. Dr. Charles H. Maahs, 6400 Glenwood St., Ste. 210, Shawnee Mission, KS 66202-4021 Tel. (913)362-0733 Fax (913) 362-0317 (M-F)

Arkansas-Oklahoma, Rev. Floyd M. Schoenhals, 6911 S. 66th E. Ave., Ste. 200, Tulsa, OK 74133-1748 Tel. (918)492-4288 Fax (918) 491-6275

Northern Texas-Northern Louisiana, Rev. Mark B. Herbener, 1230 Riverbend Dr., Ste. 105, P.O. Box 560587, Dallas, TX 75356-0587 Tel. (214)637-6865 Fax (214)637-4805

Southwestern Texas, Rev. James E. Bennett, 8919 Tesoro Dr., Ste. 109, P.O. Box 171270, San Antonio, TX 78217-8270 Tel. (210)824-0068 Fax (210)824-7009

Texas-Louisiana Gulf Coast, Rev. Paul J. Blom, 12707 N. Freeway, #580, Houston, TX 77060-1239 Tel. (281)873-5665 Fax (281)875-4716

Regional Coord., Rev. Charles H. Maahs, Central States Synod, 6400 Glenwood St., Ste. 210, Shawnee Mission, KS 66202-4021 Tel. (913)362-0733 Fax (913)362-0317 (M-F)

Region 5

Metropolitan Chicago, Rev. Kenneth R. Olsen, 1420 West Dickens St., Chicago, IL 60614 Tel. (773)248-0021 Fax (773)248-0085

Northern Illinois, Rev. Gary M. Wollersheim, 103 W. State St., Rockford, IL 61101-1105 Tel. (815) 964-9934 Fax(815)964-2295

Central/Southern Illinois, Rev. Alton Zenker, 524 S. Fifth St., Springfield, IL 62701-1822 Tel. (217)753-7915 Fax (217)753-7976

Southeastern Iowa, Rev. Philip L. Hougen, 2635 Northgate Dr., P.O. Box 3167, Iowa City, IA 52244-3167 Tel. (319)338-1273 Fax (319) 351-8677

Western Iowa, Rev. Curtis H. Miller, 318 E. Fifth St., P.O. Box 577, Storm Lake, IA 50588-0577 Tel. (712)732-4968 Fax (712)732-6540

Northeastern Iowa, Rev. Steven L. Ullestad, 201-20th St. SW, P.O. Box 804, Waverly, IA 50677-0804 Tel. (319)352-1414 Fax (319) 352-1416

Northern Great Lakes, Rev. Thomas A. Shrenes, 1029 N. Third St., Marquette, MI 49855-3588 Tel. (906)228-2300 Fax (906)228-2527

Northwest Synod of Wisconsin, Rev. Robert D. Berg, 12 W. Marshall St., P.O. Box 730, Rice Lake, WI 54868-0730 Tel. (715)234-3373 Fax (715) 234-4183

East-Central Synod of Wisconsin, Rev. John C. Beem, 16 Tri-Park Way, Appleton, WI 54914-1658 Tel. (920)734-5381 Fax (920)734-5074

Greater Milwaukee, Rev. Peter Rogness, 1212 S. Layton Blvd., Milwaukee, WI 53215-1653 Tel. (414)671-1212 Fax (414)671-1756

South-Central Synod of Wisconsin, Rev. Dr. Jon S. Enslin, 2909 Landmark Pl., Ste. 202, Madison, WI 53713-4237 Tel. (608)270-0201 Fax (608)270-0202

La Crosse Area, Rev. April Ulring Larson, 3462 Losey Blvd. S., La Crosse, WI 54601-7217 Tel. (608)788-5000 Fax (608)788-4916

Regional Coord., Rev. Carl R. Evenson, Region 5, 675 Deerwood Dr., Ste. 4., Neenah, WI 54956 Tel. (920)720-9880 Fax (920)720-9881

Region 6

Southeast Michigan, Rev. Robert A. Rimbo, 218 Fisher Bldg., 3011 W. Grand Ave., Detroit, MI 48202-3011 Tel. (313)875-1881 Fax (313) 875-1889

North/West Lower Michigan, Rev. Gary L. Hansen, 801 S. Waverly Rd., Ste. 201, Lansing, MI 48917-4254 Tel. (517)321-5066 Fax (517) 321-2612

Indiana-Kentucky, Rev. James R. Stuck, 911 E. 86th St., Ste. 200, Indianapolis, IN 46240-1840 Tel. (317)253-3522 Fax (317)254-5666

Northwestern Ohio, Rev. Marcus C. Lohrmann, 621 Bright Rd., Findlay, OH 45840-6987 Tel. (419) 423-3664 Fax (419)423-8801

Northeastern Ohio, Rev. Marcus J. Miller, 282 W. Bowery St., 3rd Fl., Akron, OH 44307-2504 Tel. (330)253-1500 Fax (330)253-2199

Southern Ohio, Rev. Dr. Callon W. Holloway, Jr., 300 S. 2nd St., Columbus, OH 43215-7102 Tel. (614)464-3532 Fax (614)464-3422

Regional Coord., Marilyn McCann Smith, Region 6, PO Box 91, 119 1/2 N. Main St. Bluffton, OH 45817 Tel. (419)369-4006 Fax (419)369-4007

Region 7

New Jersey, Rev. E. Roy Riley, Jr., 1930 State Hwy. 33, Hamilton Square, Trenton, NJ 08690-1799 Tel. (609) 586-6800 Fax (609) 586-1597

New England, Rev. Robert L. Isaksen, 20 Upland St., Worcester, MA 01607-1624 Tel. (508)791-1530 Fax (508)797-9295

Metropolitan New York, Rev. Stephen P. Bouman, 390 Park Ave., S., 7th Floor, New York, NY 10016-8803 Tel. (212)532-5369 Fax (212)532-5078

Upstate New York, Rev. Dr. Lee M. Miller, 3049 E. Genesee St., Syracuse, NY 13224-1699 Tel. (315)446-2502 Fax (315)446-4642

Northeastern Pennsylvania, Rev. Dr. David R. Strobel, 4865 Hamilton Blvd., Wescosville, PA 18106-9705 Tel. (610)395-6891 Fax (610) 398-7083

Southeastern Pennsylvania, Rev. Roy G. Almquist, 506 Haws Ave., Norristown, PA 19401-4543 Tel. (610)278-7342 Fax (610) 696-2782

Slovak Zion, Rev. Juan Cobrda, 8340 N. Oleander Ave., Niles, IL 60714 Tel. (847)965-2475 Fax (847)583-8015

Regional Coord., Rev. Caleb Harms, Lutheran Theol. Seminary at Philadelphia, Hagan Hall, 7301 Germantown Ave., Philadelphia, PA 19119-1794 Tel. (215)248-4616 Fax (215) 248-4577

Region 8

Northwestern Pennsylvania, Rev. Paull E. Spring, Rte. 257, Salina Rd., P.O. Box 338, Seneca, PA 16346-0338 Tel. (814)677-5706 Fax (814)676-8591

Southwestern Pennsylvania, Rev. Donald J. McCoid, 9625 Perry Hwy., Pittsburgh, PA 15237-5590 Tel. (412)367-8222 Fax (412) 369-8840

Allegheny, Rev. Gregory R. Pile, 701 Quail Ave., Altoona, PA 16602-3010 Tel. (814)942-1042 Fax (814)941-9259

Lower Susquehanna, Rev. Dr. Guy S. Edmiston, Jr., 900 S. Arlington Ave., Rm. 208, Harrisburg, PA 17109-5031 Tel. (717)652-1852 Fax (717)652-2504

Upper Susquehanna, Rev. Dr. A. Donald Main, Rt. 192 & Reitz Blvd., P.O. Box 36, Lewisburg, PA 17837-0036 Tel. (570)524-9778 Fax (570)524-9757

Delaware-Maryland, Rev. Dr. George P. Mocko, 7604 York Rd., Baltimore, MD 21204-7570 Tel. (410)825-9520 Fax (410)825-6745

Metropolitan Washington, D.C., Rev. Theodore F. Schneider, 1030-15th St., Ste 1010, Washington, DC 20005-1503 Tel. (202)408-8110 Fax (202)408-8114

West Virginia-Western Maryland, Rev. Ralph Dunkin, The Atrium, 503 Morgantown Avenue, Ste. 100, Fairmont, WV 26554-4374 Tel. (304)363-4030 Fax (304)366-9846

Regional Coord., Dir., Rev. James E. Miley, Lutheran Theological Sem. at Gettysburg, 61 Seminary Ridge, Gettysburg, PA 17325-1795 Tel. (717)334-6286 Ext. 2133 Fax (717)334-0323

Region 9

Virginia, Rev. James F. Mauney, Roanoke College, Bittle Hall, P.O. Drawer 70, Salem, VA 24153-0070 Tel. (540)389-1000 Fax (540)389-5962

North Carolina, Rev. Leonard H. Bolick, 1988 Lutheran Synod Dr., Salisbury, NC 28144-4480 Tel. (704)633-4861 Fax (704)638-0508

South Carolina, Rev. David A. Donges, 1003 Richland St., P.O. Box 43, Columbia, SC 29202-0043 Tel. (803)765-0590 Fax (803) 252-5558

Southeastern, Rev. Ronald B. Warren, 100 Edgewood Ave., NE, Ste. 1600, Atlanta, GA 30303 Tel. (404)589-1977 Fax (404)521-1980

Florida-Bahamas, Rev. William B. Trexler, 3838 W. Cypress St., Tampa, FL 33607-4897 Tel. (813)876-7660 Fax (813)870-0826

Caribbean, Rev. Francisco L. Sosa, Calle Constitucion 363, Puerto Nuevo, PR 00920 Tel. (787) 273-8300 Fax (787)273-7877

Regional Coord., Dr. Dorothy L. Jeffcoat, Region 9, Lutheran Theological Southern Seminary, 4201 N. Main St., Columbia, SC 29203 Tel. (803)754-2879 Fax (803)786-6499

Periodicals

The Lutheran; Lutheran Partners; Lutheran Woman Today; Seeds for the Parish

Evangelical Lutheran Synod

The Evangelical Lutheran Synod had its beginning among the Norwegian settlers who brought with them their Lutheran heritage. The Synod was organized in 1853. It was reorganized in 1918 by those who desired to adhere to the synod's principles not only in word but also in deed.

The Synod owns and operates Bethany Lutheran College and Bethany Lutheran Theological Seminary. It has congregations in 20 states and maintains foreign missions in Peru, Chile, the Czech Republic and Ukraine. It operates a seminary in Lima, Peru and in Ternopil, Ukraine.

Headquarters

6 Browns Court, Mankato, MN 56001 Tel. (507) 344-7356 Fax (507)344-7426
Media Contact, Pres., Rev. George Orvick
Email: gorvick@blc.edu
Website: http://www.EvLuthSyn.org

Officers

Pres., Rev. George Orvick

Sec., Rev. Craig Ferkenstad, Rt. 3, Box 40, St. Peter, MN 56082

Treas., LeRoy W. Meyer, 1038 S. Lewis Ave., Lombard, IL 60148

OTHER ORGANIZATIONS

Lutheran Synod Book Co., Bethany Lutheran College, Mankato, MN 56001

Bethany Lutheran Theological Seminary, 6 Browns Court, Mankato, MN 56001

Periodicals

Lutheran Sentinel; Lutheran Synod Quarterly; Young Branches; ELS Educator; Oak Leaves; Mission News

Evangelical Mennonite Church

The Evangelical Mennonite Church is an American denomination in the European free church tradition, tracing its heritage to the Reformation period of the 16th century. The Swiss Brethren of that time believed that salvation could come only by repentance for sins and faith in Jesus Christ; that baptism was only for believers; and that the church should be separate from controls of the state. Their enemies called them Anabaptists, since they insisted on rebaptizing believers who had been baptized as infants. As the Anabaptist movement spread to other countries, Menno Simons became its principal leader. In time his followers were called Mennonites.

In 1693 a Mennonite minister, Jacob Amman, insisted that the church should adopt a more conservative position on dress and style of living and should more rigidly enforce the "ban" - the church's method of disciplining disobedient members. Amman's insistence finally resulted in a division within the South German Mennonite groups; his followers became known as the Amish.

Migrations to America, involving both Mennonites and Amish, took place in the 1700s and 1800s, for both religious and economic reasons.

The Evangelical Mennonite Church was formed in 1866 out of a spiritual awakening among the Amish in Indiana. It was first known as the Egly Amish, after its founder Bishop Henry Egly. Bishop Egly emphasized regeneration, separation and nonconformity to the world. His willingness to rebaptize anyone who had been baptized without repentance created a split in his church, prompting him to gather a new congregation in 1866. The conference, which has met annually since 1895, united a number of other congregations of like mind. This group became The Defenseless Mennonite Church in 1898 and has been known as the Evangelical Mennonite Church since 1948.

Headquarters

1420 Kerrway Ct., Fort Wayne, IN 46805 Tel. (219)423-3649 Fax (219)420-1905

Media Contact, Admn. Asst., Lynette Augsburger

Officers

Pres., Rev. Donald W. Roth

Chpsn., Rev. Doug Habegger, 1050 S. Fourth St., Morton, IL 61550

Vice-Chpsn., Rev. Bryce Winteregg, 11331 Coldwater Rd., Ft. Wayne, IN 46845

Sec., Gene Rupp, c/o Taylor University, 236 W. Reade Ave., Upland, IN 46989

Treas., Elmer Lengacher, 11507 Bull Rapids Rd., Grabill, IN 46741

Periodicals

EMC Today

Evangelical Methodist Church

The Evangelical Methodist Church was organized in 1946 at Memphis, Tenn., largely as a movement of people who opposed modern liberalism and wished for a return to the historic Wesleyan position. In 1960, it merged with the Evangel Church (formerly Evangelistic Tabernacles) and with the People's Methodist Church in 1962.

Headquarters

P.O. Box 17070, Indianapolis, IN 46217 Tel. (317)780-8017 Fax (317)780-8078

Media Contact, Gen. Conf. Sec.-Treas., Rev. James A. Coulston

Officers

Gen. Supt., Dr. Edward W. Williamson

Gen. Conf. Sec.-Treas., Rev. James A. Coulston

Evangelical Presbyterian Church

The Evangelical Presbyterian Church (EPC), established in March 1981, is a conservative denomination of 9 geographic presbyteries - 8 in the United States and one in Argentina. From its inception with 12 churches, the EPC has grown to 190 churches with a membership of over 60,000.

Planted firmly within the historic Reformed tradition, evangelical in spirit, the EPC places high priority on church planting and development along with world missions. Fifty-six missionaries serve the church's mission.

Based on the truth of Scripture and adhering to the Westminster Confession of Faith plus its Book of Order, the denomination is committed to the "essentials of the faith." The historic motto "In essentials, unity; in nonessentials, liberty; in all things charity" catches the irenic spirit of the EPC, along with the Ephesians theme, "truth in love."

The Evangelical Presbyterian Church is a member of the World Alliance of Reformed Churches, National Association of Evangelicals, World Evangelical Fellowship and the Evangelical Council for Financial Accountability. Observers annually attend the North American Presbyterian and Reformed Council (NAPARC).

Headquarters

Office of the General Assembly, 29140 Buckingham Ave., Ste. 5, Livonia, MI 48154 Tel. (734)261-2001 Fax (734)261-3282

Media Contact, Stated Clk., Dr. L. Edward Davis, 29140 Buckingham Ave., Ste. 5, Livonia, MI 48154 Tel. (734)261-2001 Fax (734)261-3282
Email: EPCHURCH@aol.com
Website: http://www. epc.org

Officers

Mod., Dr. James McGuire, Ward Presbyterian Church, 40000 Six Milerd, Northville, MI 48167
Administration Committee, Chmn., Mr. Alan Smith, 5408 Galley Ct., Fairfax, VA 22032
Stated Clk., Dr. L. Edward Davis

PERMANENT COMMITTEES

Board of Pension & Benefits, Chmn., Dr. Orin Littlejohn, 100 Azelea Way, Marshall, TX 75672
Committee on Admn., Chmn., Mr. Alan Smith, 5408 Galley Ct., Fairfax, VA 22032
Committee on Fraternal Relations, Chmn., Dr. Graham Smith, 10708 Stanhope Place, Fairfax, VA 22032
Committee on National Outreach, Chmn., Rev. Rodger Woodworth, New Hope EPC, 2710 Shadeland Ave., Pittsburgh, PA 15212
Committee on Presbyterian Review, Chmn., Mr. Buck Russell, 2270 S. Joliet Way, Aurora, CO 80014
Committee on World Outreach, Chmn., Dr. Bern Draper, 8103 Saguro Ridge Rd., Parker, CO 80134
Committee on Ministerial Vocation, Chmn., Dr. William Moore, Trinity Presbyterian Church, 10101 W. Ann Arbor Rd., Plymouth, MI 48170
Comm. on Christian Educ. & Publ., Chmn., Rev. Bruce Spear, Bear Creek EPC, 3101 S. Kipling, Lakewood, CO 80227
Committee on Women's Ministries, Chmn., Anne Blackley, 323 Pine Valley Dr., Wilmington, NC 28412
Committee on Theology, Chmn., -vacant-
Committee on Student and Young Adult Ministries, Chmn.,Rev. Rick Stauffer, North Park EPC, 600 Ingomar Rd., Wexford, PA 15090

PRESBYTERIES

Central South, Stated Clk., Rev. Dennis Flach, New Covenant Evangelical Presbyterian Church, P.O. Box 842, Natchez, MS 39121
East, Stated Clk., Frank Johnson, 136 Chaucer Pl., Cherry Hills, NJ 08003
Florida, Stated Clk., Rev. Robert Garment, Trinity EPC, 5150 Oleander, Ft. Pierce, FL 34982
Mid-America, Stated Clk., Mr. Dexter Huklman, 1926 Prospector Ridge, Ballwin, MO 63011
Mid-Atlantic, Stated Clk., Dr. Howard Shockley, 58 Bear Trail, Fairview, NC 28730
Midwest, Stated Clk., Alton Bennett, 33604 Grand River, Farmington, MI 48335

Southeast, Stated Clk., Rev. Russ Ragon, Lookout Valley Pres. Church, 435 Patten Chapel Rd., Chattanooga, TN 37419
West, Stated Clk., Rev. Marc Huebl, Covenant Comm. Pres. Church, 4343 S. Buckley Rd., Aurora, CA 80015
St. Andrews, Stated Clk., Rev. Juan Jose Mejias, San Antonio de Padua Mission Church, Godoy Cruz 99, 1718 San Antonio de Padua, Pica, Buenos Aires, Argentina

Periodicals

Reflections Magazine

Fellowship of Evangelical Bible Churches

Formerly known as Evangelical Mennonite Brethren, this body emanates from the Russian immigration of Mennonites into the United States, 1873-74. Established with the emphasis on true repentance, conversion and a committed life to Jesus as Savior and Lord, the conference was founded in 1889 under the leadership of Isaac Peters and Aaron Wall. The founding churches were located in Mountain Lake, Minnesota, and in Henderson and Janzen, Nebraska. The conference has since grown to a fellowship of 39 churches with approximately 4,400 members in Argentina, Canada, Paraguay and the United States.

Foreign missions have been a vital ingredient of the total ministry. Today missions constitute about 35 percent of the total annual budget, with one missionary for every 30 members in the home churches. The conference does not develop and administer foreign mission fields of its own, but actively participates with existing evangelical "faith" mission societies. The conference has representation on several mission boards and has missionaries serving under approximately 41 different agencies around the world.

The church is holding fast to the inerrancy of Scripture, the Deity of Christ and the need for spiritual regeneration of man from his sinful natural state by faith in the death, burial and resurrection of Jesus Christ as payment for sin. Members look forward to the imminent return of Jesus Christ and retain a sense of urgency to share the gospel with those who have never heard of God's redeeming love.

Headquarters

5800 S. 14th St., Omaha, NE 68107 Tel. (402) 731-4780 Fax (402)731-1173
Admn., Robert L. Frey, 5800 S. 14th St., Omaha, NE 68107 Tel. (402)731-4780 Fax (402)731-1173
Email: febcoma@aol.com

Officers

Pres., Rev. Gerald Epp, P.O. Box 86, Waldheim, SK S0K 4R0 Tel. (306)945-2023 Email: ggepp@sk.sympatico.ca
Vice-President, Rev. Frank Wiens, P.O. Box

50773, Billings, MT 59105-0773 Tel. (406) 254-6961, Email: fcwen@aol.com

Rec. Sec., Stan Seifert, 35351 Munroe Ave., Abbotsford, BC V2S 1L4 Tel. (604)852-3253 Fax (604)852-7887

Admn., Robert L. Frey, 5800 South 14th St., Omaha, NE 68107-3584 Tel. (402)731-4780 Fax (402)731-1173
Email: febcoma@aol.com

Ministries Coordinator, Harvey Schultz, 3011 3rd Ave. East, P.O. Box 8, Waldheim, SK S0K 4R0, Tel. (306)945-2220 Fax (306)945-2088, Email: hesals@aol.com

Commission on Churches, Chpsn., Rev. Bob Vogt, 495 Evergreen Ave., Box 21861, Steinbach, MB R5G 1B5, Tel. [O](204)326-3561, [H](204)346-2642 Fax (204)326-5420, Email: sbachemb@mts.net

Commission on Education, Chpsn., Rev. Harvey Gilbert, 5112 N. 86th St., Omaha, NE 68134-2814, Tel. (402)571-3541 Email: hgilbert@ops.esu19k12.ne.us

Commission on Missions, Chpsn., Martin Fast, SR 266, Box 9, Frazer, MT 59225 Tel. (406)392-5722, Email: 2mkfast@nemontel.ne

Commission of Trustees, Chpsn., William Janzen, 6212 Country Club Rd., Omaha, NE 68152-2057 Tel. [O] (402)397-7812, [H] (402)571-2352 Fax (204)397-2113

Commission on Church Planting, Chpsn., Rev. Randy Smart, Box 111, Stuartburn, MB R0A 2B0 Tel. [O](204)425-3383 [H](204)425-3990 Email: smart@aecc.escape.ca

Comm. on Women's Ministries, Chpsn., Ruth Epp, Box 86, Waldheim, SK S0K 4R0 Tel. (306)945-2023, Email: ggepp@sk.sympatico. ca

Periodicals
Gospel Tidings

Fellowship of Fundamental Bible Churches

The churches in this body represent the 1939 separation from the Methodist Protestant Church, when some 50 delegates and pastors (approximately one-third of the Eastern Conference) withdrew to protest the union of the Methodist Protestant Church with the Methodist Episcopal Church and the Methodist Episcopal Church South, and what they considered the liberal tendencies of those churches. These churches subsequently changed their name to the Bible Protestant Church. In 1985, this group again changed its name to the Fellowship of Fundamental Bible Churches to more accurately define their position.

As fundamentalists, this group strongly adheres to the historic fundamentals of the faith, including the doctrine of separation. This group accepts a literal view of the Bible and, consequently, accepts premillennial theology and a pre-tribulational rapture.

The churches are currently located in New Jersey, New York, Pennsylvania, Virginia, Michigan, and California. It is a fellowship of independent Bible and Baptist churches. Baptism, by immersion, and the Lord's Supper, as a memorial, are recognized as ordinances. There are currently 21 churches representing 1500 members. This constituent body is a member of the American Council of Christian Churches.

The Fellowship of Fundamental Bible Churches owns and operates Tri-State Bible Camp and Conference Center in Montague, New Jersey, oversees a mission board called Fundamental Bible Missions, and conducts a Bible Institute called Fundamental Bible Institute.

Headquarters
P.O. Box 206, Penns Grove, NJ 08069
Media Contact, Sec., Rev. Edmund G. Cotton, 80 Hudson St., Port Jervis, NY 12771 Tel. (914)856-7695
Email: edgc@pikeonline.net

Officers
Pres., Rev. Mark Franklin, 284 Whig Lane, Monroeville, NJ 08343 Tel. (609)881-0057
Vice-Pres., Rev. Gary Myers, P.O. Box 191, Meshoppen, PA 18630 Tel. (717)833-4898
Sec., Rev. Edmund G. Cotton, 80 Hudson St., Port Jervis, NY 12771 Tel. (914)856-7695
Treas., Ken Thompson, 501 N. Main Street, Elmer, NJ 08318 (865)358-0515

Fellowship of Grace Brethren Churches

A division occurred in the Church of the Brethren in 1882 on the question of the legislative authority of the annual meeting. It resulted in the establishment of the Brethren Church under a legal charter requiring congregational government. This body divided in 1939 with the Grace Brethren establishing headquarters at Winona Lake, Ind., and the Brethren Church at Ashland, Ohio.

Headquarters
Media Contact, Fellowship Coord., Rev. Thomas Avey, P.O. Box 386, Winona Lake, IN 46590 Tel. (219)269-1269 Fax (219)269-4066
Email: fgbc@fgbc.org
Website:http:// www.fgbc.org

Officers
Mod., Dr. Galen Wiley, 22713 Ellsworth Ave., Minerva, OH 44657
1st Mod.-Elect, Dr. James Custer, 2515 Carriage Rd., Powell, OH 43065
2nd Mod.-Elect, Dr. Ron Manahan, 2316 E. Kemo Ave., Warsaw, IN 46580
Fellowship Coord., Rev. Thomas Avey, P.O. Box 386, Winona Lake, IN 46590 Tel. (219)269-1269 Fax (219)269-4066
Sec., Fellowship Coord., Rev. Thomas Avey, P.O. Box 386, Winona Lake, IN 46590

Treas., Thomas Staller, 2311 S. Cost-a-Plenty Drive, Warsaw, IN 46580

OTHER BOARDS

Grace Brethren International Missions, Exec. Dir., Rev. Tom Julien, P.O. Box 588, Winona Lake, IN 46590

Grace Brethren Home Missions, Exec. Dir., Larry Chamberlain, P.O. Box 587, Winona Lake, IN 46590

Grace College & Seminary, Pres., Ronald E. Manahan, 200 Seminary Dr., Winona Lake, IN 46590 Tel. (210)372-5100

Brethren Missionary Herald Co., Pub. & Gen. Mgr., James Bustram, P.O. Box 544, Winona Lake, IN 46590

CE National, Exec. Dir., Rev. Ed Lewis, P.O. Box 365, Winona Lake, IN 46590

Grace Brethren Navajo Ministries, Dir., Steve Galegor, Counselor, NM 87018

Grace Village Retirement Community, Admn., Jeff Carroll, P.O. Box 337, Winona Lake, IN 46590

Natl. Fellowship of Grace Brethren Ministries, Pres., Dr. Steve Taylor, 132 Summerall Ct., Aiken, SC 29801 Women's Missionary Council, Pres., Janet Minnix, 3314 Kenwick Tr., S.W., Roanoke, VA, 24015

Grace Brethren Men International, Pres., Morgan Burgess, 163 N. Franklin St., Delaware, OH 43015

Free Christian Zion Church of Christ

This church was organized in 1905 at Redemption, Ark., by a company of African-American ministers associated with various denominations. Its polity is in general accord with that of Methodist bodies.

Headquarters

1315 S. Hutchinson St., Nashville, AR 71852 Tel. (501)845-4933

Media Contact, Gen. Sec., Shirlie Cheatham

Officers

Chief Pastor, Willie Benson, Jr.

Free Methodist Church of North America

The Free Methodist Church was organized in 1860 in Western New York by ministers and laymen who had called the Methodist Episcopal Church to return to what they considered the original doctrines and lifestyle of Methodism. The issues included human freedom (anti-slavery), freedom and simplicity in worship, free seats so that the poor would not be discriminated against and freedom from secret oaths (societies) so the truth might be spoken freely at all times. The founders emphasized the teaching of the entire sanctification of life by means of grace through faith.

The denomination continues to be true to its founding principles. It communicates the gospel and its power to all people without discrimination through strong missionary, evangelistic and educational programs. Six colleges, a Bible college and numerous overseas schools train the youth of the church to serve in lay and ministerial roles.

Its members covenant to maintain simplicity in life, worship, daily devotion to Christ, responsible stewardship of time, talent and finance.

Headquarters

World Ministries Center: 770 N. High School Rd., Indianapolis, IN 46214 Tel. (317)244-3660 Fax (317)244-1247

Mailing Address, P.O. Box 535002, Indianapolis, IN 46253 Tel. (800)342-5531

Media Contact, Yearbook Ed., P.O. Box 535002, Indianapolis, IN 46253

Officers

Bishops: Robert Nxumalo; Noah Nzeyimana; Richard D. Snyder; Luis Uanela Nhaphale; Jim Tuan; Teodoro Reynoso; Joseph F. James; Roger W. Haskins; Leslie Krober

Gen. Conf. Sec., Melvin J. Spencer

Admn. & Finance, Gen. Dir., Gary M. Kilgore

Growth Ministries, Gen. Dir., David Harvey

Light & Life Communications, Publisher, John E. Van Valin

Light & Life Magazine, Ed.,Doug Newton

Higher Education, Gen. Sec., Timothy M. Beuthin

Men's Ministries, Exec. Dir., Lucien E. Behar

Free Methodist Foundation, Stanley B. Thompson

Women's Ministries Intl., Pres., Beth Webb

World Missions, Gen. Dir., Larry Houck

Periodicals

Light and Life Magazine; Free Methodist World Mission People

Friends General Conference

Friends General Conference is an association of fourteen yearly meetings open to all Friends meetings which wish to be actively associated with its programs and services. The General Conference includes Baltimore, Canadian, Illinois, Lake Erie, New England, New York, Northern Ohio Valley, Philadelphia, South Central and Southeaster Yearly Meetings; Central Alaska Conference, Southern Appalachian Yearly Meeting and Association, and Piedmont Friends Fellowship; and Heartland (KS), Manhattan Meetings. Friends General Conference is primarily a service organization with the stated purpose of nurturing the spiritual life within its constituency of predominantly unprogrammed Friends. FGC offers services to all Friends, but has no authority over constituent meetings. A Central Committee, to which constituent Yearly Meetings name appointees (in proportion to membership), and its Executive Committee, are responsible for the direction of FGC's program of year-round services. In the

117

1995 Central Committee approved the following Minute of Purpose:

Friends General Conference is a Quaker organization in the unprogrammed tradition of the Religious Society of Friends which primarily serves affiliated yearly and monthly meetings. It is our experience that:

**Faith is based on direct experience of God.

**Our lives witness this experience individually and corporately.

**By answering that of God in everyone, we build and sustain inclusive community.

Friends General Conference provides resources and opportunities that educate and invite members and attenders to experience, individually and corporately, God's living presence, and to discern and follow God's leadings. Friends General Conference reaches out to seekers and to other religious bodies inside and outside the Religious Society of Friends.

Headquarters
1216 Arch St., 2B, Philadelphia, PA 19107 Tel. (215)561-1700 Fax (215)561-0759
Media Contact, Gen. Sec., Bruce Birchard
Email: friends@fgc.quaker.org
Website: www.quaker.org/fgc

Officers
Gen. Sec., Bruce Birchard
Presiding Clerk, Janice Domanik
Treas., Mark Kinnucan

YEARLY MEETINGS
*Baltimore, Clerk, Lamar Matthew, 17100 Quaker Ln., Sandy Spring, MD 20860 Tel. (301)774-7663; Email: dianajbym@igc.org

*Canadian: Co-clerk, Gale Wills, 91A Fourth Ave., Ottawa, ON K1S 2L1 Tel. (613)235-8553; Email: cym@web.net Website: http://www.web.net/~cym

Central Alaska Friends Conference, Clerk, Charlotte Basham, P.O. Box 25078, Ester, AK 99725 Tel. (907)479-2006; Email: ffcsb@aurora.alaska.edu

Illinois, Clerk, Elizabeth Mertic, 21898 Brentwood Lane, Lake Villa, IL 60046, Email: jnurenberg@xcel.com

Lake Erie, Clerk, Janet Smith, 121 Cherry St., Perrysburg, OH 43551 Tel. (419) 874-6738, Email: jesmith@glasscity.net

*New England, Clerk, Betsy Muench, 24 Dewey Rd., Lexington, MA 02173 Tel. (781) 862-2839, Email: neym@ultranet.com

*New York, Clerk, Victoria B. Cooley, 15 Rutherford Pl., New York, NY 10003 Tel. (212) 673-5750, Email: hyym@compuserve. com

Northern: Co-Clerks, Lorene Ludy and Jean Eden, 510 S. Dickinson, Madison, WI 53703, Tel. (608) 251-3375, Email: ludyeden@danenet.wicip.org

Ohio Valley, Clerk, Christine Snyder, 7897 Rain Tree Rd., Centerville, OH 45459 Tel. (937)433-6204, Email: snydervc@aol.com

Philadelphia, Clerk, Martha B. Bryans, 1515 Cherry St., Philadelphia, PA 19102 Tel. (215)241-7210, Email: joang@pym.org

Piedmont Friends Fellowship, Clerk, David Bailey, 1712 Lakemont Dr., Greensboro, NC 27410 Tel. (336)854-1225, Email: DLLOYDBAI@aol.com

South Central, Clerk, Glenna Balch, 1202 Kinney Ave., Austin, TX 78704 Tel. (512)442-0554; Email: quakertx@ktc.com OR johansen@unt.edu

*southeastern, Clerk, Cecilia Yocum, Annie McPherson, Staff, 1115 NW 40 Dr., Gainsville, FL 32605-4750 Tel. (352)336-7689; Email: SEYM@juno.com

Southern Appalachian, Clerk, Penny Wright, 1106 Caldwell Lane, Nashville, TN 37204 Tel. (615)298-1385; Email: pennywright@earthlink.net

*also affiliated with Friends United Meeting

Periodicals
Friends Journal

Friends United Meeting
Friends United Meeting was organized in 1902 (the name was changed in 1963 from the Five Years Meeting of Friends) as a loose confederation of North American yearly meetings to facilitate a united Quaker witness in missions, peace work and Christian education.

Today Friends United Meeting is comprised of 27 member yearly meetings representing about half the Friends in the world. FUM's current work includes programs of mission and service and congregational renewal. FUM publishes Christian education curriculum, books of Quaker history and religious thought and a magazine, *Quaker Life*.

Headquarters
101 Quaker Hill Dr., Richmond, IN 47374-1980 Tel. (765)962-7573 Fax (765)966-1293
Media Contact, Gen. Sec., Johan Maurer
Email: fuminfo@xc.org
Website: www.fum.org

Officers
Presiding Clk., Stan Bauer
Treas., John Bell
Gen. Sec., Johan Maurer

DEPARTMENTS
World Ministries, Assoc. Sec., Retha McCutchen
Meeting Ministries, Interim Assoc. Sec., Barbara Mays
Quaker Hill Bookstore, Mgr., Sue Calhoun
Friends United Press, Ed., Barbara Mays

YEARLY MEETINGS
Baltimore Yearly Meeting, 17100 Quaker Ln., Sandy Spring, MD 20860 Tel. (301)774-7663 (800)962-4766 Fax (301)774-7084 Lamar Matthew, clerk; Frank Massey, Gen. Sec.

Bware Yearly Meeting, P.O. Box 179, Suna, Kenya; Epainitus Adego, Gen Supt.

Canadian Yearly Meeting: 91-A Fourth Ave., Ottawa ON K1S 2L1, Canada; Tel. and Fax (613)235-8553; Gale Wills, clerk

Central Yearly Meeting, P.O. Box 1510, Kakamega, Kenya, East Africa, Joseph Andugu, Gen. Sec.

Cuba Yearly Meeting, Ave. Libertad #110, Puerto Padre, Las Tunas, Cuba; Ramon Gonzalez-Longoria E., clerk.

East Africa Yearly Meeting of Friends, P.O. Box 35, Tiriki, Kenya, East Africa; Matthew Tsimbaji, Clerk, Thomas Ilote, Gen. Sec., Erastus Kesohole, Gen Supt.

East Africa Yearly Meeting of Friends (North), P.O. Box 544, Kitale, Kenya, East Africa; Henry Mayabe, Gen. Sec., Titus Adira, Gen. Supt.

East Africa Yearly Meeting of Friends (South), P.O. Box 160, Vihiga, Kenya, East Africa; Joseph Kisia, Clerk; Lam Kisanya Osodo, Gen. Sec.

Elgon East Yearly Meeting, P.O. Box 2322, Kitale, Kenya, East Africa; Maurice Simiyu, Gen. Sec.

Elgon Religious Soociety of Friends, P.O. Box 4, Wibuye, Kenya, East Africa, Tom Isiye, General Sec., John Ngoya, Gen. Supt., Charles Mbachi, Presiding Clerk

Indiana Yearly Meeting, 4715 N. Wheeling Ave., Muncie, IN 47304-1222; Tel. (765)284-6900 Fax (765)284-8925; Susan Kirkpatrick, Clerk; David Bridges, Interim Gen. Supt.

Iowa Yearly Meeting, Box 657, Oskaloosa, IA 52577; Tel. (515)673-9717 Fax (515)673-9718; Stan Bauer, Clerk, Kevin Mortimer, Gen. Superintendent

Jamaica Yearly Meeting, 4 Worthington Ave., Kingston 5, Jamaica WI; Tel. (809)926-7371; Angela Johnson, Clerk

Kakamega Yearly Meeting, P.O. Box 465, Kakamega, Kenya, East Africa; Jonathan Shisanya, Gen. Sec.

Lugari Yearly Meeting, Lugari Farmers Training Centre, P.O. Box 438, Turbo, Kenya, East Africa; Samson Atsya, Gen. Sec.

Malava Yearly Meeting, P.O. Box 26, Malava, Kenya, East Africa; Enoch Shinachi, Gen. Sec.

Nairobi Yearly Meeting, P.O. Box 8321, Nairobi, Kenya, East Africa; Stanley Ndezwa, Clerk, Aggrey Mukilima, Gen. Supt.

Nandi Yearly Meeting, P.O. Box 102, Kapsabet, Kenya, East Africa; Fredrick Inyangu, Presiding clk.

Nebraska Yearly Meeting, 423 S. Tinker St., Hominy, OK 74035; Tel. (918)885-2714; David Nagle, Clerk

New England Yearly Meeting, 901 Pleasant St., Worcester, MA 01602 Tel. (508)754-6760; Elizabeth Muench, Clerk; Jonathan Vogel-Borne, Field Secretary

New York Yearly Meeting, 15 Rutherford Pl., New York, NY 10003 Tel. (212)673-5750; Victoria B. Cooley, Clerk; Helen Garay Toppins, Admin. Sec.

North Carolina Yearly Meeting, 5506 W. Friendly Ave., Greensboro, NC 27410; Tel. (336)292-6957; Brent McKinney, Clerk; John Porter, Gen. Superintendent

Southeastern Yearly Meeting, 1115 NW 40 Dr., Gainsville, FL 32605; Tel. (904)422-1446; Cecilia Yocum, Clerk, Annie McPhearson, Sec.

Tanzania Yearly Meeting, P.O. Box 151, Mugumu, Serengeti, Tanzania; Joshua Lavuna Oguma, Gen. Sec.

Uganda Yearly Meeting, P.O. Box 605, Kampala, Uganda, East Africa; Samuel Wefwafwa, Gen. Sec.

Vokoli Yearly Meetings, P.O. Box 266, Wodanga, Vokoli, Kenya, 0331 45033; Javan Mirembe, Gen. Sec., Hannington Mbaco, Presiding Clerk, Timonakita, Gen Supt.

Western Yearly Meeting, P.O. Box 70, Plainfield, IN 46168; Tel. (317)839-2789 and 839-2849 Fax (317)839-2616; Charles Heavilin, Clerk; Curt Shaw, Gen. Superintendent

Wilmington Yearly Meeting, Pyle Center Box 1194, Wilmington, OH 45177; Tel. (937)382-2491 Fax (937)382-7077; Gary Farlow, Clerk; Rudy Haag, Ex. Sec.

Periodicals

Quaker Life

Evangelical Friends International—North American Region is listed under "E".

Philadelphia Yearly Meeting of the Religious Society of Friends is listed under "P".

Religious Society of Friends (Conservative) is listed under "R".

Religious Society of Friends (Unaffiliated Meetings) is listed under "R".

Full Gospel Assemblies International

The Full Gospel Assemblies International was founded in 1962 under the leadership of Dr. Charles Elwood Strauser. The roots of Full Gospel Assemblies may be traced to 1947 with the beginning of the Full Gospel Church of Coatesville, Pennsylvania. As an Assemblies of God Pentecostal church, the Full Gospel Church of Coatesville was active in evangelization and educational ministries to the community. In service to the ministers and students of the Full Gospel Church ministries, the Full Gospel Trinity Ministerial Fellowship was formed in 1962, later changing its name to Full Gospel Assemblies International.

Retaining its original doctrine and faith, Full Gospel Assemblies is Trinitarian and believes in the Bible as God's infallible Word to all people, in baptism in the Holy Spirit according to Acts 2, in divine healing made possible by the sufferings of our Lord Jesus Christ and in the imminent return of Christ for those who love him.

The body of Full Gospel Assemblies is an

119

evangelical missionary fellowship sponsoring ministry at home and abroad, composed of self governing ministries and churches. Congregations, affiliate ministries and clerical bodies are located throughout the United States and over 30 countries of the world.

Headquarters
3170 Lincoln Hwy, Parkesburg, PA
Mailing Address, P.O. Box 1230, Coatesville, PA 19320 Tel. (610)857-2357
Media Contact, Simeon Strauser

Officers
Gen. Supt., Dr. AnnaMae Strauser
Exec. Dir of Admn., Simeon Strauser
Exec. Dir. of Ministry, J. Victor Fisk
Exec. Sec., Betty Stewart
National Ministers Council & Trustees: Chpsn., Simeon Strauser, Sadsburyville, PA; Donald Campbell, Mt. Morris, PA; David Treat, Cape Coral, FL; Carol Strauser, Parkesburg, PA; Edward Popovich, Burgtstown, PA; Archie Neal, Pittsburgh, PA; J. Victor Fisk, Appolo, PA

Periodicals
Full Gospel Ministries Outreach Report

Full Gospel Fellowship of Churches and Ministers International

In the early 1960s a conviction grew in the hearts of many ministers that there should be closer fellowship between the people of God who believed in the apostolic ministry. At the same time, many independent churches were experiencing serious difficulties in receiving authority from the IRS to give governmentally accepted tax-exempt receipts for donations.

In September 1962 a group of ministers met in Dallas, Texas, to form a Fellowship to give expression to the essential unity of the Body of Christ under the leadership of the Holy Spirit" a unity that goes beyond individuals, churches or organizations. This was not a movement to build another denomination, but rather an effort to join ministers, churches and ministry organizations of like mind across denominational lines.

To provide opportunities for fellowship and to support the objectives and goals of local and national ministries: regional conventions and an annual international convention are held.

Headquarters
4325 W. Ledbetter Dr., Dallas, TX 75233 Tel. (214)339-1200 Fax (214)339-8790
Media Contact, Exec. Sec., Dr. Chester P. Jenkins

Officers
Pres., Dr. Don Arnold, P.O. Box 324, Gadsden, AL 35901
1st Vice-Pres., Dr. Ray Chamberlain
Exec. Sec., Dr. Chester P. Jenkins

Treas., Rev. Gene Evans P.O. Box 813 Douglasville, GA 30133
CFO, Dr. S.K. Biffle, 4325 W. Ledbetter Dr.
Ofc. Sec., Ms. Lea Ann Philpott & Nita Biffle
Vice-Pres. at Large: Rev. Maurice Hart, P.O. Box 4316, Omaha, NE 68104; Rev. Don Westbrook, 3518 Rose of Sharon Rd., Durham, NC 27705
Chmn. of Evangelism, David Ellis
Past Pres., Dr. James Helton

REGIONAL VICE-PRESIDENTS
Southeast, Rev. Gene Evans, P.O. Box 813, Douglasville, GA 30133
South Central, Rev. Robert J. Miller, P.O. Box 10621, Killeen, TX 76547
Southwest, Rev. Don Shepherd, 631 Southgate Rd., Sacramento, CA 95815
Northeast, Rev. David Ellis, 3636 Winchester Rd., Allertown, PA 18104
North Central, Rev. Raymond Rothwell, P.O. Box 367, Eaton, OH 45320
Northwest, Rev. Ralph Trask, 3212 Hyacinth NE, Salem, OR 97303

Periodicals
Fellowship Tidings

Fundamental Methodist Church, Inc.

This group traces its origin through the Methodist Protestant Church. It withdrew from The Methodist Church and organized on August 27, 1942.

Headquarters
1034 N. Broadway, Springfield, MO 65802
Media Contact, Dist. Supt., Rev. Ronnie Howerton, 1952 Highway H, Monett, MO 65708 Tel. (417)235-3849

Officers
Treas., Wayne Blades, Rt. 1, Crane, MO 65633 Tel. (417)723-8123
Sec., Betty Nicholson, Rt. 2, Box 397, Ash Grove, MO 65604 Tel. (417)672-2268
Dist. Supt., Rev. Ronnie Howerton, 1952 Highway H, Monett, MO 65708 Tel. (417)235-3849

General Assembly of the Korean Presbyterian Church in America

This body came into official existence in the United States in 1976 and is currently an ethnic church, using the Korean language.

Headquarters
P.O. Box 457, Morganville, NJ 07951 Tel. (908)591-2771 Fax (908)591-2260
Media Contact, Gen. Sec., Rev. John Woo

Officers
Stated Clk., Rev. Sang Koo Kim, 5777 Los Arcos Way, Buena Park, CA 90620 Tel. (714)826-5714 Fax (714)680-6418

General Association of General Baptists

Similar in doctrine to those General Baptists organized in England in the 17th century, the first General Baptist churches were organized on the Midwest frontier following the Second Great Awakening. The first church was established by the Rev. Benoni Stinson, in 1823 at Evansville, Ind.

Stinson's major theological emphasis was general atonement—"Christ tasted death for every man." The group also allows for the possibility of apostasy. It practices open communion and believer's baptism by immersion.

Called "liberal" Baptists because of their emphasis on the freedom of man, General Baptists organized a General Association in 1870 and invited other "liberal" Baptists (e.g., "Free Will" and Separate Baptists) to participate.

The policy-setting body is composed of delegates from local General Baptist churches and associations. Each local church is autonomous but belongs to an association. The group currently consists of more than 60 associations in 16 states, as well as several associations in the Philippines, Guam, Saipan, Jamaica and India. Ministers and deacons are ordained by a presbytery.

A number of boards continue a variety of missions, schools and other support ministries. General Baptists belong to the Baptist World Alliance, the North American Baptist Fellowship and the National Association of Evangelicals.

Headquarters

100 Stinson Dr., Poplar Bluff, MO 63901 Tel. (573)785-7746 Fax (573)785-0564
Media Contact, Exec. Dir., Rev. Ron Black

Officers

Mod., Rev. Scott Keller
Clk., Rev. Tommy Roberts
Exec. Dir., Rev. Ron Black

OTHER ORGANIZATIONS

International Missions, Dir., Rev. Jack Eberhardt
National Missions, Dir., Rev. Gene Koker
Brotherhood Bd., Pres., ""
Women's Ministries, Dir., Sandra Trivitt
Nursing Home Admn., Wanda Britt, Rt. #2, Box 230, Campbell, MO 63933
College Bd., Pres., Dr. James Murray, Oakland City College, P.O. Box 235, Oakland City, IN 47660
Congregational Ministries, Dir., Rev. Mike Warren, 100 Stinson Dr., Poplar Bluff, MO 63901
Pastoral Ministries, Dir., Rev. Fred Brittain, 100 Stinson Dr., Poplar Bluff, MO 63901
Admin./Financial Services, Financial Officer, Linda McDonough, 100 Stinson Dr., Poplar Bluff, MO 63901
Stinson Press, Inc., Pres., Rev. Sam Ramdial, 100 Stinson Dr., Poplar Bluff, MO 63901
Oakview Heights Continuing Care, Administrator, Rev. Jack Cole, 1320 West 9th St., Mt. Carmel, IL 62863
Compassionate Care Adoption Agency, Dir., Dr. John Clanton, Rt. 3, Box 12B, Oakland City, IN 47660

Periodicals

General Baptist Messenger; Capsule; Voice; The Wave

General Association of Regular Baptist Churches

This association was founded in May, 1932, in Chicago by a group of churches which had withdrawn from the Northern Baptist Convention (now the American Baptist Churches in the U.S.A.) because of doctrinal differences. Its Confession of Faith, which it requires all churches to subscribe to, is essentially the old, historic New Hampshire Confession of Faith with a premillennial ending applied to the last article.

Headquarters

1300 N. Meacham Rd., Schaumburg, IL 60173 Tel. (847)843-1600 Fax (847)843-3757
Media Contact, Natl. Rep., Dr. John Greening
Email: garbc@garbc.org
Website: http://www.garbc.org

Officers

Chpsn., Rev. Bryce Augsburger
Vice-Chpsn., Rev. David Graham
Treas.,Dr. David Gower
Sec., Rev. R. Craig Golden
Natl. Rep., Dr. John Greening

Periodicals

Baptist Bulletin

General Church of the New Jerusalem

The General Church of the New Jerusalem, also called The New Church, is the result of a reorganization in 1897 of the General Church of The Advent of the Lord. It stresses the full acceptance of the doctrines contained in the theological writings of Emanuel Swedenborg.

Headquarters

P.O. Box 711, Bryn Athyn, PA 19009 Tel. (215) 938-2620
Media Contact, Ed., Church Journal, Donald L. Rose, Box 277, Bryn Athyn, PA 19009 Tel. (215)947-6225 Fax (215)947-3078
Email: svsimpso@newchurch.edu
Website:http://www.newchurch.org

Officers

Presiding Bishop, Rt. Rev. P. M. Buss
Sec., Susan V. Simpson
Treas., Daniel T. Allen

Periodicals

New Church Life

General Conference of Mennonite Brethren Churches

A small group, requesting that closer attention be given to prayer, Bible study and a consistent lifestyle, withdrew from the larger Mennonite Church in the Ukraine in 1860. Anabaptist in origin, the group was influenced by Lutheran pietists and Baptist teachings and adopted a quasi-congregational form of church government. In 1874 and years following, small groups of these German-speaking Mennonites left Russia, settled in Kansas and then spread to the Midwest west of the Mississippi and into Canada. Some years later the movement spread to California and the West Coast. In 1960, the Krimmer Mennonite Brethren Conference merged with this body.

Today the General Conference of Mennonite Brethren Churches conducts services in many European languages as well as in Vietnamese, Mandarin and Hindi. It works with other denominations in missionary and development projects in 25 countries outside North America.

Headquarters

4812 E. Butler Ave., Fresno, CA 93727 Tel. (209)452-1713 Fax (209)452-1752
Media Contact, Exec. Sec., Marvin Hein

Officers

Mod., Ed Boschman, 12630 N. 103rd Ave., Suite 215, Sun City, AZ 85351
Asst. Mod., Herb Kopp, 200 McIvor Ave., Winnipeg, NB R20 028
Sec., Valerie Rempel
Exec. Sec., Marvin Hein

Periodicals

Christian Leader; Mennonite Bretheren Herald

Grace Gospel Fellowship

The Grace Gospel Fellowship was organized in 1944 by a group of pastors who held to a dispensational interpretation of Scripture. Most had ministries in the Midwest. Two prominent leaders were J. C. O'Hair of Chicago and Charles Baker of Milwaukee. Subsequent to 1945, a Bible Institute was founded (now Grace Bible College of Grand Rapids, Mich.), and a previously organized foreign mission (now Grace Ministries International of Grand Rapids) was affiliated with the group. Churches have now been established in most sections of the country.

The body has remained a fellowship, each church being autonomous in polity. All support for its college, mission and headquarters is on a contributory basis.

The binding force of the Fellowship has been the members'' doctrinal position. They believe in the Deity and Saviorship of Jesus Christ and subscribe to the inerrant authority of Scripture. Their method of biblical interpretation is dispensational, with emphasis on the distinctive revelation to and the ministry of the apostle Paul.

Headquarters

Media Contact, Pres., Roger G. Anderson, 2125 Martindale SW, P.O. Box 9432, Grand Rapids, MI 49509 Tel. (616)245-0100 Fax (616)241-2542
Email: ggfinc@aol.com

Officers

Pres., Roger G. Anderson

OTHER ORGANIZATIONS

Grace Bible College, Pres., Rev. Bruce Kemper, 1011 Aldon St. SW, Grand Rapids, MI 49509
Grace Ministries Intl., Exec. Dir., Dr. Samuel Vinton, 2125 Martindale Ave. SW, Grand Rapids, MI 49509
Prison Mission Association, Gen. Dir., Nathan Whitham, P.O. Box 1587, Port Orchard, WA 98366-0140
Grace Publications Inc., Exec. Dir., Roger G. Anderson, 2125 Martindale Ave. SW, Grand Rapids, MI 49509
Bible Doctrines to Live By, Exec. Dir., Lee Homoki, P.O. Box 2351, Grand Rapids, MI 49501

Periodicals

Truth

Greek Orthodox Archdiocese of America

The Greek Orthodox Archdiocese of America is under the jurisdiction of the Ecumenical Patriarchate of Constantinople in Istanbul. It was chartered in 1922 by the State of New York and has 523 parishes in the United States. The first Greek Orthodox Church was founded in New Orleans in 1864.

Headquarters

8-10 E. 79th St., New York, NY 10021 Tel. (212)570-3500 Fax (212)570-3569
Media Contact: Fr. Mark Arey, Executive Director, Dept. of Communications, Tel. (212)570-3571 Fax (212)570-3598

ARCHDIOCESAN COUNCIL

Primate of the Greek Orthodox Archdiocese of America and Exarch of the Atlantic and Pacific Oceans, His Eminence Archbishop Dimitrios

SYNOD OF BISHOPS

Most Rev. Metropolitan Iakovos of Krinis, Diocese of Chicago, 40 E. Burton Place, Chicago, IL 60610
Most Rev. Metropolitan Anthony of Dardanelles, Diocese of San Francisco, 372 Santa Clara Avenue, San Francisco, CA 94127
Most Rev. Metropolitan Maximos of Aenos, Diocese of Pittsburgh, 5201 Ellsworth Avenue, Pittsburgh, PA 15232
Most Rev. Metropolitan Methodios of Aneon, Diocese of Boston, 162 Goddard Avenue, Brookline, MA 02146
Most Reverend Metropolitan Isaiah of

Proikonisou, Diocese of Denver, 4310 E. Alameda Avenue, Denver, CO 80222

AUXILIARY BISHOPS

His Grace Bishop Alexios of Troas, Archdiocesan Vicar, Diocese of Atlanta; His Grace Bishop Dimitrios of Xanthou, Archdiocese, New York, NY; His Grace Bishop of George of Komanon, Bethesda, MD

EXECUTIVE COMMITTEE

John A. Catsimatidis, Vice Chairman, New York, NY; Peter J. Pappas, Sec., Syosset, NJ; Andrew A. Athens, Chicago, IL; George Behrakis, Tewksbury, MA; Michael G. Cantonis, Tarpon Springs, FL; Harry J. Pappas, Visalia, CA; James J. Paulos, Dallas, TX; George E. Safiol, Weston, MA

ARCHDIOCESE OF NEW YORK; Office of the Archbishop; Office of the Chief Secretariat; Office of the Chancellor: Chancellor, V. Rev. Protopresbyter George G. Passias

ARCHDIOCESAN DEPARTMENTS

Archives; Archdiocese Benefits Committee; Archons, Order of St. Andrew; Dept. of Communications: GOTelecom, Internet Ministries, News & Information, Office of Publications, ORTHODOX OBSERVER (bi-monthly publication); Education & Culture; Finance; Inter-Orthodox & Ecumenical Affairs; Internet Ministries; Ionian Village; Leadership 100 Endowment Fund; Management Information Systems; Registry; Religious Education/DOXA; Stewardship Ministries/ LOGOS; Youth & Young Adult Ministries

ORGANIZATIONS/ INSTITUTIONS

All Saints Center; Archdiocesan Presbyters Council; Diocesan and Parish Summer Camps; Greek Orthodox Young Adult League (GOYAL); Hellenic Cultural Center; Hellenic College/Holy Cross Greek Orthodox School of Theology; Holy Cross Bookstore; Inter-Church/Inter-Faith Marriage Committee; National Ladies Philoptochos Society; National Sisterhood of Presbyters; National Forum of Greek Orthodox Church Musicians; Orthodox Christian Mission Center; Patriarch Athenagoras National Institute; Patriarch Athenagoras Orthodox Institute at the Graduate Theological Union; Standing Conference of Canonical Orthodox Bishops in the Americas (SCOBA): Chairman, His Eminence Archbishop Spyridon; St. Basil Academy; St. Michael's Home- Quality Care for the Elderly; St. Nicholas Ranch and Retreat Center; St. Photios National Shrine

OTHER JURISDICTIONS OF THE ECUMENICAL PATRIARCHATE IN THE USA

Albanian Orthodox Diocese in America; Belarusian Council of Orthodox Churches in North America; American Carpatho-Russian Orthodox Greek Catholic Diocese of the USA; Ukrainian Orthodox Church of the USA

The Holy Eastern Orthodox Catholic and Apostolic Church in North America, Inc.

Called by many independents The 1927 Aftimios Church, this Church was canonically established Feburary 2, 1927 by the Russian Synod of Bishops in North America with approval of the Russian Patriarch. Archbishop Aftimios Ofiesh of the Syrian mission was appointed first Archbishop President of this Church by the Russian Synod. The Church was incorporated on Febuary 1, 1928 by Archbishop Aftimios and seven others in Boston and continues today. This Church was established to serve the English speaking Orthodox Community in the New World and to be the anchor of the orthodoxy in North America. The short name listed in our Constitution is the "American Orthodox Catholic Church" and the Synod approved the name "Orthodox Metropolitanate in North America" when the title of the Archbishop President was changed to Metropolitan. We are mainly a western rite Church today but some clergy still offer the Eastern Liturgy.

Headquarters

Presently a temporary see in Arkansas: All Saints Parish, P.O. Box 477, Mtn. View, AR 72560 Tel. (870) 269-2912

(Soon to acquire property in New Mexico for National Church Headquarters and shrine.)

Primate: Metropolitan Victor, Email: theocacna@webtv.net, Website: theocacna.org

NORTH AMERICAN HOLY SYNOD

Archbishop Victor
Mar Kepha
Archbishop Lawrence
Bishop Gerald

SYNOD ADVISORS

Archbishop Joseph
Archbishop James
Bishop Donald

Holy Ukrainian Autocephalic Orthodox Church in Exile

This church was organized in a parish in New York in 1951 by Ukrainian laymen and clergy who settled in the Western Hemisphere after World War II. In 1954 two bishops, immigrants from Europe, met with clergy and laymen and formally organized the religious body.

Headquarters

103 Evergreen St., W. Babylon, NY 11704

Officers

Admn., Rt. Rev. Serhij K. Pastukhiv, Tel. (516)669-7402

123

House of God, Which is the Church of the Living God, the Pillar and Ground of the Truth, Inc.

This body, founded by Mary L. Tate in 1919, is episcopally organized.

Headquarters

1301 N. 58th St., Philadelphia, PA 19131
Media Contact, Sec., Rose Canon, 515 S. 57th St., Philadelphia, PA 19143 Tel. (215)474-8913

Officers

Bishop, Raymond W. White, 6107 Cobbs Creek Pkwy., Philadelphia, PA 19143 Tel. (215)748-6338

Hungarian Reformed Church in America

A Hungarian Reformed Church was organized in New York in 1904 in connection with the Reformed Church of Hungary. In 1922, the Church in Hungary transferred most of its congregations in the United States to the Reformed Church in the U.S. Some, however, preferred to continue as an autonomous, self-supporting American denomination, and these formed the Free Magyar Reformed Church in America. This group changed its name in 1958 to Hungarian Reformed Church in America.

This church is a member of the World Alliance of Reformed Churches, Presbyterian and Congregational, the World Council of Churches and the National Council of Churches of Christ.

Headquarters

Bishop's Office, 13 Grove St., Poughkeepsie, NY 12601 Tel. (914)454-5735

Officers

Bishop, Rt. Rev. Alexander Forro
Chief Lay-Curator, Prof. Stephen Szabo, 464 Forest Ave., Paramus, NJ 07652
Gen. Sec. (Clergy), Rt. Rev. Stefan M. Torok, 331 Kirkland Pl., Perth Amboy, NJ 08861 Tel. (908)442-7799
Gen Sec. (Lay), Zoltan Ambrus, 3358 Maple Dr., Melvindale, MI 48122
Eastern Classes: Dean (Senior of the Deans, Chair in Bishop's absence), Very Rev. Imre Bertalan, 10401 Grosvenor Pl., #1521, Rockville, MD 20852 Tel. (301)493-5036 Fax (301)571-5111; Lay-Curator, Balint Balogh, 519 N. Muhlenberg St., Allentown, PA 18104
New York Classes: Supervisor, Rt. Rev. Alexander Forro; Lay-Curator, Laszlo B. Vanyi, 229 E 82nd St., New York, NY 10028
Western Classes: Dean, V. Rev. Andor Demeter, 3921 W. Christy Dr., Phoenix, AZ 85029; Lay-Curator, Zolton Kun, 2604 Saybrook Dr., Pittsburgh, PA 15235

Periodicals

Magyar Egyhaz

Hutterian Brethren

Small groups of Hutterites derive their names from Jacob Hutter, a 16th-century Anabaptist who taught true discipleship after accepting Jesus as Saviour, advocated communal ownership of property and was burned as a heretic in Austria in 1536.

Many believers are of German descent and still use their native tongue at home and in church. Much of the denominational literature is produced in German and English. "Colonies" share property, practice non-resistance, dress plainly, do not participate in politics and operate their own schools. There are 428 colonies with 42,000 members in North America. Each congregation conducts its own youth work through Sunday school. Until age 15, children attend German and English school which is operated by each colony. All youth ages 15 to 20 attend Sunday school. They are baptized as adults upon confession of faith, around age 20.

Headquarters

Media Contact, Philip J. Gross, 3610 N. Wood Rd., Reardon, WA 99029 Tel. (509)299-5400 Fax (509)299-3099
Email: philsjg@juno.com

Officers

Smiedleut Chmn., No. 1, Jacob Waldner—Blumengard Colony, Box 13 Plum Coulee, MB R0G 1R0 Tel. (204)829-3527
Smiedleut Chmn., No. 2, Jacob Wipf, Spring Creek Colony, 36562 102 Street, Forbes, ND 58439 Tel. (701)358-8621
Dariusleut, Chmn., No. 1, Martin Walter, Springpoint Colony, Box 249, Pincher Creek, AB T0K 1W0 Phone (403)553-4368
Lehrerleut, Chmn., Rev. John Wipf, Rosetown Colony, Box 1509, Rosetown, SK S0L 2V0 Tel. (306)882-3344

Independent Fundamental Churches of America/ IFCA International, Inc.

This group of churches was organized in 1930 at Cicero, Illinois, by representatives of the American Council of Undenominational Churches and representatives of various independent churches. The founding churches and members had separated themselves from various denominational affiliations.

The IFCA provides a way for independent churches and ministers to unite in close fellowship and cooperation, in defense of the fundamental teachings of Scripture and in the proclamation of the gospel of God's grace.

Headquarters

3520 Fairlanes, Grandville, MI 49418 Tel. (616) 531-1840 Fax (616)531-1814
Mailing Address, P.O. Box 810, Grandville, MI 49468-0810

124

Media Contact, Exec. Dir., Dr. Richard I. Gregory

Email: office@ifca.org

Website: http://www.ifca.org

Officers

Exec. Dir., Dr. Richard I. Gregory, 2684 Meadow Ridge Dr., Byron Center, MI 49315 Tel. (616)878-1285

Pres., Dr. Robert Graves, Santa Rosa, CA

1st Vice-Pres., Rev. Robert Bell, Sun City, CA

2nd Vice-Pres., Rev. Gerald Smita, Duluth, GA

Periodicals

The Voice

International Church of the Foursquare Gospel

Founded by Aimee Semple McPherson in 1927, the International Church of the Foursquare Gospel proclaims the message of Jesus Christ the Savior, Healer, Baptizer with the Holy Spirit and Soon-coming King. Headquartered in Los Angeles, this evangelistic missionary body of believers consists of nearly 1,907 churches in the United States and Canada.

The International Church of the Foursquare Gospel is incorporated in the state of California and governed by a Board of Directors who direct its corporate affairs. A Foursquare Cabinet, consisting of the Corporate Officers, Board of Directors and District Supervisors of the various districts of the Foursquare Church in the United States and other elected or appointed members, serves in an advisory capacity to the President and the Board of Directors.

Each local Foursquare Church is a subordinate unit of the International Church of the Foursquare Gospel. The pastor of the church is appointed by the Board of Directors and is responsible for the spiritual and physical welfare of the church. To assist and advise the pastor, a church council is elected by the local church members.

Foursquare Churches seek to build strong believers through Christian education, Christian day schools, youth camping and ministry, Foursquare Women International who support and encourage Foursquare missionaries abroad, radio and television ministries, the Foursquare World Advance Magazine and 276 Bible Colleges worldwide.

Worldwide missions remains the focus of the Foursquare Gospel Church with 24,473 churches and meeting places, 34,350 national Foursquare pastors/leaders and 2,863,232 members and adherents in 99 countries around the globe. The Church is affiliated with the Pentecostal/ Charismatic Churches of North America, National Association of Evangelicals and the World Pentecostal Fellowship.

Headquarters

1910 W. Sunset Blvd., Ste. 200, P.O. Box 26902, Los Angeles, CA 90026-0176 Tel. (213)989-4234 Fax (213)989-4590

Media Contact, Editor, Dr. Ron Williams

Website: www.foursquare.org

Corporate Officers

Pres., Dr. Paul C. Risser

Vice-Pres., Dr. Clifford Hanes

Gen. Supvr., Rev. Jared Roth

Interim Dir. of Missions Intl., Rev. Michael Larkin

Sec., Rev. Herbert Schneidau

Treas., Mr. Brent Morgan

Bd. of Directors: Dr. Paul C. Risser; Rev. Ralph Torres; Rev. Naomi Beard; Dr. Ron Williams; Rev. Arthur Gray; Mark Simon; Rev. Alan Eastland; Rev. Lolita Frederick

District Supervisors: Eastern, Dr. Dewey Morrow; Great Lakes, Dr. Fred Parker; Midwest, Rev. Larry Spousta; Northwest, Dr. Tom Ferguson; South Central, Dr. Sidney Westbrook; Southeast, Rev. Glenn Burris, Jr.; Southern California, Rev. James C. Scott, Jr.; Southwest, Rev. Don Long; Western, Rev. Robert Booth

Foursquare Cabinet: Composed of Corp. Officers; Board of Directors; District Supervisors, Rev. Michael J. O'Brien; Dr. Ricky R. Temple; Rev. James Machen; Dr. Sterling Brackett; Rev. Beverly Bradfford; Dr. Jack W. Hayford; Rev. Loren Houltberg; Rev. Ronald Long; Dr. Ronald Mehl; Rev. Stephen Overman; Dr. Richard Scott; Dr. Roger Whitlow

SUPPORT MINISTRIES

Natl. Dept. of Youth, Natl. Youth Minister, Rev. Jerry Dirmann

Natl. Dept. of Chr. Educ., Dir., Rev. Rick Wulfestieg

Foursquare Women International, Dir., Rev. Molly Doland

Periodicals

Foursquare World Advance

International Council of Community Churches

This body is a fellowship of locally autonomous, ecumenically minded, congregationally governed, non-creedal Churches. The Council came into being in 1950 as the union of two former councils of community churches, one formed of black churches known as the Biennial Council of Community Churches and the other of white churches known as the National Council of Community Churches.

Headquarters

21116 Washington Pky., Frankfort, IL 60423-1253 Tel. (815)464-5690 Fax (815)464-5692

Media Contact, Exec. Dir., Rev. Michael E. Livingston

Officers

Pres., Rev. Judson Souers

Vice-Pres., Abraham Wright
Vice-Pres., Grace O'Neal
Sec., Rev. Herbert Freitag
Treas., Martha Nolan

OTHER ORGANIZATIONS

Commission on Church Relations, Dr. James MacVicar
Commission on Ecumenical Relations, Rev. Herman Harmelink
Commission on Clergy Relations, Rev. Donald Ashmall
Commission on Laity Relations, Rev. Martin Singley
Commission on Faith & Order, Rev. Dr. Kate Epperly
Comm. on Theological & Human Concerns, Rev. Martha Blanchett
Commission on Missions, Rev. David Blanchett
Commission on Informational Services, Brenda Swanson
Commission on Informational Services, Helen Long
Women's Christian Fellowship, Pres., Shirley Fairley
Samaritans (Men's Fellowship), Pres., Al Albergottie
Young Adult Fellowship, Pres., Shantelle Harrell
Youth Fellowship, Pres., Jerry Jones

Periodicals

The Christian Community

The International Pentecostal Church of Christ

At a General Conference held at London, Ohio, Aug. 10, 1976, the International Pentecostal Assemblies and the Pentecostal Church of Christ consolidated into one body, taking the name International Pentecostal Church of Christ.

The International Pentecostal Assemblies was the successor of the Association of Pentecostal Assemblies and the International Pentecostal Missionary Union. The Pentecostal Church of Christ was founded by John Stroup of Flatwoods, Ketucky, on May 10, 1917 and was incorporated at Portsmouth, Ohio, in 1927. The International Pentecostal Church of Christ is an active member of the Pentecostal/Charismatic Churches of North America, as well as a member of the National Association of Evangelicals.

The priorities of the International Pentecostal Church of Christ are to be an agency of God for evangelizing the world, to be a corporate body in which people may worship God and to be a channel of God's purpose to build a body of saints being perfected in the image of His Son.

The Annual Conference is held each year during the first full week of August in London, Ohio.

Headquarters

2245 St. Rt. 42 SW, P.O. Box 439, London, OH 43140 Tel. (740)852-4722 Fax (740)852-0348

Media Contact, Gen. Overseer, Clyde M. Hughes
Email: hqipcc@aol.com

EXECUTIVE COMMITTEE

Gen. Overseer, Clyde M. Hughes, P.O. Box 439, London, OH 43140 Tel. (740)852-4722 Fax (740)852-0348
Asst. Gen. Overseer, Thomas L. Dooley, 3200 Dueber Ave. SW, Canton, OH 44706 Tel. (330)484-6053 Fax (330)484-6053
Gen. Sec., Rev. B. G. Turner, Rt. 1, Box 260L, Charles Town, WV 25414 Tel. (304)725-4346 Fax (304)535-2221
Gen. Treas., Rev. Clifford A. Edwards, P.O. Box 18145, Atlanta, GA 30316 Tel. (404)627-2681 Fax (404)627-0702
Dir. of Global Missions, Dr. James B. Keiller, P.O. Box 18145, Atlanta, GA 30316 Tel. (404) 627-2681 Fax (404)627-0702

DISTRICT OVERSEERS

Blue Ridge District, Clyde M. Hughes, P.O. Box 439, London, OH 43140 Tel. (740)852-4722 Fax (740)852-0348
Central District, Ervin Hargrave, 2279 Seminole Ave., Springfield, OH 45506 Tel. and Fax (937)323-6433
Mid-Eastern District, H. Gene Boyce, 705 W. Grubb St., Hertford, NC 27944 Tel. (252)426-5403
Mountain District, Terry Lykins, P.O. Box 131, Staffordsville, KY 41256 Tel. (606)297-3282
New River District, Calvin Weikel, Rt. 2, Box 300, Ronceverte, WV 24970 Tel. (304)647-4301
North Central District, Edgar Kent, 67473 Red Arrow Hwy., P.O. Box 275, Hartford, MI 49057 Tel. (616)621-3326
North Eastern District, Wayne Taylor, 806 8th St., Shenandoah, VA 22849 Tel. (540) 652-8090
South Eastern District, Frank Angie, 2507 Old Peachtree Rd., Duluth, GA 30097 Tel. (770) 476-5196
Tri-State District, Cline McCallister, 5210 Wilson St., Portsmouth, OH 45662 Tel. and Fax (740)776-6357

OTHER ORGANIZATIONS

Beulah Heights Bible College, Pres., Samuel R. Chand, PO Box 18145, Atlanta, GA 31306 Tel. (404)627-2681
Women's Ministries, Gen. Pres., Janice Boyce, 121 W. Hunters Tr., Elizabeth City, NC 27909 Tel. and Fax (252)338-3003
Pentecostal Ambassadors, Oustin Hughes, National Youth Dir., P.O Box 439, London, OH 43140 Tel.
(740)852-0448 Fax (740)852-0348
National Christian Education Dept., Dir., Dustin Hughes, P.O. Box 439, London, OH 43140 Tel. (740)852-0448 Fax (740)852-0348

Periodicals

The Bridegroom's Messenger; The Pentecostal Leader

126

International Pentecostal Holiness Church

This body grew out of the National Holiness Association movement of the last century, with roots in Methodism. Beginning in the South and Midwest, the church represents the merger of the Fire-Baptized Holiness Church founded by B. H. Irwin in Iowa in 1895; the Pentecostal Holiness Church founded by A. B. Crumpler in Goldsboro, North Carolina, in 1898; and the Tabernacle Pentecostal Church founded by N. J. Holmes in 1898.

All three bodies joined the ranks of the pentecostal movement as a result of the Azusa Street revival in Los Angeles in 1906 and a 1907 pentecostal revival in Dunn, N.C., conducted by G. B. Cashwell, who had visited Azusa Street. In 1911 the Fire-Baptized and Pentecostal Holiness bodies merged in Falcon, N.C., to form the present church; the Tabernacle Pentecostal Church was added in 1915 in Canon, Georgia.

The church stresses the new birth, the Wesleyan experience of sanctification, the pentecostal baptism in the Holy Spirit, evidenced by speaking in tongues, divine healing and the premillennial second coming of Christ.

Headquarters
P.O. Box 12609, Oklahoma City, OK 73157 Tel. (405)787-7110 Fax (405)789-3957
Media Contact, Admn. Asst.

Officers
Email: jdl@iphc.org (for Bishop Leggett)
Website: http://www.iphc.org
Gen. Supt., Bishop James D. Leggett
Vice Chpsn./Asst. Gen. Supt., Rev. M. Donald Duncan
Asst. Gen. Supt., Dr. Ronald Carpenter
Asst. Gen. Supt., Rev. Paul Howell
Gen. Sec.-Treas., Rev. Jack Goodson

OTHER ORGANIZATIONS
The Publishing House (LifeSprings), Gen. Admn., Greg Hearn, Franklin Springs, GA 30639
Women's Ministries, Exec. Dir., Mary Belle Johnson
Men's Ministries, General. Dir., Col. Jack Kelley, P.O. Box 53307, Fayetteville, NC 28305

Periodicals
IssacharFile; Helping Hand; Evangelism USA; Worldorama; CEM Connection

Jehovah's Witnesses

Modern-day Jehovah's Witnesses began in the early 1870s when Charles Taze Russell was the leader of a Bible study group in Allegheny City, Pennsylvania. In July 1879, the first issue of *Zion's Watch Tower* and *Herald of Christ's Presence* (now called *The Watchtower*) appeared. In 1884 Zion's Watch Tower Tract Society was incorporated, later changed to Watch Tower

Bible and Tract Society. Congregations spread into other states and followers witnessed from house to house.

By 1913, printed sermons were in four languages in 3,000 newspapers in the United States, Canada and Europe. Hundreds of millions of books, booklets and tracts were distributed. Publication of the magazine now known as *Awake!* Began in 1919. Today, it is published in more than 80 languages and has a circulation of upwards of 19,000,000. In 1931 the name Jehovah's Witnesses, based on Isaiah 43:10-12, was adopted.

During the 1930s and 1940s Jehovah's Witnesses fought many court cases in the interest of preserving freedom of speech, press, assembly and worship. They have won a total of 43 cases before the United States Supreme Court. A missionary taining school was established in 1943, and it has been a major factor in the international expansion of the Witnessess. There are now 5.6 million Witnesses in 232 lands (1997).

Jehovah's Witnesses believe in one almighty God, Jehovah, who is the Creator of all things. They believe in Jesus Christ as God's Son, the first of His creations. While Jesus is now an immortal spirit in heaven, ruling as King of God's Kingdom, he is still subject to his heavenly Father, Jehovah God. Christ's human life was sacrificed as a ransom to open up for obedient mankind the opportunity of eternal life. With Christ in heaven, 144,000 individuals chosen from among mankind will rule in righteousness over an unnumbered great crowd who will survive the destruction of wickedness and receive salvation into an earth cleansed of evil. (Rev. 7:9,10; 14:1-5). These, along with the resurrected dead, will transform the earth into a global earthly paradise and will have the prospect of living forever on it.

Headquarters
25 Columbia Heights, Brooklyn, NY 11201-2483 Tel. (718)560-5600
Media Contact, Public Affairs Office, James Pellechia

Officers
Pres. Watch Tower Bible and Tract Society of Pennsylvania, Milton G. Henschel

Korean Presbyterian Church—please see General Assembly of the Korean Presbyterian Church in America

Latter-Day Saints—please see The Church of Jesus Christ of Latter-Day Saints

The Latvian Evangelical Lutheran Church in America

This body was organized into a denomination on Aug. 22, 1975 after having existed as the Federation of Latvian Evangelical Lutheran Churches in America since 1955. This church is a regional constituent part of the Lutheran Church of

127

Latvia Abroad, a member of the Lutheran World Federation and the World Council of Churches.

The Latvian Evangelical Lutheran Church in America works to foster religious life, traditions and customs in its congregations in harmony with the Holy Scriptures, the Apostles', Nicean and Athanasian Creeds, the unaltered Augsburg Confession, Martin Luther's Small and Large Catechisms and other documents of the Book of Concord.

The LELCA is ordered by its Synod (General Assembly), executive board, auditing committee and district conferences.

Headquarters

2140 Okla Dr., Golden Valley, MN 55427 Tel. (612)722-0174

Media Contact, Juris Pulins, 9531 Knoll Top Rd., Union, IL 60180 Tel. (815)923-5919

Officers

Pres., Rev. Uldis Cepure, Tel. (612)546-3712

Vice-Pres., Rev. Anita Varsbergs, 9908 Shelburne Terr., 312, Gathersburg, MD 20878 Tel. (301) 251-4151

2nd Vice-Pres., Aivrs Ronis, 449 S. 40th St., Lincoln, NE 68510 Tel. (402)489-2776

Sec., Ansis Abele, 25182 Northrup Dr., Laguna Beach, CA 92653 Tel. (714)830-9712

Treas., Alfreds Trautmanis, 103 Rose St., Freeport, NY 11520 Tel. (516)623-2646

Periodicals

Cela Biedrs; Lelba Zinas

The Liberal Catholic Church— Province of the United States of America

The Liberal Catholic Church was founded Feb. 13, 1916 as a reorganization of the Old Catholic Church in Great Britain with the Rt. Rev. James I. Wedgwood as the first Presiding Bishop. The first ordination of a priest in the United States was Fr. Charles Hampton, later a Bishop. The first Regionary Bishop for the American Province was the Rt. Rev. Irving S. Cooper (1919-1935).

Headquarters

Pres., Rt. Rev. Lawrence J. Smith, 9740 S. Avers Ave., Evergreen Park, IL 60805 Tel. (708)424-6548 Fax (708)423-8053

Media Contact, Regionary Bishop, Rt. Rev. Lawrence J. Smith

Email: regionary@aol.com

Website: http://members.aol.com/l.catholic/ndex.htm

Officers

Pres. & Regionary Bishop, Rt. Rev. Lawrence J. Smith

Vice-Pres., Rev. L. Marshall Heminway, P.O. Box 19957 Hampden Sta., Baltimore, MD 21211-0957

Sec. (Provincial), Rev. Lloyd Worley, 1232 24th

Avenue Ct., Greeley, CO 80631 Tel. (303)356-3002

Provost, Rev. Lloyd Worley

Treas., Rev. Lloyd Worley

BISHOPS

Regionary Bishop for the American Province, Rt. Rev. Lawrence J. Smith

Aux. Bishops of the American Province: Rt. Rev. Dr. Robert S. McGinnis, Jr., 3612 N. Labarre Rd., Metaire, LA 70002; Rt. Rev. Joseph L. Tisch, P.O. Box 1117, Melbourne, FL 32901; Rt. Rev. Dr. Hein VanBeusekom, 12 Krotona Hill, Ojai, CA 93023; Rt. Rev. Ruben Cabigting, P.O. Box 270, Wheaton, IL 60189; Rt. Rev. William S.H. Downey, 1206 Ayers Ave., Ojai, CA 93023

Periodicals

Ubique

The Lutheran Church—Missouri Synod

The Lutheran Church-Missouri Synod, which was founded in 1847, has more than 6,000 congregations in the United States and works in 60 other countries. It has 2.6 million members and is the second-largest Lutheran denomination in North America.

Christian education is offered for all ages. The North American congregations operate the largest elementary and secondary school systems of any Protestant denomination in the nation, and 14,717 students are enrolled in 12 LCMS institutions of higher learning.

Traditional beliefs concerning the authority and interpretation of Scripture are important. The synod is known for mass-media outreach through "The Lutheran Hour" on radio, "This Is The Life" dramas on television, and the products of Concordia Publishing House, the third-largest Protestant publisher, whose Arch Books children's series has sold more than 58 million copies.

An extensive network of more than 1,000 volunteers in 55 work centers produces Braille, large-type, and audiocassette materials for the blind and visually impaired. Fifty-nine of the Eighty-five deaf congregations affiliated with U.S. Lutherandenominations are LCMS; and many denominations use the Bible lessons prepared for developmentally disabled persons.

The involvement of women is high, although they do not occupy clergy positions. Serving as teachers, deaconesses and social workers, women comprise approximately 48 percent of total professional workers.

The members" responsibility for congregational leadership is a distinctive characteristic of the synod. Power is vested in voters" assemblies, generally comprised of adults of voting age. Synod decision making is given to the delegates at triennial national and district conventions, where the franchise is equally divided between lay and pastoral representatives.

Headquarters

The Lutheran Church-Missouri Synod, International Center, 1333 S. Kirkwood Rd., St. Louis, MO 63122-7295

Media Contact, Dir., News & Information, Rev. David Mahsman, Tel. (314)965-9917 Ext. 1227; Director, Public Relations, Mr. David Strand, Ext. 1229; Manager, News Bureau, Mr. Joe Isenhower, Ext. 1231, Fax (314) 965-3396

Email: infocenter@lcms.org

Website: http://www.lcms.org

Officers

Pres., Dr. A.L. Barry

1st Vice-Pres., Dr. Robert T. Kuhn

2nd Vice-Pres., Dr. Robert King

3rd Vice-Pres., Dr. William C. Weinrich

4th Vice-Pres., Dr. Roger D. Pittelko

5th Vice-Pres., Dr. Wallace Schulz

Sec., Dr. Raymond L. Hartwig

Treas., Mr. Paul Middeke

Admn. Officer of Bd. of Dir., Bradford L. Hewitt

Exec. Dir., Human Resources, Barb Ryan

Bd. of Directors: Dr. Karl L. Barth, Milwaukee, WI; Rev. Roosevelt Gray, Detroit, MI; Dr. Betty Duda, Oviedo, FL; Richard Peters, Amery, WI; Clifford A. Dietrich, Fort Wayne, IN; Ernest E. Garbe, Dieterich, IL; Dr. Jean Garton, Benton, AR; Oscar H. Hanson, Lafayette, CA; Ted Kober, Billings, MT; Dr. Donald K. Muchow, Austin, TX, Chairman; Rev. Ulmer Marshall, Jr., Mobile, AL; Christian Preus, Plymouth, MN; Dr. Edwin Trapp, Jr., Dallas, TX

BOARDS AND COMMISSIONS

Communication Services, Exec. Dir., Dr. Paul Devantier

Mission Services, Exec. Dir., Dr. Glenn O'shoney

Higher Education Services, Exec. Dir., Dr. William F. Meyer

Human Care Ministries, Exec. Dir., Rev. Richard L. Krenzke

Worker Benefit Plans, Exec. Dir., Dan A. Leeman

Lutheran Church-Missouri Syno Foundation, Pres., Dr. Norman Sell

Lutheran Church Ext. Fund-Missouri Synod, Pres., Merle Freitag

Congregational Services, Exec. Dir., -vacant-

Black Ministries Services, Exec. Dir., Dr. Bryant Clancy

ORGANIZATIONS

Concordia Publishing House, Pres./CEO, Dr. Stephen Carter, 3558 S. Jefferson Ave., St. Louis, MO 63118-3968

Concordia Historical Institute, Dir., Rev. Daniel Preus, Concordia Seminary, 801 De Mun Ave., St. Louis, MO 63105

Intl. Lutheran Laymen's League, Exec. Dir., Rodger W. Hebermehl, 2185 Hampton Ave., St. Louis, MO 63139-2983

KFUO Radio, Exec. Dir., Rev. Paul Devantier

Intl. Lutheran Women's Missionary League, Pres., Virginia Von Seggern, 3558 S. Jefferson Ave., St. Louis, MO 63118-3910

Periodicals

The Lutheran Witness; Reporter

The American Association of Lutheran Churches is listed under "A".

Apostolic Lutheran Church of America is listed under "A".

Conservative Lutheran Association is listed under "C".

Evangelical Lutheran Church in America is listed under "E".

Evangelical Lutheran Synod is listed under "E".

Malankara Orthodox Syrian Church, Diocese of America

The American Diocese of the Malankara Orthodox Syrian Church is in full accord with the Mother Church- Malankara Orthodox Syrian Church, also known as the Indian Orthodox Church. The diocese is a national or missionary entity of the Indian Orthodox Church. The Malankara Orthodox Syrian Church established an American diocese in 1978 to serve her immigrant members in America. This diocese is a new phenomenon with great challenges and potentials, composed of immigrant Indian Orthodox members and their American born children. Now that some years have passed, the immigrant church is entering into an indigenous era with the second generation Indian Orthodox members. Currently there are 60 parishes, 68 clergy and about 12,000 members of this church in the United States. The diocese is still growing with immigrants and native-born members.

The Malankara Orthodox Syrian Church has claimed its roots in the Apostolic ministry of Apostle St. Thomas, who was martyred in India, since 52 AD. Although there is not much available about the early history of the Indian Church, it is known that later it was influenced by Roman Catholicism and then Protestant missionaries of the post Reformation period. During the sixteenth century, there arose an increased relationship with the Oriental churches with the arrival of Syrian Bishops. Although different segments of Christianity have been flourishing in India, the Church maintained a close faith in the Non-Chalcedonian councils.

The Malankara Orthodox Syrian Church has got its name: "Malankara" from Maliankara, a nearby town of Dodungalloor where St. Thomas is believed to have arrived in 52 AD; "Orthodox" comes from the faith of the fathers- non Chalcedonian faith; "Syrian" comes from its connection with the Syrian Orthodox Church's traditions, practices, liturgy, language, and liturgical calendar.

80-34 Commonwealth Boulevard
Bellerose, NY 11426
Tel. (718) 470-9844
Fax (718) 470-9219
Media Contact, His Grace Mathews Mar
Barnabas, Diocesan Metropolitan

Officers

Diocesan Metropolitan, His Grace Mathews Mar
Barnabas

Mar Thoma Syrian Church of India

According to tradition, the Mar Thoma Church was established as a result of the apostolic mission of St. Thomas, the apostle in 52 AD. Church history attests to the continuity of the community of faithful, throughout the long centuries in India. The liturgy and faith practices of the Church were based on the relationship between the Church in Kerala, India, which St. Thomas founded, with the East-Syrian and Persian Churches. This started in the 3rd century and continued up to the 16th century. In the 17th century, the Malabar Church of St. Thomas (as the Church in Kerala was known) renewed her relationship with the Orthodox Patriarchate of Antioch as part of the resistance to forced Latinization by the Portuguese. This process also led to the development of the Kerala Episcopacy, whereby the first Indian Bishop Mar Thoma I was consecrated in Kerala.

The Mar Thoma Church retains her Eastern Orthodoxy. She follows an Orthodox (true) worship form and liturgy, believes in the catholicity of grace, is missionary and evangelistic in approach. She derives Episcopal succession from the Syrian Orthodox Church of Antioch and follows Eastern Reformed Theology. She is independent, autonomous, and indigenous, constitutionally combining democratic values and Episcopal authority. She has been in full communion with the Anglican Church since 1954.

The Diocese of North America was organized in 1988 in order to serve the needs of the immigrant community. It has a membership of around five thousand families in sixty five parishes.

Headquarters

Sinai Mar Thoma Center, 2320 S. Merrick Avenue, Merrick, New York 11566 Tel. (516)377-3311 Fax (516)377-3322

Officers

Diocesan Bishop: The Rt. Rev. Dr. Zacharias Mar Theophilus Episcopa
Diocesan/Bishop's Sec.: The Rev. Oommen Philip
Diocesan Treasurer: Kuruvilla Cherian, CPA

Mennonite Church

The Mennonite Church is currently working with two other North American Mennonite denominations—the General Conference Mennonite Church and the Conference of Mennonites in Canada—to form the new, United Mennonite Church, organized as U.S. and Canadian bodies. The three have adopted the same vision statement and the Confession of Faith in a Mennonite Perspective. Some staff members are already jointly appointed. An Executive Board for Mennonite Church USA and a General Board for Mennonite Church Canada were elected in July 1999. Further decisions will be made in summer 2001.

The Mennonite Church in North America traces its beginnings to the Protestant Reformation. Conrad Grebel, Georg Blaurock and a small band of radical believers baptized one another in Zurich, Switzerland, on Jan. 21, 1525. First nicknamed Anabaptists (Rebaptizers) by their opponents, they preferred the term Brothers and Sisters in Christ. They later took their name from the Dutch priest Menno Simons, who joined the movement in 1536.

The Mennonites' refusal to conform to majesterial decrees, including bearing of arms and the swearing of oaths, attracted fierce animosity. Thousands were martyred for their beliefs in nearly a century of persecution. They moved to many places, including the United States and Canada, where some arrived as early as 1683.

North American Mennonites began their first home mission program in Chicago, Illinois in 1893 and their first overseas mission program in India in 1899. Since the 1920s the church has established extensive emergency relief and development services in conjunction with its mission program.

Mennonites hold that the Word of God is central and that new life in Christ is available to all who believe. Adult "Believers" baptism is practiced, symbolizing a conscious decision to follow Christ. Mennonites take seriously Christ's command to witness in word and deed. They stress that Christians need the support of a faith community for encouragement and growth. They view the teachings of Jesus as directly applicable to their lives. Mennonites generally refuse to serve in the military or to use violent resistance.

The largest body of Mennonites in North America, the Mennonite Church is a member of the Mennonite and Brethren in Christ World Conference, a worldwide fellowship, and the Mennonite Central Committee, an international relief and service agency. Individuals and program agencies participate in a variety of ecumenical activities at various levels of church life.

Headquarters

421 S. Second St., Ste. 600, Elkhart, IN 46516 Tel. (219)294-7131 Fax (219)293-3977, Email: mcgb@juno.com
Media Contact, J. Ron Byler, Associate Gen. Sec.
Email: rbyler@juno.com

Officers

Mod., Lee Snyder, 259 Brookwood Dr., Bluffton, OH 45817

Mod. Elect, Ervin Stutzman, 374 Donegal Springs Rd., Mount Joy, PA 17552

Sec., Duane Oswald, 1111 E. Herndon Ave., Suite 308, Fresno, CA 93720-3100

Member at large, James M. Harder, P.O. Box 191, North Newton, KS 67117

Member at large, Roy Williams, 22642 Newfield Ct., Land O'Lakes, FL 34639

Gen. Sec., George Stoltzfus, 421 S. 2nd St., Ste. 600, Elkhart, IN 46516

Exec. Bd., Gen. Sec., George B. Stoltzfus

Historical Cmte., Dir., John E. Sharp, 1700 S. Main, Goshen, IN 46526 Tel. (219)535-7477 Fax (219)535-7477, Email: johnes@hoshen.edu

Peace & Justice Committee, Susan Mark Landis, Minister of Peace and Justice, P.O.Box 173, Orville, OH 44667 Tel. (330) 683-6844 Fax (330) 683-6844, Email: mcpjc@ssnet.com

Bd. of Congregational Min., Pres., Everett J. Thomas, Box 1245, Elkhart, IN 46515 Tel. (219)294-7523 Fax (219)293-1892, Email: mbcma@juno.com

Bd. of Educ., Pres., Orville L. Yoder, Box 1142, Elkhart, IN 46515 Tel. (219)389-0018 Fax (219)293-7446, Email: sand.lb@juno.com

Bd. of Missions, Pres., Stanley W. Green, Box 370, Elkhart, IN 46515 Tel. (219)294-7523, Fax (219)294-8669, Email: barbara@mbm.org

Mutual Aid Bd., Pres., Howard L. Brenneman, 1110 North Main, P.O. Box 483, Goshen, IN 46526 Tel. (219)533-9511 Fax (219)533-5264, Email: mma@mma-online.org

Mennonite Publication Bd., Publisher, J. Robert Ramer, 616 Walnut Ave., Scottdale, PA 15683 Tel. (412)887-8500 Fax (412)887-3111, Email: info@mph.org

Periodicals

The Mennonite Builder; Christian Living; Rejoice!; Mennonite Historical Bulletin; Mennonite Quarterly Review; Purpose; Story Friends

Mennonite Church, The General Conference

The General Conference Mennonite Church is currently working with two other North American Mennonite denominations—the Mennonite Church and the Conference of Mennonites in Canada—to form the new, united Mennonite Church, organized as U.S. and Canadian bodies. The three have adopted the same vision statement and the Confession of Faith in a Mennonite Perspective. Some staff members are already jointly appointed. An Executive Board for Mennonite Church USA and a General Board for Mennonite Church Canada were elected in July 1999. Further decisions will be made in summer 2001.

The General Conference Mennonite Church was formed in 1860, uniting Mennonites throughout the United States who were interested in doing missionary work together. Today 65,500 Christians in 400 member congregations in Canada, the United States and three countries in South America try to follow the way of Jesus in their daily lives.

The conference consists of people of many ethnic backgrounds—Swiss and German, Russian and Dutch, Native American, African-American, Hispanic, Chinese, Vietnamese and Laotian.

The basic belief and practice of the conference come from the life and teachings of Jesus Christ, the early church of the New Testament and the Anabaptists of the 16th-century Reformation. Thus the conference seeks to be evangelical, guided by the Bible, led by the Holy Spirit and supported by a praying, discerning community of believers in congregations and fellowships. Peace, or shalom, is at the very heart of members, who seek to be peacemakers in everyday life.

The Mennonite vision statement reads, "God calls us to be followers of Jesus Christ and, by the power of the Holy Spirit, to grow as communities of grace, joy, and peace, so that God's healing and hope flow through us to the world."

Headquarters

722 Main, P.O. Box 347, Newton, KS 67114 Tel. (316)283-5100 Fax (316)283-0454

Media Contact, Dir. of Communications, David Linscheid

Email: gcmc@gcmc.org

Website: http://www2.southwind.net/~gcmc

Officers & Staff, Mennonite Church USA

Moderator, Lee Snyder, 259 Brookwood Drive, Bluffton, OH 45817

Moderator-elect, Ervin Sttzman, 374 Donegal Springs Rd., Mount Joy, PA 17552

Secretary, Duane Oswald, 1111 E. Herndon Ave., Suite 308, Fresno, CA 93720-3100

Member at Large, James M. Harder, P.O. Box 191, North Newton, KS 67117

Member at Large, Roy Williams, 22642 Newfield Ct., Land O'Lakes, FL 34639

General Secretary, George Stoltzfus, 421 S. 2nd Street, Suite 600, Elkhart, IN 46516

Gen. Sec., James Schrag

Ministerial Leadership Committee, Dir. of Ministerial Leadership, John A. Esau

OTHER ORGANIZATIONS RELATED TO GENERAL CONFERENCE MENNONITE CHURCH

Commission on Education, Exec. Sec., Dennis Good

Commission on Home Ministries, Exec., Lois Barrett

Commission on Overseas Mission, Exec. Sec., Ron Flaming

DIVISION OF GENERAL SERVICES
Business Manager and Treas., Ted Stuckey;
Communications Dir., Dave Linscheid
Faith and Life Press, Manager, Dennis Good
Mennonite Women, Exec. Coords., Susan
Jantzen and Lara Hall Blosser
Mennonite Men, Coord, Jim Gingerich

Periodicals
The Mennonite (published jointly with the
Mennonite Church)

**Church of God in Christ, Mennonite is listed
under "C".**

Evangelical Mennonite Church is listed under "E".

**General Conference of Mennonite Brethren
Churches is listed under "G".**

Evangelical Methodist Church is listed under "E".

**Fundamental Methodist Church, Inc. is listed
under "F".**

**The United Methodist Church is listed under
"U".**

The Metropolitan Church Association, Inc.
Organized after a revival movement in
Chicago in 1894 as the Metropolitan Holiness
Church, this organization was chartered as the
Metropolitan Church Association in 1899. It has
Wesleyan theology.

Headquarters
323 Broad St., Lake Geneva, WI 53147 Tel.
(414)248-6786
Media Contact, Pres., Rev. Warren W. Bitzer

Officers
Pres., Rev. Warren W. Bitzer
Vice-Pres. & Sec., Elbert L. Ison
Treas., Gertrude J. Puckhaber

Periodicals
The Burning Bush

The Missionary Church
The Missionary Church was formed in 1969
through a merger of the United Missionary
Church (organized in 1883) and the Missionary
Church Association (founded in 1898). It is evangelical and conservative with a strong emphasis
on missionary work and church planting.

There are three levels of church government
with local, district and general conferences.
There are 10 church districts in the United States.
The general conference meets every two years.
The denomination operates one college in the
United States.

Headquarters
3811 Vanguard Dr., P.O. Box 9127, Ft. Wayne,
IN 46899-9127 Tel. (219)747-2027 Fax (219)
747-5331

Media Contact, Pres., Dr. John Moran
Email: missionary.church@internetmci.com

Officers
Pres., Dr. John Moran
Vice-Pres., Rev. William Hossler
Sec., Rev. Dave Engbrecht
Treas., Milt Gerber
Director of Church Planting, Rev. Robert
Ransom
Director of World Partners sUSA: Rev. David
Mann
Director of Discipling Ministries, Rev. Tom
Swank
Dir. of Ad. Services, David Von Gunten
Director of Financial Services, Neil Rinehart
Bethel Church Services, Dir., Rev. Larry Avery
Youth Dir., Eric Liechty
Children's Dir., Ms. Frances Blankenbaker
Resource & Curriculum, Dr. Duane Beals
Family Life Dir., Christine Crocker
Marketing & Communication Dir., Murray
Young
Sunday School/Body Building Dir., Bob Keller
Senior Adult Ministry Dir., Dr. Charles Cureton
Missionary Men Liaison, Rev. Ron Phipps
Missionary Women Intl., Pres., Barbara Reffey
Missionary Church Investment Foundation, Mr.
Eric Smith

Periodicals
Emphasis on Faith and Living; Priority

Moravian Church in America (Unitas Fratrum)
In 1735 German Moravian missionaries of the
pre-Reformation faith of Jan Hus came to
Georgia, in 1740 to Pennsylvania, and in 1753 to
North Carolina. They established the American
Moravian Church, which is broadly evangelical,
ecumenical, liturgical, "conferential" in form of
government and has an episcopacy as a spiritual
office. The Northern and Southern Provinces of
the church operate on a semi-atonomous basis.

Headquarters
Denominational offices or headquarters are
called the Provincial Elders' Conference.
See addresses for Northern and Southern
Provinces:

Northern Province

Headquarters
1021 Center St., P.O. Box 1245, Bethlehem, PA
18016-1245 Tel. (610)867-7566 Fax
(610)866-9223
Media Contact, Rev. R. Burke Johnson

PROVINCIAL ELDERS' CONFERENCE
Pres., Rev. R. Burke Johnson
Vice-Pres./Sec. (Eastern Dist.), Rev. David L.
Wickmann
Vice-Pres. (Western Dist.), Rev. Lawrence
Christianson

Comptroller, Theresa E. Kunda, 1021 Center St., P.O. Box 1245, Bethlehem, PA 18016-1245

NORTHERN PROVINCE

1021 Center St., P.O. Box 1245, Bethlehem, PA 18016-1245 Tel. (610)867-7566 Fax (610)866-9223

Eastern District Pres., Rev. David L. Wickmann, P.O. Box 1245, Bethlehem, PA 18016-1245

Western District Pres., Rev. Lawrence Christianson, P.O. Box 386, Sun Prairie, WI 53590

Pacific Southwest District Pres., Rev. Larry Wetzel, 7142 W. Cherry Hills Dr., Peoria, AZ 85345 Tel. (602)979-0488

Canadian District Pres., Ruth Humphreys, 25 23332 Twp. Rd. 20, Sherwood Park, AB T8B 1L5

Email: burke@mcnp.org

Website: http://www.moravian.org

SOUTHERN PROVINCE

Headquarters

459 S. Church St., Winston-Salem, NC 27101 or Mailing address: Drawer O, Winston-Salem, NC 27108 Tel. (336)725-5811 Fax (336)723-1029

Email: rsawyer@mcsp.org

Website: www.moravian.org (for Moravian Church, Northern and Southern Province)

PROVINCIAL ELDERS' CONFERENCE

Pres., Rev. Dr. Robert E. Sawyer

Vice President, Rev. Lane A. Sapp

Sec. Mr. George Johnson

Treas., Mr. Richard Cartner, Drawer M, Salem Station, Winston-Salem, NC 27108

Other Members: Mrs. Betsy R. Bombick, Rev. Tom Shelton

Asst. to Pres., Robert Hunter

ALASKA PROVINCE

P.O. Box 545, Bethel, AK 99559

Officers

Pres., Rev. Frank Chingliak

Vice-Pres., Rev. Peter Green

Sec., Sarah Owens

Treas., Juanita Asicksik

Dir. of Theological Education, Rev. Will Updegrove

Periodicals

The Moravian

Mormons—please see The Church of Jesus Christ of Latter-Day Saints.

National Association of Free Will Baptists

This evangelical group of Arminian Baptists was organized by Paul Palmer in 1727 at Chowan, North Carolina. Another movement (teaching the same doctrines of free grace, free salvation and free will) was organized June 30,

1780, in New Durham, N.H., but there was no connection with the southern organization except for a fraternal relationship.

The northern line expanded more rapidly and extended into the West and Southwest. This body merged with the Northern Baptist Convention Oct. 5, 1911, but a remnant of churches reorganized into the Cooperative General Association of Free Will Baptists Dec. 28, 1916, at Pattonsburg, Mo.

Churches in the southern line were organized into various conferences from the beginning and finally united in one General Conference in 1921.

Representatives of the Cooperative General Association and the General Conference joined Nov. 5, 1935 to form the National Association of Free Will Baptists.

Headquarters

5233 Mt. View Rd., Antioch, TN 37013-2306 Tel. (615)731-6812 Fax (615)731-0771

Mailing Address, P.O. Box 5002, Antioch, TN 37011-5002

Media Contact, Exec. Sec., Melvin Worthington

Officers

Exec. Sec., Dr. Melvin Worthington

Mod., Rev. Carl Cheshier, PO Box 7208, Moore, TX 73153

DENOMINATIONAL AGENCIES

Free Will Baptist Foundation, Exec. Dir., William Evans

Free Will Baptist Bible College, Pres., Dr. Tom Malone

Foreign Missions Dept., Dir., Rev. James Forlines

Home Missions Dept., Dir., Rev. Trymon Messer

Bd. of Retirement, Dir., Rev. William Evans

Historical Commission, Chpsn., Dr. Thomas Marberry

Comm. for Theological Integrity, Chpsn., Rev. Leroy Forlines, P.O. Box 50117, Nashville, TN 37205

Music Commission, Chpsn., Rev. Randy Sawyer, 2316 Union Rd., Gastonia, NC 28054

Media Comm., Chpsn., Rev. Steve Faison, PO Box 295, Cedar Springs, GA 31732

Sunday School & Church Training Dept., Dir., Dr. Alton Loveless

Women Nationally Active for Christ, Exec. Sec., Majorie Workman

Master's Men Dept., Dir., Rev. Tom Dooley

Periodicals

Attack, A Magazine for Christian Men; Contact; Free Will Bible College Bulletin; Co-Laborer; Free Will Baptist Gem; Heartbeat; AIM

National Association of Congregational Christian Churches

This association was organized in 1955 in Detroit, Michigan, by delegates from Congregational Christian Churches committed to continuing

133

the Congregational way of faith and order in church life. Participation by member churches is voluntary.

Headquarters

P.O. Box 1620, Oak Creek, WI 53154 Tel. (414)764-1620 Fax (414)764-0319
Media Contact, Assoc. Exec. Sec., Rev. Dr. Donald P. Olsen, 8473 So. Howell Ave., Oak Creek, WI 53154 Tel. (414)764-1620 Fax (414)764-0319
Email: naccc@naccc.org
Website: http://www.naccc.org/

Officers

Exec. Sec., Rev. Dr. Douglas L. Lobb, 8473 South Howell Ave., Oak Creek, WI 53154
Assoc. Exec. Secs., Rev. Phil Jackson and Rev. Dr. Donald P. Olsen

Periodicals

The Congregationalist

National Baptist Convention of America, Inc.

The National Baptist Convention of America, Inc., was organized in 1880. Its mission is articulated through its history, constitution, articles of incorporation and by-laws. The Convention (corporate churches) has a mission statement with fourteen (14) objectives including: fostering unity throughout its membership and the world Christian community by proclaiming the gospel of Jesus Christ; validating and propagating the Baptist doctrine of faith and practice, and its distinctive principles throughout the world; and harnassing and encouraging the scholarly and Christian creative skills of its membership for Christian writing and publications.

Headquarters

Media Contact, Liaison Officer, Dr. Richard A. Rollins, 777 S. R.L. Thornton Fwy., Ste. 205, Dallas, TX 75203 Tel. (214)946-8913 Fax (214)946-9619

Officers

Pres., Dr. E. Edward Jones, 1327 Pierre Ave., Shreveport, LA 71103 Tel. (318)221-3701 Fax (318)222-7512
Gen. Rec. Sec., Dr. Clarence C. Pennywell, 2016 Russell Rd., Shreveport, LA 71107
Corres. Sec., Rev. E. E. Stafford, 6614 South Western Ave., Los Angeles, CA 90047
Liaison Officer, Dr. Richard A. Rollins, 777 So. R.L. Thornton Frwy., Ste. 205, Dallas, TX 75203 Tel. (214)946-8913 Fax (214)946-9619
Pres. Aide, Rev. Dr. Joe R. Gant, 5823 Ledbetter St., Shreveport, LA 77108

Periodicals

The Lantern

National Baptist Convention, U.S.A., Inc.

The older and parent convention of black Baptists, this body is to be distinguished from the National Baptist Convention of America.

Headquarters

1700 Baptist World Center Dr., Nashville, TN 37207 Tel. (615)228-6292 Fax (615)226-5935

Officers

Pres., Dr. William J. Shaw, 1700 Baptist World Center Dr., Nashville, TN 37207 Tel. (615)228-6292 Fax (615)226-5935
Gen. Sec., Dr. Roscoe Cooper, Jr., 300 Grace St., Richmond, VA 23220-4908 Tel. (804)643-0192

Periodicals

Mission Herald

National Missionary Baptist Convention of America

The National Missionary Baptist Convention of America was organized in 1988 as a separate entity from the National Baptist Convention of America, Inc., after a dispute over control of the convention's publishing efforts. The new organization intended to remain committed to the National Baptist Sunday Church School and Baptist Training Union Congress and the National Baptist Publishing Board.

The purpose of the National Missionary Baptist Convention of America is to serve as an agency of Christian education, church extension and missionary efforts. It seeks to maintain and safeguard full religious liberty and engage in social and economic development.

Headquarters

1404 E. Firestone, Los Angeles, CA 90001 Tel. (213)582-0090
Media Contact, Dr. W. T. Snead, Sr.

Officers

Pres., Dr. W. T. Snead, Sr.
Vice-Pres., At-large, Dr. Harvey E. Leggett, 866 Monroe St., Ypsilanti, MI 48197
Vice-Pres., Ecumenical Affairs, Dr. F. Benjamin Davis, 1535 Dr. A.J. Brown Blvd. N., Indianapolis, IN 46202
Vice-Pres., Auxiliaries, T. J. Prince, 2219 Sea Island Dr., Dallas, TX 75232
Vice-Pres., Boards, Dr. O. E. Piper, 4220 W. 18th St., Chicago, IL 60623
Vice-Pres., Financial Affairs, J. A. Boles, 2001 South J St., Tacoma, WA 98405
Pres., National Baptist Publishing Bd., Dr. T. B. Boyd, III, 6717 Centennial Blvd., Nashville, TN 37209
Gen. Sec., Dr. Melvin V. Wade, 4269 S. Figueroa, Los Angeles, CA 90037
Corres. Sec., Dr. H. J. Johnson, 2429 South Blvd., Dallas, TX 75215
Treas., Dr. W. N. Daniel, 415 W. Englewood Ave., Chicago, IL 60612
Rec. Sec., Dr. Lonnie Franks, Crocker, TX

National Organization of the New Apostolic Church of North America

This body is a variant of the Catholic Apostolic Church which began in England in

1830. The New Apostolic Church distinguished itself from the parent body in 1863 by recognizing a succession of Apostles.

Headquarters

3753 N. Troy St., Chicago, IL 60618
Media Contact, Sec. & Treas., Ellen E. Eckhardt, Tel. (773)539-3652 Fax (773)478-6691
Website: http://www.nak.org

Officers

Pres., Rev. Erwin Wagner, 330 Arlene Pl., Waterloo, ON N2J 2G6
First Vice-Pres., Rev. Richard C. Freund, 1 Mikel Ln., Glen Head, NY 11545-1591
Second Vice-Pres., Rev. Leonard E Kolb, 4522 Wood St., Erie, PA 16509-1639
Treas. & Sec., Ellen E. Eckhardt, 6380 N. Indian Rd., Chicago, IL 60646
Asst. Sec., Rev. John E. Doderer, 3753 N. Troy St., Chicago, IL 60618

National Primitive Baptist Convention, Inc.

Throughout the years of slavery and the Civil War, the Negro population of the South worshipped with the white population in their various churches. At the time of emancipation, their white brethren helped them establish their own churches, granting them letters of fellowship, ordaining their deacons and ministers and helping them in other ways.

The doctrine and polity of this body are quite similar to that of white Primitive Baptists, yet there are local associations and a national convention, organized in 1907.

Each church is independent and receives and controls its own membership. This body was formerly known as Colored Primitive Baptists.

Headquarters

6433 Hidden Forest Dr., Charlotte, NC 28213 Tel. (704)596-1508
Media Contact, Elder T. W. Samuels

Officers

Natl. Convention, Pres., Elder T. W. Samuels, Tel. (704)596-3153
Natl. Convention, Vice-Pres., Elder Ernest Ferrell, Tallahassee, FL
Natl. Convention, Chmn. Bd. of Dirs., Elder Ernest Ferrell, Tallahassee, FL
Natl. Church School Training Union, Pres., Jonathan Yates, Mobile, AL
Natl. Ushers Congress, Pres., Bro. Carl Batts, 21213 Garden View Dr., Maple Heights, OH 44137
Publishing Bd., Chpsn., Elder E. W. Wallace, Creamridge, NJ
Women's Congress, Pres., Betty Brown, Cocoa Beach, FL
Natl. Laymen's Council, Pres., Densimore Robinson, Huntsville, AL
Natl. Youth Congress, Pres., Robert White, Trenton, NJ

National Spiritualist Association of Churches

This organization is made up of believers that Spiritualism is a science, philosophy and religion based upon the demonstrated facts of communication between this world and the next.

Headquarters

NSAC General Offices, Rev. Sharon L. Snowman, Secretary, P.O. Box 217, Lily Dale, NY 14752-0217
Media Contact, Ms. Marrice Converson, 5341 S., Cornell, Chicago, IL 60615-6205
Email: nsac@nsac.org
Website: http://www.nsac.org

Officers

Pres., Rev. Barbara Thurman, 200 Marina Vista Rd., Larkspur, CA 94939-2144
Vice-Pres., Rev. Pamla Ashlay, 11811 Watertown Plank Rd., Milwaukee, WI 53226
Sec., Rev. Sharon L. Snowman, P.O. Box 217, Lily Dale, NY 14752 Tel. (716)595-2000 Fax (716)595-2020
Treas., Rev. Lelia Cutler, 7310 Medfield St. #1, Norfolk, VA 23505

OTHER ORGANIZATIONS

Bureau of Educ., Supt., Rev. Janet Travis, 17 Ann Court, Kings Park, NY 11754
Bureau of Public Relations, Ms. Marrice Coverson, 5341 S. Cornell, Chicago, IL 60615-6205
The Stow Memorial Foundation, Sec., Rev. Sharon L. Snowman, P.O. Box 217, Lily Dale, NY 14752 Tel. (716)595-2000 Fax (716)595-2020
Spiritualist Benevolent Society, Inc., P.O. Box 217, Lily Dale, NY 14752

Periodicals

The National Spiritualist Summit; Spotlight

Netherlands Reformed Congregations

The Netherlands Reformed Congregations organized denominationally in 1907. In the Netherlands, the so-called Churches Under the Cross (established in 1839, after breaking away from the 1834 Secession congregations) and the so-called Ledeboerian churches (established in 1841 under the leadership of the Rev. Ledeboer, who seceded from the Reformed State Church), united in 1907 under the leadership of the then 25-year-old Rev. G. H. Kersten, to form the Netherlands Reformed Congregations. Many of the North American congregations left the Christian Reformed Church to join the Netherlands Reformed Congregations after the Kuyperian presupposed regeneration doctrine began making inroads.

All Netherlands Reformed Congregations, office-bearers and members subscribe to three Reformed Forms of Unity: The Belgic

135

Confession of Faith (by DeBres), the Heidelberg Catechism (by Ursinus and Olevianus) and the Canons of Dort. Both the Belgic Confession and the Canons of Dort are read regularly at worship services, and the Heidelberg Catechism is preached weekly, except on church feast days.

Headquarters

Media Contact, Synodical Clk., Rev. C. Vogelaar, 2281 Mapleleaf Terrace, Grand Rapids, MI 49505 Tel. (616)742-5929 Fax (616)742-5930

OTHER ORGANIZATIONS

Netherlands Reformed Book and Publishing, 1233 Leffingwell NE, Grand Rapids, MI 49505

Periodicals

The Banner of Truth; Paul (mission magazine); Insight Into (for young people); Learning and Living (for school and home)

The New Church—please see General Church of the New Jerusalem

North American Baptist Conference

The North American Baptist Conference was begun by immigrants from Germany. The first church was organized by the Rev. Konrad Fleischmann in Philadelphia in 1843. In 1865 delegates of the churches met in Wilmot, Ontario, and organized the North American Baptist Conference. Today only a few churches still use the German language, mostly in a bilingual setting.

The Conference meets in general session once every three years for fellowship, inspiration and to conduct the business of the Conference through elected delegates from the local churches. The General Council, composed of representatives of the various Associations and Conference organizations and departments, meets annually to determine the annual budget and programs for the Conference and its departments and agencies. The General Council also makes recommendations to the Triennial Conference on policies, long-range plans and election of certain personnel, boards and committees.

Approximately 65 missionaries serve in Brazil, Cameroon, Japan, Mexico, Nigeria, Philippines, and Russia.

Ten homes for the aged are affiliated with the Conference and 12 camps are operated on the association level.

Headquarters

1 S. 210 Summit Ave., Oakbrook Terrace, IL 60181 Tel. (630)495-2000 Fax (630)495-3301 Media Contact, Marilyn Schaer

Officers

Mod., Mr. Wayne Wegner
Vice-Mod., Rev. Harvey Wilke

Exec. Dir., Dr. Philip Yntema
Treas., Jackie Loewer

OTHER ORGANIZATIONS

Intl. Missions Dept., Dir., Ron Salzman
Home Missions Dept., Dir., Rev. Jim Fann
Church Extension Investors Fund, Dir., Robert Mayforth

North American Old Roman Catholic Church (Archdiocese of New York)

This body is identical with the Roman Catholic Church in faith but differs from it in discipline and worship. The Mass is offered with the appropriate rite either in Latin or in the vernacular. All other sacraments are taken from the Roman Pontifical. This jurisdiction allows for married clergy.

Primatial Headquarters

Box 021647 GPO, Brooklyn, NY 11202-0036 Tel. (718)855-0600
Media Contact, Chancellor, Most Rev. Albert J. Berube

Officers

Primate, The Most Rev. Herve L. Quessy
Chancellor, Most Rev. Albert J. Berube
Diocese of New York: Ordinary, Most Rev. Albert J. Berube
Diocese of Montreal & French Canada: Ordinary, Most Rev. Herve L. Quessy

Old German Baptist Brethren

This group separated from the Church of the Brethren (formerly German Baptist Brethren) in 1881 in order to preserve and maintain historic Brethren Doctrine.

Headquarters

Vindicator Ofc. Ed., Steven L. Bayer, 6952 N. Montgomery County Line Rd., Englewood, OH 45322-9748 Tel. (937)884-7531

Periodicals

The Vindicator

Old Order (Wisler) Mennonite Church

This body arose from a separation of Mennonites dated 1872, under Jacob Wisler, in opposition to what were thought to be innovations. The group is in the Eastern United States and Canada. Each state, or district, has its own organization and holds semi-annual conferences.

Headquarters

Media Contact, Amos B. Hoover, 376 N. Muddy Creek Rd., Denver, PA 17517 Tel. (717)484-4849 Fax (717)484-104

Old Order Amish Church

The congregations of this Old Order Amish group have no annual conference. They worship in private homes. They adhere to the older forms of worship and attire. This body has bishops, ministers and deacons.

Officers
Information
Der Neue Amerikanische Calendar, c/o Raber's Book Store, 2467 C R 600, Baltic, OH 43804
Telephone Contact, LeRoy Beachy, Beachy Amish Mennonite Church, 4324 SR 39, Millersburg, OH 44654 Tel. (216)893-2883

Open Bible Standard Churches
Open Bible Standard Churches originated from two revival movements: Bible Standard Conference, founded in Eugene, Oregon, under the leadership of Fred L. Hornshuh in 1919, and Open Bible Evangelistic Association, founded in Des Moines, Iowa, under the leadership of John R. Richey in 1932.

Similar in doctrine and government, the two groups amalgamated on July 26, 1935 as "Open Bible Standard Churches, Inc." with headquarters in Des Moines, Iowa.

The original group of 210 ministers has enlarged to incorporate over 1,902 ministers and 1,069 churches in 36 countries. The first missionary left for India in 1926. The church now ministers in Asia, Africa, South America, Europe, Canada, Mexico, Central America, and the Caribbean Islands.

Historical roots of the parent groups reach back to the outpouring of the Holy Spirit in 1906 at Azusa Street Mission in Los Angeles and to the full gospel movement in the Midwest. Both groups were organized under the impetus of pentecostal revival. Simple faith, freedom from fanaticism, emphasis on evangelism and missions and free fellowship with other groups were characteristics of the growing organizations.

The highest governing body of Open Bible Standard Churches meets biennially and is composed of all ministers and one voting delegate per 100 members from each church. A National Board of Directors, elected by the national and regional conferences, conducts the business of the organization. Official Bible College is Eugene Bible College in Oregon.

Open Bible Standard Churches is a charter member of the National Association of Evangelicals and of the Pentecostal/Charismatic Churches of North America. It is a member of the Pentecostal World Conference.

NATIONAL OFFICE
2020 Bell Ave., Des Moines, IA 50315 Tel. (515)288-6761 Fax (515)288-2510
Media Contact, Exec. Dir., Communications & Resources, Jeff Farmer, Tel. (515)288-6761 Fax (515)288-2510
Email: info@openbible.org
Website: http://www. openbible.org

Officers
Pres., Jeffrey E. Farmer

Sec.-Treas., Teresa A. Beyer
Dir. of Intl. Min., Paul V. Canfield

Periodicals
Message of the Open Bible

The Orthodox Church in America
The Orthodox Church of America entered Alaska in 1794 before its purchase by the United States in 1867. Its canonical status of independence (autocephaly) was granted by its Mother Church, the Russian Orthodox Church, on April 10, 1970, and it is now known as The Orthodox Church in America.

Headquarters
P.O. Box 675, Syosset, NY 11791-0675 Tel. (516)922-0550 Fax (516)922-0954
Media Contact, Dir. of Communications, V. Rev. John Matusiak
Email: jjm@oca.org
Website: http://www.oca.org

Officers
Primate, Archbishop of Washington, Metropolitan of All America & Canada, Most Blessed Theodosius
Chancellor, V. Rev. Robert S. Kondratick, P.O. Box 675, Syosset, NY 11791 Tel. (516)922-0550 Fax (516)922-0954

SYNOD
Chpsn., His Beatitude Theodosius, P.O. Box 675, Syosset, NY 11791
Archbishop of New York, Most Rev. Peter, 33 Hewitt Ave., Bronxville, NY 10708
Archbishop of Pittsburgh & Western PA, Most Rev. Kyrill, P.O. Box R, Wexford, PA 15090
Archbishop of Dallas, Archbishop Dmitri, 4112 Throckmorton, Dallas, TX 75219
Bishop of Philadelphia, Archbishop Herman, St. Tikhon's Monastery, South Canaan, PA 18459
Aux. Bishop of Anchorage, Rt. Rev. Innocent, P.O. Box 240805, Anchorage, AK 99524-0805
Bishop of Detroit, Rt. Rev. Nathaniel, P.O. Box 309, Grass Lake, MI 49240-0309
Bishop of Midwest, Rt. Rev. Job, 605 Iowa St., Oak Park, IL 60302
Bishop of San Francisco, Rt. Rev. Tikhon, 649 North Robinson St., Los Angeles, CA 90026
Bishop of Ottawa and Canada, Rt. Rev. Seraphim, P.O. Box 179, Spencerville, ON K0E 1X0 Tel. (613)925-5226
Auxiliary Bishop, Titular Bishop of Bethesda, Rt. Rev. Mark, 9511 Sun Pointe Dr., Boynton Beach, FL 33437
Auxiliary Bishop for the Diocese of Alaska, Rt. Rev. Innocent, 513 E. 24th St., Ste. #3, Ancorage, AK 99503 Tel. (907) 279-0025

Periodicals
The Orthodox Church

The Orthodox Presbyterian Church
On June 11, 1936, certain ministers, elders and lay members of the Presbyterian Church in the

U.S.A. withdrew from that body to form a new denomination. Under the leadership of the late Rev. J. Gresham Machen, noted conservative New Testament scholar, the new church determined to continue to uphold the Westminster Confession of Faith as traditionally understood by Presbyterians and to engage in proclamation of the gospel at home and abroad.

The church has grown modestly over the years and suffered early defections, most notably one in 1937 that resulted in the formation of the Bible Presbyterian Church under the leadership of Dr. Carl McIntire. It now has congregations throughout the states of the continental United States.

The denomination is a member of the North American Presbyterian and Reformed Council and the International Council of Reformed Churches.

Headquarters
607 N. Easton Rd., Bldg. E, Box P, Willlow Grove, PA 19090-0920 Tel. (215)830-0900 Fax (215)830-0350

Media Contact, Stated Clerk, Rev. Donald J. Duff

Email: duff.1@opc.org

Website: http://www.opc.org

Headquarters
Moderator of General Assembly, The Rev. Larry G. Mininger, 818 East Harbour Ct., Ocoee, FL 34761-3116

Stated Clk., Rev. Donald J. Duff

Periodicals

New Horizons in the Orthodox Presbyterian Church

Patriarchal Parishes of the Russian Orthodox Church in the U.S.A.
This group of parishes is under the direct jurisdiction of the Patriarch of Moscow and All Russia, His Holiness Aleksy II, in the person of a Vicar Bishop, His Grace Paul, Bishop of Zaraisk.

Headquarters
St. Nicholas Cathedral, 15 E. 97th St., New York, NY 10029 Tel. (212)831-6294 Fax (212)427-5003

Media Contact, Sec. to the Bishop, Deacon Vladimir Tyschuk, Tel. (212)289-1915

Periodicals
One Church

Pentecostal Assemblies of the World, Inc.
This organization is an interracial Pentecostal holiness of the Apostolic Faith, believing in repentance, baptism in Jesus's name and being filled with the Holy Ghost, with the evidence of speaking in tongues. It originated in the early part of the century in the Middle West and has spread throughout the country.

Headquarters
3939 Meadows Dr., Indianapolis, IN 46205 Tel. (317)547-9541

Media Contact, Admin., John E. Hampton, Fax (317)543-0512

Officers
Presiding Bishop, Norman L. Wagner

Asst. Presiding Bishop, James E. Tyson

Bishops: Arthus Brazier; George Brooks; Ramsey Butler; Morris Golder; Francis L. Smith, Francis L.; Brooker T. Jones; C. R. Lee; Robert McMurray; Philip L. Scott; William L. Smith; Samuel A. Layne; Freeman M. Thomas; James E. Tyson; Charles Davis; Willie Burrell; Harry Herman; Jeremiah Reed; Jeron Johnson; Clifton Jones; Robert Wauls; Ronald L. Young; Henry L. Johnson; Leodis Warren; Thomas J. Weeks; Eugene Redd; Thomas W. Weeks, Sr.; Willard Saunders; Davis L. Ellis; Earl Parchia; Vanuel C. Little; Norman Wagner; George Austin; Benjamin A. Pitt; Markose Thopil; John K. Cole; Peter Warkie; Norman Walters; Alphonso Scott; David Dawkins

Gen. Sec, Dr. Aletha Cushinberry

Assist. Gen Sec., Suffragan Bishop Noel Jones

Gen. Treas., Elder James Loving

Asst. Treas., Dist. Eld. Charles Ellis III

Periodicals
Christian Outlook

Pentecostal Church of God
Growing out of the pentecostal revival at the turn of the century, the Pentecostal Church of God was organized in Chicago on Dec. 30, 1919, as the Pentecostal Assemblies of the U.S.A. The name was changed to Pentecostal Church of God in 1922; in 1934 it was changed again to The Pentecostal Church of God of America, Inc.; and finally the name became the Pentecostal Church of God (Inc.) in 1979.

The International Headquarters was moved from Chicago, Illinois to Ottumwa, Iowa, in 1927, then to Kansas City, Missoui, in 1933 and finally to Joplin, Missouri, in 1951.

The denomination is evangelical and pentecostal in doctrine and practice. Active membership in the National Association of Evangelicals and the Pentecostal/Charismatic Churches North America is maintained.

The church is Trinitarian in doctrine and teaches the absolute inerrancy of the Scripture from Genesis to Revelation. Among its cardinal beliefs are the doctrines of salvation, which includes regeneration; divine healing, as provided for in the atonement; the baptism in the Holy Ghost, with the initial physical evidence of speaking in tongues; and the premillennial second coming of Christ.

Headquarters
4901 Pennsylvania, P.O. Box 850, Joplin, MO 64802 Tel. (417)624-7050 Fax (417)624-7102

Media Contact, Gen. Sec., Dr. Ronald R. Minor
Email: peg@peg.org

Officers
Gen. Supt., Dr. James D. Gee
Gen. Sec., Dr. Ronald R. Minor

OTHER GENERAL EXECUTIVES
Dir. of World Missions, Rev. John K. Norvell
Dir. of Indian Missions, Dr. C. Don Burke
Dir. of Youth Ministries, Rev. Reggie O. Powers
Dir. of Home Missions/Evangelism, Dr. H. O. (Pat) Wilson

ASSISTANT GENERAL SUPERINTENDENTS
Northwestern Division, Rev. Dale G. Sage
Southwestern Division, Rev. Lloyd L. Naten
North Central Division, Rev. Donald R. Dennis
South Central Division, Rev. E. L. Redding
Northeastern Division, Rev. Thomas E. Branham
Southeastern Division, Rev. John W. Stalls

OTHER DEPARTMENTAL OFFICERS
Bus. Mgr., Rev. Alan Greagrey
Director of Women's Ministry, Diana L. Gee
Christian Educ., Dir., Mrs. Billie Palumbo

Periodicals
The Pentecostal Messenger; Spirit

Pentecostal Fire-Baptized Holiness Church

Organized in 1918, this group consolidated with the Pentecostal Free Will Baptists in 1919. It maintains rigid discipline over members.

Headquarters
P.O. Box 261, La Grange, GA 30241-0261 Tel. (706)884-7742
Media Contact, Gen. Mod., Wallace B. Pittman, Jr.

Officers
Gen. Treas., K. N. (Bill) Johnson, P.O. Box 1528, Laurinburg, NC 28352 Tel. (919)276-1295
Gen. Sec., W. H. Preskitt, Sr., Rt. 1, Box 169, Wetumpka, AL 36092 Tel. (205)567-6565
Gen. Mod., Wallace B. Pittman, Jr.
Gen. Supt. Mission Bd., Jerry Powell, Rt. 1, Box 384, Chadourn, NC 28431

Periodicals
Faith and Truth

The Pentecostal Free Will Baptist Church, Inc.

The Cape Fear Conference of Free Will Baptists, organized in 1855, merged in 1959 with The Wilmington Conference and The New River Conference of Free Will Baptists and was renamed the Pentecostal Free Will Baptist Church, Inc. The doctrines include regeneration, sanctification, the Pentecostal baptism of the Holy Ghost, the Second Coming of Christ and divine healing.

Headquarters
P.O. Box 1568, Dunn, NC 28335 Tel. (910)892-4161 Fax (910)892-6876
Media Contact, Gen. Supt., Preston Heath
Email: pheath@intrstar.net

Officers
Gen. Supt., Rev. Preston Heath
Asst. Gen. Supt., Rev. Reynolds Smith
Gen. Sec., Rev. Horace Johnson
Gen. Treas., Dr. W. L. Ellis
Christian Ed. Dir., Rev. Murray King
World Witness Dir., Rev. Dock Hobbs
Gen. Services Dir., Danny Blackman
Ministerial Council Dir., ———
Ladies' Auxiliary Dir., Dollie Davis
Heritage Bible College, Pres., Dr. W. L. Ellis
Crusader Youth Camp, Dir., Rev. Murray King

OTHER ORGANIZATIONS
Heritage Bible College
Crusader Youth Camp
Blessings Bookstore, 1006 W. Cumberland St., Dunn, NC 28334 Tel. (910)892-2401
Cape Fear Christian Academy, Rt 1 Box 139, Erwin, NC 28339 Tel. (910)897-5423

Periodicals
The Messenger

Philadelphia Yearly Meeting of the Religious Society of Friends

PYM traces its roots to the yearly meeting of 1681 in Burlington, New Jersey. For more than three centuries, PYM has served Monthly Meetings and Quarterly Meetings throughout eastern Pennsylvania, southern New Jersey, northern Maryland and Delaware. In general, the activities of PYM are organized under five Standing Committees: Standing Committee on Worship and Care; Standing Committee on Education; Standing Committee on Peace and Concerns; Standing Committee on Support and Outreach; Standing Committee on General Services.

Headquarters
Philadelphia Yearly Meeting, 1515 Cherry Street, Philadelphia, PA 19102-1479 Tel. (215)241-7000 Fax (215)567-2096
Website: www.pym.org

Officers
Gen. Sec., Thomas Jeavons
Clerk, Standing Committee on Worship and Care, D. Craig Trueblood, Email: worship@pym.org
Clerk, Standing Committee on Education, Rachel Bull (610)358-5926, Email: rabatbull@aol.com or education@pym.org Clerk, Standing Committee on Peace and Concerns, Elizabeth R. Marsh, Email: peace@pym.org
Clerk, Standing Committee on Support and Outreach, Sandra Gibbs Horne, Email: outreach@pym.org

139

Clerk, Standing Committee on General Services, Sandra Moyer, Email: services@pym.org

Pillar of Fire

The Pillar of Fire was founded by Alma Bridwell White in Denver on Dec. 29, 1901 as the Pentecostal Union. In 1917, the name was changed to Pillar of Fire. Alma White was born in Kentucky in 1862 and taught school in Montana where she met her husband, Kent White, a Methodist minister, who was a University student in Denver.

Because of Alma White's evangelistic endeavors, she was frowned upon by her superiors, which eventually necessitated her withdrawing from Methodist Church supervision. She was ordained as Bishop and her work spread to many states, to England, and since her death to Liberia, West Africa, Malawi, East Africa, Yugoslavia, Spain, India and the Philippines.

The Pillar of Fire organization has a college and two seminaries stressing Biblical studies. It operates eight separate schools for young people. The church continues to keep in mind the founder's goals and purposes.

Headquarters

P.O. Box 9159, Zarephath, NJ 08890 Tel. (908) 356-0102

Western Headquarters, 1302 Sherman St., Denver, CO 80203 Tel. (303)427-5462

Media Contact, 1st Vice Pres., Robert B. Dallenbach, 3455 W. 83 Ave., Westminster, CO 80030 Tel. (303)427-5462 Fax (303)429-0910

Officers

Pres. & Gen. Supt., Bishop Donald J. Wolfram

1st Vice-Pres. & Asst. Supt., Bishop Robert B. Dallenbach

2nd Vice-Pres./Sec.-Treas., Lois R. Stewart

Trustees: Kenneth Cope; Elsworth N. Bradford; S. Rea Crawford; Lois Stewart; Dr. Donald J. Wolfram; Robert B. Dallenbach; June Blue

Periodicals

The Pillar Monthly

Plymouth Brethren—please see Christian Brethren.

Polish National Catholic Church of America

After a number of attempts to resolve differences regarding the role of the laity in parish administration in the Roman Catholic Church in Scranton, Pennsylvania, this Church was organized in 1897. With the consecration to the episcopacy of the Most Rev. F. Hodur, this Church became a member of the Old Catholic Union of Utrecht in 1907.

Headquarters

Office of the Prime Bishop, 1004 Pittston Ave., Scranton, PA 18505 Tel. (570)346-9131

Media Contact, Prime Bishop, Most Rev. John F. Swantek, 1002 Pittston Ave., Scranton, PA 18505 Tel. (570)346-9131 Fax (570)346-2188

Officers

Prime Bishop, Most Rev. John F. Swantek, 115 Lake Scranton Rd., Scranton, PA 18505

Central Diocese: Bishop, Rt. Rev. Anthony M. Rysz, 529 E. Locust St., Scranton, PA 18505

Eastern Diocese: Bishop, Rt. Rev. Thomas J. Gnat, 166 Pearl St., Manchester, NH 03104

Buffalo-Pittsburgh Diocese: Bishop, Rt. Rev. Thaddeus S. Peplowski, 5776 Broadway, Lancaster, NY 14086

Western Diocese: Rt. Rev. Robert M. Nemkovich, 920 N. Northwest Hwy., Park Ridge, IL 60068

Canadian Diocese: Bishop, Sede Vacante, 186 Cowan Ave., Toronto, ON M6K 2N6

Ecumenical Officer, V. Rev. Stanley Skrzypek, 206 Main Street, New York Mills, NY 13416 Tel. (315)736-9757

Periodicals

God's Field; Polka

Presbyterian Church (U.S.A.)

The Presbyterian Church (U.S.A.) was organized June 10, 1983, when the Presbyterian Church in the United States and the United Presbyterian Church in the United States of America united in Atlanta. The union healed a major division which began with the Civil War when Presbyterians in the South withdrew from the Presbyterian Church in the United States of America to form the Presbyterian Church in the Confederate States.

The United Presbyterian Church in the United States of America had been created by the 1958 union of the Presbyterian Church in the United States of America and the United Presbyterian Church of North America. Of those two uniting bodies, the Presbyterian Church in the U.S.A. dated from the first Presbytery organized in Philadelphia, about 1706. The United Presbyterian Church of North America was formed in 1858, when the Associate Reformed Presbyterian Church and the Associate Presbyterian Church united.

Strongly ecumenical in outlook, the Presbyterian Church (U.S.A.) is the result of at least 10 different denominational mergers over the last 250 years. A restructure, adopted by the General Assembly meeting in June 1993, has been implemented. The Presbyterian Church (U.S.A.) dedicated its new national offices in Louisville, Kentucky in 1988.

Headquarters

100 Witherspoon St., Louisville, KY 40202 Tel. (502)569-5000 Fax (502)569-5018

Media Contact, Assoc. Dir. for Communications, Gary W. Luhr, Tel. (502)569-5515 Fax (502) 569-8073

Email: presytel@pcusa.org
Website: http://www.pcusa.org

Officers

Mod., Freda Gardner
Vice-Mod., Floyd Rhodis
Stated Clk., Clifton Kirkpatrick
Assoc. Stated Clks., C. Fred Jenkins, Eugene G. Turner

THE OFFICE OF THE GENERAL ASSEMBLY

Tel. (502)569-5360 Fax (502)569-8005
Stated Clk., Clifton Kirkpatrick
Dept. of the Stated Clerk: Dir., Loyda Aja
Dept. of Administration & Assemby Services: Dir., Richard Ferguson
Dept. of Constitutional Servicess: Dir., C. Fred Jenkins
Dept. of Governing Bodies, Ecumenical & Agency Rel.: Dir., Eugene G. Turner
Dept. of Communication& Technology: Dir., Kerry Clemmento
Dept. of Hist., Philadelphia: 425 Lombard St., Philadelphia, PA 19147 Tel. (215)627-1852 Fax (215)627-0509; Dir., Frederick J. Heuser, Jr.
Deputy Dir., Margery Sly
Deputy Dir., Michelle Francis, PO Box 849, Montreat, NC 28757

GENERAL ASSEMBLY COUNCIL

Exec. Dir., John J. Detterick, Fax (502)569-8080
Worldwide Ministries Division, Dir., Marian McClure
Congregational Ministries Division, Dir., Donald G. Campbell
National Ministries Division, Dir., Curtis A. Kearns, Jr.
Mission Support Services Dir., Joy Bailey

BOARD OF PENSIONS

Chpsn. of the Bd., Gloria Wilson
Pres., & CEO, Robert Macgo, Jr., 2000 Market St., Philadelphia, PA 19103-3298 Tel. (215) 587-7200

PRESBYTERIAN CHURCH (U.S.A.) FOUNDATION

Ofc., 200 E. Twelfth St., Jeffersonville, IN 47130 Tel. (812)288-8841 Fax (502)569-5980
Chpsn. of the Bd., John R. Adams
Pres. & CEO, James Henderson, Interim

PRESBYTERIAN CHURCH (U.S.A.) INVESTMENT/LOAN PROGRAM, INC.

Chpsn. of the Board, Ben McAnally
Pres. & CEO, Kenneth G.Y. Grant, Tel. (800)903-7457 Fax (502)569-8868

PRESBYTERIAN PUBLISHING CORPORATE

Pres. & CEO, Davis Perkins, Fax (502)569-5113
Chpsn. of the Bd., Robert Bohl

SYNOD EXECUTIVES

Alaska-Northwest, Rev.Gary Skinner, 233 6th Ave. N., Ste. 100, Seattle, WA 98109-5000 Tel. (206)448-6403

Covenant, Rev. Lowell Simms, 6172 Busch Blvd., Ste. 3000, Columbus, OH 43229-2564 Tel. (614)436-3310

Lakes & Prairies, Rev. Margaret J. Thomas, 8012 Cedar Ave. S., Bloomington, MN 55425-1210 Tel. (612)854-0144

Lincoln Trails, Rev. Verne E. Sindlinger, 1100 W. 42nd St., Indianapolis, IN 46208-3381 Tel. (317)923-3681

Living Waters, Rev. William Giles, P.O. Box 1207, Brentwood, TN 37024 Tel. (615)370-4008

Mid-America, Rev. John L. Williams, 6400 Glenwood, Ste. 111, Overland Park, KS 66202-4072 Tel. (913)384-3020

Mid-Atlantic, Rev. William Stewart, Jr. Interim, P.O. Box 27026, Richmond, VA 23261-7026 Tel. (804) 342-0016

Northeast, Rev. Robert Howell White, Jr., 5811 Heritage Landing Dr., East Syracuse, NY 13057-9360 Tel. (315)446-5990

Pacific, Rev. Philip H. Young, 8 Fourth St., Petaluma, CA 94952-3004 Tel. (707)765-1772

Puerto Rico (Boriquen in Puerto Rico), Rev. Harry Fred Del Valle, Ave. Hostos Edificio 740, Cond. Medical Center Plaza, Ste. 216, Mayaguez, PR 00680 Tel. (787)832-8375

Rocky Mountains, Rev. Richard O. Wyatt, 3025 West 37th Ave., Ste.206, Denver, CO 80211-2799 Tel. (303)477-9070

South Atlantic, Rev. John Niles Bartholomew, 118 E. Monroe St., Jacksonville, FL 32202 Tel. (904)356-6070

Southern California, Hawaii, Rev. John N. Langfitt, 1501 Wilshire Blvd., Los Angeles, CA 90017-2293 Tel. (213)483-3840

Southwest, Jane F. Odell, 4423 N. 24th St., Ste. 800, Phoenix, AZ 85016-5592 Tel. (602)468-3800

Sun, Rev. Judy R. Fletcher (Interim), 920 S. I 35 E, Denton, TX 76205-7898 Tel. (940)382-9656

Trinity, Rev. Thomas M. Johnston, Jr., 3040 Market St., Camp Hill, PA 17011-4599 Tel. (717)737-0421

Periodicals

American Presbyterians: Journal of Presbyterian History; Presbyterian News Service "News Briefs"; Church & Society Magazine; Horizons; Monday Morning; Presbyterians Today; Interpretation; Presbyterian Outlook; "Presbyterians: Being Faithful to Jesus Christ"

Presbyterian Church in America

The Presbyterian Church in America has a strong commitment to evangelism, to missionary work at home and abroad and to Christian education.

Organized in December 1973, this church was first known as the National Presbyterian Church but changed its name in 1974 to Presbyterian Church in America (PCA).

The PCA made a firm commitment on the doctrinal standards which had been significant in

141

presbyterianism since 1645, namely the Westminster Confession of Faith and Catechisms. These doctrinal standards express the distinctives of the Calvinistic or Reformed tradition.

The PCA maintains the historic polity of Presbyterian governance, namely rule by presbyters (or elders) and the graded courts which are the session governing the local church. The presbytery is responsible for regional matters and the general assembly for national matters. The PCA has taken seriously the position of the parity of elders, making a distinction between the two classes of elders, teaching and ruling.

In 1982, the Reformed Presbyterian Church, Evangelical Synod (RPCES) joined the PCA. It brought with it a tradition that had antecedents in Colonial America. It also included Covenant College in Lookout Mountain, Georgia, and Covenant Theological Seminary in St. Louis, both of which are national denominational institutions of the PCA.

Headquarters
1852 Century Pl., Atlanta, GA 30345-4305 Tel. (404)320-3366 Fax (404)329-1275
Media Contact: Rev. J. Robert Fiol
Email: info@ac.pca-atl.org
Website: http://www.pcanet.org

Officers
Mod., Rev. Kennedy Smartt
Stated Clk., Dr. L. Roy Taylor, 1852 Century Pl., Ste. 190, Atlanta, GA 30345-4305 Tel. (404)320-3366

PERMANENT COMMITTEES
Admn., Dr. L. Roy Taylor, 1852 Century Pl., Ste. 190, Atlanta, GA 30345-4305 Tel. (404) 320-3366 Fax (404)329-1275
Christian Educ. & Publ., Dr. Charles Dunahoo, 1852 Century Pl., Ste. 190, Atlanta, GA 30345-4305 Tel. (404)320-3388
Mission to North America, Dr. Cortez Cooper, 1852 Century Pl., Ste. 205, Atlanta, GA 30345-4305 Tel. (404)320-3330
Mission to the World, Dr. Paul D. Kooistra, 1852 Century Pl., Ste. 201, Atlanta, GA 30345-4305 Tel. (404)320-3373

Evangelical Presbyterian Church is listed under "E".

Primitive Advent Christian Church
This body split from the Advent Christian Church. All its churches are in West Virginia. The Primitive Advent Christian Church believes that the Bible is the only rule of faith and practice and that Christian character is the only test of fellowship and communion. The church agrees with Christian fidelity and meekness; exercises mutual watch and care; counsels, admonishes, or reproves as duty may require and receives the same from each other as becomes the household of faith. Primitive Advent Christians do not believe in taking up arms.

The church believes that three ordinances are set forth by the Bible to be observed by the Christian church: (1) baptism by immersion; (2) the Lord's Supper, by partaking of unleavened bread and wine; (3) feet washing, to be observed by the saints" washing of one another's feet.

Headquarters
Media Contact, Sec.-Treas., Roger Wines, 1971 Grapevine Rd., Sissonville, WV 25320 Tel. (304)988-2668

Officers
Pres., Herbert Newhouse, 7632 Hughart Dr., Sissonville, WV 25320 Tel. (304)984-9277
Vice-Pres., Roger Hammons, 273 Frame Rd., Elkview, WV 25071 Tel. (304)965-6247
Sec. & Treas., Roger Wines, 1971 Grapevine Rd., Sissonville, WV 25320 Tel. (304)988-2668

Primitive Baptists
This large group of Baptists, located throughout the United States, opposes all centralization and modern missionary societies. They preach salvation by grace alone.

Headquarters
P.O. Box 38, Thornton, AR 71766 Tel. (501)352-3694
Media Contact, Elder W. Hartsel Cayce

Officers
Elder W. Hartsel Cayce
Elder Lasserre Bradley, Jr., Box 17037, Cincinnati, OH 45217 Tel. (513)821-7289
Elder S. T. Tolley, P.O. Box 68, Atwood, TN 38220 Tel. (901)662-7417

Periodicals
Baptist Witness; The Christian Baptist; The Primitive Baptist; For the Poor

Primitive Methodist Church in the U.S.A.
Hugh Bourne and William Clowes, local preachers in the Wesleyan Church in England, organized a daylong meeting at Mow Cop in Staffordshire on May 31, 1807, after Lorenzo Dow, a Methodist preacher from America, told them of American camp meetings. Thousands attended and many were converted but the Methodist church, founded by the open-air preacher John Wesley, refused to accept the converts and reprimanded the preachers.

After waiting for two years for a favorable action by the Wesleyan Society, Bourne and Clowes established The Society of the Primitive Methodists. This was not a schism, Bourne said, for "we did not take one from them...it now appeared to be the will of God that we...should form classes and take upon us the care of churches in the fear of God." Primitive Methodist missionaries were sent to New York in 1829. An American conference was established in 1840.

Missionary efforts reach into Guatemala,

142

Spain and other countries. The denomination joins in federation with the Evangelical Congregational Church, the United Brethren in Christ Church and the Southern Methodist Church and is a member of the National Association of Evangelicals.

The church believes the Bible is the only true rule of faith and practice, the inspired Word of God. It believes in one Triune God, the Deity of Jesus Christ, the Deity and personality of the Holy Spirit, the innocence of Adam and Eve, the Fall of the human race, the necessity of repentance, justification by faith of all who believe, regeneration witnessed by the Holy Spirit, sanctification by the Holy Spirit, the second coming of the Lord Jesus Christ, the resurrection of the dead and conscious future existence of all people and future judgments with eternal rewards and punishments.

Headquarters
Media Contact, Pres., Rev. Wayne Yarnall, 1045 Laurel Run Rd., Wilkes-Barre, PA 18702 Tel. (717)472-3436 Fax (717)472-9283
Email: pmconf@juno.com

Officers
Pres., Rev. Wayne Yarnall, 1045 Laurel Run Rd., Wilkes-Barre, PA 18702 Tel. (717)472-3436 Fax (717)472-9283
Vice-Pres., Rev. Kerry R. Pitts, 723 Preston Ln., Hatboro, PA 19040
General. Secretary.: Rev. David Allen, Jr., 1199 Lawrence St., Lowell, MA 01522-5526 Tel. (978) 453-2052
Email: pahson@banet.net
Treas., Mr. Raymond C. Baldwin, 11012 Langton Arms Ct., Oakton, VA 22124
Email: Rbaldwin32@aol.com

Progressive National Baptist Convention, Inc.
This body held its organizational meeting in Cincinnati in November, 1961. Subsequent regional sessions were followed by the first annual session in Philadelphia in 1962.

Headquarters
601 50th Street, N.E., Washington, DC 20019 Tel. (202)396-0558 Fax (202)398-4998
Media Contact, Gen. Sec., Dr. Tyrone S. Pitts

Officers
Pres., Dr. Bennett W. Smith, Sr., St. John Baptist Church, 184 Goodell St., Buffalo, NY 14204
Gen. Sec., Dr. Tyrone S. Pitts

OTHER ORGANIZATIONS
Dept. of Christian Education, Exec. Dir., Dr. C. B. Lucas, Emmanuel Baptist Church, 3815 W. Broadway, Louisville, KY 40211
Women's Dept., Mildred Wormley, 218 Spring St., Trenton, NJ 08618
Home Mission Bd., Exec. Dir., Rev. Archie LeMone, Jr.
Congress of Christian Education, Pres., Rev. Harold S. Diggs, Mayfield Memorial Baptist

Church, 700 Sugar Creek Rd. W., Charlotte, NC 28213
Baptist Global Mission Bureau, Dr. Ronald K. Hill, 161-163 60th St., Philadelphia, PA 19139 Nannie Helen Burroughs School, Tel. (202)398-5266

Periodicals
Baptist Progress

Protestant Reformed Churches in America
The Protestant Reformed Churches (PRC) have their roots in the sixteenth century Reformation of Martin Luther and John Calvin, as it developed in the Dutch Reformed churches. The denomination originated as a result of a controversy in the Christian Reformed Church in 1924 involving the adoption of the "Three Points of Common Grace." Three ministers in the Christian Reformed Church, the Reverends Herman Hoeksema, George Ophoff, and Henry Danhof, and their consistories (Eastern Avenue, Hope, and Kalamazoo, respectively) rejected the doctrine. Eventually these men were deposed, and their consistories were either deposed or set outside the Christian Reformed Church. The denomination was formed in 1926 with three congregations. Today the denomination is comprised of some twenty-seven churches (more than 6,000 members) in the USA and Canada.

The presbyterian form of church government as determined by the Church Order of Dordt is followed by the PRC. The doctrinal standards of the PRC are the Reformed confessions " the Heidelberg Catechism, Belgic Confession of Faith, and Canons of Dordrecht. The doctrine of the covenant is a cornerstone of their teaching. They maintain an unconditional, particular covenant of grace that God establishes with His elect.

Headquarters
16511 South Park Ave., South Holland, IL 60473 Tel. (708)333-1314
Media Contact, Stat. Clk., Don Doezema, 4949 Ivanrest Ave., Grandville, MI 49418 Tel. (616) 531-1490
Email: doezema@prca.org

Officers
Stat. Clk., Don Doezema

Periodicals
The Standard Bearer

Quakers—please see Friends.

Reformed Church in America
The Reformed Church in America was established in 1628 by the earliest settlers of New York. It is the oldest Protestant denomination with a continuous ministry in North America. Until 1867 it was known as the Reformed Protestant Dutch Church.

The first ordained minister, Domine Jonas

143

Michaelius, arrived in New Amsterdam from The Netherlands in 1628. Throughout the colonial period, the Reformed Church lived under the authority of the Classis of Amsterdam. Its churches were clustered in New York and New Jersey. Under the leadership of Rev. John Livingston, it became a denomination independent of the authority of the Classis of Amsterdam in 1776. Its geographical base was broadened in the 19th century by the immigration of Reformed Dutch and German settlers in the midwestern United States. The Reformed Church now spans the United States and Canada.

The Reformed Church in America accepts as its standards of faith the Heidelberg Catechism, Belgic Confession and Canons of Dort. It has a rich heritage of world mission activity. It claims to be loyal to reformed tradition which emphasizes obedience to God in all aspects of life.

Although the Reformed Church in America has worked in close cooperation with other churches, it has never entered into merger with any other denomination. It is a member of the World Alliance of Reformed Churches, the World Council of Churches and the National Council of the Churches of Christ in the United States of America. In 1998 it also entered into a relationship of full communion with the Evangelical Lutheran Church in America, Presbyterian Church (U.S.A.), and the United Church of Christ by way of the Formula of Agreement.

Headquarters

475 Riverside Dr., New York, NY 10115 Tel. (212)870-2841 Fax (212)870-2499

Media Contact, Dir., Congregational Services, Jeffrey Japinga, 4500 60th St. SE, Grand Rapids, MI 49512, Tel. (616)698-7071 Fax (616)698-6606

Email: jjapinga@rca.org

Website: www.rca.org

Officers and Staff of General Synod

Pres., Gregg Mast, 475 Riverside Dr., 18th Floor, New York, NY 10115

Gen. Sec., Wesley Granberg- Michaelson, 475 Riverside Dr., 18th Floor, New York, NY 10115

OTHER ORGANIZATIONS

Bd. of Pensions: Pres., to be elected in October; Sec., Wesley Granberg- Michaelson

General Synod Council: Mod., Frederick Kruithof

Office of Policy, Planning & Admn. Serv., Dir. & Assistnat Sec., Kenneth R. Bradsell

Ofc. of Ministry & personnel Services, Dir., Vernon Hoffs

Office of Evangelism & Church Dev. Ser., Richard Welscott

Ofc. of Finance Services, Treas., Susan Converse

Ofc. of Congregational Ser., Dir., Jeffrey Japinga

Ofc. Of Mission Services, Dir., Bruce Menning

RCA Foundation Dir., E. Wayne Antworth

RCA Building and Extension Fund, Fund Executive, Paul Karssen

Reformed Church Women's Ministries, Exec. Dir., Arlene Waldorf

African-American Council, Exec. Dir., Glen Missick

Council for Hispanic Ministries, Natl. Sec., Luis Perez

Native American Indian Ministries Council, Interim Assoc. for, George Montanari

Council for Pacific/Asian-American Min., Natl. Sec., Ella Campbell

Periodicals

Perspectives; The Church Herald

Reformed Church in the United States

Lacking pastors, early German Reformed immigrants to the American colonies were led in worship by "readers." One reader, schoolmaster John Philip Boehm, organized the first congregations near Philadelphia in 1725. A Swiss pastor, Michael Schlatter, was sent by the Dutch Reformed Church in 1746. Strong ties with the Netherlands existed until the formation of the Synod of the German Reformed Church in 1793.

The Eureka Classis, organized in North and South Dakota in 1910 and strongly influenced by the writings of H. Kohlbruegge, P. Geyser and J. Stark, refused to become part of the 1934 merger of the Reformed Church with the Evangelical Synod of North America, holding that it sacrificed the Reformed heritage. (The merged Evangelical and Reformed Church became part of the United Church of Christ in 1957.) Under the leadership of pastors W. Grossmann and W. J. Krieger, the Eureka Classis in 1942 incorporated as the continuing Reformed Church in the United States.

The growing Eureka Classis dissolved in 1986 to form a Synod with four regional classes. An heir to the Reformation theology of Zwingli and Calvin, the Heidelberg Catechism, the Belgic Confession and the Canons of Dort are used as the confessional standards of the church. The Bible is strictly held to be the inerrant, infallible Word of God.

The RCUS supports Dordt College, Mid-America Reformed Seminary, New Geneva Theological Seminary, West Minster Theological Seminary in California, and Hope Haven. The RCUS is the official sponsor to the Reformed Confessing Church of Zaire.

Headquarters

Media Contact, Rev. Frank Walker Th.M., 5601 Spring Blossom St., Bakersfield, CA 93313-6041 Tel. (661)827-9885

Email: fhw@iname.com

Website: http://www.rcus.org

Officers

Pres., Rev. Vernon Pollema, 235 James Street, Shafter, CA 93263 Tel. (661)746-6907
Vice-Pres., Rev. Robert Grossmann, Th.M., 1905 200th St., Garner, IA 50438 Tel. (515)923-3060
Stated Clk., Rev. Frank Walker Th.M., 5601 Spring Blossom St., Bakersfield, CA 93313-6025 Tel. (661)827-9885
Treas., Clayton Greiman, 2115 Hwy. 69, Garner, IA 50438 Tel. (515)923-2950

Periodicals
Reformed Herald

Reformed Episcopal Church

The Reformed Episcopal Church was founded December 2, 1873 in New York City by Bishop George D. Cummins, an assistant bishop in the Protestant Episcopal Church from 1866 until 1873. Cummins and other evangelical Episcopalians viewed with alarm the influence of the Oxford Movement in the Protestant Episcopal Church, for the interest it stimulated in Roman Catholic ritual and doctrine and for intolerance it bred toward evangelical Protestant doctrine.

Throughout the late 1860s, evangelicals and ritualists clashed over ceremonies and vestments, exchanges of pulpits with clergy of other denominations, the meaning of critical passages in the Book of Common Prayer, interpretation of the sacraments and validity of the Apostolic Succession.

In October, 1873, other bishops publicly attacked Cummins in the church newspapers for participating in an ecumenical Communion service sponsored by the Evangelical Alliance. Cummins resigned and drafted a call to Episcopalians to organize a new Episcopal Church for the "purpose of restoring the old paths of their fathers." On Dec. 2, 1873, a Declaration of Principles was adopted and Dr. Charles E. Cheney was elected bishop to serve with Cummins. The Second General Council, meeting in May 1874 in New York City, approved a Constitution and Canons and a slightly amended version of the Book of Common Prayer. In 1875, the Third General Council adopted a set of Thirty-Five Articles.

Cummins died in 1876. The church had grown to nine jurisdictions in the United States and Canada at that time. The Reformed Episcopal Church is a member of the National Association of Evangelicals.

Headquarters
7372 Henry Ave., Philadelphia, PA 19128-1401 Tel. (215)483-1196 Fax (215)483-5235
Media Contact, Rt. Rev. Leonard Riches
Media Contact, Rt. Rev. Royal U. Grote, Jr., Church Growth Office, 211 Byrne Ave., Houston, TX 77009 Tel. (713)862-4929
Email: nicaea@aol.com
Website: http://www.geopages.com/capitolhill/1125/

Officers

Pres. & Presiding Bishop, Rt. Rev. Leonard W. Riches
Vice-Pres., Rt. Rev. Royal U. Grote, Jr.
Sec., Rev. Walter Banek
Treas., Rev. Jon W. Abboud

OTHER ORGANIZATIONS
Bd. of Foreign Missions: Pres., Dr. Barbara J. West, 316 Hunters Rd., Swedesboro, NJ 08085 Tel. (609) 467-1641
Bd. of Natl. Church Extension: Pres., Rt. Rev. Royal U. Grote, Jr., 211 Byrne Ave., Houston, TX 77009 Tel. (713)862-4929
Publication Society: Pres., Rt. Rev. Gregory K. Hotchkiss, 318 Main St., Somerville, NJ 08876 Tel. (908)725-2678 Fax (908)725-4641; Orders, Rev. Jonathan S. Riches, 7372 Henry Ave., Philadelphia, PA 19128 25-956-0655
The Reapers: Pres., Susan Higham, 472 Leedom St., Jenkintown, PA 19046
Committee on Women's Work: Pres., Joan Workowski, 1162 Beverly Rd., Rydal, PA 19046

BISHOPS
William H.S. Jerdan, Jr., 414 W. 2nd South St., Summerville, SC 29483
Sanco K. Rembert, P.O. Box 20068, Charleston, SC 29413
Franklin H. Sellers, Sr., 81 Buttercup Ct., Marco Island, FL 33937-3480
Leonard W. Riches, Sr., 85 Smithtown Rd., Pipersville, PA 18947 Tel. (215)483-1196 Fax (215)294-8009
Royal U. Grote, Jr., 211 Byrne Ave., Houston, TX 77009
James C. West, Sr., 408 Red Fox Run, Summerville, SC 29485
Robert H. Booth, 1611 Park Ave., #212, Quakertown, PA 18951
Gregory K. Hotchkiss, 318 E. Main St., Somerville, NJ 08876
George B. Fincke, 155 Woodstock Circle, Vacaville, CA 95687-3381
Daniel R. Morse, 11259 Wexford Dr., Eads, TN 38025
Michael Fedechko, Box 2532, New Liskeard, ON P0J 1P0
Charles W. Dorrington, 626 Blanshard St., Victoria, BC V8W 3G6
Ted Follows, 626 Blanshard St., Victoria, BC V8W 3G6
Daniel G. Cox, 9 Hilltop Pl., Baltimore, MD 21228
Ray R. Sutton, 3421 Madison Park Blvd., Shreveport, LA 71104

Periodicals
Reformed Episcopalians

Reformed Mennonite Church

This is a small group of believers in Pennsylvania, Ohio, Michigan, Illinois, and

US RELIGIOUS BODIES

145

Ontario, Canada who believe in non-resistance of evil, and non-conformity to the world and who practice separation from unfaithful worship. They believe that Christian unity is the effect of brotherly love and are of one mind and spirit. Their church was established in 1812 by John Herr who agreed with the teachings of Menno Simon as well as those of Jesus Christ.

Headquarters

Lancaster County only, Reformed Mennonite Church, 602 Strasburg Pike, Lancaster, PA 17602

Media Contact, Bishop, Glenn M. Gross, Tel. (717)697-4623

Officers

Bishop Glenn M. Gross, 906 Grantham Rd., Mechanicsburg, PA 17055

Reformed Methodist Union Episcopal Church

The Reformed Methodist Union Episcopal church was formed after a group of ministers withdrew from the African Methodist Episcopal Church following a dispute over the election of ministerial delegates to the General Conference.

These ministers organized the Reformed Methodist Union church during a four-day meeting beginning on January 22, 1885 at Hills Chapel (now known as Mt. Hermon RMUE church), in Charleston, South Carolina. The Rev. William E. Johnson was elected president of the new church. Following the death of Rev. Johnson in 1896, it was decided that the church would conform to regular American Methodism (the Episcopacy). The first Bishop, Edward Russell Middleton, was elected, and "Episcopal" was added to the name of the church. Bishop Middleton was consecrated on Dec. 5, 1896, by Bishop P. F. Stephens of the Reformed Episcopal Church.

Headquarters

1136 Brody Ave., Charleston, SC 29407

Media Contact, Gen. Secretary, Brother Willie B. Oliver, P.O. Box 1995, Orangeburg, SC 29116 Tel. (803)536-3293

Officers

Bishop, Rt. Rev. Leroy Gethers, Tel. (803)766-3534
Asst. Bishop, Rt. Rev. Jerry M. DeVoe, Jr.
Gen. Sec., Brother Willie B. Oliver
Treas., Rev. Daniel Green
Sec. of Education, Rev. William Polite
Sec. of Books Concerns, Sister Ann Blanding
Sec. of Pension Fund, Rev. Joseph Powell
Sec. of Church Extension, Brother William Parker
Sec. of Sunday School Union, Sister Wine
Sec. of Mission, Rev. Warren Hatcher

Reformed Presbyterian Church of North America

Also known as the Church of the Covenanters, this church's origin dates back to the Reformation days of Scotland when the Covenanters signed their "Covenants" in resistance to the king and the Roman Church in the enforcement of state church practices. The Church in America has signed two "Covenants" in particular, those of 1871 and 1954.

Headquarters

Media Contact, Stated Clk., Louis D. Hutmire, 7408 Penn Ave., Pittsburgh, PA 15208 Tel. (412)731-1177 Fax (412)731-8861

Officers

Mod., Rev. William J. Edgar, 25 Lawrence Rd., Broomall, PA 19008 Tel. (610) 353-1371
Clk., J. Bruce Martin, 310 Main St., Ridgefield Park, NJ 07660 Tel. (201) 440-5993
Asst. Clk., Raymond E. Morton, 411 N. Vine St., Sparta, IL 62286 Tel. (618)443-3419
Stated Clk., Louis D. Hutmire, 7408 Penn Ave., Pittsburgh, PA 15208 Tel. (412)731-1177

Periodicals

The Covenanter Witness

Reformed Zion Union Apostolic Church

This group was organized in 1869 at Boydton, Va., by Elder James R. Howell of New York, a minister of the A.M.E. Zion Church, with doctrines of the Methodist Episcopal Church.

Headquarters

Rt. 1, Box 64D, Dundas, VA 23938 Tel. (804)676-8509
Media Contact, Bishop G. W. Studivant

Officers

Exec. Brd., Chair, Rev. Hilman Wright, Tel. (804)447-3988
Sec., Joseph Russell, Tel. (804)634-4520

Religious Society of Friends (Conservative)

These Friends mark their present identity from separations occurring by regions at different times from 1845 to 1904. They hold to a minimum of organizational structure. Their meetings for worship, which are unprogrammed and based on silent, expectant waiting upon the Lord, demonstrate the belief that all individuals may commune directly with God and may share equally in vocal ministry.

They continue to stress the importance of the Living Christ and the experience of the Holy Spirit working with power in the lives of individuals who obey it.

YEARLY MEETINGS

North Carolina YM, Robert Gosner, P.O. Box 489, Woodland, NC 27897 Tel. (252)587-2571
Iowa YM: Deborah Frisch, Clerk, 916 41st Street, Des Moines, Iowa 50312-2612
Ohio YM, S. S. Smith, Clerk, 61830 Sandy Ridge Road, Barnesville, OH 43713

146

Religious Society of Friends (Unaffiliated Meetings)

Though all groups of Friends acknowledge the same historical roots, 19th-century divisions in theology and experience led to some of the current organizational groupings. Many newer yearly meetings, often marked by spontaneity, variety and experimentation and hoping for renewed Quaker unity, have chosen not to identify with past divisions by affiliating in traditional ways with the larger organizations within the Society. Some of these unaffiliated groups have begun within the past 25 years.

YEARLY MEETINGS

Central Yearly Meeting (I), Supt., Cecil Hinshaw, Rt. 2, Box 232, Winchester, IN 46394 Tel. (317)584-1089

Intermountain Yearly Meeting(I), Clerk, Chuck Rostkowski, 962 26th St., Ogden, UT 84401 Tel. (801)399-9491

North Pacific Yearly Meeting (I), Contact:, Helen Dart, 3311 NW Polk, Corvallis, OR 97330 Tel. (206)633-4860

Pacific Yearly Meeting (I), Clerk, Eric Moon, 2314 Eighth St., Apt. B, Berkeley, CA 94710 Tel. (510) 841-5471

Periodicals

Friends Bulletin

Reorganized Church of Jesus Christ of Latter Day Saints

This church was founded April 6, 1830, by Joseph Smith, Jr., and reorganized under the leadership of the founder's son, Joseph Smith III, in 1860. The church, with headquarters in Independence, Missouri, is established in 36 countries in addition to the United States and Canada. A biennial world conference is held in Independence, Missouri. The current president is W. Grant McMurray. The church has a worldwide membership of approximately 245,000.

Headquarters

World Headquarters, P.O. Box 1059, Independence, MO 64051 Tel. (816)833-1000 Fax (816)521-3096

Media Contact, Publ. Rel. Commissioner, Susan Naylor

Officers

First Presidency: Pres., W. Grant McMurray; Counselor, Howard S. Sheehy, Jr.; Counselor, Kenneth N. Robinson

Council of 12 Apostles, Pres., A. Alex Kahtava

Presiding Bishopric: Presiding Bishop, Larry R. Norris; Counselor, Orval G. Fisher; Counselor, Stephen M. Jones

Presiding Evangelist, Everett S. Graffeo

World Church Sec., A. Bruce Lindgren

Public Relations, Susan Naylor

Periodicals

Saints Herald; Restoration Witness

The Roman Catholic Church

The largest single body of Christians in the United States, the Roman Catholic Church, is under the spiritual leadership of His Holiness the Pope. Its establishment in America dates back to the priests who accompanied Columbus on his second voyage to the New World. A settlement, later discontinued, was made at St. Augustine, Florida. The continuous history of this Church in the Colonies began at St. Mary's in Maryland, in 1634.

(The following information has been furnished by the editor of The Official Catholic Directory, published by P. J. Kenedy & Sons, 3004 Glenview Rd., Wilmette, IL 60091. Reference to this complete volume will provide additional information.)

INTERNATIONAL ORGANIZATION

His Holiness the Pope, Bishop of Rome, Vicar of Jesus Christ, Supreme Pontiff of the Catholic Church.

Pope John Paul II, Karol Wojtyla (born May 18, 1920; installed Oct. 22, 1978)

APOSTOLIC PRO NUNCIO TO THE UNITED STATES

Archbishop Gabriel Montalvo, 3339 Massachusetts Ave., N.W., Washington, DC 20008 Tel. (202)333-7121 Fax (202)337-4036

U.S. ORGANIZATION

National Conference of Catholic Bishops, 3211 Fourth St., Washington, DC 20017-1194. (202)541-3000

The National Conference of Catholic Bishops (NCCB) is a canonical entity operating in accordance with the Vatican II Decree, Christus Dominus. Its purpose is to foster the Church's mission to mankind by providing the Bishops of this country with an opportunity to exchange views and insights of prudence and experience and to exercise in a joint manner their pastoral office.

Officers

Pres., Bishop Joseph A. Fiorenza

Vice-Pres., Bishop Wilton D. Gregory

Treas., Bishop Robert J. Banks

Sec., Archbishop Harry J. Flynn

NCCB GENERAL SECRETARIAT

Gen. Sec., Rev. Msgr.Dennis M. Schnurr

Assoc. Gen. Sec., Rev. William P. Fay, Sr. Sharon A. Euart, R.S.M., Mr. Bruce Egnew

Sec. for Communication, Rev. Msgr. Francis J. Maniscalco

NCCB COMMITTEES

Administrative Committee: Chmn., Bishop Joseph A. Fiorenza

Executive Committee: Chmn., Bishop Joseph A. Fiorenza

Committee on Budget and Finance: Chmn., Bishop Robert J. Banks

Committee on Personnel: Bishop Wilton D. Gregory

147

Committee on Priorities and Plans: Chmn., Bishop Joseph A. Fiorenza

American College Louvain: Chmn., Bishop Edward K. Braxton

Bishop's Welfare Emergency Relief: Chmn., Bishop Anthony M. Pilla

Aid to the Church in Central and Eastern Europe: Chmn., Adam Cardinal Meida

Diaconate: Chmn., Bishop Gerald F. Kicanas

African American Catholics: Chmn., Bishop George V. Murray

Bishop's Life and Ministry: Chmn. Bishop William S. Skylstad

Catholic Charismatic Renewal: Chmn., Bishop Sam G. Jacobs

Canonical Affairs: Chmn., Bishop David E. Fellhauer

Church in Latin America: Chmn., Bishop Roberto O. Cronzalez, OFM

Consecrated Life: Chmn., Bishop Joseph J. Gerry, OSB

Doctrine: Chmn., Archbishop Daniel E. Pilarczyk

Economic Concerns of the Holy See: Chmn. Archbishop James P. Keleher

Ecumenical and Interreligious Affairs: Chmn., Archbishop Alexander Brunett

Evangelization: Chmn., Archbishop Michael J. Sheehan

Hispanic Affairs: Chmn., Bishop Gerald R. Barnes

Home Missions: Chmn., Bishop Edward J. Slattery

Laity: Chmn. Bishop G. Patrick Ziemann

Lay Ministry Subcommittee: Chmn., Bishop Phillip R. Straling

Liturgy: Chmn., Archbishop Jerome G. Hanus, O.S.B.

Marriage and Family Life: Chmn., Bishop Thomas J. O'Brien

Migration: Chmn., Bishop Nicholas A. DiMarzio

Native American Catholics: Chmn. Bishop Donald Pelotte, SSS

Nomination of Conference Officers: Chmn. Archbishop James P. Keleher

North American College Rome: Chmn., Bishop Donald W. Wuerl

Pastoral Practices: Chmn., Bishop Stephen E. Blaire

Priestly Formation: Chmn., Archbishop John C. Favalora

Priestly Life and Ministry: Chmn.,Bishop Richard C. Hanifen

Pro-Life Activities: Chmn., William Cardinal Keeler

Relationship Between Eastern and Latin Catholic Churches: Chmn., Bishop Andrew Pataki

Review of Scripture Translations: Chmn., Bishop Richard J. Sklba

Ex Corde Ecclesiae: Chmn., Bishop John J. Leibrecht

Forum on the Principles of Translation: Chmn., Archbishop Jerome G. Hanus

Healthcare Issues and the Church: Chmn., Bishop Donald W. Wuerl

Oversee and Use of the Catechism: Chmn., Archbishop Daniel M. Buechlein

Science and Human Values: Chmn., Bishop Edward M. Egan

Selection of Bishops: Chmn., Bishop Joseph A. Fiorenza

Sexual Abuse: Chmn. Bishop John F. Kinney

Shrines: Chmn. Archbishop James P. Keleher

Stewardship: Chmn. Bishop Sylvester D. Ryan

Subcommittee on Youth: Bishop Roger L. Schweitz, OMI

Vocations: Chmn. Bishop Roger L. Schwietz

Women in Society and in the Church: Chmn., Archbishop John G. Vlazny

World Missions: Chmn., Bishop Curtis J. Guillory

United States Catholic Conference, 3211 Fourth St., Washington, DC 20017, Tel. (202)541-3000

The **United States Catholic Conference** (USCC) is a civil entity of the American Catholic Bishops assisting them in their service to the Church in this country by uniting the people of God where voluntary, collective action on a broad diocesan level is needed. The USCC provides an organizational structure and the resources needed to insure coordination, cooperation and assistance in the public, educational and social concerns of the church at the national, regional, state and, as appropriate, diocesan levels.

Officers

Pres., Bishop Joseph A. Fiorenza
Vice-Pres., Bishop Wilton D. Gregory
Treas., Bishop Robert J. Banks
Sec., Archbishop Harry J. Flynn

GENERAL SECRETARIAT

Gen. Sec., Dennis M. Schnurr

Assoc. Gen. Sec., Rev. William P. Fay, Sr. Sharon A. Euart, R.S.M., Mr. Bruce Egnew

Sec. for Communications, Rev. Msgr. Francis J. Maniscalco

USCC COMMITTEES AND DEPARTMENTS

Administrative Board: Chmn., Bishop Joseph A. Fiorenza

Executive Committee: Chmn., Bishop Joseph A. Fiorenza

Committee on Budget and Finance: Chmn. Bishop Robert J. Banks

Committee on Personnel: Chmn., Bishop Wilton D. Gregory

Committee on Priorities and Plans: Chmn., Bishop Joseph A. Fiorenza

Catholic Campaign for Human Development: Chmn., Bishop John J. Leibrecht

Committee on Communications: Chmn., Bishop Robert N. Lynch

Committee on Education: Chmn., Archbishop Francis B. Schulte

Bishops and Catholic College and University Presidents: Chmn., Archbishop Francis B. Schulte

Advisory Committee on Public Policy and Catholic Schools: Chmn., Archbishop Francis B. Schulte

Sapientia Christiana: Chmn., Bishop John P. Boles

Committee of Domestic Policy: Chmn., Roger Cardinal Mahony

Committee on International Policy: Chmn., Archbishop Theodore E. McCarrick

For information on related organizations and individual dioceses, consult the Official Catholic Directory (published annually by P.J. Kenedy and Sons) and the NCCB/USCC website (www.nccbuscc.org).

Periodicals

Nuestra Parroquia; The Pilot; Clarion Herald; Our Sunday Visitor; The New World; The Criterion; Commonweal; Maryknoll; Columbia; Clarion Herald; The Evangelist; Catholic Universe Bulletin; National Catholic Reporter; Catholic Worker; The Catholic Transcript; Catholic Standard and Times; Liguorian; The Catholic Review; Catholic Light; Homiletic and Pastoral Review; Catholic Herald; Extension; Catholic Digest; Catholic Chronicle; New Oxford Review; The Long Island Catholic; Pastoral Life; Columban Mission; Salt of the Earth; The Pilot; Praying; Providence Visitor; The Tidings; Worship; Saint Anthony Messenger; Review for Religious; The Tablet; Theology Digest; U.S. Catholic

The Romanian Orthodox Church in America

The Romanian Orthodox Church in America is an autonomous Archdiocese chartered under the name of "Romanian Orthodox Archdiocese in America."

The diocese was founded in 1929 and approved by the Holy Synod of the Romanian Orthodox Church in Romania in 1934. The Holy Synod of the Romanian Orthodox Church of July 12, 1950, granted it ecclesiastical autonomy in America, continuing to hold only dogmatical and canonical ties with the Holy Synod and the Romanian Orthodox Patriarchate of Romania.

In 1951, approximately 40 parishes with their clergy from the United States and Canada separated from this church. In 1960, they joined the Russian Orthodox Greek Catholic Metropolia, now called the Orthodox Church in America, which reordained for these parishes a bishop with the title "Bishop of Detroit and Michigan."

The Holy Synod of the Romanian Orthodox Church, on June 11, 1973, elevated the Bishop of Romanian Orthodox Missionary Episcopate in America to the rank of Archbishop.

Headquarters

19959 Riopelle St., Detroit, MI 48203 Tel. (313) 893-8390

Media Contact, Archdiocesan Dean & Secretary, V. Rev. Fr. Nicholas Apostola, 44 Midland St.,

Worcester, MA 01602-4217 Tel. (508)799-0040 Fax (508)756-9866

Officers

Archbishop, His Eminence Victorin Ursache

Vicar, V. Rev. Archim. Dr. Vasile Vasilachi, 45-03 48th Ave., Woodside, Queens, NY 11377 Tel. (718)784-4453

Inter-Church Relations, Dir., Rev. Fr. Nicholas Apostola, 14 Hammond St., Worcester, MA 01610 Tel. (617)799-0040

Sec., V. Rev. Fr. Nicholas Apostola, 44 Midland St., Worcester, MA 01602 Tel. (508)756-9866 Fax (508)799-0040

Periodicals

Credinta-The Faith

The Romanian Orthodox Episcopate of America

This body of Eastern Orthodox Christians of Romanian descent was organized in 1929 as an autonomous Diocese under the jurisdiction of the Romanian Patriarchate. In 1951 it severed all relations with the Orthodox Church of Romania. Now under the canonical jurisdiction of the autocephalous Orthodox Church in America, it enjoys full administrative autonomy and is headed by its own Bishop.

Headquarters

P.O. Box 309, Grass Lake, MI 49240 Tel. (517) 522-4800 Fax (517)522-5907

Media Contact, Ed./Sec., Dept. of Publications, Rev. Deacon David Oancea, P.O. Box 185, Grass Lake, MI 49240-0185 Tel. (517)522-3656 Fax (517)522-5907

Email: roeasolia@aol.com

Website: http://www.roea.org

Officers

Ruling Bishop, His Grace Bishop Nathaniel Popp

Dean of Western Canada, V. Rev. Daniel Nenson, 2855 Helmsing St., Regina, SK S4V 0W7, Canada

Dean of Eastern Canada, V. Rev. Dumitru Paun, 200 Sandringham Crescent, Apt. 816, London, ON N6C 5B6, Canada

OTHER ORGANIZATIONS

The American Romanian Orthodox Youth, Pres., Tom Rosco, 625 Centralia St., Dearborn Heights, MI 48127-3736

Assoc. of Romanian Orthodox Ladies" Aux., Pres., Mary Ellen Rosco, 625 Centralia St., Dearborn Hts., MI 48127-3736

Orthodox Brotherhood U.S.A., Pres., Valer Pufescu, 40558 Aynesley St., Mount Clemens, MI 48044-2166

Orthodox Brotherhood of Canada, Pres., Gloria Buchanan, 26 Mill Bay, Regina, SK S4N 1L6, Canada

Periodicals

Solia-The Herald; Calendarul Solia (annual)

149

The Russian Orthodox Church Outside of Russia

This group was organized in 1920 to unite in one body of dioceses the missions and parishes of the Russian Orthodox Church outside of Russia. The governing body, set up in Constantinople, was sponsored by the Ecumenical Patriarchate. In November 1950, it came to the United States. The Russian Orthodox Church Outside of Russia emphasizes being true to the old traditions of the Russian Church. It is not in communion with the Moscow Patriarchate.

Headquarters

75 E. 93rd St., New York, NY 10128 Tel. (212)534-1601 Fax (212)426-1086
Media Contact, Dep. Sec., Bishop Gabriel

SYNOD OF BISHOPS

Pres., His Eminence Metropolitan Vitaly
Sec., Archbishop of Syracuse and Trinity, Laurus
Dep. Sec., Bishop of Manhattan, Gabriel, Tel. (212)722-6577

Periodicals

Living Orthodoxy; Orthodox Family; Orthodox Russia (Russian); Orthodox Voices; Pravoslavnaya Rus; Pravoslavnaya Zhisn; Orthodox America

Patriarchal Parishes of the Russian Orthodox Church in the U.S.A. is listed under "P".

The Salvation Army

The Salvation Army, founded in 1865 by William Booth (1829-1912) in London, England, and introduced into America in 1880, is an international religious and charitable movement organized and operated on a paramilitary pattern and is a branch of the Christian church. To carry out its purposes, The Salvation Army has established a widely diversified program of religious and social welfare services which are designed to meet the needs of children, youth and adults in all age groups.

Headquarters

615 Slaters Ln., Alexandria, VA 22313 Tel. (703)684-5500 Fax (703)684-5538
Media Contact, Community Relations & Devel., Lt. Colonel Tom Jones, Tel. (703)684-5521 Fax (703)684-5538

Officers

Natl. Commander, Commissioner John A. Busby
Natl. Chief Sec., Col. John M. Bate
Natl. Community Relations, Dir., Lt. Colonel Tom Jones

TERRITORIAL ORGANIZATIONS

Central Territory: 10 W. Algonquin Rd., Des Plaines, IL 60016 Tel. (847)294-2000 Fax (847)294-2299; Territorial Commander, Commissioner Harold D. Hinson
Eastern Territory: 440 W. Nyack Rd., P.O. Box C-635, West Nyack, NY 10994 Tel. (914)620-7200 Fax (914)620-7766; Territorial Commander, Commissioner Joe Noland
Southern Territory: 1424 Northeast Expressway, Atlanta, GA 30329 Tel. (404)728-1300 Fax (404)728-1331; Territorial Commander, Commissioner Raymond A. Cooper
Western Territory: 30840 Hawthorne Blvd., Rancho Palos Verdes, CA 90275 Tel. (310)541-4721 Fax (310)544-1674; Territorial Commander, Commissioner David Edwards

Periodicals

The War Cry

The Schwenkfelder Church

The Schwenkfelders are the spiritual descendants of the Silesian nobleman Caspar Schwenkfeld von Ossig (1489-1561), a scholar, reformer, preacher and prolific writer who endeavored to aid in the cause of the Protestant Reformation. A contemporary of Martin Luther, John Calvin, Ulrich Zwingli and Phillip Melanchthon, Schwenkfeld sought no following, formulated no creed and did not attempt to organize a church based on his beliefs. He labored for liberty of religious belief, for a fellowship of all believers and for one united Christian church.

He and his cobelievers supported a movement known as the Reformation by the Middle Way. Persecuted by state churches, ultimately 180 Schwenkfelders exiled from Silesia emigrated to Pennsylvania. They landed at Philadelphia Sept. 22, 1734. In 1782, the Society of Schwenkfelders, the forerunner of the present Schwenkfelder Church, was formed. The church was incorporated in 1909.

The General Conference of the Schwenkfelder Church is a voluntary association for the Schwenkfelder Churches at Palm, Worcester, Lansdale, Norristown and Philadelphia, Pennsylvania.

They practice adult baptism and dedication of children, and observe the Lord's Supper regularly with open Communion. In theology, they are Christo-centric; in polity, congregational; in missions, world-minded; in ecclesiastical organization, ecumenical.

The ministry is recruited from graduates of colleges, universities and accredited theological seminaries. The churches take leadership in ecumenical concerns through ministerial associations, community service and action groups, councils of Christian education and other agencies.

Headquarters

105 Seminary St., Pennsburg, PA 18073 Tel. (215)679-3103
Media Contact, Dennis Moyer

Officers

Mod., John Graham, Collegeville, PA 19426
Sec., Frances Witte, Central Schwenkfelder Church, Worcester, PA 19490

150

Treas., Syl Rittenhouse, 1614 Kriebel Rd., Lansdale, PA 19446

Periodicals
The Schwenkfeldian

Separate Baptists in Christ

The Separate Baptists in Christ are a group of Baptists found in Indiana, Ohio, Kentucky, Tennessee, Virginia, West Virginia, Florida and North Carolina dating back to an association formed in 1758 in North Carolina and Virginia.

Today this group consists of approximately 100 churches. They believe in the infallibility of the Bible, the divine ordinances of the Lord's Supper, feetwashing, baptism and that those who endureth to the end shall be saved.

The Separate Baptists are Arminian in doctrine, rejecting both the doctrines of predestination and eternal security of the believer.

At the 1991 General Association, an additional article of doctrine was adopted. "We believe that at Christ's return in the clouds of heaven all Christians will meet the Lord in the air, and time shall be no more," thus leaving no time for a literal one thousand year reign. Seven associations comprise the General Association of Separate Baptists.

Headquarters
Media Contact, Clk., Greg Erdman, 10102 N. Hickory Ln., Columbus, IN 47203 812-526-2540
Email: mail@separatebaptist.org
Website: www.separatebaptist.org

Officers
Mod., Rev. Jim Goff, 1020 Gagel Ave., Louisville, KY 40216
Asst. Mod., Rev. Jimmy Polston, 785 Kitchen Rd., Mooresville, IN 46158 Tel. (317)831-6745
Clk., Greg Erdman, 10102 N. Hickory Ln., Columbus, IN 47203 Tel. (812)526-2540
Asst. Clk., Rev. Mark Polston, 787 Kitchen Rd., Mooresville, IN 46158 Tel. (317)834-0286

Serbian Orthodox Church in the U.S.A. and Canada

The Serbian Orthodox Church is an organic part of the Eastern Orthodox Church. As a local church it received its autocephaly from Constantinople in 1219 A.D.

In 1921, a Serbian Orthodox Diocese in the United States of America and Canada was organized. In 1963, it was reorganized into three dioceses, and in 1983 a fourth diocese was created for the Canadian part of the church. The Serbian Orthodox Church in the USA and Canada received its administrative autonomy in 1928. However, it remains canonically an integral part of the Serbian Orthodox Patriarchate with its see in Belgrade. The Serbian Orthodox Church is in absolute doctrinal unity with all other local Orthodox Churches.

Headquarters
St. Sava Monastery, P.O. Box 519, Libertyville, IL 60048 Tel. (847)367-0698

BISHOPS
Metropolitan of Midwestern America, Most Rev. Metropolitan Christopher
Bishop of Canada, Georgije, 5A Stockbridge Ave., Toronto, ON M8Z 4M6 Tel. (416)231-4009
Bishop of Eastern America, Rt. Rev. Bishop Mitrophan, P.O. Box 368, Sewickley, PA 15143 Tel. (412)741-5686
Diocese of Western America, Bishop Jovan, 2541 Crestline Terr., Alhambra, CA 91803 Tel. (818)264-6825

OTHER ORGANIZATIONS
Brotherhood of Serbian Orth. Clergy in U.S.A. & Canada, Pres., V. Rev. Lazar Kostur, Merrilville, IN
Federation of Circles of Serbian Sisters
Serbian Singing Federation

Periodicals
The Path of Orthodoxy

Seventh-day Adventist Church

The Seventh-day Adventist Church grew out of a worldwide religious revival in the mid-19th century. People of many religious persuasions believed Bible prophecies indicated that the second coming or advent of Christ was imminent.

When Christ did not come in the 1840s, a group of these disappointed Adventists in the United States continued their Bible studies and concluded they had misinterpreted prophetic events and that the second coming of Christ was still in the future. This same group of Adventists later accepted the teaching of the seventh-day Sabbath and became known as Seventh-day Adventists. The denomination organized formally in 1863.

The church was largely confined to North America until 1874, when its first missionary was sent to Europe. Today, over 42,000 congregations meet in 204 countries. Membership exceeds 9 million and increases between five and six percent each year.

In addition to a mission program, the church has the largest worldwide Protestant parochial school system with approximately 5,500 schools with more than 914,000 students on elementary through college and university levels.

The Adventist Development and Relief Agency (ADRA) helps victims of war and natural disasters, and many local congregations have community service facilities to help those in need close to home.

The church also has a worldwide publishing ministry with 55 printing facilities producing magazines and other publications in over 230 languages and dialects. In the United States and Canada, the church sponsors a variety of radio

151

and television programs, including *Christian Lifestyle Magazine*, *It Is Written*, *Breath of Life*, *Ayer, Hoy, y Mañana*, *Voice of Prophecy*, and *La Voz de la Esperanza*.

The North American Division of Seventh-day Adventist includes 58 Conferences which are grouped together into 9 organized Union Conferences. The various Conferences work under the general direction of these Union Conferences.

Headquarters

12501 Old Columbia Pike, Silver Spring, MD 20904-6600 Tel. (301)680-6000

Media Contact, Act. Dir., Archives & Statistics, Bert Haloviak

World-Wide Officers

Pres., Jan Paulsen
Sec., G. Ralph Thompson
Treas., Robert L. Rawson

WORLD-WIDE DEPARTMENTS

Adventist Chaplaincy Ministries, Dir., Richard O. Stenbakken
Children's Ministries, Dir., Virginia L. Smith
Education, Dir., Humberto M. Rasi
Communication, Dir., Rajmund Dabrowski
Family Ministries, Dir., Ronald M. Flowers
Health and Temperance, Dir., Allan R. Handysides
Ministerial Assoc., Dir., James A. Cress
Public Affairs & Religious Liberty, Dir., John Graz
Publishing, Dir., Ronald E. Appenzeller
Sabbath School & Personal Ministries, James W. Zackrison
Stewardship, Dir., Benjamin C. Maxson
Trust Services, G. Tom Carter
Women's Ministries, Ardis D. Stenbakken
Youth, Baraka G. Muganda

North American Officers

Pres., Alfred C. McClure
Vice-Pres.: Debra Brill; Clarence E. Hodges; Cyril Miller; Richard C. Osborn; Rose M. Otis; Manuel Vasquez
Sec., Harold W. Baptiste
Assoc. Sec., Rosa T. Banks
Treas., Juan R. Prestol
Assoc. Treas.: Marshall Chase; Del L. Johnson; Kenneth W. Osborn

NORTH AMERICAN ORGANIZATIONS

Atlantic Union Conf.: P.O. Box 1189, South Lancaster, MA 01561-1189; Pres., Theodore T. Jones
Canada: Seventh-day Adventist Church in Canada (see Ch. 4)
Columbia Union Conf.: 5427 Twin Knolls Rd., Columbia, MD 21045; Pres., Harold L. Lee
Lake Union Conf.: P.O. Box C, Berrien Springs, MI 49103; Pres., Don C. Schneider
Mid-America Union Conf.: P.O. Box 6128, Lincoln, NE 68506; Pres., Charles Sandefur

North Pacific Union Conf.: Pres., Jere D. Patzer, P.O. Box 16677, Portland, OR 97216;
Pacific Union Conf.: P.O. Box 5005, Westlake Village, CA 91359; Pres., Thomas J. Mostert, Jr
Southern Union Conf.: P.O. Box 849, Decatur, GA 30031; Pres., Malcolm B. Gordon
Southwestern Union Conf.: P.O. Box 4000, Burleson, TX 76097; Pres., Max A. Trevino

Periodicals

Collegiate Quarterly; Adra Today; Sabbath School Leadership; Adventist Review; Christian Record; Cornerstone Connections; Guide; Insight; Journal of Adventist Education; Liberty; Listen; Message; Ministry; Adult, Youth, and Children's Editions Mission; Our Little Friend; Primary Treasure; Signs of the Times; Vibrant Life; Youth Ministry Accent; Children's Friend; The Student; Women of Spirit; Young & Alive; Lifeglow; Vida Radiante

Seventh Day Baptist General Conference, USA and Canada

Seventh Day Baptists emerged during the English Reformation, organizing their first churches in the mid-1600s. The first Seventh Day Baptists of record in America were Stephen and Ann Mumford, who emigrated from England in 1664. Beginning in 1665 several members of the First Baptist Church at Newport, R.I. began observing the seventh day Sabbath, or Saturday. In 1671, five members, together with the Mumfords, formed the first Seventh Day Baptist Church in America at Newport.

Beginning about 1700, other Seventh Day Baptist churches were established in New Jersey and Pennsylvania. From these three centers, the denomination grew and expanded westward. They founded the Seventh Day Baptist General Conference in 1802.

The organization of the denomination reflects an interest in home and foreign missions, publications and education. Women have been encouraged to participate. From the earliest years religious freedom has been championed for all and the separation of church and state, advocated.

Seventh Day Baptists are members of the Baptist World Alliance and Baptist Joint Committee. The Seventh Day Baptist World Federation has 17 member conferences on six continents.

Headquarters

Seventh Day Baptist Center, 3120 Kennedy Rd., P.O. Box 1678, Janesville, WI 53547-1678 Tel. (608)752-5055 Fax (608)752-7711
Media Contact, Ex. Sec., Calvin Babcock
Email: sdbgen@inwave.com
Website: http://www.seventhdaybaptist.org

OTHER ORGANIZATIONS

Seventh Day Baptist Missionary Society, Exec. Dir., Kirk Looper, 119 Main St., Westerly, RI 02891

Seventh Day Bapt. Bd. of Christian Ed., Exec. Dir., Dr. Ernest K. Bee, Jr., Box 115, Alfred Station, NY 14803

Women's Soc. of the Gen. Conference, Pres., Mrs. Ruth Probasco, 858 Barrett Run Rd., Bridgeton, NJ 08302

American Sabbath Tract & Comm. Council, Dir. of Communications, Rev. Kevin J. Butler, 3120 Kennedy Rd., P.O. Box 1678, Janesville, WI 53547

Seventh Day Baptist Historical Society, Historian, Don A. Sanford, 3120 Kennedy Rd., P.O. Box 1678, Janesville, WI 53547

Seventh Day Baptist Center on Ministry, Dir. of Pastoral Services, Rev. Rodney Henry, 3120 Kennedy Rd., P.O. Box 1678, Janesville, WI 53547

Periodicals
Sabbath Recorder

Southern Baptist Convention

The Southern Baptist Convention was organized on May 10, 1845, in Augusta, Georgia. Cooperating Baptist churches are located in all 50 states, the District of Columbia, Puerto Rico, American Samoa and the Virgin Islands. The members of the churches work together through 1,212 district associations and 39 state conventions and/or fellowships. The Southern Baptist Convention has an Executive Committee and 12 national agencies—four boards, six seminaries, one commission, and one associated organization.

The purpose of the Southern Baptist Convention is "to provide a general organization for Baptists in the United States and its territories for the promotion of Christian missions at home and abroad and any other objects such as Christian education, benevolent enterprises, and social services which it may deem proper and advisable for the furtherance of the Kingdom of God". (Constitution, Article II)

The Convention exists in order to help the churches lead people to God through Jesus Christ.

From the beginning, there has been a mission desire to share the Gospel with the peoples of the world. The Cooperative Program is the basic channel of mission support. In addition, the Lottie Moon Christmas Offering for Foreign Missions and the Annie Armstrong Easter Offering for Home Missions support Southern Baptists' world mission programs.

In 1998, there were over 4,200 foreign missionaries serving in 127 foreign countries and over 5,654 home missionaries serving within the United States.

In 1987, the Southern Baptist Convention adopted themes and goals for the major denominational emphasis of Bold Mission Thrust for 1990-2000. Bold Mission Thrust is an effort to enable every person in the world to have opportunity to hear and to respond to the Gospel of Christ by the year 2000.

Headquarters
901 Commerce St., Ste. 750, Nashville, TN 37203 Tel. (615)244-2355

Media Contact, Vice-Pres. for Convention Relations, A. William Merrell, Tel. (615)244-2355 Fax (615)782-8684

Email: bmerrell@sbc.net

Website: www.sbc.net

Officers
Pres., Paige Patterson, P.O. Box 1889, Wake Forest, NC 27588-1889 Tel. (919)556-3101

Recording Sec., John Yeats, P.O. Box 12130, Oklahoma City, OK 73112

Executive Committee: Pres., Morris H. Chapman; Vice-Pres., Business & Finance, Jack Wilkerson; Vice-Pres., Convention News, Herb V. Hollinger; Vice-Pres., Convention Relations, A. William Merrell; Vice-Pres., Convention Policy, Augie Boto; Vice-Pres., Cooperative Program, David E. Hankins

GENERAL BOARDS AND COMMISSION
International Mission Board: Pres., Jerry A. Rankin, Box 6767, Richmond, VA 23230 Tel. (804)353-6655

North American Mission Board: Pres., Robert E. Reccord, 4200 No. Point Pkwy., Alpharetta, GA 30202 Tel. (770) 410-6519

Annuity Board: Pres., O. S. Hawkins, P.O. Box 2190, Dallas, TX 75221 Tel. (214)720-0511

LifeWay Christian Resources: Pres., James T. Draper, Jr. 127 Ninth Ave. N., Nashville, TN 37234 Tel. (615)251-2605

Ethics and Religious Liberty Commission: Pres., Richard D. Land, 901 Commerce St., Nashville, TN 37203 Tel. (615)244-2495

STATE CONVENTIONS
Alabama, Rick Lance, 2001 E. South Blvd., Montgomery, AL 36116 Tel. (334)288-2460

Alaska, Cloyd Sullins, 1750 O'Malley Rd., Anchorage, AK 99516 Tel. (907)344-9627

Arizona, Steve Bass, 3031 W. Northern Ave., Ste. 131, Phoenix, AZ 85052 Tel. (602)864-0337

Arkansas, Emil Turner, P.O. Box 552, Little Rock, AR 72203 Tel. (501)376-4791

California, Fermin A. Whittaker, 678 E. Shaw Ave., Fresno, CA 93710 Tel. (209)229-9533

Colorado, David T. Bunch, 7393 So. Alton Way, Englewood, CO 80112 Tel. (303)771-2480

District of Columbia, W. Jere Allen, 1628 16th St. NW, Washington, DC 20009 Tel. (202)265-1526

Florida, John Sullivan, 1230 Hendricks Ave., Jacksonville, FL 32207 Tel. (904)396-2351

Georgia, Dr. J. Robert White, 2930 Flowers Rd., S, Atlanta, GA 30341 Tel. (770)455-0404

Hawaii, O. W. Efurd, 2042 Vancouver Dr., Honolulu, HI 96822 Tel. (808)946-9581

Illinois, Bob Wiley, P.O. Box 19247, Springfield, IL 62794 Tel. (217)786-2600

Indiana, Charles W. Sullivan, P.O. Box 24189, Indianapolis, IN 46224 Tel. (317)241-9317

Iowa Southern Baptist Convention, O. Wyndell Jones, Suite #27, 2400 86th St., Des Moines, IA 50322 Tel. (515)278-4369

Kansas-Nebraska, R. Rex Lindsay, 5410 W. Seventh St., Topeka, KS 66606 Tel. (785)273-4880

Kentucky, Bill Mackey, P.O. Box 43433, Middletown, KY 40243 Tel. (502)245-4101

Louisiana, Dean Doster, P.O. Box 311, Alexandria, LA 71309 Tel. (318)448-3402

Maryland-Delaware, Charles R. Barnes, 10255 Old Columbia Rd., Columbia, MD 21046 Tel. (410)290-5290

Michigan, Michael Collins, 15635 W. 12 Mile Rd., Southfield, MI 48076 Tel. (248)557-4200

Minnesota-Wisconsin, William C. Tinsley, 519 16th St. SE, Rochester, MN 55904 Tel. (507)282-3636

Mississippi, James R. Futral, P.O. Box 530, Jackson, MS 39205 Tel. (601)968-3800

Missouri, James L. Hill, 400 E. High Street, Jefferson City, MO 65101 Tel. (573)635-7931

Nevada, David F. Meacham, 406 California Ave., Reno, NV 89509 Tel. (702)786-0406

New England, Kenneth R. Lyle, 5 Oak Ave., Northboro, MA 01532 Tel. (508)393-6013

New Mexico, Claude W. Cone, P.O. Box 485, Albuquerque, NM 87103 Tel. (505)924-2300

New York, J. B. Graham, 6538 Collamer Rd., East Syracuse, NY 13057 Tel. (315)433-1001

North Carolina, James H. Royston, 205 Convention Dr., Cary, NC 27511 Tel. (919)467-5100

Northwest, Jeff Iorg, 3200 NE 109th Ave., Vancouver, WA 98682 Tel. (360)882-2100 x. 121

Ohio, Exec. Dir., Jack P. Kwok, 1680 E. Broad St., Columbus, OH 43203 Tel. (614)258-8491

Oklahoma, Anthony L. Jordan, 3800 N. May Ave., Oklahoma City, OK 73112 Tel. (405)942-3800

Pennsylvania-South Jersey, David C. Waltz, 4620 Fritchey St., Harrisburg, PA 17109 Tel. (717)652-5856

South Carolina, B. Carlisle Driggers, 190 Stoneridge Dr., Columbia, SC 29210 Tel. (803)765-0030

Tennessee, James M. Porch, P.O. Box 728, Brentwood, TN 37024 Tel. (615)371-2090

Texas, William M. Pinson, 333 N. Washington, Dallas, TX 75246 Tel. (214)828-5300

Utah-Idaho, Jim Harding, P.O. Box 1347, Draper, UT 84020 Tel. (801)572-5350

Virginia, Reginald M. McDonough, P.O. Box 8568, Richmond, VA 23226 Tel. (804)672-2100

West Virginia, Jere L. Phillips, Number One Missions Way, Scott Depot, WV 25560 Tel. (304)757-0944

Wyoming, John W. Thomason, P.O. Box 4779, Casper, WY 82604 Tel. (307)472-4087

FELLOWSHIPS

Dakota Southern Baptist Fellowship, W.D. "Doc" Lindsey, Interim, P.O. Box 7187, Bismarck, ND 58502 Tel. (701)255-3765

Montana Southern Baptist Fellowship, C. Clyde Billingsley, P.O. Box 99, Billings, MT 59103 Tel. (406)252-7537

Canadian Convention of Southern Baptists, Gerry Taillon, Postal Bag 300, Cochrane, Alberta T0L 0W0 Tel. (403)932-5688

Periodicals

The Commission; SBC Life; MissionsUSA

Southern Methodist Church

Organized in 1939, this body is composed of congregations desirous of continuing in true Biblical Methodism and preserving the fundamental doctrines and beliefs of the Methodist Episcopal Church, South. These congregations declined to be a party to the merger of the Methodist Episcopal Church, The Methodist Episcopal Church, South and the Methodist Protestant Church into The Methodist Church.

Headquarters

P.O. Box 39, Orangeburg, SC 29116-0039 Tel. (803)536-1378 Fax (803)535-3881

Media Contact, Pres., Rev. Bedford F. Landers Email: smchq@juno.com

Officers

Pres., Rev. Bedford F. Landers

Admn. Asst. to Pres., Philip A. Rorabaugh

Director of Foreign Missions, Rev. Franklin D. McLellan, P.O. Box 39, Orangeburg, SC 29116-0039

Southern Methodist College Pres., Rev. Daniel H. Shapley, PO Box 1027, Orangeburg, SC 29116-1027

The Eastern Conf., Vice-Pres., Rev. John T. Hucks, Jr., 221 Pinewood Dr., Rowesville, SC 29133

Alabama-Florida-Georgia Conf., Vice-Pres., Rev. Glenn A Blank, 2275 Scenic Highway, Apt. 109, Pensacola, FL 32502

Mid-South Conf., Vice-Pres., Rev. Dr. Ronald R. Carrier, 5030 Hillsboro Rd., Nashville, TN 37215

South-Western Conf., Vice-Pres., Rev. Ira Schilling, 106 Albert Dr., Haughton, LA 71037

Gen. Conf., Treas., Rev. Philip A. Rorabaugh, P.O. Drawer A, Orangeburg, SC 29116-0039

Periodicals

The Southern Methodist

Sovereign Grace Believers

The Sovereign Grace Believers are a contemporary movement which began its stirrings in the mid-1950s when some pastors in traditional Baptist churches returned to a Calvinist-theological perspective.

The first "Sovereign Grace" conference was held in Ashland, Kentucky, in 1954 and since then, conferences of this sort have been sponsored by various local churches on the West Coast, Southern and Northern states and Canada. This movement is a spontaneous phenomenon concerning reformation at the local church level. Consequently, there is no interest in establishing a Reformed Baptist "Convention" or "Denomination." Each local church is to administer the keys to the kingdom.

Most Sovereign Grace Believers formally or informally relate to the "First London" (1646), "Second London" (1689) or "Philadelphia" (1742) Confessions.

There is a wide variety of local church government in this movement. Many Calvinist Baptists have a plurality of elders in each assembly. Other Sovereign Grace Believers, however, prefer to function with one pastor and several deacons.

Membership procedures vary from church to church but all require a credible profession of faith in Christ, and proper baptism as a basis for membership.

Calvinistic Baptists financially support gospel efforts (missionaries, pastors of small churches at home and abroad, literature publication and distribution, radio programs, etc.) in various parts of the world.

Headquarters
Media Contact, Corres., Jon Zens, P.O. Box 548, St. Croix Falls, WI 54024 Tel. (651)465-6516 Fax (651)465-5101
Email: jon@searchingtogether.org
Website: www.searchingtogether.org

Periodicals
Reformation Today; Kindred Minds; Searching Together

The Swedenborgian Church

Founded in North America in 1792 as the Church of the New Jerusalem, the Swedenborgian Church was organized as a national body in 1817 and incorporated in Illinois in 1861. Its biblically-based theology is derived from the spiritual, or mystical, experiences and exhaustive biblical studies of the Swedish scientist and philosopher Emanuel Swedenborg (1688-1772).

The church centers its worship and teachings on the historical life and the risen and glorified present reality of the Lord Jesus Christ. It looks with an ecumenical vision toward the establishment of the kingdom of God in the form of a universal Church, active in the lives of all people of good will who desire and strive for freedom, peace and justice for all. It is a member of the NCCC and active in many local councils of churches.

With churches and groups throughout the United States and Canada, the denomination's central administrative offices and its seminary" Swedenborg School of Religion" are located in Newton, Massachusetts. Affiliated churches are found in Africa, Asia, Australia, Canada, Europe,

the United Kingdom, Japan, South Korea and South America. Many philosophers and writers have acknowledged their appreciation of Swedenborg's teachings.

Headquarters
11 Highland Ave., Newtonville, MA 02460 Tel. (617)969-4240 Fax (617)964-3258
Media Contact, Central Ofc. Mgr., Martha Bauer
Email: manager@centraloffice.swedenborg.org
Website: http://www.swedenborg.org

Officers
Pres., Rev. Ronald P. Brugler, 489 Franklin St., N., Kitchener, ON, Canada N2A 1Z2
Vice-Pres., Christine Laitner, 10 Hanna Court, Midland, MI 48642
Rec. Sec., Gloria Toot, 10280 Gentlewind Dr., Montgomery, OH 45242
Treas., Polly Baxter, 4720 Bel Pre Rd., Rockville, MD 20853
Ofc. Mgr., Martha Bauer

Periodicals
The Messenger; Our Daily Bread

Syrian Orthodox Church of Antioch

The Syrian Orthodox Church of Antioch traces its origin to the Patriarchate established in Antioch by St. Peter the Apostle. It is under the supreme ecclesiastical jurisdiction of His Holiness the Syrian Orthodox Patriarch of Antioch and All the East, now residing in Damascus, Syria. The Syrian Orthodox Church" composed of several archdioceses, numerous parishes, schools and seminaries" professes the faith of the first three Ecumenical Councils of Nicaea, Constantinople and Ephesus, and numbers faithful in the Middle East, India, the Americas, Europe and Australia.

The first Syrian Orthodox faithful came to North America during the late 1800s, and by 1907 the first Syrian Orthodox priest was ordained to tend to the community's spiritual needs. In 1949, His Eminence Archbishop Mor Athanasius Y. Samuel came to America and was soon appointed Patriarchal Vicar. The Archdiocese was officially established in 1957. In 1995, the Archdiocese of North America was divided into three separate Patriarchal Vicariates (Eastern United States, Western United States and Canada), each under a hierarch of the Church.

There are 18 official archdiocesan parishes and three mission congregations in the United States, located in California, District of Columbia, Florida, Illinois, Massachusetts, Michigan, New Jersey, New York, Oregon, Rhode Island and Texas. In Canada, there are five official parishes: three in the Province of Ontario and two in the Province of Quebec and a mission congregation in the Province of Alberta.

Headquarters
Archdiocese for the Eastern U.S., 260 Elm

Avenue, Teaneck, NJ 07666 Tel. (201)801-0660 Fax (201)801-0603

Email: syrianoc@syrianorthodoxchurch.org

Website: www.syrianorthodoxchurch.org

Archdiocese of Los Angeles and Environs, 417 E. Fairmont Rd., Burbank, CA 91501 Tel. (818)845-5089 Fax (818)845-5436

Media Contact, Archdiocesan Gen. Sec., V. Rev. Choreepiscopus John Meno, 260 Elm Ave., Teaneck, NJ 07666 Tel. (201)907-0122 Fax (201)907-0551

Officers

Archdiocese for Eastern U.S.: Archbishop, Mor Cyril Aphrem Karim

Archdiocese of Los Angeles and Environs: Archbishop, Mor Clemis Eugene Kaplan

Triumph the Church and Kingdom of God in Christ Inc. (International)

This church was given through the wisdom and knowledge of God to the Late Apostle Elias Dempsey Smith on Oct. 20, 1897, in Issaquena County, Mississippi, while he was pastor of a Methodist church.

The Triumph Church, as this body is more commonly known, was founded in 1902. Its doors opened in 1904 and it was confirmed in Birmingham, Alabama, with 225 members in 1915. It was incorporated in Washington, D.C., in 1918 and currently operates in 31 states and overseas. The General Church is divided into 13 districts, including the Africa District.

Triumphant doctrine and philosophy are based on the principles of life, truth and knowledge; the understanding that God is in man and expressed through man; the belief in manifested wisdom and the hope for constant new revelations. Its concepts and methods of teaching the second coming of Christ are based on these and all other attributes of goodness.

Triumphians emphasize that God is the God of the living, not the God of the dead.

Headquarters

213 Farrington Ave. S.E., Atlanta, GA 30315

Media Contact, Bishop C. W. Drummond, 7114 Idlewild, Pittsburg, PA 15208 Tel. (412)731-2286

Officers

Chief Bishop, Bishop C. W. Drummond, 7114 Idlewild, Pittsburgh, PA 15208 Tel. (412)731-2286

Gen. Bd of Trustees, Chmn., Bishop Leon Simon, 1028 59th St., Oakland, CA 94608 Tel. (415)652-9576

Gen. Treas., Bishop Hosea Lewis, 1713 Needlewood Ln., Orlando, FL 32818 Tel. (407)295-5488

Gen. Rec. Sec., Bishop Zephaniah Swindle, Box 1927, Shelbyville, TX 75973 Tel. (409)598-3082

True Orthodox Church of Greece (Synod of Metropolitan Cyprian), American Exarchate

The American Exarchate of the True (Old Calendar) Orthodox Church of Greece adheres to the tenets of the Eastern Orthodox Church, which considers itself the legitimate heir of the historical Apostolic Church.

When the Orthodox Church of Greece adopted the New, or Gregorian, Calendar in 1924, many felt that this breach with tradition compromised the Church's festal calendar, based on the Old, or Julian, Calendar, and its unity with world Orthodoxy. In 1935, three State Church Bishops returned to the Old Calendar and established a Synod in Resistance, the True Orthodox Church of Greece. When the last of these Bishops died, the Russian Orthodox Church Abroad consecrated a new Hierarchy for the Greek Old Calendarists and, in 1969, declared them a Sister Church.

In the face of persecution by the State Church, some Old Calendarists denied the validity of the Mother Church of Greece and formed two synods, now under the direction of Archbishop Chrysostomos of Athens and Archbishop Andreas of Athens. A moderate faction under Metropolitan Cyprian of Oropos and Fili does not maintain communion with the Mother Church of Greece, but recognizes its validity and seeks a restoration of unity by a return to the Julian Calendar and traditional ecclesiastical polity by the State Church. About 1.5 million Orthodox Greeks belong to the Old Calendar Church.

The first Old Calendarist communities in the United States were formed in the 1930s. The Exarchate under Metropolitan Cyprian was established in 1986. Placing emphasis on clergy education, youth programs, and recognition of the Old Calendarist minority in American Orthodoxy, the Exarchate has encouraged the establishment of monastic communities and missions. Cordial contacts with the New Calendarist and other Orthodox communities are encouraged. A center for theological training and Patristic studies has been established at the Exarchate headquarters in Etna, California.

In July 1994, the True Orthodox Church of Greece (Synod of Metropolitan Cyprian), the True Orthodox Church of Romania, the True Orthodox Church of Bulgaria, and the Russian Orthodox Church Abroad entered into liturgical union, forming a coalition of traditionalist Orthodox bodies several million strong.

Headquarters

St. Gregory Palamas Monastery, P.O. Box 398, Etna, CA 96027-0398 Tel. (530)467-3228 Fax (530) 467-5228

Media Contact, Exarch in America, His Eminence, Archbishop Chrysostomos

Officers

Acting Synodal Exarch in America, His Grace Bishop Auxentios

Chancellor of the Exarchate, The Very Rev. Raphael Abraham, 3635 Cottage Grove Ave., S.E., Cedar Rapids, IA 52403-1612

Periodicals
Orthodox Tradition (quarterly theological journal)

Ukrainian Orthodox Church of America (Ecumenical Patriarchate)

This body was organized in the United States in 1928, when the first convention was held. In 1932, Dr. Joseph Zuk was consecrated as first Bishop. His successor was the Most Rev. Bishop Bohdan, Primate, who was consecrated by the order of the Ecumenical Patriarchate of Constantinople in 1937, in New York City. He was succeeded by the Most Rev. Metropolitan Andrei Kuschak, consecrated by the blessing of Ecumenical Patriarch by Archbishop Iakovos, Metropolitan Germanos and Bishop Silas of the Greek-Orthodox Church, in 1967. His successor is Bishop Vsevolod, ordained in 1987 by Archbishop Iakovos, Metropolitan Silas and Bishops Philip and Athenagoras.

Headquarters
Ukrainian Orthodox Church of America, 3 Davenport Ave., Ste. 2A, New Rochelle, NY 10805 Tel. (914)636-7813 Fax (914)636-7813
Media Contact, Very Rev. Arihimandrite Lev, 10 Oakwood St., Bridgeport, CT 06006

Officers
Primate, Rt. Rev. Bishop Vsevolod

Periodicals
Ukrainian Orthodox Herald

Ukrainian Orthodox Church of the U.S.A.

The church was formally organized in the United States in 1919. Archbishop John Theodorovich arrived from Ukraine in 1924.

Headquarters
P.O. Box 495, South Bound Brook, NJ 08880 Tel. (908)356-0090 Fax (908)356-5556
135 Davidson Ave., Somerset, NJ 08873
Media Contact, Archbishop, His Eminence Antony

Officers
Metropolitan, His Beatitude Constantine [Buggan], Archbishop of Chicago & Philadelphia
Archbishop, His Eminence Antony

Unitarian Universalist Association of Congregations

The Unitarian Universalist Association (UUA), created in 1961 through a merger of the Universalist Church of America with the American Unitarian Association, combines two liberal religious traditions. The religion traces its roots back to Europe where in 1569, the Transylvanian king, John Sigismund (1540-1571), issued an edict of religious freedom. The religious philosophy led to the organization of the Universalists in this country in 1793, and the Unitarians (organized here in 1825).

Founders of Universalism believed in universal salvation, while founders of Unitarianism believed in the unity of God (as opposed to the Trinity). Today, Unitarian Universalism is a liberal, creedless religion with Judeo-Christian roots. It draws also from Eastern, humanist, and other religious traditions, and encourages its members to seek religious truth out of their own reflection and experience. The denomination teaches tolerance and respect for other religious viewpoints, and affirms the worth and dignity of every person.

The Unitarian Universalist Association consists of over 1,040 congregations located principally in the United States and Canada, with over 214,000 members, and is served by more than 1,150 ministers. The Association is the fastest-growing liberal religion in North America, and this year completed its sixteenth consecutive year of growth. Each member congregation within the UUA is governed independently. The Association is made up of 23 Districts (served by a District Executive who is a member of the UUA staff) in North America, with each congregation having district affiliation. The Association is governed by an elected Board of Trustees, chaired by an elected Moderator. An elected President, three vice presidents, and directors of five departments form the Executive Staff which administers the daily activities of the Association.

The General Assembly, held each June in a different UUA District, serves as the Association's annual business meeting. The UUA includes Departments of Ministry; Religious Education; Congregational, District and Extension Services; Communications; Development; and Faith in Action. *The World*, published bi-monthly, is the denominational journal. Beacon Press, an internationally honored publishing house, is wholly owned by the Unitarian Universalist Association.

Headquarters
25 Beacon Street, Boston, MA 02108, Tel. (617) 742-2100, Fax (617) 367-323
Media Contact, John Hurley, Director of Information, Tel. (617)-742-2100 x. 131
Email: jhurley@uua.org
Website: www.uua.org

Officers
President, The Rev. Dr. John A. Buehrens
Moderator, Denise T. Davidoff
Executive Vice President, Kathleen C. Montgomery

United Christian Church

The United Christian Church originated about 1864. There were some ministers and laymen in

157

the United Brethren in Christ Church who disagreed with the position and practice of the church on infant baptism, voluntary bearing of arms and belonging to oath-bound secret combinations. This group developed into United Christian Church, organized at a conference held in Campbelltown, Pennsylvania, on May 9, 1877. The principal founders of the denomination were George Hoffman, John Stamn and Thomas Lesher. Before they were organized, they were called Hoffmanites.

The United Christian Church has district conferences, a yearly general conference, a general board of trustees, a mission board, a board of directors of the United Christian Church Home, a camp meeting board, a young peoples" board and local organized congregations.

It believes in the Holy Trinity and the inspired Holy Scriptures with the doctrines they teach. The church practices the ordinances of Baptism, Holy Communion and Foot Washing.

It welcomes all into its fold who are born again, believe in Jesus Christ as Savior and Lord and have received the Holy Spirit.

Headquarters

c/o John P. Ludwig, Jr., 523 W. Walnut St., Cleona, PA 17042 Tel. (717)273-9629
Media Contact, Presiding Elder, John P. Ludwig, Jr.

Officers

Presiding Elder, Elder John P. Ludwig, Jr.
Conf. Sec., Mr. Lee Wenger, 1625 Thompson Ave., Annville, PA 17003
Conf. Moderator, Elder Gerald Brinser, 2360 Horseshoe Pike, Annville, PA 17003

OTHER ORGANIZATIONS

Mission Board: Pres., Elder John P. Ludwig, Jr.; Sec., Elder David Heagy, 4129 Oak St., Lebanon, PA 17042; Treas., LeRoy Bomgardner, 1000 Bomgardner Lane, Annville, PA 17003

United Church of Christ

The United Church of Christ was constituted on June 25, 1957 by representatives of the Congregational Christian Churches and of the Evangelical and Reformed Church, in Cleveland, Ohio.

The Preamble to the Constitution states: "The United Church of Christ acknowledges as its sole head, Jesus Christ...It acknowledges as kindred in Christ all who share in this confession. It looks to the Word of God in the Scriptures, and to the presence and power of the Holy Spirit...It claims...the faith of the historic Church expressed in the ancient creeds and reclaimed in the basic insights of the Protestant Reformers. It affirms the responsibility of the Church in each generation to make this faith its own in...worship, in honesty of thought and expression, and in purity of heart before God....it recognizes two sacraments: Baptism and the Lord's Supper."

The creation of the United Church of Christ brought together four unique traditions:

(1) Groundwork for the Congregational Way was laid by Calvinist Puritans and Separatists during the late 16th-early 17th centuries, then achieved prominence among English Protestants during the civil war of the 1640s. Opposition to state control prompted followers to emigrate to the United States, where they helped colonize New England in the 17th century. Congregationalists have been self-consciously a denomination from the mid-19th century.

(2) The Christian Churches, an 18th-century American restorationist movement emphasized Christ as the only head of the church, the New Testament as their only rule of faith, and "Christian" as their sole name. This loosely organized denomination found in the Congregational Churches a like disposition. In 1931, the two bodies formally united as the Congregational Christian Churches.

(3) The German Reformed Church comprised an irenic aspect of the Protestant Reformation, as a second generation of Reformers drew on the insights of Zwingli, Luther and Calvin to formulate the Heidelberg Catechism of 1563. People of the German Reformed Church began immigrating to the New World early in the 18th century, the heaviest concentration in Pennsylvania. Formal organization of the American denomination was completed in 1793. The church spread across the country. In the Mercersburg Movement, a strong emphasis on evangelical catholicity and Christian unity was eveloped.

(4) In 19th-century Germany, Enlightenment criticism and Pietist inwardness decreased longstanding conflicts between religious groups. In Prussia, a royal proclamation merged Lutheran and Reformed people into one United Evangelical Church (1817). Members of this new church way migrated to America. The Evangelicals settled in large numbers in Missouri and Illinois, emphasizing pietistic devotion and unionism; in 1840 they formed the German Evangelical Church Society in the West. After union with other Evangelical church associations, in 1877 it took the name of the German Evangelical Synod of North America.

On June 25, 1934, this Synod and the Reformed Church in the U.S. (formerly the German Reformed Church) united to form the Evangelical and Reformed Church. They blended the Reformed tradition's passion for the unity of the church and the Evangelical tradition's commitment to the liberty of conscience inherent in the gospel.

Headquarters

700 Prospect Avenue, Cleveland, OH 44115 Tel. (216)736-2100 Fax (216)736-2120
Media Contact, UCC-Sec., Edith A. Guffey, 700 Prospect Ave., Cleveland, OH 44115 Tel. (216)736-2110 Fax (216)736-2120
Email: langa @ucc.org
Website: www.ucc.org

Officers

Pres., The Rev. John H. Thomas
Sec., Edith A. Guffey
Dir. of Fin. & Treas., Rev. Doris R. Powell
Exec. Assoc. to Pres., Rev. Vilma M. Machin
Asst. to Pres. for Ecumenical Concerns, Rev. John H. Thomas
Asst. to Pres., Lorin W. Cope
Chpsn. Exec. Council, Rev. Linda S. Gruber
Vice-Chpsn., Ms. Iris M. Branch
Mod., Rev. Nancy S. Taylor
Asst. Mod.: Mr. Marc D. Benoist; Mr. Richard Harter

ORGANIZATIONS

United Church Board for World Min.: 700 Prospect Ave., Cleveland, OH 44115 Tel. (216)736-3200; 475 Riverside Dr., New York, NY 10115 Tel. (212)870-2637; Exec. Vice-Pres., Mr. Dale L. Bishop; Mission Program Unit, Gen. Sec.; Support Services Unit, Treas., Bruce Bergquist

United Church Board for Homeland Min.: 700 Prospect Ave., Cleveland, OH 44115 Tel. (216)736-3800 Fax (216)736-3803; Office of Exec. Vice-Pres., Exec. Vice-Pres., Rev. Thomas E. Dipko; Gen. Sec., Rev. Robert P. Noble, Jr.; Office of the Treasurer, Acting Treas., Kathy Houston; Div. of Evangelism & Local Church Dev., Gen. Sec., Rev. Jose A. Malayang; Div. of Education & Publication, Gen. Sec., Audrey Miller; Div. of American Missionary Association, Gen. Sec., Rev. F. Allison Phillips

Commission for Racial Justice: 700 Prospect Ave., Cleveland, OH 44115; Ofc. for Urban & Natl. Racial Justice, 5113 Georgia Ave. NW, Washington, DC 20011 Tel. (202)291-1593; Ofc. for Constituency Dev./Rural Racial Justice, Franklinton Center, P.O. Box 187, Enfield, NC 27823 Tel. (919)437-1723; Ofc. for Ecumenical Racial Justice, 475 Riverside Dr., Room 1948, New York, NY 10115 Tel. (212) 870-2077; Exec. Dir., Bernice Powell Jackson

Council for American Indian Ministry: 471 3rd Street, Box 412, Excelsior, MN 55331 Tel. (612)474-3532; Exec. Dir., Rev. Armin L. Schmidt

Council for Health & Human Service Min.: 700 Prospect Ave., Cleveland, OH 44115 Tel. (216)736-2250; Exec. Dir., Rev. Bryan Sickbert

Coord. Center for Women in Church & Soc.: 700 Prospect Ave., Cleveland, OH 44115 Tel. (216)736-2150; Exec. Dir., Rev. Lois M. Powell

Office for Church in Society: Exec. Dir., Rev. Wallace Ryan Kuroiwa, 700 Prospect Ave., Cleveland, OH 44115; 110 Maryland Ave. NE, Washington, DC 20002, Tel. 202-543-1517; Dir., Washington Ofc., Rev. Jay E. Lintner

Office for Church Life & Leadership: 700 Prospect Ave., Cleveland, OH 44115, Tel. 202-543-1517; Exec. Dir., Rev. William A. Hulteen, Jr.

Office of Communication: 700 Prospect Ave., Cleveland, OH 44115 Tel. (216)736-2222 Fax (216)736-2223; 475 Riverside Dr., 16th Fl., New York, NY 10115 Tel. (212)870-2137; Dir., Rev. Robert Chase

Stewardship Council: 700 Prospect Ave., Cleveland, OH 44115; 412 Orange St., New Haven, CT 06511; Exec. Dir., Rev. Earl D. Miller

Commission on Development: Dir. Planned Giving, Rev. Donald G. Stoner

Historical Council: Office of Archivist, 700 Prospect Ave., Cleveland, OH 44115

Pension Boards: 475 Riverside Dr., New York, NY 10115; Exec. Vice-Pres., Joan F. Brannick

United Church Foundation, Inc.: 475 Riverside Dr., New York, NY 10115; Financial Vice-Pres. & Treas., Donald G. Hart

CONFERENCES

Western Region

California, Nevada, Northern, Rev. Mary Susan Gast, 9260 Alcosta Blvd.,#C18, San Ramon, CA 94583-4143

California, Southern, Rev. Daniel F. Romero, 2401 N. Lake St., Altadena, CA 91001

Hawaii, Rev. David P. Hansen, 15 Craigside Pl., Honolulu, HI 96817

Montana-Northern Wyoming, Rev. John M. Schaeffer, 2016 Alderson Ave., Billings, MT 59102

Central Pacific, Rev. Hector Lopez, 0245 SW Bancroft St., Ste. E, Portland, OR 97201

Rocky Mountain, Rev. William A. Dalke, 7000 Broadway, Ste. 420, ABS Bldg., Denver, CO 80221

Southwest, Rev. Ann C. Rogers-Witte, 4423 N. 24th St., Ste. 600, Phoenix, AZ 85016

Washington-North Idaho, Rev. Lynne S. Fitch, 720 14th Ave. E., Seattle, WA 98102; Rev. Randall Hyvonen, S. 412 Bernard St., Spokane, WA 99204

West Central Region

Iowa, Rev. Susan J. Ingham, 600 42nd St., Des Moines, IA 50312

Kansas-Oklahoma, Rev. John H. Krueger, 1248 Fabrique, Wichita, KS 67218

Minnesota, Rev. William Kaseman, 122 W. Franklin Ave., Rm. 323, Minneapolis, MN 55404

Missouri, Rev. A. Gayle Engel, 461 E. Lockwood Ave., St. Louis, MO 63119

Nebraska, Rev. George S. Worcester, 825 M St., Lincoln, NE 68508

North Dakota, Rev. Jack J. Seville, Jr., 227 W. Broadway, Bismarck, ND 58501

South Dakota, Rev. Gene E. Miller, 3500 S. Phillips Ave., #121, Sioux Falls, SD 57105-6864

159

Great Lakes Region

Illinois, Rev. Charlene Burch, 1840 Westchester Blvd., Westchester, IL 60154

Illinois South, Rev. Ronald L. Eslinger, Box 325, 1312 Broadway, Highland, IL 62249

Indiana-Kentucky, Rev. Stephen C. Gray, 1100 W. 42nd St., Indianapolis, IN 46208

Michigan, Rev. Kent J. Ulery, P.O. Box 1006, East Lansing, MI 48826

Ohio, Rev. Ralph C. Quellhorst, 6161 Busch Blvd.,#95, Columbus, OH 43229

Wisconsin, Rev. Frederick R. Trost, 4459 Gray Rd., Box 495, De Forest, WI 53532-0495

Southern Region

Florida, Rev. M. Douglas Borko, 222 E. Welbourne Ave., Winter Park, FL 32789

South Central, Rev. Mark H. Miller, 6633 E. Hwy. 290, #200, Austin, TX 78723-1157

Southeast, Rev. Timothy C. Downs, 756 W. Peachtree St., NW, Atlanta, GA 30308

Southern, Rev. Emmett O. FLoyd, 217 N. Main St., Box 658, Graham, NC 27253

Middle Atlantic Region

Central Atlantic, Rev. John R. Deckenback, 916 S. Rolling Rd., Baltimore, MD 21228

New York, Rev. C. Jack Richards, The Church Center, Rm. 202, 3049 E. Genesee St., Syracuse, NY 13224

Penn Central, Rev. Lyle J. Weible, The United Church Center, Rm. 126, 900 S. Arlington Ave., Harrisburg, PA 17109

Penn Northeast, Rev. Daniel A. Vander PLOEG, 431 Delaware Ave., P.O. Box 177, Palmerton, PA 18071

Penn Southeast, Rev. Franklin R. Mittman, Jr., 505 Second Ave., P.O. Box 400, Collegeville, PA 19426

Penn West, Rev. Paul L. Westcoat, Jr., 320 South Maple Ave., Greensburg, PA 15601

Puerto Rico, Rev. Osvaldo Malave-Rivera, Box 8609, Caguas, PR 00762

New England Region

Connecticut, Rev. Davida Foy Crabtree, 125 Sherman St., Hartford, CT 06105

Maine, Rev. Jean M. Alexander, Rev. David R. Gaewski, 68 Main St., P.O. Box 966, Yarmouth, ME 04096

Massachusetts, Rev. Bennie E. Whiten, Jr., P.O. Box 2246, 1 Badger Rd., Framingham, MA 01701

New Hampshire: Rev. Carole C. Carlson; Rev. Benjamin C. L. Crosby; Rev. John W. Lynes, 314 S. Main, P.O. Box 465, Concord, NH 03302

Rhode Island, Rev. H. Dahler Hayes, 56 Walcott St., Pawtucket, RI 02860

Vermont, Rev. Arnold I. Thomas, 285 Maple St., Burlington, VT 05401

Nongeographic

Calvin Synod, Rev. Louis Medgyesi, 607 Plum St., Fairport Harbor, OH 44077

Periodicals

United Church News; Common Lot; Courage in the Struggle for Justice and Peace

United Holy Church of America, Inc.

The United Holy Church of America, Inc. is an outgrowth of the great revival that began with the outpouring of the Holy Ghost on the Day of Pentecost. The church is built upon the foundation of the Apostles and Prophets, Jesus Christ being the cornerstone.

During a revival of repentence, regeneration and holiness of heart and life that swept through the South and West, the United Holy Church was born. The founding fathers had no desire to establish a denomination but were pushed out of organized churches because of this experience of holiness and testimony of the Spirit-filled life.

On the first Sunday in May 1886, in Method, North Carolina, what is today known as the United Holy Church of America, Inc. was born. The church was incorporated on Sept. 25, 1918.

Baptism by immersion, the Lord's Supper and feet washing are observed. The premillennial teaching of the Second Coming of Christ, Divine healing, justification by faith, sanctification as a second work of grace and Spirit baptism are accepted.

Headquarters

5104 Dunstan Rd., Greensboro, NC 27405 Tel. (336)621-0669

Media Contact, Gen. Statistician, Ms. Jacquelyn B. McCain, 1210 N. Euclid Ave., Apt. A, St. Louis, MO 63113-2012, Tel. 314-367-8351 Fax 314-367-1835; Email: books@mohistory.org

GENERAL ADMINISTRATION

Gen. Pres., The Rt. Rev. Odell McCollum, 707 Woodmark Run, Gahanna, OH 43230, Tel. 614-475-4713, Rax 614-475-4713

Gen. Vice Pres., Bishop Elijah Williams, 901 Briarwood St., Reidsville, NC 27320 Tel. (919) 349-7275

Gen. 2nd Vice-Pres., The Rt. Rev. Kenneth O. Robinson, Sr., 33 Springbrook Road, Nanuet, NY 10954-4423, Tel. 914-425-8311, Fax 914-352-2686

Gen. Rec. Sec., Rev. Mrs. Elsie harris, 2304 Eighth Street, Portsmouth, VA 23704, Tel. 757-399-0926

Asst. Rec. Sec., Mrs. Cassandra Jones, 3869 JoAnn Drive, Cleveland, OH 44122, Tel. 216-921-0097

Gen. Fin. Sec., Vera Perkins-Hughes, P.O. Box 6194, Cleveland, OH Tel. (216) 851-7448

Asst. Fin. Sec., Bertha Williams, 4749 Shaw Dr., Wilmington, NC 28405 Tel. (919)395-4462

Gen. Corres. Sec., Ms. Gwendolyn Lane, 3069 Hudson Street, Columbus, OH 43219

Gen. Treas., Louis Bagley, 8779 Wales Dr., Cincinnati, OH 45249 Tel. (513)247-0588

GENERAL OFFICERS

Gen Pres. Missionary Dept., Rev. Ardelia M. Corbett, 519 Madera Dr., Youngstown, OH 44504 Tel. (216)744-3284

Gen. Evangelism & Extension Dept., Pres., Elder Clifford R. Pitts, 3563 North 14th St., Milwaukee, WI 53206, Tel. 414-244-1319

Gen. Bible Church School Dept., Superintendent, Robert L. Rollins, 1628 Avondale Ave., Toledo, OH 43607 Tel. (419)246-4046

Gen. Y.P.H.A., Pres., Elder James W. Brooks, Rt. 3 Box 105, Pittsboro, NC 27312 Tel. (919)542-5357

Gen. Ushers Department, Pres., Ms. Sherly M. Hughes, 1491 East 191st Street, #H-604, Euclid, OH 44117, Te. 216-383-0038

Gen. Educ. Dept., Elder Roosevelt Alston, 168 Willow Creek Run, Henderson, NC 27636, Tel, 919-438-5854

Gen. Music Dept., Chair, Rosie Johnson, 2009 Forest Dale Dr., Silver Spring, MD 20932

Gen. Historian, Dr. Chester Gregory, Sr., 1302 Lincoln Woods Dr., Baltimore, MD 21228, Tel. 410-788-5144

Gen. Counsel, Mr. Joe L. Webster, Esquire, Attorney-At-Law, P.O. Box 2301, Chapel Hill, NC 27515-2301, Tel. 919-542-5150

UHCA Academy, Dir., Ms. Stephanie Davis, The United Holy Church of America, Inc., 5104 Dunstan Road, Greensboro, NC 27405, Tel. 336-621-0069

Gen. Statistician, Ms. Jacquelyn B. McCain, 1210 N. Euclid Ave., Apt. A, St. Louis, MO 63113-2012, Tel. 314-367-8351 Fax 314-367-1835

PRESIDENTS OF CONVOCATIONAL DISTRICTS

Barbados District; The Rt. Rev. Jestina Gentles, 5 West Ridge St., Britton's Hill, St. Michael, BH2 Barbados, West Indies, Tel. 246-427-7185

Bermuda Dist., The Rt. Rev. Calvin Armstrong, P.O. Box 234, Paget, Bermuda, Tel. 441-296-0828 or 441-292-8383

Central Western Dist., Bishop Bose Bradford, 6279 Natural Bridge, Pine Lawn, MO 63121 Tel. (314)355-1598

Ghana, West Africa Dist., The Rt. Rev. Robert Blount, 231 Arlington Av., Jersey City, NJ 07035, Tel. 201-433-5672

New England Dist., The Rt. Rev. Lowell Edney, 85 Woodhaven St., Mattapan, MA 02126, Tel. 617-296-5366

Northern Dist., The Rt. Rev. Kenneth O. Robinson, Sr., 33 Springbrook Rd., Nanuet, NY 10954, Tel. 914-425-8311

Northwestern Dist., The Rt. Rev. M. Daniel Borden, 8655 North Melody Lane, Macedonia, OH 44056, Tel. 330-468-0270

Pacific Coast Dist., The Rt. Rev. Irvin Evans, 235 Harvard Rd., Linden, NJ 07036, Tel. 908-925-6138

Southeastern Dist., The Rt. Rev. James C. Bellamy, 1825 Rockland Dr., SE, Atlanta, GA 30316, Tel. 404-241-1821

Southern Dist.—Goldsboro, The Rt. Rev. Ralph E. Love, Sr., 200 Barrington Rd., Greenville, NC 27834, Tel. 252-353-0495

Southern Dist.- Henderson, The Rt. Rev. Jesse Jones, 608 Cecil Street, Durham, NC 27707, Tel. 919-682-8249

St. Lucia Dist., The Rt. Rev. Carlisle Collymore, P.O. Box 51, Castries, St. Lucia, West Indies, Tel. 758-452-5835

Virginia Dist., The Rt. Rev. Albert Augson, 1406 Melton Ave., Richmond, VA 23223, Tel. 804-222-0463

West Virginia Dist., The Rt. Rev. Alvester McConnell, Route 3, Box 263, Bluefield, WV 24701, Tel. 304-248-8046

Western North Carolina Dist., The Rt. Rev. Elijah Williams, 901 Briarwood St., Reidsville, NC 27320-7020, Tel. 336-349-7275

Periodicals

The Holiness Union; The United Holy Church General Church Organ

United House of Prayer

The United House of Prayer was founded and organized as a hierarchical church in the 1920s by the late Bishop C. M. Grace, who had built the first House of Prayer in 1919 in West Wareham, MA, with his own hands. The purpose of the organization is to establish, maintain and perpetuate the doctrine of Christianity and the Apostolic Faith throughout the world among all people; to erect and maintain houses of prayer and worship where all people may gather for prayer and to worship the almighty God in spirit and in truth, irrespective of denomination or creed, and to maintain the Apostolic faith of the Lord and Savior, Jesus Christ.

Headquarters

1117 7th St. NW, Washington, DC 20001 Tel. (202)289-0238 Fax (202)289-8058

Media Contact, Apostle S. Green

Officers

CEO, Bishop S. C. Madison, 1665 N. Portal Dr. NW, Washington, DC 20012 Tel. (202)882-3956 Fax (202)829-4717

NATIONAL PROGRAM STAFF

The General Assembly, Presiding Officer, Bishop S. C. Madison, 1665 N. Portal Dr. NW, Washington, DC 20012 Tel. (202)882-3956 Fax (202)829-4717

General Council Ecclesiastical Court, Clerk, Apostle R. Price, 1665 N. Portal Dr. NW, Washington, DC 20012 Tel. (202)882-3956 Fax (202)829-4717

Annual Truth & Facts Publication, Exec. Editor, Bishop S. C. Madison, 1665 N. Portal Dr. NW, Washington, DC 20012 Tel. (202)829-4717

Nationwide Building Program, General Builder, Bishop S. C. Madison, 1665 N. Portal Dr. NW,

Washington, DC 20012 Tel. (202)882-3956 Fax (202)829-4717
Special Projects, Dir., Apostle S. Green

The United Methodist Church

The United Methodist Church was formed April 23, 1968, in Dallas by the union of The Methodist Church and The Evangelical United Brethren Church. The two churches shared a common historical and spiritual heritage. The Methodist Church resulted in 1939 from the unification of three branches of Methodism—the Methodist Episcopal Church, the Methodist Episcopal Church, South, and the Methodist Protestant Church.

The Methodist movement began in 18th-century England under the preaching of John Wesley, but the Christmas Conference of 1784 in Baltimore is regarded as the date on which the organized Methodist Church was founded as an ecclesiastical organization. It was there that Francis Asbury was elected the first bishop in this country.

The Evangelical United Brethren Church was formed in 1946 with the merger of the Evangelical Church and the Church of the United Brethren in Christ, both of which had their beginnings in Pennsylvania in the evangelistic movement of the 18th and early 19th centuries. Philip William Otterbein and Jacob Albright were early leaders of this movement among the German-speaking settlers of the Middle Colonies.

Headquarters

Information InfoServ, Dir., Mary Lynn Holly, Tel. 1-800-251-8140
Email: infoserv@umcom.umc.org
Website: http://www.umc.org
Media Contact, Dir., United Methodist News Service, Thomas S. McAnally,
Tel. (615)742-5470 Fax (615)742-5469

Headquarters

Gen. Conference, Sec., Carolyn M. Marshall, 204 N. Newlin St., Veedersburg, IN 47987
Council of Bishops: Pres., Bishop George W. Bashore, 1204 Freedom Rd., Cranberry Township, PA 16066; Sec., Bishop Sharon Zimmerman Rader, 750 Windsor St., Ste. 303, Sun Prairie, WI 53590

BISHOPS AND CONFERENCE COUNCIL DIRECTORS

North Central Jurisdiction
Sec., Judith McCartney, 240 N. Sandusky St., Delaware, OH 43015 Tel. (614)363-0864
Dakotas: Bishop Michael J. Coyner, 815 25th St. S., Fargo, ND 58103-2303 Tel. (701)232-2241 Fax (701)232-2615; Richard W. Fisher, 1331 W. University Ave., P.O. Box 460, Mitchell, SD 57301-0460 Tel. (605)996-6552 Fax (605) 996-1766
Detroit: Bishop Donald A. Ott, Tel. (248)559-7000 Fax (248)569-4830; Jeffery Regan,

21700 Northwestern Hwy., Ste. 1200, Southfield, MI 48075-4917 Tel. (248)559-7000 Fax (248)569-4830
East Ohio: Bishop Jonathan D. Keaton, Tel. (330)499-3972 Fax (330)499-3279; Judith A. Olin, 8800 Cleveland Ave. NW, P.O. Box 2800, North Canton, OH 44720 Tel. (330)499-3972 Fax (330)499-3279
Illinois Great Rivers: Bishop Sharon Brown Christopher, 400 Chatham Rd., Ste. 100, Springfield, IL 62704 Tel. (217)726-8071 Fax (217)726-8074; Rev. Raymond P. Owens, P.O. Box 515, Bloomington, IL 61702-0515 Tel. (309)828-5092 Fax (309)829-8369
Iowa: Bishop Charles W. Jordan, Tel. (515)283-1991 Fax (515)283-8672; Don Mendenhall, 500 E. Court Ave., Ste. C, Des Moines, IA 50309-2019 Tel. (515)283-1991 Fax (515) 288-1906
Minnesota: Bishop John L. Hopkins, Tel. (612)870-4007 Fax (612)870-3587; James H. Perry, 122 W. Franklin Ave., #400, Minneapolis, MN 55404-2472 Tel. (612)870-0058 Fax (612) 870-1260
North Indiana: Bishop Woodie W. White, 1100 W. 42nd St., Indianapolis, IN 46208 Tel. (317)924-1321 Fax (317)924-4859; Steven Burris, P.O. Box 869, Marion, IN 46952 Tel. (765)664-5138 Fax (765)664-2307
Northern Illinois: Bishop C. Joseph Sprague, 77 W. Washington St., Ste. 1820, Chicago, IL 60602 Tel. (312)346-9766 Fax (312)214-9031; Phillip Blackwell, 8765 W. Higgins Rd., Ste. 650, Chicago, IL 60631 Tel. (773)380-5060 Fax (773)380-5067
South Indiana: Bishop Woodie W. White, 1100 W. 42nd St., Indianapolis, IN 46208 Tel. (317)924-1321 Fax (317)924-4859; Susan W.N. Ruach, Box 5008, Bloomington, IN 47407-5008 Tel. (812)336-0186 Fax (812)336-0216
West Michigan: Bishop Donald A. Ott, 21700 Northwestern Hwy., Ste. 1200, Southfield, MI 48075-4917 Tel. (248)559-7000 Fax (810) 569-4830; John R. Thompson, P.O. Box 6247, Grand Rapids, MI 49516-6247 Tel. (616)459-4503 Fax (616)459-0191
West Ohio: Bishop Judith Craig, Tel. (614)844-6200 Fax (614)781-2625; Stanley T. Ling, 32 Wesley Blvd., Worthington, OH 43085 Tel. (614)844-6200 Fax (614)781-2642
Wisconsin: Bishop Sharon Z. Rader, 750 Windsor St., Ste. 303, Sun Prairie, WI 53590 Tel. (608)837-8526 Fax (608)837-0281; Jane Follmer Zekoff, P.O. Box 620, Sun Prairie, WI 53590-0620 Tel. (608)837-7328 Fax (608) 837-8547

Northeastern Jurisdiction
Baltimore-Washington: Bishop Felton Edwin May, 110 Maryland Ave., NE, Ste. 311, Washington, DC 20002 Tel. (202)546-3110 Fax (202)546-3186; Marcus Matthews, 9720 Patuxent Woods Dr., Ste. 100, Columbus, MD 21046 Tel. (410)309-3400 Fax (410)309-9430

Central Pennsylvania: Bishop Neil L. Irons, Tel. (717)652-6705 Fax (717)652-5109; G. Edwin Zeiders, 900 S. Arlington Ave., Harrisburg, PA 17109-5086 Tel. (717)652-0460 Fax (717)652-3499

Eastern Pennsylvania: Bishop Peter D. Weaver, Tel. (610)666-9090 Fax (610)666-9181; Michelle Barlow, P.O. Box 820, Valley Forge, PA 19482-0820 Tel. (610)666-9090 Fax (610) 666-9093

New England: Bishop Susan W. Hassinger, PO Box 249, Lawrence, MA 01842-0449 Tel. (978)682-7555 Fax (978)682-9555; Lornagrace Stuart, PO Box 249, Lawrence, MA 01842-0449 Tel. (978)682-7555 Fax (978)682-9555

New York: Bishop Ernest S. Lyght, Tel. (914) 684-6922 Fax (914)997-1628; Clayton Miller, 252 Bryant Ave., White Plains, NY 10605 Tel. (914)997-1570 Fax (914)684-6874

North Central New York: Bishop Hae-Jong Kim, 1010 East Ave., Rochester, NY 14607 Tel. (716)271-3400 Fax (716)271-3404; c/o CCOM Director, P.O. Box 1515, Cicero, NY 13039 Tel. (315)699-8715 Fax (315)699-8774

Northern New Jersey: Bishop Alfred Johnson, 112 W. Delaware Ave., Pennington, NJ 08534 Tel. (609)737-3940 Fax (609)737-6962; Sherrie Dobbs, 22 Madison, Madison, NJ 07940 Tel. (201)377-3800 Fax (201)765-9868

Peninsula-Delaware: Bishop Peter D. Weaver, P.O. Box 820, Valley Forge, PA 19482-0820 Tel. (610)666-9090 Fax (610)666-9181; Jonathan Baker, 139 N. State St., Dover, DE 19901 Tel. (302)674-2626 Fax (302)674-1573

Southern New Jersey: Bishop Alfred Johnson, 112 W. Delaware Ave., Pennington, NJ 08534 Tel. (609)737-3940 Fax (609)737-6962; John A. Janka, 1995 E. Marlton Pike East, Cherry Hill, NJ 08003-1893 Tel. (609)424-1700 Fax (609)424-9282

Troy: Bishop Susan M. Morrison, 215 Lancaster St., Albany, NY 12210-1131 Tel. (518)426-0386 Fax (518)426-0347; Garry Campbell, P.O. Box 560, Saratoga Springs, NY 12866 Tel. (518)584-8214 Fax (518)584-8378

West Virginia: Bishop S. Clifton Ives, 900 Washington St., East, Charleston, WV 25301 Tel. (304)344-8330 Fax (304)344-8330; Randall Flanagan, P.O. Box 2313, Charleston, WV 25328 Tel. (304)344-8331 Fax (304)344-8338

Western New York: Bishop Hae-Jong Kim, 1010 East Ave., Rochester, NY 14607 Tel. (716)271-3400 Fax (716)271-3404; James M. Pollard, 8499 Main St., Buffalo, NY 14221 Tel. (716)633-8558 Fax (716)633-8581

Western Pennsylvania: Bishop George W. Bashore, Tel. (724)776-2300 Fax (724)776-1355; Larry Homitsky, PO Box 5002, Cranberry Township, PA 16066 Tel. (724)776-2300 Fax (724)776-1355

Wyoming: Bishop Susan M. Morrison, 215 Lancaster St., Albany, NY 12210-1131 Tel. (518) 426-0386 Fax (518)426-0347; Charles Johns, 1700 Monroe St., Endicott, NY 13761-0058 Tel. (607)757-0608 Fax (607)757-0752

South Central Jurisdiction

Exec. Sec.: Thalia Matherson, 5646 Milton St., #240, Dallas, TX 75206 Tel. (214)692-9081

Central Texas: Bishop Joe A. Wilson, Tel. (817) 877-5222 Fax (817)332-4609; Henry Radde, 464 Bailey, Ft. Worth, TX 76107-2153 Tel. (817)877-5222 Fax (817)338-4541

Kansas East: Bishop Albert F. Mutti, Tel. (913) 272-0587 Fax (913)272-9135; Dale L. Fooshee, P.O. Box 4187, Topeka, KS 66604-0187 Tel. (913)272-9111 Fax (913)272-9135

Kansas West: Bishop Albert F. Mutti, P.O. Box 4187, Topeka, KS 66604 Tel. (913)272-0587 Fax (913)272-9135; Barbara Sheldon, 9440 E. Boston, #150, Wichita, KS 67207-3600 Tel. (316)684-0266 Fax (316)684-0044

Little Rock: Bishop Janice K. Riggle Huie, 723 Center St., Little Rock, AR 72201-4399 Tel. (501)324-8019 Fax (501)324-8018; Lewis T. See, Jr., 715 Center St., Ste. 202, Little Rock, AR 72201 Tel. (501)324-8027 Fax (501)324-8018

Louisiana: Bishop Dan E. Solomon, Tel. (504) 346-1646 Fax (504)387-3662; Leslie Nichols Akin, 527 North Blvd., Baton Rouge, LA 70802-5720 Tel. (504)346-1646 Fax (504)383-2652

Missouri East: Bishop Ann B. Sherer, PO Box 6039, Chesterfield, MO 63006 Tel. (314) 891-8001 Fax (314)891-8003; Elmer E. Revelle, 870 Woods Mill Rd., #400, Ballwin, MO 63011 Tel. (314)891-1207 Fax (314)891-1211

Missouri West: Bishop Ann B. Sherer, PO Box 6039, Chesterfield, MO 63006 Tel. (314)891-8001 Fax (314)891-8003; Keith T. Berry, 1512 Van Brunt Blvd., Kansas City, MO 64127 Tel. (816)241-7650 Fax (816)241-4086

Nebraska: Bishop Joel L. Martinez, Tel. (402) 466-4955 Fax (402)466-7931; Mel Luetchens, P.O. Box 4553, Lincoln, NE 68504 Tel. (402)464-5994 Fax (402)466-7931

New Mexico: Bishop Alfred L. Norris, Tel. (505)255-8786 Fax (505)255-8738; James E. Large, 7920 Mountain Rd. NE, Albuquerque, NM 87110-7805 Tel. (505)255-8786 Fax (505) 255-8738

North Arkansas: Bishop Janice K. Riggle Huie, 723 Center St., Little Rock, AR 72201-4399 Tel. (501)324-8019 Fax (501)324-8018; Lewis T. See, 715 Center St., Ste. 202, Little Rock, AR 72201 Tel. (501)324-8034 Fax (501) 324-8018

North Texas: Bishop William B. Oden, 3300 Mockingbird Ln., P.O. Box 600127, Dallas, TX 75360-0127 Tel. (214)522-6741 Fax (214)528-4435; Mary Brooke Casad, P.O. Box 516069, Dallas, TX 75251-6069 Tel. (972)490-3438 Fax (972) 490-7216

Northwest Texas: Bishop Alfred L. Norris, 7920

163

Mountain Rd. NE, Albuquerque, NM 87110-7805 Tel. (505)255-8786 Fax (505)255-8738; Louise Schock, 1415 Ave. M, Lubbock, TX 79401-3939 Tel. (806)762-0201 Fax (806)762-0205

Oklahoma: Bishop Bruce P. Blake, Tel. (405)525-2252 Fax (405)525-2216; David Severe, 2420 N. Blackwelder, Oklahoma City, OK 73106-1499 Tel. (405)525-2252 Fax (405)525-4164

Oklahoma Indian Missionary: Bishop Bruce P. Blake, 2420 N. Blackwelder Ave., Oklahoma City, OK 73106-1499 Tel. (405)525-2252 Fax (405)525-2216; David L. Severe, 2420 N. Blackwelder Ave., Oklahoma City, OK 73106-1499 Tel. (405)525-2252 Fax (405)525-2216

Rio Grande: Bishop Raymond H. Owen, P.O. Box 781688, San Antonio, TX 78278 Tel. (210)408-4500 Fax (210)408-4515; Francisco Estrada, P.O. Box 781974, San Antonio, TX 78278 Tel. (210)408-5313 Fax (210)408-4515

Southwest Texas: Bishop Raymond H. Owen, P.O. Box 781688, San Antonio, TX 78278 Tel. (210)408-4500 Fax (210)408-4501; Jerry Jay Smith, P.O. Box 78149, San Antonio, TX 78278 Tel. (210)408-4500 Fax (210)408-4501

Texas: Bishop J. Woodrow Hearn, Tel. (713)529-7736 Fax (713)521-3724; James Foster, 5215 Main St., Houston, TX 77002-9792 Tel. (713) 521-9383 Fax (713)521-3724

Southeastern Jurisdiction

Exec. Dir.: Gordon C. Goodgame, P.O. Box 67, Lake Junaluska, NC 28745 Tel. (704)452-2881

Alabama-West Florida: Bishop William W. Morris, 424 Interstate Park Dr., Montgomery, AL 36109 Tel. (334)277-1787 Fax (334)277-0109; James William Carpenter, P.O. Drawer 700, Andalusia, AL 36420-0700 Tel. (334)222-3127 Fax (334)222-0469

Florida: Bishop Cornelius L. Henderson, P.O. Box 1747, Lakeland, FL 33802-1747 Tel. (941) 688-4427 Fax (941)687-0568; James Jennings, P.O. Box 3767, Lakeland, FL 33802 Tel. (941) 688-5563 Fax (941)680-1912

Holston: Bishop Ray W. Chamberlain, Jr., P.O. Box 51787, Knoxville, TN 37950-1787 Tel. (423)525-1809 Fax (423)673-4474; Calvin W. Maas, P.O. Box 1178, Johnson City, TN 37605-1178 Tel. (423)928-2156 Fax (423)928-8807

Kentucky: Bishop Robert C. Morgan, 2000 Warrington Way, #280, Louisville, KY 40222 Tel. (502)425-4240 Fax (502)426-5181; Rhoda Peters, 2000 Warrington Way, #280, Louisville, KY 40222 Tel. (502)425-3884 Fax (502)426-5181

Memphis: Bishop Kenneth L. Carder, 520 Commerce St., Ste. 201, Nashville, TN 37203 Tel. (615)742-8834 Fax (615)742-3726; Benny Hopper, PO Box 1257, Jackson, TN 38302 Tel. (901)427-8589 Fax (901)423-2419

Mississippi: Bishop Marshall L. Meadows, Jr.,

P.O. Box 931, Jackson, MS 39205-0931 Tel. (601)948-4561 Fax (601)948-5981; c/o CCOM Dir., P.O. Box 1147, Jackson, MS 39215 Tel. (601) 354-0515 Fax (601)948-5982

North Alabama: Bishop Robert E. Fannin, Tel. (205)322-8665 Fax (205)322-8938; Michael Stewart, 898 Arkadelphia Rd., Birmingham, AL 35204 Tel. (205)226-7954 Fax (205)226-7975

North Carolina: Bishop Marion M. Edwards, P.O. Box 10955, Raleigh, NC 27605-0955 Tel. (919)832-9560 Fax (919)834-7989; Hope Morgan Ward, P.O. Box 10955, Raleigh, NC 27605-0955 Tel. (919)832-9560 Fax (919) 834-7989

North Georgia: Bishop G. Lindsey Davis, Tel. (404)659-0002 Fax (404)577-0068; Douglas Brantley, 159 Ralph McGill Blvd. NE, Atlanta, GA 30308 Tel. (404)659-0002 Fax (404) 577-0131

Red Bird Missionary: Bishop Robert C. Morgan, 2000 Warrington Way, #280, Louisville, KY 40222 Tel. (502)425-4240 Fax (502)426-5181; Ruth Wiertzema, 6 Queendale Ctr., Beverly, KY 40913 Tel. (606)598-5915 Fax (606)598-6405

South Carolina: Bishop J. Lawrence McCleskey, Tel. (803)786-9486 Fax (803)754-9327; Charles L. Johnson, Sr., 4908 Colonial Dr., Columbia, SC 29203 Tel. (803)786-9486 Fax (803)691-0220

South Georgia: Bishop Richard C. Looney, P.O. Box 13616, Macon, GA 31208-3616 Tel. (912) 738-0048 Fax (912)738-9033; James T. Pennell, P.O. Box 20408, St. Simons Island, GA 31522-0008 Tel. (912)638-8626 Fax (912)638-5258

Tennessee: Bishop Kenneth L. Carder, 520 Commerce St., Ste. 201, Nashville, TN 37203 Tel. (615)742-8834 Fax (615)742-3726; Randall C. Ganues, P.O. Box 120607, Nashville, TN 37212 Tel. (615)329-1177 Fax (615)329-0884

Virginia: Bishop Joe E. Pennel, Jr., Tel. (804) 359-9451 Fax (804)358-7736; F. Douglas Dillard, P.O. 11367, Richmond, VA 23230-1367 Tel. (804)359-9451 Fax (804)359-5427

Western North Carolina: Bishop Charlene P. Kammerer, P.O. Box 18750, Charlotte, NC 28218 Tel. (704)535-2260 Fax (704)567-6117; Thomas R. Sigmon, P.O. Box 18005, Charlotte, NC 28218-0005 Tel. (704)535-2260 Fax (704) 567-6117

Western Jurisdiction

Alaska Missionary: Bishop Edward W. Paup, 1505 SW 18th Ave., Portland, OR 97201-2599 Tel. (503)226-1530 Fax (503)228-3189; Dale Kelley, 3402 Wesleyan Dr., Anchorage, AK 99508-4866 Tel. (907)333-5050 Fax (907) 333-2304

California-Nevada: Bishop Melvin G. Talbert, Tel. (916)374-1510 Fax (916)372-5544; James H. Corson, P.O. Box 980250, West

Sacramento, CA 95798-0250 Tel. (916)374-1516 Fax (916)372-5544

California-Pacific: Bishop Roy I. Sano, Tel. (626)568-7300 Fax (626)796-7297; Marilynn Huntington, P.O. Box 6006, Pasadena, CA 91102 Tel. (626)568-7300 Fax (626)796-7297

Desert Southwest: Bishop William W. Dew, Jr., Tel. (602)266-6956 Fax (602)266-5343; Thomas G. Butcher, 1550 E. Meadowbrook Ave., Ste. 200, Phoenix, AZ 85014-4040 Tel. (602)266-6956 Fax (602)266-5343

Oregon-Idaho: Bishop Edward W. Paup, 1505 SW 18th Ave., Portland, OR 97201-2599 Tel. (503) 226-7931 Fax (503)228-3189; James Wenger-Monroe, 1505 SW 18th Ave., Portland, OR 97201-2599 Tel. (503) 226-7931 Fax (503)226-4158

Pacific Northwest: Bishop Elias G. Galvan, 2112 Third Ave. Ste. 301, Seattle, WA 98121-2333 Tel. (206)728-7674 Fax (206)728-8442; Daniel P. Smith, 2112 Third Ave., Ste. 300, Seattle, WA 98121-2333 Tel. (206)728-7462 Fax (206) 728-8442

Rocky Mountain: Bishop Mary Ann Swenson, Tel. (303)733-5035 Fax (303)733-5047; Gary M. Keene, 2200 S. University Blvd., Denver, CO 80210-4797 Tel. (303)733-3736 Fax (303)733-1730

Yellowstone: Bishop Mary Ann Swenson, 2200 S. University Blvd., Denver, CO 80210-4797 Tel. (303)733-5035 Fax (303)733-5047; Thomas Boller, P.O. Box 2540, Billings, MT 59103 Tel. (406)256-1385 Fax (406)256-4948

AGENCIES

Judicial Council: Pres., Tom Matheny; Sec., Sally Curtis AsKew, P.O. Box 58, Bogart, GA 30622 Tel. (770)725-1543 Fax (770)725-1685

Council on Finance & Administration: Pres., Bishop Richard C. Looney; Gen. Sec., Sandra Kelley Lackore, 1200 Davis St., Evanston, IL 60201-4193 Tel. (847)869-3345 Fax (847) 869-6972

Council on Ministries: Pres., Bishop J. Woodrow Hearn; Gen. Sec., C. David Lundquist, 601 W. Riverview Ave., Dayton, OH 45406 Tel. (937) 227-9400 Fax (937)227-9407

Board of Church & Society: Pres., Bishop Charles W. Jordan; Gen. Sec., Thomas White Wolf Fassett, 100 Maryland Ave. NE, Washington, DC 20002 Tel. (202)488-5623 Fax (202)488-5619

Board of Discipleship: Pres., Bishop Mary Ann Swenson; Gen. Sec., Ezra Earl Jones, P.O. Box 840, Nashville, TN 37202 Tel. (615)340-7200 Fax (615)304-7006

Board of Global Ministries: Pres., Bishop Dan E. Solomon; Gen. Sec., Randolph Nugent, 475 Riverside Dr., New York, NY 10115 Tel. (212)870-3600 Fax (212)870-3748

Board of Higher Education & Ministry: Pres., Bishop William B. Oden; Gen. Sec., Roger Ireson, P.O. Box 871, Nashville, TN 37202 Tel. (615)340-7400 Fax (615)340-7048

Board of Pension & Health Benefits: Pres., Bishop Bruce P. Blake; Gen. Sec., Barbara Boigegrain, 1201 Davis St., Evanston, IL 60201 Tel. (847) 869-4550 Fax (847)475-5061

Board of Publications: Chpsn., W. Randolph Smith; United Methodist Publishing House, Pres. & Publisher, Neil M. Alexander, P.O. Box 801, Nashville, TN 37202 Tel. (615)749-6000 Fax (615)749-6079

Commission on Archives & History: Pres., Bishop Emilio de Carvalho; Gen. Sec., Charles Yrigoyen, P.O. Box 127, Madison, NJ 07940 Tel. (973)408-3189 Fax (973)408-3909

Comm. Christian Unity/Interrel. Concerns: Pres., Bishop Roy I. Sano; Gen. Sec., Bruce Robbins, 475 Riverside Dr., Rm. 1300, New York, NY 10115 Tel. (212)749-3553 Fax (212)749-3556

Comm. on Communication/UM Communications: Pres., Bishop Sharon Z. Rader; Gen. Sec., Judith Weidman, 810 12th Ave. S., Nashville, TN 37203 Tel. (615)742-5400 Fax (615)742-5469

Commission on Religion & Race: Pres., Bishop S. Clifton Ives; Gen. Sec., Barbara R. Thompson, 100 Maryland Ave. NE, Washington, DC 20002 Tel. (202)547-2271 Fax (202)547-0358

Commission on the Status & Role of Women: Pres., Joyce Waldon Bright; Gen. Sec., Stephanie Anna Hixon; Cecelia M. Long, 1200 Davis St., Evanston, IL 60201 Tel. (847)869-7330 Fax (847)869-1466

Commission of United Methodist Men: Pres., Bishop Raymond H. Owen; Gen. Sec., Joseph L. Harris, PO Box 860, Nashville, TN 37202-0860 Tel. (615)340-7145 Fax (615)340-1770

Periodicals

Mature Years; El Intérprete; New World Outlook; Newscope; Interpreter; Methodist History; Christian Social Action; Pockets; Response; Social Questions Bulletin; United Methodist Reporter; United Methodist Review; Quarterly Review; Alive Now; Circuit Rider; El Aposento Alto; Weavings:A Journal of the Christian Spiritual Life; The Upper Room

United Pentecostal Church International

The United Pentecostal Church International came into being through the merger of two one-ness Pentecostal organizations - the Pentecostal Church, Inc., and the Pentecostal Assemblies of Jesus Christ. The first of these was known as the Pentecostal Ministerial Alliance from its inception in 1925 until 1932. The second was formed in 1931 by a merger of the Apostolic Church of Jesus Christ with the Pentecostal Assemblies of the World.

The church contends that the Bible teaches that there is one God who manifested himself as the Father in creation, in the Son in redemption and as the Holy Spirit in regeneration; that Jesus is the name of this absolute deity and that water

165

baptism should be administered in his name, not in the titles Father, Son and Holy Ghost (Acts 2:38, 8:16, and 19:6).

The Fundamental Doctrine of the United Pentecostal Church International, as stated in its Articles of Faith, is "the Bible standard of full salvation, which is repentance, baptism in water by immersion in the name of the Lord Jesus Christ for the remission of sins, and the baptism of the Holy Ghost with the initial sign of speaking with other tongues as the Spirit gives utterance."

Further doctrinal teachings concern a life of holiness and separation, the operation of the gifts of the Spirit within the church, the second coming of the Lord and the church's obligation to take the gospel to the whole world.

Headquarters

8855 Dunn Rd., Hazelwood, MO 63042 Tel. (314)837-7300 Fax (314)837-4503

Media Contact, Gen. Sec.-Treas., Rev. C. M. Becton

Officers

Gen. Supt., Rev. Nathaniel A. Urshan

Asst. Gen. Supts.: Rev. Kenneth Haney, 7149 E. 8 Mile Rd., Stockton, CA 95212; Jesse Williams, P.O. Box 64277, Fayetteville, NC 28306

Gen. Sec.-Treas., Rev. C. M. Becton

Dir. of Foreign Missions, Rev. Harry Scism

Gen. Dir. of Home Missions, Rev. Jack Cunningham

Editor-in-Chief, Rev. J. L. Hall

Gen. Sunday School Dir., Rev. E. J. McClintock

OTHER ORGANIZATIONS

Pentecostal Publishing House, Mgr., Rev. Marvin Curry

Youth Division (Pentecostal Conquerors), Pres., Brian Kinsey, Hazelwood, MO 63042

Ladies Auxiliary, Pres., Gwyn Oakes, P.O. Box 247, Bald Knob, AR 72010

Harvestime Radio Broadcast, Dir., Rev. J. Hugh Rose, 698 Kerr Ave., Cadiz, OH 43907

Stewardship Dept., Contact Church Division, Hazelwood, MO 63042

Education Division, Supt., Rev. Arless Glass, 4502 Aztec, Pasadena, TX 77504

Public Relations Division, Contact Church Division, Hazelwood, MO 63042

Historical Society & Archives

Periodicals

World Harvest Today; The North American Challenge; Homelife; Conqueror; Reflections; Forward

The United Pentecostal Churches of Christ

In a time when the Church of Jesus Christ is challenged to send the "Evening Light Message" to the uppermost part of the Earth, a group of men and women came together on May 29, 1992 at the Pentecostal Church of Christ in Cleveland,

Ohio to form what is now called The United Pentecostal Churches of Christ.

Organized and established by Bishop Jesse Delano Ellis, II, the United Pentecostal Churches of Christ is about the business of preparing people to see the Lord of Glory. The traditional barriers of yesteryear must not keep saints or like faith apart ever again and this fellowship of Pentecostal, Apostolic Independent Churches have discovered the truth of Our Lord's Prayer in the seventeenth chapter of Saint John: "that they may all be One."

The United Pentecostal Churches of Christ is a fellowship of holiness assemblies which has membership in the universal Body of Christ. As such, we preserve the message of Christ's redeeming love through His atonement and declare holiness of life to be His requirement for all men who would enter into the Kingdom of God. We preach repentence from sin, baptism in the Name of Jesus Christ, a personal indwelling of the Holy Spirit, a daily walk with the Lord and life after death. Coupled with the cardinal truths of the Church are the age old customs of ceremony and celebration.

Headquarters

10515 Chester Ave., (at University Circle), Cleveland, OH 44106 Tel. (216)721-5935 Fax (216)721-6938

Contact Person, Asst. Gen. Sec., Rev. W. Michelle James Williams

REGIONAL OFFICE

493-5 Monroe St., Brooklyn, New York 11221 Tel. (718)574-4100 Fax (718)574-8504

Contact Person, Asst. Gen. Sec., Rev. Rodney McNeil Johnson

Officers

Presiding Bishop and Gen. Overseer, Bishop J. Delano Ellis, II, Cleveland, OH

Asst. Presiding Bishop, Bishop Carl Halloway Montgomery, II, Baltimore, MD

Secretary Gen., Bishop James R. Chambers, Brookyn, NY

Supervisor of Women's Department, Rev. Sabrina J. Ellis, Cleveland, OH

Pres. Of Pentecostal Youth Congress, Overseer Gregory Dillard, Chicago, IL

Periodicals

THE PENTACOSTAL FLAME

United Zion Church

A branch of the Brethren in Christ which settled in Lancaster County, Pennsylvania, the United Zion Church was organized under the leadership of Matthias Brinser in 1855.

Headquarters

United Zion Retirement Community, 722 Furnace Hills Pk., Lititz, PA 17543

Media Contact, Bishop, Carl Eberly, 270 Clay School Rd., Ephrata, PA 17522 Tel. (717)733-3932

Officers

Gen. Conf. Mod., Bishop Carl Eberly, 270 Clay School Rd., Ephrata, PA 17522 Tel. (717)733-3932

Asst. Mod., Rev. John Leisey

Gen. Conf. Sec., Rev. Clyde Martin

Gen. Conf. Treas., Kenneth Kleinfelter, 919 Sycamore Lane, Lebanon, PA 17042

Periodicals

Zion's Herald

Unity of the Brethren

Czech and Moravian immigrants in Texas (beginning about 1855) established congregations which grew into an Evangelical Union in 1903, and with the accession of other Brethren in Texas, into the Evangelical Unity of the Czech-Moravian Brethren in North America. In 1959, it shortened the name to the original name used in 1457, the Unity of the Brethren (Unitas Fratrum, or Jednota Bratrska).

Headquarters

4009 Hunter Creek, College Station, TX 77845

Media Contact, Sec. of Exec. Committee, Ginger McKay, 148 N. Burnett, Baytown, TX 77520

Officers

Pres., Kent Laza, 4009 Hunter Creek, College Station, TX 77845

1st Vice Pres., Rev. Michael Groseclose, 902 Church St., Belleville, TX 77418 Tel. (512)365-6890

Sec. of Exec. Committee, Ginger McKay, 148 N. Burnett, Baytown, TX 77520

Fin. Sec., Rev. Joseph Polasek, 4241 Blue Heron, Bryan, TX 77807

Treas., Arranna Jakubik, P.O. Box 408, Snook, TX 77878

OTHER ORGANIZATIONS

Bd. of Christian Educ., Dr., Donald Ketcham, 900 N. Harrison, West, TX 76691

Brethren Youth Fellowship, Pres., Jamie Brooke Bryan, 1231 Four Corners, West, TX 76691

Friends of the Hus Encampment, Jim Baletka, 727 San Benito, College Station, TX 77845

Christian Sisters Union, Pres., Janet Pomykal, P.O. Box 560, Brenham, TX 77834

Sunday School Union, Pres., Dorothy Kocian, 107 S. Barbara Dr., Waco, TX 76705

Youth Director, Kimberly Stewart, 1500 Lawnmont Dr., Apt. 208, Round Rock, TX 78664

Periodicals

Brethren Journal, Editor, Rev.Milton Maly, 6703 FM 2502, Brenham, TX 77833; Bus Mngr., Jean Maly, 6703 FM 2502, Brenham, TX 77833

Universal Fellowship of Metropolitan Community Churches

The Universal Fellowship of Metropolitan Community Churches was founded Oct. 6, 1968 by the Rev. Troy D. Perry in Los Angeles, with a particular but not exclusive outreach to the gay community. Since that time, the Fellowship has grown to include congregations throughout the world.

The group is trinitarian and accepts the Bible as the divinely inspired Word of God. The Fellowship has two sacraments, baptism and holy communion, as well as a number of traditionally recognized rites such as ordination.

This Fellowship acknowledges "the Holy Scriptures interpreted by the Holy Spirit in conscience and faith, as its guide in faith, discipline, and government." The government of this Fellowship is vested in its General Council (consisting of Elders and District Coordinators), clergy and church delegates, who exert the right of control in all of its affairs, subject to the provisions of its Articles of Incorporation and By-Laws.

Headquarters

8704 Santa Monica Blvd. 2nd Floor, West Hollywood, CA 90069-4548 Tel. (310)360-8640 x. 215 Fax (310)360-8680

Media Contact, Dir. of Communications, Maaza Mengiste

Email: communications@ufmcchq.com or mmen giste@ufmcchq.com

Website: http://www.ufmcchq.com

Officers

Mod., Rev. Elder Troy D. Perry

Vice-Mod., Rev. Elder Nancy L. Wilson

Treas., Rev. Elder Donald Eastman

Clk., Rev. Elder Darlene Garner

Elder Carlee Friesen, P.O. Box 90685, Tucson, AZ 85752

Rev. Elder Nori Rost, 214 S. Prospect St., Colorado Springs, CO 80903

Rev. Elder Hong Kia Tan, 72 Fleet Rd., Hampstead, London, NW3 2QT England

Deputy Chief Executive Officer, Margaret Mahlman, 8704 Santa Monica Blvd., 2nd Floor, West Holywood, CA 90069-4548

Press Officer, Maaza Mengiste, 8704 Santa Monica Blvd., 2nd Floor, West Hollywood, CA 90069-4548

US National Ecumenical Officer, Rev. Gwynne Guibord, 4311 Wilshire Blvd., Ste. 308, Los Angeles, CA 90010 Tel. (213)932-1516

DISTRICT COORDINATORS

Australian District, Rev. Greg Smith, MCC Sydney, P.O. Box 1237, Darlinghurst NSW 2010, Australia

Eastern Canadian District, Rev. Diane Fisher, 179 Palmer Rd. No. 411, Belleville, ON K8P 4S8 Canada

European District, Ms. Cecilia Eggleston, Email: c.m.e@btinternet.com

Great Lakes District, Judy Dale, 1300 Ambridge Dr., Louisville, KY 40207-2410 Tel. (502)897-3821

Gulf Lower Atlantic District, Rev. Jay Neely, c/o

167

First MCC of Atlanta, 1379 Tullie Rd., Atlanta, GA 30329

Mid-Atlantic District, Rev. Arlene Ackerman, P.O. Box 276, Landsville, PA 17538

Mountains & Plains District, Rev. Ken Pilot, P.O. Box 1028, St. Louis, MO 63188

Northeast District, Rev. Diane Fisher, 179 Palmer Rd. No. 411, Belleville, ON K8P 4S8 Canada

Northwest District, Mr. Chuck Harvey, 4051 E. Burnside, Portland, OR 97214

South Central District, Rev. Eleanor Nealy, P.O. Box 8231, Ft. Worth, TX 76124

Southeast District, Rev. Judy Davenport, P.O. Box 12768, St. Petersburg, FL 33733-2768

Southwest District, Don Pederson, 3600 S. Harbor Blvd., No. 183, Oxnard, CA 93035-4136

OTHER COMMISSIONS & COMMITTEES

Min. of Global Outreach, Field Dir., Rev. Judy Dahl

Commission on the Laity, Chpsn., Mel Johnson

Clergy Credentials & Concerns, Admn., Rev. Justin Tanis

Bd. of Pensions, Admn., Margaret Mahlman, 8704 Santa Monica Blvd. 2nd Floor, West Hollywood, CA 90069-4548

Ecumenical Witness & Ministry: Dir., Rev. Elder Nancy L. Wilson

UFMCC AIDS Ministry: AIDS Liaison., Rev. Elder Don Eastman

Periodicals

Keeping in Touch; UFMCC E-Mail News Service (FREE)

Volunteers of America

Volunteers of America, founded in 1896 by Ballington and Maud Booth, provides spiritual and material aid for those in need in more than 300 communities across the United States. As one of the nation's largest and most diversified human-service organizations, Volunteers of America offers more than 400 programs for the elderly, families, youth, alcoholics, drug abusers, offenders and the disabled.

Headquarters

110 South Union St., Alexandria, VA 22314-3324 Tel. (800)899-0089

Officers

Chpsn., Jean Galloway

Pres., Charles W. Gould

Periodicals

Spirit

The Wesleyan Church

The Wesleyan Church was formed on June 26, 1968, through the union of the Wesleyan Methodist Church of America (1843) and the Pilgrim Holiness Church (1897). The headquar-ters was established at Marion, Ind., and relocated to Indianapolis in 1987.

The Wesleyan movement centers around the beliefs, based on Scripture, that the atonement in Christ provides for the regeneration of sinners and the entire sanctification of believers. John Wesley led a revival of these beliefs in the 18th century.

When a group of New England Methodist ministers led by Orange Scott began to crusade for the abolition of slavery, the bishops and others sought to silence them. This led to a series of withdrawals from the Methodist Episcopal Church. In 1843, the Wesleyan Methodist Connection of America was organized and led by Scott, Jotham Horton, LaRoy Sunderland, Luther Lee and Lucius C. Matlack.

During the holiness revival in the last half of the 19th century, holiness replaced social reform as the major tenet of the Connection. In 1947 the name was changed from Connection to Church and a central supervisory authority was set up.

The Pilgrim Holiness Church was one of many independent holiness churches which came into existence as a result of the holiness revival. Led by Martin Wells Knapp and Seth C. Rees, the International Holiness Union and Prayer League was inaugurated in 1897 in Cincinnati. Its purpose was to promote worldwide holiness evangelism and the Union had a strong missionary emphasis from the beginning. It developed into a church by 1913.

The Wesleyan Church is now spread across most of the United States and Canada and 58 other countries. The Wesleyan World Fellowship was organized in 1972 to unite Wesleyan mission bodies developing into mature churches. The Wesleyan Church is a member of the Christian Holiness Partnership, the National Association of Evangelicals and the World Methodist Council.

Headquarters

P.O. Box 50434, Indianapolis, IN 46250 Tel. (317)842-0444

Email: gensecoff@aol.com

Website: http://www.wesleyan.org

Media Contact, Gen. Sec., Dr. Ronald R. Brannon, Tel. (317)570-5154 Fax (317)570-5280

Officers

Gen. Supts.: Dr. Earle L. Wilson; Dr. Lee M. Haines; Dr. Thomas E. Armiger

Gen. Sec., Dr. Ronald R. Brannon

Gen. Treas., Donald M. Frase

Gen. Director of Communications, Dr. Norman G. Wilson

Gen. Publisher, Mr. Don Cady

Evangelism & Church Growth, Gen. Dir., Dr. B. Marlin Mull

World Missions, Gen. Dir., Dr. Donald L. Bray

Local Church Educ., Gen. Dir., Dr. Ray E. Barnwell, Sr.

Student Ministries, Gen. Dir., Rev. Ross DeMerchant

Education & the Ministry, Gen. Dir., Rev. Kerry D. Kind

Estate Planning, Gen. Dir., Rev. Howard B. Castle

Wesleyan Pension Fund, Gen. Dir., Mr. Bobby L. Temple

Wesleyan Investment Foundation, Gen. Dir., Dr. John A. Dunn

Periodicals

Wesleyan Woman; The Wesleyan Advocate; Wesleyan World

Wesleyan Holiness Association of Churches

This body was founded Aug. 4, 1959 near Muncie, Indiana by a group of ministers and laymen who were drawn together for the purpose of spreading and conserving sweet, radical, scriptural holiness. These men came from various church bodies. This group is Wesleyan in doctrine and standards.

Headquarters

RR 2, Box 9, Winchester, IN 47394 Tel. (765)584-3199 Fax (717)966-4147

Media Contact, Gen. Sec.-Treas., Rev. Robert W. Wilson, R.D. 1, Box 98A, Mifflinburg, PA 17844

Officers

Gen. Supt., Rev. John Brewer

Asst. Gen. Supt., Rev. Jack W. Dulin, Rt. 2, Box 309, Milton, KY 40045 Tel. (502)268-5826

Gen. Sec.-Treas., Rev. Robert W. Wilson, R D 1, Box 98A, Mifflinburg, PA 17844 Tel. (717)966-4147

Gen. Youth Pres., Rev. Nathan Shockley, 504 W. Tyrell St., St. Louis, MI 48880 Tel. (517)681-2591

Periodicals

Eleventh Hour Messenger

Wisconsin Evangelical Lutheran Synod

Organized in 1850 at Milwaukee, Wisconsin, by three pastors sent to America by a German mission society, the Wisconsin Evangelical Lutheran Synod still reflects its origins, although it now has congregations in 50 states and three Canadian provinces. It supports missions in 26 countries.

The Wisconsin Synod federated with the Michigan and Minnesota Synods in 1892 in order to more effectively carry on education and mission enterprises. A merger of these three Synods followed in 1917 to give the Wisconsin Evangelical Lutheran Synod its present form.

Although at its organization in 1850 WELS turned away from conservative Lutheran theology, today it is ranked as one of the most conservative Lutheran bodies in the United States. WELS confesses that the Bible is the verbally inspired, infallible Word of God and subscribes without reservation to the confessional writings of the Lutheran Church. Its interchurch relations are determined by a firm commitment to the principle that unity of doctrine and practice are the prerequisites of pulpit and altar fellowship and ecclesiastical cooperation. It does not hold membership in ecumenical organizations.

Headquarters

2929 N. Mayfair Rd., Milwaukee, WI 53222 Tel. (414)256-3888 Fax (414)256-3899

Email: webbin@sab.wels.net

Website: http://www.wels.net

Dir. of Communications, Rev. Gary Baumler

Officers

Pres., Rev. Karl R. Gurgel

1st Vice-Pres., Rev. Richard E. Lauersdorf

2nd Vice-Pres., Rev. Jon Mahnke, 6001 Blossom Ave., San Jose CA 95123

Sec., Rev. Douglas L. Bode, 1005 E. Broadway, Prairie du Chien, WI 53821

OTHER ORGANIZATIONS

Executive Dir. Of Support Services, (to be named)

Bd. for Ministerial Education, Admn., Rev. John Lawrenz

Bd. for Parish Services, Admn., Rev. Wayne Mueller

Bd. for Home Missions, Admn., Rev. Harold J. Hagedorn

Bd. for World Missions, Admn., Rev. Daniel Koelpin

Periodicals

Wisconsin Lutheran Quarterly; Lutheran Parent; Lutheran Parent's Wellspring; Northwestern Lutheran; The Lutheran Educator; Mission Connection

Religious Bodies in the United States Arranged by Families

The following list of religious bodies appearing in the Directory Section of the *Yearbook* shows the "families," or related clusters into which American religious bodies can be grouped. For example, there are many communions that can be grouped under the heading "Baptist" for historical and theological reasons. It should not be assumed, however, that all denominations under one family heading are necessarily consistent in belief or practice. The family clusters tend to represent historical factors more often than theological or practical ones. These family categories provide one of the major pitfalls when compiling church statistics because there is often a tendency to combine the statistics by families for analytical and comparative purposes. Such combined totals are deeply flawed, even though they are often used as variables for sociological analysis. The arrangement by families offered here is intended only as a general guide for conceptual organization when viewing the broad sweep of American religious culture.

Religious bodies that cannot be categorized under family headings appear alphabetically and are not indented in the following list.

Adventist Bodies

Advent Christian Church
Church of God General Conference (Oregon, IL and Morrow, GA)
Primitive Advent Christian Church
Seventh-day Adventist Church

American Catholic Church
American Evangelical Christian Churches
American Rescue Workers

Anglican Bodies

The Anglican Orthodox Church
Episcopal Church
Reformed Episcopal Church

Apostolic Christian Church (Nazarene)
Apostolic Christian Churches of America
Apostolic Episcopal Church

Baptist Bodies

The American Baptist Association
American Baptist Churches in the U.S.A.
Baptist Bible Fellowship International
Baptist General Conference
Baptist Missionary Association of America
Conservative Baptist Association of America
General Association of General Baptists
General Association of Regular Baptist Churches
National Association of Free Will Baptists
National Baptist Convention of America, Inc.
National Baptist Convention, U.S.A., Inc.
National Missionary Baptist Convention of America
National Primitive Baptist Convention, Inc.
North American Baptist Conference
Primitive Baptists
Progressive National Baptist Convention, Inc.
Separate Baptists in Christ
Seventh Day Baptist General Conference, USA and Canada

Southern Baptist Convention
Sovereign Grace Believers

Berean Fundamental Church

Brethren (German Baptists)

Brethren Church (Ashland, Ohio)
Church of the Brethren
Fellowship of Grace Brethren Churches
Old German Baptist Brethren

Brethren, River

Brethren in Christ Church
United Zion Church

Christ Community Church (Evangelical-Protestant)
Christadelphians
Christian Brethren (also known as Plymouth Brethren)
The Christian Congregation, Inc.
The Christian and Missionary Alliance
Christian Union
The Church of Christ (Holiness) U.S.A.
Church of Christ, Scientist
The Church of Illumination
Church of the Living God
Church of the Nazarene

Churches of Christ—Christian Churches

Christian Church (Disciples of Christ)
Christian Churches and Churches of Christ
Churches of Christ
Churches of Christ in Christian Union

Churches of God

Church of God (Anderson, Indiana)
The Church of God (Seventh Day), Denver, Colorado

Church of God by Faith, Inc.
Churches of God, General Conference

Churches of the New Jerusalem

General Church of the New Jerusalem
The Swedenborgian Church

Conservative Congregational Christian Conference

Eastern Orthodox Churches

Albanian Orthodox Archdiocese in America
Albanian Orthodox Diocese of America
The American Carpatho-Russian Orthodox Greek Catholic Church
The Antiochian Orthodox Christian Archdiocese of North America
Apostolic Catholic Assyrian Church of the East, North American Dioceses
Apostolic Orthodox Catholic Church
Greek Orthodox Archdiocese of America
The Holy Eastern Orthodox Catholic and Apostolic Church in North America, Inc.
Holy Ukrainian Autocephalic Orthodox Church in Exile
The Orthodox Church in America
Patriarchal Parishes of the Russian Orthodox Church in the U.S.A.
The Romanian Orthodox Church in America
The Romanian Orthodox Episcopate of America
The Russian Orthodox Church Outside of Russia
Serbian Orthodox Church in the U.S.A. and Canada
True Orthodox Church of Greece (Synod of Metropolitan Cyprian), American Exarchate
Ukrainian Orthodox Church of America (Ecumenical Patriarchate)
Ukrainian Orthodox Church of the U.S.A.

The Evangelical Church Alliance
The Evangelical Church
The Evangelical Congregational Church
The Evangelical Covenant Church
The Evangelical Free Church of America
Fellowship of Fundamental Bible Churches
Free Christian Zion Church of Christ

Friends

Evangelical Friends International—North American Region
Friends General Conference
Friends United Meeting
Philadelphia Yearly Meeting of the Religious Society of Friends
Religious Society of Friends (Conservative)
Religious Society of Friends (Unaffiliated Meetings)

Grace Gospel Fellowship
House of God, Which is the Church of the Living God, the Pillar and Ground of the Truth, Inc
Independent Fundamental Churches of America/ IFCA International, Inc.
International Council of Community Churches
Jehovah's Witnesses

Latter Day Saints (Mormons)

Church of Christ
The Church of Jesus Christ of Latter-day Saints
The Church of Jesus Christ (Bickertonites)
Reorganized Church of Jesus Christ of Latter Day Saints

The Liberal Catholic Church" Province of the United States of America

Lutheran Bodies

The American Association of Lutheran Churches
Apostolic Lutheran Church of America
The Association of Free Lutheran Congregations
Church of the Lutheran Brethren of America
Church of the Lutheran Confession
Conservative Lutheran Association
The Estonian Evangelical Lutheran Church
Evangelical Lutheran Church in America
Evangelical Lutheran Synod
The Latvian Evangelical Lutheran Church in America
The Lutheran Church—Missouri Synod
Wisconsin Evangelical Lutheran Synod

Mennonite Bodies

Beachy Amish Mennonite Churches
Bible Fellowship Church
Church of God in Christ, Mennonite
Evangelical Mennonite Church
Fellowship of Evangelical Bible Churches
General Conference of Mennonite Brethren Churches
Hutterian Brethren
Mennonite Church
Mennonite Church, The General Conference
Old Order (Wisler) Mennonite Church
Old Order Amish Church
Reformed Mennonite Church

Methodist Bodies

African Methodist Episcopal Church
African Methodist Episcopal Zion Church
Allegheny Wesleyan Methodist Connection (Original Allegheny Conference)
Bible Holiness Church
Christian Methodist Episcopal Church
Evangelical Methodist Church

Free Methodist Church of North America
Fundamental Methodist Church, Inc.
Primitive Methodist Church in the U.S.A.
Reformed Methodist Union Episcopal Church
Reformed Zion Union Apostolic Church
Southern Methodist Church
The United Methodist Church
The Wesleyan Church

The Metropolitan Church Association, Inc.
The Missionary Church

Moravian Bodies

Moravian Church in America (Unitas Fratrum)
Unity of the Brethren

National Association of Congregational Christian Churches
National Organization of the New Apostolic Church of North America
National Spiritualist Association of Churches
North American Old Roman Catholic Church (Archdiocese of New York)

Old Catholic Churches

Christ Catholic Church

Oriental Orthodox Churches

Armenian Apostolic Church of America
Armenian Apostolic Church, Diocese of America
Coptic Orthodox Church
Syrian Orthodox Church of Antioch

Pentecostal Bodies

Apostolic Faith Mission of Portland, Oregon
Apostolic Faith Mission Church of God
Apostolic Overcoming Holy Church of God, Inc.
Assemblies of God
Assemblies of God International Fellowship (Independent/Not affiliated)
The Bible Church of Christ, Inc.
Bible Way Church of Our Lord Jesus Christ World Wide, Inc.
Christian Church of North America, General Council
Church of God of Prophecy
Church of God (Cleveland, Tennessee)
Church of God in Christ, International
The Church Of God In Christ
The (Original) Church of God, Inc.
Church of God, Mountain Assembly, Inc.
Church of Our Lord Jesus Christ of the Congregational Holiness Church
Elim Fellowship
Full Gospel Assemblies International
Full Gospel Fellowship of Churches and Ministers Internationa
International Church of the Foursquare Gospel

The International Pentecostal Church of Christ
International Pentecostal Holiness Church
Open Bible Standard Churches
Pentecostal Assemblies of the World, Inc.
Pentecostal Church of God
Pentecostal Fire-Baptized Holiness Church
The Pentecostal Free Will Baptist Church, Inc.
Pillar of Fire
United Holy Church of America, Inc.
United Pentecostal Church International
The United Pentecostal Churches of Christ

Polish National Catholic Church of America

Presbyterian Bodies

Associate Reformed Presbyterian Church (General Synod)
Cumberland Presbyterian Church
Cumberland Presbyterian Church in America
Evangelical Presbyterian Church
General Assembly of the Korean Presbyterian Church in America
The Orthodox Presbyterian Church
Presbyterian Church (U.S.A.)
Presbyterian Church in America
Reformed Presbyterian Church of North America

Reformed Bodies

Christian Reformed Church in North America
Hungarian Reformed Church in America
Netherlands Reformed Congregations
Protestant Reformed Churches in America
Reformed Church in America
Reformed Church in the United States
United Church of Christ

The Roman Catholic Church
The Salvation Army
The Schwenkfelder Church

Thomist Churches

Malankara Orthodox Syrian Church, Diocese of America
Mar Thoma Syrian Church of India

Triumph the Church and Kingdom of God in Christ Inc. (International)
Unitarian Universalist Association of Congregations

United Brethren Bodies

Church of the United Brethren in Christ
United Christian Church

United House of Prayer
Universal Fellowship of Metropolitan Community Churches
Volunteers of America
Wesleyan Holiness Association of Churches

4. Religious Bodies in Canada

A large number of Canadian religious bodies were organized by immigrants from Europe and elsewhere, and a smaller number sprang up originally on Canadian soil. In the case of Canada, moreover, many denominations that overlap the U.S.-Canada border have headquarters in the United States.

A final section in this directory lists churches according to denominational families. This can be a helpful tool in finding a particular church if you don't know the official name. Complete statistics for Canadian churches are found in the statistical section in chapter 3: Table 1 contains membership figures, and Table 4 contains giving figures. Addresses for periodicals are found in the directory entitled "Religious Periodicals in Canada."

Amish—please see Old Order Amish Church

The Anglican Church of Canada

Anglicanism came to Canada with the early explorers such as Martin Frobisher and Henry Hudson. Continuous services began in Newfoundland about 1700 and in Nova Scotia in 1710. The first Bishop, Charles Inglis, was appointed to Nova Scotia in 1787. The numerical strength of Anglicanism was increased by the coming of American Loyalists and by massive immigration both after the Napoleonic wars and in the later 19th and early 20th centuries.

The Anglican Church of Canada has enjoyed self-government for over a century and is an autonomous member of the worldwide Anglican Communion. The General Synod, which normally meets triennially, consists of the Archbishops, Bishops and elected clerical and lay representatives of the 30 dioceses. Each of the Ecclesiastical Provinces—Canada, Ontario, Rupert's Land and British Columbia—is organized under a Metro-politan and has its own Provincial Synod and Executive Council. Each diocese has its own Diocesan Synod.

Headquarters

Church House, 600 Jarvis St., Toronto, ON M4Y 2J6 Tel. (416)924-9192 Fax (416)968-7983, Website: www.anglican.ca

Media Contact, Dir. of Information Resources, Douglas Tindal

Email: dtindal@national.anglican.ca

GENERAL SYNOD

Primate of the Anglican Church of Canada, Most Rev. Michael G. Peers

Prolocutor, Ven. Rodney O. Andrews, Box 1168, Sault Ste. Marie, ON P6A 5N7

Gen. Sec., Ven. James B. Boyles

Treas., Gen. Synod, Mr. James Cullen

DEPARTMENTS AND DIVISIONS

Faith, Worship & Ministry, Dir., Rev. Canon Alyson Barnett-Cowan

Financial Management and Dev., Dir., Mr. James Cullen

Inform. Resources Dir., Mr. Douglas Tindal

Partnerships, Dir., Dr. Eleanor Johnson

Pensions, Dir., Mrs. Jenny Mason

Primate's World Relief and Dev. Fund, Dir., Mr. Andrew Ignatieff

METROPOLITANS (ARCHBISHOPS)

Ecclesiastical Province of: Canada, The Most Rev. Arthur G. Peters, 5732 College St., Halifax, NS B3H 1X3; Rupert's Land, -vacant-; British Columbia, The Most Rev. David P. Crawley, 1876 Richter St., Kelowna, BC V1Y 2M9 Tel. (250)762-3306 Fax (250)762-4150; Ontario, The Most Rev. Percy R. O'Driscoll, One London Place, 903-255 Queens Ave., London, ON N6A 5R8 Tel. (519)434-6893 Fax (519)673-4151

DIOCESAN BISHOPS

Algoma: The Rt. Rev. Ronald Ferris, Box 1168, Sault Ste. Marie, ON P6A 5N7 Tel. (705)256-5061 Fax (705)946-1860, Email: dioceseofalgoma@on.aibn.com

Arctic: The Rt. Rev. Christopher Williams, 4910 51st St., Box 1454, Yellowknife, NT X1A 2P1 Tel. (867)873-5432 Fax (867)873-8478, Email: cwill@internorth.com

Athabasca: The Right Rev. John R. Clarke, Box 6868, Peace River, AB T8S 1S6 Tel. (780)624-2767 Fax (780)624-2365, Email: bpath@telus planet.net

Brandon: The Rt. Rev. Malcolm A.W. Harding, Box 21009 WEPO, Brandon, MB R7B 3W8 Tel. (204)727-7550 Fax (204)727-4135, Email: bishopbdn@techplus.com

British Columbia: The Rt. Rev. Barry Jenks, 900 Vancouver St., Victoria, BC V8V 3V7 Tel. (250)386-7781 Fax (250)386-4013, Email: bishop@acts.bc.ca

Caledonia: The Rt. Rev. John E. Hannen, Box 278, Prince Rupert, BC V8J 3P6 Tel. (250)624-6013 Fax (250)624-4299, Email: bishopj@citytel.net

Calgary: Archbishop, -vacant-, #560, 1207 11th Ave., SW, Salgary, AB T3C 0M5, Tel. (403)243-3673 Fax (403)243-2182, Diocesan Email: synod@calgary.anglican.ca

Cariboo: The Right Rev. James D. Cruickshank, 5-618 Tranquille Rd., Kamloops, BC V2B 3H6 Tel. (250)376-0112 Fax (250)376-1984, Email: cariboo@sage.ark.com

Central Newfoundland: The Rt. Rev. Edward Marsh, 34 Fraser Rd., Gander, NF A1V 2E8 Tel. (709)256-2372 Fax (709)256-2396

Eastern Newfoundland and Labrador: The Rt. Rev. Donald F. Harvey, 19 King's Bridge Rd., St. John's, NF A1C 3K4 Tel. (709)576-6697 Fax (709)576-7122

Edmonton: The Rt. Rev. Victoria Matthews, 10033 - 84 Ave., Edmonton, AB T6E 2G6 Tel. (780)439-7344 Fax (780)439-6549

Fredericton: The Rt. Rev. William J. Hockin, 115 Church St., Fredericton, NB E3B 4C8 Tel. (506)459-1801 Fax (506)459-8475, Email: bishfton@nbnet.nb.ca

Huron: The Most Rev. Percy R. O'Driscoll, One London Place, 903-255 Queens Ave., London, ON N6A 5R8 Tel. (519)434-6893 Fax (519)673-4151, Email: huron@wwdc.com

Keewatin: The Rt. Rev. Gordon Beardy, 915 Ottawa St., Keewatin, ON P0X 1C0 Tel. (807)547-3353 Fax (807)547-3356

Kootenay: Archbishop, The Most Rev. David P. Crawley, 1876 Richter St., Kelowna, BC V1Y 2M9 Tel. (250)762-3306 Fax (250)762-4150, Email: diocese_of_kootenay@bc.sympatico.ca

Montreal: The Rt. Rev. Andrew S. Hutchison, 1444 Union Ave., Montreal, QC H3A 2B8 Tel. (514)843-6577 Fax (514)843-3221, Email: bishops.office@montreal.anglican.ca

Moosonee: The Rt. Rev. Caleb J. Lawrence, Box 841, Schumacher, ON P0N 1G0 Tel. (705)360-1129 Fax (705)360-1120, Email: lawrence@ntl.sympatico.ca

New Westminster: The Rt. Rev. Michael C. Ingham, 580-401 W. Georgia St., Vancouver, BC V6B 5A1 Tel. (604)684-6306 Fax (604)684-7017

Niagara: The Rt. Rev. Ralph Spence, 252 James St. N., Hamilton, ON L8R 2L3 Tel. (905)527-1278 Fax (905)527-1281

Nova Scotia: The Most Rev. Arthur G. Peters, 5732 College St., Halifax, NS B3H 1X3 Tel. (902)420-0717 Fax (902)425-0717, Email: diocese@fox.nstn.ca

Ontario: The Rt. Rev. Peter Mason, 90 Johnson St., Kingston, ON K7L 1X7 Tel. (613)544-4774 Fax (613)547-3745, Email: pmason@ontario.anglican.ca

Ottawa: The Rt. Rev. Peter R. Coffin, 71 Bronson Ave., Ottawa, ON K1R 6G6 Tel. (613)232-7124 Fax (613)232-7088

Qu'Appelle: The Rt. Rev. Duncan D. Wallace, 1501 College Ave., Regina, SK S4P 1B8 Tel. (306)522-1608 Fax (306)352-6808, Email: quappelle@sk.sympatico.ca

Quebec: The Rt. Rev. Bruce Stavert, 31 rue des Jardins, Quebec, QC G1R 4L6 Tel. (418)692-3858 Fax (418)692-3876, Email: bdstav-que@msn.com

Rupert's Land: -vacant-, 935 Nesbitt Bay, Winnipeg, MB R3T 1W6 Tel. (204)453-6130 Fax (204)452-3915, Email: diocese@escape.ca

Saskatchewan: The Rt. Rev. Anthony Burton, 1308 5th Ave. East, Prince Albert, SK S6V 2H7 Tel. (306)763-2455 Fax (306)764-5172, Email: burton@sk.sympatico.ca

Saskatoon: The Rt. Rev. Thomas O. Morgan, Box 1965, Saskatoon, SK S7K 3S5 Tel. (306)244-5651 Fax (306)933-4606

Toronto: The Rt. Rev. Terence E. Finlay, 135 Adelaide St. East, Toronto, ON M5C 1L8 Tel. (416)363-6021 Fax (416)363-3683, Email: tfinlay@toronto.anglican.ca

Western Newfoundland: The Rt. Rev. Leonard Whitten, 25 Main St., Corner Brook, NF A2H 1C2 Tel. (709)639-8712 Fax (709)639-1636, Email: dsown@nf.sympatico.ca

Yukon: The Rt. Rev. Terry Buckle, Box 4247, Whitehorse, YT Y1A 3T3 Tel. (867)667-7746 Fax (867)667-6125, Email: dioyuktb@yukon. net

Periodicals

Anglican Journal (National Newspaper); Ministry Matters

The Antiochian Orthodox Christian Archdiocese of North America

The approximately 100,000 members of the Antiochian Orthodox community in Canada are under the jurisdiction of the Antiochian Orthodox Christian Archdiocese of North America with headquarters in Englewood, N.J. There are churches in Edmonton, Winnipeg, Halifax, London, Ottawa, Toronto, Windsor, Montreal Saskatoon, Hamilton, Vancouver, Charlottestown, PEI.

Headquarters

Metropolitan Philip Saliba, 358 Mountain Rd., Englewood, NJ 07631 Tel. (201)871-1355 Fax (201)871-7954

Website: http://www.antiochian.com

Media Contact, Rev. Fr. Thomas Zain, 52 78th St., Brooklyn, NY 11209 Tel. (718)748-7940 Fax (718)855-3608

Periodicals

The Word; Again; Handmaiden

Apostolic Christian Church (Nazarene)

This church was formed in Canada as a result of immigration from various European countries. The body began as a movement originated by the Rev. S. H. Froehlich, a Swiss pastor, whose followers are still found in Switzerland and Central Europe.

Headquarters

Apostolic Christian Church Foundation, 1135 Sholey Rd., Richmond, VA 23231 Tel. (804)222-1943

Media Contact, James Hodges

Officers

Exec. Dir., James Hodges

The Apostolic Church in Canada

The Apostolic Church in Canada is affiliated with the worldwide organization of the Apostolic

Church with headquarters in Great Britain. A product of the Welsh Revival (1904 to 1908), its Canadian beginnings originated in Nova Scotia in 1927. Today its main centers are in Nova Scotia, Ontario and Quebec. This church is evangelical, fundamental and Pentecostal, with special emphasis on the ministry gifts listed in Ephesians 4:11-12.

Headquarters
27 Castlefield Ave., Toronto, ON M4R 1G3
Media Contact, Pres., Rev. John Kristensen, 685 Park St. S., Peterborough, ON K9J 3S9 Tel. (705)742-1618

Officers
Pres., Rev. John Kristensen, 685 Park St. S., Peterborough, ON K9J 3S9 Tel. (705)742-1618
Natl. Sec., Rev. J. Karl Thomas, 22 Malamute Cres., Scarborough, ON M1T 2C7 Tel. (416)298-0977

Apostolic Church of Pentecost of Canada Inc.

This body was founded in 1921 at Winnipeg, Manitoba, by Pastor Frank Small. Doctrines include belief in eternal salvation by the grace of God, baptism of the Holy Spirit with the evidence of speaking in tongues, water baptism by immersion in the name of the Lord Jesus Christ.

Headquarters
#119-2340 Degasus Way NE, Calgary, AB T2E 8M5
Email: acop@compuserve.com
Website: www.acop.ca
Media Contact, Admn., Rev. Wes Mills, Tel. (403)273-5777 Fax (403)273-8102

Officers
Mod., Rev. G. Killam
Admin., Rev. Wes Mills

Periodicals
Fellowship Focus; Harvest Time

Armenian Holy Apostolic Church—Canadian Diocese

The Canadian branch of the ancient Church of Armenia founded in A.D. 301 by St. Gregory the Illuminator was established in Canada at St. Catharines, Ontario, in 1930. The diocesan organization is under the jurisdiction of the Holy See of Etchmiadzin, Armenia. The Diocese has churches in St. Catharines, Hamilton, Toronto, Ottawa, Vancouver, Mississauga, Montreal, Laval, Windsor, Halifax, Winnipeg, Edmonton and Calgary.

Headquarters
Diocesan Offices: Primate, Canadian Diocese, Archbishop Hovnan Derderian, 615 Stuart Ave., Outremont, QC H2V 3H2 Tel. (514)276-9479 Fax (514)276-9960, Email: adiocese@aol.com; Website: www.canarmdiocese.org

Media Contact, Exec. Dir., ArminÈ Keuchgerian; Silva Mangassarian, Secretary

Officers
Exec. Dir, Armine Keuchgerian
Sec., Silva Mangassarian
Webmaster, Garen Migirditzian

Armenian Evangelical Church

Founded in 1960 by immigrant Armenian evangelical families from the Middle East, this body is conservative doctrinally, with an evangelical, biblical emphasis. The polity of churches within the group differ with congregationalism being dominant, but there are presbyterian Armenian Evangelical churches as well. Most of the local churches have joined main-line denominations. All of the remaining Armenian Evangelical (congregational or presbyterian) local churches in the United States and Canada have joined with the Armenian Evangelical Union of North America.

Headquarters
Armenian Evangelical Church of Toronto, 2851 John St., P.O. Box 42015, Markham, ON L3R 5R0 Tel. (905)305-8144
Media Contact, Chief Editor, Rev. Yessayi Sarmazian

A.E.U.N.A. Officers
Min. to the Union, Rev. Karl Avakian, 1789 E. Frederick Ave., Fresno, CA 93720
Mod., Rev. Bernard Geulsgeugian

Officers
Min., Rev. Yessayi Sarmazian

Periodicals
Armenian Evangelical Church

Associated Gospel Churches

The Associated Gospel Churches (AGC) traces its historical roots to the 1890s. To counteract the growth of liberal theology evident in many established denominations at this time, individuals and whole congregations seeking to uphold the final authority of the Scriptures in all matters of faith and conduct withdrew from those denominations and established churches with an evangelical ministry. These churches defended the belief that "all Scripture is given by inspiration of God" and also declared that the Holy Spirit gave the identical word of sacred writings of holy men of old, chosen by Him to be the channel of His revelation to man.

At first this growing group of independent churches was known as the Christian Workers' Churches of Canada, and by 1922 there was desire for forming an association for fellowship, counsel and cooperation. Several churches in southern Ontario banded together under the leadership of Dr. P. W. Philpott of Hamilton and Rev. H. E. Irwin, K. C. of Toronto.

When a new Dominion Charter was obtained

on March 18, 1925, the name was changed to Associated Gospel Churches. Since that time the AGC has steadily grown, spreading across Canada by invitation to other independent churches of like faith and by actively beginning new churches.

Headquarters

3228 South Service Rd., Burlington, ON L7N 3H8 Tel. (905)634-8184 Fax (905)634-6283 Email: admin@agcofcanada.com
Website: http://www.agcofcanada.com/home
Media Contact, Rev. Tim Davis, c/o 3228 South Service Rd., Burlington, ON L7N 3H8 Tel. (905)634-8184 Fax (905)634-6283

Officers

Pres., —
Mod., Rev. Vern Trafford, 55 Leonard St., Kitchener, ON N2H 6C7 Tel. (519)744-8061
Sec.-Treas., Rev. Don Ralph, Box 3203, Stn. C, Hamilton, ON L8H 7K6 Tel. (905)549-4516

Association of Regular Baptist Churches (Canada)

The Association of Regular Baptist Churches was organized in 1957 by a group of churches for the purpose of mutual cooperation in missionary activities. The Association believes the Bible to be God's word, stands for historic Baptist principles, and opposes modern ecumenism.

Headquarters

130 Gerrard St. E., Toronto, ON M5A 3T4 Tel. (416)925-3261
Media Contact, Sec., Rev. W. P. Bauman, Tel. (416)925-3263 Fax (416)925-8305

Officers

Chmn., Rev. S. Kring, 67 Sovereen St., Delhi, ON N4B 1L7
Sec., Rev. W. P. Bauman

Baptist General Conference of Canada

The Baptist General Conference was founded in Canada by missionaries from the United States. Originally a Swedish body, BGC Canada now includes people of many nationalities and is conservative and evangelical in doctrine and practice.

Headquarters

4306-97 St. NW, Edmonton, AB T6E 5R9 Tel. (780)438-9127 Fax (780)435-2478
Media Contact, Exec. Dir., Rev. Abe Funk

Officers

Exec. Dir., Rev. Abe Funk, 4306-97 St. NW, Edmonton, AB T6E 5R9 Tel. (780)438-9127 Fax (780)435-2478

DISTRICTS

Central Canada Baptist Conference: Exec. Min., Rev. Alf Bell, 19-130 Ulster St., Winnipeg, MB R3T 3A2 Tel. (204)261-9113 Fax (204)261-9176

Baptist General Conference in Alberta: Exec. Min., Dr. Cal Netterfield, 5011 122nd A St., Edmonton, AB T6H 3S8 Tel. (780)438-9126 Fax (780)438-5258
British Columbia Baptist Conference: Exec. Min., Rev. Walter W. Wieser, 7600 Glover Rd., Langley, BC V2Y 1Y1 Tel. (604)888-2246 Fax (604)888-0046
Baptist General Conf. in Saskatchewan: Exec

Periodicals

BGC Canada News

The Bible Holiness Movement

The Bible Holiness Movement, organized in 1949 as an outgrowth of the city mission work of the late Pastor William James Elijah Wakefield, an early-day Salvation Army officer, has been headed since its inception by his son, Evangelist Wesley H. Wakefield, its bishop-general.

It derives its emphasis on the original Methodist faith of salvation and scriptural holiness from the late Bishop R. C. Horner. It adheres to the common evangelical faith in the Bible, the Deity and the atonement of Christ. It stresses a personal experience of salvation for the repentant sinner, of being wholly sanctified for the believer and of the fullness of the Holy Spirit for effective witness.

Membership involves a life of Christian love and evangelistic and social activism. Members are required to totally abstain from liquor and tobacco. They may not attend popular amusements or join secret societies. Divorce and remarriage are forbidden. Similar to Wesley's Methodism, members are, under some circumstances, allowed to retain membership in other evangelical church fellowships. Interchurch affiliations are maintained with a number of Wesleyan-Arminian Holiness denominations.

Year-round evangelistic outreach is maintained through open-air meetings, visitation, literature and other media. Noninstitutional welfare work, including addiction counseling, is conducted among minorities. There is direct overseas famine relief, civil rights action, environment protection and antinuclearism. The movement sponsors a permanent committee on religious freedom and an active promotion of Christian racial equality.

The movement has a world outreach with branches in the United States, India, Nigeria, Philippines, Ghana, Liberia, Cameroon, Kenya, Zambia, South Korea, Mulawi, and Tanzania. It also ministers to 89 countries in 42 languages through literature, radio and audiocassettes.

Headquarters

Box 223, Postal Stn. A, Vancouver, BC V6C 2M3 Tel. (250)492-3376
Media Contact, Bishop-General, Evangelist Wesley H. Wakefield, P.O. Box 223, Postal Station A, Vancouver, BC V6C 2M3 Tel. (250)492-3376

Bishop-General, Evangelist Wesley H. Wakefield, (Intl. Leader)

Evangelist M. J. Wakefield, Penticton, BC

Pastor Vincente & Mirasal Hernando, Phillipines

Pastor & Mrs. Daniel Stinnett, 1425 Mountain View W., Phoenix, AZ 85021

Evangelist I. S. Udoh, Abak, Akwalbom, Nigeria, West Africa

Pastor Richard & Laura Wesley, Protem, Monrovia, Liberia

Pastor Choe Chong Dee, Cha Pa Puk, S. Korea

Pastor S. A. Samuel, Andra, India

Pastors Heinz and Catherine Speitelsbach, Sardis, BC V2R 3W2

Pastor and Mrs. Daniel Vandee, Ghana, W. Africa

Periodicals

Hallelujah!

Brethren in Christ Church, Canadian Conference

The Brethren in Christ, formerly known as Tunkers in Canada, arose out of a religious awakening in Lancaster County, Pennsylvania late in the 18th century. Representatives of the new denomination reached Ontario in 1788 and established the church in the southern part of the present province. Presently the conference has congregations in Ontario, Alberta, Quebec and Saskatchewan. In theology they have accents of the Pietist, Anabaptist, Wesleyan and Evangelical movements.

Headquarters

Brethren in Christ Church, Gen. Ofc., P.O. Box A, Grantham, PA 17027-0901 Tel. (717)697-2634 Fax (717)697-7714

Canadian Headquarters, Bishop's Ofc., 2619 Niagara Pkwy., Ft. Erie, ON L2A 5M4 Tel. (905)871-9991

Media Contact, Mod., Dr. Warren L. Hoffman, Brethren in Christ Church Gen. Ofc.

Officers

Mod., Bishop Darrell S. Winger, 2619 Niagara Pkwy., Ft. Erie, ON L2A 5M4 Tel. (905)871-9991

Sec., Betty Albrecht, RR 2, Petersburg, ON N0B 2H0

Periodicals

Evangelical Visitor; "Yes", Shalom

British Methodist Episcopal Church of Canada

The British Methodist Episcopal Church was organized in 1856 in Chatham, Ontario and incorporated in 1913. It has congregations across the Province of Ontario.

Headquarters

430 Grey Street, London, ON N6B 1H3 Tel. Media Contact, Gen. Sec., Rev. Jacqueline

Collins, 47 Connolly St., Toronto, ON M6N 4Y5 Tel. (416)653-6339

Officers

Gen. Supt., Rt. Rev. Dr. Douglas Birse, R.R. #5, Thameswille, ON N0P 2K0, Tel. (519)692-3628

Asst. Gen. Supt., Maurice M. Hicks, 3 Boxdene Ave., Scarborough, ON M1V 3C9 Tel. (416)298-5715

Gen. Sec., Rev. Jacqueline Collins, 47 Connolly St., Toronto, ON M6N 4Y5 Tel. (416)653-6339

Gen. Treas., Ms. Hazel Small, 7 Wood Fernway, North York, ON M2J 4P6, Tel. (416)491-0313

Periodicals

B.M.E. Church Newsletter

Canadian and American Reformed Churches

The Canadian and American Reformed Churches accept the Bible as the infallible Word of God, as summarized in The Belgic Confession of Faith (1561), The Heidelberg Cathechism (1563) and The Canons of Dordt (1618-1619). The federation was founded in Canada in 1950 and in the United States in 1955.

Headquarters

Synod: 607 Dynes Rd., Burlington, ON L7N 2V4

Canadian Reformed Churches: Ebenezer Canadian Reformed Church, 607 Dynes Rd., Burlington, ON L7N 2V4

American Reformed Churches: American Reformed Church, 3167-68th St. S.E., Caledonia, MI 46316

Theological College, Dr. N. H. Gootjes, 110 W. 27th St., Hamilton, ON L9C 5A1 Tel. (905)575-3688 Fax (905)575-0799

Media Contact, Rev. G. Nederveen, 3089 Woodward Ave., Burlington, ON L7N 2M3 Tel. (905)681-7055 Fax (905)681-7055

Periodicals

Reformed Perspective: A Magazine for the Christian Family; In Holy Array; Evangel: The Good News of Jesus Christ; Clarion: The Canadian Reformed Magazine; Diakonia-A Magazine of Office-Bearers

Canadian Baptist Ministries

The Canadian Baptist Ministries has four federated member bodies: (1) Baptist Convention of Ontario and Quebec, (2) Baptist Union of Western Canada, (3) the United Baptist Convention of the Atlantic Provinces, (4) Union d'...glises Baptistes FranÁaises au Canada (French Baptist Union). Its main purpose is to act as a coordinating agency for the four groups for mission in all five continents.

Headquarters

7185 Millcreek Dr., Mississauga, ON L5N 5R4 Tel. (905)821-3533 Fax (905)826-3441

CANADIAN RELIGIOUS BODIES

Website: www.cbmin.org
Media Contact, Communications, David
Rogelstad
Email: daver@cbmin.org

Officers
Pres., Dr. Carmen Moir
Gen. Sec., Rev. David Phillips
Email: dphillips@cbmin.org

Baptist Convention of Ontario and Quebec

The Baptist Convention of Ontario and
Quebec is a family of 386 churches in Ontario
and Quebec, united for mutual support and
encouragement and united in missions in Canada
and the world.

The Convention was formally organized in
1888. It has two educational institutions-
McMaster Divinty College founded in 1887, and
the Baptist Leadership Education Centre at
Whitby. The Convention works through the all-
Canada missionary agency, Canadian Baptist
Ministries. The churches also support the
Sharing Way, its relief and development arm of
Canadian Baptist Ministries.

Headquarters
195 The West Mall, Ste. 414, Etobicoke, ON
M9C 5K1 Tel. (416)622-8600 Fax (416)622-
2308
Media Contact, Exec. Min., Dr. Ken Bellous

Officers
Pres., Mr. Keith Hillyer
1st Vice-Pres., Rev. Don Crisp
2nd Vice-Pres., Rev. Ian Dixon
Treas./Bus. Admn., Nancy Bell
Exec. Min., Dr. Ken Bellous
Past Pres., Rev. Rosetta O'Neal

Periodicals
The Canadian Baptist

Baptist Union of Western Canada

Headquarters
302,902-11 Ave., SW, Calgary, AB T2R 0E7
Media Contact, Exec. Min., Dr. Gerald Fisher

Officers
Pres., Mr. Bill Mains, 4576 Rainer Crescent,
Prince George, BC V2K 1X4
Exec. Min., Dr. Rev. Gerald Fisher, 302,902-11
Ave., SW, Calgary, AB T2R 0E7
Area Min., Alberta, Dr. Keith Churchill, 307,
10328-81 Ave., Edmonton, AB T6E 1X2
Area Min., British Columbia, Rev. Paul Pearce,
201, 20349-88th Ave., Langley, BC VIM 2K5
Area Min., Saskatchewan, Rev. Wayne Larson,
2155 Cross Pl., Regina, SK S4S 4C8
Carey Theological College, Principal, Dr. Brian
Stelck, 5920 Iona Dr., Vancouver, BC V6T 1J6
Baptist Resources Centre, Dr. Bernie Potrin,

Director of Learning Services, 605, 999-8
Street SW, Calgary, AB T2R 1J5

United Baptist Convention of the Atlantic Provinces

The United Baptist Convention of the Atlantic
Provinces is the largest Baptist Convention in
Canada. Through the Canadian Baptist Ministries,
it is a member of the Baptist World Alliance.

In 1763 two Baptist churches were organized
in Atlantic Canada, one in Sackville, New
Brunswick and the other in Wolfville, Nova
Scotia. Although both these churches experienced crises and lost continuity, they recovered
and stand today as the beginning of organized
Baptist work in Canada.

Nine Baptist churches met in Lower Granville,
Nova Scotia in 1800 and formed the first Baptist
Association in Canada. By 1846 the Maritime
Baptist Convention was organized, consisting of
169 churches. Two streams of Baptist life merged
in 1905 to form the United Baptist Convention.
This is how the term "United Baptist" was
derived. Today there are 554 churches within 21
associations across the Convention.

The Convention has two educational institutions: Atlantic Baptist University in Moncton,
New Brunswick, a Christian Liberal Arts
University, and Acadia Divinity College in
Wolfville, Nova Scotia, a Graduate School of
Theology. The Convention engages in world
mission through Canadian Baptist Ministries, the
all-Canada mission agency. In addition to an
active program of home mission, evangelism,
training, social action and stewardship, the
Convention operates ten senior citizen complex-
es and a Christian bookstore.

Headquarters
1655 Manawagonish Rd., Saint John, NB E2M
3Y2 Tel. (506)635-1922 Fax (506)635-0366
Email: ubcap@fundy.net
Media Contact, Interim Dir. of Communications,
Dr. Eugene M. Thompson

Officers
Pres., Dr. Robert Wilson
Vice-Pres., Dr. Rick Thomas
Exec. Min., Dr. Harry G. Gardner
Dir. of Admn. & Treas., Daryl MacKenzie
Dir. of Home Missions & Church Planting, Dr.
David Cook
Dir. of Evangelism, Dr. Malcolm Beckett
Dir. of Training, Rev. Marilyn McCormick

Union d'Eglises Baptistes Françaises au Canada

Baptist churches in French Canada first came
into being through the labors of two missionaries
from Switzerland, Rev. Louis Roussy and Mme.
Henriette Feller, who arrived in Canada in 1835.
The earliest church was organized in Grande
Ligne (now St.-Blaise), Quebec in 1838.

By 1900 there were 7 churches in the province of Quebec and 13 French-language Baptist churches in the New England states. The leadership was totally French Canadian.

By 1960, the process of Americanization had caused the disappearance of the French Baptist churches. During the 1960s, Quebec as a society, began rapidly changing in all its facets: education, politics, social values and structures. Mission, evangelism and church growth once again flourished. In 1969, in response to the new conditions, the Grande Ligne Mission passed control of its work to the newly formed Union of French Baptist Churches in Canada, which then included 8 churches. By 1990 the French Canadian Baptist movement had grown to include 25 congregations.

The Union d'Églises Baptistes FranÁaises au Canada is a member body of the Canadian Baptist Ministries and thus is affiliated with the Baptist World Alliance.

Headquarters

2285 avenue Papineau, Montreal, QC H2K 4J5 Tel. (514)526-6643 Fax (514)526-9269
Media Contact, Gen. Sec., Rev. David Affleck

Officers

Sec. Gen., Rev. David Affleck

Periodicals

Le Trait d'Union

Canadian Conference of Mennonite Brethren Churches

The conference was incorporated November 22, 1945.

Headquarters

3-169 Riverton Ave., Winnipeg, MB R2L 2E5 Tel. (204)669-6575 Fax (204)654-1865
Media Contact, Conf. Min., Reuben Pauls

Officers

Mod., Ike Bergen, 32025 Bahlstrom Ave., Rm. 302, Abbotsford, BC V2T 2K7 Tel. (604)853-6959 Fax (604)853-6990
Asst. Mod., Ralph Gliege, Box 67, Hepburn, SK S0K 1Z0 Tel. (306)947-2030
Sec., Diana MacFarlane, 46100 Chilliwack Central Rd., Chilliwack, BC V2P 1J6 Tel. (604)792-8037 Fax (604)792-4145

Periodicals

Mennonite Brethren Herald; Mennonitische Rundschau; IdeaBank; Le Lien; Expression; Chinese Herald

Canadian Convention of Southern Baptists

The Canadian Convention of Southern Baptists was formed at the Annual Meeting, May 7-9, 1985, in Kelowna, British Columbia. It was formerly known as the Canadian Baptist Conference, founded in Kamloops, British Columbia, in 1959 by pastors of existing churches.

Headquarters

Postal Bag 300, Cochrane, AB T0L 0W0 Tel. (403)932-5688 Fax (403)932-4937
Email: 70420.2230@compuserve.com
Media Contact, Exec. Dir.-Treas., Rev. Allen E. Schmidt

Officers

Exec. Dir.-Treas., Allen E. Schmidt, 128 Riverview Cir., Cochrane, AB T0L 0W4
Pres., Mr. Clarke Cremer, 2 Timmins Ave., Winnipeg, MB R2R 2M2

Periodicals

The Baptist Horizon

Canadian District of the Moravian Church in America, Northern Province

The work in Canada is under the general oversight and rules of the Moravian Church, Northern Province, general offices for which are located in Bethlehem, Pennsylvania. For complete information, see "Religious Bodies in the United States" section of the Yearbook.

Headquarters

1021 Center St., P.O. Box 1245, Bethlehem, PA 18016-1245
Media Contact, Rev. R. Burke Johnson

Officers

Pres., Ruth Humphreys, 25-23332 Twp. Rd. 520, Sherwood Park, AB T8B 1L5 Tel. (403)467-6745 Fax (403)467-0411

Canadian Evangelical Christian Churches

The Canadian Evangelical Christian Churches are associated through a common doctrine that is a combination of Calvinistic and Arminian beliefs.

Each congregation is managed independently, however ordination is supervised by the national body.

Headquarters

General Superintendent, Rev. David P. Lavigne, 410-125 Lincoln Rd., Waterloo, ON N2J J2N, Tel. (519)725-5578, Email: cecc@global serve.net

Officers

Exec. Dir., Rev. Otto Ferber
Gen. Sec., Rev. Steve Thompson
Gen. Supt., Rev. David P. Lavigne

Canadian Yearly Meeting of the Religious Society of Friends

Canadian Yearly Meeting of the Religious Society of Friends was founded in Canada as an offshoot of the Quaker movement in Great Britain and colonial America. Genesee Yearly Meeting, founded 1834, Canada Yearly Meeting (Orthodox), founded in 1867, and Canada Yearly Meeting, founded in 1881, united in 1955 to form

179

the Canadian Yearly Meeting. Canadian Yearly Meeting is affiliated with Friends United Meeting and Friends General Conference. It is also a member of Friends World Committee for Consultation.

Headquarters
91A Fourth Ave., Ottawa, ON K1S 2L1 Tel. (613)235-8553 OR (613)296-3222 Fax (613)235-1753
Email: cym@web.net
Website: http://www.web.net/-cym
Media Contact, Gen. Sec.-Treas., -

Officers
Gen. Sec.-Treas.,———
Clerk: Gale Wills
Archivist, Jane Zavitz Bond
Archives, Arthur G. Dorland, Pickering College, 389 Bayview St., Newmarket, ON L3Y 4X2 Tel. (416)895-1700

Periodicals
The Canadian Friend; Quaker Concern

The Roman Catholic Church is listed under "R".

Christ Catholic Church International

The Christ Catholic Church International, with Cathedral, churches, missions and oratories in Canada, the United States, Norway, Australia, Bosnia and Colombia South America, is an Orthodox-Catholic Communion tracing Apostolic Succession through the Old Catholic and Orthodox Catholic Churches.

The church ministers to a growing number of people seeking an experiential relationship with their Lord and Savior Jesus Christ in a Sacramental and Scripture based church. As one of the three founding members of FOCUS: Federation of Orthodox Catholic Churches United Sacramentally, CCCI is working to bring together Old and Orthodox Catholicism into one united church under the headship of Jesus Christ.

Headquarters
5165 Palmer Ave., P.O. Box 73, Niagara Falls, ON L2E 6S8 Tel. (905)354-2329 Fax (905)354-9934
Email: dwmullan@sympatico.ca
Website: http://www3.sympatico.ca/dwmullan
Media Contact, The Rt. Rev. John W. Brown, 1504-75 Queen St., Hamilton, ON L8R 3J3 Tel. (905)527-9089 Fax (905)354-9934

Officers
Presiding Bishop, The Most Rev. Donald Wm. Mullan, 6190 Barker St., Niagara Falls, ON L2E 1Y4
Archbishop, The Most Rev. Jose Ruben Garcia Matiz, Calle 52 Sur #24 A-35 - Bq. #1, Ap. 301, Santa Fe de Bogota, D.C., Colombia, South America
Episcopal Vicar, The Rt. Rev. John Wm. Brown, 1504-75 Queen St. N., Hamilton, ON L8R 3J3

Auxiliary Bishop, The Rt. Rev. Acie Angel, 1085 Wiethaupt Rd., Florissant, MO 63031
Auxiliary Bishop, The Rt. Rev. Curtis Bradley, 145 S. Garfield St., Denver, CO 80209
Auxiliary Bishop, The Rt. Rev. Gerard Laplante, 715 E. 51st Ave., Vancouver, BC V5X 1E2
Auxiliary Bishop, The Rt. Rev. Luis Fernando Hoyos Maldonado, A.A. 2437 Santa Fe de Bogota, D.C., Colombia, South America
Auxiliary Bishop, The Rt. Rev. L.M. McFerran, #206-6020 East Boulevard, Vancouver, BC C6M 3V5
Auxiliary Bishop, The Rt. Rev. Ronald K. Pace, 1411 Nursery Rd., Clearwater, FL 33756
Auxiliary Bishop, The Rt. Rev. Jose Moises Moncada Quevedo, A.A. 2437 Santa Fe de Bogota, D.C., Colombia, South America
Auxiliary Bishop, The Rt. Rev. Roger Robberstad, Pb 2624 St. Hanshaugen N-0131 Oslo, Norway

SEMINARY
St. Mary's Seminary: The Very Rev. Del Baier, 8287 Lamont, Niagara Falls, ON L2G 7L4 (offering on-site and correspondence programs)
The New Order of St. Francis: (Priests, Brothers and Sisters), Sec. General, Rev. Bro. Sean Ross, 5768 Summer St., Niagara Falls, ON L2G 1M2

Periodicals
St. Luke Magazine; The Franciscan

Christian and Missionary Alliance in Canada

A Canadian movement, dedicated to the teaching of Jesus Christ the Saviour, Sanctifier, Healer and Coming King, commenced in Toronto in 1887 under the leadership of the Rev. John Salmon. Two years later, the movement united with The Christian Alliance of New York, founded by Rev. A. B. Simpson, becoming the Dominion Auxiliary of the Christian Alliance, Toronto, under the presidency of the Hon. William H. Howland. Its four founding branches were Toronto, Hamilton, Montreal, and Quebec. By Dec. 31, 1997, there were 386 churches across Canada, with 1211 official workers, including a worldwide missionary force of 240.

In 1980, the Christian and Missionary Alliance in Canada became autonomous. Its General Assembly is held every two years.

NATIONAL OFFICE
Box 7900 Stn. B, Willowdale, ON M2K 2R6 Tel. (905)771-6747 Fax (905) 771-9874
Email: nationaloffice@cmacan.org
Media Contact, Vice-Pres. General Services, Kenneth Paton

Officers
Pres., Dr. Arnold Cook, Box 7900, Postal Sta. B, Willowdale, ON M2K 2R6

Vice-Pres./Personnel & Missions, Rev. Wallace C.E. Albrecht

Vice-Pres./Fin., Paul D. Lorimer

Vice-Pres./Canadian Ministries, Rev. C. Stuart Lightbody

Vice-Pres./Gen. Services, Kenneth Paton

DISTRICT SUPERINTENDENTS

Canadian Pacific: Rev. Brian Thom

Western Canadian: Rev. Arnold Downey

Canadian Midwest: Rev. Bob Peters

Central Canadian: Rev. David Lewis

East Canadian District: Rev. Doug Wiebe

St. Lawrence: Rev. Yvan Fournier

Christian Brethren (also known as Plymouth Brethren)

The Christian Brethren are a loose grouping autonomous local churches, often called "assemblies." They are firmly committed to the inerrancy of Scripture and to evangelical doctrine of salvation by faith alone apart from works or sacrament. Characteristics and common elements are a weekly Breaking of Bread and freedom of ministry without a requirement of ordination. For their history, see "Religious Bodies in the United States" in the Directories section of this Yearbook.

CORRESPONDENT

James A Stahr, 327 W. Prairie Ave., Wheaton, IL 60187-3408 Tel. (630)665-3757

RELATED ORGANIZATIONS

Christian Brethren Church in the Province of Quebec, Exec. Sec., Marj Robbins, P.O. Box 1054, Sherbrooke, QC J1H 5L3 Tel. (819)820-1693 Fax (819)821-9287

MSC Canada, Administrator, William Yuille, 509-3950 14th Ave., Markham, ON L3R 0A9 Tel. (905)947-0468 Fax (905)947-0352

Vision Ministries Canada, Dir., Gord Martin, P.O. Box 28032, Waterloo, ON N2L 6J8 Tel. (519)725-1212 Fax (519)725-9421

Periodicals

News of Quebec

Christian Church (Disciples of Christ) in Canada

Disciples have been in Canada since 1810, and were organized nationally in 1922. This national church seeks to serve the Canadian context as part of the whole Christian Church (Disciples of Christ) in the United States and Canada.

Headquarters

128 Woolwich St., #202, P.O. Box 64, Guelph, ON N1H 6J6 Tel. (519)823-5190 Fax (519)823-5766

Media Contact, Exec. Min., Robert W. Steffer

Officers

Mod., Mervin Bailey, 1205 Jubilee Ave., Regina, SK S4S 3S7

Vice-Mod., John Dick, RR#4, Thamesdill, ON N0P 2K0

Exec. Min., Rev. Dr. Robert W. Steffer, P.O. Box 30013, 2 Quebec St., Guelph, ON N1H 8J5

Periodicals

Canadian Disciple

Christian Reformed Church in North America

Canadian congregations of the Christian Reformed Church in North America have been formed since 1908. For detailed information about this denomination, please refer to the listing for the Christian Reformed Church in North America in Chapter 3, "Religious Bodies in the United States."

Headquarters

United States Office: 2850 Kalamazoo Ave., S.E., Grand Rapids, MI 49560 Tel. (616)224-0744 Fax (616)224-5895

Canadian Office: 3475 Mainway, P.O. Box 5070 STN LCR 1, Burlington, ON L7R 3Y8 Tel. (905)336-2920 Fax (905)336-8344

Website: http://www.crcna.org

Media Contact, Gen. Sec., Dr. David H. Engelhard, U.S. Office

Officers

Gen. Sec., Dr. David H. Engelhard, U.S. Office

Exec. Dir./Ministries, Dr. Peter Borgdorff, U.S.Office

Canadian Ministries Director, Raymond Elgersma, Canadian Office

Dir. of Fin.& Administration, Kenneth Horjus, U.S. Office

Periodicals

The Banner

Church of God (Anderson, Indiana)

This body is one of the largest of the groups which have taken the name "Church of God." Its headquarters are at Anderson, Indiana. It originated about 1880 and emphasizes Christian unity.

Headquarters

Western Canada Assembly, Chpsn., Hilda Nauenburg, 4717 56th St., Camrose, AB T4V 2C4 Tel. (780)672-0772 Fax (780)672-6888

Eastern Canada Assembly, Chpsn., Jim Wiebe, 38 James St., Dundas, ON L9H 2J6

Email: wcdncog@cable-lynx.net

Website: http://www.cable-lynx.net/~wcdncog

Media Contact for Western Canada, Church Service/Mission Coordinator, John D. Campbell, 4717 56th St., Camrose, AB T4V 2C4 Tel. (780)672-0772 Fax (780)672-6888

Periodicals

College News & Updates; The Gospel Contact; The Messenger

Church of God (Cleveland, Tennessee)

It is one of America's oldest Pentecostal churches founded in 1886 as an outgrowth of the holiness revival under the name Christian Union. In 1907 the church adopted the organizational name Church of God. It has its foundation upon the principles of Christ as revealed in the Bible. The Church of God is Christian, Protestant, foundational in its doctrine, evangelical in practice and distinctively Pentecostal. It maintains a centralized form of government and a commitment to world evangelization.

The first church in Canada was established in 1919 in Scotland Farm, Manitoba. Paul H. Walker became the first overseer of Canada in 1931.

Headquarters

Intl. Offices: 2490 Keith St., NW, Cleveland, TN 37320 Tel. (423)472-3361 Fax (423)478-7066
Media Contact, Dir. of Communications, Michael L. Baker, P.O. Box 2430, Cleveland, TN 37320-2430 Tel. (423)478-7112 Fax (423)478-7066

EXECUTIVES

Genearl Overseer: Paul L. Walker
Assistant Genearl Overseers: R. Lamar Vest, G. Dennis McGuire, T.L. Lowery
Genearl Secretary/Treasurer: Bill F. Sheeks
Canada-Eastern, Rev. Canute Blake, P.O. Box 2036, Brampton, ON L6T 3TO Tel. (905)793-2213 Fax (905)793-9173
Canada-Western, Rev. Raymond W. Wall, Box 54055, 2640 52 St. NE, Calgary, AB T1Y 6S6 Tel. (403)293-8817 Fax (403)293-8832
Canada-Quebec/Maritimes, Rev. Jacques Houle, 19 Orly, Granby, QC J2H 1Y4 Tel. (514)378-4442 Fax (514)378-8646

Periodicals

Church of God Evangel, Editorial Evangelica

Church of God in Christ (Mennonite)

The Church of God in Christ, Mennonite was organized by the evangelist-reformer John Holdeman in Ohio. The church unites with the faith of the Waldenses, Anabaptists and other such groups throughout history. Emphasis is placed on obedience to the teachings of the Bible, including the doctrine of the new birth and spiritual life, noninvolvement in government or the military, a head-covering for women, beards for men and separation from the world shown by simplicity in clothing, homes, possessions and lifestyle. The church has a worldwide membership of about 17,800, largely concentrated in the United States and Canada.

Headquarters

P.O. Box 313, 420 N. Wedel Ave., Moundridge, KS 67107 Tel. (316)345-2532 Fax (316)345-2582
Media Contact, Dale Koehn, P.O.Box 230, Moundridge, KS 67107 Tel. (316)345-2532 Fax (316)345-2582

Periodicals

Messenger of Truth

The Church of God of Prophecy in Canada

In the late 19th century, people seeking God's eternal plan as they followed the Reformation spirit began to delve further for scriptural light concerning Christ and his church. A small group of people emerged which dedicated and covenanted themselves to God and one another to be the Church of God. On June 13, 1903, A.J. Tomlinson joined them during a period of intense prayer and Bible study. Under Tomlinson's dynamic leadership, the church enjoyed tremendous growth.

In 1923 two churches emerged. Those that opposed Tomlinson's leadership are known today in Canada as the New Testament Church of God. Tomlinson's followers are called the Church of God of Prophecy.

In Canada, the first Church of God of Prophecy congregation was organized in Swan River, Manitoba, in 1937. Churches are now established in British Columbia, Manitoba, Alberta, Saskatchewan, Ontario, Quebec and all 50 states.

The church accepts the whole Bible rightly divided, with the New Testament as the rule of faith and practice, government and discipline. The membership upholds the Bible as the inspired Word of God and believes that its truths are known by the illumination of the Holy Spirit. The Trinity is recognized as one supreme God in three persons-Father, Son and Holy Ghost. It is believed that Jesus Christ, the virgin-born Son of God, lived a sinless life, fulfilled his ministry on earth, was crucified, resurrected and later ascended to the right hand of God. Believers now await Christ's return to earth and the establishment of the millenial kingdom.

Headquarters

World Headquarters: Bible Place, P.O. Box 2910, Cleveland, TN 37320-2910
National Office: Bishop Adrian L. Varlack, P.O. Box 457, Brampton, ON L6V 2L4 Tel. (905)843-2379 Fax (905)843-3990
Media Contact, Bishop Mirriam Bailey, P.O. Box 457, Brampton, ON L6V 2L4 Tel. (905)843-2379 Fax (905)843-3990

Officers

Pres., Bishop Adrian L. Varlack
V. Pres & Sec., Aston R. Morrison
Asst. Sec. & Treas., Mirriam Bailey

Periodicals

Canada Update

The Church of Jesus Christ of Latter-Day Saints in Canada

The Church has had a presence in Canada since the early 1830's. Joseph Smith and Brigham Young both came to Eastern Canada as missionaries. There are now 157,000 members in Canada in more than 400 congregations.

Leading the Church in Canada are the presidents of over 40 stakes (equivalent to a diocese). World headquarters is in Salt Lake City, UT (See U.S. Religious Bodies chapter of the Directories section of this Yearbook).

Headquarters

50 East North Temple St., Salt Lake City, UT 84150
Media Contact, Public Affairs Dir., Bruce Smith, 1185 Eglinton Ave., Box 116, North York, ON M3C 3C6 Tel. (416)424-2485 Fax (416)424-3326

Church of Jesus Christ of Latter Day Saints (Reorganized)—please see the Reorganized Church of Jesus Christ of Latter Day Saints.

Church of the Lutheran Brethren

The Church of the Lutheran Brethren of America was organized in December 1900. Five independent Lutheran congregations met together in Milwaukee, Wisconsin, and adopted a constitution patterned very closely to that of the Lutheran Free Church of Norway.

The spiritual awakening in the Midwest during the 1890s crystallized into convictions that led to the formation of a new church body. Chief among the concerns were church membership practices, observance of Holy Communion, confirmation practices and local church government.

The Church of the Lutheran Brethren practices a simple order of worship with the sermon as the primary part of the worship service. It believes that personal profession of faith is the primary criterion for membership in the congregation. The Communion service is reserved for those who profess faith in Christ as savior. Each congregation is autonomous and the synod serves the congregations in advisory and cooperative capacities.

The synod supports a world mission program in Cameroon, Chad, Japan and Taiwan. Approximately 40 percent of the synodical budget is earmarked for world missions. A growing home mission ministry is planting new congregations in the United States and Canada. Affiliate organizations operate several retirement/nursing homes, conference and retreat centers.

Headquarters

1020 Alcott Ave., W., P.O. Box 655, Fergus Falls, MN 56538 Tel. (218)739-3336 Fax (218)739-5514
Email: rmo@clba.org
Website: www.clba.org
Media Contact, Rev. David Rinden

Officers

Pres., Rev. Arthur Berge, 72 Midridge Close SE, Calgary, AB T2X 1G1
Vice-Pres., Rev. Luther Stenberg, PO Box 75, Hagen, SK S0J 1B0
Sec., Mr. Alvin Herman, 3105 Taylor Street E., Saskatoon, SK S7H 1H5

Treas., Edwin Rundbraaten, Box 739, Birch Hills, SK S0J 0G0
Youth Coord., Rev. Harold Rust, 2617 Preston Ave. S., Saskatoon, SK S7J 2G3

Periodicals

Faith and Fellowship

Church of the Nazarene in Canada

The first Church of the Nazarene in Canada was organized in November, 1902, by Dr. H. F. Reynolds. It was in Oxford, Nova Scotia. The Church of the Nazarene is Wesleyan Arminian in theology, representative in church government and warmly evangelistic.

Headquarters

20 Regan Rd., Unit 9, Brampton, ON L7A 1C3 Tel. (905)846-4220 Fax (905)846-1775
Email: nazarene@interlog.com
Website: http://web.1-888.com.nazarene/national/
Media Contact, Gen. Sec., Dr. Jack Stone, 6401 The Paseo, Kansas City, MO 64131 Tel. (816)333-7000 Fax (816)822-9071

Officers

Natl. Dir., Dr. William E. Stewart, 20 Regan Rd. Unit 9, Brampton, ON L7A 1C3 Tel. (905)846-4220 Fax (905)846-1775
Exec. Asst., John T. Martin, 20 Regan Rd. Unit 9, Brampton, ON L7A 1C3 Tel. (905)846-4220 Fax (905)846-1775
Chmn., Rev. Wesley G. Campbell, #205, 1255 56th St., Delta, BC V4L 2B9
Vice-Chmn., Rev. Ronald G. Fry, 1280 Finch Ave. W. Ste. 416, North York, ON M3J 3K6
Sec., Rev. Larry Dahl, 14320 94th St., Edmonton, AL T5E 3W2

Churches of Christ in Canada

Churches of Christ are autonomous congregations, whose members appeal to the Bible alone to determine matters of faith and practice. There are no central offices or officers. Publications and institutions related to the churches are either under local congregational control or independent of any one congregation.

Churches of Christ shared a common fellowship in the 19th century with the Christian Churches/Churches of Christ and the Christian Church (Disciples of Christ). Fellowship was broken after the introduction of instrumental music in worship and centralization of church-wide activities through a missionary society. Churches of Christ began in Canada soon after 1800, largely in the middle provinces. The few pioneer congregations were greatly strengthened in the mid-1800s, growing in size and number.

Members of Churches of Christ believe in the inspiration of the Scriptures, the divinity of Jesus Christ, and immersion into Christ for the remission of sins. The New Testament pattern is followed in worship and church organization.

Headquarters

Media Contact, Man. Ed., Gospel Herald,

Eugene C. Perry, 4904 King St., Beansville, ON L0R 1B6 Tel. (416)563-7503 Fax (416)563-7503
Email: eperry9953@aol.com

Periodicals
Gospel Herald; Sister Triangle

Conference of Mennonites in Canada

The Conference of Mennonites in Canada began in 1902 as an organized fellowship of Mennonite immigrants from Russia clustered in southern Manitoba and around Rosthern, Saskatchewan. The first annual sessions were held in July, 1903. Its members hold to traditional Christian beliefs, believer's baptism and congregational polity. They emphasize practical Christianity: opposition to war, service to others and personal ethics. Further immigration from Russia in the 1920s and 1940s increased the group which is now located in all provinces from New Brunswick to British Columbia. In recent years a variety of other ethnic groups, including native Canadians, have joined the conference. This conference is affiliated with the General Conference Mennonite Church whose offices are at Newton, Manitoba.

Headquarters
600 Shaftesbury Blvd., Winnipeg, MB R3P 0M4 Tel. (204)888-6781 Fax (204)831-5675
Media Contact, Roma Quapp

Officers
Chpsn., Ron Sawatsky, 134 Woodbend Cresc., Waterloo, ON N2T 1G9
Vice-Chpsn., Gerd Bartel, 6250 49 Ave., Delta, BC V4K 4S5
Sec., Mary Anne Loeppky, Box 973, Altona, MB R0G 0B0
Gen. Sec., Helmut Harder

Periodicals
Mennonite Reporter; NEXUS

Congregational Christian Churches in Canada

This body originated in the early 18th century when devout Christians within several denominations in the northern and eastern United States, dissatisfied with sectarian controversy, broke away from their own denominations and took the simple title "Christians." First organized in 1821 at Keswick, Ontario, the Congregational Christian Churches in Canada was incorporated on Dec. 4, 1989, as a national organization. In doctrine the body is evangelical, being governed by the Bible as the final authority in faith and practice. It believes that Christian character must be expressed in daily living; it aims at the unity of all true believers in Christ that others may believe in Him and be saved. In church polity, the body is democratic and autonomous. It is also a member of The World Evangelical Congregational Fellowship.

Headquarters
241 Dunsdon St. Ste. 405, Brantford, ON N3R 7C3 Tel. (519)751-0606 Fax (519)751-0852
Media Contact, Pres., Jim Potter, 8 Church St., Waldemar, ON L0N 1G0 Tel. (519)928-561

Officers
Pres., Jim Potter
Exec. Dir., Rev. Bruce Robertson
Sec., Rev. Alan McInnes

Periodicals
Spirit Catalyst Bi Monthly
Editor, Rev. Russ Bailey

The Coptic Orthodox Church in Canada

The Coptic Orthodox Church in North America was begun in Canada in 1964 and was registered in the province of Ontario in 1965. The Coptic Orthodox Church has spread rapidly since then. The total number of local churches in both Canada and the USA have reached seventy-four. Besides two dioceses were established a monastery with a bishop, monks and novices, as well as two theological seminaries.

The Coptic Orthodox Church is a hierarchical church and the administrative governing body of each local church is an elected Board of Deacons approved by the Bishop.

Headquarters
St. Mark's Coptic Orthodox Church, 41 Glendinning Ave., Scarborough, ON M1W 3E2 Tel. (416)494-4449 Fax (416)494-2631
Media Contact, Fr. Ammonius Guirguis, Tel. (416)494-4449 Fax (416)494-2631

Officers
Archpriest, Fr. Marcos A. Marcos
Officer, Fr. Ammonius Guirguis, 41 Glendinning Ave., Agincourt, ON M1W 3E2 Tel. (416)494-4449
Officer, Fr. Misael Ataalla

Disciples of Christ—please see Christian Church (Disciples of Christ) in Canada.

Doukhobars—please see Union of Spiritual Communities in Christ.

Elim Fellowship of Evangelical Churches and Ministers

The Elim Fellowship of Evangelical Churches and Ministers, a Pentecostal body, was established in 1984 as a sister organization of Elim Fellowship in the United States.

This is an association of churches, ministers and missionaries seeking to serve the whole body of Christ. It is Pentecostal and has a charismatic orientation.

Headquarters
379 Golf Road, RR#6, Brantford, ON N3T 5L8, Tel. (519)753-7266 Fax (519)753-5887

184

Email: elim@bfree.on.ca
Website: http://Bfree.ON.ca/comdir/churchs/elim
Ofc. Mgr., Larry Jones

Officers
Pres., Errol Alchin
Vice-Pres., John Woods, 3G Crestlea Cres. Nepean, ON N2G 4N1
Sec., Howard Ellis, 102 Ripley Cres., Kitchener, ON N2N 1V4
Treas., Aubrey Phillips, P.O. Box 208, Blairsville, GA 30512
President Emeritus, Carlton Spencer

COUNCIL OF ELDERS
Errol Alchin, Tel. (519)753-7266
Howard Ellis, Tel. (519)579-9844
Claude Favreau (819)477-7421
Aubrey Phillips, Tel. (706)745-2473
John Woods, Tel. (613)228-1796
Bernard Evans, Tel. (716)528-2790
Howard Ellis

The Estonian Evangelical Lutheran Church
The Estonian Evangelical Lutheran Church (EELC) was founded in 1917 in Estonia and reorganized in Sweden in 1944. The teachings of the EELC are based on the Old and New Testaments, explained through the Apostolic, Nicean and Athanasian confessions, the unaltered Confession of Augsburg and other teachings found in the Book of Concord.

Headquarters
383 Jarvis St., Toronto, ON M5B 2C7 Tel. (416)925-5465 Fax (416)925-5688
Media Contact, Archbishop, Rev. Udo Petersoo

Officers
Archbishop, The Rev. Udo Petersoo
Gen. Sec., Dean Edgar Heinsoo

Periodicals
Eesti Kirik

The Evangelical Covenant Church of Canada
A Canadian denomination organized in Canada at Winnipeg in 1904 which is affiliated with the Evangelical Covenant Church of America and with the International Federation of Free Evangelical Churches, which includes 31 federations in 26 countries.

This body believes in the one triune God as confessed in the Apostles' Creed, that salvation is received through faith in Christ as Saviour, that the Bible is the authoritative guide in all matters of faith and practice. Christian Baptism and the Lord's Supper are accepted as divinely ordained sacraments of the church. As descendants of the 19th century northern European pietistic awakening, the group believes in the need of a personal experience of commitment to Christ, the development of a virtuous life and the urgency of spreading the gospel to the "ends of the world."

Headquarters
2791 Pembina Highway, Winnipeg, MB R3T 2H5
Media Contact, Supt., Jeff Anderson

Officers
Supt., Rev. Jerome W. Johnson
Chpsn., Les Doell, RR 2, Wetaskiwin, AB T9A 1W9
Sec., Lori Koop, 6568 Claytonwood Pl., Surrey, BC V3S 7T5
Treas., Rod Johnson, Box 196, Norquay, SK S0A 2V0

Periodicals
The Covenant Messenger

Evangelical Free Church of Canada
The Evangelical Free Church of Canada traces its beginning back to 1917 when the church in Enchant, Alberta opened its doors. Today the denomination has nearly 144 churches from the West Coast to Quebec. Approximately 45 missionaries are sponsored by the EFCC in 10 countries. The Evangelical Free Church is the founding denomination of Trinity Western University in Langley, British Columbia. Church membership is 7,123, average attendance is 16,375.

Headquarters
Mailing Address, P.O. Box 850 LCD1, Langley, BC V3A 8S3 Tel. (604)888-8668 Fax (604) 888-3108
Location, 7600 Glover Rd., Langley, BC
Email: efcc@twu.ca
Website: www.twu.ca/efcc/efcc.htm
Media Contact, Exec. Sec., Wilma Oddsson, P.O. Box 850 LCD1, Langley, BC V3A 8S3 Tel. (604)888-8668 Fax (604)888-3108

Officers
Pres., Dr. Richard J. Penner
Mod., William Dyck, Box 170, Fosston, SK, S0E 0V0

Periodicals
The Pulse

Evangelical Lutheran Church in Canada
The Evangelical Lutheran Church in Canada was organized in 1985 through a merger of The Evangelical Lutheran Church of Canada (ELCC) and the Lutheran Church in America-Canada Section.

The merger is a result of an invitation issued in 1972 by the ELCC to the Lutheran Church in America-Canada Section and the Lutheran Church-Canada. Three-way merger discussions took place until 1978 when it was decided that only a two-way merger was possible. The ELCC was the Canada District of the ALC until autonomy in 1967.

The Lutheran Church in Canada traces its history back more than 200 years. Congregations

185

were organized by German Lutherans in Halifax and Lunenburg County in Nova Scotia in 1749. German Lutherans, including many United Empire Loyalists, also settled in large numbers along the St. Lawrence and in Upper Canada. In the late 19th century, immigrants arrived from Scandinavia, Germany and central European countries, many via the United States. The Lutheran synods in the United States have provided the pastoral support and help for the Canadian church.

Headquarters

302-393 Portage Avenue, Winnipeg, MB R3B 3H6 Tel. (204)984-9150 Fax (204)984-9185
Media Contact, Bishop, Rev. Telmor G. Sartison

Officers

Bishop, Rev. Telmor G. Sartison
Vice-Pres., Janet Morley
Sec., Mr. Robert H. Granke
Treas., William C. Risto

ASSISTANTS TO THE BISHOPS

Rev. Cynthia Halmarson
Rev. Richard Stetson

DIVISIONS AND OFFICES

Evangelical Lutheran Women, Pres., Carolyn Hertzberger
Exec. Dir., Diane Doth

SYNODS

Alberta and the Territories: Bishop, Rev. Stephen P. Kristenson, 10014-81 Ave., Edmonton, AB T6E 1W8 Tel. (403)439-2636 Fax (403)433-6623
Eastern: Bishop, Rev. Michael J. Pryse, 50 Queen St. N., Kitchener, ON N2H 6P4 Tel. (519)743-1461 Fax (519)743-4291
British Columbia: Bishop, Rev. Raymond L. Schultz, 80-10th Ave., E., New Westminster, BC V3L 4R5 Tel. (604)524-1318 Fax (604)524-9255
Manitoba/Northwestern Ontario: Bishop, Rev. Richard M. Smith, 201-3657 Roblin Blvd., Winnipeg, MB R3G 0E2 Tel. (204)889-3760 Fax (204)869-0272
Saskatchewan: Bishop, Rev. Allan A. Grundahl, Bessborough Towers, Rm. 707, 601 Spadina Cres. E., Saskatoon, SK S7K 3G8 Tel. (306)244-2474 Fax (306)664-8677

Periodicals

Canada Lutheran; Esprit

The Evangelical Mennonite Conference

The Evangelical Mennonite Conference began as a renewal movement among a small group of Dutch-German (DG) Mennonites in Southern Russia. Klaas Reimer, a Mennonite minister, was concerned about what he saw as a decline of spiritual life and discipline in the church, and inappropriate involvement in the Napoleonic War. Around 1812, Reimer and several others began

separate worship services, emphasizing a stricter discipline and separation from values and beliefs seen as dangerous. By 1814, they were organized as a separate group, called the Kleine Gemeinde (KG, small church).

Increasing pressure from the government, particularly about military conscription, led to the group's migration to North America in 1874 to 1875. Fifty families settled in Manitoba and 36 families settled in Nebraska. Ties between the two groups weakened, and eventually the U.S. group gave up its KG identity.

The KG passed through pioneer hardships and then suspicions, because of its pacifism, during times of war. It survived several schisms and migrations. Beginning in the 1940s, the church began to move away from a pattern of isolation. It developed a vision for foreign missions, began to support higher education (initially, in the area of Bible School Training), developed congregations in non-DG communities, and began to work in cooperation with other evangelical denominations and missions. It is a supporting member of Mennonite Central Committee, the relief, development, and education agency.

There has been a growing rural to urban shift. The cultural make-up of congregations is changing, though the DG background is still dominant nationally. Ten churches have pastors or ministers of non-DG background. Some churches have a multiple leadership pattern; others have new patterns. Most churches now support the leading minister full-time.

A German language magazine was published from 1935 to 1984. An English language magazine began in 1963 and continues today. The common language used in worship is English. Among churches developed among people of DG Mennonite background returning from Mexico, services can be in a mixture of Low German, High German, and English.

The church's name was changed to Evangelical Mennonite Church in 1952 and Evangelical Mennonite Conference in 1960. The conference has roughly 134 mission workers in 20 countries of the world. It has 52 congregations across British Columbia to Ontario, with 33 being in Manitoba. In 1997 its membership passed 6,600. Membership is for people baptized on confession of faith (not infants). Children are considered safe in Christ until they reach the age of accountability and opt out.

Headquarters

Box 1268, 440 Main St., Steinbach, MB R0A 2A0 Tel. (204)326-6401 Fax (204)326-1613
Email: emconf@mts.net
Media Contact, Conf. Pastor, John Koop

Officers

Acting Conf. Mod., Ralph Unger, Box 18, Grp. 3 R.R. 1, Steinbach, MB R0A 2A0
Bd. of Missions, Exec. Sec., Henry Klassen
Bd. of Missions, Foreign Sec., Lester Olfert

Bd. of Church Ministries, Exec. Sec./Editor,
Terry M. Smith
Canadian Sec., Conf. Pastor, John Koop
Conference Youth Minister, Gerald Reimer

Periodicals

The Messenger

Evangelical Mennonite Mission Conference

This group was founded in 1936 as the Rudnerweider Mennonite Church in Southern Manitoba and organized as the Evangelical Mennonite Mission Conference in 1959. It was incorporated in 1962. The Annual Conference meeting is held in July.

Headquarters

Box 52059, Niakwa P.O., Winnipeg, MB R2M 5P9 Tel. (204)253-7929 Fax (204)256-7384
Email: emmc@mb.sympatico.ca
Media Contact, John Bergman, Box 206, Niverville, MB R0A 1E0 Tel. (204)388-4775 Fax (204)388-4775
Email: jbergman@mb.sympatico.ca

Officers

Mod., David Penner, 906-300 Sherk St., Leamington, ON N8H 4N7
Vice-Mod., Carl Zacharias, R.R. 1, Box 205, Winkler, MB R6W 4A1
Sec., Darrell Dyck, R.R. 1, Box 186, Winkler, MB R6W 4A1
Dir. of Conference Ministries, Jack Heppner
Dir. of Missions, Rev. Leonard Sawatzky
Business Admin., Henry Thiessen

OTHER ORGANIZATIONS

The Gospel Message: Box 1622, Saskatoon, SK S7K 3R8 Tel. (306)242-5001 Fax (306)242-6115; 210-401-33rd St. W., Saskatoon, SK S7L 0V5 Tel. (306)242-5001;
Radio Pastor, Rev. Ed Martens

Periodicals

EMMC Recorder

The Evangelical Missionary Church of Canada

This denomination was formed in 1993 with the merger of The Evangelical Church of Canada and The Missionary Church of Canada. The Evangelical Missionary Church of Canada maintains fraternal relations with the worldwide body of the Missionary Church, Inc. and with the Evangelical Church of North America.The Evangelical Church of Canada was among those North American Evangelical United Brethren Conferences which did not join the EUB in merging with the Methodist Church in 1968. The Missionary Church of Canada is Anabaptist in heritage. Its practices and theology were shaped by the Holiness Revivals of the late 1800s. The Evangelical Missionary Church consists of 135 churches in two conferences in Canada.

Headquarters

#550 1212-31st Ave. NE, Calgary, AB T2E 7S8 Tel. (403)250-2759 Fax (403)291-4720
Media Contact, Exec. Dir., Missions and Administration, G. Keith Elliott
Email: evanmiss@emcc.ca

Officers

Pres., Rev. Mark Bolender, #550, 1212-31st Ave. NE, Calgary, AB T2E 7S8 Tel. (403)250-2759 Fax (403)291-4720
Canada East District, Dist. Supt., Rev. Phil Delsaut, 130 Fergus Ave., Kitchener, ON N2A 2H2 Tel. (519)894-9800
Canada West District, Dist. Supt., Rev. Walter Erion, #550, 1212-31st Ave. NE, Calgary, AB T2E 7S8 Tel. (403)291-5525

The Fellowship of Evangelical Baptist Churches in Canada

This organization was founded in 1953 by the merging of the Union of Regular Baptist Churches of Ontario and Quebec with the Fellowship of Independent Baptist Churches of Canada.

Headquarters

679 Southgate Dr., Guelph, ON N1G 4S2 Tel. (519)821-4830 Fax (519)821-9829
Media Contact, Pres., Rev. Terry D. Cuthbert
Email: president@fellowship.ca

Officers

Pres., Rev. Terry D. Cuthbert
Chmn., Rev. James A. Reese

Periodicals

B.C. Fellowship Baptist; The Evangelical Baptist; Intercom

Foursquare Gospel Church of Canada

The Western Canada District was formed in 1964 with the Rev. Roy Hicks as supervisor. Prior to 1964 it had been a part of the Northwest District of the International Church of the Foursquare Gospel with headquarters in Portland, Oregon.

A Provincial Society, the Church of the Foursquare Gospel of Western Canada, was formed in 1976; a Federal corporation, the Foursquare Gospel Church of Canada, was incorporated in 1981 and a national church formed.

Headquarters

#100 8459 160th St., Surrey, BC V3S 3T9
Email: fgcc@portal.ca
Media Contact, Pres. & Gen. Supervisor, Timothy J. Peterson, #100-8459 160th St., Surrey, BC V4N 1B4 Tel. (604)543-8414 Fax (604)543-8417

Officers

Pres. & Gen. Supervisor, Timothy J. Peterson

Periodicals

VIP Communique

187

Free Methodist Church in Canada

The Free Methodist Church was founded in New York in 1860 and expanded in 1880. It is Methodist in doctrine, evangelical in ministry and emphasizes the teaching of holiness of life through faith in Jesus Christ.

The Free Methodist Church in Canada was incorporated in 1927 after the establishment of a Canadian Executive Board. In 1959 the Holiness Movement Church merged with the Free Methodist Church. Full autonomy for the Canadian church was realized in 1990 with the formation of a Canadian General Conference. Mississauga, Ontario, continues to be the location of the Canadian Headquarters.

The Free Methodist Church ministers in 50 countries through its World Ministries Center in Indianapolis, Indiana.

Headquarters

4315 Village Centre Ct., Mississauga, ON L4Z 1S2 Tel. (905)848-2600 Fax (905)848-2603
Email: fmccan@inforamp.net
Website: http://www.fmc-canada.org
Media Contact, Mary-Elsie Fletcher

Officers

Bishop, Rev. Keith Elford
Dir. of Admn. Ser., Norman Bull
Dir. of Ministry Advancement, Rev. Mary-Elsie Fletcher
Supt., Personnel, Rev. Alan Retzman
Supt., Growth Ministries, Rev. Dr. Ron Bonar

Periodicals

The Free Methodist Herald

Free Will Baptists

As revival fires burned throughout New England in the mid- and late 1700s, Benjamin Randall proclaimed his doctrine of Free Will to large crowds of seekers. In due time, a number of Randall's converts moved to Nova Scotia. One such believer was Asa McGray, who was to become instrumental in the establishment of several Free Baptist churches. Local congregations were organized in New Brunswick. After several years of numerical and geographic gains, disagreements surfaced over the question of music, Sunday school, church offerings, salaried clergy and other issues. Adherents of the more progressive element decided to form their own fellowship. Led by George Orser, they became known as Free Christian Baptists.

The new group faithfully adhered to the truths and doctrines which embodied the theological basis of Free Will Baptists. Largely through Archibald Hatfield, contact was made with Free Will Baptists in the United States in the 1960s. The association was officially welcomed into the Free Will Baptist family in July 1981, by the National Association.

Headquarters

5233 Mt. View Rd., Antioch, TN 37013-2306 Tel. (615)731-6812 Fax (615)731-0771

Media Contact, Mod., Dwayne Broad, RR 3, Bath, NB E0J 1E0 Tel. (506)278-3771

Officers

Mod., Dwayne Broad
Promotional Officer, Dwayne Broad

General Church of the New Jerusalem

The Church of the New Jerusalem, also called The New Church, is a Christian Church founded on the Bible and the Writings of Emanuel Swedenborg (1688-1772). These Writings were first brought to Ontario in 1835 by Christian Enslin.

Headquarters

c/o Olivet Church, 279 Burnhamthorpe Rd., Etobicoke, ON M9B 1Z6 Tel. (416)239-3054 Fax (416)239-4935
Email: Mgladish@interlog.com
Website: http://www.newchurch.org
Media Contact, Exec. Vice-Pres., Rev. Michael D. Gladish

Officers

Pres., Rt. Rev. P. M. Buss, Bryn Athyn, PA 19009
Exec. Vice-Pres., Rev. Michael D. Gladish
Sec., Suzanna Hill, 55 Chapel Hill Dr., Kitchener, ON N2G 3W5
Treas., James Bellinger, 2 Shaver Court, Etobicoke, ON M9B 4P5

Periodicals

New Church Canadian

Greek Orthodox Metropolis of Toronto (Canada)

Greek Orthodox Christians in Canada are under the jurisdiction of the Ecumenical Patriarchate of Constantinople (Istanbul).

Headquarters

86 Overlea Blvd., Toronto, ON M4H 1C6 Tel. (416)429-5757 Fax (416)429-4588
Email: gocanada@total.net
Media Contact, Orthodox Way Committee

Officers

Metropolitan Archbishop of the Metropolis of Toronto (Canada), His Eminence Metropolitan Archbishop Sotirios

Periodicals

Orthodox Way

Independent Assemblies of God International (Canada)

This fellowship of churches has been operating in Canada for over 52 years. It is a branch of the Pentecostal Church in Sweden. Each church within the fellowship is completely independent.

Headquarters

1211 Lancaster St., London, ON N5V 2L4 Tel. (519)451-1751 Fax (519)453-3258
Media Contact, Gen. Sec., Rev. Harry Wuerch
Email: rwuerch@odyssey.on.ca

Officers

Gen. Sec., Rev. Harry Wuerch

Treas., Rev. David Ellyatt, 1795 Parkhurst Ave., London, ON N5V 2C4

Email: david.ellyatt@odyssey.on.ca

Periodicals

The Mantle

Independent Holiness Church

The former Holiness Movement of Canada merged with the Free Methodist Church in 1958. Some churches remained independent of this merger and they formed the Independent Holiness Church in 1960, in Kingston, Ontario. The doctrines are Methodist and Wesleyan. The General Conference is every three years, next meeting in 1998.

Headquarters

Rev. R. E. Votary, 1564 John Quinn Rd., R.R.1, Greely, ON K4P 1J9 Tel. (613)821-2237

Media Contact, Gen. Sec., Dwayne Reaney, 5025 River Rd. RR #1, Manotick, ON K4M 1B2 Tel. (613)692-3237

Officers

Gen. Supt., Rev. R. E. Votary, 1564 John Quinn Rd., Greeley, ON K4P 1J9

Gen. Sec., Dwayne Reaney

Additional Officers: E. Brown, 104-610 Pesehudoff Cresc., Saskatoon, SK S7N 4H5; D. Wallace, 1456 John Quinn Rd., R#1, Greely, ON K4P 1J9

Periodicals

Gospel Tidings

The Italian Pentecostal Church of Canada

This body had its beginnings in Hamilton, Ontario, in 1912 when a few people of an Italian Presbyterian Church banded themselves together for prayer and received a Pentecostal experience of the baptism in the Holy Spirit. Since 1912, there has been a close association with the teachings and practices of the Pentecostal Assemblies of Canada.

The work spread to Toronto, then to Montreal, where it also flourished. In 1959, the church was incorporated in the province of Quebec. The early leaders of this body were the Rev. Luigi Ippolito and the Rev. Ferdinand Zaffuto. The churches carry on their ministry in both the English and Italian languages.

Headquarters

6724 Fabre St., Montreal, QC H2G 2Z6 Tel. (514)593-1944 Fax (514)593-1835

Media Contact, Gen. Sec., Rev. John DellaForesta, 12216 Pierre Baillargeon, Montreal, QC H1E 6K1 Tel. (514)494-6969

Officers

Gen. Supt., Rev. Daniel Ippolito, 46 George Anderson Dr., Toronto, ON M6M 2Y8 Tel. (416)244-4005 Fax (416)244-0381

Gen. Sec., Rev. John DellaForesta, 12216 Pierre Baillargeon, Montreal, QC H1E 6K1 Tel. (514)494-6969

Gen. Treas., Rev. David Mortelliti, 6724 Fabre St., Montreal, QC H2G 2Z6 Tel. (514)593-1944 Fax (514)593-1835

Overseer, Rev. Mario Spiridigliozzi, 23 Wildwood Dr., Port Moody, BC V3H 4M4 Tel. (604)469-0788

Overseer, Rev. Tom Ciccarella, 1235 Minto Ave., LaSalle, ON N9J 3H0 Tel. (519)734-1340

Periodicals

Voce Evangelica/Evangel Voice

Jehovah's Witnesses

For details on Jehovah's Witnesses see "Religious Bodies in United States" in this edition of the Yearbook.

Headquarters

25 Columbia Heights, Brooklyn, NY 11201-2483 Tel. (718)560-5600 Fax (718)560-5619

Canadian Branch Office: Box 4100, Halton Hills, ON L7G 4Y4

Media Contact, Director, Public Affairs Office, James N. Pellechia

Media Contact, Public Affairs Office in Canada, Dennis Charland

Latter-Day Saints—please see The Church of Jesus Christ of Latter-day Saints in Canada

Lutheran Church—Canada

Lutheran Church-Canada was established in 1959 at Edmonton, Alberta, as a federation of Canadian districts of the Lutheran Church - Missouri Synod; it was constituted in 1988 at Winnipeg, Manitoba, as an autonomous church.

The church confesses the Bible as both inspired and infallible, the only source and norm of doctrine and life and subscribes without reservation to the Lutheran Confessions as contained in the Book of Concord of 1580.

Headquarters

3074 Portage Ave., Winnipeg, MB R3K 0Y2 Tel. (204)895-3433 Fax (204)897-4319

Media Contact, Dir. of Comm., Ian Adnams

Officers

Pres., Rev. Ralph Mayan, 8631 Wagner Dr., Richmond, BC V7A 4N2

Vice-Pres., Rev. Dennis Putzman, 24 Valencia Dr., St. Catharines, ON L2T 3X8

2nd Vice-Pres., Rev. Daniel Rinderknecht, Box 1 Site 11 R.R. 4, Stony Plain, AB T7Z 1X4

3rd Vice-Pres., Rev. James Fritsche, 30 Dayton Dr., Winnipeg, MB R2J 3N1

Sec., Rev. William Ney, 4906 55th Ave., Stony Plain, AB T7Z 1B5

Treas., Allan Webster, C.A.

DISTRICT OFFICES

Alberta-British Columbia: Pres., Dr. H. Ruf,

7100 Ada Blvd., Edmonton, AB T5B 4E4 Tel. (403)474-0063 Fax (403)477-9829

Central: Pres., Dr. R. Holm, 1927 Grant Dr., Regina, SK S4S 4V6 Tel. (306)586-4434 Fax (306)586-0656

East: Pres., Dr. R. Winger, 275 Lawrence Ave., Kitchener, ON N2M 1Y3 Tel. (519)578-6500 Fax (519)578-3369

Periodicals
The Canadian Lutheran

Evangelical Lutheran Church in Canada is listed under "E".

Mennonite Church (Canada)

This body has its origins in Europe in 1525 as an outgrowth of the Anabaptist movement. It was organized in North America in 1898.(See: Mennonite Church description in the section "Religious Bodies in the United States")

Headquarters
421 S. Second St., Ste. 600, Elkhart, IN 46516 Tel. (219)294-7131 Fax (219)293-3977

Email: mcgb@juno.com

Media Contact, J. Ron Byler, Associate General Secretary, Email: rbyler@juno.com

Periodicals
Canadian Mennonite (published jointly with Conference of Mennonites in Canada)

Canadian Conference of Mennonite Brethren Churches is listed under "C".

Conference of Mennonites in Canada is listed under "C".

Evangelical Mennonite Conference is listed under "E".

Evangelical Mennonite Mission Conference is listed under "E".

Reinland Mennonite Church is listed under "R".

Moravian Church—please see Canadian District of the Moravian Church in America, Northern Province

Mormons—please see The Church of Jesus Christ of Latter-Day Saints in Canada

North American Baptist Conference

Churches belonging to this conference emanated from German Baptist immigrants of more than a century ago. Although scattered across Canada and the U.S., they are bound together by a common heritage, a strong spiritual unity, a Bible-centered faith and a deep interest in missions.

Note: The details of general organization, officers, and periodicals of this body will be found in the North American Baptist Conference directory in the "Religious Bodies in the United States" section of this Yearbook.

Headquarters
1 S. 210 Summit Ave., Oakbrook Terrace, IL 60181 Tel. (630)495-2000 Fax (630)495-3301 Media Contact, Marilyn Schaer

Officers
Exec. Dir., Dr. Philip Yntema

Periodicals
N.A.B. Today

The Old Catholic Church of Canada

The church was founded in 1948 in Hamilton, Ontario. The first bishop was the Rt. Rev. George Davis. The Old Catholic Church of Canada accepts all the doctrines of the Eastern Orthodox Churches and, therefore, not Papal Infallibility or the Immaculate Conception. The ritual is Western (Latin Rite) and is in the vernacular language. Celibacy is optional.

Headquarters
RR #1, Midland, ON L4R 4K3 Tel. (705)835-6940 Media Contact, Bishop, The Most Rev. David Thomson

Officers
Vicar General and Auxiliary Bishop, The Rt. Rev. A.C. Keating, PhD., 5066 Forest Grove Crest, Burlington, ON L7L GG6 Tel. (905)331-1113

Old Order Amish Church

This is the most conservative branch of the Mennonite Church and direct descendants of Swiss Brethren (Anabaptists) who emerged from the Reformation in Switzerland in 1525. The Amish, followers of Bishop Jacob Ammann, became a distinct group in 1693. They began migrating to North America about 1720; all of them still reside in the United States or Canada. They first migrated to Ontario in 1824 directly from Bavaria, Germany and also from Pennsylvania and Alsace-Lorraine. Since 1953 some Amish have migrated to Ontario from Ohio, Indiana and Iowa.

In 1998 there were 22 congregations in Ontario, each being autonomous. No membership figures are kept by this group, and there is no central headquarters. Each congregation is served by a bishop, two ministers and a deacon, all of whom are chosen from among the male members by lot for life.

CORRESPONDENT
Pathway Publishers, David Luthy, Rt. 4, Aylmer, ON N5H 2R3

Periodicals
Blackboard Bulletin; Herold der Wahreit; The Budget; The Diary; Die Botschaft; Family Life; Young Companion

Open Bible Faith Fellowship of Canada

This is an Evangelical, Full Gospel Fellowship of Churches and Ministries emphasizing evangelism, missions and the local church for success in the present harvest of souls. OBFF was chartered January 7, 1982.

Headquarters

Word of Life Church, 310 Scott St., St. Catharines, ON L2R 6Z4 Tel. (905)646-0970
Media Contact, Exec. Dir., Randy Neilson

Officers

Pres., Peter Youngren
Exec. Dir., Randy Neilson
Sec., George Woodward
Treas., Ron Cosby, 1100 Gorham St., Ste. 11B, Newmarket, ON L3Y 7V1 Tel. (905)836-9337

Orthodox Church in America (Canada Section)

The Archdiocese of Canada of the Orthodox Church in America was established in 1916. First organized by St. Tikhon, martyr Patriarch of Moscow, previously Archbishop of North America, it is part of the Russian Metropolia and its successor, the autocephalous Orthodox Church in America.

The Archdiocesan Council meets twice yearly, the General Assembly of the Archdiocese takes place every three years. The Archdiocese is also known as "Orthodox Church in Canada."

Headquarters

P.O. Box 179, Spencerville, ON K0E 1X0 Tel. (613)925-5226 Fax (613)925-1521
Email: zoe@recorder.ca

Officers

Bishop of Ottawa & Canada, The Rt. Rev. Seraphim Chancellor, V. Rev. Dennis Pinach, 17319
Treas., Nikita Lopoukhine, 55 Clarey Ave., Ottawa, ON K1S 2R6
Eastern Sec., Olga Jurgens, P.O. Box 179, Spencerville, ON K0E 1X0
Western Sec., Deacon Andrew Piasta,

ARCHDIOCESAN COUNCIL

Clergy Members: Rev. Lawrence Farley; V. Rev. Nicolas Boldireff; Rev. R.S. Kennaugh; Rev. Larry Reinheimer; V. Rev. John Tkachuk
Lay Members: Audrey Ewanchuk; Nicholas Ignatieff; David Grier; John Hadjinicolaou; Denis Lessard; Sister Theodora (Zion); David Rystephanuk
Ex Officio: Chancellor; Treas.; Eastern Sec.; Western Sec.

REPRESENTATIVES TO METROPOLITAN COUNCIL

V. Rev. John Tkachuk
Richard Schneider

Periodicals

Canadian Orthodox Messenger

Patriarchal Parishes of the Russian Orthodox Church in Canada

This is the diocese of Canada of the former Exarchate of North and South America of the Russian Orthodox Church. It was originally founded in 1897 by the Russian Orthodox Archdiocese in North America.

Headquarters

St. Barbara's Russian Orthodox Cathedral, 10105 96th St., Edmonton, AB T5H 2G3
Media Contact, Sec.-Treas., Victor Lopushinsky, #303 9566-101 Ave., Edmonton, AB T5H 0B4 Tel. (780)455-9071

Officers

Admn., Archbishop of Kashira, Most Rev. Mark, 10812-108 St., Edmonton, AB T5H 3A6 Tel. (780)420-9945

The Pentecostal Assemblies of Canada

This body is incorporated under the Dominion Charter of 1919 and is also recognized in the Province of Quebec as an ecclesiastical corporation. Its beginnings are to be found in the revivals at the turn of the century, and most of the first Canadian Pentecostal leaders came from a religious background rooted in the Holiness movements.

The original incorporation of 1919 was implemented among churches of eastern Canada only. In the same year, a conference was called in Moose Jaw, Saskatchewan, to which the late Rev. J. M. Welch, general superintendent of the then-organized Assemblies of God in the U.S., was invited. The churches of Manitoba and Saskatchewan were organized as the Western District Council of the Assemblies of God. They were joined later by Alberta and British Columbia. In 1921, a conference was held in Montreal, to which the general chairman of the Assemblies of God was invited. Eastern Canada also became a district of the Assemblies of God, joining Eastern and Western Canada as two districts in a single organizational union.

In 1920, at Kitchener, Ontario, eastern and western churches agreed to dissolve the Canadian District of the Assemblies of God and unite under the name The Pentecostal Assemblies of Canada.

Today the Pentecostal Assemblies of Canada operates throughout the nation and in about 30 countries around the world. Religious services are conducted in more than 25 different languages in the 1,100 local churches in Canada. Members and adherents number about 230,000. The number of local churches includes approximately 100 Native congregations.

Headquarters

6745 Century Ave., Mississauga, ON L5N 6P7 Tel. (905)542-7400 Fax (905)542-7313
Media Contact, Public Relations, Rev. W. A. Griffin
Email: wgriffin@paoc.org

Officers

Gen. Supt., Rev. William D. Morrow
Asst. Gen. Supt., Rev. E. Stewart Hunter
Gen. Sec.-Treas., Rev. David Ball

DISTRICT SUPERINTENDENTS

British Columbia: Rev. William R. Gibson, 5641 176 A St., Surrey, BC V3S 4G8 Tel. (604)576-9421 Fax (604)576-1499

Alberta: Rev. Lorne D. McAlister, 10585-111 St., #101, Edmonton, AB T5H 3E8 Tel. (403)426-0084 Fax (403)420-1318

Saskatchewan: Rev. Samuel O. Biro, 3488 Fairlight Dr., Saskatoon, SK S7M 3Z4 Tel. (306)652-6088 Fax (306)652-0199

Manitoba: Rev. Gordon V. Peters, 187 Henlow Bay, Winnipeg, MB R3Y 1G4 Tel. (204)488-6800 Fax (204)489-0499

Western Ontario: Rev. David Shepherd, 3214 S. Service Rd., Burlington, ON L7M 3J2 Tel. (905)637-5566 Fax (905)637-7558

Eastern Ontario and Quebec: Rev. Richard Hilsden, Box 13250, Kanata, ON K2K 1X4 Tel. (613)599-3422 Fax (613)599-7284

Maritime Provinces: Rev. David C. Slauenwhite, Box 1184, Truro, NS B2N 5H1 Tel. (902)895-4212 Fax (902)897-0705

BRANCH CONFERENCES

German Conference: Rev. Philip F. Kniesel, #310, 684 Belmont Ave., W, Kitchener, ON N2M 1N6

Slavic Conferences: Eastern District, Rev. A. Muravski, 44 Glenabbey Dr. Courtice, ON L1E 1B7; Western District, Rev. Michael Brandebura, 4108-134 Ave., Edmonton, AB T5A 3M2

Finnish Conference: Rev. E. Ahonen, 1920 Argyle Dr., Vancouver, BC V5P 2A8

Periodicals

Pentecostal Testimony; Resource: The National Leadership Magazine

Pentecostal Assemblies of Newfoundland

This body began in 1911 and held its first meetings at Bethesda Mission at St. John's. It was incorporated in 1925 as The Bethesda Pentecostal Assemblies of Newfoundland and changed its name in 1930 to The Pentecostal Assemblies of Newfoundland.

Headquarters

57 Thorburn Rd., Box 8895, Stn. "A", St. John's, NF A1B 3T2 Tel. (709)753-6314 Fax (709)753-4945

Email: paon@paon.nf.ca

Media Contact, Gen. Sup't., A. Earl Batstone, 57 Thorburn Rd., Box 8895, Stn. "A", St. John's, NF A1B 3T2

EXECUTIVE OFFICERS

Gen. Sup't. A. Earl Batstone, 57 Thorburn Rd., Box 8895, Stn. "A", St. John's, NF A1B 3T2

Gen. Sec.-Treas., Clarence Buckle, 57 Thorburn Box 8895, Stn. "A", St. John's, NF A1B 3T2

Ex. Dir. of Home Missions, Barry Q. Grimes, 57 Thorburn Rd., Box 8895, Stn. "A", St. John's, NF A1B 3T2

Ex. Dir. of Ch. Ministries, Robert H. Dewling, 57 Thorburn Rd., Box 8895, Stn. "A", St. John's, NF A1B 3T2

PROVINCIAL DIRECTORS

Sunday school Ministry, Eric A. Dawe, Box 299, Deer Lake, NF A0K 2E0

Children's Ministry, Lorinda R. Moulton, 669 Tamarack Dr., Apt. 304, Labrador City, Labrador A2V 2V2

Women's Ministries, Nancy L. Hunter, 12 Harp Place, Paradise, NF A1L 1G9

Men's Ministries, Norman C. Joy, 54 Premier Dr., Corner Brook, NF A2H 1S4

Youth Ministry, B. Dean Brenton, 14 Wickham Place, St. John's, NF A1B 3L5

Mature Adult Ministry, Clayton Rice, 29 Diana Rd., St. John's, NF A1B 1H7

Family Ministry, Eva M. Winsor, 26 Ireland Dr., Grand Falls-Windsor, NF A2A 2S6

AUXILIARY SERVICES

Chaplain for Institutions, Roy A. Burden, 293 Frecker Dr., St. John's NF A1E 5T8

Pentecostal Senior Citizens Home Administrator, Beverly Bellefleur, Box 130, Clarke's Beach, NF A0A 1W0

Evergreen Manor, Summerford, NF A0G 4E0

Pastoral Enrichment Ministry, Gary D. & Eva M. Winsor, 26 Ireland Dr., Grand Falls-Windsor NF A2A 2S6

Chaplain, Memorial University of Newfoundland, -not yet named-, Thompson Student Centre, Room T 3036, Memorial University of Newfoundland, Box 102, St. John's, NF A1C 5S7

Emmanuel Convention Centre Administrator, Ronald M. Dicks, Box 248, Lewisporte, NF A0G 3A0

World Missions Promotions, A. Scott Hunter, 12 Harp Place, Paradise, NF A1L 1G9

Periodicals

Good Tidings

Plymouth Brethren—please see Christian Brethren.

Presbyterian Church in America (Canadian Section)

Canadian congregations of the Reformed Presbyterian Church, Evangelical Synod, became a part of the Presbyterian Church in America when the RPCES joined PCA in June 1982. Some of the churches were in predecessor bodies of the RPCES, which was the product of a 1965 merger of the Reformed Presbyterian Church in North America, General Synod and the Evangelical Presbyterian Church. Others came into existence later as a part of the home missions work of RPCES. Congregations are located in seven provinces, and the PCA is continuing church extension work in Canada. The denomination is committed to world evangelization and to a continuation of historic Presbyterianism. Its officers are required to subscribe to the Reformed faith as set forth in the Westminster Confession of Faith and Catechisms.

Headquarters
Media Contact, Correspondent, Doug Codling, Faith Reformed Presbyterian Church, 2581 E. 45th St., Vancouver, BC V5R 3B9 Tel. (604)438-8755

Periodicals
Equip for Ministry; Multiply; Network

Presbyterian Church in Canada
This is the nonconcurring portion of the Presbyterian Church in Canada that did not become a part of The United Church of Canada in 1925.

Headquarters
50 Wynford Dr., North York, ON M3C 1J7 Tel. (416)441-1111 Fax (416)441-2825
Website: http://www.presbycan.cal
Media Contact, Principal Clk., Rev. Stephen Kendall

Periodicals
Channels; The Presbyterian Message; Presbyterian Record; Glad Tidings; La Vie Chrétienne

Reformed Church in Canada
The Canadian branch of the Reformed Church in America consists of 41 churches organized under the Council of the Reformed Church in Canada and within the classis of Ontario (24 churches), British Columbia (10 churches), Canadian Prairies (7 churches). The Reformed Church in America was established in 1628 by the earliest Dutch settlers in America as the Reformed Protestant Dutch Church. It is evangelical in theology and presbyterian in government.

Headquarters
Gen. Sec., Rev. Wesley Granberg- Michaelson, 475 Riverside Dr., Rm. 1812, New York, NY 10115 Tel. (212)870-2841 Fax (212)870-2499

Officers
Council of the Reformed Church in Canada, Exec. Sec., Rev. James Moerman, Reformed Church Center, RR #4, Cambridge, ON N1R 5S5 Tel. (519)622-1777
Media Contact, Dir., Stewardship & Communication Services, Rev. E. Wayne Antworth, 475 Riverside Dr., Rm. 1815, New York, NY 10115 Tel. (212)870-2954 Fax (212)870-2499

The Reformed Episcopal Church of Canada
The Reformed Episcopal Church is a separate entity. It was established in Canada by an act of incorporation given royal assent on June 2, 1886. It maintains the founding principles of episcopacy (in historic succession from the apostles), Anglican liturgy and Reformed doctrine and evangelical zeal. In practice it continues to recognize the validity of certain nonepiscopal orders of evangelical ministry. The Church has reunited with the Reformed Episcopal Church and is now composed of two Dioceses in this body - the Diocese of Central and Eastern Canada and the Diocese of Western Canada and Alaska. The current Presiding Bishop is Bishop Leonard Riches in Philadelphia.

Headquarters
Box 2532, New Liskeard, ON P0J 1P0 Tel. (705)647-4565 Fax (705)647-4565
Email: fed@nt.net
Website: http://www.recus.org
Media Contact, Pres., Rt. Rev. Michael Fedechko, M.Div., D.D.

Officers
Pres., Rt. Rev. Michael Fedechko, 320 Armstrong St., New Liskeard, ON P0J 1P0
Sec., Janet Dividson, 224 Haliburton,New Liskeard, ON P0J 1P0

BISHOPS
Diocese of Central & Eastern Canada: Rt. Rev. Michael Fedechko, 320 Armstrong St., New Liskeard, ON P0J 1P0 Tel. (705)647-4565 Fax (705)647-4565
Diocese of Western Canada & Alaska: Rt. Rev. Charles W. Dorrington, 54 Blanchard St., Victoria, BC V8X 4R1 Tel. (604)744-5014 Fax (604)388-5891

Periodicals
The Messenger

Reinland Mennonite Church
This group was founded in 1958 when 10 ministers and approximately 600 members separated from the Sommerfelder Mennonite Church. In 1968, four ministers and about 200 members migrated to Bolivia. The church has work in five communities in Manitoba and one in Ontario

Headquarters
Bishop William H. Friesen, P.O. Box 96, Rosenfeld, MB R0G 1X0 Tel. (204)324-6339
Media Contact, Deacon, Henry Wiebe, Box 2587, Winkler, MB R6W 4C3 Tel. (204)325-8487

Reorganized Church of Jesus Christ of Latter Day Saints
Founded April 6, 1830, by Joseph Smith, Jr., the church was reorganized under the leadership of the founder's son, Joseph Smith III, in 1860. The Church is established in 38 countries including the United States and Canada, with nearly a quarter of a million members. A biennial world conference is held in Independence, Missouri. The current president is W. Grant McMurray.

Headquarters

World Headquarters Complex: P.O. Box 1059, Independence, MO 64051 Tel. (816)833-1000 Fax (816)521-3095

Ontario Regional Ofc.: 390 Speedvale Ave. E., Guelph, ON N1E 1N5

Media Contact, Public Relations Coordinator, Susan Naylor

Officers
CANADIAN REGIONS AND DISTRICTS

North Plains & Prairie Provinces Region: Regional Admn., Kenneth Barrows, 84 Hidden Park NW, Calgary, AB T3A 5K5; Alberta District, R.A.(Ryan) Levitt, #325, 51369 Range Rd., Sherwood Park, AB T8C 1H3; Saskatchewan District, Robert G. Klombies, 202 Saskatchewan Crescent W., Saskatoon, SK S7M 0A4

Pacific Northwest Region: Regional Admn., Raymond Peter, P.O. Box 18469, 4820 Morgan, Seattle, WA 98118; British Columbia District, E. Carl Bolger, 410-1005 McKenzie Ave., Victoria, BC V8X 4A9

Ontario Region: Regional Admn., Larry D. Windland, 390 Speedvale Ave. E., Guelph, ON N1E 1N5; Chatham District, David R. Wood, 127 Mount Pleasant Crescent, Wallaceburg, ON N8A 5A3; Grand River District, C. Allen Taylor, R R 2, Orangeville, ON L9W 2Y9; London District, William T. Leney, Jr., 18 Glendon Road, Stratford, ON N5A 5B3; Niagara District, Willis L. Hopkin, 765 Rymal Rd. E., Hamilton, ON L8W 1B6; Northern Ontario District, Douglas G. Bolger, 482 Timmins St., North Bay, ON P1B 4K7; Ottawa District, Marion Smith, 70 Mayburry St., Hull, QC J9A 2E9; Owen Sound District, Robin M. Duff, P.O. Box 52, Owen Sound, ON N1K 5P1; Toronto Metropole, Kerry J. Richards, 74 Parkside Dr., Brampton, ON L6Y 2G9

Periodicals
Saints Herald

The Roman Catholic Church in Canada

The largest single body of Christians in Canada, the Roman Catholic Church is under the spiritual leadership of His Holiness the Pope. Catholicism in Canada dates back to 1534, when the first Mass was celebrated on the GaspÈ Peninsula on July 7, by a priest accompanying Jacques Cartier. Catholicism had been implanted earlier by fishermen and sailors from Europe. Priests came to Acadia as early as 1604. Traces of a regular colony go back to 1608 when Champlain settled in Quebec City. The Recollets (1615), followed by the Jesuits (1625) and the Sulpicians (1657), began the missions among the native population. The first official Roman document relative to the Canadian missions dates from March 20, 1618. Bishop FranÁois de Montmorency-Laval, the first bishop, arrived in Quebec in 1659. The church developed in the East, but not until 1818 did systematic missionary work begin in western Canada.

In the latter 1700s, English-speaking Roman Catholics, mainly from Ireland and Scotland, began to arrive in Canada's Atlantic provinces. After 1815 Irish Catholics settled in large numbers in what is now Ontario. The Irish potato famine of 1847 greatly increased that population in all parts of eastern Canada.

By the 1850s the Catholic Church in both English- and French-speaking Canada had begun to erect new dioceses and found many religious communities. These communities did educational, medical and charitable work among their own people as well as among Canada's native peoples. By the 1890s large numbers of non-English and non-French-speaking Catholics had settled in Canada, especially in the Western provinces. In the 20th century the pastoral horizons have continued to expand to meet the needs of what has now become a very multiracial church.

Headquarters

Media Contact, Dir. Communications Service, Rev. Mr. William Kokesch, Email: kokesch@ccb.ca

Dir. Service des Communications, Sylvain Salvas, Email: salvas@cccb.ca

Officers

General Secretariat of the Episcopacy

Secrétaire général (French Sector), Father Émilius Goulet

General Secretary (English Sector), Msgr. Peter Schonenbach

Assistant General Secretary (English Sector), Bede Martin Hubbard

Secrétaire général adjoint (French Sector), M. Gérald Baril

CANADIAN ORGANIZATION

Canadian Conference of Catholic Bishops/ Conférence des évêques catholiques du Canada, 90 Parent Ave., Ottawa, ON K1N 7B1 Tel. (613)241-9461 Fax (613)241-8117, Email: cecc@cccb.ca, Website: www.cccb.ca

EXECUTIVE COMMITTEE
National Level

Pres., His Eminence Jean-Claude Cardinal Turcotte (Montreal)

Vice-Pres., Most Rev. Gerald Wiesner, o.m.i. (Prince George)

Co-Treas.: Most Rev. Anthony F. Tonnos (Hamilton)

EPISCOPAL COMMISSIONS
National Level

Social Affairs, Mgr. Francois Thibodeau

Canon Law, Most Rev. Francis J. Spence

Relations with Assoc. of Priests, Religious, & Laity, Most Rev. Terrence Prendergast

Evangelization of Peoples, Mgr. AndrÈ Gaumond

Ecumenism, Most Rev. Brendan O'Brien

Theology, ———

Sector Level
Comm. sociales, Mgr. Robert Lebel
Social Comm., Most Rev. Fred Colli
Éducation chrétienne, Mgr. Paul Marchand
Christian Education, Most Rev. Anthony Tonnos
Liturgie, Mgr. Antoine Hacault
Liturgy, Most Rev. Marcel A.J. Gervais

OFFICES
Secteur français
Evangélisation des peuples, Dir., Mme. Adéle Bolduc
Office des communications sociales, Dir. général, M. Bertrand Ouellet
Office national de liturgie, coordonnateur, M. l'abbé Paul Boily, 3530, rue Adam, Montréal, QC H1W 1Y8 Tel. (514)522-4930 Fax (514)522-1557
Oecuménisme, Sr. Donna Geernaert
Services des communications, Dir., M. Sylvain Salvas
Service des Editions, Dir., Mme Johanne Gnassi
Théologie, Dir., P. Gilles Langevin
Tribunal d'appel du Canada, P. Pierre Allard, s.m.
Éducation chrétienne Dir., F. Jean-Claude Éthier
Affaires sociales, Dir., M. Joseph Gunn
English Sector
Natl. Liturgical Ofc., Dir., Sr. Donna Kelly, c.n.d.
Natl. Ofc. of Religious Educ., Dir., Bernadette Tourangeau
Evangelization of peoples, Dir., Ms. Adéle Bolduc
Ecumenism, Sr. Donna Geernaert
Theology Dir., P. Gilles Langevin, S.J.
Canadian Appeal Tribunal, P. Pierre Allard, s.m.
Communications Service, Dir., Rev. William Kokesch
Social Affairs, Dir., Joseph Gunn

REGIONAL EPISCOPAL ASSEMBLIES
Atlantic Episcopal Assembly: Pres., Mgr. André Richard; Vice-Pres., Most Rev. Raymond Lahey et Mgr. Francois Thibodeau; Sec.-Treas., Daniel Deveau, c.s.c., Tel. (506)758-2589 Fax (506)758-2580
Assemblée des évêques du Que: Prés., Mgr. Pierre Morissette; Vice-Pres., Mgr. Robert Ébacher; Sécrétaire général, M. Guy St. Onge, prêtre; Secrétariat, 1225 Boulevard Saint Joseph est, Montréal, QC H2J 1L7 Tel. (514)274-4323 Fax (514)274-4383
Email: aeq@eveques.qc.ca
Ontario Conference of Catholic Bishops: Pres., Bishop Anthony Tonnos; Vice-Pres., Most Rev. Brendan O'Brien; Sec., Thomas J. Reilly; Secretariat, Ste. 800, 10 St. Mary St., Toronto, ON M4Y 1P9 Tel. (416)923-1423 Fax (416)923-1509
Email: occb@pathcom.com
Western Catholic Conference: Pres., Bishop Blaise Morand; Vice-Pres., Mgr. Raymond Roussin; Sec., Abbot Peter Novecosky, O.S.B., P.O. Box 10, Muenster, SK S0K 2Y0 Tel. (306)682-1788 Fax (306)682-1766

MILITARY ORDINARIATE
Ordinaire aux forces canadiennes: Mgr. Donald Thériault, National Defence Headquarters, Ottawa, ON K1A 0K2 Tel. (613)990- 7824 Fax (613)990-7824
Canadian Religious Conference: Sec. Gen., Sr. Hélène Robitaille, F.D.L.S., 219 Argyle St., Ottawa, ON K2P 2H4 Tel. (613)236-0824 Fax (613)236-0825
Email: crcn@web.net

Periodicals
Cahiers de Spiritualité Ignatienne; The Catholic Register; The Catholic Times (Montreal); Companion Magazine; Global Village Voice; Discover the Bible; L'Église Canadienne; The Monitor; National Bulletin on Liturgy; The New Freeman; Messenger (of the Sacred Heart); Foi et Culture (Bulletin natl. de liturgie) Liturgie; Prairie Messenger; Vie Liturgique; La Vie des Communautés religieuses; Relations; Présence; The Communicator; Scarboro Missions; Missions Today

Romanian Orthodox Church in America (Canadian Parishes)

The first Romanian Orthodox immigrants in Canada called for Orthodox priests from their native country of Romania. Between 1902 and 1914, they organized the first Romanian parish communities and built Orthodox churches in different cities and farming regions of western Canada (Alberta, Saskatchewan, Manitoba) as well as in the eastern part (Ontario and Quebec).

In 1929, the Romanian Orthodox parishes from Canada joined with those of the United States in a Congress held in Detroit, Michigan, and asked the Holy Synod of the Romanian Orthodox Church of Romania to establish a Romanian Orthodox Missionary Episcopate in America. The first Bishop, Policarp (Morushca), was elected and consecrated by the Holy Synod of the Romanian Orthodox Church and came to the United States in 1935. He established his headquarters in Detroit with jurisdiction over all the Romanian Orthodox parishes in the United States and Canada.

In 1950, the Romanian Orthodox Church in America (i.e. the Romanian Orthodox Missionary Episcopate in America) was granted administrative autonomy by the Holy Synod of the Romanian Orthodox Church of Romania, and only doctrinal and canonical ties remain with this latter body.

In 1974 the Holy Synod of the Romanian Orthodox Church of Romania recognized and approved the elevation of the Episcopate to the rank of the Romanian Orthodox Archdiocese in America and Canada.

Headquarters
Canadian Office: Descent of the Holy Ghost, Romanian Orthodox Church, 2895 Seminole St., Windsor, ON N8Y 1Y1

Media Contact, Most Rev. Archbishop Victorin, 19959 Riopelle St., Detroit, MI 48203 Tel. (313)893-8390

Officers

Archbishop, Most Rev. Archbishop Victorin, 19959 Riopelle St., Detroit, MI 48203 Tel. (313)893-8390

Vicar, V. Rev. Archim., Dr. Vasile Vasilachi, 45-03 48th Ave., Woodside, Queens, NY 11377 Tel. (718)784-4453

Cultural Councilor, Very Rev. Fr. Nicolae Ciurea, 19 Murray St. W., Hamilton, ON L8L 1B1 Tel. (416)523-8268

Admn. Councilor, V. Rev. Fr. Mircea Panciuk, 11024-165th Ave., Edmonton, AB T5X 1X9

Sec., Rev. Fr. Simion John Catau, 31227 Roan Dr., Warren, MI 48093 Tel. (810)264-1924

The Romanian Orthodox Episcopate of America (Jackson, MI)

This body of Eastern Orthodox Christians of Romanian descent is part of the Autocephalous Orthodox Church in America. For complete description and listing of officers, please see chapter 3, "Religious Bodies in the United States."

Headquarters

2522 Grey Tower Rd., Jackson, MI 49201 Tel. (517)522-4800 Fax (517)522-5907
Email: roeasolia@aol.com
Website: http://www.roea.org
Mailing Address, P.O. Box 309, Grass Lake, MI 49240-0309
Media Contact, Ed./Sec., Rev. Dea. David Oancea, P.O. Box 185, Grass Lake, MI 49240-0185 Tel. (517)522-3656 Fax (517)522-5907

Officers

Ruling Bishop, Rt. Rev. Nathaniel Popp
Deans for the Deanery of Canada, Western Provinces, Very Rev. Daniel Nenson, 2855 Helmsing St., Regina, SK S4V 0W7 Tel. (306)761-2379; Eastern Provinces, Very Rev. Dumitru Paun, 47 Adelaide S., London, ON N5Z 3K1 Tel. (519)858-4065

Periodicals

Solia —The Herald

Russian Orthodox Church—please see the Patriarchal Parishes of the Russian Orthodox Church in Canada

The Salvation Army in Canada

The Salvation Army, an evangelical branch of the Christian Church, is an international movement founded in 1865 in London, England. The ministry of Salvationists, consisting of clergy (officers) and laity, comes from a commitment to Jesus Christ and is revealed in practical service, regardless of race, color, creed, sex or age.

The goals of The Salvation Army are to preach the gospel, disseminate Christian truths, instill Christian values, enrich family life and improve the quality of all life.

To attain these goals, The Salvation Army operates local congregations, provides counseling, supplies basic human needs and undertakes spiritual and moral rehabilitation of any needy people who come within its influence.

A quasi-military system of government was set up in 1878, by General William Booth, founder (1829-1912). Converts from England started Salvation Army work in London, Ontario, in 1882. Two years later, Canada was recognized as a Territorial Command, and since 1933 it has included Bermuda. An act to incorporate the Governing Council of The Salvation Army in Canada received royal assent on May 19, 1909.

Headquarters

2 Overlea Blvd., Toronto, ON M4H 1P4 Tel. (416)425-2111
Media Contact, Major Robert MacKenzie, Tel. (416)425-6153 Fax (416)425-6157
Email: bob.mackenzie@sallynet.org
Website: http://www.sallynet.org

Officers

Territorial Commander, Commissioner Norman Howe
Territorial Pres., Women's Organizations, Commissioner Marian Howe
Chief Sec., Col. Clyde Moore
Sec. for Personnel, Lt. Col. Merv Leach
Bus. Adm. Sec., Lt. Col. Peter Wood
Fin. Sec., Major Susan McMillan
Program Sec., Lt. Col. David Luginbuhl
Community Rel. and Communications Secretary, Major Robert Mac Kenzie
Property Sec., Col. Donald Copple

Periodicals

The War Cry; Faith & Friends; En Avant!; The Young Soldier; The Edge; Catherine; Horizons

Serbian Orthodox Church in the U.S.A. and Canada, Diocese of Canada

The Serbian Orthodox Church is an organic part of the Eastern Orthodox Church. As a local church it received its autocephaly from Constantinople in A.D. 1219. The Patriarchal seat of the church today is in Belgrade, Yugoslavia. In 1921, a Serbian Orthodox Diocese in the United States of America and Canada was organized. In 1963, it was reorganized into three dioceses, and in 1983 a fourth diocese was created for the Canadian part of the church. The Serbian Orthodox Church is in absolute doctrinal unity with all other local Orthodox Churches.

Headquarters

7470 McNiven Rd., RR 3, Campbellville, ON L0P 1B0 Tel. (905)878-0043 Fax (905)878-1909
Email: vladika@istocnik.com
Website: http://www. istocnik.com
Media Contact, Rt. Rev. Georgije

Serbian Orthodox Bishop of Canada, Rt. Rev.
Georgije
Dean of Western Deanery, V. Rev. Mirko
Malinovic, 924 13th Ave., Regina, SK S4N
0K7 Tel. (306)352-2917
Dean of Eastern Deanery, V. Rev. Zivorad
Subotic, 351 Mellville Ave., Westmount, QC
H3Z 2Y7 Tel. + Fax (514)931-6664

Periodicals

*Istocnik, Herald of the Serbian Orthodox
Church— Canadian Diocese*

Seventh-day Adventist Church in Canada

The Seventh-day Adventist Church in Canada
is part of the worldwide Seventh-day Adventist
Church with headquarters in Washington, D.C.
(See "Religious Bodies in the United States" section of this Yearbook for a fuller description.)
The Seventh-day Adventist Church in Canada
was organized in 1901 and reorganized in 1932.

Headquarters

1148 King St., E., Oshawa, ON L1H 1H8 Tel.
(905)433-0011 Fax (905)433-0982
Media Contact, Orville Parchment

Officers

Pres., Orville Parchment
Sec., Claude Sabot
Treas., Donald Upson

DEPARTMENTS

Under Treas., Brian Christenson
Asst. Treas., Clarelene Ivany
Computer Services, Brian Ford
Coord. of Ministries, John Howard
Education, Mike Lekic
Public Affairs/Religious Liberty Trust, Karnik
Doukmetzian

Periodicals

Canadian Adventist Messenger

**Southern Baptists—please see Canadian
Convention of Southern Baptists.**

Syrian Orthodox Church of Antioch

The Syrian Orthodox Church professes the
faith of the first three ecumenical councils of
Nicaea, Constantinople and Ephesus and num-
bers faithful in the Middle East, India, the
Americas, Europe and Australia. It traces its ori-
gin to the Patriarchate established in Antioch by
St. Peter the Apostle and is under the supreme
ecclesiastical jurisdiction of His Holiness the
Syrian Orthodox Patriarch of Antioch and All the
East, now residing in Damascus, Syria.

The Archdiocese of the Syrian Orthodox
Church in the U.S. and Canada was formally
established in 1957. In 1995, the Archdiocese of
North America was divided into three separate

Patriarchal Vicariates, including one for Canada.
The first Syrian Orthodox faithful came to
Canada in the 1890s and formed the first
Canadian parish in Sherbrooke, Quebec. Today
five official parishes of the Archdiocese exist in
Canada-two in Quebec and three in Ontario.
There is also an official mission congregation in
Calgary, Alberta.

Headquarters

Archdiocese of Canada, The New Archdiocesan
Centre, 4375 Henri-Bourassa Ouest, St.-
Laurent, Quebec H4L 1A5, Canada Tel.
(514)334-6993 Fax (514)334-8233

Officers

Archbishop Mor Timotheos Aphrem Aboodi

Ukrainian Orthodox Church of Canada

Toward the end of the 19th century many
Ukrainian immigrants settled in Canada. In 1918, a
group of these pioneers established the Ukrainian
Orthodox Church of Canada (UOCC), today the
largest Ukrainian Orthodox Church beyond the
borders of Ukraine. In 1990, the UOCC entered
into a eucharistic union with the Ecumenical
Patriarchate at Constantinople (Istanbul).

Headquarters

Ukrainian Orthodox Church of Canada, Office of
the Consistory, 9 St. Johns Ave., Winnipeg,
MB R2W 1G8 Tel. (204)586-3093 Fax
(204)582-5241
Email: consistory@uocc.ca
Website: www. uocc.ca
Media Contacts, Rev. Fr. Andrew Jarmus, 9st.
John's Ave., Winnipeg, MB R2W 1G8, Tel.
(204)586-3093 Fax (204)582-5241; Ms. M.
Zurek, 9 St. Johns Ave., Winnipeg, MB R2W
1G8 Tel. (204)586-3093 Fax (204)582-5241

Officers

Primate, Most Rev. Metropolitan Wasyly Fedak,
9 St. Johns Ave., Winnipeg, MB R2W 1G8
Tel. (204)586-3093 Fax (204)582-5241
Chancellor, Rt. Rev. Dr. Oleg Krawchenko

Periodicals

Visnyk/The Herald/Le Messager (newspaper)
Ridna Nyva (almanac/annual)

Union of Spiritual Communities of Christ (Orthodox Doukhobors in Canada)

The Doukhobors are groups of Canadians of
Russian origin living in the western provinces of
Canada, but their beginnings in Russia are
unknown. The name "Doukhobors," or "Spirit
Wrestlers," was given in derision by the Russian
Orthodox clergy in Russia as far back as 1785.
Victims of decades of persecution in Russia, about
7,500 Doukhobors arrived in Canada in 1899.

The teaching of the Doukhobors is penetrated
with the Gospel spirit of love. Worshiping God in

197

the spirit, they affirm that the outward church and all that is performed in it and concerns it has no importance for them; the church is where two or three are gathered together, united in the name of Christ. Their teaching is founded on tradition, which they call the "Book of Life," because it lives in their memory and hearts. In this book are sacred songs or chants, partly composed independently, partly formed out of the contents of the Bible, and these are committed to memory by each succeeding generation. Doukhobors observe complete pacifism and non-violence.

The Doukhobors were reorganized in 1938 by their leader, Peter P. Verigin, shortly before his death, into the Union of Spiritual Communities of Christ, commonly called Orthodox Doukhobors. It is headed by a democratically elected Executive Committee which executes the will and protects the interests of the people.

At least 99 percent of the Doukhobors are law-abiding, pay taxes, and "do not burn or bomb or parade in the nude" as they say a fanatical off-shoot called the "Sons of Freedom" does.

Headquarters
USCC Central Office, Box 760, Grand Forks, BC V0H 1H0 Tel. (250)442-8252 Fax (250)442-3433

Media Contact, John J. Verigin, Sr.

Officers
Hon. Chmn. of the Exec. Comm., John J. Verigin, Sr.

Chpsn., Andrew Evin

Periodicals
ISKRA

United Brethren Church in Canada

Founded in 1767 in Lancaster County, Pennsylvania, missionaries came to Canada about 1850. The first class was held in Kitchener in 1855, and the first building was erected in Port Elgin in 1867.

The Church of the United Brethren in Christ had its beginning with Philip William Otterbein and Martin Boehm, who were leaders in the revivalistic movement in Pennsylvania and Maryland during the late 1760s.

Headquarters
302 Lake St., Huntington, IN 46750 Tel. (219) 356-2312 Fax (219)356-4730

General Officers
Pres., Rev. Brian Magnus, 120 Fife Rd., Guelph, ON N1H 6Y2 Tel. (519)836-0180

Treas., Brian Winger, 2233 Hurontario St., Apt. 916, Mississauga, ON L5A 2E9 Tel. (905)275-8140

The United Church of Canada

The United Church of Canada was formed on June 10, 1925, through the union of the Methodist Church, Canada, the Congregational Union of Canada, the Council of Local Union Churches and 70 percent of the Presbyterian Church in Canada. The union culminated years of negotiation between the churches, all of which had integral associations with the development and history of the nation.

In fulfillment of its mandate to be a uniting as well as a United Church, the denomination has been enriched by other unions during its history. The Wesleyan Methodist Church of Bermuda joined in 1930. On January 1, 1968, the Canada Conference of the Evangelical United Brethren became part of The United Church of Canada. At various times, congregations of other Christian communions have also become congregations of the United Church.

The United Church of Canada is a full member of the World Methodist Council, the World Alliance of Reformed Churches (Presbyterian and Congregational), and the Canadian and World Councils of Churches.

The United Church is the largest Protestant denomination in Canada.

NATIONAL OFFICES
The United Church House, 3250 Bloor St. W., Ste. 300, Etobicoke, ON M8X 2Y4 Tel. (416)231-5931 Fax (416)231-3103

Email: info@uccan.org

Website: http://www.uccan.org

Media Contact, Manager Public Relations & Info. Unit, Mary-Frances Denis

GENERAL COUNCIL
Mod., William F. Phipps

Gen. Sec., K. Virginia Coleman

Human Resources, Sec., Anne Shirley Sutherland

Theology, Faith & Ecumenism, Sec., Rev. S. Peter Wyatt

Archivist, 73 Queen's Park Cr., E., Toronto, ON M5C 1K7 Tel. (416)585-4563 Fax (416)585-4584

Email: uccvu.archives@utoronto.ca

Website: http://www. vicu.utoronto.ca/archives/archives.htm

ADMINISTRATIVE DIVISIONS
Communication: Gen. Sec., Linda E. Slough

Finance: Gen. Sec., Steven Adams

Ministry Personnel & Education: Gen. Sec., Rev. Steven Chambers

Mission in Canada: Gen. Sec., Rev. David Iverson

World Outreach: Gen. Sec., -vacant-

CONFERENCE EXECUTIVE SECRETARIES
Alberta and Northwest: Rev. George H. Rodgers, 9911-48 Ave., Edmonton, AB T6E 5V6 Tel. (780)435-3995 Fax (780)438-3317

Email: anwconf@web.net

All Native Circle: Speaker, Rev. Arlene J. Granbois, 367 Selkirk Ave., Winnipeg, MB

R2W 2N3 Tel. (204)582-5518 Fax (204)582-6649

Email: ancc@mb.sympatico.ca

Bay of Quinte: Rev. Wendy Bulloch, P.O. Box 700, 67 Mill St., Frankford, ON K0K 2C0 Tel. (613)398-1051 Fax (613)398-8894

Email: bayq.conference@sympatico.ca

British Columbia: Rev. Brian D. Thorpe, 4383 Rumble St., Burnaby, BC V5J 2A2 Tel. (604)431-0434 Fax (604)431-0439

Email: bcconf@infoserve.net

Hamilton: Rev. Roslyn A. Campbell, Box 100, Carlisle, ON L0R 1H0 Tel. (905)659-3343 Fax (905)659-7766

Email: office@hamconf.org

London: W. Peter Scott, 359 Windermere Rd., London, ON N6G 2K3 Tel. (519)672-1930 Fax (519)439-2800

Email: lonconf@execulink.com

Manitoba and Northwestern Ontario: Rev. Roger A. Coll, 170 Saint Mary's Rd., Winnipeg, MB R2H 1H9 Tel. (204)233-8911 Fax (204)233-3289

Email: confmnwo@mb.sympatico.ca

Manitou: Rev. Rev. Jim Sinclair, 1402 Regina St., North Bay, ON P1B 2L5 Tel. (705)474-3350 Fax (705)497-3597

Email: manitou@efni.com

Maritime: Rev. Catherine H. Gaw, 32 York St., Sackville, NB E4L 4R4 Tel. (506)536-1334 Fax (506)536-2900

Email: marconf@nbnet.nb,ca

Montreal and Ottawa: Rev. Gordon J. Roberts, 225-50 Ave., Lachine, QC H8T 2T7 Tel. (514)634-7015 Fax (514)634-2489

Email: lachine@istar.ca

Newfoundland and Labrador: Rev. Clarence R. Sellers, 320 Elizabeth Ave., St. John's, NF A1B 1T9 Tel. (709)754-0386 Fax (709)754-8336

Email: newlab@seascape.com

Saskatchewan: Rev. Wilbert R. Wall, 418 A. McDonald St., Regina, SK S4N 6E1 Tel. (306)721-3311 Fax (306)721-3171

Email: ucskco@sk.sympatico.ca

Toronto: Rev. David W. Allen, 65 Mayall Ave., Downsview, ON M3L 1E7 Tel. (416)241-2677 Fax (416)241-2689

Email: torconf@web.net

Periodicals

Fellowship Magazine; United Church Observer; Mandate; Aujourd'hui Credo

United Pentecostal Church in Canada

This body, which is affiliated with the United Pentecostal Church, International, with headquarters in Hazelwood, Missouri, accepts the Bible standard of full salvation, which is repentance, baptism by immersion in the name of the Lord Jesus Christ for the remission of sins and the baptism of the Holy Ghost, with the initial signs of speaking in tongues as the Spirit gives utterance. Other tenets of faith include the Oneness of God in Christ, holiness, divine healing and the second coming of Jesus Christ.

Headquarters

United Pentecostal Church Intl., 8855 Dunn Rd., Hazelwood, MO 63042 Tel. (314)837-7300 Fax (314)837-4503

Media Contact, Gen. Sec.-Treas., Rev. C. M. Becton

DISTRICT SUPERINTENDENTS

Atlantic: Rev. Harry Lewis, P.O. Box 1046, Perth Andover, NB E0J 1V0

British Columbia: Rev. Paul V. Reynolds, 13447-112th Ave., Surrey, BC V3R 2E7

Canadian Plains: Rev. Johnny King, 615 Northmount Dr., NW, Calgary, AB T2K 3J6

Central Canadian: Rev. Clifford Heaslip, 4215 Roblin Blvd., Winnipeg, MB R3R 0E8

Newfoundland: Jack Cunningham

Nova Scotia: Superintendent, Rev. John D. Mean, P.O. Box 2183, D.E.P.S., Dartmouth, NS B2W 3Y2

Ontario: Rev. Carl H. Stephenson, 63 Castlegrove Blvd., Don Mills, ON M3A 1L3

Universal Fellowship of Metropolitan Community Churches

The Universal Fellowship of Metropolitan Community Churches is a Christian church which directs a special ministry within, and on behalf of, the gay and lesbian community. Involvement, however, is not exclusively limited to gays and lesbians; U.F.M.C.C. tries to stress its openness to all people and does not call itself a "gay church."

Founded in 1968 in Los Angeles by the Rev. Troy Perry, the U.F.M.C.C. has over 300 member congregations worldwide. Congregations are in Vancouver, Edmonton, Windsor, London, Toronto, Ottawa (2), Guelph, Fredericton, Winnipeg, Halifax, Barrie and Belleville.

Theologically, the Metropolitan Community Churches stand within the mainstream of Christian doctrine, being "ecumenical" or "inter-denominational" in stance (albeit a "denomination" in their own right).

The Metropolitan Community Churches are characterized by their belief that the love of God is a gift, freely offered to all people, regardless of sexual orientation and that no incompatibility exists between human sexuality and the Christian faith.

The Metropolitan Community Churches in Canada were founded in Toronto in 1973 by the Rev. Robert Wolfe.

Headquarters

Media Contact, Marcie Wexler, 33 Holly St., #1117, Toronto, ON M4S 2G8 Tel. (416)487-8429 Fax (416)932-1836

Eastern Canadian District: Rev. Marcie Wexler,
33 Holly St., #1117, Toronto, ON M4S 2G8
Tel. (416)487-8429

The Wesleyan Church of Canada

This group is the Canadian portion of The
Wesleyan Church which consists of the Atlantic
and Central Canada districts. The Central Canada
District of the former Wesleyan Methodist
Church of America was organized at Winchester,
Ontario, in 1889 and the Atlantic District was
founded in 1888 as the Alliance of the Reformed
Baptist Church, which merged with the Wesleyan
Methodist Church in July, 1966.

The Wesleyan Methodist Church and the
Pilgrim Holiness Church merged in June, 1968,
to become The Wesleyan Church. The doctrine is
evangelical and Wesleyan Arminian and stresses
holiness beliefs. For more details, consult the
U.S. listing under The Wesleyan Church.

Headquarters

The Wesleyan Church Intl. Center, P.O. Box
50434, Indianapolis, IN 46250-0434

Media Contact, Dist. Supt., Central Canada, Rev.
Donald E. Hodgins, 3 Applewood Dr., Ste.
101, Belleville, ON K8P 4E3 Tel. (613)966-
7527 Fax (613)968-6190

DISTRICT SUPERINTENDENTS

Central Canada: Rev. Donald E. Hodgins, 3
Applewood Dr., Ste.101, Belleville, ON K8P
4E3

Email: central.canada.district@sympatico.ca

Atlantic: Rev. Dr. H. C. Wilson, P.O. Box 20, 41
Summit Ave., Sussex, NB E0E 1P0 Tel.
(506)433-1007

Email: ncwilson@nbnet.nb.ca

Periodicals

Central Canada; The Clarion

Religious Bodies in Canada Arranged by Families

The following list of religious bodies appearing in the Directory Section of the Yearbook shows the "families," or related clusters into which Canadian religious bodies can be grouped. For example, there are many communions that can be grouped under the heading "Baptist" for historical and theological reasons. It should not be assumed, however, that all denominations under one family heading are necessarily consistent in belief or practice. The family clusters tend to represent historical factors more often than theological or practical ones. These family categories provide one of the major pitfalls when compiling church statistics because there is often a tendency to combine the statistics by families for analytical and comparative purposes. Such combined totals are deeply flawed, even though they are often used as variables for sociological analysis. The arrangement by families offered here is intended only as a general guide for conceptual organization when viewing the broad sweep of Canadian religious culture.

Religious bodies that can not be categorized under family headings appear alphabetically and are not indented in the following list.

The Anglican Church of Canada
Apostolic Christian Church (Nazarene)
Armenian Evangelical Church
Associated Gospel Churches

Baptist Bodies

Association of Regular Baptist Churches (Canada)
Baptist Convention of Ontario and Quebec
Baptist General Conference of Canada
Baptist Union of Western Canada
Canadian Baptist Ministries
Canadian Convention of Southern Baptists
The Fellowship of Evangelical Baptist Churches in Canada
Free Will Baptists
North American Baptist Conference
Union d'Eglises Baptistes Franáaises au Canada
United Baptist Convention of the Atlantic Provinces

Brethren in Christ Church, Canadian Conference
Canadian District of the Moravian Church in America, Northern Province
Canadian Evangelical Christian Churches
Canadian Yearly Meeting of the Religious Society of Friends
Christ Catholic Church International
Christian Brethren (also known as Plymouth Brethren)
Christian and Missionary Alliance in Canada
Church of God (Anderson, Ind.)
Church of the Nazarene in Canada

Churches of Christ—Christian Churches

Christian Church (Disciples of Christ) in Canada
Churches of Christ in Canada

Congregational Christian Churches in Canada

Eastern Orthodox Churches

The Antiochian Orthodox Christian Archdiocese of North America
Greek Orthodox Metropolis of Toronto (Canada)
Orthodox Church in America (Canada Section)
Patriarchal Parishes of the Russian Orthodox Church in Canada
Romanian Orthodox Church in America (Canadian Parishes)
The Romanian Orthodox Episcopate of America (Jackson, MI)
Serbian Orthodox Church in the U.S.A. and Canada, Diocese of Canada
Ukrainian Orthodox Church of Canada

The Evangelical Covenant Church of Canada
Evangelical Free Church of Canada
The Evangelical Missionary Church of Canada
General Church of the New Jerusalem
Jehovah's Witnesses

Latter-Day Saints (Mormons)

The Church of Jesus Christ of Latter-Day Saints in Canada
Reorganized Church of Jesus Christ of Latter Day Saints

Lutheran Bodies

Church of the Lutheran Brethren
The Estonian Evangelical Lutheran Church
Evangelical Lutheran Church in Canada
Lutheran Church—Canada

Mennonite Bodies

Canadian Conference of Mennonite Brethren Churches

Church of God in Christ (Mennonite)
Conference of Mennonites in Canada
The Evangelical Mennonite Conference
Evangelical Mennonite Mission Conference
Mennonite Church (Canada)
Old Order Amish Church
Reinland Mennonite Church

Methodist Bodies

British Methodist Episcopal Church of
  Canada
Free Methodist Church in Canada
Independent Holiness Church
The Wesleyan Church of Canada

The Old Catholic Church of Canada
Open Bible Faith Fellowship of Canada

Oriental Orthodox Churches

Armenian Holy Apostolic Church - Canadian
  Diocese
The Coptic Orthodox Church in Canada
Syrian Orthodox Church of Antioch

Pentecostal Bodies

The Apostolic Church in Canada
Apostolic Church of Pentecost of Canada Inc.
The Bible Holiness Movement
Church of God (Cleveland, Tenn.)
The Church of God of Prophecy in Canada
Elim Fellowship of Evangelical Churches and
  Ministers
Foursquare Gospel Church of Canada
Independent Assemblies of God International
  (Canada)
The Italian Pentecostal Church of Canada
The Pentecostal Assemblies of Canada
Pentecostal Assemblies of Newfoundland
United Pentecostal Church in Canada

Presbyterian Bodies

Presbyterian Church in America (Canadian
  Section)
Presbyterian Church in Canada

Reformed Bodies

Canadian and American Reformed Churches
Christian Reformed Church in North America
Reformed Church in Canada

The Reformed Episcopal Church of Canada
The Roman Catholic Church in Canada
The Salvation Army in Canada
Seventh-day Adventist Church in Canada
Union of Spiritual Communities of Christ
  (Orthodox Doukhobors in Canada)
United Brethren Church in Canada
The United Church of Canada
Universal Fellowship of Metropolitan
  Community Churches

5. The Emerging Electronic Church

Information by and about religious bodies in Canada and the United States is increasingly available on line and in electronic form. With increasing speed and at an ever lower cost one can access church-related news, music, graphic images (including video), disaster reports, speeches, pastoral letters and sermons, historic and biographical data, program information, bulletin notes, or contact information for staff members of a local church or a regional, national, or international body.

The World Wide Web (www) addresses listed here are but the tip of the iceberg. From one web page you will most often find links to a variety of additional resources. For example, a visit to the home page of the Evangelical Lutheran Church in America (www.elca.org) will allow you click on a link labeled "Congregations" to find the name and map location of the local ELCA congregation nearest your home. You may also find that congregation has created its own page providing specific information about itself. Another example is provided by The United Methodist Church Board for Church and Society. From their home page you can link to the text for all of the legislation currently being considered in the House and Senate of the United States. From the National Council of the Churches of Christ in the U.S.A. (www.ncccusa.org) home page you can link to the *Yearbook* pages, Church World Service, the World Council of Churches and from these to many other sites as you will see below.

Specialized church-related discussion services (such as Ecunet) and some Internet service providers that also provide content (America Online, for example) list a variety of sources on religion including a variety of email and real time chat rooms or discussion groups where one can meet to discuss spirituality, theology, or any other topic of interest. Further, Internet search sites, such as Yahoo and Alta Vista, can return vast numbers of links to Roman Catholic, Buddhist, Muslim, evangelical, and interfaith groups. Using email one can conveniently contact denominational staff, mission organizations, teen groups, women's groups, and other special interest groups.

Space here is limited, so only a few key addresses are being provided. Additional and updated email and website information pertaining to U.S. and Canadian religious organizations is provided online at our new Electronic Church website (**www.ElectronicChurch.org.**) With these addresses and the links they provide to other resources, your accessibility to church-related information is virtually limitless.

In this directory, online databases and search engines are listed first, followed by addresses for U.S. religious bodies.

Helpful Databases and Search Engines for Local Churches and Denominations

A more thorough and frequently updated listing of church related links may be found at **www.ElectronicChurch.org.** Another excellent link to church-related electronic resources is available at the World Council of Churches site (www.wcc-coe.org). Another place to begin your search for specific information is with one of the following search engines:

All-in-one Christian Index—Website: http://allinone.crossdaily.com/
   This resource provides links to extensive Internet church resources, including search engines, indices, software, and best-site lists.
Christian Connection—Websit: www.christianconnection.net
   This resource includes links to recorded music, live radio broadcasts, online Bibles, commentaries and concordances, newsgroups, clip art, commercial links, and a local congregation directory of local churches.
Christianity.Net Church Locator—Website: www.christianity.net/churchlocator/CLhelp.html
   Sponsored by Christianity.Net, this resource lets one browse all the United States churches by region, denomination and key word searches, provides registry for persons wishing to add churches to the list, and offers help with building church websites.
Christian Web Directory—Churches—Website: http://www.goshen.net/WebDirectory/den.html
   Sponsored by Goshen.Net, this resource offers a limited list of denominations and independent churches, but also offers free web space for churches wishing to add their pages to the Internet. The grouping of denominations into categories is at times misleading or confusing. It has a church locator to help in finding local churches by region, tradition and denomination.
Cross Search Church and Denominational Resources—Website: http://www.crosssearch.com/Church_and_Denominational_Resources/
   This site has listings for congregations, denominations, church service and related organizations. Social and community groups are also included in this partial listing.
Ecunet—Website: http://www.ecunet.org
   A pioneer in church-related electronic discussion forums. The interface can be somewhat difficult to master, but the church-related discussions and shared resources are top drawer, anyone can begin a

new discussion topic, and, because secure discussions are possible, Ecunet is ideal for church groups/committees to work efficiently over long distances.

For Ministry—Website: http://www.forministry.com

An Internet ministry of the American Bible Society (formerly Houses of Worship). This site provides perhaps the most thorough listing of USA congregations. ForMinistry.com provides churches with free starter web sites, links to more than 15,000 ForMinistry.com church web sites, template-based web pages with interactive features, and resources and tools to aid in church ministry.

In the Footsteps of the Lord Churches and Organizations—Website: http://www.xensei.com/users/ Angel/Churches.html

A worldwide general listing of Christian organizations, evangelism outreaches, denominations and ministries.

Net Ministries Church Directory—Website: http://netministries.org/churches.htm#denoms

Consists primarily of lists of congregations and local churches, mainly in the United States, but some worldwide. Relatively extensive listings are given by region and denomination.

Yahoo! Society and Culture Directory—Website: http://www.yahoo.com/Society_and_Culture/ Religion/Faiths_and_Practices/Christianity.

This is a large, high-level resource that is rather thorough, though the links relate mostly to United States churches and may not always be active.

Electronic Addresses of Denominations listed in the US Religious Bodies Chapter of this *Yearbook*

Advent Christian Church (Official)—Email: acpub@adventchristian.org
Web: www.adventchristian.org/index.htm

African Methodist Episcopal Church (Official)—Email:gball@dhvx20.csudh.edu
Web: www.amenet.org/ame.htm

African Methodist Episcopal Zion Church (Official)—Email: info@amezion.org
Web: www.amezion.org

Albanian Orthodox Archdiocese of America (Official)—Web: www.oca.org/OCA/AL

Allegheny Wesleyan Methodist Connection (Original Allegheny Conference)—
Email: AWMC@JUNO.COM
Web: c1web.com/local_info/churches/aw.html (List of Churches)

American Baptist Churches in the U. S. A. (Official)—Email: richard.schramm@abc-usa.org
Web: www.abc-usa.org

The American Carpatho-Russian Orthodox Greek Catholic Church—
Email: archdiocese@goarch.org
Web: www.goarch.org

American Catholic Church (Official)—Email: berzol@apollo3.com
Web: www.geocities.com/WestHollywood/4136

American Evangelical Christian Churches—Email: alpha@strato.net
Web: www.aeccministries.com

American Rescue Workers (Official)—Email: amerscwk@pcspower.net
Web: www.arwus.com

The Antiochian Orthodox Christian Archdiocese of North America—
Email: archdiocese@antiochian.org
Web: www.antiochian.org

Apostolic Catholic Assyrian Church of the East, North American Dioceses (Official)—
Web: www.cired.org/ace.html

Apostolic Christian Church (Nazarene) (Official)—Email: webmaster@bibleviews.com
Web: www.mich.com/~lhaines/index.html

Apostolic Christian Churches of America (Official)—Email: Questions@ApostolicChristian.org
Web: www.apostolicchristian.org

Apostolic Episcopal Church (Official)—Email:HCCAEC@ix.netcom.com

Apostolic Faith Mission of Portland, Oregon (Official)—Email: webmaster@apostolicfaith.org
Web: www.apostolicfaith.org

Apostolic Lutheran Church of America (Official)—Email: webmaster@Apostolic-Lutheran.org
Web: www.apostolic-lutheran.org/

Apostolic Orthodox Catholic Church (Official)—Email: idyll@pe.net
Web: www.pe.net/~idyll/para1.htm

Apostolic Overcoming Holy Church of God, Inc. (Unofficial)—Email: AOH@PDNT.com
   Web: www.prairienet.org/staoh/
Armenian Apostolic Church of America (Official)—Email: prelacy@gis.net
   Web: www.armprelacy.org
Assemblies of God (Official)—Email: opr@ag.org
   Web: www.ag.org
Assemblies of God International Fellowship (Independent/Not Affiliated) (Official)—
   Email: info@agifellowship.org
   Web: agifellowship.org
Associate Reformed Presbyterian Church (General Synod) (Official)—
   Email: leland@arpsynod.org
   Web: www.arpsynod.org
The Association of Free Lutheran Congregations (Official)—Email: hqmail@aflc.org
   Web: www.aflc.org
Baptist Bible Fellowship International (Official)—Email: Info@bbfi.org
   Web: www.bbfi.org
Baptist General Conference (Official)—Email:GMBGCSTD@aol.com
   Web: www.bgc.bethel.edu
Baptist Missionary Association of America (Official)—Email: pzhgrx@bmaa-missions.cnchost.com
   Web: bmaa-missions.cnchost.com
The Bible Church of Christ, Inc. (Official)—Web: www.tbcc.org
Bible Fellowship Church (Official)—Email:EricClontz@juno.com
   Web: www.bfc.org
Bible Way Church of Our Lord Jesus Christ World Wide, Inc. (Official)—
   Email: LADYAGNES@email.msn.com
   Web: www.biblewaychurch.org
Brethren in Christ Church (Official)—Email:Khoke@messiah.edu
   Web: www.bic-church.org/main/index.htm
Brethren in Christ Church (Ashland, Ohio) (Official)—Email:brethren@bright.net
   Web: www.apollotrust.com/~brethren
Christ Catholic Church (Official)—Web: christcatholic.org
Christadelphians (Official)—Email:bible@islandnet.com
   Web: www.christadelphia.org
The Christian and Missionary Alliance (Official)—Email:info@cmalliance.org
   Web: www.cmalliance.org
Christian Brethren (AKA: Plymouth Brethren) (Unofficial FAQ)—
   Web: www.storm.ca/~sabigail/faqs/brethren.htm
Christian Church (Disciples of Christ) (Official)—Email:cmiller@oc.disciples.org
   Web: www.disciples.org
Christian Church of North America, General Council (Official)—Email:ccna@nauticom.net
   Web: www.ccna.org
Christian Churches and Churches of Christ (Unofficial)—Email:jowston@cwv.edu
   Web: www.cwv.net/christ'n
Christian Methodist Episcopal Church (Official)—Email:ljames5@bellsouth.net
   Web: www.c-m-e.org
Christian Reformed Church in North America (Official)—Email:Email: btgh@crcna.org
   Web: www.crcna.org
Church of Christ (Official)—Web: church-of-christ.com
Church of Christ, Scientist (Official)—Web: www.tfccs.com
Church of God (Anderson, Indiana) (Official)—Email:BPearson@chog.org
   Web: www.chog.org
Church of God (Cleveland, Tennessee) (Official)—Email: cogmedia@aol.com
   Web: www.chofgod.org
Church of God by Faith, Inc. (Official)—Web: www.cogbf.org
Church of God General Conference (Oregon, Il and Morrow, GA) (Official)—
   Email:info@abc-coggc.org
   Web: www.abc-coggc.org

The Church of God in Christ—Web: www.cogic.org

Church of God in Christ, Mennonite (Unofficial)—Email:webmaster@bibleviews.com
Web: www.bibleviews.com/holdeman.html

Church of God of Prophecy (Official)—Email:cogopinfo@cogop.org
Web: www.cogop.org

Church of God, Mountain Assembly, Inc. (Official)—Email: cgmahdq@jellico.com
Web: michael.padgett.net/cgma

Church of God (Seventh Day), Denver (Official)—Email:cofgsd@denver.net
Web: www.denver.net/~cofgsd

The Church of Illumination (Official)—Email:bevhall@mail.comcat.com
Web: www.soul.org

The Church of Jesus Christ of Latter-day Saints (Official)—Web: www.lds.org

Church of Our Lord Jesus Christ of the Apostolic Faith, Inc. (Churches Directory)
Web: www.churchsurf.com/churches/apostol.htm

Church of the Brethren (Official)—Email:ssnyder_gb@brethren.org
Web: www.brethren.org

Church of Christ (Holiness) U.S.A. (Official)—Email:Everything@cochusa.com
Web: www.cochusa.com

Church of the Lutheran Brethren in America (Official)—Email:clba@clba.org
Web: www.clba.org

Church of the Lutheran Confession (Official)—Email:JohnHLau@juno.com
Web: www.primenet.com/~clcpub/clc/clc.html

Church of the Nazarene (Official)—Email:webmaster@nazarene.org
Web: www.nazarene.org

Church of the United Brethren in Christ (Official)—Email:sdennie@ub.org
Web: www.ub.org

Churches of Christ in Christian Union (Official)—Web: www.bright.net/~cccuhq

Churches of God, General Conference (Official)—Email:comptech@cggc.org
Web: www.cggc.org

Congregational Holiness Church (Official)—Email:chchurch@bellsouth.net
Web: chchurch.com

Conservative Baptist Association of America (Official)—Email:CBAmerica@aol.com
Web: www.cbamerica.org

Conservative Congregational Christian Conference (Official)—Email:CCCC4@juno.com
Web: www.ccccusa.org

Conservative Lutheran Association—Email: PastorPJ@ix.netcom.com
Web: www.tlcanaheim.com/CLA

Coptic Orthodox Church—Email: Webmaster@coptic.org
Web: www.coptic.org

Cumberland Presbyterian Church (Official)—Email:pmj@cumberland.org
Web: www.cumberland.org

Cumberland Presbyterian Church in America (Official)—Email:mleslie598@aol.com
Web: www.cumberland.org/cpca

Diocese of the Armenian Church of America (Official)—
Web: www.canarmdiocese.org/directory.htm

Elim Fellowship—Email:75551.743@compuserve.com
Web: www.elim.edu/ef/efexec.htm

Episcopal Church (Official)—Email:pam.darling@ecunet.org
Web www.ecusa.anglican.org

The Estonian Evangelical Lutheran Church— Email:EELK.Toronto@churchoffice.com
Web: www.churchoffice.com/eelk/eelkto.html

The Evangelical Church Alliance (Official)—Email:ECA@keynet.net
Web: www.keynet.net/~eca

The Evangelical Congregational Church (Official)—Email:eccenter@eccenter.com
Web: www.eccenter.com/church

The Evangelical Covenant Church (Official)—Email:CovCom@compuserve.com
Web: www.covchurch.org

The Evangelical Episcopal Church International (Official)—Web: www.eeci.org

The Evangelical Free Church of America (Official)—Email:webmaster@efca.org
Web: www.efca.org

Evangelical Friends International—North American Region (Official)—
Email:carym@earthlink.net
Web: www.evangelical-friends.org

Evangelical Lutheran Church in America (Official)—Email:info@elca.org
Web: www.elca.org

Evangelical Lutheran Synod (Official)—Email:gorvick@blc.edu
Web: www.evluthsyn.org

Evangelical Mennonite Church (Official)—Email:emcintlmin@aol.com
Web: www.brookside.org/emc.htm

Evangelical Methodist Church (Official)—Email:headquarters@emchurch.org
Web: www.emchurch.org

Evangelical Presbyterian Church (Official)—Email:EPCHURCH@aol.com
Web: www.epc.org

Fellowship of Evangelical Bible Churches—Email:febcoma@aol.com
Web: members.aol.com/febcoma

Fellowship of Fundamental Bible Churches—Email:info@churches-ffbc.org
Web: www.churches-ffbc.org

Fellowship of Grace Brethren Churches (Official)—Email:fgbc@fgbc.org
Web: www.fgbc.org

Free Methodist Church of North America (Official)—Email:infor@fmcna.org
Web: www.fmcna.org

Friends General Conference (Official)—Email:friends@fgc.quaker.org
Web: www.quaker.org/fgc

Friends United Meeting (Official)—Email:fuminfo@xc.org
Web: www.fum.org

Full Gospel Fellowship of Churches and Ministers International (Official)
Email:fgfcmi@aol.com
Web: www.fgfcmi.org

General Assembly of the Korean Presbyterian Church in America—Web: www.kapc.org

General Association of General Baptists (Unofficial)—
Web: www.angelfire.com/mo/genbap/gagb.html

General Association of Regular Baptist Churches (Official)—Email:garbc@garbc.org
Web: www.garbc.org

General Church of the New Jerusalem (Official)—Email:svsimpso@newchurch.edu
Web: www.newchurch.org

General Conference of Mennonite Brethren Churches (Official)—Email:mhein1@fresno.edu
Web: www.mbconf.org

Grace Gospel Fellowship (Official)—Email:ggfinc@aol.com
Web: www.ggfusa.org

Greek Orthodox Archdiocese of America (Official)—Email:archdiocese@goarch.org
Web: www.goarch.org

The Holy Eastern Orthodox Catholic and Apostolic Church in North America, Inc.—
Email:info@theocacna.org
Web: www.theocacna.org

Holy Ukrainian Autocephalic Orthodox Church in Exile—Web: www.stmichaelacademy.org

Independent Fundamental Churches of America/IFCA International, Inc. (Official)—
Email:office@ifca.org
Web: www.ifca.org

International Church of the Foursquare Gospel (Official)—Email:nco@foursquare.org
Web: www.foursquare.org

International Council of Community Churches (Official)—
Web: www.akcache.com/community/iccc-nat.html

The International Pentecostal Church of Christ (Official)—Email:hqipcc@aol.com
Web: members.aol.com/hqipcc/index.htm

International Pentecostal Holiness Church (Official)—Email:jdl@iphc.org
Web: www.iphc.org

Jehovah's Witnesses (Official)—Web: www.watchtower.org

The Liberal Catholic Church (Official)—Email:ldworle@bentley.univnorthco.edu
Web: members.aol.com/lcatholic

Lutheran Church—Missouri Synod (Official)—Email:infocenter@lcms.org
Web: www.lcms.org

Malankara Orthodox Syrian Church, Diocese of America (Official)—
Email:Malankara@malankara.org
Web: www.malankara.org/american.htm

Mar Thoma Syrian Church of India (Official)—Email:thirumeni@marthomachurch.org
Web: www.marthomachurch.org

Mennonite Church (Official)—Email:rbyler@juno.com
Web: www.mennonites.org

Mennonite Church, General Conference (Official)—Email: gcmcinfo@gcmc.org
Web: www2.southwind.net/~gcmc

The Missionary Church (Official)—Email: mcdenomusa@aol.com
Web: www.sweetwater.com/mcusa

Moravian Church in America (Unitas Fratrum) (Official)—
Email: burke@mcnp.org (Northern Province)
Email: rsawyer@mcsp.org (Southern Province)
Web: www.moravian.org

National Association of Congregational Christian Churches (Official)—Email: naccc@naccc.org
Web: www.naccc.org

National Association of Free Will Baptists (Official)—Web: www.nafwb.org

National Baptist Convention of America, Inc. (Official)—Email: nbyc1@aol.com
Web: members.aol.com/nbyc1/nbca.html

National Organization of the New Apostolic Church of North America—Web: www.nak.org

National Spiritualist Association of Churches (Official)—Email: nsac@nsac.org
Web: www.nsac.org

North American Baptist Conference (Official)—Email: serve@NABConference.org
Web: www.nabconference.org

Open Bible Standard Churches (Official)—Email: info@openbible.org
Web: www.openbible.org

The Orthodox Church in America (Official)—Email: jjm@oca.org
Web: www.oca.org

The Orthodox Presbyterian Church (Official)—Web: www.opc.org

Pentecostal Church of God (Official)—Email: pcg@pcg.org
Web: www.pcg.org

Presbyterian Church (U.S.A.) (Official)—Email: presytel@pcusa.org
Web: www.pcusa.org

Presbyterian Church in America—Email: info@ac.pca-atl.org
Web: www.pcanet.org

Primitive Methodist Church in the U. S. A. (Official)—Email: pmconf@juno.com

Progressive National Baptist Convention, Inc. (Official)—Email: info@pnbc.org
Web: www.pnbc.org

Protestant Reformed Churches in America (Official)—Email: doezema@prca.org
Web: www.prca.org

Reformed Church in America (Official)—Email: japinga@rca.org
Web: www.rca.org

Reformed Church in the United States (Official)—Email: fhw@iname.com
Web: www.rcus.org

Reformed Episcopal Church (Official)—Email: nicaea@aol.com
Web: www.geopages.com/capitolhill/1125

Reformed Presbyterian Church of North America (Official)—Web: www.reformed.com/rpcna

Religious Society of Friends (Unaffiliated Meetings) (Official)—Web: www.quaker.org/fwcc

Reorganized Church of Jesus Christ of Latter Day Saints—Email:snaylor@rlds.org
Web: www.rlds.org

The Roman Catholic Church (Official)—Web: www.vatican.va

The Romanian Orthodox Episcopate of America (Official)—Email: roeasolia@aol.com
Web: www.roea.org

The Russian Orthodox Church Outside of Russia (Official)—Web: www.synod.com

The Salvation Army (Official)—Email: websa@SalvationArmy.org
Web: www.sarmy.org

Separate Baptists in Christ (Official)—Email: mail@separatebaptist.org
Web: www.separatebaptist.org

Serbian Orthodox Church in the U. S. A. and Canada (Official)—Email: gsladic@mcs.com

Seventh-day Adventist Church (Official)—Email: northamerica.adventist.org
Web: www.adventist.org

Seventh Day Baptist General Conference, USA and Canada (Official)—
Email: sdbgen@inwave.com
Web: www.seventhdaybaptist.org

Southern Baptist Convention (Official)—Email:bmerrell@sbc.net
Web: www.sbc.net

Southern Methodist Church—Email: smchq@juno.com

Sovereign Grace Believers—Email: libcfl@aol.com
Web: www.searchingtogether.org

The Swedenborgian Church (Official)—Email: manager@centraloffice.swedenborg.org
Web: www.swedenborg.org

Syrian Orthodox Church of Antioch (Official)—Email: Syrianoc@syrianorthodoxchurch.org
Web: www.syrianorthodoxchurch.org

Unitarian Universalist Association of Congregations (Official)—Email: jhurley@uua.org
Web: www.uua.org

United Church of Christ (Official)—Email: langa@ucc.org
Web: www.ucc.org

United Methodist Church (Official)—Email: infoserv@umcom.umc.org
Web: www.umc.org

United Pentecostal Church, International (Official)—Web: www.upci.org

United Zion Church (Official)—Email: archbishopgregory@usa.net

Universal Fellowship of Metropolitan Community Churches (Official)—
Email: communications@ufmcchq.com
Web: www.ufmcchq.com

Volunteers of America (Official)—Email: voa@voa.org
Web: www.voa.org

The Wesleyan Church (Official)—Web: www.wesleyan.org

Wisconsin Evangelical Lutheran Synod (Official)—Email: pres@sab.wels.net
Web: www.wels.net

For additional website information pertaining to U.S. and Canadian religious organizations, try our new electronic church website at www.ElectronicChurch.org.

THE EMERGING
ELECTRONIC CHURCH

Sources of Religion-related Research

The editorial office of the *Yearbook of American & Canadian Churches* receives innumerable requests for data about churches, religious organizations, attendance patterns, and comparative religion concerns. Sometimes we are able to furnish the requested data, but more often we refer the inquirer to other research colleagues in the field. We are always interested in and aided by such requests, and we find ourselves informed by each question.

In response to such inquiries, the "Sources in Religion-related Research" directory was initiated in the 1999 edition of the *Yearbook*. It was quite well received, and as a result, this year we have decided to expand this directory in the 2000 edition of the *Yearbook*. Not only is the list of organizations now larger than it was last year, this year we provide a much more detailed description of the kinds of research performed by these organizations. In addition to asking each organization to provide a brief overall description, each was also asked to indicate any special research foci (i.e. denominational, congregational, interfaith, gender, etc.). Further, each organization was asked to identify the sociological, methodological, or theological approaches that serve to guide their research, and to describe any current or recent research projects. Last, we asked for a list of recurrent publications. Below the organizations' responses to these questions are reported as clearly and completely as is possible. Contact information appears just beneath the title of each organization. In most cases the organizations' websites provide very detailed information about current research projects.

Numerous other research centers in the area of American religious life, each with specific areas of concern, conduct timely and significant research. We hope that readers will find utility in this directory, and we invite them to identify additional sources by email at yearbook@ncccusa.org or by fax: (212) 870-2817.

American Academy of Religion (AAR)

AAR Executive Office
825 Houston Mill Rd., Ste. 300
Atlanta, GA 30329
Tel. (404)727-7920
Email: aar@emory.edu
Website: www.aar-site.org
President: Dr. Lawrence E. Sullivan
Exec. Dir.: Dr. Barbara DeConcini

The AAR is the major learned society and professional association for scholars whose object of study is religion. Its mission" in a world where religion plays so central a role in social, political and economic events, as well as in the lives of communities and individuals" is to meet a critical need for ongoing reflection upon and understanding of religious traditions, issues, questions and values. As a learned society and professional association of teachers and research scholars, the American Academy of Religion has over 8000 members who teach in some 1,500 colleges, universities, seminaries, and schools in North America and abroad. The Academy is dedicated to furthering knowledge of religion and religious institutions in all their forms and manifestations. This is accomplished through Academy-wide and regional conferences and meetings, publications, programs, and membership services. Within a context of free inquiry and critical examination, the Academy welcomes all disciplined reflection on religion, "both from within and outside of communities of belief and practice" and seeks to enhance its broad public understanding.

The AAR's annual meeting, over 7,500 scholars gather to share research and collaborate on scholarly projects. The annual meeting sessions are grouped into over 70 program units, each representing an ongoing community of scholars who are collectively engaged in pursuing knowledge about a specific religious tradition or a specific aspect of religion. In addition, the AAR's ten regional organizations sponsor smaller annual meetings that are similar in structure to the Academy-wide meeting. All of the world's major religious traditions, as well as indigenous and historical religions, are explored in the work of AAR members.

Current or Recent Research

Currently, for example, the AAR offers teaching workshops for both junior and senior scholars. It is organizing efforts to gather data on the field to facilitate departmental planning and funding. A full explanation of the many current research projects is available on the AAR website, which is listed above.

Periodicals

The *Journal of the American Academy of Religion* is the scholarly periodical of the AAR. In addition, the AAR publishes a semi-annual periodical titled "Spotlight on Teaching" in the society's newsletter, *Religious Studies News*.

American Religion Data Archive (ARDA)

Department of Sociology / Anthropology
Purdue University
1365 Stone Hall
West Lafayette, IN 47907-1476
Tel. (765) 494-0081
Fax (765) 496-1476
Email: archive@sri.soc.purdue.edu
Website: www.TheARDA.com
Director: Dr. Roger Finke

The American Religion Data Archive (ARDA) is an Internet-based data archive that stores and distributes quantitative data sets from the leading studies on American religion" free of charge. Supported by the Lilly Endowment and housed at Purdue University, ARDA strives to *preserve* data files for future use, *prepare* the data files for immediate public use, and make the data files easily *accessible* to all. Data files can be downloaded from the Internet site or they can be analyzed online.

The ARDA includes national surveys on American and Canadian religion, regional surveys, surveys sampling the membership of specific denominations, and surveys of religions professionals. The 1952, 1971, 1980, and 1990 church and church membership surveys for counties and states are also included in the ARDA.

Association of Theological Schools (ATS)

10 Summit Park Dr.
Pittsburgh, PA 15275-1103
Tel. (412) 788-6505
Fax (412) 788-6510
Email: ats@ats.edu
Website: www.ats.edu
Exec. Dir.: Daniel O. Aleshire
Contact: Nancy Merrill, Dir. of Communications and Membership Services

The Association of Theological Schools (ATS) is the accrediting and program agency for graduate theological education in North America. Its 237 member institutions represent the broad spectrum of denominational, ecclesiastical, and theological perspectives evident in North America today, making it the most broad-based religious organization of its kind. The Association comprises Protestant, Roman Catholic, and Orthodox schools of theology, both university-related divinity schools and freestanding seminaries. A full list of members is available on the above website.

The primary purpose of the Association is the improvement of theological schools, which ATS seeks to attain by accrediting schools and by providing programs and service to its membership, such as, among others, a data center of statistical information on the member schools; leadership education for seminary presidents, academic deans, trustees, and development officers; grants for faculty scholarship and research; faculty development programs sponsored by the Faculty Resource Center; student information resources; a program of globalization in theological education; efforts to enhance the participation of under-represented constituencies in theological education; and various publications. In addition, the Association provides a venue for addressing the critical and emerging issues in North American theological education

Current or Recent Research

The current discussion focuses on identifying the nature, characteristics, and related issues related to the "Public Character of Theological Education." The major activities of the project include convening five study groups to explore the issue from varying ecclesial and institutional contexts; a regranting program to provide the stimulus for schools to experiment with programs to establish a greater civic presence in their communities; and opportunities to focus though and conversation about the public character of theological education broadly among faculties and administrative leaders of ATS schools. The discussion will explore how more rigorous theological thinking about the public issues that face democratic cultures can contribute not only to the intellectual life of the theological school but to the broader society as well.

Periodicals

Fact Book on Theological Education is published annually and provides statistical data on theological education in the U.S. and Canada. Also, the Association publishes a journal, *Theological Education* bi-annually, a newsletter bimonthly called *Colloquy*, and the formal institutional documents of the Association entitled the *Bulletin*. The *Bulletin* also contains an ATS directory and a membership list.

Auburn Theological Seminary

3041 Broadway
New York, NY 10027
Tel. (212) 662-4314
Fax (212) 662-4315
Email: mnw@auburn.org
Website: www.auburnsem.org
Director: Dr. Barbara G. Wheeler
Contact: Dr. Mark N. Wilhelm

Auburn Theological Seminary's mission is to strengthen religious leadership. It carries out its mission through programs of non-degree theological education for clergy and laity; through programs for Presbyterian students enrolled at its partner institution, Union Seminary in New York City; and by conducting research on theological education at its Center for the Study of Theological Education. Auburn was founded in 1818 in Auburn, New York; it is currently located on Union Seminary's campus.

Auburn Seminary is related by covenant agreement with Presbyterian Church (U.S.A.), but most of its programs are ecumenical, and many have a multi-faith focus. The Center for the Study of Theological Education includes rabbinical schools and Protestant and Roman Catholic seminaries and divinity schools in its studies.

Research is conducted using a variety of methods, including survey and ethnographic research, structured interview and documentary research, research reports on surveys and case studies. Reports of findings are frequently published with accompanying information on the history of the issue being studied and with theological commentaries written from a variety of perspectives.

Current or Recent Research

Currently, the Center is completing studies of seminary students, of public perceptions of theological education and church leadership, and of history of religion and urban America. The Center is about to begin a study of seminary trustees and senior administrators.

Periodicals

Auburn Studies, an occasional bulletin in which the Center publishes its research results. Research reports are also available on Auburn's website (listed above).

Barna Research Group, Ltd.

5528 Everglades
Ventura, CA 93003
Tel. (805) 658-8885
Fax (805) 658-7298
Website: www.barna.org
President: George Barna
Contact: David Kinnaman, Vice President

Barna Research Group works with Christian churches and parachurch ministries throughout the nation by providing primary research data related to cultural change, people's lifestyles, values, attitudes, beliefs and religious practices. Its vision is to provide current accurate and reliable information, in bite-sized pieces and at reasonable costs, to ministries who will use the information to make better strategic decisions. They conduct primary research for ministries that commission such research, studying their community, their church or special population. Barna also produces many research-based books, reports, and ministry tools to help churches understand the national context of ministry. Barna Research conducts seminars in many markets across the nation to inform church leaders of its findings, and to train church leaders in the application of that information. The organization works with churches from all Christian denominations.

Barna Research has no special research focus. It conducts projects based upon existing needs in the church at large, or for its clients specifically, and analyzes all of its findings in relation to a minimum of three dozen population subgroups involved in the survey interviews. Methodologically, Barna Research uses both qualitative approaches (focus groups, depth interviews) and quantitative approaches (cross-sectional surveys, longitudinal studies, panel research). Data collection methods include telephone surveys, mail surveys, in-person interviews, on-line surveys, self-administered surveys, focus groups.

Current or Recent Research

Barna Research conducts more than 50 studies each year, covering a broad range of topics. Some of the recent non-proprietary studies completed are focused on understanding the state of the church;

the habits of highly effective churches; worship efficacy; the unchurched; strategies and techniques for developing lay leaders; understanding effective discipleship processes; pastoral profiles; beliefs and core attitudes of religious donors; biblical knowledge, and many others.

Periodicals

Barna Research offers a bi-weekly update on current information related to faith matters from its national non-proprietary research. This information is free to those who register for it at the website (listed above).

Center for the Study of Religion and American Culture

Indiana University
Purdue University at Indianapolis
425 University Blvd, Room 341
Indianapolis, IN 46202-5140
Tel. (317) 274-8409
Fax (317) 278-3354
Email: Ccherry@iupui.edu
Website: www.iupui.edu/it/raac
Director: Dr. Conrad Cherry

The Center for the Study of Religion and American Culture is a research and public outreach institute devoted to the promotion of the understanding of the relation between religion and other features of American culture. Research methods are both inter-disciplinary and multi-disciplinary. Established in 1989, the Center is based in the School of Liberal Arts and Indiana University-Purdue University at Indianapolis. Center activities include national conferences and symposia, commissioned books, essays, bibliographies, and research projects, fellowships for younger scholars, data based communication about developments in the field of American religion, a newsletter devoted to the promotion of Center activities, and the semi-annual scholarly periodical, *Religion and American Culture: A Journal of Interpretation*.

Current or Recent Research

The Center is currently conducting research on the "public dimensions of American Religion," and on "Religion in Higher Education."

Periodicals

Religion and American Culture: A Journal of Interpretation. Center books include the series, "The Public Expressions of Religion in America."

empty tomb, inc.

301 North Fourth Street
P.O. Box 2404
Champaign, IL 61825-2404
Tel. (217)356-9519
Fax (217)356-2344
Website: www.emptytomb.org
CEO: John L. Ronsvalle
Exec.Vice-Pres.: Sylvia Ronsvalle

empty tomb, inc. is a Christian research and service organization. On a local level, it coordinates direct services to people in need in cooperation with area congregations. On a national level, it studies church member giving patterns of historically Christian churches, including Roman Catholic, mainline and evangelical Protestant, Anabaptist, Pentecostal, Orthodox, and fundamentalist communions. empty tomb publishes the annual *State of Church Giving* series. Staff also work with a select number of congregations, discovering ways to reverse the negative giving trends indicated by national data, through its project, The National Money for Mission Program.

Current or Recent Research

Current research monitors and analyzes church member giving patters, and is published in *The State of Church Giving* series produced by empty tomb, inc. The description of dynamics affecting current giving patterns is presented in *Behind The Stained Glass Windows: Money Dynamics in The Church (*Grand Rapids, MI: Baker Books, 1996).

Periodicals

The State of Church Giving series is an annual publication. It considers denominational giving data, analysis of giving and membership trends, and other estimates of charitable giving. Each edition has featured a special focus chapter, which discusses giving issues relevant to a broad audience. Selected data tables are posted on the empty tomb website (listed above).

The Hartford Institute for Religious Research of Hartford Seminary

Hartford Seminary
77 Sherman Street
Hartford, CT 06105
Tel. (860)509-9543
Fax (860)509-9559
Email: hirr@hartsem.edu Website: www.hartsem.edu/csrr/

The Hartford Institute for Religion Research of Hartford Seminary was established in 1981, formalizing a research program initiated by the Seminary in 1974. Until recently it was known as The Center for Social and Religious Research. The Institute's work is guided by a disciplined understanding of the interrelationship between (a) the inner life and resources of American religious institutions and (b) the possibilities and limits placed on those institutions by the social and cultural context into which God has called them.

Its twenty-year record of rigorous, policy-relevant research, anticipation of emerging issues, commitment to the creative dissemination of learning, and strong connections to both theological education and the church has earned the Institute an international reputation as an important bridge between the scholarly community and the practice of ministry.

Current or Resent Research

Some of the titles of current projects at the Institute are: "Organizing Religious Work for the 21st Century: Exploring "Denominationalism;" "Cooperative Congregational Studies Project;" "Congregational Consulting Services;" "New England Religion Discussion Society (NERDS);" "Congregational Studies Team." Descriptions of these programs are available on the Institute's website, listed above.

Periodicals

Praxis is Hartford Seminary's magazine, which focuses on the activities and faculty of the Institute.

Institute for Ecumenical and Cultural Research

P.O. Box 6188
Collegeville, MN 56321-6188
Tel. (320) 363-3366
Fax (320) 363-3313
Email: iecr@csbsju.edu
Website: www.csbsju.edu/iecr
Exec. Dir.: Dr. Patrick Henry

The Institute for Ecumenical and Cultural Research brings together well-trained, creative, articulate men and women for careful thought and dialogue in a place of inquiry and prayer. The Resident scholars Program welcomes researchers and their families for either individual semesters or for an entire academic year. Resident scholars work on their own projects but meet once a week for seminars, and have other occasions for conversation. Each scholar presents a public lecture. Ecumenism happens at the Institute as people come to know one another in community. The Institute is an independent corporation, but shares in the Benedictine and academic life of Saint John's Abbey and University, and of nearby Saint Benedict's Monastery and the College of Saint Benedict. In the summer the Institute uses its facilities for invitational consultations on subjects considered by the Board of Directors to be of special ecumenical interest.

In the Resident Scholars Program, the subjects of research are determined by the interests of the applicants who are invited to come by the Admissions Committee. While most of the work tends to be in traditional theological areas, we encourage people in all fields to consider applying, both because ecumenism is of concern across the spectrum of disciplines, and because the term "cultural" in our title extends our reach beyond theology and religious studies. In particular cases, work done here may have a denominational, congregational, or interfaith focus, but the Institute does not prescribe or delimit, in any narrow way, what is appropriate.

Current or Recent Research

Recent summer consultations have had the following titles: "Prayer in the Ecumenical Movement"; "Virtues for an Ecumenical Heart"; "The Price of Disunity"; "Living Faithfully in North America Today." Among subjects dealt with in earlier years are "Orthodoxy at Home in North America"; "transmitting Tradition to Children and Young People"; "The Nature of Christian Hope";

"Women and the Church"; Jewish and Christian Relatedness to Scripture"; "Confessing Christian Faith in a Pluralistic Society."

Periodicals

Ecumenical People, Programs, Papers is a biannual newsletter containing brief sketches of resident scholars, reports on Institute programs, and, in nearly every issue, an "An Occasional Paper" on a subject of ecumenical interest. The newsletter is free.

Institute for the Study of American Evangelicals (ISAE)

Wheaton College
Wheaton, IL 60187
Tel. (630) 752-5437
Fax (630) 752-5916
Email: isae@wheaton.edu
Website: www.wheaton.edu/isae
Director: Dr. Edith Blumhofer

Founded in 1982, the Institute for the Study of American Evangelicals is a center for research and functions as a program of Wheaton College. The purpose of the ISAE is to encourage and support research on evangelical Christianity in the United States and Canada. The institute seeks to help evangelicals develop a mature understanding of their own heritage and to inform others about evangelicals" historical significance and contemporary role. For the most part, the ISAE focuses on historical research, with occasional sociological or economic researchers participating in the projects.

Current or Recent Research

One recent project entitled, "Hymnody in American Protestantism" is a research project focusing on the history of hymnology in American religious life.

Periodicals

Evangelical Studies Bulletin (*ESB*) is designed to aid both the scholar and the layman in his or her education and research of evangelicalism. Issued quarterly, the bulletin contains articles, book reviews, notices, a calendar of events, and bibliographic information on the latest dissertations, articles and books related to the study of evangelicalism.

Institute for the Study of American Religion

P.O. Box 90709
Santa Barbara, CA 93190-0709
Tel. (805)967-7721
Fax (805)961-0141
Website: www.americanreligion.org

The Institute for the Study of American Religion was founded in 1969 in Evanston, Illinois as a religious studies research facility with a particular focus upon the smaller religions of the United States. Those groups which it has concentrated upon have been known under a variety of labels including sect, cult, minority religion, alternative religion, non-conventional religion, spiritual movement, and new religious movement. It quickly extended its attention to Canada developed a worldwide focus in the 1990s. In 1985, the institute moved to its present location in Santa Barbara, California.

Over the years the institute built a large collection of both primary and secondary materials on the religious groups and movements it studied. In 1985 this collection of more than 40,000 volumes and thousands of periodicals and archival materials was deposited to the Davidson Library at the University of California in Santa Barbara. The reference material exists today as the *American Religious Collection* and is open to scholars and the interested public. The institute continues to support the collection with donations of additional materials.

Current or Recent Research

Today the institute has two main foci. It monitors all of the religious denominations, organizations, and movements functioning in North America and regularly publishes reports drawing from that activity in a series of reference books. The most important of these reference books is the *Encyclopedia of American Religions* (Detroit: Gale research, 5th edition, 1996). Among the most called for information is factual data on the many new and more controversial religious movements, which are popularly labeled as "cults." The institute's second focus developed out of its more recent refocusing on the international scene, provoked by the international life of most of the religious groups which it has studied in previous decades. With support from the Institute of World Spirituality in Chicago, Illinois, the institute launched the International Religions Directory Project in 1996, a massive five year project that aims to create a full directory of religious bodies, interfaith organizations, and other religious groups world-wide. Please see the above website for more information.

J.W. Dawson Institute of Church-State Studies at Baylor University

P.O. Box 97308
Waco, TX 76798-7308
Tel. (254) 710-1510
Fax (254) 710-1571
Email: dere_davis@baylor.edu
Website: www.baylor.edu/~Church_State
Director: Dr. Derek Davis

Baylor University established the J.M. Dawson Institute of Church-State Studies in 1957, so named in honor of an outstanding alumnus, an ardent advocate of religious liberty, and a distinguished author of publications on church and state. The Institute is the oldest and most well-established facility of its kind located in a university setting. It is exclusively devoted to research in the broad field of church and state and the advancement of religious liberty around the world.

From its inception in 1957, the stated purpose of the Institute has been to stimulate academic interest and encourage research and publication in the broad area of church/state relations. In carrying out its statement of purpose, the Institute has sought to honor a threefold commitment: to be interfaith, interdisciplinary, and international.

Current or Recent Research

Some current research includes: government persecution of minority religions in Europe; original intent of founding fathers regarding religion and public life; Christian Right views on political activism; conservative versus moderate Baptist views on church/state relations; role of civil religion in America; international treaties and religious liberty.

Periodicals

Journal of Church and State is the only scholarly journal expressly devoted to church/state relations.

The Louisville Institute

1044 Alta Vista Road
Louisville, KY 40205-1798
Tel. (502) 895-3411 ext. 487
Fax (502) 894-2286
Email: info@louisville-institute.org
Website: www.louisville-institute.org
Exec. Dir.: Dr. James W. Lewis

The Louisville Institute is a Lilly Endowment program for the study of American religion based at the Louisville Presbyterian Seminary. As a program of Lilly Endowment, the Louisville Institute builds upon the Endowment's long-standing support of both leadership education and scholarly research on American religion, focusing on American Protestantism, American Catholicism, the historic African American churches, and the Hispanic religious experience. The distinctive mission of the Louisville Institute is to enrich the religious life of American Christians and to encourage the revitalization of their institutions by bringing together those who lead religious institutions with those who study them, so that the work of each might stimulate and inform the other. The Louisville Institute seeks to fulfill its mission through a program of grantmaking and conferences.

The work of the Louisville Institute focuses on religion in North America, with particular attention to three issues. The first, Christian faith and life, concerns the character and role of the theology and spirituality that are effectively at work in the lives of American Christians. The second, religious institutions, asks how America's religious institutions might respond most constructively in the midst of the bewildering institutional reconfiguration occurring in American society. The third, pastoral leadership, explores various strategies for improving the quality of religious leadership in North America. The various research projects employ a variety of disciplinary perspectives, including but not limited to, theology, history, ethics, and the social sciences. They may also be interdisciplinary in nature.

Current or Recent Research

Please see the Louisville Institute website (listed above) for lists of recent grants made by the Louisville Institute.

The Pluralism Project

Harvard University
201 Vanserg Hall
25 Francis Avenue
Cambridge, MA 02138
Tel. (617)496-2481
Fax (617)496-2428
Email: pluralsm@fas.harvard.edu
Website: www.fas.harvard.edu/~pluralsm
Director: Dr. Diana L. Eck
Project Manager: Ellie J. Pierce

The Pluralism Project was developed by Dr. Diana L. Eck at Harvard University to study and document the growing religions diversity of the United States, with a special view to its new immigrant religious communities. The religious landscape of the U.S. has radically changed in the past 30 years; in light of these changes, how Americans of all faiths begin to engage with one another in shaping a positive pluralism is one of the most important questions American society faces in the years ahead. In addressing these phenomena, the Project has three goals: 1) to document some further changes taking place in America's cities and towns by beginning to map their new religious demography with old and new mosques and Islamic centers, Sikh gurdwaras, Hindu and Jain temples, Buddhist temples and meditation centers, Zoroastrian and Taoist religious centers. 2) To begin to study how these religious traditions are changing as they take root in American soil and develop in a new context. How are they beginning to recreate their community life, religious institutions, rites and rituals, and forms of transmission in the cultural environment of the United States? 3) To explore how the United States is changing as we begin to appropriate this new religious diversity in our public life and institutions and in emerging forms of interfaith relationships.

The Pluralism Project has the most comprehensive archive anywhere of the print materials of America's new immigrant religious communities: newsletters, serial publications, anniversary programs, handbooks, prayer books, calendars, and educational materials. The Project files also include research papers as well as a variety of materials donated directly by centers.

The Pluralism Project On-Line Directory maintains an extensive directory of religious centers in the United States. At present, this directory exists in a sortable database, with listings of nearly 3,000 centers across the U.S.

Current or Recent Research

The Pluralism Project produced a CD-ROM, *On Common Ground: World Religions in America*, to present some of the wide range of work that had emerged from three years of research. A further grant from the Ford Foundation has enabled the Project to extend its research on the American religious landscape.

Princeton Religion Research Center (PRRC)

47 Hulfish Street
P.O. Box 389
Princeton, NJ 08542
Tel. (609) 279-2255
Fax (609) 924-0228
Email: marie_swirsky@gallup.com
Website: www.prrc.com
Exec. Dir.: George Gallup, Jr.
Contact: Marie Swirsky

The Princeton Religion Research Center is a venerable interfaith, non-denominational organization founded by George Gallup, Jr. and Dr. Miriam Murphy in 1977. The PRRC specializes in creative, practical research, utilizing the worldwide Gallup survey facilities. The purpose of the PRRC is to gain a better understanding of the nature and depth of religious commitment, and to explore the factors behind spiritual growth and decline. The research employs qualitative and quantitative Gallup survey research using scientifically-selected samples of people.

Current or Recent Research

The Princeton Religion Research Center, the Gallup Organization, the Gallup Poll, and the Gallup Youth Survey have conducted surveys for more than 100 denominations or religious groups.

Periodicals

Emerging Trends, published since 1979, provides up-to-date Gallup survey information on reli-

SOURCES

217

gion and society. The six-page monthly keeps readers abreast of national issues facing church and society, as well as the latest findings on religious belief, practice, and knowledge. *Religion in America* is a bi-annual report.

The Public Religion Project

919 North Michigan Ave.
Suite 540
Chicago, IL 60611-1681
Tel. (312)397-6400
Email: prp-info@publicreligionproj.org
Website: www.publicreligionproj.org
Director: Dr. Martin E. Marty

Building on the strength of personal and private expressions of religious faith, the Public Religion Project addresses the issue of public expressions of faith in a diverse civil society. The Chicago-based directors, staff, and advisors of the Project cooperate internationally with the many agencies, academies, and individuals who would bridge the gap between public and private articulations and actions. It is through this cooperation that the Public Religion Project seeks to contribute to the improved quality of life in the republic. The Public Religion Project has no particular ideological bias, and its only agenda is to help assure that the role of religion is given a representative hearing. The Project's leadership listens carefully for expressions by people of profound conviction and institutions that represent the ever-growing variety of religious impulses in America. It seeks to promote that expression in public life. The role of The Public Religion Project is to provide public access to experts; it does not do original research.

Current or Recent Research

The Public Religion Project maintains a comprehensive database of contact information for individuals who can address questions about religion and about the role it plays in public life. The database consists of internationally recognized scholars, experts, spokespersons and authorities who have agreed to be listed as resources. The database serves a great variety of researchers, including academics, politicians, religious leaders, and many others.

7. United States Regional and Local Ecumenical Bodies

One of the many ways Christians and Christian churches relate to one another locally and regionally is through ecumenical bodies. The membership in these ecumenical organizations is diverse. Historically, councils of churches were formed primarily by Protestants, but many local and regional organizations now include Orthodox and Roman Catholics. Many are made up of congregations or judicatory units of churches. Some have a membership base of individuals. Others foster cooperation between ministerial groups, community ministries, coalitions, or church agencies. While "council of churches" is a term still commonly used to describe this form of cooperation, other terms such as "conference of churches," "ecumenical councils," "churches united," "metropolitan ministries," are coming into use. Ecumenical organizations that are national in scope are listed in Directory 1, "United States Cooperative Organizations."

An increasing number of ecumenical bodies have been exploring ways to strengthen the interreligious aspect of life in the context of religious pluralism in the U.S. today. Some organizations in this listing are fully interfaith agencies primarily through the inclusion of Jewish congregations in their membership. Other organizations nurture partnerships with a broader base of religious groups in their communities, especially in the areas of public policy and interreligious dialogue.

This list does not include all local and regional ecumenical and interfaith organizations in existence today. For information about other groups, contact the Ecumenical Networks Commission of the National Council of Churches of Christ in the U.S.A., 475 Riverside Drive, New York, NY 10115-0050. Tel. (212)870-2155 Fax (212)870-2690.

The terms "regional" and "local" are relative, making identification somewhat ambiguous. Regional councils may cover sections of large states or cross state borders. Local councils may be made up of several counties, towns, or clusters of congregations. State councils or state-level ecumenical contacts exist in 43 of the 50 states. These state-level or multi-state organizations are marked with a "*". The organizations are listed alphabetically by state.

ALABAMA

Greater Birmingham Ministries

2304 12th Ave. N, Birmingham, AL 35234-3111
Tel. (205) 326-6821 Fax (205) 252-8458
Media Contact, Scott Douglas
Exec. Dir., Scott Douglas
Economic Justice, Co-Chpsn., Helen Holdefer; Karnie Smith
Direct Services, Chpsn., Benjamin Greene
Finance & Fund-Raising, Chpsn., Dick Sales
Pres., Richard Ambrose
Sec., Lois Martin
Treas., Chris Hamlin
Major Activities: Direct Service Ministries (Food, Utilities, Rent and Nutrition Education, Shelter); Alabama Arise (Statewide legislative network focusing on low income issues); Economic Justice Issues (Low Income Housing and Advocacy, Health Care, Community Development, Jobs Creation, Public Transportation); Faith in Community Ministries (Interchurch Forum, Interpreting and Organizing, Bible Study)

Interfaith Mission Service

411-B Holmes Ave. NE, Huntsville, AL 35801
Tel. (256) 536-2401 Fax (256) 536-2284
Email: ims@traveller.com
Website: www.hsv.tis.net/~ims
Exec. Dir., Susan J. Smith
Pres., Rev. William McWeeny
Major Activities: Foodline & Food Pantry; Emergency Funds; Local FEMA Committee; Ministry Development; Clergy Luncheon; Workshops; Response to Community Needs; Information and Referral; Interfaith Understanding; Christian Unity; Homeless Needs

ALASKA

Alaska Christian Conference

Episcopal Diocese of Alaska, 1205 Denali Way, Fairbanks, AK 99701-4178
Tel. (907) 452-3040
Email: MARK_MACDONALD.parti@ecunet.org
Media Contact, Rt. Rev. Mark MacDonald
Pres., Rt. Rev. Mark MacDonald
Vice-Pres., Rev. David I. Blanchett, 1100 Pullman Drive, Wasilla, AK 99654 Tel. (907) 352-2517
Sec., Rev. Dianne A. O'Connell, 9851 Basher Avenue, Anchorage, AK 99507-1279 Tel. (907) 261-5053
Treas., Carolyn M. Winters, 2133 Bridgewater Drive, Fairbanks, AK 99709-4101 Tel. (907) 456-8555
Major Activities: Legislative & Social Concerns; Resources and Continuing Education; New Ecumenical Ministries; Communication; Alcoholism (Education & Prevention); Family Violence (Education & Prevention); Native Issues; Ecumenical/ Theological Dialogue; HIV/AIDS Education and Ministry; Criminal Justice

ARIZONA

*Arizona Ecumenical Council

4423 N. 24th St., Ste. 750, Phoenix, AZ 85016
Tel. (602) 468-3818 Fax (602) 468-3839
Media Contact, Exec. Dir., Dr. Paul Eppinger,
Tel. (602)967-6040 Fax (602)468-3839
Exec. Dir., Dr. Paul Eppinger
Pres., Rev. Gail Davis, 4423 N. 24th St. Ste. 700,
Phoenix, AZ 85016
Major Activities: Donohoe Ecumenical Forum
Series; Political Action Team; Legislative
Workshop; Arizona Ecumenical Indian
Concerns Committee; Mexican/ American
Border Issues; ISN-TV; Disaster Relief; Break
Violence-Build Community; Truckin' for
Kids; "Souper Bowl"; Gun Information and
Safety Program

ARKANSAS

*Arkansas Interfaith Conference

P.O. Box 151, Scott, AR 72142
Tel. (501) 961-2626 Fax (501) 961-1040
Email: aicark@aol.com
Media Contact, Conf. Exec., Mimi Dortch
Conf. Exec., Mimi Dortch
Pres., Rabbi Eugene Levy, 3700 Rodney Park
Ave., Little Rock, AR 72212
Sec., Rev. Thurston Lamb, Bethel AME Church,
Little Rock, AR 72202
Treas., Jim Davis, Box 7239, Little Rock, AR
72217
Major Activities: Institutional Ministry; Inter-
faith Executives' Advisory Council; Interfaith
Relations; Church Women United; IMPACT;
AIDS Task Force; Our House-Shelter;
Legislative Liaison; Ecumenical Choir Camp;
Tornado Disaster Relief; Camp for Jonesboro
School Children Massacre; Welfare Reform
Work

CALIFORNIA

*California Council of Churches/
California Church Impact

2700 L Street, Sacramento, CA 95816
Tel. (916) 442-5447 Fax (916) 442-3036
Email: cccinfo@calchurches.org
Website: www.calchurches.org
Media Contact, Exec. Dir., Scott D. Anderson
Exec. Dir., Scott D. Anderson
Major Activities: Monitoring State Legislation;
California IMPACT Network; Legislative
Principles; Food Policy Advocacy; Family
Welfare Issues; Health; Church/State Issues;
Violence Prevention; Child Care Program/
Capacity Coordinator to Increase Quality Child
Care within California for the Working Poor, etc.

The Council of Churches of Santa
Clara County

1710 Moorpark Avenue, San Jose, CA 95128
Tel. (408) 297-2660 Fax (408) 297-2661

Email: ccscc@aol.com
Media Contact, Ex. Dir., Rev. Vaughn F.
Beckman
Exec. Dir., Rev. Vaughn F. Beckman
Pres., Rev. John L. Freesemann
Assoc. Dir., ———
Major Activities: Social Education/ Action;
Ecumenical and Interfaith Witness; Affordable
Housing; Environmental Ministry; Family/
Children; Refugee Immigration Ministry;
Interfaith Study Project; Convale-scent
Hospital Ministries; Gay Ministry

The Ecumenical Council of
Pasadena Area Churches

P.O. Box 41125, 444 E. Washington Blvd.,
Pasadena, CA 91114-8125
Tel. (626) 797-2402 Fax (626) 797-7353
Email: zyhv76@prodigy.com
Exec. Dir., Rev. Frank B. Clark
Major Activities: Christian Education; Community
Worship; Community Concerns; Christian Unity;
Ethnic Ministries; Hunger; Peace; Food, Clothing
Assistance for the Poor; Emergency Shelter

Ecumenical Council of San Diego
County

1880 Third Ave., San Diego, CA 92101
Website: http://home.earthlink.net/~searay1/
Exec. Dir., Rev. Glenn S. Allison
Admn., Patricia R. Munley
Pres., George Mitrovich
Treas., Joseph Ramsey
Major Activities: Interfaith Shelter Network/El
Nido Transitional Living Program; Emerging
Issues; Faith Order & Witness; Worship &
Celebration; Ecumenical Tribute Dinner;
Advent Prayer Breakfast; AIDS Chaplaincy
Program; Third World Opportunities; Seminars
and Workshops; Called to Dance Assn.; S.D.
Names Project Quilt; Children's Sabbath
Workshops and events; Edgemoor Chaplaincy;
Stand for Children events; Continuing
Education for clergy and laypersons

Fresno Metro Ministry

1055 N. Van Ness, Ste. H, Fresno, CA 93728
Tel. (559) 485-1416 Fax (559) 485-9109
Email: metromin@qnis.net
Media Contact, Exec. Dir., Rev. Walter P. Parry
Exec. Dir., Rev. Walter P. Parry
Admn. Asst., Linda Jimenez
Pres., Rev. Delman Howard
Major Activities: Hunger Relief Advocacy;
Human Relations and Anti-Racism; Health
Care Advocacy; Public Education Concerns;
Children's Needs; Biblical and Theological
Education For Laity; Ecumenical & Interfaith
Celebrations & Cooperation; Youth Needs;
Community Network Building; Human
Services Facilitation; Anti-Poverty Efforts;
Hate Crime Prevention and Response

Interfaith Council of Contra Costa County

1543 Sunnyvale Ave., Walnut Creek, CA 94596
Tel. (925) 933-6030 Fax (925) 952-4554
Media Contact, Dir., Rev. Machrina L. Blasdell
Dir., Rev. Machrina L. Blasdell
Chaplains: Rev. Charles Tinsley; Rev. Duane Woida; Rev. Harold Wright; Laurie Maxwell
Pres., Rev. Steve Harms
Treas., Robert Bender
Major Activities: Institutional Chaplaincies, Community Education, Interfaith Cooperation; Social Justice

Interfaith Service Bureau

3720 Folsom Blvd., Sacramento, CA 95816
Tel. (916) 456-3815 Fax (916) 456-3816
Media Contact, Interim Dir., Dexter McNamara
Interim Dir., Dexter McNamara
Pres., Rabbi Brad Bloom
Vice-Pres., Patricia Hill
Major Activities: Welfare Reform Concerns; Refugee Resettlement & Support; Religious Cable Television; Violence Prevention; Graffiti Abatement; Religious and Racial Cooperation and Understanding

Marin Interfaith Council

650 Las Gallinas, San Rafael, CA 94903
Tel. (415) 492-1052 Fax (415) 492-8907
Media Contact, Exec. Dir., Rev. Kevin F. Tripp
Exec. Dir., Rev. Kevin F. Tripp
Major Activities: Interfaith Dialogue; Education; Advocacy; Convening; Interfaith Worship Services & Commemorations

*Northern California Interreligious Conference

965 Mission St., #711, San Francisco, CA 94103
Tel. (415) 512-7110 Fax (415) 512-1172
Email: NCIC@igc.org
Media Contact, Charlene Tschirhart
Exec. Dir., Charlene Tschirhart
Pres., Rev. Phil Lawson
Vice-Pres., Nancy Nielsen
Sec., Robert Forsberg
Treas., John Lanehart
Major Activities: Peace with Justice Commission; Interreligious Relationships Commission; Public Policy Advocacy; Same Gender marriage Education Campaign

Pacific and Asian American Center for Theology and Strategies (PACTS)

Graduate Theological Union, 2400 Ridge Rd., Berkeley, CA 94709
Tel. (510) 849-0653
Media Contact, Dir., Deborah Lee
Dir., Deborah Lee
Pres., Ron Nakasone
Major Activities: Collect and Disseminate Resource Materials; Training Conferences; Public Seminars; Women in Ministry; Racial and Ethnic Minority Concerns; Journal and Newsletter; Hawaii & Greater Pacific Programme; Sale of Sadao Watanabe Calendars; Informational Forums on Peace & Social Justice in Asian Pacific American Community and Asia/Pacific Internationally; Forums & Conferences for Seminarians Asian Pacific Heritage

Pomona Inland Valley Council of Churches

1753 N. Park Ave., Pomona, CA 91768
Tel. (909) 622-3806 Fax (909) 622-0484
Media Contact, Dir. of Development, Mary Kashmar
Pres., The Rev. Henry Rush
Acting Exec. Dir., The Rev. La Quetta Bush-Simmons
Sec., Ken Coates
Treas., Anne Ashford
Major Activities: Advocacy and Education for Social Justice; Ecumenical Celebrations; Hunger Advocacy; Emergency Food and Shelter Assistance; Farmer's Market; Affordable Housing; Transitional Housing

San Fernando Valley Interfaith Council

10824 Topanga Canyon Blvd., No. 7, Chatsworth, CA 91311
Tel. (818) 718-6460 Fax (818) 718-0734
Email: sfvic@earthlink.net
Media Contact, Communications Coord., Dyanne Hendrix, ext. 3002
Exec. Dir., Barry Smedberg; Ext. 3011
Pres., Dr. William Huling
Major Activities: Seniors Multi-Purpose Centers; Nutrition & Services; Meals to Homebound; Meals on Wheels; Interfaith Reporter; Interfaith Relations; Social Adult Day Care; Hunger/Homelessness; Volunteer Care-Givers; Clergy Gatherings; Food Pantries and Outreach; Social Concerns; Aging; Hunger; Human Relations; Child Abuse Program; Medical Service; Homeless Program; Disaster Response Preparedness; Immigration Services; Self-Sufficiency Program for Section 8 Families

South Coast Ecumenical Council

3300 Magnolia Ave., Long Beach, CA 90806
Tel. (562) 595-0268 Fax (562) 490-9920
Email: SCECI@aol.com
Website: http://members.aol.com/scec1/
Media Contact, Exec. Dir., Rev. Ginny Wagener
STAFF
Exec. Dir., Rev. Ginny Wagener
Farmers' Markets, Rev. Dale Whitney
Pres., Fr. Nicholas Milatos
Centro Shalom, Amelia Nieto
Women & Children First, Dr. Anneka Davidson
New Communion, David Satchwell

Bulgarian Children's Fund, Molly Byer

Major Activities: Homeless Support Services; Farmers' Markets; Hunger Projects; Church Athletic Leagues; Community Action; Hunger Walks; Easter Sunrise Worships; Interreligious Dialogue; Justice Advocacy; Martin Luther King, Jr. Celebration; Violence Prevention; Long Beach Church Women United; Long Beach Interfaith Clergy; Publishing Area Religious Directories; Longbeach Nonprofit Partnership

*Southern California Ecumenical Council

54 N. Oakland Ave., Pasadena, CA 91101-2086
Tel. (626) 578-6371 Fax (626) 578-6358
Email: scec@loop.com
Media Contact, Exec. Dir., Rev. Albert G. Cohen
Exec. Dir., Rev. Albert G. Cohen
Pres., Rev. Donald Smith
Treas., Fr. Arshag Khatchadourian
V.P. Finance, Rev. Dr. Mildred Gilmore
V.P. Communications, Ms. Mila LaDuke
V.P. Faith & Tradition, Rev. Wil Tyrrell, S.A.
V.P. Special Events, Dr. Gwynne Guibord
Member at Large, Rev. Dr. Efstathios Mylonas
Faith and Order Chair, Rev. Dr. Rod Parrott
Major Activities: Consultation with the regional religious sector concerning the well being and spiritual vitality of this most diverse and challenging area

Westside Interfaith Council

P.O. Box 1402, Santa Monica, CA 90406
Tel. (310) 394-1518 Fax (310) 576-1895
Media Contact, Rev. Janet A. Bregar
Exec. Dir., Rev. Janet A. Bregar
Major Activities: Meals on Wheels; Community Religious Services; Convalescent Hospital Chaplaincy; Homeless Partnership; Hunger & Shelter Coalition

COLORADO

*Colorado Council of Churches

1234 Bannock St., Denver, CO 80204-3631
Tel. (303) 825-4910 Fax (303) 534-1266
Email: council@diac.com
Media Contact, Exec. Dir., Rev. Lucia Guzman
Pres., Rev. Louise Barger
Staff Assoc, Robert Hunter
Major Activities: Institutional Ministries; Human Needs and Economic Issues (Includes Homelessness, Migrant Ministry, Justice in the Workplace); World Peace and Global Affairs; Religion in the Media; Interreligious Dialogue; Covenant with Children

Interfaith Council of Boulder

3700 Baseline Rd., Boulder, CO 80303
Tel. (303) 494-8094
Media Contact, Pres., Stan Grotegut, 810 Kalma Ave., Boulder, CO 80304 Tel. (303)443-2291
Pres., Stan Grotegut

Major Activities: Interfaith Dialogue and Programs; Thanksgiving Worship Services; Food for the Hungry; Share-A-Gift; Monthly Newsletter

CONNECTICUT

Association of Religious Communities

325 Main St., Danbury, CT 06810
Tel. (203) 792-9450 Fax (203) 792-9452
Email: arc325@aol.com
Media Contact, Exec. Dir., Samuel E. Deibler, Jr.
Exec. Dir., Samuel E. Deibler, Jr.
Pres., The Rev. Mark Lingle
Major Activities: Refugee Resettlement; Family Counseling; Family Violence Prevention; Affordable Housing

The Capitol Region Conference of Churches

30 Arbor St., Hartford, CT 06106
Tel. (860) 236-1295 Fax (860) 236-8071
Media Contact, Exec. Dir., Rev. Roger W. Floyd
Exec. Dir., Rev. Roger W. Floyd
Pastoral Care & Training, Dir., Rev. Kathleen Davis
Aging Project, Dir., Barbara Malcolm
Community Organizer, Joseph Wasserman
Broadcast Ministry Consultant, Ivor T. Hugh
Pres., Rev. Kenneth Monroe
Major Activities: Organizing for Peace and Justice; Aging; Legislative Action; Cooperative Broadcast Ministry; Ecumenical Cooperation; Interfaith Reconciliation; Chaplaincies; Low-Income Senior Empowerment; Anti-Racism Education

Center City Churches

100 Constitution Plaza, Suite 721, Hartford, CT 06103-1721
Tel. (860) 728-3201 Fax (860) 549-8550
Media Contact, Exec. Dir., Paul C. Christie
Exec. Dir., Paul C. Christie
Pres., The Rev. Dr. Jay Terbush
Sec., John Hunt
Treas., Ann Thomas
Major Activities: Senior Services; Family Support Center; Energy Bank; Crisis Intervention; After School Tutoring; Summer Day Camp; Housing for persons with AIDS; Mental Health Residence; Community Soup Kitchen; Job Training for Homeless

Christian Community Action (Norwalk)

98 S. Main St., South Norwalk, CT 06854
Tel. (203) 854-1811 Fax (203) 854-1870
Dir., Jacquelyn P. Miller
Major Activities: Emergency Food Program; Used Furniture; Loans for Emergencies; Loans for Rent, Security

Christian Community Action (New Haven)

168 Davenport Ave., New Haven, CT 06519
Tel. (203) 777-7848 Fax (203) 777-7923
Email: cca168@aol.com
Media Contact, Exec. Dir., The Rev. Bonita Grubbs
Exec. Dir., The Rev. Bonita Grubbs
Major Activities: Emergency Food Program; Used Furniture & Clothing; Security and Fuel; Emergency Housing for Families; Advocacy; Transitional Housing for Families

*Christian Conference of Connecticut (CHRISCON)

60 Lorraine St., Hartford, CT 06105
Tel. (860) 236-4281 Fax (860) 236-9977
Email: chconf@aol.com
Media Contact, Exec. Dir., Rev. Stephen J. Sidorak, Jr.
Exec. Dir., Rev. Stephen J. Sidorak, Jr.
Pres., The Rt. Rev. Clarence N. Coleridge
Vice-Pres., Most Rev. Daniel A. Cronin
Sec., The Rev. Dr. Lowell H. Fewster
Treas., Thomas F. Sarubbi
Major Activities: Communications; Institutional Ministries; Conn. Bible Society; Connecticut Council on Alcohol Problems; Ecumenical Forum; Faith & Order; Social Concerns; Public Policy; Peace and Justice Convocation

Council of Churches of Greater Bridgeport, Inc.

180 Fairfield Ave., Bridgeport, CT 06604
Tel. (203) 334-1121 Fax (203) 367-8113
Email: ccgb@snet.net
Website: www.ccgb.com
Media Contact, Exec. Dir., Rev. John S. Kidd
Exec. Dir., Rev. John S. Kidd
Pres., Rev. Kevin Agee
Sec., Dorothy Allsop
Treas., Carolyn Jackson
Major Activities: Youth in Crisis; Safe Places; Youth Shelter; Criminal Justice; Nursing Home and Jail Ministries; Local Hunger; Ecumenical Relations, Prayer and Celebration; Covenantal Ministries; Homework Help; Summer Programs; Race Relations/Bridge Building; Good Jobs / First Jobs; Faith Based Community Development Consortium

Council of Churches and Synagogues of Southwestern Connecticut

628 Main St., Stamford, CT 06901
Tel. (203) 348-2800 Fax (203) 358-0627
Email: council@flvax.ferg.lib.ct.us
Website: www.interfaithcouncil.org
Media Contact, Communications Ofc., Lois Alcosser
Exec. Dir., Jack Penfield, Interim Director
Major Activities: Partnership Against Hunger; The Food Bank of Lower Fairfield County; Friendly Visitors and Friendly Shoppers; Senior Neighborhood Support Services; Christmas in April; Interfaith Programming; Prison Visitation; Friendship House; Help a Neighbor; Operation Fuel; Teaching Place

Greater Waterbury Interfaith Ministries, Inc.

84 Crown St., Waterbury, CT 06704
Tel. 203-756-7831 Fax 203-419-0024
Media Contact, Exec. Dir., Carroll E. Brown
Exec. Dir., Carroll E. Brown
Pres., The Rev. Dr. James G. Bradley
Major Activities: Emergency Food Program; Emergency Fuel Program; Soup Kitchen; Ecumenical Worship; Christmas Toy Sale; Annual Hunger Walk

Manchester Area Conference of Churches

P.O. Box 773, Manchester, CT 06045-0773
Tel. (860) 649-2093
Media Contact, Exec. Dir., Denise Cabana
Exec. Dir., Denise Cabana
Dir. of Community Ministries, Joseph Piescik
Dept.of Ministry Development, Dir., Karen Bergin
Pres., Rev. Charles Ericson
Vice-Pres., Theresa Ghabrial
Sec., Jean Richert
Treas., Clive Perrin
Major Activities: Provision of Basic Needs (Food, Fuel, Clothing, Furniture); Emergency Aid Assistance; Emergency Shelter; Soup Kitchen; Reentry Assistance to Sex-Offenders; Pastoral Care in Local Institutions; Interfaith Day Camp; Advocacy for the Poor; Ecumenical Education and Worship

New Britain Area Conference of Churches (NEWBRACC)

830 Corbin Ave., New Britain, CT 06052
Tel. (860) 229-3751 Fax (860) 223-3445
Media Contact, Exec. Dir., Michael Gorzoch
Exec. Dir., Michael Gorzoch
Pastoral Care/Chaplaincy, Rev. Ron Smith; Rev. Will Baumgartner; Rev. Rod Rinnel
Pres., Alton Brooks
Treas., Lynne Alexander
Major Activities: Worship; Social Concerns; Emergency Food Bank Support; Communications —Mass Media; Hospital; Elderly Programming; Homelessness and Hunger Programs; Telephone Ministry; Thanks- giving Vouchers

DELAWARE

*The Christian Council of Delaware and Maryland's Eastern Shore

Diocese of Delaware, 2020 N. Tatnall Street, Wilmington, DE 19802
Tel. 302-656-5441 Fax 302-656-7342

223

Media Contact, Pres., Bishop Wayne P. Wright, Diocese of Delaware, 2020 N. Tatnall Street, Wilmington, DE 19802

Pres., Bishop Wayne P. Wright, Diocese of Delaware, 2020 N. Tatnall Street, Wilmington, DE 19802

Moderator, The Rev. Patricia McClurg, Presbyterian Church (USA), E-62 Omega Drive, Newark, DE 19713

Major Activities: Exploring Common Theological, Ecclesiastical and Community Concerns; Racism; Prisons

DISTRICT OF COLUMBIA

The Council of Churches of Greater Washington

5 Thomas Circle N.W., Washington, DC 20005
Tel. (202) 722-9240 Fax (202) 722-9241
Media Contact, Exec. Dir., The Rev. Rodger Hall Reed, Sr.
Pres., The Rev. Lewis Anthony
Exec. Dir., The Rev. Rodger Hall Reed, Sr.
Program Officer, Daniel M. Thompson
Major Activities: Promotion of Christian Unity/ Ecumenical Prayer & Worship; Coordination of Community Ministries; Summer Youth Employment; Summer Camping/Inner City Youth; Supports wide variety of social justice concerns

InterFaith Conference of Metropolitan Washington

1419 V St. NW, Washington, DC 20009
Tel. (202) 234-6300 Fax (202) 234-6303
Email: ifc@interfaith-metrodc.org
Website: www.interfaith-metrodc.org
Media Contact, Exec. Dir., Rev. Dr. Clark Lobenstine
Exec. Dir., Rev. Dr. Clark Lobenstine
Admn. Sec., Najla Robinson
Pres., Rev. Elizabeth Orens
1st Vice-Pres., Ms. Amrit Kaur
Chpsn., Mr. Jack Serber
Sec., Janice Sadeghian, Ph.D.
Treas., Ms. Frances B. Albers
Major Activities: Interfaith Dialogue; Interfaith Concert; Racial and Ethnic Polarization; Youth Leadership Training; Hunger; Homelessness; Church-State Zoning Issues

FLORIDA

Christian Service Center for Central Florida, Inc.

808 W. Central Blvd., Orlando, FL 32805-1809
Tel. (407) 425-2523 Fax (407) 425-9513
Media Contact, Exec. Dir., Robert F. Stuart
Exec. Dir., Robert F. Stuart
Family Emergency Services, Dir., LaVerne Sainten
Alzheimers Respite, Dir., Mary Ellen Ort-Marvin
Fresh Start, Dir., Rev. Haggeo Gautier

Dir. of Mktg., Margaret Ruffier-Farris
Pres., Dr. Charles Horton
Treas., Rick Crandall
Sec., Annie Harris
Major Activities: Provision of Basic Needs (food, clothing, shelter); Emergency Assistance; Noon-time Meals; Sunday Church Services at Walt Disney World; Collection and Distribution of Used Clothing; Shelter & Training for Homeless; Respite for Caregivers of Alzheimers

*Florida Council of Churches

924 N. Magnolia Ave., Ste. 301, Orlando, FL 32803
Tel. (407) 839-3454 Fax (407) 246-0019
Email: fced@aol.com
Website: www.floridachurches.org
Media Contact, Exec. Dir., Rev. Fred Morris
Exec. Dir., Rev. Fred Morris
Associate Dir., H. Basil Nichols
Project Director, Cherishing the Creation, Brian Hinkman
Major Activities: Justice and Peace; Disaster Response; Legislation & Public Policy; Local Ecumenism; Farmworker Ministry; Cherishing the Creation (Environmental Stewardship)

GEORGIA

Christian Council of Metropolitan Atlanta

465 Boulevard, S.E., Atlanta, GA 30312
Tel. (404) 622-2235 Fax (404) 627-6626
Email: dojccma@aol.com
Media Contact, Dir. of Development & Communication, Jane Hopson Enniss
Exec. Dir., Rev. Dr. David O. Jenkins
Assoc. Dir., -vacant-
Pres., Rev. Elizabeth Rechter
Major Activities: Refugee Services; Commission on Children and Youth, Supervised Ministry; Homeless; Ecumenical and Interreligious Events; persons with Handicapping Conditions; Women's Concerns; Task Force on Prison Ministry; Quarterly Forums on Ecumenical Issues; Faith and Order Concerns; Interracial & Intercultural Emphasis

*Georgia Christian Council

P.O. Box 7193, Macon, GA 31209-7193
Tel. (912) 743-2085 Fax (912) 743-2085
Email: lccollins@juno.com
Website: georgiachurches.org
Media Contact, Exec. Dir., Rev. Leland C. Collins
Exec. Dir., Rev. Leland C. Collins
Pres., Bishop McKinley Young, 700 Martin Luther King Drive, SW, Atlanta, GA 30314
Sec., Rev. Scudder Edwards, 6865 Turner Ct., Cumming, GA 30131
Major Activities: Local Ecumenical Support and Resourcing; Legislation; Rural Development;

Racial Justice; Networking for Migrant Coalition; Aging Coalition; GA To GA With Love; Medical Care; Prison Chaplaincy; Training for Church Development; Souper Bowl; Disaster Relief; Clustering; Development of Local Ecumenism

IDAHO

The Regional Council for Christian Ministry, Inc.
237 N. Water, Idaho Falls, ID 83403
Tel. (208) 524-9935
Exec. Sec., Wendy Schoonmaker
Major Activities: Island Park Ministry; Community Food Bank; Community Observances; Community Information and Referral Service; F.I.S.H.

ILLINOIS

Churches United of the Quad City Area
630 9th St., Rock Island, IL 61201
Tel. (309) 786-6494 Fax (309) 786-5916
Email: clandon@revealed.net OR awachal@revealed.net
Media Contact, Exec. Dir., Rev. Charles R. Landon, Jr.
Exec. Dir., Rev. Charles R. Landon, Jr.
Program Manager, Anne E. Wachal
Pres., Dr. Chris J. Fragley, D.C.
Treas., Rev. Robert Pearson
Major Activities: Jail Ministry; Hunger Projects; Minority Enablement; Criminal Justice; Radio-TV; Peace; Local Church Development

Contact Ministries of Springfield
1100 E. Adams, Springfield, IL 62703
Tel. (217) 753-3939 Fax (217) 753-8643
Media Contact, Exec. Dir., Ethel Butchek
Exec. Dir., Ethel Butchek
Major Activities: Information; Referral and Advocacy; Ecumenical Coordination; Low Income Housing Referral; Food Pantry Coordination; Prescription & Travel Emergency; Low Income Budget Counseling; 24 hours on call; Emergency On-site Family Shelter

Evanston Ecumenical Action Council
P.O. Box 1414, Evanston, IL 60204
Tel. (847) 475-1150 Fax (847) 475-1150
Website: http://members.aol.com/eeachome/eeac.html
Media Contact, Comm. Chpsn., Donna Spicuzza
Dir. Hospitality Cntr. for the Homeless, Sue Murphy
Co-Pres., Rev. Mark Adams; Rev. Hardist Lane
Treas., James Lindholm
Admn. Dir., Thomas Sullivan, M.DIV.
Major Activities: Interchurch Communication

and Education; Peace and Justice Ministries; Coordinated Social Action; Soup Kitchens; Multi-Purpose Hospitality Center for the Homeless; Worship and Renewal

Greater Chicago Broadcast Ministries
112 E. Chestnut St., Chicago, IL 60611-2014
Tel. (312) 988-9001 Fax (312) 988-9004
Media Contact, Exec. Dir., Lydia Talbot
Pres., Bd. of Dir., Eugene H. Winkler
Exec. Dir., Lydia Talbot
Admn. Asst., Margaret Early
Major Activities: Television, Cable, Interfaith/Ecumenical Development; Social/Justice Concerns

The Hyde Park & Kenwood Interfaith Council
1448 E. 53rd St., Chicago, IL 60615
Tel. (773) 752-1911 Fax (773) 752-2676
Media Contact, Exec. Dir., Lesley M. Radius
Exec. Dir., Lesley M. Radius
Pres., Rev. David Grainger
Sec., Barbara Krell
Major Activities: Interfaith Work; Hunger Projects; Community Development

*Illinois Conference of Churches
615 S. 5th St., Springfield, IL 62703
Tel. (217) 544-3423 Fax (217) 544-9307
Email: ILCOCH@juno.com
Media Contact, Exec. Dir., Rev. David A. Anderson
Exec. Dir., Rev. David A. Anderson
Assoc. Dir., Nancy Tegtmeier
Pres., Rev. C. Bruce Naylor Tel. (309)467-2369
Major Activities: Unity and Relationships Commission; Church and Society Commission; Public Policy Ecumenical Network; Harvesting Hope; Disaster Relief; Annual Clergy Ecumenical Forum; Triennial Statewide Ecumenical Assembly

Oak Park-River Forest Community of Congregations
P.O. Box 3365, Oak Park, IL 60303-3365
Tel. (708) 386-8802 Fax (708) 386-1399
Website: http://www.mcs.net/~grossman/comcong.htm
Media Contact, , Patricia C. Koko
Admn. Sec., Patricia C. Koko
Pres., Rev. Joseph Ruiz
Treas., Sue Rizzo
Major Activities: Community Affairs; Ecumenical/Interfaith Affairs; Youth Education; FOOD PANTRY; Senior Citizens Worship Services; Interfaith Thanksgiving Services; Good Friday Services; UNICEF Children's Fund Drive; ASSIST (Network); Blood Drive; Literacy Training; CROP/CWS Hunger Walkathon; Work with Homeless Through PADS (Public

225

Action to Deliver Shelter); Senior Resource Coordinator Program

Peoria Friendship House of Christian Service

800 N.E. Madison Ave., Peoria, IL 61603
Tel. (309) 671-5200 Fax (309) 671-5206
Media Contact, Exec. Dir., Beverly Isom
Pres. of Bd., David Dadds
Major Activities: Children's After-School; Teen Programs; Recreational Leagues; Senior Citizens Activities; Emergency Food/Clothing Distribution; Emergency Payments for Prescriptions, Rent, Utilities; Community Outreach; Economic Development; Neighborhood Empowerment; GED Classes; Family Literacy; Mother's Group; Welfare to Work Programs

INDIANA

The Associated Churches of Fort Wayne & Allen County, Inc.

602 E. Wayne St., Fort Wayne, IN 46802
Tel. (219) 422-3528 Fax (219) 422-6721
Email: Vernchurch@aol.com
Media Contact, Exec. Dir., Rev. Vernon R. Graham
Exec. Dir., Rev. Vernon R. Graham
Sec., Jenny Varecha
Foodbank: Ellen Graham; John Kaiser; John Lassen
Prog. Development, Ellen Graham
WRE Coord., Kathy Rolf
Pres., Rev. Sam Summer 836 E. Jefferson Blvd., Ft. Wayne, IN 46803
Treas., Ann Frellick, 170 Curdes Avenue, Ft. Wayne, IN 46805
Major Activities: Weekday Religious Ed.; Radio & TV; Church Clusters; Church and Society Commission; Overcoming Racism; A Baby's Closet; Widowed-to-Widowed; CROP; Campus Ministry; Feeding the Babies; Food Bank System; Peace & Justice Commission; Welfare Reform; Endowment Development; Habitat for Humanity; Child Care Advocacy; Advocates Inc.; Ecumenical Dialogue; Feeding Children; Vincent House (Homeless); A Learning Journey (Literacy); Reaching Out in Love; The Jail Ministry

Christian Ministries of Delaware County

401 E. Main St., Muncie, IN 47305
Tel. (317) 288-0601 Fax (317) 282-4522
Media Contact, Exec. Dir., Susan Hughes
Exec. Dir., Susan Hughes
Pres., Sue Klein
Treas., Dr. J. B. Black
Major Activities: Baby Care Program; Youth Ministry at Detention Center; Community Church Festivals; Community Pantry; Community Assistance Fund; CROP Walk;

Social Justice; Family Life Education; Combined Clergy; Homeless Shelter (sleeping room only); Clothing and household items available free; workshops for low income clients; homeless people apartments available" short stays only at no cost; provide programs and workshops for pastors and churches in community; work with schools sponsoring programs such as Teen Mom Program; plays about child abuse/conflict resolution

Church Community Services

1703 Benham Ave., Elkhart, IN 46516
Tel. (219) 295-3673
Media Contact, Dir., Trisha Leasor
Exec. Dir., Rosalie J. Day
Major Activities: Advocacy for Low Income persons; Financial Assistance for Emergencies; Food Pantry; Used Furniture; Information and Referral; Clothing Referral; Laundry Voucher; Medication; Transportation Vouchers; Rent Funds; Classes on Cooking; Budget and Money; Credit; Managing a Checking Account

The Church Federation of Greater Indianapolis, Inc.

1100 W. 42nd St., Ste. 345, Indianapolis, IN 46208
Tel. (317) 926-5371 Fax (317) 926-5373
Email: churches@churchfederationindy.org
Website: www.churchfederationindy.org
Media Contact, Comm. Consultant, Julie Foster
Exec. Dir., Rev. Dr. Angelique Walker-Smith
Pres., Rev. James Clark
Treas., R. Wayne Reynolds
Major Activities: "Sacred Spaces" (A Christian Partnership of Neighborhood Action) Reclaiming Our Neighborhoods through Community Formation, Community Resourcing, Community Education, and Communications; The Sanctuary Church Movement; "Loving Our Children": An Educational Partnership Between Church and Public Schools for "at risk" Children; Indianapolis Prayer Network to Stop the Violence; Racial Reconciliation; Clearinghouse Ministry; Ecumenical Project for Reconciliation and Healing

Evansville Area Community of Churches, Inc.

414 N.W. Sixth St., Evansville, IN 47708-1332
Tel. (812) 425-3524 Fax (812) 425-3525
Media Contact, Dir. of Programs & Church Relations, Barbara G. Gaisser
Dir. of Programs/Ofc. Mgr., Barbara G. Gaisser
Exec. Dir., Rev. William F. Bower
Weekday Dir., Linda M. Schenk
Pres., Rev. Steve Lintzench
V. Pres., John Musgrove
Sec., Rev. Shane O'Neill
Treas., Ms. Julia Wood

226

Major Activities: Christian Education; Community Responsibility & Service; Public Relations; Interpretation; Church Women United; Institutional Ministries; Interfaith Dialogue; Earth Care Ethics; Public Education Support; Disaster Preparedness; Job Loss Networking Support Group; Interfaith TV Program; Women in Ministry Support Group; International Women's Day Celebration Events

Indiana Partners for Christian Unity and Mission

P.O. Box 88790, Indianapolis, IN 46208-0790
Tel. (800) 746-2310 Fax (317) 927-0957
Email: indunity@aol.com
Website: www.IPCUM.org
Media Contact, James Dougans
Pres., Rev. Robert Kirk
Treas., Rev. Alan Overstreet
Major Activities: Spring Celebration of Christian Unity; Fall Educational Conference; Network the 117 ministerial Associations in Indiana; Initiate dialogue and the building of relationships between ecumenical officers and judicatory leaders; Task Force on Racial Reconciliation

Interfaith Community Council, Inc.

702 E. Market St., New Albany, IN 47150
Tel. (812) 948-9248 Fax (812) 948-9249
Email: interfaithcouncil@juno.com
Media Contact, Exec. Dir., M. Christopher Boyer
Exec. Dir., M. Christopher Boyer
Programs/Emergency Assistance, Jane Alcorn
RSVP, Dir., Ceil Sperzel
Major Activities: Emergency Assistance; Retired Senior Volunteer Program; New Clothing and Toy Drives; Convalescent Sitter & Mother's Aides; Senior Day College; Emergency Food Distribution; Homeless Prevention

Lafayette Urban Ministry

525 N. 4th St., Lafayette, IN 47901
Tel. (317) 423-2691 Fax (317) 423-2693
Media Contact, Exec. Dir., Joseph Micon
Exec. Dir., Joseph Micon
Advocate Coord., Rebecca Smith
Public Policy Coord., Harry Brown
Pres., John Wilson
Major Activities: Social Justice Ministries with and among the Poor

United Religious Community of St. Joseph County

2015 Western Ave., South Bend, IN 46629
Tel. (219) 282-2397 Fax (219) 282-8014
Media Contact, Exec. Dir., Dr. James J. Fisko
Exec. Dir., Dr. James J. Fisko
Pres., John Reese
Victim Offender Reconciliation Prog., Victim Impact Panel Coord., Martha Sallows
Volunteer Advocacy Project: Coord., Sara Goetz; Coord., Linda Jung-Zimmerman

Major Activities: Religious Understanding; Interfaith/Ecumenical Education; CROP Walk; Hunger Education; Housing and Homelessness Issues; Clergy Education and Support; Refugee Resettlement; Victim Assistance; Advocacy for the Needy

West Central Neighborhood Ministry, Inc.

1316 Broadway, Fort Wayne, IN 46802-3304
Tel. (219) 422-6618 Fax (219) 422-9319
Media Contact, Exec. Dir., Andrea S. Thomas
Exec. Dir., Andrea S. Thomas
Ofc. Mgr., J. R. Stopperich
Neighborhood Services Dir., Carol Salge
Senior Citizens Dir., Gayle Mann
Youth Director, Michael Ganaway
Major Activities: After-school Programs; Teen Drop-In Center; Summer Day Camp; Summer Overnight Camp; Information and Referral Services; Food Pantry; Nutrition Program for Senior Citizens; Senior Citizens Activities; Tutoring; Developmental Services for Families & Senior Citizens; Parent Club

IOWA

Churches United, Inc.

866 4th Ave. SE, Cedar Rapids, IA 52403
Tel. (319) 366-7163
Media Contact, Admn. Sec., Marcey Luxa
Admn. Sec., Marcey Luxa
Pres., Rev. Carroll Brown
Treas., Joseph Luxa, 450 19th St. NW, Cedar Rapids, IA 52405
Major Activities: Communication/ resource center for member churches; Community Information and Referral; Community Food Bank; L.E.A.F. (Local Emergency Assistance Fund; Care Center Ministry; Radio/TV Ministry; Ecumenical City-wide Celebrations; CROP/World Hunger; Jail Chaplaincy Ministry

Des Moines Area Religious Council

3816 - 36th St., Des Moines, IA 50310
Tel. (515) 277-6969 Fax (515) 274-8389
Email: dmreligious@mcleodusa.net
Media Contact, Exec. Dir., Forrest Harms
Exec. Dir., Forrest Harms
Pres., Sharon Baker
Treas., Bill Corwin
Major Activities: Outreach and Nurture; Education; Social Concerns; Mission; Emergency Food Pantry; Ministry to Widowed; Child Care Assistance

*Ecumenical Ministries of Iowa (EMI)

3816-36th St., Ste. 202, Des Moines, IA 50310-4722
Tel. (515) 255-5905 Fax (515) 255-1421
Email: emofiowa@aol.com

227

Media Contact, Exec. Dir., Rev. Sarai Schnucker Beck

Exec. Dir., Rev. Sarai Schnucker Beck

Admn. Asst., Martha E. Hedberg

Major Activities: Facilitating the denominations—cooperative agenda of resourcing local expression of the church; Assess needs & develop responses through Justice and Unity Commissions

*Iowa Religious Media Services
3816 36th St., Des Moines, IA 50310

Tel. (515) 277-2920

Media Contact, Dir., Sue Sonner

Educ. Consultant, Joanne Talarico, CHM

Production Mgr., Dr. Richard Harbart

Major Activities: Media Library for Churches in 6 Denominations in Iowa; Provide Video Production Services for Churches, Non-profit & Educational organizations

KANSAS

Cross-Lines Cooperative Council
736 Shawnee Ave., Kansas City, KS 66105

Tel. (913) 281-3388 Fax (913) 281-2344

Email: xlines@TFS.net

Media Contact, Dir. of Dev., Bill Scholl

Exec. Dir., Marilynn Rudell

Dir. of Programs, Rev. Robert L. Moore

Major Activities: Emergency Assistance; Family Support Advocacy; Crisis Heating/Plumbing Repair; Thrift Store; Workcamp Experiences; Adult Education (GED and Basic English Literacy Skills); School Supplies; Christmas Store; Institute for Poverty and Empowerment Studies (Education on poverty for the non-poor)

Inter-Faith Ministries—Wichita
829 N. Market, Wichita, KS 67214-3519

Tel. (316) 264-9303 Fax (316) 264-2233

Media Contact, Exec. Dir., Sam Muyskens

Exec. Dir., Rev. Sam Muyskens

Adm. Asst.- Kathy Freed

Care Coordination Team: Dir., Cody Patton

Inter-Faith Inn (Homeless Shelter), Dir., Sandy Swank

Operation Holiday, Dir., Sally Dewey

Dev./Communications, Dir., James D. Marler

Campaign to End Childhood Hunger, Connie Pace

Community Ministry, Cammie Funston

Racial Justice, Coord., Cammie Funston

Major Activities: Communications; Urban Education; Inter-religious Understanding; Community Needs and Issues; Theology and Worship; Hunger; HIV/AIDS Ministry; Family Life; Multi-Cultural Concerns

*Kansas Ecumenical Ministries
5833 SW 29th St., Topeka, KS 66614-2499

Tel. (785) 272-9531 Fax (785) 272-9533

Email: kemstaff@cjnetworks.com

Media Contact, Exec. Dir., Dr. Joe M. Hendrixson, Email: joe_hendrixson@ecunet.org

Exec. Dir., Dr. Joe M. Hendrixson

Pres., Rev. Art Jaggard

Vice-Pres., Rev. Sally Fahrenthold

Sec., Rev. Jane Ireland

Major Activities: State Council of Churches; Legislative Activities; Program Facilitation and Coordination; Education; Mother-to-Mother Program; Rural Concerns; Health Care; Hate group monitoring; Children & Families; AIDS/HIV Programs; Domestic Violence; Faith and Order

KENTUCKY

Eastern Area Community Ministries
P.O. Box 43049, Louisville, KY 40253-0049

Tel. (502) 244-6141 Fax (502) 254-5141

Media Contact, Exec. Dir., Rev. Sue Eaton

Exec. Dir., Rev. Sue Eaton

Board Pres., Marcia Lile

Board Sec., Betsy Wilborn

Board Treas., Homer Lacy, Jr.

Youth and Family Services, Prog. Dir.

Older Adult Services, Associate Program Dir., Sharon Eckler

Neighborhood Visitor Program, Prog. Dir.

Major Activities: Food Pantry; Clothes Closet; Meals on Wheels; Teen Court; Community Worship Services; Good Start for Kids; Juvenile Court Diversion; Community Development; Transient Fund; Ministerial Association

Fern Creek/Highview United Ministries
7502 Tangelo Dr., Louisvlle, KY 40228

Tel. (502) 239-7407 Fax (502) 239-7454

Email: FernCreek.Ministries@crnky.org

Media Contact, Exec. Dir., Kay Sanders, 7502 Tangelo Dr., Louisville, KY 40228 Tel. (502)239-7407

Exec. Dir., Kay Sanders

Pres., Katherine Games

Major Activities: Ecumenically supported social service agency providing services to the community, including Emergency Financial Assistance, Food/Clothing, Health Aid Equipment Loans, Information/Referral, Advocacy, Monthly Blood-Pressure Checks; Holiday Programs, Life Skills Training; Mentoring; Case Management; Adult Day-Care Program

Hazard-Perry County Community Ministries, Inc.
P.O. Box 1506, Hazard, KY 41702-1506

Tel. (606) 436-0051 Fax (606) 436-0071

Media Contact, Gerry Feamster-Roll

Exec. Dir., Gerry Feamster-Roll

Chpsn., Sarah Hughes

V. Chpsn., Susan Duff

Sec., Virginia Campbell

Treas., Margaret Adams

Major Activities: Food Pantry/Crisis Aid Program; Day Care; Summer Day Camp; After-school Program; Christmas Tree; Family Support Center; Adult Day Care; Transitional Housing

Highlands Community Ministries

1140 Cherokee Rd., Louisville, KY 40204
Tel. (502) 451-3695
Email: IFADIR@iglou.com
Media Contact, Exec. Dir., Stan Esterle
Exec. Dir., Stan Esterle
Major Activities: Welfare Assistance; Day Care; Counseling with Youth, Parents and Adults; Adult Day Care; Social Services for Elderly; Housing for Elderly and Handicapped; Ecumenical Programs; Community Classes; Activities for Children; Neighborhood and Business organization

Kentuckiana Interfaith Community

1113 South 4th St., Suite 200, Louisville, KY 40203
Tel. (502) 587-6265 Fax (502) 540-5017
Email: kic@crnky.org
Pres., Annette Turner
Vice-Pres., David L. Kohn
Sec., Geoffrey Ellis
Treas., Arthur Clark
Executive Dir., Reba S. Cobb
Major Activities: Christian/Jewish Ministries in KY, Southern IN; Consensus Advocacy; Interfaith Dialogue; Community Hunger Walk; Racial Justice Forums; Network for Neighborhood-based Ministries; Hunger & Racial Justice Commission; Faith Channel-Cable TV Station, Horizon News Paper; Police/Comm. Relations Task Force; Ecumenical Strategic Planning; Networking with Seminaries & Religious-Affiliated Institutions

*Kentucky Council of Churches

2549 Richmond Road, Suite 302, Lexington, KY 40509
Tel. (606) 269-7715 Fax (606) 269-1240
Email: kcc@kycouncilofchurches.org
Website: www.kycouncilofchurches.org
Media Contact, Exec. Dir., Nancy Jo Kemper
Exec. Dir., Rev. Nancy Jo Kemper
Pres., Fr. Jude Weisenbeck
Kentucky Interchurch Disaster Recovery Program Coodinator., Rev. John Kays
Program Associate for Local Ecumenism, Rev. W. Chris Benham Skidmore
Program Associate for Anti-Racism Projects, Cathy J. Cox
Major Activities: Christian Unity; Public Policy; Justice; Disaster Response; Peace Issues; Anti-Racism; Health Care Issues; Local Ecumenism; Rural Land/Farm Issues; Gambling; Capital Punishment

Ministries United South Central Louisville (M.U.S.C.L., Inc.)

1207 Hart Avenue, Louisville, KY 42013
Tel. (502) 363-9087 Fax (502) 363-9087
Media Contact, Ex. Dir., Rev. Antonio (Tony) Aja, M.Div. Tel. (502)363-2383, Email: Tony_Aja@pcusa.org
Ex. Dir., Rev. Antonio (Tony) Aja, M.Div.
Airport Relocation Ombudsman, Rev. Phillip Garrett, M.Div. Tel. (502)361-2706; Email: philombud@aol.com
Senior Adults Programs, Dir., Mrs. Jeannine Blakeman, BSSW
Emergency Assistance, Dir., Mr. Michael Hundley
Low-Income Coord., Ms. Wanda Irvio
Youth Services, Dir., Rev. Bill Sanders, M.Div.
Volunteers Coord., Mrs. Carol Stemmle

Northern Kentucky Interfaith Commission, Inc.

901 York St., Newport, KY 41072
Tel. (606) 581-2237 Fax (606) 261-6041
Media Contact, Exec. Dir., Rev. William C. Neuroth
Pres., Rev. Donald Smith
Sec., Ms. Jo Shade
Treas., Sister Marilyn Hoffman
Admin. Asst., Pat McDermott
Major Activities: Understanding Faiths; Meeting Spiritual and Human Needs; Enabling Churches to Greater Ministry

Paducah Cooperative Ministry

1359 S. 6th St., Paducah, KY 42003
Tel. (270) 442-6795 Fax (270) 442-6812
Media Contact, Dir., Heidi Suhrheinrich
Dir., Heidi Suhrheinrich
Chpsn., Dr. Rick C. Dye
Vice-Chpsn., Father Brian Johnson
Major Activities: Programs for: Hungry, Elderly, Poor, Homeless, Handicapped, Undereducated

St. Matthews Area Ministries

201 Biltmore Rd., Louisville, KY 40207
Tel. (502) 893-0205 Fax (502) 893-0206
Media Contact, Exec. Dir., Dan G. Lane
Exec. Dir., Dan G. Lane
Child Care, Dir., Janet Hennessey
Dir. Assoc., Eileen Bartlett
Major Activities: Child Care; Emergency Assistance; Youth Services; Interchurch Worship and Education; Housing Development; Counseling; Information & Referral; Mentor Program; Developmentally Disabled

South East Associated Ministries (SEAM)

6500 Six Mile Ln., Ste.A, Louisville, KY 40218
Tel. (502) 499-9350
Media Contact, Mary Beth Helton
Exec. Dir., Mary Beth Helton

Life Skills Center, Dir., Robert Davis
Youth Services, Dir., Bill Jewel
Pres., David Ehresman
Treas., Bill Trusty
Major Activities: Emergency Food, Clothing and Financial Assistance; Life Skills Center (Programs of Prevention and Case Management and Self-Sufficiency Through Education, Empowerment, Support Groups, etc.); Bloodmobile; Ecumenical Education and Worship; Juvenile Court Diversion; TEEN Court; Teen Crime & the Community

South Louisville Community Ministries
Peterson Social Services Center, 204 Seneca Trail, Louisville, KY 40214
Tel. (502) 367-6445 Fax (502) 361-4668
Email: slcm@crnky.org
Media Contact, Exec. Dir., J. Michael Jupin
Bd. Chair., Jane Davis
Bd. Vice-Chair., Cyndi Marlow
Bd. Treas., Eugene Wells
Exec. Dir., Rev. J. Michael Jupin
Major Activities: Food, Clothing & Financial Assistance; Home Delivered Meals; Transportation; Refugee Resettlement; Ecumenical Worship; Juvenile Diversion Program; Affordable Housing; Adult Day Care; Truancy Prevention; Case Management

LOUISIANA

Greater Baton Rouge Federation of Churches and Synagogues
P.O. Box 626, Baton Rouge, LA 70821
Tel. (225) 925-3414 Fax (225) 925-3065
Media Contact, Exec. Dir., Rev. Jeff Day
Exec. Dir., Rev. Jeff Day
Admn. Asst., Marion Zachary
Pres., Bette Lavine
Pres.-Elect, Tom Sylvest
Treas., Randy Trahan
Major Activities: Combating Hunger; Housing (Helpers for Housing); Interfaith Relations; Interfaith Concert; Race Relations

Greater New Orleans Federation of Churches
4640 S. Carrollton Ave, Suite 2B, New Orleans, LA 70119-6077
Tel. (504) 488-8788 Fax (504) 488-8823
Exec. Dir., Rev. J. Richard Randels
Major Activities: Information and Referral; Food Distribution(FEMA); Forward Together TV Program; Sponsors seminars for pastors (e.g. church growth, clergy taxes,etc.); Police Chaplaincy; Fire Chaplaincy

*Louisiana Interchurch Conference
660 N. Foster Dr., Ste. A-225, Baton Rouge, LA 70806

Tel. (225) 924-0213 Fax (225) 927-7860
Email: dan_krutz@ecunet.org
Media Contact, Exec. Dir., Rev. C. Dana Krutz
Exec. Dir., Rev. C. Dana Krutz
Pres., The Most Rev. Michael Jarrell, Bishop
Major Activities: Ministries to Aging; Prison Reform; Liaison with State Agencies; Ecumenical Dialogue; Institutional Chaplains; Racism

MAINE

*Maine Council of Churches
15 Pleasant Ave., Portland, ME 04103
Tel. (207) 772-1918 Fax (207) 772-2947
Email: mecchurchs@aol.com
Website: www.mainecouncilofchurches.com
Media Contact, Communications Director, Karen Caouette
Exec. Dir., Thomas C. Ewell
Assoc. Dir., Douglas Cruger
Admin. Asst., M. Sue Dermond
Pres., Rev. Charles Whiston
Sec., ————
Treas., Rev. Thomas Merrill
Major Activities: Criminal Justice Reform and Restorative Justice; Legislative Work and Coalition Work in Health, Homelessness, and Children; Advocacy

MARYLAND

*Central Maryland Ecumenical Council
Cathedral House, 4 E. University Pkwy., Baltimore, MD 21218
Tel. (410) 467-6194 Fax (410) 554-6387
Media Contact, Admn., Martha Young
Pres., Rev. H.J. Siegfried Otto
Major Activities: Interchurch Communications and Collaboration; Information Systems; Ecumenical Relations; Urban Mission and Advocacy; Staff for Judicatory Leadership Council; Commission on Dialogue; Commission on Church & Society; Commission on Admin. & Dev.; Ecumenical Choral Concerts; Ecumenical Worship Services

The Christian Council of Delaware and Maryland's Eastern Shore
(see listing under Delaware)

Community Ministries of Rockville
114 West Montgomery Ave., Rockville, MD 20850
Tel. (301) 762-8682 Fax (301) 762-2939
Email: cmr114mr@aol.com
Media Contact, Managing Dir., Agnes Saenz
Exec. Dir. & Comm. Min., Mansfield M. Kaseman
Managing Dir., Agnes Aaenz
Major Activities: Shelter Care; Emergency Assistance; Elderly Home Care; Affordable Housing; Political Advocacy; Community Education; Education to Recent Immigrants

Community Ministry of Montgomery County

114 West Montgomery Ave., Rockville, MD 20850
Tel. (301) 762-8682 Fax (301) 762-2939
Media Contact, Exec. Dir., Rebecca Wagner
Exec. Dir., Rebecca Wagner
Major Activities: Interfaith Clothing Center; Emergency Assistance Coalition; The Advocacy Function; Information and Referral Services; Friends in Action; The Thanksgiving Hunger Drive; Thanksgiving in February; Community Based Shelter

MASSACHUSETTS

Attleboro Area Council of Churches, Inc.

505 N. Main St., Attleboro, MA 02703
Tel. (508) 222-2933 Fax (508) 222-2933
Media Contact, Executive Director, Carolyn L. Bronkar
Exec. Dir., Carolyn L. Bronkar
Admn. Sec.-vacant-
Staff Asst., Emergency Food Program, Lynne F. Sias
Hosp. Chplns., Rev. Dr. William B. Udall and Rev. Janet Long
Pres., Rev. David Hill, 52 Glendale Rd., Attleboro, MA 02703
Treas., Ray Larson, 33 Watson Ave., Attleboro, MA 02703
Major Activities: Hospital Chaplaincy; personal Growth/Skill Workshops; Ecumenical Worship; Media Resource Center; Referral Center; Communications/ Publications; Community Social Action; Food'n Friends Kitchens; Nursing Home Volunteer Visitation Program; Lay School of Christian Theology; Clergy Fellowship/ Learning Events

The Cape Cod Council of Churches, Inc.

320 Main St., P.O. Box 758, Hyannis, MA 02601
Tel. (508) 775-5073
Media Contact, Exec. Dir., Rev. Susan Royce Scribner
Exec. Dir., Rev. Susan Royce Scribner
Pres., Mr. Barry Jones-Henry, Sr.
Chaplain, Cape Cod Hospital, Rev. William Wilcox
Chaplain, Falmouth Hospital, Rev. Allen Page
Chaplain, House of Correction & Jail, Rev. Thomas Shepherd
Chaplain, Rehabilitation Hospital of the Cape and Islands, Mrs. Elizabeth Stommel
Service Center & Thrift Shop: P.O. Box 125, Dennisport, MA 02639 Tel. (508)394-6361
Major Activities: Pastoral Care; Social Concerns; Religious Education; Emergency Distribution of Food, Clothing, Furniture; Referral and Information; Church World Service; Interfaith Relations; Media Presence; Hospital & Jail Chaplaincy; Arts & Religion

Cooperative Metropolitan Ministries

474 Centre St., Newton, MA 02158
Tel. (617) 244-3650 Fax (617) 244-0569
Media Contact, Exec. Dir., Claire Kashuck
Exec. Dir., Claire Kashuck
Bd. Pres., Sr. Joyceyn McMullen
Treas., Karen Gunn
Clk., Fran Grady
Major Activities: Low Income; Suburban/Urban Bridges; Racial and Economic Justice

Council of Churches of Greater Springfield

39 Oakland St., Springfield, MA 01108
Tel. (413) 733-2149 Fax (413) 733-9817
Media Contact, Asst. to Dir., Sr. John Bridgid
Exec. Dir., Rev. Ann Geer
Community Min., Dir., Rev. L. Edgar Depaz
Pres., The Rev. Dr. David Hunter
Treas., John Pearson, Esq
Major Activities: Christian Education Resource Center; Advocacy; Emergency Fuel Fund; Peace and Justice Division; Community Ministry; Task Force on Racism; Hospital and Jail Chaplaincies; Pastoral Service; Crisis Counseling; Christian Social Relations; Relief Collections; Ecumenical and Interfaith Relations; Ecumenical Dialogue with Roman Catholic Diocese; Mass Media; Church/Community Projects and Community Dialogues

Greater Lawrence Council of Churches

117A S. Broadway, Lawrence, MA 01843
Tel. (508) 686-4012
Email: glcclawrence@juno.com
Media Contact, Exec. Dir., David Edwards
Exec. Dir., David Edwards
Pres., Carol Rabs
Vice-Pres., Rev. Michael Graham
Admn. Asst., Linda Sullivan
Major Activities: Ecumenical Worship; Radio Ministry; Hospital and Nursing Home Chaplaincy; Church Women United; After-school Children's Program; Vacation Bible School

Inter-Church Council of Greater New Bedford

412 County St., New Bedford, MA 02740-5096
Tel. (508) 993-6242 Fax (508) 991-3158
Email: icc@ma.ultranet.com
Website: www.ultranet.com/~icc
Media Contact, Min., Rev. Edward R. Dufresne, Ph.D.
Exec. Min., Rev. Edward R. Dufresne, Ph.D.
Pres., Pamela Pollock
Treas., Christopher Bunnell
Major Activities: Pastoral Counseling; Spiritual Direction; Chaplaincy; Housing for Elderly;

231

Urban Affairs; Community Development; Parish Nurse Ministry; Accounting for the Developmentally Challenged; Prison Chaplaincy

Massachusetts Commission on Christian Unity

82 Luce St., Lowell, MA 01852-3034
Tel. (978) 453-5423 Fax (978) 453-5423
Media Contact, Exec. Dir., Rev. K. Gordon White
Exec. Sec., Rev. K. Gordon White
Major Activities: Faith and Order Dialogue with Church Judicatories; Guidelines & Pastoral Directives for Inter-Church Marriages

*Massachusetts Council of Churches

14 Beacon St., Rm. 416, Boston, MA 02108
Tel. (617) 523-2771 Fax (617) 523-1483
Email: ecumass@juno.com
Media Contact, Dir., Rev. Diane C. Kessler
Exec. Dir., Rev. Diane C. Kessler
Assoc. Dir., -vacant-
Adjunct Assoc., Rev. Betsy Sowers
Pres., Mrs. Mary Alice Stahleker
Vice-Pres., Rev. Canon Edward Rodman
Sec., Eden Grace
Treas., Robert Sarly
Major Activities: Christian Unity; Education and Evangelism; Defend Social Justice & Individual Rights; Ecumenical Worship; Services and Resources for Individuals and Churches

Worcester County Ecumenical Council

4 Caroline St., Worcester, MA 01604
Tel. (508) 757-8385 Fax (508) 795-7704
Email: worcecumen@aol.com
Media Contact, Sec., Eleanor G. Bird
Dir., Rev. Steven Alspach
Interim Pres., Rev. Dr. Paul D. Kennedy
Major Activities: Ecumenical worship and dialogue networking congregations together in partnerships of mission, education and spiritual renewal. Clusters of Churches; Ecumenical Worship and Dialogue; Interfaith Activities; Resource Connection for Churches; Group Purchasing Consortium

MICHIGAN

Bay Area Ecumenical Forum

103 E. Midland St., Bay City, MI 48706
Tel. (517) 686-1360
Media Contact, Rev. Karen Banaszak
Major Activities: Ecumenical Worship; Community Issues; Christian Unity; Education; CROP Walk

Berrien County Association of Churches

275 Pipestone, P.O. Box 1042, Benton Harbor, MI 49023-1042

Tel. (616) 926-0030
Media Contact, Sec., Mary Ann Hinz
Pres., Rev. Skip MacCarty
Dir., Street Ministry, Rev. James Atterberry
Major Activities: Street Ministry; CROP Walk; Community Issues; Fellowship; Christian Unity; Hospital Chaplaincy Program; Publish Annual County Church Directory and Monthly Newsletter; Resource Guide for Helping Needy; Distribution of Worship Opportunity—Brochure for Tourists

Christian Communication Council of Metropolitan Detroit Churches

1300 Mutual Building, 28 W. Adams, Detroit, MI 48226
Tel. (313) 962-0340
Email: councilweb@aol.com
Website: http://users.aol.com/councilweb/index.htm
Media Contact, Rev. Richard Singleton
Exec. Dir., Rev. Richard Singleton
Meals for Shut-ins, Prog. Dir., John Simpson
Major Activities: Theological and Social Concerns; Ecumenical Worship; Educational Services; Electronic Media; Print Media; Meals for Shut-Ins; Summer Feeding Program

Grand Rapids Area Center for Ecumenism (GRACE)

38 Fulton West, Grand Rapids, MI 49503-2628
Tel. (616) 774-2042 Fax (616) 774-2883
Email: dbaak@ecunet.org
Website: http://www.grcmc.org/grace
Media Contact, Exec. Dir., Rev. David P. Baak
Exec. Dir., Rev. David P. Baak
Prog. Dir., Lisa H. Mitchell
Major Activities: AIDS Pastoral Care Network (Client Services Education/ Volunteer Coordination); Hunger Walk ; Education/ Relationships; (Ecumenical Lecture, Christian Unity Worship/Events, Interfaith Dialogue Conference, Prayer Against Violence); (Affiliates: ACCESS-All County Churches Emergency Support System, FISH for My People-transportation); Publications (Religious Community Directory, Grace Notes); Racial Justice Institute; Project Zero Mentoring (Welfare Reform Response)

Greater Flint Association of Christian Churches

310 E. Third Ave., Suite 600, Flint, MI 48502
Tel. (810) 238-3691 Fax (810) 238-4463
Media Contact, Mrs. Constance D. Neely
President, Rev. James F. Offrink
Major Activities: Christian Education; Christian Unity; Christian Missions; Nursing Home Visitors; Church in Society; American Bible Society Materials; Interfaith Dialogue; Church Teacher Exchange Sunday; Directory of Area Faiths and Clergy; Thanksgiving & Easter Sunrise Services; CROP Walks

In One Accord

312 Capital Ave., NE, Battle Creek, MI 49017
Tel. (616) 966-2500 Fax (616) 660-6665
Pres., Rev. Erick Johnson
Vice-Pres., Haleyon Liew
Secretary: Sally Goss
Major Activities: CROP Walk; Food Closet;
Christian Sports; Week of Prayer for Christian
Unity; Ecumenical Worship

The Jackson County Interfaith Council

425 Oakwood, P.O. Box 156, Clarklake, MI
49234-0156
Tel. (517) 529-9721
Media Contact, Exec. Dir., Rev. Loyal H. Wiemer
Exec. Dir., Rev. Loyal H. Wiemer
Major Activities: Chaplaincy at Institutions and
Senior Citizens Residences; Martin L. King,
Jr. Day Celebrations; Ecumenical Council
Representation; Radio and TV Programs;
Food Pantry; Interreligious Events; Clergy
Directory

*Michigan Ecumenical Forum

809 Center St., Ste. 5, Lansing, MI 48906
Tel. (517) 485-4395 Fax (517) 482-8751
Email: ecumenical@earthlink.net
Media Contact, Coord./Exec. Dir., Rev. Steven
L. Johns-Boehme
Coord./Exec. Dir., Rev. Steven L. Johns-Boehme
Major Activities: Communication and Coordi-
nation; Support and Development of Regional
Ecumenical Fora; Ecumenical Studies;
Fellowship and Celebration; Church and
Society Issues; Continuing Education

Muskegon County Cooperating Churches

2525 Hall Road, Muskegon, MI 49442-1520
Tel. 231-777-2888 Fax 231-773-4007
Media Contact, Program Coordinator, Delphine
Hogston
President, Rev. Tim Vander Haar
Major Activities: Racial Reconciliation, Dialogue,
& Healing; Ecumenical Worship; Faith News
TV Ministry; CROP Walk; Community Issues;
Prison Ministry; Jewish-Christian Dialogue;
Tutoring; Senior Issues
SUBSIDIARY ORGANIZATION
Institute for Healing Racism—Muskegon
2525 Hall Road, Muskegon, MI 49442-1520,
Tel. 231-777-7883 Fax. 231-773-4007
Media Contact, Gordon Rinard, Dir.
Major Activities: Racial Reconciliation,
Dialogue, & Healing

MINNESOTA

*Arrowhead Interfaith Council

230 E. Skyline Pkwy., Duluth, MN 55811
Tel. (218) 727-5020 Fax (218) 727-5022

Media Contact, Pres., Alan Cutter
Pres., Alan Cutter
Vice-Pres., Amy Berstein
Sec., John H. Kemp
Major Activities: InterFaith Dialogue; Joint
Religious Legislative Coalition; Corrections
Chaplaincy; Human Justice and Community
Concerns; Community Seminars; Children's
Concerns

Community Emergency Assistance Program (CEAP)

7231 Brooklyn Blvd., Brooklyn Center, MN
55429
Tel. (612) 566-9600 Fax (612) 566-9604
Media Contact, Exec. Dir., Tia Henry-Johnson
Exec. Dir., Tia Henry-Johnson
Major Activities: Provision of Basic Needs
(Food, Clothing); Emergency Financial
Assistance for Shelter; Home Delivered Meals;
Chore Services and Homemaking Assistance;
Family Loan Program; Volunteer Services

Greater Minneapolis Council of Churches

1001 E. Lake St., P.O. Box 7509, Minneapolis,
MN 55407-0509
Tel. (612) 721-8687 Fax (612) 722-8669
Email: info@gmcc.org
Website: www.gmcc.org
Media Contact, Dir. of Communications, Darcy
Hanzlik
President and CEO, Rev. Dr. Gary B. Reierson
Email: reierson@gmcc.org
Chair, Barbara Koch
Treas., Dorothy Bridges
Indian Work: Sr. Vice President & Exec. Dir., Mary
Ellen Dumas; Assoc. Ex. Dir., Noya Woodrich
Programs, Vice President., Edward L. Duren, Jr.
Minnesota FoodShare, Dir., Rev. Christopher
Morton
Handyworks, Dir., Mary Jo Tarasar
Correctional Chaplains: Rev. Susan Allers
Hatlie; Rev. Thomas Van Leer; Imam Charles
El-Amin; Susan Jourdain
Congregations In Community, Dir., Rev. Bruce
Bjork
Shared Ministries Tutorial Program, Coord.
Div. of Indian Work: Family Violence Prog., Dir.,
Herb Grant; Teen Parents Prog., Dir., Jaime
Windyboy.; Youth Leadership Dev. Prog., Dir.,
Vivinnie Crowe; Horizons Unlimited, Dir.,
Monica Melanie Thompson; AnpaWaste (New
Beginnings) House for Teen Indian Parents,
Dir., Jaime Windyboy
Finance & Admin., Vice President and CFO.,
Dennis Anderson
Institutional Advancement: Vice President., Don
R. Riggs
Metro Paint-A-Thon, Dir., Beth Storey
Minnesota Churches Anti-Racism Initiative, Dir.,
James and Nadine Addington

233

Congregations Concerned for Children Child Advocacy Network, Coord., Norma Bourland
Project Restoration, Dir., Rev. Bruce Bjork
Center for Urban Service, Dir., Rev. Bruce Bjork
Child Care Center Challenge Grant Fund, President and CEO, Rev. Dr. Gary B. Reierson
Major Activities: Indian Work (Emergency Assistance, Youth Leadership, self-sufficiency, Jobs Program, Teen Indian Parents Program, and Family Violence Program); Minnesota FoodShare; Metro Paint-A-Thon; Shared Ministries Tutorial Program; Congregations In Community; Correctional Chaplaincy Program; HandyWorks; Anti-racism Initiative; Child Advocacy; Social Justice Advocacy; Child Care Center Start-up; Home Renovation; Affordable Housing; Urban Immersion Service Retreats; Welfare Reform; Economic Self-Sufficiency; Discover Support Groups; Job Readiness

The Joint Religious Legislative Coalition

122 W. Franklin Ave., Rm. 315, Minneapolis, MN 55404
Tel. (612) 870-3670 Fax (612) 870-3671
Email: jrlc@ecunet.org
Website: www.jrlc.org
Media Contact, Exec. Dir., Brian A. Rusche
Exec. Dir., Brian A. Rusche
Research Dir., Dr. James Casebolt
Congregational Organizer, Rev. Becky Myrick
Major Activities: Lobbying at State Legislature; Researching Social Justice Issues and Preparing Position Statements; Organizing Grassroots Citizen's Lobby

Metropolitan Interfaith Council on Affordable Housing (MICAH)

122 W. Franklin Ave., #310, Minneapolis, MN 55404
Tel. (612) 871-8980 Fax (612) 813-4501
Email: info@micah.org
Website: www.micah.org
Media Contact, Ex. Dir., Joy Sorensen Navarre
Ex. Dir., Joy Sorensen Navarre
Assoc. Dir., JosÇ Trejo
Congregational Organizer, Jodi Nelson, Jean Pearson, Rev. John Buzza, Gloria Little
Pres., Sue Watlov Phillips
Sec., Rev. Paul Robinson
Vice Pres., Dick Little
Treas., Joseph Holmberg
Pres. Elect, Kristine Gentilini
Major Activities: MICAH is a regional advocacy organization made up of over 100 Catholic, Islamic, Jewish, and Protestant congregations dedicated to ensuring decent, safe, and affordable housing for everyone in our community. Its central organizing motto is, "To think regionally, act locally, and live faithfully." In partnership with its members and other

groups, MICAH has created community support for 200 new apartment homes in the past two years. In addition it has preserved over 1,000 structurally sound apartments at risk of demolition.

*Minnesota Council of Churches

122 W. Franklin Ave., Rm. 100, Minneapolis, MN 55404
Tel. (612) 870-3600 Fax (612) 870-3622
Email: mcc@mnchurches.org
Website: www.mnchurches.org
Media Contact, Exec. Dir., Rev. Peg Chemberlin, Email: Pegchemberlin@mn.churches.org
Officers and Staff
Exec. Dir., Rev. Peg Chemberlin, Pegchemberlin @mn.churches.org
Life & Work, Dir., Robert Hulteen, bobhulteen@ecunet.org
Unity & Relationships, Dir., Rev. Lydia Veliko, Email: veliko@ecunet.org
Refugee Services, Dir.,
Indian Ministry, Field Organizer, Sandy Berlin
Communications, Dir., Dr. Robert M. Frame, III
Facilities, Dir., Cynthia Darrington-Ottinger
Tri-Council Coordinating Commission: Co-Dirs., James and Nadine Addington
Research Dir. & Admn. Asst., James Casebolt
Joint Religious Legislative Coalition, Exec., Brian A. Rusche
Pres., Bishop Mark Hanson
Renewing the Public Church, Field Organizer, Karen Roles
Major Activities: Minnesota Church Center; Local Ecumenism; Life & Work: Rural Life-Ag Crisis; Racial Reconciliation; Indian Ministry; Legislative Advocacy; Refugee Services; Service to Newly Legalized/ Undocumented persons; Unity & Relationships: Sexual Exploitation within the Religious Community; Chaplaincy; Clergy Support; Consultation on Church Union; Ecumenical Study & Dialogue; Jewish-Christian Relations; Muslim-Christian Relations; State Fair Ministry; Tri-Council Coordinating Commission (Minnesota Churches Anti-Racism Initiative, Religious Initiative for Gender Justice); Active Non-Violence; No-Interest Small Loan Program; Child Labor Discussions

St. Paul Area Council of Churches

1671 Summit Ave, St. Paul, MN 55105
Tel. (651) 646-8805 Fax (651) 646-6866
Email: rwalz@pioneerplanet.infi.net
Website: www.center.hamline.edu/spacc
Media Contact, Sandy Lucas
Exec. Dir., Rev. Thomas A. Duke
Dir. of Development, Kristi Anderson
Congregations in Community, Bob Walz
Congregations Concerned for Children, Peg Wangensteen
Project Spirit, Rev. Paulette Ajavon

234

Project Home, Margaret Lovejoy
Dept. of Indian Work, Sheila White Eagle
Criminal Justice Care Services, Rev. Kathleen Gatson
Pres. of the Board, Rev. Dick Goebel
Treas., Bert Nienaber
Sec., Charles Hawkins
Major Activities: Chaplaincy at Detention and Corrections Authority Institutions; Police Chaplaincy; Education and Advocacy Regarding Children and Poverty; Assistance to Churches Developing Children's Parenting Care Services; Ecumenical Encounters and Activities; Indian Ministries; Leadership in Forming Cooperative Ministries for Children and Youth; After School Tutoring; Assistance to Congregations Developing Shared Ministry Activities; Training Programs in Anti-racism; Shelters for homeless

Tri-Council Coordinating Commission
122 W. Franklin, Rm. 100, Minneapolis, MN 55404
Tel. (612) 871-0229 Fax (612) 870-3622
Website: www.amcc.org/tcc.html
Media Contact, Co-Dir., Nadine Addington OR Co-Dir., R. James Addington
Co-Dir., R. James Addington
Co-Dir., Nadine Addington
Pres., Rev. Thomas Duke, 1671 Summit Ave., St. Paul, MN 55105
Major Activities: Anti-Racism Training; Organizing & Resource; Anti-Sexism Education and Resource Center

MISSISSIPPI

*Mississippi Religious Leadership Conference
P.O. Box 68123, Jackson, MS 39286-8123
Tel. (601) 948-5954 Fax (601) 354-3401
Media Contact, Exec. Dir., Rev. Canon Thomas E. Tiller, Jr.
Exec. Dir., Rev. Canon Thomas E. Tiller, Jr.
Chair, Bishop Marshall Meadors
Treas., Rev. Tom Clark
Major Activities: Cooperation among Religious Leaders; Lay/Clergy Retreats; Social Concerns Seminars; Disaster Task Force; Advocacy for Disadvantaged

MISSOURI

Council of Churches of the Ozarks
P.O. Box 3947, Springfield, MO 65808-3947
Tel. (417) 862-3586 Fax (417) 862-2129
Email: ccozarks@ccozarks.org
Website: www.ccozarks.org
Media Contact, Comm. Dir., Susan Jackson
Exec. Dir., Rev. Jesse Thorton
Dev. Officer, Trudy Pischer
Program Dir., Barbara Gardner

Major Activities: Ministerial Alliance; Retired Sr. Volunteer Prog.; Treatment Center for Alcohol and Drug Abuse; Helping Elderly Live More Productively; Daybreak Adult Day Care Services; Ombudsman for Nursing Homes; Homesharing; Family Day Care Homes; USDA Food Program; Youth Ministry; Disaster Aid and Counseling; Homebound Shoppers; Food and Clothing Pantry; Ozarks Food Harvest

Ecumenical Ministries
#2 St. Louis Ave., Fulton, MO 65251
Tel. (573) 642-6065
Email: em_fulton@ecunet.org
Website: www.coin.missouri.edu/region/call-away/em.html
Media Contact, Ofc. Mgr., Karen Luebbert
Exec. Dir., Andrea Langton
Pres., William Jessop
Major Activities: Kingdom Hospice; CROP Hunger Walk; Little Brother and Sister; Unity Service; Senior Center Bible Study; County Jail Ministry; Fulton High School Baccalaureate Service, HAVEN House; Missouri Youth Treatment Center Ministry

Interfaith Community Services
200 Cherokee St., P.O. Box 4038, St. Joseph, MO 64504-0038
Tel. (816) 238-4511 Fax (816) 238-3274
Email: DaveB@PonyExpress.net
Website: www.inter-serv.org
Media Contact, Exec. Dir., David G. Berger
Exec. Dir., David G. Berger
Major Activities: Child Development; Neighborhood Family Services; Group Home for Girls; Retired Senior Volunteer Program; Nutrition Program; Mobile Meals; Southside Youth Program; Church and Community; Housing Development; Homemaker Services to Elderly; Emergency Food, Rent, Utilities; AIDS Assistance; Family Respite; Family and Individual Casework

MONTANA

*Montana Association of Churches
Andrew Square, Ste. G, 180 24th St. W., Billings, MT 59102
Tel. (406) 656-9779 Fax (406) 656-2156
Email: zmac@wtp.net
Website: www.wtp.net/~zmac
Media Contact, Exec. Dir., Margaret MacDonald
Exec. Dir., Margaret E. MacDonald
Admn. Asst., Larry D. Drane
Pres., Rev. Jessica Crist, 401 4th Ave. N., Great Falls, MT 59401-2310
Treas., Rev. Paul Everett, 401 Riverview, Glendive, MT 59330
Sec., Rev. Gretchen Knapp, P.O. Box 794, Hilger, MT 59451
Christian Witness for Humanity, Mark Nagasawa
Christian Advocates Network, Betty Waddell

Major Activities: Montana Christian Advocates Network; Christian Unity; Junior Citizen Camp; Public Information; Ministries Development; Social Ministry; Faith Responses to Extremism and Racism through Christian Witness For Humanity

Project; Crop Walk for Hunger; Unicef Drive; New Clergy Orientation; Directory of Clergy, Congregations & Religious Resources; Multi-Faith Planning Calendar Publication; "Faith Report" on KOLN/KGIN-TV (Nation's oldest religious TV news program)

NEBRASKA

*Interchurch Ministries of Nebraska
215 Centennial Mall S., Rm. 411, Lincoln, NE 68508-1888
Tel. (402) 476-3391 Fax (402) 476-9310
Email: im50427@navix.net
Media Contact, Exec., Mrs. Marilyn P. Mecham
Pres.,Bishop James E. Krotz
Treas., Mrs. Shirley Mac Marsh
Exec., Mrs. Marilyn Mecham
Admin. Asst., Sharon K. Kalcik
Major Activities: Interchurch Planning and Development; Comity; Indian Ministry; Rural Church Strategy; United Ministries in Higher Education; Disaster Response; Rural Response Hotline; Pantry Network; Rural Health; Community Organizing Initiative Planning; Peace with Justice; Ministry with Lesbian & Gay Persons & Their Families

Lincoln Interfaith Council
140 S. 27th St., Ste. B, Lincoln, NE 68510-1301
Tel. (402) 474-3017 Fax (402) 475-3262
Email: Li92630@navix.net
Media Contact, David Hancock
Exec. Dir., Rev. Dr. Norman E. Leach
Pres., Dr. William Caldwell
Vice-Pres., Rev. Dr. Roger Harp
Sec., Barbara Dewey
Treas., The Rev. Clip Higgins
Media Specialist, David Hancock
Urban Ministries, Rev. Dr. Norman E. Leach
Admn. Asst., Jean Scali
Fiscal Mgr., Jean Scali
Family Outreach Workers:Bich Tang; Tan Pham
Police Community Liaison,Toan Tran
Migrant Child Education Outreach, Marina Wray
Faces of the Middle East, Mohammed Al-Bezerji
Major Activities: Emergency Food Pantries System; MLK, Jr. Observance; Interfaith Passover Seder; Week of Prayer Christian Unity; Center for Spiritual Growth; Festival of Faith & Culture; Holocaust Memorial Observance; Citizens Against Racism & Discrimination; HIV/AIDS Healing Worship Services; Community organization; Anti-Drug & Anti-Alcohol Abuse Projects; Youth Gang & Violence Prevention; Domestic Abuse Prevention; Migrant Child Education; American Citizenship Classes; Survival English for Pre-literate AmerAsians and Elderly Refugees; Ecumenical Deaf Ministry; Multi-Faith & Multi-Cultural Training; Faces of the Middle East Project; Communities Helping Immigrants & Refugees Progress

NEW HAMPSHIRE

*New Hampshire Council of Churches
316 S. Main St., P.O. Box 1087, Concord, NH 03302
Tel. (603) 224-1352 Fax (603) 224-9161
Email: churchesnh@aol.com
Website: www.nhchurches.org
Media Contact, Exec. Sec., David Lamarre-Vincent, Email:davidlv@aol.com
Exec. Sec., David Lamarre-Vincent
Pres., Rev. Benjamin C. L. Crosby, 314 S. Main St., Concord, NH 03301-3468
Treas., Richard Couser
Major Activities: Ecumenical Work

NEW JERSEY

Bergen County Council of Churches
165 Burton Ave., Hasbrouck Hts., NJ 07604
Tel. (201) 288-3784
Media Contact, Pres., Rev. Stephen Giordano, Clinton Avenue Reformed Church, Clinton Ave. & James St., Bergenfield, NJ 07621 Tel. (201)384-2454 Fax (201)384-2585
Exec. Sec., Anne Annunziato
Major Activities: Ecumenical and Religious Institute; Brotherhood/Sisterhood Breakfast; Center for Food Action; Homeless Aid; Operation Santa Claus; Aging Services; Boy & Girl Scouts; Easter Dawn Services; Music; Youth; Ecumenical Representation; Support of Chaplains in Jails & Hospitals

Council of Churches of Greater Camden
P.O. Box 1208, Merchantville, NJ 08109
Tel. (856) 985-5162
Media Contact, Exec. Sec., Rev. Dr. Samuel A. Jeanes, Braddock Bldg., 205 Tuckerton Road, Medford, NJ 08055 Tel. (609)985-7724
Exec. Sec., Rev. Dr. Samuel A. Jeanes
Pres., Rev. Lawrence L. Dunn
Treas., William G. Mason
Major Activities: Radio & T.V.; Hospital Chaplaincy; United Services; Good Friday Breakfast; Mayors" Prayer Breakfast; Public Affairs; Easter Sunrise Service

Ecclesia
1001 Pennnington Rd., Trenton, NJ 08618-2629
Tel. (609) 882-5942
Media Contact, Exec. Dir., Rev. Dr. John R. Norwood, Jr.

236

Exec. Dir., Rev. Dr. John R. Norwood, Jr.
Pres., Rev. Donald Brash
Campus Chaplains: Rev. Nancy Schulter; Rev. Joanne B. Bullock
Sec., Tina Swan
Major Activities: Racial Justice; Children & Youth Ministries; Advocacy; CROP Walk; Ecumenical Worship; Hospital Chaplaincy; Church Women United; Campus Chaplaincy; Congregational Empowerment; Prison Chaplaincy; Substance Abuse Ministry Training

Metropolitan Ecumenical Ministry
525 Orange St., Newark, NJ 07107
Tel. (201) 481-6650 Fax (201) 481-7883
Media Contact, Pam Smith
Exec. Dir., C. Stephen Jones
Major Activities: Community Advocacy (education, housing, environment); Church Mission Assistance; Community and Clergy Leadership Development; Economic Development; Affordable Housing

Metropolitan Ecumenical Ministry Community Development Corp.
525 Orange St., Newark, NJ 07107
Tel. (201) 481-6650 Fax (201) 481-7883
Email: memcdc@juno.com
Exec. Dir., Jacqueline Jones
Major Activities: Housing Development; Neighborhood Revitalization; Commercial/ Small Business Development; Economic Development; Community Development; Credit Union; Home Ownership Counseling; Credit Repair; Mortgage Approval; Technical Assitance To Congregations

*New Jersey Council of Churches
176 W. State St., Trenton, NJ 08608
Tel. (609) 396-9546 Fax (609) 396-7646
Media Contact, Public Policy Dir., Joan Diefenbach, Esq.
Pres., Rev. Jack Johnson
Vice-Pres., —
Sec., Beverly McNally
Treas., Marge Christie
Major Activities: Racial Justice; Children's Issues; Theological Unity; Ethics Public Forums; Advocacy; Economic Justice

NEW MEXICO

Inter-Faith Council of Santa Fe, New Mexico
PO Box 4637, Santa Fe, NM 87502
Tel. (505) 983-2892 Fax (505) 473-5637
Media Contact, Barbara A. Robinson
Treas., Marcia Mize
Major Activities: Faith Community Assistance Center; Interfaith Dialogues/ Celebrations/ Visitations; Peace Projects; Understanding Hispanic Heritage; Newsletter

*New Mexico Conference of Churches
124 Hermosa SE, Albuquerque, NM 87108-2610
Tel. (505) 255-1509 Fax (505) 256-0071
Email: wford@ecunet.org
Website: www.rt66.com/~nmcc
Media Contact, Exec. Sec., Dr. Wallace Ford
Pres., The Rev. Ann Calvin Rogers-Witte
Treas., Ruth Tribeou
Exec. Sec., Rev. Dr. Wallace Ford
Major Activities: Ecumenical Institute for Ministry; Affordable Housing; Social Justice Coalitions; Spiritual Life & Ministries

NEW YORK

Brooklyn Council of Churches
125 Ft. Greene Pl., Brooklyn, NY 11217
Tel. (718) 625-5851 Fax 718-522-1231
Media Contact, Dir., Charles Henze
Program Dir., Charles Henze
Pres., Rev. John L. Pratt., Sr.
Treas., Rev. Charles H. Straut , Jr.
Major Activities: Education Workshops; Food Pantries; Welfare Advocacy; Hospital and Nursing Home Chaplaincy; Church Women United; Legislative Concerns

Broome County Council of Churches, Inc.
81 Main St., Binghamton, NY 13905
Tel. (607) 724-9130 Fax (607) 724-9148
Email: bccouncil@juno.com
Website: www.tier.net/bccc
Media Contact, Assoc. Dir., Jan Aerie
Exec. Dir., William H. Stanton
Assoc. Dir., Jan Aerie
Hospital Chaplains: Betty Pomeroy; Rev. Nadine Ridley
Jail Chaplain, Rev. Philip Singer; Pat Dillon
Aging Ministry Coord., Linda McCalgin
CHOW Prog. Coord., Heidi Kowalchyk
Pres., Rev. Art Suggs
Treas., Rachel Light
Caregiver Program Coord., Rebecca Mebert
Major Activities: Hospital and Jail Chaplains; Youth and Aging Ministries; Broome Bounty (Food Rescue Program); CHOW (Emergency Hunger Program); Faith & Family Values; Ecumenical Worship and Fellowship; Media; Community Affairs; Peace with Justice; Day by Day Marriage Prep Program; Interfaith Coalition; Interfaith Volunteer Caregiver Program

Capital Area Council of Churches, Inc.
646 State St., Albany, NY 12203-3815
Tel. (518) 462-5450 Fax (518) 462-5450
Media Contact, Admn. Asst.,Kitt Jackson
Exec. Dir., Rev. Dr. Robert C. Lamar
Admn. Asst.,Kitt Jackson

Pres.,Marlene Shilling
Treas.,Edward Cameron
Major Activities: Hospital Chaplaincy; Food Pantries; CROP Walk; Jail and Nursing Home Ministries; Martin Luther King Memorial Service and Scholarship Fund; Emergency Shelter for the Homeless; Campus Ministry; Ecumenical Dialogue; Forums on Social Concerns; Peace and Justice Education; Inter-Faith Programs; Legislative Concerns; Comm. Thanksgiving Day and Good Friday Services; Annual Ecumenical Musical Celebration

CAPITAL Region Ecumenical Organization (CREO)

Box 2199, Scotia, NY 12302
Tel. (518) 382-7505 Fax (518) 382-7505
Email: TishMurph@aol.com
Media Contact, Coord., Jim Murphy
Coord., Jim Murphy
Major Activities: Promote Cooperation/ Coordination Among Member Judicatories and Ecumenical Organizations in the Capital Region in Urban Ministries, Social Action

Chautaugua County Rural Ministry

127 Central Ave., P.O. Box 362, Dunkirk, NY 14048
Tel. (716) 366-1787
Media Contact, Exec. Dir., Kathleen Peterson
Exec. Dir., Kathleen Peterson
Major Activities: Chautaugua County Food Bank; Collection/Distribution of Furniture, Clothing, & Appliances; Homeless Services; Advocacy for the Poor; Soup Kitchen; Emergency Food Pantry; Thrift Store

Concerned Ecumenical Ministry to the Upper West Side

286 LaFayette Ave., Buffalo, NY 14213
Tel. (716) 882-2442 Fax (716) 882-2477
Email: catrg@banet.net
Media Contact, Exec. Dir., The Rev. Catherine Rieley-Goddard
Interim Exec. Dir., The Rev. Catherine Rieley-Goddard
Pres., The Rev. Robert Grimm
Major Activities: Community Center Serving Youth, Young Families, Seniors and the Hungry

Cortland County Council of Churches, Inc.

7 Calvert St., Cortland, NY 13045
Tel. (607) 753-1002
Media Contact, Office Mgr., Joy Niswender
Exec. Dir., Rev. Donald M. Wilcox
Major Activities: College Campus Ministry; Hospital Chaplaincy; Nursing Home Ministry; Newspaper Column; Interfaith Relationships; Hunger Relief; CWS; Crop Walk; Leadership Education; Community Issues; Mental Health Chaplaincy; Grief Support; Jail Ministry

Council of Churches of Chemung County, Inc.

330 W. Church St., Elmira, NY 14901
Tel. (607) 734-2294
Media Contact, Exec. Dir., Joan Geldmacher, Tel. (607)734-7622
Exec. Dir., Joan Geldmacher
Pres., Rev. Doris Washington, Tel. (607)733-6155
Major Activities: CWS Collection; CROP Walk; UNICEF; Institutional Chaplaincies; Radio, Easter Dawn Service; Communications Network; Produce & Distribute Complete Church Directories; Representation on Community Boards and Agencies; Ecumenical Services; Interfaith Coalition; Taskforce on Children & Families; Multicultural Committee; Compeer

Council of Churches of the City of New York

475 Riverside Dr., Rm. 720, New York, NY 10115
Tel. (212) 367-4222 Fax (212) 367-4280
Email: JEHiemstra@aol.com
Media Contact, Exec. Dir., Dr. John E. Hiemstra
Exec. Dir., Dr. John E. Hiemstra
Pres., Rev. Calvin O. Butts
1st Vice-Pres., Friend Carol Holmes
2nd Vice-Pres., Rev. Carolyn Holloway
3rd Vice-Pres., Ven. Michael Kendall
Sec., Rev.N.J. L'Heureux
Treas., Dr. John Blackwell
Major Activities: Radio & TV; Pastoral Care; Protestant Chapel, Kennedy International Airport; Coordination and Strategic Planning; Religious Conferences; Referral & Advocacy; Youth Development; Building Great Minds Tutoring Program; Directory of Churches and Database Available

Dutchess Interfaith Council, Inc.

9 Vassar St., Poughkeepsie, NY 12601
Tel. (914) 471-7333
Media Contact, Exec. Dir., Rev. Gail A. Burger
Exec. Dir., Rev. Gail A. Burger
Pres.,Rev. Dr. Brian E. McWeeney
Treas., Elizabeth M. DiStefano
Major Activities: CROP Hunger Walk; Interfaith Music Festival; Public Worship Events; Interfaith Dialogue; Christian Unity; Interfaith Youth Evening; Oil Purchase Group; HIV/AIDS Work; Weekly Radio Program; Racial Unity Work

Genesee County Churches United, Inc.

P.O. Box 547, Batavia, NY 14021
Tel. (716) 343-6763
Media Contact, Pres.,Captain Leonard Boynton, Salvation Army, 529 East Main St., Batavia, NY 14020 Tel. (716)343-6284

Pres.,Leonard Boynton
Exec. Sec., Helen H. Mullen
Chaplain, Rev. Bert Tidlund
Major Activities: Jail Ministry; Food Pantries; Serve Needy Families; Radio Ministry; Pulpit Exchange; Community Thanksgiving; Ecumenical Services at County Fair

Genesee-Orleans Ministry of Concern

118 S. Main St., Box 245, Albion, NY 14411-0245
Tel. (716) 589-9210
Media Contact, Exec. Dir., Marian M. Adrian, GNSH
Exec. Dir., Marian M. Adrian, GNSH
Advocates: JoAnn McCowan; Heather Cook
Pres., John W. Cebula, Esq.
Chaplains: Orleans County Jail, Rev. Wilford Moss; Orleans Albion Correctional Facility, Sr. Dolores O'Dowd
Major Activities: Advocacy Services for the Disadvantaged, Homeless, Ill, Incarcerated and Victims of Family Violence; Emergency Food, Shelter, Utilities, Medicines

Graymoor Ecumenical & Interreligious Institute

475 Riverside Dr., Rm. 1960, New York, NY 10115-1999
Tel. (212) 870-2330 Fax (212) 870-2001
Email: 104075,2312@compuserve.com
Media Contact, Walter Gange, SA, Graymoor, Route 9, PO Box 300, Garrison, NY 10524-0300 Tel. (914)424-3671 ext. 3540 Fax (914)424-3433
Major Activities: (See Listing in US Cooperative Directory)

Greater Rochester Community of Churches

2 Riverside St., Rochester, NY 14613-1222
Tel. (716) 254-2570 Fax (716) 254-6551
Email: grcc@juno.com
Media Contact, Coord., Marie E. Gibson
Major Activities: Ecumenical Worship; Refugee Resettlement; Chaplaincy Services; Christian Unity; Beyond Racism Project; Interfaith Cooperation; Community Economic Development; Annual Faith in Action Celebration; Rochester's Religious Community Directory; Religious Information/Resources

InterReligious Council of Central New York

3049 E. Genesee St., Syracuse, NY 13224
Tel. (315) 449-3552 Fax (315) 449-3103
Email: IRCCNY@aol.com
Media Contact, Chrissie Rizzo
Executive Dir., The Rev. Robert E. Hanson
Pres., The Rev. Emily S. Gibson

Bus. Mgr., Arthur A. West
Director for Resource Development, Chrissie Rizzo
Pastoral Care Prog., Dir., The Rev. Terry Culbertson
Refugee Resettlement Prog., Dir., Nona Stewart
Senior Companion Prog., Dir., Virginia Frey
Long Term Ombudsman Prog., Dir., Linda Kashdin
Covenant Housing Prog., Dir., Kimberlee Dupcak
Southeast Asia Center, Acting Dir., Hoang Nguyen
Community Wide Dialogue on Racism, Race Relations and Racial Healing, Dir., Milady Andrews
Major Activities: Pastoral Ministries; Community Ministries; Interreligious and Ecumenical Relations; Diversity Education; Worship; Community Advocacy and Planning

The Long Island Council of Churches

1644 Denton Green, Hempstead, NY 11550
Tel. (516) 565-0290 Fax (call first)
Email: tgoodhue@suffolk.lib.ny.us
Website: www.homestead.com/licc
Media Contact, Admn. Asst., Barbara McLaughlin
Exec. Dir., Rev. Thomas W. Goodhue
Admn. Asst., Barbara McLaughlin
Pastoral Care, Interim Dir., Rev. Richard Lehman
Clinical Pastoral Educ., Dir.,"
Social Services, Dir., Cynthia Morrow, Tel. (516)565-0390
Nassau County Ofc., Social Services Sec., Loretta Tysinger
Suffolk County Ofc., Food Program & Family Support, Carolyn Gumbs
Nassau County Blood Prog. Coord., Rose Lee Davis
Suffolk County Blood Prog. Coord., Gloria Weiss
Dev. Dir.,,Kenneth Lewis
Major Activities: Pastoral Care in Hospitals and Jails; Clinical Pastoral Education; Emergency Food; Family Support & Advocacy; Advocacy for Domestic and International Peace & Justice; Blood Donor Coordination; Church World Service; Multifaith Cooperation; Clergy/Laity Training; Newsletter; Church Directory; AIDS Interfaith of Long Island; Special Projects
Eastern Office, 235 Sweezy Ave., Riverhead, NY 11901 Tel. (516)727-2210

Network of Religious Communities

1272 Delaware Ave., Buffalo, NY 14209-2496
Tel. (716) 882-4793 Fax (716) 882-7671
Email: ReligiousNet@aol.com
Website: ReligiousNet.org
Media Contact, Co-Exec. Dir., Rev. Dr. G. Stanford Bratton

239

Co-Exec. Dir. & COO, Rev. Dr. G. Stanford Bratton

Co-Exec. Dir., Rev. Francis X. Mazur

Pres.,Rev. Jeff Carter (Church of God in Christ)

Vice-Pres. For Program, The Rev. Dr. David McKee (General Presbyter, Presbytery of WNY)

Vice-Pres. For Administration, Ms. Marlene Glickman (Dir., American Jewish Committee)

Secretary, Ms. Barbara Arnold (Baha'i)

Treasurer, Mr. Terry Gensler (Evangelical Luterhan Church in America)

Chpsn., Interreligious Concerns, Rev. Dr. Kenneth Neal (Christian Church, Disciples of Christ)

Chpsn., Personnel, The Rev. James Croglio (Diocese of Buffalo- Roman Catholic)

Chpsn., Membership, The Rev. Robert Grimm (United Church of Christ)

Chpsn., Riefler Enablement Fund, Mrs. Thelma Lanier (African Methodist Episcopal Church)

Chpsn., Public Issues, Rev. Merle Showers (United Methodist Church)

Chpsn., Religious Leaders Forum, Rev. Paul Litwin (Diocese of Buffalo -Roman Catholic)

Chpsn., Church Women United, Mrs. Roberta Grimm

STAFF (Other than Executive Directors)

Communications Coordinator, Ms. Maureen Gensler

Office Coordinator, Ms. Sally Giordano

Director of Food For All, Patricia Griffin

Nutrition Outreach and Education Coordinator, Ms. Carolyn Williams

Staff Assistant, Mr. Lamont Gist

Major Activities: Regionwide Interreligious Conversation, Hunger Advocacy, Food Distribution, Roll Call Against Racism, Buffalo Coalition for Common Ground, Ecumenical and Interreligious Relations and Celebrations, Radio-TV Broadcast and Production, Church Women United, Lay/Religious Leaders Education, Community Development, Chaplaincy, Yom Hashoah Commemoration Service, Aids Memorial Service, Police/Community Relations, CROP Walks

*New York State Community of Churches, Inc.

362 State St, Albany, NY 12210-1202

Tel. (518) 436-9319 Fax (518) 427-6705

Email: nyscoc@aol.com

Media Contact, The Rev., Daniel Hahn

Executive Dir., Ms. Mary Lu Bowen

Pres., The Rev. Dr. Robert White

Corp. Sec., The Rev. Dr. Jon Norton

Treas., Bishop Susan M. Morrison

Convener, Bishop Lee M. Miller

Coordinator of Chaplaincy Services, Ms. Damaris McGuire

Public Policy Advocate, The Rev. Daniel Hahn

Admin. Asst., Sylvenia F. Cochran

Major Activities: Faith & Order; Interfaith Dialogue; State Chaplaincy and Public Policy Advocacy in the following areas: Anti-Racism; Campaign Reform; Criminal Justice System Reform; Disability; Ecomomic/Social Justice; Environmental; Health care; Homelessness/ Shelter; Hunger/Foode Programs; Immigrant Issues; Public Education; Rural Issues; Substance Abuse; Violence; Women's Issues

The Niagara Council of Churches Inc.

St. Paul UMC, 723 Seventh St., Niagara Falls, NY 14301

Tel. (716) 285-7505

Media Contact, Pres., Nessie S. Bloomquist, 7120 Laur Rd., Niagara Falls, NY 14304 Tel. (716)297-0698 Fax (716)298-1193

Exec. Dir., Ruby Babb

Pres., Nessie S. Bloomquist

Treas., Shirley Bathurst

Trustees Chpsn., Rev. Vincent Mattoni, 834 19th St., Niagara Falls, NY 14304

Major Activities: Ecumenical Worship; Bible Study; Christian Ed. & Social Concerns; Church Women United; Evangelism & Mission; Institutional Min. Youth Activities; Hymn Festival; Week of Prayer for Christian Unity; CWS Projects; Audio-Visual Library; UNICEF; Food Pantries and Kitchens; Community Missions, Inc.; Political Refugees; Eco-Justice Task Force; Migrant/ Rural Ministries; Interfaith Coalition on Energy

Niagara County Migrant Rural Ministry

6507 Wheeler Rd., Lockport, NY 14094

Tel. (716) 434-4405

Media Contact, Exec. Dir., Grayce M. Dietz

Chpsn., Lois Farley

Vice-Chpsn., Beverly Farnham

Sec., Anne Eifert

Treas., Rev. Patricia Ludwig

Major Activities: Migrant Farm Worker Program; Assist with Immigration Problems and Application Process for Social Services; Monitor Housing Conditions; Assist Rural Poor; Referrals to Appropriate Service Agencies; Children's Daily Enrichment Program

Queens Federation of Churches

86-17 105th St., Richmond Hill, NY 11418-1597

Tel. (718) 847-6764 Fax (718) 847-7392

Email: qfc@ecunet.org

Media Contact, Rev. N. J. L'Heureux, Jr.

Exec. Dir., Rev. N. J. L'Heureux, Jr.

York College Chaplain, Rev. Dr. Hortense Merritt

Pres., Rev. Allen D. Maclean

Treas.,Annie Lee Phillips

240

Major Activities: Emergency Food Service; York College Campus Ministry; Blood Bank; Scouting; Christian Education Workshops; Planning and Strategy; Church Women United; Community Consultations; Seminars for Church Leaders; Directory of Churches and Synagogues; Christian Relations (Prot/RC); Chaplaincies; Public Policy Issues; N.Y.S. Interfaith Commission on Landmarking of Religious Property; Queens Interfaith Hunger Network

Rural Migrant Ministry
P.O. Box 4757, Poughkeepsie, NY 12601
Tel. (914) 485-8627 Fax (914) 485-1963
Email: rmmyage@aol.com
Media Contact, Exec. Dir., Rev. Richard Witt
Exec. Dir., Rev. Richard Witt
Pres., Karen Maxwell
Major Activities: Serving the Rural Poor and Migrants Through a Ministry of Advocacy & Empowerment; Youth Program; Latino Committee; Organization and Advocacy with and for Rural Poor and Migrant Farm Workers

Schenectady Inner City Ministry
930 Albany St., Schenectady, NY 12307-1514
Tel. (518) 374-2683 Fax (518) 382-1871
Email: sicm@crisny.org
Website: www. crisny.org/not-for-profit/sicm
Media Contact, Marianne Comfort
Urban Agent, Rev. Phillip N. Grigsby
Off. Mgr., Vjucna Anderson
Fiscal Officer, Joan LaMonica
Emergency Food Liaison, Patricia Obrecht
Church/Community Worker, Jim Murphy
Pres., Judy DePasquale
Save and Share, Cathy Bryson
Damien Center, Laurie Bacheldor
Improvisational Teen Theatre, Laurie Bacheldar
Jobs, Etc., David Coplon, Cynthia Blair
Summer Food, Joan LaMonica, Melissa MacKinnon
Major Activities: Food Security; Advocacy; Housing; Neighborhood and Economic Issues; Ecumenical Worship and Fellowship; Community Research; Education in Churches on Faith Responses to Social Concerns; Legislative Advocacy; Food Buying Coop; Homelessness Prevention; CROP Walk; HIV/AIDS Ministry; Teen Theatre; Job Training and Placement Center; Summer Lunch for Youth; Study Circles Initiative on Embracing Diversity; EPRUS/Americorps

Southeast Ecumenical Ministry
25 Westminster Rd., Rochester, NY 14607
Tel. (716) 271-5350 Fax (716) 271-8526
Email: sem@frontiernet.net
Media Contact, Laurie Kennedy
Dir., Laurie Kennedy
Pres., Rev. James Widboom

Major Activities: Transportation of Elderly & Disabled; Emergency Food Cupboard; Supplemental Nutrition Program

Staten Island Council of Churches
2187 Victory Blvd., Staten Island, NY 10314
Tel. (718) 761-6782
Media Contact, Exec. Sec., Mildred J. Saderholm, 94 Russell St., Staten Island, NY 10308 Tel. (718)761-6782
Pres., Rev. Dr. Claude A. Knight
Exec. Sec., Mildred J. Saderholm
Major Activities: Support; Christian Education; Pastoral Care; Congregational Concerns; Urban Affairs

Troy Area United Ministries
17 First St., #2, Troy, NY 12180
Tel. (518) 274-5920 Fax (518) 271-1909
Email: TAUMMS@juno.com OR TAUM@crisny.org
Media Contact, Exec. Dir., Margaret T. Stoner
Exec. Dir., Margaret T. Stoner
Pres., Dorcas Rose
Chaplain, R.P.I., Rev. Paul Fraser
Chaplain, Russell Sage College, Rev. Paul Fraser
Major Activities: Community Dispute Settlement (mediation) Program; College Ministry; Nursing Home Ministry; CROP Walk; Homeless and Housing Concerns; Weekend Meals Program at Homeless Shelter; Community Worship Celebrations; Racial Relations; Furniture Program; Damien Center of Troy Hospitality for persons with HIV/AIDS; Computer Ministries

Wainwright House
260 Stuyvesant Ave., Rye, NY 10580
Tel. (914) 967-6080 Fax (914) 967-6114
Media Contact, Exec. Dir., Judith W. Milinowski
Exec. Dir., Judith W. Milinowski
Pres., Dr. Robert A. Rothman
Exec. Vice-Pres., Beth Adams Smith
Major Activities: Educational Program and Conference Center; Intellectual, Psychological, Physical and Spiritual Growth; Healing and Health

NORTH CAROLINA

Asheville-Buncombe Community Christian Ministry (ABCCM)
30 Cumberland Ave., Asheville, NC 28801
Tel. (704) 259-5300 Fax (704) 259-5923
Media Contact, Exec. Dir., Rev. Scott Rogers, Fax (704)259-5323
Exec. Dir., Rev. Scott Rogers
Pres., Dr. John Grant
Major Activities: Crisis Ministry; Jail/Prison Ministry; Shelter Ministry; Medical Ministry

Greensboro Urban Ministry
305 West Lee St., Greensboro, NC 27406

241

Tel. (910) 271-5959 Fax (910) 271-5920
Email: Guministry@aol.com
Website: www.greensboro.com/gum
Media Contact, Exec. Dir., Rev. Mike Aiken
Exec. Dir., Rev. Mike Aiken
Major Activities: Emergency Financial Assistance; Emergency Housing; Hunger Relief; Inter-Faith and Inter-Racial Understanding; Justice Ministry; Chaplaincy with the Poor

*North Carolina
Council of Churches
Methodist Bldg., 1307 Glenwood Ave., Ste. 162, Raleigh, NC 27605-3258
Tel. (919) 828-6501
Email: nccck@aol.com
Media Contact, Exec. Dir., Rev. S. Collins Kilburn
Exec. Dir., Rev. S. Collins Kilburn
Program Associates,Sr. Evelyn Mattern, Rev. George Reed
Pres., Bridget Johnson, 1208 Hounslow Dr., Greensboro, NC 27410
Treas., Dr. James W. Ferree, 5108 Huntcliff Tr., Winston-Salem, NC 27104
Major Activities: Children and Families; Health Care Justice; Christian Unity; Equal Rights; Legislative Program; Criminal Justice; Farmworker Ministry; Rural Crisis; Racial Justice; Disaster Response; AIDS Ministry; Death Penalty; Poverty and Response to Welfare Changes

NORTH DAKOTA

*North Dakota Conference of Churches
227 W. Broadway, #1, Bismarck, ND 58501
Tel. (701) 255-0604 Fax (701) 223-6075
Media Contact, Executive Sec., Renee Gopal
Pres., Bishop Andrew Fairfield
Treas., Christopher Dodson
Executive Sec., Renee Gopal
Major Activities: Prison Chaplaincy; Rural Life Ministry; Faith and Order; North Dakota 101; Current Ecumenical Proposals

OHIO

Akron Area Association of Churches
350 S. Portage Path, Akron, OH 44320
Tel. (330) 535-3112 Fax (330) 374-5041
Email: aaac1@juno.com
Website: www.triple-ac.org
Media Contact, Admin. Asst., Chloe Ann Kriska
Exec. Dir., Rev. Dennis D. Sparks
Bd. of Trustees, Pres., Rev. Raymond Kovach
Vice-Pres., Rev. J. Waman Butts
Sec., Dale Kline
Treas., Dr. Stephen Laning
Program Dir., Rev. Dennis D. Sparks
Christian Ed., Dir., Chloe Ann Kriska

Major Activities: Messiah Sing; Interfaith Council; Newsletters; Resource Center; Community Worship; Training of Local Church Leadership; Radio Programs; Clergy and Lay Fellowship Luncheons; Cable TV; Interfaith Caregivers; Neighborhood Development; Community Outreach; Church Inter-racial Partnerships

Alliance of Churches
470 E. Broadway, Alliance, OH 44601
Tel. (330) 821-6648
Media Contact, Dir., Lisa A. Oyster
Dir., Lisa A. Oyster
Pres., Rev. Bud Hoffman
Treas., Betty Rush
Major Activities: Christian Education; Community Relations & Service; Ecumenical Worship; Community Ministry; Peacemaking; Medical Transportation for Anyone Needing It; Emergency Financial Assistance

Churchpeople for Change and Reconciliation
326 W. McKibben, Box 488, Lima, OH 45802
Tel. (419) 229-6949
Media Contact, Exec. Dir., Richard Keller
Exec. Dir., Richard Keller
Major Activities: Developing Agencies for Minorities, Poor, Alienated and Despairing; Community Kitchens

Council of Christian Communions of Greater Cincinnati
42 Calhoun St., Cincinnati, OH 45219-1525
Tel. (513) 559-3151
Media Contact, Exec. Dir., Joellen W. Grady
Exec. Dir., Joellen W. Grady
Justice Chaplaincy, Assoc. Dir., Rev. Jack Marsh
Educ., Assoc., Lillie D. Bibb
Pres., Rev. Damon Lynch III
Major Activities: Christian Unity & Interfaith Cooperation; Justice Chaplaincies; Police-Clergy Team; Adult and Juvenile Jail Chaplains; Religious Education

Greater Dayton Christian Connection
601 W. Riverview Ave., Dayton, OH 45406
Tel. (513) 227-9485 Fax (513) 227-9407
Media Contact, Exec. Dir., James S. Burton
Exec. Dir., James S. Burton
Jail Ministry, Dir., Nancy Haas
Reconciliation Ministry, Dir., James S. Burton
Pres., Rev. Robert Thornton
Major Activities: Communications: Service to Churches and Community; Race Relations Advocacy; Jail Chaplaincy; CROP Walk; Saturday Meals for Seniors; Newsletter; Martin Luther King Activities; Workplace Reconnections

Interchurch Council of Greater Cleveland

2230 Euclid Ave., Cleveland, OH 44115
Tel. (216) 621-5925 Fax (216) 621-0588
Media Contact, Janice Giering
Exec. Dir., Dr. Dennis N. Paulson, Tel. (216)621-5925
Church & Society, Dir., Rev. Mylion Waite
Communications, Dir., Janice Giering, Karen Drasler
Chmn. of the Assembly, Rev. Jeremiah Pryce
Dir. Of Development, Lynn Paulin
Major Activities: Church and Society; Communications; Hunger; Christian Education; Legislation; Faith and Order; Public Education; Interchurch News; Tutoring; Parent-Child First Teachers Program; Shelter for Homeless Women and Children; Radio & TV; Interracial Cooperation; Interfaith Cooperation; Adopt-A-School; Women of Hope; Leadership Development; Religious Education; Center for Peace & Reconciliation—Youth and the Courts; Support Services to Local Churches

Mahoning Valley Association of Churches

25 W. Rayen Ave., Youngstown, OH 44503
Tel. (330) 744-8946 Fax (330) 774-0018
Media Contact, Exec. Dir., Elsie L. Dursi
Exec. Dir., Elsie L. Dursi
Pres., Rev. Connie Sassanella
Treas., Paul Fryman
Major Activities: Communications; Christian Education; Ecumenism; Social Action; Advocacy

Metropolitan Area Church Council

760 E. Broad St., Columbus, OH 43205
Tel. (614) 461-7103
Media Contact, Exec. Dir., Rev. Burton Cantrell
Exec. Dir., Rev. Burton Cantrell
Chpsn. of Bd., Alvin Hadley
Sec./Treas., Lily Schlichter
Major Activities: Newspaper; Liaison with Community organizations; Assembly; Week of Prayer for Christian Unity; Support for Ministerial Associations and Church Councils; Seminars for Church Leaders; Prayer Groups; CROP Walk; Social Concerns Hearings

Metropolitan Area Religious Coalition of Cincinnati

Ste. 1035, 617 Vine St., Cincinnati, OH 45202-2423
Tel. (513) 721-4843 Fax (513) 721-4891
Media Contact, Dir., Rev. Duane Holm
Dir., Rev. Duane Holm
Pres., Burton Perlman
Major Activities: Local social policy decisions chosen annually.
1999: Public Education, Welfare Reform.

*Ohio Council of Churches

6877 N. High St., Ste. 206, Columbus, OH 43085-2516
Tel. (614) 885-9590 Fax (614) 885-6097
Email: mail@ohcouncilchs.org
Website: www.ohcouncilchs.org
Exec. Dir., Rev. Rebecca J. Tollefson
Public Policy, Dir., Tom Smith
Ecumenical Issues Dir., Rev. Ronald Botts
Pres., Rev. George Lambert
Vice Pres., Jack Davis
Treas., Sr. Barbara Niehaus
Major Activities: Agricultural Issues; Economic & Social Justice; Ecumenical Relations; Health Care Reform; Public Policy Issues; Theological Dialogue; Racial Relations; Education/Funding; Childcare/ Children Issues; Poverty/Welfare; Rural Life/Farm Crisis and Environment

Pike County Outreach Council

122 E. North St., Waverly, OH 45690-1146
Tel. (614) 947-7151
Dir., Judy Dixon
Major Activities: Emergency Service Program; Self Help Groups; Homeless Shelter

Toledo Ecumenical Area Ministries

444 Floyd St., Toledo, OH 43620
Tel. (419) 242-7401 Fax (419) 242-7404
Media Contact, Admn., Nancy Lee Atkins
Metro-Toledo Churches United, Admn., Nancy Lee Atkins
Toledo Metropolitan Mission, Exec. Dir., Nancy Lee Atkins
Major Activities: Ecumenical Relations; Interfaith Relations; Food Program; Housing Program; Social Action-Public Education; Health Care; Urban Ministry; Employment; Welfare Rights; Housing; Mental Retardation; Voter Registration/Education; Substance Abuse Treatment; Youth Leadership; Children At-risk; Elimination of Discrimination

Tuscarawas County Council for Church and Community

107 West High , Ste. B, New Philadelphia, OH 44663
Tel. (330) 343-6012 Fax (330) 343-9845
Media Contact, Barbara E. Lauer
Exec. Dir., Barbara E. Lauer
Pres., Zoe Ann Kelley, 201 E. 12th St., Dover, OH 44622
Treas., James Barnhouse, 120 N. Broadway, New Philadelphia, OH 44663
Major Activities: Human Services; Health; Family Life; Child Abuse; Housing; Educational Programs; Emergency Assistance; Legislative Concerns; Juvenile Prevention Program; Character Formation; Prevention Program for High Risk Children; Bimonthly newsletter The Pilot

243

West Side Ecumenical Ministry

5209 Detroit Ave, Cleveland, OH 44102
Tel. (216) 651-2037 Fax (216) 651-4145
Email: wsem@stratos.net
Media Contact, Exec. Dir., Elving F. Otero
Exec. Dir., Elving F. Otero
Director of Operations, Adam Roth
Major Activities: Emergency Food Centers;
Senior Meals Programs; Youth Services;
Advocacy, Empowerment Programs; Church
Clusters; Employment Assistance Program;
Head Start Centers; Theatre; Teen Centers

OKLAHOMA

*Oklahoma Conference of Churches

301 Northwest 36th St., Oklahoma City, OK
73118
Tel. (405) 525-2928 Fax (405) 525-2636
Email: okconfch@flash.net
Website: www.flash.net/~okconfch
Media Contact, Deborah Canary-Marshall
Exec. Dir., The Rev. Dr. Rita K. Newton
Pres., The Rev. Melvin E. Truiett
Treas., The Rev. Lura Cayton
Major Activities: Christian Unity Issues;
Community Building Among Members; Rural
Community Care; Ecumenical Decade with
Women; Children's Advocacy; Day at the
Legislature; Impact; Criminal Justice; Hunger
& Poverty; Legislative Advocacy

Tulsa Metropolitan Ministry

221 S. Nogales, Tulsa, OK 74127
Tel. (918) 582-3147 Fax (918) 582-3159
Email: TMM@ionet.com
Website: www. TUMM.org
Media Contact, Sr. Sylvia Schmidt
Exec. Dir., Sr. Sylvia Schmidt, S.F.C.C.
Operations Dir., James Robinson
Day Center for the Homeless, Dir., Sandra
Holden
Corrections Min. Coordinator, Rev. Mary
McAnnally
Pres., Dr. James W. Johnson
Vice-Pres., Dr. Sandra Rana
Sec., Rev. John McLemore
Treas., Sara Jo Waggoner
Major Activities: Corrections Ministry;
Religious Understanding; Shelter for the
Homeless; Women's Issues; U.N. Decade on
Indigenous People; Legislative Issues;
Interfaith Dialogue TV Series; Christian
Issues; Justice and Peace Issues; Immigration
Concerns; Communications; Task Force
Against Racism; Metro. Comm. Building;
Directory of Metro. Religious Community

OREGON

*Ecumenical Ministries of Oregon

0245 S.W. Bancroft St., Ste. B, Portland, OR
97201

Tel. (503) 221-1054 Fax (503) 223-7007
Email: emo@emoregon.org
Website: www.emoregon.org
Media Contact, Teri Ruch, EMO Communications Manager
Exec. Dir., David A. Leslie
Community Ministry/Development, Dir., Janet
Miller
Finance and Administrative Services, Dir., Gary
B. Logsdon
Alcohol Polcy Initiative Program, Nigel Wrangham
Refugees & Immigration Ministries Division,
Dir., Penny Strauss
Basic Human Needs, Dir., Rick Stoller
Russian Oregon Social Services, Yelena Sergeva
Intl. Learning Program, Jackie Sandquist
Public Policy, Dir., Enid Edwards
Interfaith Network for Earth Concerns, Jenny
Holmes
Parent Mentor Program, Sylvia Hart-Landsberg
Shared Housing, Lowen Berman
Northeast Emergency Food Program, Drew
Hudson
Pres., Charles Jordan
Major Activities: Theological Education and
Dialogue; Public Policy Advocacy and
Community Ministries including "Basic
Human Needs" (Drug Education, HIV Day
Center, NE Emergency Food, Old Town Clinic,
Parent Mentor, Shared Housing); "Refugee and
Immigration Ministries" (International Learning Program, Russian Oregon Social Services,
Sponsors Organized to Assist Refugees); and
"Compassionate Care & Education" (Hopewell
House Hospice services)

PENNSYLVANIA

Allegheny Valley Association of Churches

1333 Freeport Rd., P.O. Box 236, Natrona
Heights, PA 15065
Tel. (724) 226-0606 Fax (724) 226-3197
Email: avac@salsgiver.com
Media Contact, Exec. Dir., Karen Snair
Exec. Dir., Karen Snair
Pres., Rev. Dr. W. James Legge, 232 Tarentum-
Culmerville Rd., Tarentum, PA 15084
Treas., Libby Grimm, 312 Butternut Ln.,
Tarentum, PA 15084
Major Activities: Ecumenical Services; Dial-a-
Devotion; CROP Walk for Hunger; Food
Bank; Emergency Aid; Cross-on-the-Hill;
AVAC Hospitality Network for Homeless
Families; AVAC Volunteer Caregivers; Senior
Citizen Housing

Christian Associates of Southwest Pennsylvania

204 37th St., Suite 201, Pittsburgh, PA 15201
Tel. (412) 688-9070 Fax (412) 688-9091
Email: casp1817@aol.com
Website: www.casp.org

244

Media Contact, Dir. of Communications, Bruce J. Randolph
Chair of Council, Rev. Robert Russell
Pres., Board of Delegates, Fr. Roger A. Statnick
Executive Director, Fr. Gregory C. Wingenbach, Past./Ecum. Th.D.
Director of Communications, Bruce J. Randolph
Cable-TV Coordinator, Earl C. Hartman, Jr.
Jail Chaplaincy Services Director, Rev. Ulli Klemm
Exec. Admin. Assistant, Nancy Raymond
Major Activities: Christian Associates TV, Media Ministries; Special/Cooperative/ Volunteer Ministries; Jail & Youth-Incarceration Chaplaincies; Church & Community/Social Service Ministries; Theological Dialogue/ Religious Education/ Witness; Racism/ Interracial Understanding

Christian Churches United of the Tri-County Area

P.O. Box 60750, Harrisburg, PA 17106-0750
Tel. (717) 230-9550 Fax (717) 230-9554
Email: ccuhbg@aol.com
Media Contact, Exec. Dir., Jaqueline P. Rucker
Exec. Dir., Jaqueline P. Rucker
Pres., Joe Fiedler
Treas., James Smeltzer
Vice-Pres., Betty Ann Funk
Sec., Lenore Cameron, Esq.
HELP & LaCasa Ministries, Dir., Victoria Hess, PO Box 60750, Harrisburg, PA 17106-0750 Tel. (717)238-2851 Fax (717)238-1916
Major Activities: Volunteer Ministries to Prisons; Aging; HELP (Housing, Rent, Food, Medication, Transportation, Home Heating, Clothing); La Casa de Amistad (The House of Friendship) Social Services; AIDS Outreach; Prison Chaplaincy; Lend-A-Hand (Disaster Rebuilding)

Christians United in Beaver County

1098 Third St., Beaver, PA 15009
Tel. (724) 774-1446
Media Contact, Exec. Sec., Lois L. Smith
Exec. Sec., Lois L. Smith
Chaplains: Rev. Bernard Tench; Erika Bruner; Rev. Anthony Massey; Rev. Frank Churchill; John Pusateri
Pres., Rev. Bernard Tench, 2322 10th Street, Beaver Falls, PA 15010
Treas., Ima Moldovon, 302 Lynn Dr., New Brighton, PA 15066
Major Activities: Christian Education; Evangelism; Social Action; Church Women United; United Church Men; Ecumenism; Hospital, Detention Home and Jail Ministry

East End Cooperative Ministry

250 N. Highland Ave., Pittsburgh, PA 15206
Tel. (412) 361-5549 Fax (412) 361-0151
Email: eecm@usaor.net

Media Contact, Michele Griffiths, Community Development Director
Exec. Dir., Myrna Zelenitz
Ass. Dir., Rev. Darnell Leonard
Major Activities: Food Pantry; Soup Kitchen; Men's Emergency Shelter; Drop-In Shelter for Homeless; Meals on Wheels; Casework and Supportive Services for Elderly; Information and Referral; Programs for Children and Youth; Bridge Housing Program for Men and PennFree for Women in Recovery and Their Children

Ecumenical Conference of Greater Altoona

1208 - 13th St., P.O. Box 305, Altoona, PA 16603
Tel. (814) 942-0512
Email: eilbeck@aol.com
Media Contact, Exec. Dir., Eileen Becker
Exec. Dir., Eileen Becker
Major Activities: Religious Education; Workshops; Ecumenical Activities; Religious Christmas Parade; Campus Ministry; Community Concerns; Peace Forum; Religious Education for Mentally Challenged; Inter-faith Committee; Prison Ministry

Greater Bethlehem Area Council of Churches

1021 Center St., P.O. Box 1245, Bethlehem, PA 18016-1245
Tel. (610) 867-8671 Fax (610) 866-9223
Exec. Dir., ———
Pres., Robert D. Romeril
Treas., Robert Gerst, 900 Wedgewood Rd., Bethlehem, PA 18017
Major Activities: Support Ministry; Institutional Ministry to Elderly and Infirm; Family Concerns; Scripture Center; Social Concerns; World Local Hunger Projects; Elderly Ministry; Ecumenical worship/cooperation; Mentoring— youth prisoners and other persons at risk

Hanover Area Council of Churches

136 Carlisle St., Hanover, PA 17331-2406
Tel. (717) 633-6353 Fax (717) 633-1992
Email: nicknonick@aol.com
Website: www. netrax.net/~bouchord/hacc.htm
Exec. Dir., Cathy Ferree
Major Activities: Meals on Wheels, Provide a Lunch Program, Fresh Air Program, Clothing Bank, Hospital Chaplaincy Services; Congregational & Interfaith Relations, Public Ecumenical Programs and Services, State Park Chaplaincy Services & Children's Program; Compeer; Faith at Work; CROP Walk; Stolte Scholarship Fund; Community Needs

Inter-Church Ministries of Erie County

2216 Peach St., Erie, PA 16502
Tel. (814) 454-2411

245

Voucher Program, Mary Stewart
Pres., Rev. Stephen E. Morse, 3642 W. 26th St., Erie, PA 16506
Treas., Ernest O. Wood, 11471 Scotland Ave., North East, PA 16428
Major Activities: Local Ecumenism; Ministry with Aging; Social Ministry; Continuing Education; North West Pennsylvania Conference of Bishops and Judicatory Execs.; Theological Dialogue; Coats for Kids; Voucher Program for Emergency Assistance

Lancaster County Council of Churches

134 E. King St., Lancaster, PA 17602
Tel. (717) 291-2261 Fax (717) 291-6403
Media Contact, Executive Dir., Rev. John Smaligo
Pres., Armon Snowden
Prescott House, Dir., John Stoudt
Asst. Admn., Kim Y. Wittel
Child Abuse, Dir., Louise Schiraldi
CONTACT, Dir., Lois Gascho
Service Ministry, Dir., Adela Dohner
Major Activities: Social Ministry; Residential Ministry to Youthful Offenders; CONTACT; Advocacy; Child Abuse Prevention

Lebanon County Christian Ministries

818 Water St., P.O. Box 654, Lebanon, PA 17046
Tel. (717) 274-2601
Media Contact, Exec. Dir., Lillian Morales
Exec. Dir., Lillian Morales
Noon Meals Coord., Elaine Zapata
Major Activities: H.O.P.E. (Helping Our People in Emergencies); Food & Clothing Bank; Free Meal Program; Commodity Distribution Program; Ecumenical Events

Lehigh County Conference of Churches

534 Chew St., Allentown, PA 18102
Tel. (610) 433-6421 Fax (610) 439-8039
Email: LCCCED@aol.com
Media Contact, Exec. Dir., Rev. William A. Seaman
Assoc. Dir., Marlene Merz
Pres., Dr. Pat Murray
1st Vice-Pres., Mr. Tony Muir
Sec., Rita Sparrow
Treas., David Schumacher
Major Activities: Chaplaincy Program; Social Concerns and Action; Clergy Dialogues; Drop-In-Center for De-Institutionalized Adults; Ecumenical Soup Kitchen; Housing Advocacy Program; Pathways (Reference to Social Services); Street Contact; Linkage; Guardianship

Metropolitan Christian Council of Philadelphia

1501 Cherry St., Philadelphia, PA 19102-1429
Tel. (215) 563-7854 Fax (215) 563-6849
Email: rev_geiger@mccp.org
Website: www.mccp.org

Media Contact, Assoc. Communications, Nancy L. Nolde
Exec. Dir., Rev. C. Edward Geiger
Assoc. Communications, Nancy L. Nolde
Office Mgr., Joan G. Shipman
Pres., Rev. Janet K. Hess
First Vice-Pres., Rev. Steve B. Lawrence
Treas., A. Louis Denton, Esq.
Major Activities: Congregational Clusters; Public Policy Advocacy; Communication; Interfaith Dialogue

North Hills Youth Ministry Counseling Center

802 McKnight Park Dr., Pittsburgh, PA 15237
Tel. (412) 366-1300
Email: NHYM@SGI.NET
Media Contact, Exec. Dir., Rev. Ronald B. Barnes
Exec. Dir., Ronald B. Barnes
Major Activities: Elementary, Junior and Senior High School Individual and Family Counseling; Elementary Age Youth Early Intervention Counseling; Educational Programming for Churches and Schools; Youth Advocacy; Parent Education; Marital Counseling

Northside Common Ministries

P.O. Box 99861, Pittsburgh, PA 15233
Tel. (412) 323-1163 Fax (412) 323-1749
Email: NCM@citynet.com
Media Contact, Exec. Dir., Mark Stephen Bibro
Exec. Dir., Mark Stephen Bibro
Pres., Rev. Robert J. Wilde, MSW
Major Activities: Pleasant Valley Shelter for Homeless Men; Advocacy around Hunger, Housing, Poverty, and Racial Issues; Community Food Pantry and Service Center; Supportive Housing

Northwest Interfaith Movement

6757 Greene St., Philadelphia, PA 19119
Tel. (215) 843-5600 Fax (215) 843-2755
Email: nim@libertynet.org
Media Contact, Exec. Dir., Rev. Richard R. Fernandez
Exec. Dir., Rev. Richard R. Fernandez
Chpsn., Elaine Dushoff
Long Term Care Program, Dir., Donald Carlin
Neighborhood Child Care Resource Prog., Dir., Amy Gendall
School Age Ministry, Dir., Brenda Rochester
Major Activities: Resources amd Technical Assistance for Child Care Programs; Conflict Mediation and Support for Nursing and Boarding Home Residents; Development of After-School Programs

*Pennsylvania Conference on Interchurch Cooperation

P.O. Box 2835, 223 North St., Harrisburg, PA 17105
Tel. (717) 238-9413 Fax (717) 238-1473
Website: www.pacatholic.org

Media Contact, Carolyn Astfalk

Co-Staff: Dr. Robert J. O'Hara, Jr., Rev, Gart Harke

Co-Chpsns.: Bishop Nicolas C. Datillo; Bishop Robert D. Rowley, Jr.

Major Activities: Theological Consultation; Social Concerns; Inter-Church Planning; Conferences and Seminars; Disaster Response Preparedness

*The Pennsylvania Council of Churches

900 S. Arlington Ave., Ste. 100, Harrisburg, PA 17109-5089

Tel. (717) 545-4761 Fax (717) 545-4765

Email: pcc@pachurches.org

Website: www.pachurches.org

Media Contact, Exec. Dir., Rev. Gary L. Harke

Exec. Dir., Rev. Gary L. Harke

Public Policy, Dir., Rev. K. Joy Kaufmann

Coord. for Contract Chaplaincy, -vacant-

Coord. for Leisure Ministries, Rev. Robert W. Brown

Coord. for Farmworker Ministries, Rev. Ray L. Kauffman

Coord. for Save Our Youth Program, Antoinette Hodge

Consultant for Trucker/Travel Ministries, Rev. Benjamin E. Nevin, Jr.

Pres., Rev. Dr. Lyle J. Weible

Vice-Pres., Bishop A. Donald Main

Sec., Mrs. Nancy S. Ritter

Treas., Barry R. Herr

Bus. Mgr., Janet A. Gollick

Major Activities: Institutional Ministry; Migrant Ministry; Truck Stop Chaplaincy; Social Ministry; Leisure Ministry; Inter-Church Planning and Dialogue; Conferences; Disaster Response; Trade Association Activities; Church Education; Ethnic Cooperation

Project of Easton, Inc.

330 Ferry St., Easton, PA 18042

Tel. (215) 258-4361

Pres., Dr. John H. Updegrove

Vice-Pres. Public Relations, Rev. Charles E. Staples

Vice-Pres. Operations, Don Follett

Sec., Rosemary Reese

Treas., Steve Barsony

Exec. Dir., Maryellen Shuman

Major Activities: Food Bank; Adult Literacy Program; English as a Second Language; Children's Programs; Parents as Student Support; CROP Walk; Interfaith Council; Family Literacy; Emergency Assistance; Even Start Family Literacy

Reading Berks Conference of Churches

54 N. 8th St., Reading, PA 19601

Tel. (610) 375-6108 Fax (610) 375-6205

Media Contact, Exec. Dir., Rev. Calvin Kurtz

Exec. Dir., Rev. Calvin Kurtz

Pres., John Roland, Esq.

Treas., William Maslo

Major Activities: Institutional Ministry; Social Action; Migrant Ministry; CWS; CROP Walk for Hunger; Emergency Assistance; Prison Chaplaincy; AIDS Hospice Development; Hospital Chaplaincy; Interchurch/Intercultural Services; Children & Youth Ministry

Reading Urban Ministry

134 N. Fifth St., Reading, PA 19601

Tel. (610) 374-6917 Fax (610) 371-9791

Media Contact, Beth Bitler

Exec. Dir., Beth Bitler

Pres., Edward Robertson

Vice-Pres., Sarah Walters

Sec., Jill Braun

Treas., Karen Good

Major Activities: Youth Ministry Program; Family Action Support Team (Child Abuse Prevention)

South Hills Interfaith Ministries

1900 Sleepy Hollow Rd., Library, PA 15129

Tel. (412) 854-9120 Fax (412) 854-9123

Media Contact, Exec. Dir., Donald Guinn

Prog. Dir., Susan Simons

Psychological Services, Don Zandier

Family Assistance Coordinator, Sherry Kotz

Business Mgr., Jeff Walley

Volunteer Coordinator, Kristin Snodgrass

Major Activities: Basic Human Needs; Community Organization and Development; Inter-Faith Cooperation; Personal Growth; At-Risk Youth Development; Women in Transition; Elderly Support

United Churches of Lycoming County

202 E. Third St., Williamsport, PA 17701

Tel. (570) 322-1110

Email: gwen_bernstine.parti@ecunet.org

Media Contact, Exec. Dir., Gwen Nelson Bernstine

Exec. Dir., Gwen Nelson Bernstine

Ofc. Sec., Linda Winter

Pres., The Rev. Robert L. Driesen, 324 Howard St., S. Williamsport, PA 17701

Treas., Raymond Fisher, 145 Linden St., S. Williamsport, PA 17701

Shepherd of the Streets, Rev. Wilbur L. Scranton, III, 130 E. 3rd St., Williamsport, PA 17701

Ecumenism, Dir., Rev. Morris Smith, P.O. Box 58 Ralston, PA 17763-0058

Educ. Ministries, Dir., Rev. Bruce Druckenmiller, 202 E. Third St., Williamsport, PA 17701

Institutional Ministry, Dir., Linda Leonard, 12 E. Water St., Hughesville, PA 17737

Radio-TV, Dir., Rev. Jean Moyer, 513 Spruce Street, Montoursville, PA 17754

Prison Ministry, Dir., Jane Russell, 1200 Almond St., Williamsport, PA 17701

Christian Social Concerns, Dir., Dr. Dan Doyle, 301 South Main St., Muney, PA 17756

Major Activities: Ecumenism; Educational Ministries; Church Women United; Church World Service and CROP; Prison Ministry; Radio-TV; Nursing Homes; Fuel Bank; Food Pantry; Family Life; Shepherd of the Streets Urban Ministry; Peace Concerns; Housing Initiative; Interfaith Dialogue

Wilkinsburg Community Ministry

710 Mulberry St., Pittsburgh, PA 15221
Tel. (412) 241-8072 Fax (412) 241-8315
Email: wcm@trfn.clpgh.org/wcm
Website: http://trfn.clpgh.org/wcm
Media Contact, Dir., Rev. Vivian Lovingood
Dir., Rev. Vivian Lovingood
Pres. of Bd., Roger Schneider
Major Activities: Hunger Ministry; After School Children's Programs; Summer Reading Camp; Teen-Moms Infant Care; Meals on Wheels; Church Camp Scholarships; Utility Assistance; Clothing/Furniture Assistance; Case Management for Elderly Homebound Persons and Families

Wyoming Valley Council of Churches

35 S. Franklin St., Wilkes-Barre, PA 18701
Tel. (570) 825-8543
Media Contact, Exec. Dir., Susan Grine Harper
Exec. Dir., Susan Grine Harper
Ofc. Sec., Sandra Karrott
Pres., Dn. Sergei Kapral
Treas., H. Merritt Hughes
Major Activities: Nursing Home Chaplaincy; Martin Luther King, Jr. Fuel Drive in Association with Local Agencies; Hospital Referral Service; Choral Festival of Faith; Migrant Ministry; Ecumenical Pulpit Exchange, Int.; CROP Hunger Walk; Pastoral Care Ministries; Clergy Retreats and Seminars

York County Council of Churches

P.O. Box 1865, York, PA 17405-1865
Tel. (717) 854-9504 Fax (717) 843-5295
Email: yccc@juno.com
Media Contact, Exec. Dir., Rev. Patrick B. Walker
Pres., Rev. Stephany Sechrist
Exec. Dir., Rev. Patrick B. Walker
Major Activities: Educational Development; Spiritual Growth and Renewal; Worship and Witness; Congregational Resourcing; Outreach and Mission

RHODE ISLAND

*The Rhode Island State Council of Churches

734 Hope St., Providence, RI 02906
Tel. (401) 861-1700 Fax (401) 331-3080
Email: ricouncil@aol.com

Media Contact, Exec. Min., Rev. James C. Miller
Exec. Min., Rev. James C. Miller
Admn. Asst., Peggy MacNie
Pres., Rev. Quinton Ivy
Treas., George Weavill
Major Activities: Urban Ministries; TV; Institutional Chaplaincy; Advocacy/Justice & Service: Legislative Liaison; Faith & Order; Leadership Development; Campus Ministries

SOUTH CAROLINA

*South Carolina Christian Action Council, Inc.

P.O. Drawer 3248, Columbia, SC 29230
Tel. (803) 786-7115 Fax (803) 786-7116
Email: sc.council@ecunet.org
Media Contact, Exec. Min., Dr. L. Wayne Bryan
Exec. Min., Dr. L. Wayne Bryan
Pres., Rev. Dr. Lewis Galloway
Major Activities: Advocacy and Ecumenism; Continuing Education; Interfaith Dialogue; Citizenship and Public Affairs; Publications

United Ministries

606 Pendleton St., Greenville, SC 29601
Tel. (864) 232-6463 Fax (864) 370-3518
Media Contact, Exec. Dir., Rev. Beth Templeton
Exec. Dir., Rev. Beth Templeton
Pres., Ellen Gower
Vice-Pres., The Rev. David Chandler
Sec., Don Pilzer
Treas., Robert Clanton
Major Activities: Survival Programs (Emergency Assistance, Place of Hope, a Day Shelter for Homeless, Travelers Aid); Stabilization Program (Transitions); Barrier Removal Programs (Employment Readiness); Magdalene Project (Women in Crisis); Life Skills (Educational Classes, Living Skills)

SOUTH DAKOTA

*Association of Christian Churches

1320 S. Minnesota Ave., Ste. 210, Sioux Falls, SD 57105-0657
Tel. (605) 334-1980 Fax (605) 996-1766
Email: rwfisher@midco.net
Media Contact, Pres., Rev. Richard Fisher, P.O. Box 460, Mitchell, SD 57301 Tel. (605)996-6552
Pres., Rev. Richard Fisher
Ofc. Mgr., Pat Willard
Major Activities: Ecumenical Forums; Continuing Education for Clergy; Legislative Information; Resourcing Local Ecumenism; Native American Issues; Ecumenical Fields Ministries; Rural Economic Development

TENNESSEE

Metropolitan Inter Faith Association (MIFA)

P.O. Box 3130, Memphis, TN 38173-0130
Tel. (901) 527-0208 Fax (901) 527-3202

Media Contact, Dir., Media Relations, Kim Gaskill

Exec. Dir., Allie Prescott

Major Activities: Emergency Housing; Emergency Services (Rent, Utility, Food, Clothing Assistance); Home-Delivered Meals and Senior Support Services; Youth Services

*Tennessee Association of Churches

103 Oak St., Ashland City, TN 37015

Tel. (615) 792-4631

Ecumenical Admn., -*

Pres., Rev. Steve Mosley

Treas., Paul Milliken

Major Activities: Faith and Order; Christian Unity; Social Concern Ministries; Governmental Concerns; Governor's Prayer Breakfast

Volunteer Ministry Center

103 South Gay St., Knoxville, TN 37902

Tel. (423) 524-3926 Fax (423) 524-7065

Media Contact, Exec. Dir., Angelia Moon

Exec. Dir., Angelia Moon

Pres., David Leech

Vice-Pres., John Moxham

Treas., Doug Thompson

Major Activities: Homeless Program; Food Line; Crisis Referral Program; Subsidized Apartment Program; Counselling Program; Parenting Education for Single Parents

TEXAS

Austin Metropolitan Ministries

2026 Guadalupe, Ste. 226, Austin, TX 78705

Tel. (512) 472-7627 Fax (512) 472-5274

Email: amm@ammaustin.org

Website: www.ammaustin.org

Media Contact, Exec. Dir., Patrick Flood

Exec. Dir., Patrick Flood

Pres., Rev. James Mayfield

Treas., Camille Miller

Program Director, Carole Hatfield

Admn., Carole Hatfield

Major Activities: Broadcast Ministry; Older Adult Connection; Youth at Risk Mentoring; Interfaith Dialogues; Family Issues; Housing Rehabilitation; Homeless Issues; Hunger Issues; Refugee Resettlement, Racial Reconciliation

Border Association for Refugees from Central America (BARCA), Inc.

P.O. Box 715, Edinburg, TX 78540

Tel. (210) 631-7447 Fax (210) 687-9266

Media Contact, Exec. Dir., Ninfa Ochoa-Krueger

Exec. Dir, Ninfa Ochoa-Krueger

Refugee Children Services, Dir., Bertha de la Rosa

Major Activities: Food, Shelter, Clothing to Newly Arrived Indigent Immigrants & Refugees; Medical and Other Emergency Aid;

Special Services to Children; Speakers on Refugee and Immigrant Concerns for Church Groups; Orientation, Advocacy and Legal Services for Immigrants and Refugees

Corpus Christi Metro Ministries

1919 Leopard St., P.O. Box 4899, Corpus Christi, TX 78469-4899

Tel. (361) 887-0151 Fax (361) 887-7900

Email: edseeger@electrotex.com

Media Contact, Exec. Dir., Rev. Edward B. Seeger

Exec. Dir., Rev. Edward B. Seeger

Admn. Dir., Ginger Flewelling-Leeds

Volunteer Dir., Ann Walters

Fin. Coord., Sue McCown

Loaves & Fishes Dir., Ray Gomez

Emergency Services Mgr., Dannette Valdez

Employment Dir., Larry Curtis

Adopt A Caseworker Dir., Jo Flindt

Health and Human Services, Dir., Ann Walters

Major Activities: Free Cafeteria;Transitional Shelters; Job Readiness; Job Placement; Primary Health Care; Community Service Restitution; Emergency Clothing; Information and Referral; Case Management

East Dallas Cooperative Parish

P.O. Box 720305, Dallas, TX 75372-0305

Tel. (214) 823-9149 Fax (214) 823-2015

Email: edcp@swbell.net

Media Contact, Larry Cox

Pres., Ford Keith

Sec., Norma Worrall

Major Activities: Emergency Food, Clothing, Job Bank; Medical Clinic; Legal Clinic, Tutorial Education; Home Companion Service; Pre-School Education; Developmental Learning Center; Asian Ministry; Hispanic Ministry; Activity Center for Low Income Older Adults; Pastoral Counseling; English Language Ministry

Greater Dallas Community of Churches

624 N. Good-Latimer #100, Dallas, TX 75204-5818

Tel. (214) 824-8680 Fax (214) 824-8726

Email: gdcc@churchcommunity.org

Media Contact, Interim Exec. Dir., Ray Flachmeier

Interim Exec. Dir., Ray Flachmeier

Assoc. Dirs.: The Rev. Holsey Hickman; John Stoesz

AmeriCorps/Building Blocks Dir., Wendy Hodges-Kent

Development Dir., Mary Sue Foster

Pres., Rev. George Mason, Ph.D.

Treas., Jerry McNabb

Major Activities: Interdenominational, Interfaith and Interracial Understanding and Joint Work; AmeriCorps/Building Blocks (Direct Service to Develop Inner City Children, Youth & Families); Summer Food & Reading; Hunger; Peacemaking; Public Policy; Social Justice; Faith & Life

Interfaith Ministries for Greater Houston
3217 Montrose Blvd., Houston, TX 77006
Tel. (713) 522-3955 Fax (713) 520-4663
Media Contact, Exec. Dir., Betty P. Taylor
Exec. Dir., Betty P. Taylor
Pres., Charles R. Erickson
Development, Dir., Sharon Ervine
Assoc. Exec. Dir., Larry Norton
Treas., Fort D. Flowers, Jr.
Sec., Darlene Alexander
Major Activities: Community Concerns: Hunger; Older Adults; Families; Youth; Child Abuse; Refugee Services; Congregational Relations and Development; Social Service Programs: Refugee Services; Hunger Coalition; Youth Victim Witness; Family Connection; Meals on Wheels; Senior Health; RSVP; Foster Grandparents

North Dallas Shared Ministries
2530 Glenda Ln., #500, Dallas, TX 75229
Tel. (214) 620-8696 Fax (214) 620-0433
Media Contact, Exec. Dir., J. Dwayne Martin
Exec. Dir., J. Dwayne Martin
Pres., ———
Major Activities: Emergency Assistance; Job Counseling; ESL

Northside Inter-Church Agency (NICA)
1600 Circle Park Blvd., Fort Worth, TX 76106
Tel. (817) 626-1102 Fax (817) 626-9043
Media Contact, Exec. Dir., Judy Gutierrez
Exec. Dir., Judy Gutierrez
Major Activities: Food; Clothing; Counseling; Information and Referral; Furniture and Household Items; Nutrition Education and Teen Program; Employment Services; Thanksgiving Basket Program; "Last Resort" Christmas Program; Community Networking; Ecumenical Worship Services; Volunteer Training; Newsletter

San Antonio Community of Churches
1101 W. Woodlawn, San Antonio, TX 78201
Tel. (210) 733-9159 Fax (210) 733-5780
Media Contact, Exec. Dir., Dr. Kenneth Thompson
Exec. Dir., Dr. Kenneth Thompson
Pres., Fr. Jose De La Rosa
Major Activities: Christian Education; Missions; Infant Formula and Medical Prescriptions for Children of Indigent Families; Continuing Education For Clergy and Laity; Media Resource Center; Social Issues; Aging

Concerns; Youth Concerns; Family Concerns; Sponsor annual CROP Walk for Hunger; Peace and Anti-Violence Initiatives

San Antonio Urban Ministries
535 Bandera Rd., San Antonio, TX 78228
Media Contact, Sue Kelly
Exec. Dir., Sue Kelly
Pres., Rev. Leslie Ellison
Major Activities: Homes for Discharged Mental Patients; After School Care for Latch Key Children; Christian Based Community Ministry

Southeast Area Churches (SEARCH)
P.O. Box 51256, Fort Worth, TX 76105
Tel. (817) 531-2211
Media Contact, Exec. Dir., Dorothy Anderson-Develrow
Dir., Dorothy Anderson-Develrow
Major Activities: Emergency Assistance; Advocacy; Information and Referral; Community Worship; School Supplies; Direct Aid to Low Income and Elderly

Southside Area Ministries, Inc. (SAM)
305 W. Broadway, Fort Worth, TX 76104
Tel. (817) 332-3778 Fax (817) 332-3781
Media Contact, Linda Freeto
Exec. Dir., Linda Freeto
Major Activities: Assisting Children for Whom English is a Second Language; Tutoring Grades K-5; Mentoring Grades 6-8; Programs for Senior Citizens

Tarrant Area Community of Churches
P.O. Box 11471, Fort Worth, TX 76110-0471
Tel. (817) 534-1790 Fax (817) 534-1995
Email: revkm@flash.net
Pres., Regina Taylor
Treas., Don Hoak
Exec. Dir., Dr. Kenneth W. McIntosh
Major Activities: Eldercare Program; Children's Sabbath Sponsorship; Week of Prayer for Christian Unity; CROP Walk for Hunger Relief; Community Issues Forums; Family Pathfinders

*Texas Conference of Churches
1033 La Posada, Ste. 225, Austin, TX 78752
Tel. (512) 451-0991 Fax (512) 451-5348
Email: tcc@prismnet.com
Media Contact, Exec. Dir., Dr. Carol M. Worthing
Exec. Dir., Dr. Carol M. Worthing
Admin., Keitha Hatfield
Pres., Michael Pfeifer
Major Activities: Faith & Order; Related Ecumenism; Christian-Jewish Relations; Church and Society Issues

United Board of Missions

1701 Bluebonnet Ave., P.O. Box 3856, Port Arthur, TX 77643-3856
Tel. (409) 982-9412 Fax (409) 985-3668
Media Contact, Admn. Asst., Carolyn Schwarr
Exec. Dir., Clark Moore
Pres., Glenda McCoy
Major Activities: Emergency Assistance (Food and Clothing, Rent and Utility, Medical, Dental, Transportation); Share a Toy at Christmas; Counseling; Back to School Clothing Assistance; Information and Referral; Hearing Aid Bank; Meals on Wheels; Super Pantry; Energy Conservation Programs; Job Bank Assistance to Local Residents Only

VERMONT

*Vermont Ecumenical Council and Bible Society

285 Maple St., Burlington, VT 05401
Tel. (802) 864-7723
Email: vecumen@together.net
Media Contact, Admn. Asst., Betsy Wackernagel
Exec. Sec., Mr. Philip C. Kimball
Pres., Most Rev. Kenneth A. Angell
Vice-Pres., Rev. Dr. Lawrence R. Curtis
Treas., Rev. E. Lon Schneider
Major Activities: Christian Unity; Bible Distribution; Social Justice; Committee on Faith and Order; Committee on Peace, Justice and the Integrity of Creation

VIRGINIA

*Virginia Council of Churches, Inc.

1214 W. Graham Rd., Richmond, VA 23220-1409
Tel. (804) 321-3300 Fax (804) 329-5066
Email: vcc-net@aol.com
Website: www. vcc-net.org
Media Contact, Gen. Min., Rev. James F. McDonald
Gen. Min., Rev. James F. McDonald
Assoc. Gen. Min., Dr. Judith Fa Galde Bennett
Migrant Head Start, Dir., Richard D. Cagan
Refugee Resettlement, Dir., Rev. Richard D. Cline
Weekday Rel. Educ., Coord., Evelyn W. Simmons, P.O. Box 245, Clifton Forge, VA 24422
Campus Ministry Forum, Coord., Rev. Steve Darr, c/o Community College Ministries, 305 Washington St., N.W., Blacksburg, VA 24060-4745
Major Activities: Faith and Order; Network Building & Coordination; Ecumenical Communications; Justice and Legislative Concerns; Educational Development; Rural Concerns; Refugee Resettlement; Migrant Ministries and Migrant Head Start; Disaster Coordination; Infant Mortality Prevention

WASHINGTON

Associated Ministries of Tacoma-Pierce County

1224 South I St., Tacoma, WA 98405-5021
Tel. (253) 383-3056 Fax (253) 383-2672
Email: info@associatedministries.org
Website: www. associatedministries.org
Media Contact, Exec. Dir., Rev. David T. Alger
Exec. Dir., Rev. David T. Alger, 4510 Defiance, Tacoma, WA 98407
Assoc. Dir., Janet Leng, 1809 N. Lexington, Tacoma, WA 98406
Dir. of Mental Health Chaplaincy, Diane Shepard
Dir. of Anti-Poverty Resource Center, Maria Johnson
Dir. of Paint Tacoma/Pierce Beautiful, Sallie Shawl
Dir. of Face of Hunger, Maureen Fife
Dir. of Hilltop Action Coalition, Jacquie Hackett
Pres., Rev. Richard Tietjen
Sec., Dorothy Diers
Treas., Dr. Judy Thompson
Major Activities: County-wide Hunger Walk; Hunger Awareness; Economic Justice; Religious Education; Social Service Program Advocacy; Communication and Networking of Churches; Housing; Paint Tacoma/Pierce Beautiful; Anti-Poverty Resource Center; Mental Health Chaplaincy; Theological Dialogue; Welfare to Work Mentoring; Hilltop Action Coalition; ComPeer

Associated Ministries of Thurston County

P.O. Box 895, Olympia, WA 98507
Tel. (360) 357-7224
Email: AMofThurstonCo@juno.com
Media Contact, Exec. Dir., Cheri Gonyaw
Exec. Dir., Cheri Gonyaw
Pres., George Hinkel
Treas., Bob McCoy
Major Activities: Church Information and Referral; Interfaith Relations; Social and Health Concerns; Community Action; Social Justice

Center for the Prevention of Sexual and Domestic Violence

936 N. 34th St., Ste. 200, Seattle, WA 98103
Tel. (206) 634-1903 Fax (206) 634-0115
Email: cpsdv@cpsdv.org
Website: www.cpsdv.org
Media Contact, Rev. Dr. Marie M. Fortune
Founder/Senior Analyst, Rev. Dr. Marie M. Fortune
Exec. Dir., Rev. Kathryn J. Johnson
Program Staff, Jean Anton; Rev. Thelma B. Burgonio-Watson; Sandra Barone; Ellen Johanson; Rev. Aubra Love
Finance Director, Marion J. Ward
Major Activities: Prevention and Response Education; Clergy and Lay Training; Video and Print Resources; Bi-national Educational Ministry

251

Church Council of Greater Seattle

4759 15th Ave. NE, Seattle, WA 98105-4404
Tel. (206) 525-1213 Fax (206) 525-1218
Email: CCGSea@aol.com
Website: www.churchcouncilseattle.org
Media Contact, President-Director, Rev. Tom
Quigley
Pres./Dir., Rev. Thomas H. Quigley
Assocociate Dir. for Program & Public Witness,
Alice M. Woldt
Assocociate Dir. for Development, Meredith E.
Brown, CFRE
Admin. Asst., Mary Rolston
Emergency Feeding Prog., Dir., Arthur Lee
Friend-to-Friend, Dir., Marilyn Soderquist
Youth Chaplaincy Program, Rev. Vera Diggins,
Rev. Suzanne Seaton, Chaplain
The Sharehouse, Dir., Young Kim
Homelessness Project, Dir., Nancy Dorman
Mission for Music & Healing, Dir., Susan
Gallaher
Sound Youth-Americorps, Dir., Sara Foster
Interfaith Relations, Coord., Rev. Joyce Manson
Academy of Religious Broadcasting, Dir., Rev. J.
Graley Taylor
Board Chair, Rev. Anne Hall
Board Treas., Steve Faust
Homestead Organizing Project, Dir., Bob
Kubiniec
Commisson on Children, Youth & Families, Dir.,
Rachel Allen
Young Adult Living Project, Dir., Michelle
Reitan
Editor, The Source, Leanne Skooglund Hofford
Seattle Youth Garden Works, Dir., Margaret
Hauptman
SW King County Mental Health Ministry, Dir.,
Rev. Richard Lutz
JOY Initiative, Dir., Katie Bagby
Global Economy Working Group Chair, Bill Aal
St. Petersburg- Seattle Sister Churches Program
Chair, Irene Barinoff
Asia Pacific Task Force, Chair Rev. Bill
Malcomson
Commission on Racial Justice Chair, Natasha
Brubaker
Commission on Public Witness Staff, Alice
Woldt
Major Activities: Children; Youth & Families;
Hunger Relief; Global Peace and Justice;
Housing and Homelessness; Pastoral Care;
Services for the Aging; Public Witness;
Interfaith and Ecumenical Relations

The Interfaith Association of Snohomish County

2301 Hoyt, P.O. Box 12824, Everett, WA 98206
Tel. (206) 252-6672
Media Contact, Exec. Dir., Pam W. Estes
Exec. Dir., Pam W. Estes
Pres., Evie Stegath
Major Activities: Housing and Shelter; Economic

Justice; Hunger; Interfaith Worship and
Collaboration

Northwest Harvest/E. M. M.

P.O. Box 12272, Seattle, WA 98102
Tel. (206) 625-0755 Fax (206) 625-7518
Email: nharvest@blarg.net
Website: www. northwestharvest.org
Media Contact, Comm. Affairs Dir., Ellen
Hansen
Exec. Dir., Ruth M. Velozo
Chpsn., Robert Raphael
Major Activities: Northwest Harvest (Statewide
Hunger Response); Cherry Street Food Bank
(Community Hunger Response); Northwest
Infants Corner (Special Nutritional Products
for Infants and Babies)

Spokane Council of Ecumenical Ministries

E. 245-13th Ave., Spokane, WA 99202
Tel. (509) 624-5156
Email: scem@tincan.org
Website: www. tincan.org/~scem
Media Contact, Editor & Comm. Dir., Mary
Stamp, Tel. (509)535-1813
Exec. Dir., Rev. John Olson
Chair,The Rev. Jim Burford
Vice-Chair, Pat Copeland-Malone
Treas., Barbara Shaffer
Sec., Judy Butler
Vice-Chair, Barbara Schaffer
Major Activities: Greater Spokane Coalition
Against Poverty; Camp PEACE: Multi-
Cultural Human Relations- High School Youth
Camp; Night Walk Ministry; Clergy Families
in Crisis Project; Fig Tree Newspaper; Dir. of
Churches & Community Agencies; Interfaith
Thanksgiving Worship; Easter Sunrise
Service; Friend to Friend Visitation with
Nursing Home Patients; CROP Walk; Eastern
Washington Legislative Conference; Inland
Northwest Disaster Response; Ecumenical
Sunday; Churches Against Racism

*Washington Association of Churches

419 Occidental Ave. S., Ste. 201, Seattle, WA
98104
Tel. (206) 625-9790 Fax (206) 625-9791
Email: wac@thewac.org
Website: www.thewac.org
Media Contact, John C. Boonstra, Email: boon-
stra@thewac.org
Exec. Min., Rev. John C. Boonstra
Public Policy Associate, Sara Fleming
Public Church Associate, Michael Ramos
Admn. Assoc., Bette Schneider
Native American Network, Shelley Means
Major Activities: Faith and Order; Justice
Advocacy; Confronting Poverty; Hunger Action;
Legislation; Denominational Ecumenical

Coordination; Theological Formation; Leadership Development; Refugee Advocacy; Racial Justice Advocacy; International Solidarity

Greater Fairmont Council of Churches

P.O. Box 108, Fairmont, WV 26554
Tel. (304) 367-0962
Media Contact, President, Rev. Jeremiah Jasper
President, Rev. Jeremiah Jasper
Major Activities: Community Ecumenical Services; Youth and Adult Sports Leagues; CROP Walk Sponsor; Weekly Radio Broadcasts

The Greater Wheeling Council of Churches

1060 Chapline St., 110 Methodist Building, Wheeling, WV 26003
Tel. (304) 232-5315
Media Contact, Exec. Dir., Kathy J. Burley
Exec. Dir., Kathy J. Burley
Hospital Notification Sec., Anna Lou Lenz
Pres., Rev. Martha J. Morris
Finance Chpn., Rev. Robert P. Johnson/ Doug Clatterbuck
Major Activities: Christian Education; Evangelism; Christian Heritage Week Celebration; Institutional Ministry; Regional Jail Chaplaincy; Church Women United; Volunteer Chaplaincy Care at OVMC Hospital; School of Religion; Hospital Notification; Hymn Sing in the Park; Anti-Gambling Crusade; Pentecost Celebration; Clergy Council; Easter Sunrise Service; Community Seder; Church Secretaries Fellowship; National Day of Prayer Service; Videotape Library/Audiotape Library; Flood Relief Network of the Upper Ohio Valley

*West Virginia Council of Churches

1608 Virginia St. E., Charleston, WV 25311
Tel. (304) 344-3141 Fax (304) 342-1506
Website: www.wvcc.org
Media Contact, Exec. Dir., The Rev. Nathan D. Wilson, Email: nathanwilson@wvcc.org
Pres., Dr. William B. Allen, CC (DOC)
Vice-Pres., Bishop S. Clifton Ives, UMC
Sec., The Rev. Peggy Scharff, UMC
Treas., The Very Rev. Frederick P. Annie, RC
Major Activities: Leisure Ministry; Disaster Response; Faith and Order; Family Concerns; Inter-Faith Relations; Peace and Justice; Government Concerns; Support Services Network

Center for Community Concerns

1501 Villa St., Racine, WI 53403
Tel. (414) 637-9176 Fax (414) 637-9265

Email: ccc1501@miliserv.net
Media Contact, Exec. Dir., Sr. Michelle Olley
Exec. Dir., Sr. Michelle Olley
Skillbank Coord., Eleanor Sorenson
RSVP (Retired Senior Volunteer Program), Chris Udell-Sorberg, Elaine Segedy, Cathy Townsend
Volunteer Today (55 and under), Janet LeSuer
Major Activities: Advocacy; Direct Services; Research; Community Consultant; Criminal Justice; Volunteerism; Senior Citizen Services; CROP Walk, Referral

Christian Youth Council

1715-52nd St., Kenosha, WI 53140
Tel. (414) 652-9543 Fax (414) 652-4461
Media Contact, Exec. Dir., Steven L. Nelson
Exec. Dir., Steven L. Nelson
Sports Dir., Jerry Tappen
Outreach Dir., Linda Osborne
Accountant, Debbie Cutts
Class Director, Jill Cox
Pres. & Chmn. of Board, Lon Knoedler
Gang Prevention Dir., Sam Sauceda
Major Activities: Leisure Time Ministry; Institutional Ministries; Ecumenical Committee; Social Concerns; Outreach Sports(with a Christian Philosophy)

Interfaith Conference of Greater Milwaukee

1442 N. Farwell Ave., Ste. 200, Milwaukee, WI 53202
Tel. (414) 276-9050 Fax (414) 276-8442
Email: IFCGM@aol.com
Media Contact, Exec. Dir., Jack Murtaugh
Chpsn., Rev. Velma Smith
First Vice-Chair, Archbishop Rembert G. Weakland
Second Vice-Chair, Rev. Charles Graves
Sec., Paula Simon
Treas., Rev. Mary Ann Neevel
Exec. Dir., Jack Murtaugh
Associate Dir., Marcus White
Consultant in Communications, Rev. Robert P. Seater
Major Activities: Economic Issues; Racism; CROP Walk; Public Policy; Suburban and Urban Partnerships; TV Programming; Peace and International Issues Committee; Annual Membership Luncheon; Substance Abuse, Violence Prevention

Madison Urban Ministry

1127 University Ave., Madison, WI 53715
Tel. (608) 256-0906 Fax (608) 256-4387
Media Contact, Office Manager, Jennifer Harrington
Exec. Dir., Mary K. Baum
Program Mgr., Judy Collison & Richard Wildermuth
Major Activities: Community Projects; Dialogue/ Forums; Social & Economic Justice

US ECUMENICAL BODIES

*Wisconsin Council of Churches

750 Windsor St. Ste. 301, Sun Prairie, WI 53590-2149
Tel. (608) 837-3108 Fax (608) 837-3038
Email: wcoc@mailbag.org
Media Contact, Comm. Coord., Jeanette Johnson
Exec. Dir., Rev. Jerry Folk
Assoc. Dir., -vacant-
Ofc. Mgr., Jeanette Johnson
Millenium Project Coordinator, Melinda Storey
Peace & Justice Committee Coordinator, Catherine Coy
AIDS/HIV Faith in Action Volunteer Coordinator, John Keegan
Pres., Bishop Sharon Zimmerman Rader
Treas., Dr. Robert Book
Major Activities: Social Witness; Migrant Ministry; Aging; Wisconsin Interfaith IMPACT; Institutional Chaplaincy; Peace and Justice; Faith and Order; Rural Concerns; American Indian Ministries Council; Park Ministry; RoundTable Events: All Women in Ministry; Wisconsin Housing Partnership

WYOMING

*Wyoming Church Coalition

P.O. Box 20812, Cheyenne, WY 82003-7017
Tel. (307) 635-4251 Fax (307) 778-9060
Email: Dan_Monson@ecunet.org
Media Contact, Rev. Daniel E. Monson, 1032 Melton St., Cheyenne, WY 82009 Tel. (307)635-4251
Dir., Rev. Daniel E. Monson
Assoc. Dir., Mary A. Monson
Chair, Chesie Lee
Penitentiary Chaplain, Rev. Lynn Schumacher, P.O. Box 400, Rawlins, WY 82301
Major Activities: Death Penalty; Empowering the Poor and Oppressed; Peace and Justice; Prison Ministry; Malicious Harassment; Domestic Violence, Public Health Issues; Welfare Reform

254

Index of Select Programs for U.S. Regional and Local Ecumenical Bodies

For many years the *Yearbook of American & Canadian Churches* has published a directory of U.S. Ecumenical Bodies, each entry of which contains a brief description of the diverse programs offered by each agency. Researchers, pastors, service organizations, and theological seminaries often inquire about specific programs and which agencies carry out such programs. In the 1999 *Yearbook of American & Canadian Churches*, we initiated an index listing agencies that provide programs in the five areas that were most frequently the subject of inquiry. In the 2000 edition of the *Yearbook*, we have expanded this index to include 25 different types of programs. We have collected this program information directly from these organizations by means of a simple response form. There is an enormous diversity of ministries and missions conducted by these diverse organizations. Most organizations pursue several kinds of programs at once. However, some of these may focus their efforts most especially on only one of their programs; their other programs may be less well developed than their specialty. Consequently, the extent to which any of these ministries is a priority for any particular organization cannot be inferred from this list. For detailed information about the nature and extent of any particular ministry, the reader is urged to contact the organization directly using the directory of "U.S. Regional and Local Ecumenical Bodies," which is found in the pages just prior to this index.

The twenty-five program areas listed in this index are: AIDS/HIV Programs; Anti-racism Programs; Christian Education Programs; Clothing Distribution Programs; CROP Walks; Programs with/for Persons with Disabilities; Domestic Violence Programs; Economic/Social Justice Programs; Employment Assistance Programs; Environmental Programs; Faith and Order Programs; Healthcare Issues; Homelessness/Shelter Programs; Hunger/Food Programs; Immigration Issues; Interfaith Dialogue/Relationships; Prison Chaplaincy; Public Education Advocacy; Refugee Assistance Programs; Rural Issues; Senior Citizen Programs; Substance Abuse Programs; Theology and Worship Programs; Women's Issues; Youth Activities.

AIDS/HIV Programs

Arkansas Interfaith Conference, Scott, AR
Center City Churches, Hartford, CT
Christian Churches United of the Tri-County Area, Harrisburg, PA
Council of Churches of Greater Springfield, Springfield, MA
Dutchess Interfaith Council, Inc., Poughkeepsie, NY
East End Cooperative Ministry, Pittsburgh, PA
Ecumenical Ministries, Fulton, MO
Grand Rapids Area Center for Ecumenism (GRACE), Grand Rapids, MI
Interfaith Community Services, St. Joseph, MO
Inter-Faith Ministries-Wichita, Wichita, KS
Kansas Ecumenical Ministries, Topeka, KS
Lincoln Interfaith Council, Lincoln, NE
The Long Island Council of Churches, Hempstead, NY
Network of Religious Communities, Buffalo, NY
New Britain Area Conference of Churches (NEWBRACC), New Britain, CT
New Hampshire Council of Churches, Concord, NH
New Mexico Conference of Churches, Albuquerque, NM
Northern California Interreligious Conference, San Francisco, CA
The Rhode Island State Council of Churches, Providence, RI
Schenectady Inner City Ministry, Schenectady, NY
South Carolina Christian Action Council, Inc., Columbia, SC
Southeast Ecumenical Ministry, Rochester, NY
Toledo Ecumenical Area Ministries, Toledo, OH
Troy Area United Ministries, Troy, NY
Wisconsin Council of Churches, Sun Prairie, WI
York County Council of Churches, York, PA

Anti-racism Programs

Akron Area Association of Churches, Akron, OH
Arkansas Interfaith Conference, Scott, AR
The Associated Churches of Fort Wayne & Allen County, Inc., Fort Wayne, IN
Associated Ministries of Tacoma-Pierce County, Tacoma, WA
Association of Religious Communities, Danbury, CT
Austin Metropolitan Ministries, Austin, TX
Brooklyn Council of Churches, Brooklyn, NY
California Council of Churches/California Church Impact, Sacramento, CA
Capital Area Council of Churches, Inc., Albany, NY
The Capitol Region Conference of Churches, Hartford, CT
Christian Council of Metropolitan Atlanta, Atlanta, GA
The Church Federation of Greater Indianapolis, Inc., Indianapolis, IN

255

Washington Association of Churches, Seattle, WA

West Virginia Council of Churches, Charleston, WV

Wisconsin Council of Churches, Sun Prairie, WI

Christian Education Programs

Akron Area Association of Churches, Akron, OH

Allegheny Valley Association of Churches, Natrona Heights, PA

The Associated Churches of Fort Wayne & Allen County, Inc., Fort Wayne, IN

Associated Ministries of Tacoma-Pierce County, Tacoma, WA

Brooklyn Council of Churches, Brooklyn, NY

Broome County Council of Churches, Inc., Binghamton, NY

The Church Federation of Greater Indianapolis, Inc., Indianapolis, IN

Churches United of the Quad City Area, Rock Island, IL

Council of Christian Communions of Greater Cincinnati, Cincinnati, OH

Council of Churches of Greater Springfield, Springfield, MA

Council of Churches and Synagogues of Southwestern Connecticut, Stamford, CT

East End Cooperative Ministry, Pittsburgh, PA

Ecclesia, Trenton, NJ

Ecumenical Conference of Greater Altoona, Altoona, PA

Georgia Christian Council, Macon, GA

Greater Fairmont Council of Churches, Fairmont, WV

Greater New Orleans Federation of Churches, New Orleans, LA

The Greater Wheeling Council of Churches, Wheeling, WV

Greensboro Urban Ministry, Greensboro, NC

In One Accord, Battle Creek, MI

Lincoln Interfaith Council, Lincoln, NE

The Long Island Council of Churches, Hempstead, NY

Network of Religious Communities, Buffalo, NY

New Hampshire Council of Churches, Concord, NH

New Mexico Conference of Churches, Albuquerque, NM

Oklahoma Conference of Churches, Oklahoma City, OK

The Pennsylvania Council of Churches, Harrisburg, PA

Peoria Friendship House of Christian Service, Peoria, IL

Queens Federation of Churches, Richmond Hill, NY

Tarrant Area Community of Churches, Fort Worth, TX

Toledo Ecumenical Area Ministries, Toledo, OH

United Churches of Lycoming County, Williamsport, PA

Washington Association of Churches, Seattle, WA

West Virginia Council of Churches, Charleston, WV

Wisconsin Council of Churches, Sun Prairie, WI

York County Council of Churches, York, PA

Clothing Distribution Programs

Arkansas Interfaith Conference, Scott, AR

Associated Ministries of Tacoma-Pierce County, Tacoma, WA

Community Ministry of Montgomery County, Rockville, MD

Concerned Ecumenical Ministry to the Upper West Side, Buffalo, NY

Cooperative Metropolitan Ministries, Newton, MA

Council of Churches of the Ozarks, Springfield, MO

East End Cooperative Ministry, Pittsburgh, PA

Eastern Area Community Ministries, Louisville, KY

Fern Creek/Highview United Ministries, Louisvlle, KY

Greater Fairmont Council of Churches, Fairmont, WV

Greensboro Urban Ministry, Greensboro, NC

Inter-Church Ministries of Erie County, Erie, PA

Interfaith Community Council, Inc., New Albany, IN

Interfaith Community Services, St. Joseph, MO

Lancaster County Council of Churches, Lancaster, PA

Lebanon County Christian Ministries, Lebanon, PA

Lincoln Interfaith Council, Lincoln, NE

The Long Island Council of Churches, Hempstead, NY

Northside Inter-Church Agency (NICA), Fort Worth, TX

Peoria Friendship House of Christian Service, Peoria, IL

South Coast Ecumenical Council, Long Beach, CA

South East Associated Ministries (SEAM), Louisville, KY

South Hills Interfaith Ministries, Library, PA

Southside Area Ministries, Inc. (SAM), Fort Worth, TX

Wilkinsburg Community Ministry, Pittsburgh, PA

CROP Walks

Akron Area Association of Churches, Akron, OH

Allegheny Valley Association of Churches, Natrona Heights, PA

The Associated Churches of Fort Wayne & Allen County, Inc., Fort Wayne, IN

257

Associated Ministries of Tacoma-Pierce County, Tacoma, WA

Associated Ministries of Thurston County, Olympia, WA

Attleboro Area Council of Churches, Inc., Attleboro, MA

Austin Metropolitan Ministries, Austin, TX

Broome County Council of Churches, Inc., Binghamton, NY

Capital Area Council of Churches, Inc., Albany, NY

Center for Community Concerns, Racine, WI

The Church Federation of Greater Indianapolis, Inc., Indianapolis, IN

Churches United of the Quad City Area, Rock Island, IL

Council of Churches of Chemung County, Inc., Elmira, NY

Council of Churches of the City of New York, New York, NY

Council of Churches of Greater Bridgeport, Inc., Bridgeport, CT

Council of Churches of Greater Springfield, Springfield, MA

Council of Churches of the Ozarks, Springfield, MO

Dutchess Interfaith Council, Inc., Poughkeepsie, NY

East End Cooperative Ministry, Pittsburgh, PA

Eastern Area Community Ministries, Louisville, KY

Ecclesia, Trenton, NJ

Ecumenical Ministries, Fulton, MO

Evanston Ecumenical Action Council, Evanston, IL

Florida Council of Churches, Orlando, FL

Grand Rapids Area Center for Ecumenism (GRACE), Grand Rapids, MI

Greater Bethlehem Area Council of Churches, Bethlehem, PA

Greater Dallas Community of Churches, Dallas, TX

Greater Dayton Christian Connection, Dayton, OH

Greater Fairmont Council of Churches, Fairmont, WV

Greater Waterbury Interfaith Ministries, Inc., Waterbury, CT

Greensboro Urban Ministry, Greensboro, NC

In One Accord, Battle Creek, MI

Interfaith Community Services, St. Joseph, MO

Interfaith Conference of Greater Milwaukee, Milwaukee, WI

Inter-Faith Ministries-Wichita, Wichita, KS

Lancaster County Council of Churches, Lancaster, PA

Lincoln Interfaith Council, Lincoln, NE

The Long Island Council of Churches, Hempstead, NY

Network of Religious Communities, Buffalo, NY

New Britain Area Conference of Churches (NEWBRACC), New Britain, CT

New Mexico Conference of Churches, Albuquerque, NM

Northside Inter-Church Agency (NICA), Fort Worth, TX

Oak Park-River Forest Community of Congregations, Oak Park, IL

Peoria Friendship House of Christian Service, Peoria, IL

San Fernando Valley Interfaith Council, Chatsworth, CA

Schenectady Inner City Ministry, Schenectady, NY

South Coast Ecumenical Council, Long Beach, CA

Southeast Ecumenical Ministry, Rochester, NY

Tarrant Area Community of Churches, Fort Worth, TX

Toledo Ecumenical Area Ministries, Toledo, OH

Troy Area United Ministries, Troy, NY

United Churches of Lycoming County, Williamsport, PA

United Religious Community of St. Joseph County, South Bend, IN

Wilkinsburg Community Ministry, Pittsburgh, PA

Worcester County Ecumenical Council, Worcester, MA

York County Council of Churches, York, PA

Programs with/for Persons with Disabilities

Austin Metropolitan Ministries, Austin, TX

Broome County Council of Churches, Inc., Binghamton, NY

Christian Council of Metropolitan Atlanta, Atlanta, GA

Council of Churches of Chemung County, Inc., Elmira, NY

Council of Churches of the Ozarks, Springfield, MO

Des Moines Area Religious Council, Des Moines, IA

Greater Minneapolis Council of Churches, Minneapolis, MN

The Joint Religious Legislative Coalition, Minneapolis, MN

Lincoln Interfaith Council, Lincoln, NE

Massachusetts Council of Churches, Boston, MA

New York State Community of Churches, Inc., Albany, NY

Northside Inter-Church Agency (NICA), Fort Worth, TX

Southeast Ecumenical Ministry, Rochester, NY

Toledo Ecumenical Area Ministries, Toledo, OH

Domestic Violence Programs

The Associated Churches of Fort Wayne & Allen County, Inc., Fort Wayne, IN

258

Association of Religious Communities, Danbury, CT

California Council of Churches/California Church Impact, Sacramento, CA

Center for the Prevention of Sexual and Domestic Violence, Seattle, WA

Churches United of the Quad City Area, Rock Island, IL

Council of Churches of Chemung County, Inc., Elmira, NY

Council of Churches of Greater Springfield, Springfield, MA

Evanston Ecumenical Action Council, Evanston, IL

Florida Council of Churches, Orlando, FL

Georgia Christian Council, Macon, GA

Greater Bethlehem Area Council of Churches, Bethlehem, PA

Greater Minneapolis Council of Churches, Minneapolis, MN

Indiana Partners for Christian Unity and Mission, Indianapolis, IN

Inter-Church Ministries of Erie County, Erie, PA

Kansas Ecumenical Ministries, Topeka, KS

Lancaster County Council of Churches, Lancaster, PA

Lincoln Interfaith Council, Lincoln, NE

The Long Island Council of Churches, Hempstead, NY

Madison Urban Ministry, Madison, WI

North Carolina Council of Churches, Raleigh, NC

Oklahoma Conference of Churches, Oklahoma City, OK

Peoria Friendship House of Christian Service, Peoria, IL

The Rhode Island State Council of Churches, Providence, RI

Toledo Ecumenical Area Ministries, Toledo, OH

West Virginia Council of Churches, Charleston, WV

Economic/Social Justice Programs

Akron Area Association of Churches, Akron, OH

The Associated Churches of Fort Wayne & Allen County, Inc., Fort Wayne, IN

Associated Ministries of Tacoma-Pierce County, Tacoma, WA

Associated Ministries of Thurston County, Olympia, WA

Association of Religious Communities, Danbury, CT

Brooklyn Council of Churches, Brooklyn, NY

Broome County Council of Churches, Inc., Binghamton, NY

California Council of Churches/California Church Impact, Sacramento, CA

Capital Area Council of Churches, Inc., Albany, NY

The Capitol Region Conference of Churches, Hartford, CT

Christian Community Action, New Haven, CT

Christian Conference of Connecticut (CHRISCON), Hartford, CT

Christian Council of Metropolitan Atlanta, Atlanta, GA

Church Council of Greater Seattle, Seattle, WA

The Church Federation of Greater Indianapolis, Inc., Indianapolis, IN

Churches United of the Quad City Area, Rock Island, IL

Community Ministry of Montgomery County, Rockville, MD

Concerned Ecumenical Ministry to the Upper West Side, Buffalo, NY

Cooperative Metropolitan Ministries, Newton, MA

Council of Churches of Chemung County, Inc., Elmira, NY

Council of Churches of the City of New York, New York, NY

Council of Churches of Greater Bridgeport, Inc., Bridgeport, CT

Council of Churches of Greater Springfield, Springfield, MA

Des Moines Area Religious Council, Des Moines, IA

Eastern Area Community Ministries, Louisville, KY

Ecclesia, Trenton, NJ

Ecumenical Ministries, Fulton, MO

Ecumenical Ministries of Iowa (EMI), Des Moines, IA

Evanston Ecumenical Action Council, Evanston, IL

Florida Council of Churches, Orlando, FL

Georgia Christian Council, Macon, GA

Grand Rapids Area Center for Ecumenism (GRACE), Grand Rapids, MI

Greater Bethlehem Area Council of Churches, Bethlehem, PA

Greater Chicago Broadcast Ministries, Chicago, IL

Greater Dallas Community of Churches, Dallas, TX

Greater Dayton Christian Connection, Dayton, OH

Greater Minneapolis Council of Churches, Minneapolis, MN

Illinois Conference of Churches, Springfield, IL

In One Accord, Battle Creek, MI

Interchurch Ministries of Nebraska, Lincoln, NE

Interfaith Community Council, Inc., New Albany, IN

Interfaith Community Services, St. Joseph, MO

Interfaith Conference of Greater Milwaukee, Milwaukee, WI

Interfaith Council of Contra Costa County, Walnut Creek, CA

259

Interfaith Mission Service, Huntsville, AL

InterReligious Council of Central New York, Syracuse, NY

The Joint Religious Legislative Coalition, Minneapolis, MN

Kansas Ecumenical Ministries, Topeka, KS

Kentucky Council of Churches, Lexington, KY

Lancaster County Council of Churches, Lancaster, PA

Lincoln Interfaith Council, Lincoln, NE

The Long Island Council of Churches, Hempstead, NY

Madison Urban Ministry, Madison, WI

Massachusetts Council of Churches, Boston, MA

Metropolitan Christian Council of Philadelphia, Philadelphia, PA

Metropolitan Interfaith Council on Affordable Housing (MICAH), Minneapolis, MN

Michigan Ecumenical Forum, Lansing, MI

Minnesota Council of Churches, Minneapolis, MN

Montana Association of Churches, Billings, MT

Network of Religious Communities, Buffalo, NY

New Britain Area Conference of Churches (NEWBRACC), New Britain, CT

New Hampshire Council of Churches, Concord, NH

New Mexico Conference of Churches, Albuquerque, NM

New York State Community of Churches, Inc., Albany, NY

North Carolina Council of Churches, Raleigh, NC

Northern California Interreligious Conference, San Francisco, CA

Northside Common Ministries, Pittsburgh, PA

Northside Inter-Church Agency (NICA), Fort Worth, TX

Oak Park-River Forest Community of Congregations, Oak Park, IL

Ohio Council of Churches, Columbus, OH

Oklahoma Conference of Churches, Oklahoma City, OK

The Pennsylvania Council of Churches, Harrisburg, PA

Peoria Friendship House of Christian Service, Peoria, IL

Queens Federation of Churches, Richmond Hill, NY

The Rhode Island State Council of Churches, Providence, RI

San Fernando Valley Interfaith Council, Chatsworth, CA

Schenectady Inner City Ministry, Schenectady, NY

South Carolina Christian Action Council, Inc., Columbia, SC

South Coast Ecumenical Council, Long Beach, CA

South East Associated Ministries (SEAM), Louisville, KY

Southern California Ecumenical Council, Pasadena, CA

Tarrant Area Community of Churches, Fort Worth, TX

Toledo Ecumenical Area Ministries, Toledo, OH

United Churches of Lycoming County, Williamsport, PA

United Religious Community of St. Joseph County, South Bend, IN

Washington Association of Churches, Seattle, WA

West Virginia Council of Churches, Charleston, WV

Wisconsin Council of Churches, Sun Prairie, WI

Worcester County Ecumenical Council, Worcester, MA

Employment Assistance Programs

The Associated Churches of Fort Wayne & Allen County, Inc., Fort Wayne, IN

Association of Religious Communities, Danbury, CT

Council of Churches of Greater Bridgeport, Inc., Bridgeport, CT

East End Cooperative Ministry, Pittsburgh, PA

Evanston Ecumenical Action Council, Evanston, IL

Fern Creek/Highview United Ministries, Louisvlle, KY

Florida Council of Churches, Orlando, FL

Genesee-Orleans Ministry of Concern, Albion, NY

Grand Rapids Area Center for Ecumenism (GRACE), Grand Rapids, MI

Greater Dayton Christian Connection, Dayton, OH

Greater Minneapolis Council of Churches, Minneapolis, MN

Greensboro Urban Ministry, Greensboro, NC

Interfaith Community Council, Inc., New Albany, IN

The Joint Religious Legislative Coalition, Minneapolis, MN

Lincoln Interfaith Council, Lincoln, NE

The Long Island Council of Churches, Hempstead, NY

Network of Religious Communities, Buffalo, NY

Northern California Interreligious Conference, San Francisco, CA

Northside Inter-Church Agency (NICA), Fort Worth, TX

Peoria Friendship House of Christian Service, Peoria, IL

San Fernando Valley Interfaith Council, Chatsworth, CA

Schenectady Inner City Ministry, Schenectady, NY

South East Associated Ministries (SEAM), Louisville, KY

Toledo Ecumenical Area Ministries, Toledo, OH

United Ministries, Greenville, SC
West Virginia Council of Churches, Charleston, WV

Environmental Programs

Council of Churches of Chemung County, Inc., Elmira, NY
Council of Churches of the Ozarks, Springfield, MO
Ecumenical Ministries of Iowa (EMI), Des Moines, IA
Florida Council of Churches, Orlando, FL
Georgia Christian Council, Macon, GA
Grand Rapids Area Center for Ecumenism (GRACE), Grand Rapids, MI
Interfaith Conference of Greater Milwaukee, Milwaukee, WI
The Joint Religious Legislative Coalition, Minneapolis, MN
Kansas Ecumenical Ministries, Topeka, KS
Lincoln Interfaith Council, Lincoln, NE
The Long Island Council of Churches, Hempstead, NY
Marin Interfaith Council, San Rafael, CA
Michigan Ecumenical Forum, Lansing, MI
Network of Religious Communities, Buffalo, NY
New Hampshire Council of Churches, Concord, NH
New Mexico Conference of Churches, Albuquerque, NM
New York State Community of Churches, Inc., Albany, NY
Northern California Interreligious Conference, San Francisco, CA
Ohio Council of Churches, Columbus, OH
The Pennsylvania Council of Churches, Harrisburg, PA
The Rhode Island State Council of Churches, Providence, RI
South Carolina Christian Action Council, Inc., Columbia, SC
South Coast Ecumenical Council, Long Beach, CA
Southern California Ecumenical Council, Pasadena, CA
Toledo Ecumenical Area Ministries, Toledo, OH
United Churches of Lycoming County, Williamsport, PA
Washington Association of Churches, Seattle, WA
West Virginia Council of Churches, Charleston, WV

Faith and Order Programs

Akron Area Association of Churches, Akron, OH
Allegheny Valley Association of Churches, Natrona Heights, PA
Associated Ministries of Tacoma-Pierce County, Tacoma, WA
Attleboro Area Council of Churches, Inc., Attleboro, MA

Broome County Council of Churches, Inc., Binghamton, NY
Capital Area Council of Churches, Inc., Albany, NY
The Capitol Region Conference of Churches, Hartford, CT
Christian Conference of Connecticut (CHRISCON), Hartford, CT
The Christian Council of Delaware and Maryland's Eastern Shore, Wilmington, DE
Christian Council of Metropolitan Atlanta, Atlanta, GA
Church Council of Greater Seattle, Seattle, WA
Churches United of the Quad City Area, Rock Island, IL
Council of Churches of the City of New York, New York, NY
Council of Churches of Greater Springfield, Springfield, MA
Council of Churches and Synagogues of Southwestern Connecticut, Stamford, CT
East End Cooperative Ministry, Pittsburgh, PA
Ecclesia, Trenton, NJ
Ecumenical Ministries of Iowa (EMI), Des Moines, IA
Florida Council of Churches, Orlando, FL
Georgia Christian Council, Macon, GA
Grand Rapids Area Center for Ecumenism (GRACE), Grand Rapids, MI
Greater New Orleans Federation of Churches, New Orleans, LA
Greater Waterbury Interfaith Ministries, Inc., Waterbury, CT
Illinois Conference of Churches, Springfield, IL
Indiana Partners for Christian Unity and Mission, Indianapolis, IN
Interchurch Ministries of Nebraska, Lincoln, NE
Interfaith Community Services, St. Joseph, MO
Interfaith Council of Contra Costa County, Walnut Creek, CA
Kansas Ecumenical Ministries, Topeka, KS
Kentucky Council of Churches, Lexington, KY
Lancaster County Council of Churches, Lancaster, PA
Lincoln Interfaith Council, Lincoln, NE
The Long Island Council of Churches, Hempstead, NY
Massachusetts Commission on Christian Unity, Lowell, MA
Massachusetts Council of Churches, Boston, MA
Metropolitan Christian Council of Philadelphia, Philadelphia, PA
Michigan Ecumenical Forum, Lansing, MI
Minnesota Council of Churches, Minneapolis, MN
Montana Association of Churches, Billings, MT
Network of Religious Communities, Buffalo, NY

261

New Hampshire Council of Churches, Concord, NH

New Mexico Conference of Churches, Albuquerque, NM

New York State Community of Churches, Inc., Albany, NY

North Carolina Council of Churches, Raleigh, NC

North Dakota Conference of Churches, Bismarck, ND

Northern California Interreligious Conference, San Francisco, CA

Northern Kentucky Interfaith Commission, Inc., Newport, KY

Ohio Council of Churches, Columbus, OH

Oklahoma Conference of Churches, Oklahoma City, OK

Queens Federation of Churches, Richmond Hill, NY

The Rhode Island State Council of Churches, Providence, RI

South Carolina Christian Action Council, Inc., Columbia, SC

Southern California Ecumenical Council, Pasadena, CA

Texas Conference of Churches, Austin, TX

Toledo Ecumenical Area Ministries, Toledo, OH

Vermont Ecumenical Council and Bible Society, Burlington, VT

Washington Association of Churches, Seattle, WA

West Virginia Council of Churches, Charleston, WV

Wisconsin Council of Churches, Sun Prairie, WI

Healthcare Issues

Associated Ministries of Thurston County, Olympia, WA

Association of Religious Communities, Danbury, CT

Broome County Council of Churches, Inc., Binghamton, NY

California Council of Churches/California Church Impact, Sacramento, CA

Community Ministries of Rockville, Rockville, MD

Council of Churches of Greater Springfield, Springfield, MA

Council of Churches of the Ozarks, Springfield, MO

Eastern Area Community Ministries, Louisville, KY

Ecumenical Ministries, Fulton, MO

Ecumenical Ministries of Iowa (EMI), Des Moines, IA

Greensboro Urban Ministry, Greensboro, NC

Illinois Conference of Churches, Springfield, IL

In One Accord, Battle Creek, MI

Interchurch Ministries of Nebraska, Lincoln, NE

Interfaith Council of Contra Costa County, Walnut Creek, CA

The Joint Religious Legislative Coalition, Minneapolis, MN

Kansas Ecumenical Ministries, Topeka, KS

Lincoln Interfaith Council, Lincoln, NE

The Long Island Council of Churches, Hempstead, NY

Marin Interfaith Council, San Rafael, CA

Massachusetts Council of Churches, Boston, MA

Metropolitan Ecumenical Ministry Community Development Corp., Newark, NJ

New Mexico Conference of Churches, Albuquerque, NM

New York State Community of Churches, Inc., Albany, NY

North Carolina Council of Churches, Raleigh, NC

Northern California Interreligious Conference, San Francisco, CA

Ohio Council of Churches, Columbus, OH

Peoria Friendship House of Christian Service, Peoria, IL

The Rhode Island State Council of Churches, Providence, RI

South Carolina Christian Action Council, Inc., Columbia, SC

Tarrant Area Community of Churches, Fort Worth, TX

Toledo Ecumenical Area Ministries, Toledo, OH

United Churches of Lycoming County, Williamsport, PA

Washington Association of Churches, Seattle, WA

West Virginia Council of Churches, Charleston, WV

Homelessness/Shelter Programs

Allegheny Valley Association of Churches, Natrona Heights, PA

Arkansas Interfaith Conference, Scott, AR

The Associated Churches of Fort Wayne & Allen County, Inc., Fort Wayne, IN

Associated Ministries of Tacoma-Pierce County, Tacoma, WA

Associated Ministries of Thurston County, Olympia, WA

Association of Religious Communities, Danbury, CT

Austin Metropolitan Ministries, Austin, TX

Capital Area Council of Churches, Inc., Albany, NY

The Capitol Region Conference of Churches, Hartford, CT

Christian Churches United of the Tri-County Area, Harrisburg, PA

Christian Community Action, New Haven, CT

Christian Council of Metropolitan Atlanta, Atlanta, GA

Church Council of Greater Seattle, Seattle, WA

Churches United of the Quad City Area, Rock Island, IL

Community Ministries of Rockville, Rockville, MD

Community Ministry of Montgomery County, Rockville, MD

Council of Churches of Greater Bridgeport, Inc., Bridgeport, CT

Council of Churches of Greater Springfield, Springfield, MA

East End Cooperative Ministry, Pittsburgh, PA

Ecumenical Ministries, Fulton, MO

Evanston Ecumenical Action Council, Evanston, IL

Florida Council of Churches, Orlando, FL

Genesee-Orleans Ministry of Concern, Albion, NY

Grand Rapids Area Center for Ecumenism (GRACE), Grand Rapids, MI

Greater Minneapolis Council of Churches, Minneapolis, MN

Greensboro Urban Ministry, Greensboro, NC

Interfaith Community Council, Inc., New Albany, IN

Interfaith Community Services, St. Joseph, MO

Interfaith Conference of Greater Milwaukee, Milwaukee, WI

InterFaith Conference of Metropolitan Washington, Washington, DC

Inter-Faith Ministries-Wichita, Wichita, KS

Interfaith Mission Service, Huntsville, AL

InterReligious Council of Central New York, Syracuse, NY

The Joint Religious Legislative Coalition, Minneapolis, MN

Lincoln Interfaith Council, Lincoln, NE

The Long Island Council of Churches, Hempstead, NY

Metropolitan Interfaith Council on Affordable Housing (MICAH), Minneapolis, MN

New Britain Area Conference of Churches (NEWBRACC), New Britain, CT

New Mexico Conference of Churches, Albuquerque, NM

New York State Community of Churches, Inc., Albany, NY

Northern California Interreligious Conference, San Francisco, CA

Northern Kentucky Interfaith Commission, Inc., Newport, KY

Northside Common Ministries, Pittsburgh, PA

Oak Park-River Forest Community of Congregations, Oak Park, IL

Peoria Friendship House of Christian Service, Peoria, IL

The Rhode Island State Council of Churches, Providence, RI

San Fernando Valley Interfaith Council, Chatsworth, CA

Schenectady Inner City Ministry, Schenectady, NY

Tarrant Area Community of Churches, Fort Worth, TX

Toledo Ecumenical Area Ministries, Toledo, OH

Troy Area United Ministries, Troy, NY

United Churches of Lycoming County, Williamsport, PA

United Ministries, Greenville, SC

United Religious Community of St. Joseph County, South Bend, IN

Wisconsin Council of Churches, Sun Prairie, WI

Hunger/Food Programs

Allegheny Valley Association of Churches, Natrona Heights, PA

The Associated Churches of Fort Wayne & Allen County, Inc., Fort Wayne, IN

Associated Ministries of Tacoma-Pierce County, Tacoma, WA

Associated Ministries of Thurston County, Olympia, WA

Association of Religious Communities, Danbury, CT

Attleboro Area Council of Churches, Inc., Attleboro, MA

Brooklyn Council of Churches, Brooklyn, NY

Broome County Council of Churches, Inc., Binghamton, NY

California Council of Churches/California Church Impact, Sacramento, CA

Capital Area Council of Churches, Inc., Albany, NY

Center City Churches, Hartford, CT

Christian Churches United of the Tri-County Area, Harrisburg, PA

Christian Community Action, New Haven, CT

Church Council of Greater Seattle, Seattle, WA

The Church Federation of Greater Indianapolis, Inc., Indianapolis, IN

Churches United of the Quad City Area, Rock Island, IL

Community Ministry of Montgomery County, Rockville, MD

Concerned Ecumenical Ministry to the Upper West Side, Buffalo, NY

Council of Churches of Chemung County, Inc., Elmira, NY

Council of Churches of Greater Bridgeport, Inc., Bridgeport, CT

Council of Churches of Greater Springfield, Springfield, MA

Council of Churches of the Ozarks, Springfield, MO

Council of Churches and Synagogues of Southwestern Connecticut, Stamford, CT

Des Moines Area Religious Council, Des Moines, IA

East End Cooperative Ministry, Pittsburgh, PA

Eastern Area Community Ministries, Louisville, KY

Ecclesia, Trenton, NJ

Evanston Ecumenical Action Council, Evanston, IL

263

Fern Creek/Highview United Ministries, Louisvlle, KY

Florida Council of Churches, Orlando, FL

Genesee County Churches United, Inc., Batavia, NY

Genesee-Orleans Ministry of Concern, Albion, NY

Grand Rapids Area Center for Ecumenism (GRACE), Grand Rapids, MI

Greater Bethlehem Area Council of Churches, Bethlehem, PA

Greater Dallas Community of Churches, Dallas, TX

Greater Dayton Christian Connection, Dayton, OH

Greater Minneapolis Council of Churches, Minneapolis, MN

Greater New Orleans Federation of Churches, New Orleans, LA

Greater Waterbury Interfaith Ministries, Inc., Waterbury, CT

Greensboro Urban Ministry, Greensboro, NC

Illinois Conference of Churches, Springfield, IL

In One Accord, Battle Creek, MI

Inter-Church Ministries of Erie County, Erie, PA

Interchurch Ministries of Nebraska, Lincoln, NE

Interfaith Community Council, Inc., New Albany, IN

Interfaith Community Services, St. Joseph, MO

Interfaith Conference of Greater Milwaukee, Milwaukee, WI

Inter-Faith Ministries-Wichita, Wichita, KS

Interfaith Mission Service, Huntsville, AL

The Joint Religious Legislative Coalition, Minneapolis, MN

Kansas Ecumenical Ministries, Topeka, KS

Kentuckiana Interfaith Community, Louisville, KY

Lancaster County Council of Churches, Lancaster, PA

Lebanon County Christian Ministries, Lebanon, PA

Lincoln Interfaith Council, Lincoln, NE

The Long Island Council of Churches, Hempstead, NY

Madison Urban Ministry, Madison, WI

Minnesota Council of Churches, Minneapolis, MN

Network of Religious Communities, Buffalo, NY

New Britain Area Conference of Churches (NEWBRACC), New Britain, CT

New York State Community of Churches, Inc., Albany, NY

Northern Kentucky Interfaith Commission, Inc., Newport, KY

Northside Common Ministries, Pittsburgh, PA

Northside Inter-Church Agency (NICA), Fort Worth, TX

Oak Park-River Forest Community of Congregations, Oak Park, IL

Oklahoma Conference of Churches, Oklahoma City, OK

Peoria Friendship House of Christian Service, Peoria, IL

Queens Federation of Churches, Richmond Hill, NY

The Rhode Island State Council of Churches, Providence, RI

San Fernando Valley Interfaith Council, Chatsworth, CA

Schenectady Inner City Ministry, Schenectady, NY

South Coast Ecumenical Council, Long Beach, CA

South East Associated Ministries (SEAM), Louisville, KY

South Hills Interfaith Ministries, Library, PA

Southeast Ecumenical Ministry, Rochester, NY

Southside Area Ministries, Inc. (SAM), Fort Worth, TX

Toledo Ecumenical Area Ministries, Toledo, OH

United Churches of Lycoming County, Williamsport, PA

United Ministries, Greenville, SC

United Religious Community of St. Joseph County, South Bend, IN

Washington Association of Churches, Seattle, WA

West Central Neighborhood Ministry, Inc., Fort Wayne, IN

West Virginia Council of Churches, Charleston, WV

Wilkinsburg Community Ministry, Pittsburgh, PA

York County Council of Churches, York, PA

Immigration Issues

Association of Religious Communities, Danbury, CT

Christian Council of Metropolitan Atlanta, Atlanta, GA

Churches United of the Quad City Area, Rock Island, IL

Community Ministries of Rockville, Rockville, MD

Concerned Ecumenical Ministry to the Upper West Side, Buffalo, NY

Council of Churches of Chemung County, Inc., Elmira, NY

Eastern Area Community Ministries, Louisville, KY

Ecumenical Ministries of Iowa (EMI), Des Moines, IA

The Joint Religious Legislative Coalition, Minneapolis, MN

Lincoln Interfaith Council, Lincoln, NE

The Long Island Council of Churches, Hempstead, NY

Minnesota Council of Churches, Minneapolis, MN

New York State Community of Churches, Inc., Albany, NY

Peoria Friendship House of Christian Service, Peoria, IL

The Rhode Island State Council of Churches, Providence, RI

Rural Migrant Ministry, Poughkeepsie, NY

San Fernando Valley Interfaith Council, Chatsworth, CA

South Coast Ecumenical Council, Long Beach, CA

Southside Area Ministries, Inc. (SAM), Fort Worth, TX

West Virginia Council of Churches, Charleston, WV

Interfaith Dialogue/ Relationships

Akron Area Association of Churches, Akron, OH

Arkansas Interfaith Conference, Scott, AR

The Associated Churches of Fort Wayne & Allen County, Inc., Fort Wayne, IN

Associated Ministries of Tacoma-Pierce County, Tacoma, WA

Associated Ministries of Thurston County, Olympia, WA

Association of Christian Churches, Sioux Falls, SD

Association of Religious Communities, Danbury, CT

Attleboro Area Council of Churches, Inc., Attleboro, MA

Austin Metropolitan Ministries, Austin, TX

Brooklyn Council of Churches, Brooklyn, NY

Broome County Council of Churches, Inc., Binghamton, NY

Capital Area Council of Churches, Inc., Albany, NY

Christian Churches United of the Tri-County Area, Harrisburg, PA

Christian Conference of Connecticut (CHRISCON), Hartford, CT

The Christian Council of Delaware and Maryland's Eastern Shore, Wilmington, DE

Christian Council of Metropolitan Atlanta, Atlanta, GA

Church Council of Greater Seattle, Seattle, WA

Churches United of the Quad City Area, Rock Island, IL

Community Ministries of Rockville, Rockville, MD

Community Ministry of Montgomery County, Rockville, MD

Concerned Ecumenical Ministry to the Upper West Side, Buffalo, NY

Cooperative Metropolitan Ministries, Newton, MA

Council of Churches of Chemung County, Inc., Elmira, NY

Council of Churches of the City of New York, New York, NY

Council of Churches of Greater Springfield, Springfield, MA

Council of Churches and Synagogues of Southwestern Connecticut, Stamford, CT

Des Moines Area Religious Council, Des Moines, IA

Dutchess Interfaith Council, Inc., Poughkeepsie, NY

East End Cooperative Ministry, Pittsburgh, PA

Eastern Area Community Ministries, Louisville, KY

Ecclesia, Trenton, NJ

Ecumenical Conference of Greater Altoona, Altoona, PA

Evanston Ecumenical Action Council, Evanston, IL

Florida Council of Churches, Orlando, FL

Georgia Christian Council, Macon, GA

Grand Rapids Area Center for Ecumenism (GRACE), Grand Rapids, MI

Greater Chicago Broadcast Ministries, Chicago, IL

Greater Dayton Christian Connection, Dayton, OH

Greater New Orleans Federation of Churches, New Orleans, LA

Greater Rochester Community of Churches, Rochester, NY

Greater Waterbury Interfaith Ministries, Inc., Waterbury, CT

Greensboro Urban Ministry, Greensboro, NC

In One Accord, Battle Creek, MI

Inter-Church Ministries of Erie County, Erie, PA

Interchurch Ministries of Nebraska, Lincoln, NE

Interfaith Community Council, Inc., New Albany, IN

Interfaith Community Services, St. Joseph, MO

Interfaith Conference of Greater Milwaukee, Milwaukee, WI

InterFaith Conference of Metropolitan Washington, Washington, DC

Interfaith Council of Contra Costa County, Walnut Creek, CA

Inter-Faith Ministries-Wichita, Wichita, KS

Interfaith Mission Service, Huntsville, AL

InterReligious Council of Central New York, Syracuse, NY

Kentuckiana Interfaith Community, Louisville, KY

Lancaster County Council of Churches, Lancaster, PA

Lincoln Interfaith Council, Lincoln, NE

The Long Island Council of Churches, Hempstead, NY

Marin Interfaith Council, San Rafael, CA

Massachusetts Council of Churches, Boston, MA

Metropolitan Christian Council of Philadelphia, Philadelphia, PA

Metropolitan Interfaith Council on Affordable Housing (MICAH), Minneapolis, MN

265

Minnesota Council of Churches, Minneapolis, MN

Montana Association of Churches, Billings, MT

Network of Religious Communities, Buffalo, NY

New Britain Area Conference of Churches (NEWBRACC), New Britain, CT

New Hampshire Council of Churches, Concord, NH

New Mexico Conference of Churches, Albuquerque, NM

New York State Community of Churches, Inc., Albany, NY

North Carolina Council of Churches, Raleigh, NC

Northern California Interreligious Conference, San Francisco, CA

Northern Kentucky Interfaith Commission, Inc., Newport, KY

Northwest Interfaith Movement, Philadelphia, PA

Oak Park-River Forest Community of Congregations, Oak Park, IL

Ohio Council of Churches, Columbus, OH

Oklahoma Conference of Churches, Oklahoma City, OK

Peoria Friendship House of Christian Service, Peoria, IL

The Rhode Island State Council of Churches, Providence, RI

San Fernando Valley Interfaith Council, Chatsworth, CA

South Carolina Christian Action Council, Inc., Columbia, SC

South Coast Ecumenical Council, Long Beach, CA

South Hills Interfaith Ministries, Library, PA

Southern California Ecumenical Council, Pasadena, CA

Toledo Ecumenical Area Ministries, Toledo, OH

United Religious Community of St. Joseph County, South Bend, IN

Vermont Ecumenical Council and Bible Society, Burlington, VT

Washington Association of Churches, Seattle, WA

West Virginia Council of Churches, Charleston, WV

Wisconsin Council of Churches, Sun Prairie, WI

Worcester County Ecumenical Council, Worcester, MA

York County Council of Churches, York, PA

Prison Chaplaincy

The Associated Churches of Fort Wayne & Allen County, Inc., Fort Wayne, IN

Association of Christian Churches, Sioux Falls, SD

Broome County Council of Churches, Inc., Binghamton, NY

Christian Churches United of the Tri-County Area, Harrisburg, PA

Christian Conference of Connecticut (CHRISCON), Hartford, CT

Christians United in Beaver County, Beaver, PA

Church Council of Greater Seattle, Seattle, WA

The Church Federation of Greater Indianapolis, Inc., Indianapolis, IN

Council of Christian Communions of Greater Cincinnati, Cincinnati, OH

Council of Churches of the City of New York, New York, NY

Council of Churches of Greater Springfield, Springfield, MA

Ecclesia, Trenton, NJ

Ecumenical Conference of Greater Altoona, Altoona, PA

Ecumenical Ministries, Fulton, MO

Ecumenical Ministries of Iowa (EMI), Des Moines, IA

Genesee County Churches United, Inc., Batavia, NY

Georgia Christian Council, Macon, GA

Greater Bethlehem Area Council of Churches, Bethlehem, PA

Greater Dayton Christian Connection, Dayton, OH

Greater Minneapolis Council of Churches, Minneapolis, MN

The Greater Wheeling Council of Churches, Wheeling, WV

Interfaith Council of Contra Costa County, Walnut Creek, CA

InterReligious Council of Central New York, Syracuse, NY

Lincoln Interfaith Council, Lincoln, NE

The Long Island Council of Churches, Hempstead, NY

Madison Urban Ministry, Madison, WI

Minnesota Council of Churches, Minneapolis, MN

Network of Religious Communities, Buffalo, NY

New Hampshire Council of Churches, Concord, NH

North Dakota Conference of Churches, Bismarck, ND

Northern Kentucky Interfaith Commission, Inc., Newport, KY

Ohio Council of Churches, Columbus, OH

The Pennsylvania Council of Churches, Harrisburg, PA

The Rhode Island State Council of Churches, Providence, RI

Toledo Ecumenical Area Ministries, Toledo, OH

United Churches of Lycoming County, Williamsport, PA

West Virginia Council of Churches, Charleston, WV

Wisconsin Council of Churches, Sun Prairie, WI

York County Council of Churches, York, PA

Public Education Advocacy

Akron Area Association of Churches, Akron, OH

Arkansas Interfaith Conference, Scott, AR

The Associated Churches of Fort Wayne & Allen County, Inc., Fort Wayne, IN

California Council of Churches/California Church Impact, Sacramento, CA

The Capitol Region Conference of Churches, Hartford, CT

Christian Community Action~, New Haven, CT

Church Council of Greater Seattle, Seattle, WA

Community Ministries of Rockville, Rockville, MD

Community Ministry of Montgomery County, Rockville, MD

Council of Churches of the City of New York, New York, NY

Council of Churches of Greater Springfield, Springfield, MA

East End Cooperative Ministry, Pittsburgh, PA

Ecclesia, Trenton, NJ

Ecumenical Ministries, Fulton, MO

Ecumenical Ministries of Iowa (EMI), Des Moines, IA

Evanston Ecumenical Action Council, Evanston, IL

Greater Bethlehem Area Council of Churches, Bethlehem, PA

Greater Fairmont Council of Churches, Fairmont, WV

Greater Minneapolis Council of Churches, Minneapolis, MN

Greater Rochester Community of Churches, Rochester, NY

Greater Waterbury Interfaith Ministries, Inc., Waterbury, CT

In One Accord, Battle Creek, MI

Interchurch Ministries of Nebraska, Lincoln, NE

Interfaith Conference of Greater Milwaukee, Milwaukee, WI

Interfaith Council of Contra Costa County, Walnut Creek, CA

Lincoln Interfaith Council, Lincoln, NE

The Long Island Council of Churches, Hempstead, NY

Madison Urban Ministry, Madison, WI

Marin Interfaith Council, San Rafael, CA

Massachusetts Council of Churches, Boston, MA

Metropolitan Christian Council of Philadelphia, Philadelphia, PA

Metropolitan Interfaith Council on Affordable Housing (MICAH), Minneapolis, MN

Minnesota Council of Churches, Minneapolis, MN

Network of Religious Communities, Buffalo, NY

New Hampshire Council of Churches, Concord, NH

New York State Community of Churches, Inc., Albany, NY

North Carolina Council of Churches, Raleigh, NC

Northern California Interreligious Conference, San Francisco, CA

Pennsylvania Conference on Interchurch Cooperation, Harrisburg, PA

The Pennsylvania Council of Churches, Harrisburg, PA

Peoria Friendship House of Christian Service, Peoria, IL

South Carolina Christian Action Council, Inc., Columbia, SC

Tarrant Area Community of Churches, Fort Worth, TX

Toledo Ecumenical Area Ministries, Toledo, OH

United Churches of Lycoming County, Williamsport, PA

Washington Association of Churches, Seattle, WA

West Virginia Council of Churches, Charleston, WV

Wisconsin Council of Churches, Sun Prairie, WI

Refugee Assistance Programs

Association of Religious Communities, Danbury, CT

Austin Metropolitan Ministries, Austin, TX

Christian Council of Metropolitan Atlanta, Atlanta, GA

Churches United of the Quad City Area, Rock Island, IL

Eastern Area Community Ministries, Louisville, KY

Greater Rochester Community of Churches, Rochester, NY

InterReligious Council of Central New York, Syracuse, NY

The Joint Religious Legislative Coalition, Minneapolis, MN

Lincoln Interfaith Council, Lincoln, NE

The Long Island Council of Churches, Hempstead, NY

Minnesota Council of Churches, Minneapolis, MN

Network of Religious Communities, Buffalo, NY

Southside Area Ministries, Inc. (SAM), Fort Worth, TX

United Churches of Lycoming County, Williamsport, PA

United Religious Community of St. Joseph County, South Bend, IN

West Virginia Council of Churches, Charleston, WV

Rural Issues

Alaska Christian Conference, Fairbanks, AK

Association of Christian Churches, Sioux Falls, SD

267

Ecumenical Ministries of Iowa (EMI), Des Moines, IA

Florida Council of Churches, Orlando, FL

Georgia Christian Council, Macon, GA

Illinois Conference of Churches, Springfield, IL

Interchurch Ministries of Nebraska, Lincoln, NE

Interfaith Conference of Greater Milwaukee, Milwaukee, WI

The Joint Religious Legislative Coalition, Minneapolis, MN

Kansas Ecumenical Ministries, Topeka, KS

Kentucky Council of Churches, Lexington, KY

Lincoln Interfaith Council, Lincoln, NE

Madison Urban Ministry, Madison, WI

Michigan Ecumenical Forum, Lansing, MI

Minnesota Council of Churches, Minneapolis, MN

New York State Community of Churches, Inc., Albany, NY

North Carolina Council of Churches, Raleigh, NC

North Dakota Conference of Churches, Bismarck, ND

Ohio Council of Churches, Columbus, OH

Oklahoma Conference of Churches, Oklahoma City, OK

The Pennsylvania Council of Churches, Harrisburg, PA

The Rhode Island State Council of Churches, Providence, RI

United Churches of Lycoming County, Williamsport, PA

Washington Association of Churches, Seattle, WA

West Virginia Council of Churches, Charleston, WV

Wisconsin Council of Churches, Sun Prairie, WI

Senior Citizen Programs

Allegheny Valley Association of Churches, Natrona Heights, PA

Association of Religious Communities, Danbury, CT

Attleboro Area Council of Churches, Inc., Attleboro, MA

Austin Metropolitan Ministries, Austin, TX

Broome County Council of Churches, Inc., Binghamton, NY

Capital Area Council of Churches, Inc., Albany, NY

The Capitol Region Conference of Churches, Hartford, CT

Center City Churches, Hartford, CT

Center for Community Concerns, Racine, WI

Christians United in Beaver County, Beaver, PA

Church Council of Greater Seattle, Seattle, WA

Community Ministries of Rockville, Rockville, MD

Concerned Ecumenical Ministry to the Upper West Side, Buffalo, NY

Council of Churches of the Ozarks, Springfield, MO

Council of Churches and Synagogues of Southwestern Connecticut, Stamford, CT

Eastern Area Community Ministries, Louisville, KY

Fern Creek/Highview United Ministries, Louisvlle, KY

Florida Council of Churches, Orlando, FL

Genesee-Orleans Ministry of Concern, Albion, NY

Georgia Christian Council, Macon, GA

Greater Dayton Christian Connection, Dayton, OH

Greater Minneapolis Council of Churches, Minneapolis, MN

Inter-Church Ministries of Erie County, Erie, PA

Interfaith Community Council, Inc., New Albany, IN

Interfaith Community Services, St. Joseph, MO

Interfaith Council of Contra Costa County, Walnut Creek, CA

InterReligious Council of Central New York, Syracuse, NY

The Joint Religious Legislative Coalition, Minneapolis, MN

Lincoln Interfaith Council, Lincoln, NE

The Long Island Council of Churches, Hempstead, NY

Marin Interfaith Council, San Rafael, CA

North Carolina Council of Churches, Raleigh, NC

Northside Inter-Church Agency (NICA), Fort Worth, TX

Northwest Interfaith Movement, Philadelphia, PA

Oak Park-River Forest Community of Congregations, Oak Park, IL

Peoria Friendship House of Christian Service, Peoria, IL

The Rhode Island State Council of Churches, Providence, RI

San Fernando Valley Interfaith Council, Chatsworth, CA

South Hills Interfaith Ministries, Library, PA

Southeast Ecumenical Ministry, Rochester, NY

Southside Area Ministries, Inc. (SAM), Fort Worth, TX

Tarrant Area Community of Churches, Fort Worth, TX

Toledo Ecumenical Area Ministries, Toledo, OH

United Churches of Lycoming County, Williamsport, PA

West Central Neighborhood Ministry, Inc., Fort Wayne, IN

West Virginia Council of Churches, Charleston, WV

Wisconsin Council of Churches, Sun Prairie, WI

Substance Abuse Programs

Christian Conference of Connecticut (CHRISCON), Hartford, CT
Community Ministries of Rockville, Rockville, MD
Council of Churches of Greater Springfield, Springfield, MA
Council of Churches of the Ozarks, Springfield, MO
East End Cooperative Ministry, Pittsburgh, PA
Georgia Christian Council, Macon, GA
Greensboro Urban Ministry, Greensboro, NC
The Joint Religious Legislative Coalition, Minneapolis, MN
Lincoln Interfaith Council, Lincoln, NE
The Long Island Council of Churches, Hempstead, NY
Metropolitan Ecumenical Ministry Community Development Corp., Newark, NJ
New Hampshire Council of Churches, Concord, NH
New York State Community of Churches, Inc., Albany, NY
Northside Common Ministries, Pittsburgh, PA
Toledo Ecumenical Area Ministries, Toledo, OH
United Religious Community of St. Joseph County, South Bend, IN
York County Council of Churches, York, PA

Theology and Worship Programs

Akron Area Association of Churches, Akron, OH
Associated Ministries of Tacoma-Pierce County, Tacoma, WA
Attleboro Area Council of Churches, Inc., Attleboro, MA
Broome County Council of Churches, Inc., Binghamton, NY
Capital Area Council of Churches, Inc., Albany, NY
Christian Council of Metropolitan Atlanta, Atlanta, GA
Church Council of Greater Seattle, Seattle, WA
The Church Federation of Greater Indianapolis, Inc., Indianapolis, IN
Churches United of the Quad City Area, Rock Island, IL
Council of Churches and Synagogues of Southwestern Connecticut, Stamford, CT
Eastern Area Community Ministries, Louisville, KY
Ecclesia, Trenton, NJ
Ecumenical Conference of Greater Altoona, Altoona, PA
Ecumenical Ministries, Fulton, MO
Ecumenical Ministries of Iowa (EMI), Des Moines, IA
Georgia Christian Council, Macon, GA

Grand Rapids Area Center for Ecumenism (GRACE), Grand Rapids, MI
Greater Bethlehem Area Council of Churches, Bethlehem, PA
Greater Dayton Christian Connection, Dayton, OH
Greater Fairmont Council of Churches, Fairmont, WV
Greater New Orleans Federation of Churches, New Orleans, LA
Greater Rochester Community of Churches, Rochester, NY
The Greater Wheeling Council of Churches, Wheeling, WV
Greensboro Urban Ministry, Greensboro, NC
Illinois Conference of Churches, Springfield, IL
In One Accord, Battle Creek, MI
Indiana Partners for Christian Unity and Mission, Indianapolis, IN
Interchurch Ministries of Nebraska, Lincoln, NE
Interfaith Council of Contra Costa County, Walnut Creek, CA
Interfaith Mission Service, Huntsville, AL
Kentucky Council of Churches, Lexington, KY
Lincoln Interfaith Council, Lincoln, NE
The Long Island Council of Churches, Hempstead, NY
Marin Interfaith Council, San Rafael, CA
Massachusetts Council of Churches, Boston, MA
Metropolitan Christian Council of Philadelphia, Philadelphia, PA
Michigan Ecumenical Forum, Lansing, MI
Network of Religious Communities, Buffalo, NY
New Britain Area Conference of Churches (NEWBRACC), New Britain, CT
New Mexico Conference of Churches, Albuquerque, NM
North Carolina Council of Churches, Raleigh, NC
Northern Kentucky Interfaith Commission, Inc., Newport, KY
Oak Park-River Forest Community of Congregations, Oak Park, IL
The Rhode Island State Council of Churches, Providence, RI
Schenectady Inner City Ministry, Schenectady, NY
South Coast Ecumenical Council, Long Beach, CA
South East Associated Ministries (SEAM), Louisville, KY
Southern California Ecumenical Council, Pasadena, CA
Tarrant Area Community of Churches, Fort Worth, TX
Toledo Ecumenical Area Ministries, Toledo, OH
United Churches of Lycoming County, Williamsport, PA

269

United Religious Community of St. Joseph County, South Bend, IN

Washington Association of Churches, Seattle, WA

West Virginia Council of Churches, Charleston, WV

Wisconsin Council of Churches, Sun Prairie, WI

Worcester County Ecumenical Council, Worcester, MA

Women's Issues

The Associated Churches of Fort Wayne & Allen County, Inc., Fort Wayne, IN

Center for the Prevention of Sexual and Domestic Violence, Seattle, WA

Christian Council of Metropolitan Atlanta, Atlanta, GA

The Church Federation of Greater Indianapolis, Inc., Indianapolis, IN

Churches United of the Quad City Area, Rock Island, IL

Community Ministries of Rockville, Rockville, MD

Concerned Ecumenical Ministry to the Upper West Side, Buffalo, NY

Council of Churches of the City of New York, New York, NY

Council of Churches of Greater Springfield, Springfield, MA

East End Cooperative Ministry, Pittsburgh, PA

Ecclesia, Trenton, NJ

Georgia Christian Council, Macon, GA

The Greater Wheeling Council of Churches, Wheeling, WV

The Joint Religious Legislative Coalition, Minneapolis, MN

Lincoln Interfaith Council, Lincoln, NE

The Long Island Council of Churches, Hempstead, NY

Marin Interfaith Council, San Rafael, CA

Massachusetts Council of Churches, Boston, MA

Metropolitan Christian Council of Philadelphia, Philadelphia, PA

Network of Religious Communities, Buffalo, NY

New Mexico Conference of Churches, Albuquerque, NM

New York State Community of Churches, Inc., Albany, NY

North Carolina Council of Churches, Raleigh, NC

Oklahoma Conference of Churches, Oklahoma City, OK

Peoria Friendship House of Christian Service, Peoria, IL

The Rhode Island State Council of Churches, Providence, RI

South Carolina Christian Action Council, Inc., Columbia, SC

South Coast Ecumenical Council, Long Beach, CA

South Hills Interfaith Ministries, Library, PA

Toledo Ecumenical Area Ministries, Toledo, OH

United Churches of Lycoming County, Williamsport, PA

United Ministries, Greenville, SC

Washington Association of Churches, Seattle, WA

Wisconsin Council of Churches, Sun Prairie, WI

Youth Activities

Arkansas Interfaith Conference, Scott, AR

The Associated Churches of Fort Wayne & Allen County, Inc., Fort Wayne, IN

Attleboro Area Council of Churches, Inc., Attleboro, MA

Austin Metropolitan Ministries, Austin, TX

Brooklyn Council of Churches, Brooklyn, NY

Broome County Council of Churches, Inc., Binghamton, NY

Center City Churches, Hartford, CT

Christian Council of Metropolitan Atlanta, Atlanta, GA

Church Council of Greater Seattle, Seattle, WA

The Church Federation of Greater Indianapolis, Inc., Indianapolis, IN

Churches United of the Quad City Area, Rock Island, IL

Concerned Ecumenical Ministry to the Upper West Side, Buffalo, NY

Council of Churches of Greater Bridgeport, Inc., Bridgeport, CT

East End Cooperative Ministry, Pittsburgh, PA

Eastern Area Community Ministries, Louisville, KY

Ecclesia, Trenton, NJ

Ecumenical Ministries, Fulton, MO

Fern Creek/Highview United Ministries, Louisvlle, KY

Georgia Christian Council, Macon, GA

Grand Rapids Area Center for Ecumenism (GRACE), Grand Rapids, MI

Greater Fairmont Council of Churches, Fairmont, WV

Greater Minneapolis Council of Churches, Minneapolis, MN

The Greater Wheeling Council of Churches, Wheeling, WV

Interfaith Community Services, St. Joseph, MO

Interfaith Council of Contra Costa County, Walnut Creek, CA

Lincoln Interfaith Council, Lincoln, NE

The Long Island Council of Churches, Hempstead, NY

Marin Interfaith Council, San Rafael, CA

Metropolitan Ecumenical Ministry Community Development Corp., Newark, NJ

Network of Religious Communities, Buffalo, NY

New Britain Area Conference of Churches (NEWBRACC), New Britain, CT

8. Canadian Regional and Local Ecumenical Bodies

Most of the organizations listed below are councils of churches in which churches participate officially, whether at the parish or judicatory level. They operate at the city, metropolitan area, or county level. Parish clusters within urban areas are not included.

Canadian local ecumenical bodies operate without paid staff, with the exception of a few that have part-time staff. In most cases the name and address of the president or chairperson is listed. As these offices change from year to year, some of this information may be out of date by the time the *Yearbook of American & Canadian Churches* is published. Up-to-date information may be secured from the Canadian Council of Churches, 40 St. Clair Ave. E., Ste. 201, Toronto, ON M4T 1M9.

ALBERTA

Calgary Council of Churches
Stephen Kendall, Treas. 1009 - 15 Ave. SW, Calgary, Alberta T3R 0S5

Calgary Inter-Faith Community Association
Rev. V. Hennig, 7515 7th St.SW, Calgary, Alberta T2V 1G1

Calgary Inter-Faith SAWDAP
Mrs. Caroline Brown, #240-15 Ave. SW, Calgary, Alberta T2R 0P7

ATLANTIC PROVINCES

Atlantic Ecumenical Council of Churches
Pres., Rev. John E. Boyd, Box 637, 90 Victoria St., Amherst, Nova Scotia B4H 4B4

Pictou Council of Churches
Rev. D. J. Murphy, Sec., P.O. Box 70, Pictou, Nova Scotia B0K 1H0

BRITISH COLUMBIA

Canadian Ecumenical Action
Co-ordinator, 1410 West 12th Ave., Vancouver, British Columbia V6H 1M8

Greater Victoria Council of Churches
c/o Rev. Edwin Taylor, St. Alban's Church, 1468 Ryan St. at Balmont, Victoria, British Columbia V8R 2X1

Vancouver Council of Churches
Murray Moerman, 700 Kingsway, Vancouver, British Columbia V5V 3C1 Tel. (604)420-0761

MANITOBA

Association of Christian Churches in Manitoba
The Rev. Ted Chell, President, 484 Maryland St., Winnipeg, Manitoba R3G 1M5 Tel. (204)774-3143 or (204)775-3536

NEW BRUNSWICK

First Miramichi Inter-Church Council
Pres., Ellen Robinson, Doaktown, New Brunswick E0C 1G0

Moncton Area Council of Churches
Rev. Yvon Berrieau, Visitation Ministry, Grande Digue, New Brunswick E0A 1SO

UC Maritime Conference ICIF Com.
The Rev. Leslie Robinson, P.O. Box 174, Chipman, New Brunswick, E0E 1C0 Tel. (506)339-6626 Email: maronf@nbnet.nb.ca

NOVA SCOTIA

Amherst and Area Council of Churches
Mrs. Jean Miller, President, R.R.#3 1065 HWY 204, Amherst, Nova Scotia B4H 3Y1 Tel. (902)667-8107

Atlantic Ecumenical Council of Churches
The Rev. P.A. Sandy MacDonald, 4 Pinehill Road, Dartmouth, Nova Scotia B3A 2E6 Tel.(902)469-4480 or (902)466-6247

Bridgewater Inter-Church Council
Pres., Wilson Jones, 30 Parkdale Ave., Bridgewater, Nova Scotia B4V 1L8

Cornwallis District Inter-Church Council
Pres., Mr. Tom Regan, Centreville, R.R. #2, Kings County, Nova Scotia BOT 1JO

Halifax-Dartmouth Council of Churches
Mrs. Betty Short, 3 Virginia Avenue, Dartmouth, Nova Scotia B2W 2Z4

Industrial Cape Breton Council of Churches
Rev. Karen Ralph, 24 Huron Ave., Sydney Mines, Nova Scotia B1S 1V2

Kentville Council of Churches
Rev. Canon S.J.P. Davies, 325-325 Main St., Kentville, Nova Scotia B4N 1C5

Lunenburg Queens BA Association
Mrs. Nilda Chute, 56 Hillside Dr., R.R.#4, Bridgewater, Nova Scotia B4V 2W3

Mahone Bay Interchurch Council
Patricia Joudrey, R.R. #1., Blockhouse, Nova Scotia BOJ1EO

Queens County Association of Churches
Mr. Donald Burns, Box 537, Liverpool, Nova Scotia BOT 1K6

ONTARIO

Burlington Inter-Church Council
Mr. Fred Townsend, 425 Breckenwood, Burlington, Ontario L7L 2J6

Christian Council—Capital Area
Fr. Peter Shonenback, 1247 Kilborn Ave., Ottawa, Ontario K1H 6K9

Christian Leadership Council of Downtown Toronto
Ken Bhagan, Chair, 40 Homewood Ave, #509, Toronto, Ontario M4Y 2K2

Ecumenical Committee
Rev. William B. Kidd, 76 Eastern Ave., Sault Ste. Marie, Ontario P6A 4R2

Glengarry-Prescott-Russell Christian Council
Pres., Rev. G. Labrosse, St. Eugene's, Prescott, Ontario KOB 1PO

Hamilton & District Christian Churches Association
The Rev. Dr. John Johnston, 147 Chedoke Avenue, Hamilton, Ontario L8P 4P2 Tel. (905)529-6896, [O] (905)528-2730 Fax (509)521-2539

Ignace Council of Churches
Box 5, 205 Pine St., St. Ignace, Ontario P0T 1H0

Inter Church Council of Burlington
Michael Bittle, Box 62120 Burlington Mall R.P.O., Burlington, Ontario L7R 4K2 Tel. (905)526-1523 Fax(509)526-9056
Email: mbittle@istar.ca
Website: http://home.istar.cal/mbittle/eo_schl.htm

Kitchener-Waterloo Council of Churches
Rev. Clarence Hauser, CR, 53 Allen St. E., Waterloo, Ontario N2J 1J3

London Inter-City Faith Team
David Carouthers, Chair, c/o United Church, 711 Colbourne St., London, Ontario N6A 3Z4

Massey Inter-Church Council
The Rev. Hope Jackson, Box 238, Massey, Ontario P0P 1P0 Tel. (705)865-2630

Ottawa Christian Council of the Capital Area
1247 Kilborn Ave., Ottawa, Ontario K1H 6K9

St. Catharines & Dist. Clergy Fellowship
Rev. Victor Munro, 663 Vince4 St., St. Catharines, Ontario L2M 3V8

Spadina-Bloor Interchurch Council
Rev. Frances Combes, Chair, c/o Bathurst St. United Church, 427 Bloor St. W, Toronto, Ontario M5S 1X7

Stratford & District Council of Churches
Rev. Ted Heinze, Chair, 202 Erie St., Stratford, Ontario N5A 2M8

Thorold Inter-Faith Council
1 Dunn St., St. Catharines, Ontario L2T 1P3

Thunder Bay Council of Churches
Rev. Richard Darling, 1800 Moodie St. E., Thunder Bay, Ontario P7E 4Z2

PRINCE EDWARD ISLAND

Atlantic Ecumenical Council
The Rev. Arthur Pendergast, Secretary, Immaculate Conception Church, St. Louis, Prince Edward Island C0B 1Z0 Tel. (902)963-2202 or (902) 822-2622

Summerside Christian Council
Ms. A. Kathleen Miller, P.O. Box 1551, Summerside, Prince Edward Island C1N 4K4

QUEBEC

Canadian Centre for Ecumenism/ Centre d'oecuménisme
Fr. Emmanuel Lapierre, 2065 Sherbrooke Street West, Montreal, Quebec H3H 1G6 Tel. (514)937-9176 Fax (514)937-2684

Christian Direction
The Rev. Glen Smith, #3602-465 St. Antoine St. W., Montreal, Quebec H2Z 1J1

The Ecumenical Group
c/o Mrs. C. Haten, 1185 Ste. Foy, St. Bruno, Quebec J3V 3C3

Hemmingford Ecumenical Committee

c/o Catherine Priest, Box 300, Hemmingford, Quebec J0L 1H0

Montréal Council of Churches

The Rev. Ralph Watson, 4995 Coronation Avenue, Montréal, QuÇbec H4V 2E1 Tel. (514)484-7196

Mtl. Association for the Blind Foundation

The Rev. Dr. John A. Simms, 7000 Sherbrooke St. W., Montreal, Quebec H4B 1R3 Tel. (514)489-8201

SASKATCHEWAN

Humboldt Clergy Council

Fr. Leo Hinz, OSB, Box 1989, Humboldt, Saskatchewan S0K 2A0

Melville Association of Churches

Attn., Catherine Gaw, Box 878, Melville, Saskatchewan S0A 2P0

Regina Council of Churches

The Rev. Bud Harper, 5 Robinson Crescent, Regina, Saskatchewan S4R 3R1 Tel. (306)545-3375

Saskatoon Centre for Ecumenism

Nicholas Jesson, 1006 Broadway, Saskatoon, Saskatchewas S7N 1B9 Tel. (306)553-1633 Fax (306)242-8916
Email: sce@sfn.saskatoon.sk.ca

Saskatoon Council of Churches

Dr. Colin Clay, 812 Colony St., Saskatoon, Saskatchewan S7H 0S1

9. Theological Seminaries and Bible Colleges in the United States

The following list includes theological seminaries and departments in colleges and universities in which ministerial training is given. Many denominations have additional programs. The lists of "Religious Bodies in the United States" (Directory 3) should be consulted for the address of denominational headquarters.

Inclusion in or exclusion from this list implies no judgment about the quality or accreditation of any institution. Those schools that are members (both accredited and affiliated) of the Association of Theological Schools are marked with a "*". Additional information about enrollment in ATS member schools can be found in the "Trends in Seminary Enrollment" section of chapter III.

Each of the listings include: the institution name, denominational sponsor when appropriate, location, the president or dean of the institution, telephone and fax numbers, and email and website addresses when available.

Abilene Christian University, (Churches of Christ), ACU Station Box 29100, Abilene, TX 79699-9100. Royce Money, Ph.D. Tel. (915) 674-2412 Fax (915) 674-2958
Email: moneyr@nicanor.acu.edu
Website: http://www.acu.edu

Alaska Bible College, (Nondenominational), P.O. Box 289, Glennallen, AK 99588. Steven J. Hostetter Tel. (907) 822-3201 Fax (907) 822-5027
Email: info@akbible.edu
Website: www.akbible.edu

Alliance Theological Seminary,* (The Christian and Missionary Alliance), 350 N. Highland Ave., Nyack, NY 10960-1416. David L. Rambo Tel. (914) 353-2020 Fax (914) 358-2651

American Baptist College, (National Baptist Convention U.S.A., Inc.), 1800 Baptist World Center Dr., Nashville, TN 37207. Bernard Lafayette Tel. (615) 262-1369 Fax (615) 226-7855

American Baptist Seminary of the West,* (American Baptist Churches in the U .S.A.), 2606 Dwight Way, Berkeley, CA 94704-3029. Dr. Keith A. Russell Tel. (510) 841-1905 Fax (510) 841-2446
Email: dschirer@absw.edu
Website: www.absw.edu

Anderson University School of Theology,* (Church of God- Anderson, Indiana), Anderson University, Anderson, IN 46012-3495. David Sebastian Tel. (765) 641-4032 Fax (765) 641-3005

Andover Newton Theological School,* (American Baptist Churches in the U .S.A.; United Church of Christ), 210 Herrick Rd., Newton Centre, MA 02459. Benjamin Griffin Tel. (617) 964-1100 Fax (617) 965-9756
Email: admissions@ants.edu
Website: www.ants.edu

Appalachian Bible College, (Nondenominational), P.O. Box ABC, Bradley, WV 25818. Daniel L. Anderson Tel. (304) 877-6428 or (800)6789 ABC Fax (304) 877-5082
Email: abc@appbibco.edu
Website: www.abc.edu

Aquinas Institute of Theology,* (The Roman Catholic Church), 3642 Lindell Blvd., St. Louis, MO 63108. Charles E. Bouchard Tel. (314) 977-3882 Fax (314) 977-7225
Email: aquinas@slu.edu
Website: www.ai.edu

Arizona College of the Bible, (Interdenominational), 2045 W. Northern Ave., Phoenix, AZ 85021-5197. Douglas K. Winn Tel. (602) 995-2670 Fax (602) 864-8183

Arlington Baptist College, (Baptist), 3001 W. Division, Arlington, TX 76012-3425. David Bryant Tel. (817) 461-8741 Fax (817) 274-1138

Asbury Theological Seminary,* (Interdenominational), 204 N. Lexington Ave., Wilmore, KY 40390-1199. Maxie D. Dunnam Tel. (606) 858-3581 Fax
Website: www.ats.wilmore.ky.us

Ashland Theological Seminary,* (Brethren Church-Ashland, Ohio), 910 Center St., Ashland, OH 44805. Frederick J. Finks Tel. (419) 289-5161 Fax (419) 289-5969

Assemblies of God Theological Seminary,* (Assemblies of God), 1435 North Glenstone Avenue, Springfield, MO 65802-2131. Byron D. Klaus Tel. (417) 268-1000 Fax (417) 268-1001

Associated Mennonite Biblical Seminary,* (Mennonite Church; General Conference Mennonite Church), 3003 Benham Ave., Elkhart, IN 46517-1999. J. Nelson Kraybill Tel. (219) 295-3726 Fax (219) 295-0092
Email: nkraybill@ambs.edu
Website: www.ambs.edu

275

Athenaeum of Ohio,* (The Roman Catholic Church), 6616 Beechmont Ave., Cincinnati, OH 45230-2091. Robert J. Mooney Tel. (513) 231-2223 Fax (513) 231-3254

Atlanta Christian College, (Christian Churches and Churches of Christ), 2605 Ben Hill Rd., East Point, GA 30344. R. Edwin Groover Tel. (404) 761-8861 Fax (404) 669-2024
Website: www.acc.edu

Austin Presbyterian Theological Seminary,* (Presbyterian Church- U.S.A.), 100 E. 27th St., Austin, TX 78705-5797. Robert M. Shelton Tel. (512) 472-6736 Fax (512) 479-0738
Website: www.austinseminary.edu

Azusa Pacific University,* (Interdenominational), 901 E. Alosta, P.O. Box APU, Azusa, CA 91702. Richard Felix Tel. (818) 969-3434 Fax (818) 969-7180

Bangor Theological Seminary,* (United Church of Christ), 300 Union St., Bangor, ME 04401. President Ansley Coe Throckmorton Tel. (207) 942-6781 Fax (207) 942-4914
Email: jwiebe@bts.edu
Website: www.bts.edu

Baptist Bible College, (Baptist Bible Fellowship International), 628 E. Kearney, Springfield, MO 65803. Leland Kennedy Tel. (417) 268-6060 Fax (417) 268-6694

Baptist Bible College and Seminary, (Baptist), 538 Venard Rd., Clarks Summit, PA 18411. Milo Thompson Tel. (570) 586-2400 Fax (570) 586-1753
Email: bbc@bbc.edu
Website: www.bbc.edu

Baptist Missionary Association Theological Seminary, (Baptist Missionary Association of America), 1530 E. Pine St., Jacksonville, TX 75766. Charley Holmes Tel. (903) 586-2501 Fax (903) 586-0378
Email: bmaisem@flash.net-
Website: www.geocities.com/Athens/Acropolis/3386

Baptist Theological Seminary at Richmond,* (Cooperative Baptist Fellowship), 3400 Brook Rd., Richmond, VA 23227. Thomas H. Graves Tel. (804) 355-8135 Fax (804) 355-8182
Email: btsr@mindspring.com

Barclay College, (Interdenominational), P.O. Box 288, Haviland, KS 67059. Walter E. Moody Tel. (316) 862-5252 Fax (316) 862-5403
Email: barclaycollege@havilandtalco.com

Bay Ridge Christian College, (Church of God-Anderson, Indiana), P.O. Box 726, Kendleton, TX 77451. Charles Denniston Tel. (409) 532-3982 Fax (409) 532-4352

Beeson Divinity School of Samford University,* (Interdenominational), 800 Lakeshore Dr., Birmingham, AL 35229-2252. Timothy George, Dean Tel. (205) 726-2991 Fax (205) 726-2260
Email: tfgeorge@samford.edu
Website: http://beeson.samford.edu

Bethany College, (Assemblies of God), 800 Bethany Dr., Scotts Valley, CA 95066. Tom Duncan Tel. (408) 438-3800 Fax (408) 438-4517

Bethany Lutheran Theological Seminary, (Evangelical Lutheran Synod), 6 Browns Ct., Mankato, MN 56001. G. R. Schmeling Tel. (507) 344-7354 Fax (507) 344-7426
Email: gschmeli@blc.edu
Website: http://sem-09.blc.edu/default.html

Bethany Theological Seminary,* (Church of the Brethren), 615 National Rd. W., Richmond, IN 47374. Eugene F. Roop Tel. (765) 983-1800 Fax (765) 983-1840
Email: roopge@earlham.edu

Bethel Theological Seminary,* (Baptist General Conference), 3949 Bethel Dr., St. Paul, MN 55112. George K. Brushaber Tel. (651) 638-6230 Fax (651) 638-6008
Email: webmaster@bethel.edu
Website: www.bethel.edu

Beulah Heights Bible College, (The International Pentecostal Church of Christ), 892 Berne St. SE, Atlanta, GA 30316. Samuel R. Chand Tel. (404) 627-2681 Fax (404) 627-0702
Email: b.h.b.c@beulah.org
Website: www.beulah.org

Bible Church of Christ Theological Institute, (Nondenominational), 1358 Morris, Bronx, NY 10456-1402. Roy Bryant; Sr. Tel. (718)588-2284 Fax (718)992-5597

Biblical Theological Seminary, (Interdenominational), 200 N. Main St., Hatfield, PA 19440. David G. Dunbar Tel. (215) 368-5000 Fax (215) 368-7002

Boise Bible College, (Christian Churches and Churches of Christ), 8695 Marigold St., Boise, ID 83714. Dr. Charles A. Crane Tel. (208) 376-7731 Fax (208) 376-7743
Email: boibible@micron.net
Website: netnow.micron.net/~boibible

Boston University (School of Theology),* (The United Methodist Church), 745 Commonwealth Ave., Boston, MA 02215. Robert C. Neville Tel. (617) 353-3050 Fax (617) 353-3061
Website: web.bu.edu

Brite Divinity School, Texas Christian University, (Christian Church- Disciples of Christ), TCU Box 298130, Ft. Worth, TX 76129. Leo G. Perdue Tel. (817) 921-7575 Fax (817) 921-7305
Email: L.Perdue@tcu.edu
Website: www.brite.tcu.edu/brite/

Calvary Bible College and Theological Seminary, (Independent Fundamental Churches of America), 15800 Calvary Rd., Kansas City, MO 64147-1341. James L. Anderson Tel. (800) 326-3960 Fax (816) 331-4474

Calvin Theological Seminary,* (Christian Reformed Church in North America), 3233 Burton St. S.E., Grand Rapids, MI 49546. President James A. DeJong Tel. (616) 957-6036 Fax (616) 957-8621
Email: kprg@calvin.edu
Website: www.calvin.edu/seminary

Candler School of Theology, Emory University,* (The United Methodist Church), 500 Kilgo Circle N.E., Emory Univ., Atlanta, GA 30322. Charles R. Foster, Interim Dean Tel. (404) 727-6324 Fax (404) 727-3182
Email: candler@emory.edu
Website: www.emory.edu/candler

Catholic Theological Union at Chicago,* (The Roman Catholic Church), 5401 S. Cornell Ave., Chicago, IL 60615-5698. Norman Bevan Tel. (312) 324-8000 Fax (312) 324-8490

Catholic University of America,* (The Roman Catholic Church), 113 Caldwell Hall, Cardinal Sta., Washington, DC 20064. Rev. Raymond F. Collins, STD Dean Tel. (202) 319-5683 Fax (202) 319-4967
Email: cua-deansrs@cua.edu
Website: www.cua.edu/www/srs/

Central Baptist College, (Baptist Missionary Association of Arkansas), 1501 College Ave., Conway, AR 72032. Charles Attebery Tel. (501) 329-6872 Fax (501) 329-2941
Email: CaHebery@admin.cbc.edu
Website: www.cbc.edu

Central Baptist Theological Seminary,* (Baptist), 741 N. 31st St., Kansas City, KS 66102-3964. Thomas E. Clifton Tel. (913) 371-5313 Fax (913) 371-8110
Email: central@cbts.edu
Website: www.cbts.edu

Central Baptist Theological Seminary in Indiana, (National Baptist Convention U.S.A., Inc.), 1535 Dr. A. J. Brown Ave. N., Indianapolis, IN 46202. F. Benjamin Davis Tel. (317) 636-6622 Fax

Central Bible College, (Assemblies of God), 3000 N. Grant Ave., Springfield, MO 65803. H. Maurice Lednicky Tel. (417) 833-2551 Fax (417) 833-5141

Central Christian College of the Bible, (Christian Churches and Churches of Christ), 911 E. Urbandale, Moberly, MO 65270. Lloyd M. Pelfrey Tel. (816) 263-3900 Fax (816) 263-3936
Email: develop@ccb.edu
Website: www.ccb.edu

Central Indian Bible College, (Assemblies of God), P.O. Box 550, Mobridge, SD 57601. Robert Koscak Tel. (605) 845-7801 Fax (605) 845-7744

Chicago Theological Seminary,* (United Church of Christ), 5757 South University Ave., Chicago, IL 60637-1507. Susan Brooks Thistlethwaite Tel. (773) 752-5757 Fax (773) 752-5925
Email: sthistle@chgosem.edu
Website: www.chgosem.edu

Christ the King Seminary,* (The Roman Catholic Church), 711 Knox Rd., P.O. Box 607, East Aurora, NY 14052-0607. Richard W. Siepka Tel. (716) 652-8900 Fax (716) 652-8903

Christ the Savior Seminary, (The American Carpatho-Russian Orthodox Greek Catholic Church), 225 Chandler Ave., Johnstown, PA 15906. Nicholas Smisko Tel. (814) 539-8086 Fax (814) 536-4699

Christian Theological Seminary,* (Christian Church- Disciples of Christ), 1000 W. 42nd St., Indianapolis, IN 46208. Dr. Edward L. Wheeler Tel. (317) 931-2305 Fax (317) 923-1961

Church Divinity School of the Pacific,* (Episcopal Church), 2451 Ridge Rd., Berkeley, CA 94709. Donn F. Morgan Tel. (510) 204-0700 Fax (510) 644-0712
Email: rateaver@cdsp.edu

Church of God Theological Seminary,* (Church of God-Cleveland, Tennessee), P.O. Box 3330, Cleveland, TN 37320-3330. Cecil B. Knight Tel. (423) 478-1131 Fax (423) 478-7711
Email: cogseminary@wingnet.com
Website: www.wingnet.net/~cogseminary

Cincinnati Bible College and Seminary, (Christian Churches and Churches of Christ), 2700 Glenway Ave., Cincinnati, OH 45204-3200. David A. Grubbs Tel. (513) 244-8100 Fax (513) 244-8140
Email: info@cincybible.edu
Website: www.cincybible.edu

Circleville Bible College, (Churches of Christ in Christian Union), P.O. Box 458, Circleville, OH 43113. John Conley Tel. (614) 474-8896 Fax (614) 477-7755
Email: cbc@biblecollege.edu
Website: www.biblecollege.edu

Claremont School of Theology,* (The United Methodist Church), 1325 N. College Ave., Claremont, CA 91711. Robert W. Edgar Tel. (800) 626-7821 Fax (909) 626-7062
Email: admissions@cst.edu
Website: www.cst.edu

Clear Creek Baptist Bible College, (Southern Baptist Convention), 300 Clear Creek Rd.,

Pineville, KY 40977. President Bill Whittaker Tel. (606) 337-3196 Fax (606) 337-2372 Email: ccbbc@ccbbc.edu Website: www.ccbbc.edu

Colegio Biblico Pentecostal de Puerto Rico, (Church of God-Cleveland, Tennessee), P.O. Box 901, Saint Just, PR 00978. Luz M. Rivera Tel. (787) 761-0640 Fax (787) 748-9228

Colgate Rochester/Bexley Hall/Crozer Theological Seminary,* (American Baptist Churches in the USA, Episcopal Church), 1100 S. Goodman St., Rochester, NY 14620. James H. Evans, Jr. Tel. (716) 271-1320 Fax (716) 271-8013 Website: www.crds.edu

Colorado Christian University, (Nondenominational), 180 S. Garrison St., Lakewood, CO 80226. Larry R. Donnithorne Tel. (303) 202-0100 Fax (303) 274-7560 Website: www.ccu.edu

Columbia International University, (Multi-denominational), P.O. Box 3122, Columbia, SC 29230-3122. Johnny V. Miller Tel. (803) 754-4100 Fax (803) 786-4209

Columbia Theological Seminary, (Presbyterian Church- U.S.A.), 701 Columbia Dr., P.O. Box 520, Decatur, GA 30031. Douglas Oldenburg Tel. (404) 378-8821 Fax (404) 377-9696

Concordia Seminary,* (The Lutheran Church-Missouri Synod), 801 De Mun Ave., St. Louis, MO 63105. John F. Johnson Tel. (314) 505-7000 Fax (314) 505-7001

Concordia Theological Seminary,* (The Lutheran Church-Missouri Synod), 6600 N. Clinton St., Ft. Wayne, IN 46825-4996. Dean O. Wenthe Tel. (219) 452-2100 Fax (219) 452-2121 Email: sem_relations@ctsfw.edu Website: www.ctsfw.edu

Covenant Theological Seminary,* (Prebyterian Church in America), 12330 Conway Rd., St. Louis, MO 63141-8697. Bryan Chapell Tel. (314) 434-4044 Fax (314) 434-4819 Email: admissions@covenantseminary.edu Website: www.covenantseminary.edu

Cranmer Seminary, (The Anglican Orthodox Church; The Anglican Rite Synod in the Americas), 2558 Hickory Tree Rd, Winston Salem, NC 27127-9145. The Most Rev. Robert J. Godfrey, Ph.D. Tel. (336)775-9866 Fax (336)775-9867 Email: AOCCRanmer@aol.com Website: www.divinityschool.org

Criswell Center for Biblical Studies, (Southern Baptist Convention), 4010 Gaston Ave., Dallas, TX 75246. Tel. (214) 821-5433 Fax (214) 818-1320

Crown College, (The Christian and Missionary Alliance), 6425 County Rd. 30, St. Bonifacius, MN 55375. Gary M. Benedict Tel. (612) 446-4100 Fax (612) 446-4149 Email: crown@gw.crown.edu Website: www.crown.edu

Cummins Theological Seminary, (Reformed Episcopal Church), 705 S. Main St., Summerville, SC 29483. James C. West Tel. (843) 873-3451 Fax (843) 875-6200 Email: jcw121@aol.com

Dallas Christian College, (Christian Churches and Churches of Christ), 2700 Christian Pkwy, Dallas, TX 75234. Dr. John Derry Tel. (972) 241-3371 Fax (972) 241-8021 Email: dcc@dallas.edu Website: www.dallas.edu

Dallas Theological Seminary,* (Interdenominational), 3909 Swiss Ave., Dallas, TX 75204. Charles R. Swindoll Tel. (214) 824-3094 Fax (214) 841-3625 Website: www.dts.edu

Denver Seminary,* (Conservative Baptist Association of America), Box 10,000, Denver, CO 80250-0100. Clyde B. McDowell, President Tel. (303) 761-2482 Fax (303) 761-8060 Email: info@densem.edu Website: www.gospelcom.net/densem/

The Disciples Divinity House of the University of Chicago, (Christian Church-Disciples of Christ), 1156 E. 57th St., Chicago, IL 60637. Kristine A. Culp, Dean Tel. (773) 643-4411 Fax (773) 643-4413 Email: ddh.uchicago.admin@ibm.net Website: www.uchicago.edu/aff/ddh

Dominican House of Studies,* (The Roman Catholic Church), 487 Michigan Ave. N.E., Washington, DC 20017-1585. Thomas McCreesh, O.P. Tel. (202) 529-5300 Fax (202) 636-4460 Website: www.op-dhs.org

Dominican School of Philosophy and Theology,* (The Roman Catholic Church), 2401 Ridge Rd., Berkeley, CA 94709. Gregory Rocca Tel. (510) 849-2030 Fax (510) 849-1372

Dominican Study Center of Bayamon Central University, (The Roman Catholic Church), Apartado Postal 1968, Bayamon, PR 00960-1968. P. Felix Struik, O.P. Tel. (787) 787-1826 Fax (787) 798-2712

Drew University (Theological School),* (The United Methodist Church), 36 Madison Ave., Madison, NJ 07940-4010. Leonard I. Sweet Tel. (973) 408-3258 Fax (973) 408-3534 Website: www.drew.edu

Duke University (Divinity School),* (The United Methodist Church), Box 90968,

Durham, NC 27708-0968. Dean L. Gregory Jones Tel. (919) 660-3400 Fax (919) 660-3473 Email: lgjones@mail.duke.edu
Website: divinity.duke.edu

Earlham School of Religion,* (Interdenominational-Friends), 228 College Ave., Richmond, IN 47374. Dean Andrew P. Grannell Tel. (800) 432-1377 Fax (765) 983-1688
Email: woodna@earlham.edu
Website: www.esr.earlham.edu/esr

East Coast Bible College, (Church of God-Cleveland, Tennessee), 6900 Wilkinson Blvd., Charlotte, NC 28214. T. David Sustar Tel. (704) 394-2307 Fax (704) 393-3689

Eastern Baptist Theological Seminary,* (American Baptist Churches in the U.S.A.), 6 Lancaster Ave., Wynnewood, PA 19096. Manfred T. Brauch Tel. (800) 220-3487 Fax (610) 649-3834
Website: www.ebts.edu

Eastern Mennonite Seminary,* (Mennonite Church), Eastern Mennonite Seminary, Harrisonburg, VA 22802. George R. Brunk Tel. (540) 432-4260 Fax (540) 432-4444
Email: info@emu.edu
Website: www.emu.edu/units/sem/sem.htm

Eden Theological Seminary,* (United Church of Christ), 475 E. Lockwood Ave., St. Louis, MO 63119. President David M. Greenhaw Tel. (314) 961-3627 Fax (314) 961-9063
Website: www.eden.edu

Emmanuel School of Religion,* (Christian Churches and Churches of Christ), One Walker Dr., Johnson City, TN 37601. C. Robert Wetzel Tel. (423) 926-1186 Fax (423) 926-6198
Email: emmanuel.johnson-city.tn.us
Website: www.esr.edu

Emmaus Bible College, (Christian Brethren—also known as Plymouth Brethren), 2570 Asbury Rd., Dubuque, IA 52001. Daniel H. Smith Tel. (319) 588-8000 Fax (319) 588-1216
Email: info@emmaus.edu
Website: www.emmaus.edu

Episcopal Divinity School,* (Episcopal Church), 99 Brattle St., Cambridge, MA 02138-3494. The Rt. Rev. Steven Charleston, President and Dean Tel. (617) 868-3450 Fax (617) 864-5385
Email: jgerloff@episdivschool.org
Website: www.episdivschool.org

Episcopal Theological Seminary of the Southwest,* (Episcopal Church), P.O. Box 2247, Austin, TX 78768-2247. Durstan R. McDonald Tel. (512) 472-4133 Fax (512) 472-3098

Erskine Theological Seminary,* (Associate Reformed Presbyterian Church—General Synod), Drawer 668, Due West, SC 29639.

John L. Carson Tel. (864) 379-8885 Fax (864) 379-2171
Email: carson@erskine.edu
Website: www.erskine.edu/seminary/

Eugene Bible College, (Open Bible Standard Churches, Inc.), 2155 Bailey Hill Rd., Eugene, OR 97405. Robert L. Whitlow Tel. (503) 485-1780 Fax (503) 343-5801

Evangelical School of Theology,* (The Evangelical Congregational Church), 121 S. College St., Myerstown, PA 17067. Kirby N. Keller Tel. (717) 866-5775 Fax (717) 866-4667
Website: www.evangelical.edu

Faith Baptist Bible College and Theological Seminary, (General Association of Regular Baptist Churches), 1900 N.W. 4th St., Ankeny, IA 50021-2152. Richard W. Houg Tel. (515) 964-0601 Fax (515) 964-1638
Website: www.faith.edu

Faith Evangelical Lutheran Seminary, (Conservative Lutheran Association), 3504 N. Pearl St., Tacoma, WA 98407. R. H. Redal Tel. (206) 752-2020 Fax (206) 759-1790
Email: fsinfo@faithseminary.edu
Website: www.faithseminary.edu

Florida Christian College, (Christian Churches and Churches of Christ), 1011 Bill Beck Blvd., Kissimmee, FL 34744. A. Wayne Lowen Tel. (407) 847-8966 Fax (407) 847-3925
Email: fcc@fcc.edu

Franciscan School of Theology, (The Roman Catholic Church), 1712 Euclid Ave., Berkeley, CA 94709. William M. Cieslak Tel. (510) 848-5232 Fax (510) 549-9466

Free Will Baptist Bible College, (National Association of Free Will Baptists), 3606 West End Ave., Nashville, TN 37205. Tom Malone Tel. (615) 383-1340 Fax (615) 269-6028
Email: president@fwbbc.edu
Website: www.fwbcc.edu

Fuller Theological Seminary,* (Interdenominational), 135 N. Oakland Ave., Pasadena, CA 91182. Richard J. Mouw Tel. (626) 584-5200 Fax (626) 795-8767
Email: jam@fuller.edu
Website: www.fuller.edu

Garrett-Evangelical Theological Seminary,* (The United Methodist Church), 2121 Sheridan Rd., Evanston, IL 60201. Neal F. Fisher Tel. (847) 866-3900 Fax (847) 866-3957
Email: seminary@nwu.edu
Website: www.garrett.nwu.edu

General Theological Seminary, The,* (Episcopal Church), 175 Ninth Ave., New York, NY 10011-4977. Ward B. Ewing Tel. (212) 243-5150 Fax (212) 727-3907
Website: www.gts.edu

George Mercer Jr. Memorial School of Theology, (Episcopal Church), 65 Fourth St., Garden City, NY 11530. -vacant- Tel. (516) 248-4800 Fax (516) 248-4883

God's Bible School and College, (Nondenominational), 1810 Young St., Cincinnati, OH 45210. Michael Avery Tel. (513) 721-7944 Fax (513) 721-3971
Email: GBS.po@juno.com
Website: www.gbs.edu

Golden Gate Baptist Theological Seminary,* (Southern Baptist Convention), 201 Seminary Dr., Mill Valley, CA 94941-3197. William O. Crews Tel. (415) 380-1300 Fax (415) 380-1302
Email: seminary@ggbts.edu
Website: www.ggbts.edu/index.html

Gonzaga University,* (The Roman Catholic Church), Spokane, WA 99258-0001. Fr. Robert Spitzer, S.J. Tel. (509) 328-4220 Fax (509) 323-5718
Email: large@gonzaga.edu

Gordon-Conwell Theological Seminary,* (Interdenominational), 130 Essex St., South Hamilton, MA 01982. Walter C. Kaiser, Jr. Tel. (978) 468-7111 Fax (978) 468-6691
Email: -info@gcts.edu
Website: www.gcts.edu

Grace Bible College, (Grace Gospel Fellowship), P.O. Box 910, Grand Rapids, MI 49509. Bruce Kemper Tel. (616) 538-2330 Fax (616) 538-0599
Email: gbc@gbcol.edu
Website: www.gbcol.edu

Grace Theological Seminary, (Fellowship of Grace Brethren Churches), 200 Seminary Dr., Winona Lake, IN 46590-1294. Ronald E. Manahan Tel. (219) 372-5100 Fax (219) 372-5139
Website: www.grace.edu

Grace University, (Independent), 1311 South 9th St., Omaha, NE 68108. Neal F. McBride Tel. (402) 449-2809 Fax (402) 341-9587

Graduate Theological Union,* (Inter-denominational), 2400 Ridge Rd., Berkeley, CA 94709. John Dillenberger Tel. (510) 649-2400 Fax (510) 649-1417
Email: gtuadm@gtu.edu
Website: www.gtu.edu

Great Lakes Christian College, (Christian Churches and Churches of Christ), 6211 W. Willow Hwy., Lansing, MI 48917. Larry Carter Tel. (517) 321-0242 Fax (517) 321-5902

Greenville College, (Free Methodist Church of North America), 315 E. College Ave., P.O. Box 159, Greenville, IL 62246. President Robert E. Smith Tel. (618) 664-2800 Fax (618) 664-1748
Email: rsmith@Greenville.edu
Website: www.greenville.edu

Harding University Graduate School of Religion, (Churches of Christ), 1000 Cherry Rd., Memphis, TN 38117. Bill Flatt Tel. (901) 761-1352 Fax (901) 761-1358

Hartford Seminary,* (Interdenominational), 77 Sherman St., Hartford, CT 06105-2260. Barbara Brown Zikmund Tel. (860) 509-9502 Fax (860) 509-9509
Email: info@hartsem.edu
Website: www.hartsem.edu

Harvard Divinity School,* (Nondenominational), 45 Francis Ave., Cambridge, MA 02138. J. Pryan Hehir, Chair of the Executive Committee Tel. (617) 495-5761 Fax (617) 495-9489
Website: www.hds.harvard.edu

Hebrew Union College—Jewish Institute of **Religion, NY,** (Jewish), 1 W. 4th St., New York, NY 10012. Sheldon Zimmerman Tel. (212) 674-5300 Fax (212) 533-0129

Hebrew Union College—Jewish Institute of Religion, (Jewish), 3077 University Ave., Los Angeles, CA 90007. Sheldon Zimmerman Tel. (213) 749-3424 Fax (213) 747-6128

Hebrew Union College-Jewish Institute of Religion, OH, (Jewish), 3101 Clifton Ave., Cincinnati, OH 45220. Sheldon Zimmerman Tel. (513) 221-1875 Fax (513) 221-4652
Email: rabbiz@cn.huc.edu
Website: www.huc.edu

Hobe Sound Bible College, (Nondenominational), P.O. Box 1065, Hobe Sound, FL 33475. P. Daniel Stetler Tel. (407) 546-5534 Fax (407) 545-1421

Holy Cross Greek Orthodox School of Theology,* (Greek Orthodox Archdiocese of America), 50 Goddard Ave., Brookline, MA 02445-7495. Very Reverend Damaskinos V. Ganas Tel. (617) 731-3500 Fax (617) 850-1460
Email: admissions@hchc.edu
Website: www.hchc.edu

Holy Trinity Orthodox Seminary, (The Russian Orthodox Church Outside of Russia), P.O. Box 36, Jordanville, NY 13361. Archbishop Laurus Skurla Tel. (315) 858-0940 Fax (315) 858-0505

Hood Theological Seminary,* (African Methodist Episcopal Zion Church), 800 W. Thomas St., Salisbury, NC 28144. Albert J.D. Aymer Tel. (704) 797-1113 Fax (704) 797-1897
Website: www.catawba.edu/html/businf/living/html/hood.htm

Houston Graduate School of Theology,* (Friends), 1311 Holman, Ste. 200, Houston, TX 77004-3833. Dr. David Robinson Tel. (713) 942-9505 Fax (713) 942-9506
Email: hgstinfo@hgst.edu
Website: www.hgst.edu

Howard University School of Divinity,* (Nondenominational), 1400 Shepherd St. N.E., Washington, DC 20017. Clarence G. Newsome Tel. (202) 806-0500 Fax (202) 806-0711

Huntington College, Graduate School of Christian Ministries, (Church of the United Brethren in Christ), 2303 College Ave., Huntington, IN 46750. G. Blair Dowden Tel. (219) 356-6000 Fax (219) 358-3700
Email: gscm@huntington.edu
Website: www.huntington.edu/academics/gscm

Iliff School of Theology,* (The United Methodist Church), 2201 S. University Blvd., Denver, CO 80210. Donald E. Messer Tel. (303) 744-1287 Fax (303) 777-0164
Website: www.iliff.edu

Immaculate Conception Seminary School of Theology,* (The Roman Catholic Church), 400 S. Orange Ave., South Orange, NJ 07079. John W. Flesey Tel. (201) 761-9575 Fax (201) 761-9577

Indiana Wesleyan University, (The Wesleyan Church), 4201 S. Washington, Marion, IN 46953-4999. James Barnes Tel. (765) 674-6901 Fax (765) 677-2499
Email: jbarnes@indwes.edu
Website: www.indwes.edu

Interdenominational Theological Center,* (Interdenominational), 700 Martin L. King, Jr. Dr. S.W., Atlanta, GA 30314. Dr. Robert M. Franklin Tel. (404) 527-7702 Fax (404) 527-7770
Email: rfranklin@itc.edu

International School of Theology,* (non-denominational), 7623 East Avenue, Fontana, CA 92336. Donald A. Weaver Tel. 909-770-4000 Fax 909-770-4001
Website: www.leaderu.com/isot

Jesuit School of Theology at Berkeley,* (The Roman Catholic Church), 1735 LeRoy Ave., Berkeley, CA 94709. T. Howland Sanks Tel. (510) 841-8804 Fax (510) 841-8536

Jewish Theological Seminary of America, (Jewish), 3080 Broadway, New York, NY 10027-4649. Ismar Schorsch Tel. (212) 678-8000 Fax (212) 678-8947
Email: webmaster@jtsa.edu
Website: www.jtsa.edu

John Wesley College, (Interdenominational), 2314 N. Centennial St., High Point, NC 27265. Brian C. Donley Tel. (336) 889-2262 Fax (336) 889-2261
Email: admissions@johnwesley.edu
Website: www.johnwesley.edu

Johnson Bible College, (Christian Churches and Churches of Christ), 7900 Johnson Dr., Knoxville, TN 37998. David L. Eubanks Tel. (423) 573-4517 Fax (423) 251-2336
Email: jbc@jbc.edu
Website: www.jbc.edu

Kansas City College and Bible School, (Church of God- Holiness), 7401 Metcalf Ave., Overland Park, KS 66204. Gayle Woods Tel. (913) 722-0272 Fax (913) 722-2135

Kenrick-Glennon Seminary,* (The Roman Catholic Church), 5200 Glennon Dr., St. Louis, MO 63119. Rev. Msgr. George Lucas Tel. (314) 644-0266 Fax (314) 644-3079

Kentucky Christian College, (Christian Churches and Churches of Christ), 100 Academic Parkway, Grayson, KY 41143. Keith P. Keeran Tel. (606) 474-3246 Fax (606) 474-3155
Email: pres@kcc.edu
Website: www.kcc.edu

Kentucky Mountain Bible College, (Interdenominational), Box 10, Vancleve, KY 41385. Philip Speas Tel. (606) 666-5000 Fax (606) 666-7744

La Sierra University, (Seventh-day Adventist Church), 4700 Pierce St., Riverside, CA 92515-8247. Lawrence T. Geraty Tel. (909) 785-2000 Fax (909) 785-2901
Website: www.lasierra.edu

Lancaster Bible College, (Nondenominational), 901 Eden Rd., Lancaster, PA 17601. Gilbert A. Peterson Tel. (717) 569-7071 Fax (717) 560-8213
Website: www.lbc.edu

Lancaster Theological Sem. of the United Church of Christ,* (United Church of Christ), 555 W. James St., Lancaster, PA 17603-2897. Peter Schmiechen Tel. (717) 393-0654 Fax (717) 393-0423
Email: dean@lts.org
Website: www.lts.org

Lexington Theological Seminary,* (Christian Church—Disciples of Christ), 631 S. Limestone St., Lexington, KY 40508. Richard L. Harrison Tel. (606) 252-0361 Fax (606) 281-6042
Website: www.lextheo.edu

Liberty Baptist Theological Seminary,* (Independent Baptist), 1971 University Blvd., Lynchburg, VA 24502-2269. A. Pierre Guillermin Tel. (804) 582-2000 Fax (804) 582-2304

L.I.F.E. Bible College, (International Church of the Foursquare Gospel), 1100 Covina Blvd., San Dimas, CA 91773. Dick Scott Tel. (909) 599-5433 Fax (909) 599-6690

Lincoln Christian College and Seminary,* (Christian Churches and Churches of Christ), 100 Campus View Dr., Lincoln, IL 62656. Keith H. Ray Tel. (217) 732-3168 Fax (217) 732-4078
Email: psnyder@lccs.edu
Website: www.lccs.edu

281

Logos Evangelical Seminary,* (Evangelical Formosan Church), 9358 Telstar Ave., El Monte, CA 91731. Felix Liu Tel. (626) 571-5110 Fax (626) 571-5119 Email: logos@sprynet.com Website: www.les.edu

Louisville Presbyterian Theological Seminary,* (Presbyterian Church-U.S.A.), 1044 Alta Vista Rd., Louisville, KY 40205. John M. Mulder Tel. (502) 895-3411 Fax (502) 895-1096 Website: www.lpts.edu

Loyola Univiversity Chicago Institute of Pastoral Studies,* (The Roman Catholic Church), 6525 North Sheridan Rd., Chicago, IL 60626. Camilla Burns, SND, Ph.D., Director Tel. (773) 508-2320 Fax (773) 508-2319 Website: www.luc.edu/depts/ips

Luther Seminary,* (Evangelical Lutheran Church in America), 2481 Como Ave., St. Paul, MN 55108. President David L. Tiede Tel. (651) 641-3456 Fax (651) 641-3425 Email: sbooms@luthersem.edu Website: www.luthersem.edu/

Lutheran Bible Institute in California,* (Intersynodical Lutheran), 5321 University Dr., Ste. H, Irvine, CA 92612-2938. Benjamin Johnson Tel. (949) 262-9222 Fax (949) 262-0283 Email: LBIC@aol.com

Lutheran Brethren Seminary, (Church of the Lutheran Brethren of America), 815 W. Vernon, Fergus Falls, MN 56537. Dean Eugene L. Boe, Ph.D. Tel. (218) 739-3375 Fax (218) 739-1259 Email: lbs@clba.org Website: www.lbs.edu

Lutheran School of Theology at Chicago,* (Evangelical Lutheran Church in America), 1100 E. 55th St., Chicago, IL 60615-5199. James Kenneth Echols Tel. (773) 256-0700 Fax (773) 256-0782 Website: www.istc.edu

Lutheran Theological Seminary,* (Evangelical Lutheran Church in America), 61 Seminary Ridge, Gettysburg, PA 17325-1795. Darold H. Beekmann Tel. (717) 334-6286 Fax (717) 334-3469 Email: info@ltsg.edu Website: www.ltsg.edu

Lutheran Theological Seminary at Philadelphia,* (Evangelical Lutheran Church in America), 7301 Germantown Ave., Philadelphia, PA 19119. Robert G. Hughes Tel. (215) 248-4616 Fax (215) 248-4577 Email: mtairy@ltsp.edu Website: www.ltsp.edu

Lutheran Theological Southern Seminary,* (Evangelical Lutheran Church in America), 4201 North Main St., Columbia, SC 29203. H. Frederick Reisz Tel. (803) 786-5150 Fax (803) 786-6499 Email: Freisz@ltss.edu Website: www.ltss.edu

Magnolia Bible College, (Churches of Christ), P.O. Box 1109, Kosciusko, MS 39090-1620. Cecil May Tel. (662) 289-2896 Fax (601) 288-2612

Manhattan Christian College, (Christian Churches and Churches of Christ), 1415 Anderson Ave., Manhattan, KS 66502. Kenneth Cable Tel. (785) 539-3571 Fax (785) 539-0832 Website: www.mccks.edu

McCormick Theological Seminary,* (Presbyterian Church-U.S.A.), 5555 S. Woodlawn Ave., Chicago, IL 60637. Cynthia M. Campbell Tel. (773) 947-6300 Fax (773) 947-0376 Website: www.mccormick.edu

Meadville/Lombard Theological School,* (Unitarian Universalist Association), 5701 S. Woodlawn Ave., Chicago, IL 60637. William R. Murry Tel. (773) 256-3000 Fax (773) 256-3008 Email: bmurry@meadville.edu Website: www.meadville.edu

Memphis Theological Seminary of the Cumberland Presbyterian Church,* (Cumberland Presbyterian Church), 168 E. Parkway S at Union, Memphis, TN 38104-4395. Larry A. Blakeburn Tel. (901) 458-8232 Fax (901) 452-4051 Email: lblakeburn@mtscampus.edu Website: www.mtscampus.edu

Mennonite Brethren Biblical Seminary,* (General Conference of Mennonite Brethren Churches), 4824 E. Butler Ave. (at Chestnut Ave.), Fresno, CA 93727-5097. President Henry J. Schmidt Tel. (559) 251-8628 Fax (559) 251-7212 Email: mbseminary@aol.com Website: www.fresno.edu/MBSeminary

Methodist Theological School in Ohio,* (The United Methodist Church), 3081 Columbus Pike, P.O. Box 8004, Delaware, OH 43015-8004. President Norman E. Dewire Tel. (740) 363-1146 Fax (740) 362-3135 Email: pres@mtso.edu Website: www.mtso.edu

Mid-America Bible College, (The Church of God), 3500 S.W. 119th St., Oklahoma City, OK 73170. Forrest R. Robinson Tel. (405) 691-3800 Fax (405) 692-3165

Midwestern Baptist Theological Seminary,* (Southern Baptist Convention), 5001 N. Oak

Trafficway, Kansas City, MO 64118. Mark Coppenger Tel. (816) 414-3700 Fax (816) 414-3799
Website: www.mbts.edu

Minnesota Bible College, (Christian Churches and Churches of Christ), 920 Mayowood Rd. S.W., Rochester, MN 55902. Robert W. Cash Tel. (507) 288-4563 Fax (507) 288-9046
Email: academic@mnbc.edu
Website: www.mnbc.edu

Moody Bible Institute, (Interdenominational), 820 N. La Salle Blvd., Chicago, IL 60610. Joseph M. Stowell Tel. (312) 329-4000 Fax (312) 329-4109

Moravian Theological Seminary,* (Moravian Church in America- Unitas Fratrum), 1200 Main St., Bethlehem, PA 18018. David A. Schattschneider Tel. (610) 861-1516 Fax (610) 861-1569
Email: seminary@moavian.edu
Website: www.moravian.edu

Moreau Seminary (Congregation of Holy Cross), (The Roman Catholic Church), Moreau Seminary, Notre Dame, IN 46556. Richard Gribble, C.S.C. Tel. (219) 631-7735 Fax (219) 631-9233

Morehouse School of Religion, (Interdenominational Baptist), 645 Beckwith St. S.W., Atlanta, GA 30314. William T. Perkins Tel. (404) 527-7777 Fax (404) 681-1005

Mount Angel Seminary,* (The Roman Catholic Church), St. Benedict, OR 97373. Patrick S. Brennan Tel. (503) 845-3951 Fax (503) 845-3126
Website: www.mtangel.edu

Mt. St. Mary's Seminary,* (The Roman Catholic Church), Emmitsburg, MD 21727-7797. Very Rev. Kevin C. Rhoades Tel. (301) 447-5295 Fax (301) 447-5636
Email: rhoades@msmary.edu
Website: www.msmary.edu

Mt. St. Mary's Seminary of the West,* (The Roman Catholic Church), 6616 Beechmont Ave., Cincinnati, OH 45230. Gerald R. Haemmerle Tel. (513) 231-2223 Fax (513) 231-3254
Email: jhaemmer@mtsm.org
Website: mtsm.org

Multnomah Bible College and Biblical Seminary,* (Interdenominational), 8435 N.E. Glisan St., Portland, OR 97220. Dr. Daniel R. Lockwood Tel. (503) 255-0332 Fax (503) 254-1268
Website: www.multnomah.edu

Mundelein Seminary of the Univ. of St. Mary-of-the-Lake,* (The Roman Catholic Church), 1000 E. Maple, Mundelein, IL 60060-1174. John Canary Tel. (847) 566-6401 Fax (847) 566-7330

Nashotah House (Theological Seminary),* (Episcopal Church), 2777 Mission Rd., Nashotah, WI 53058-9793. Gary W. Kriss Tel. (414) 646-6500 Fax (414) 646-6504
Email: nashotah@nashotah.edu
Website: www.nashotah.edu

Nazarene Bible College, (Church of the Nazarene), 1111 Academy Park Loop, Colorado Springs, CO 80910-3717. Hiram Sanders Tel. (719) 596-5110 Fax (719) 550-9437
Email: nbc@rmii.com
Website: www.members.aol.com/nazbibleco

Nazarene Theological Seminary,* (Church of the Nazarene), 1700 E. Meyer Blvd., Kansas City, MO 64131. A. Gordon Wetmore Tel. (816) 333-6254 Fax (816) 333-6271

Nebraska Christian College, (Christian Churches and Churches of Christ), 1800 Syracuse Ave., Norfolk, NE 68701. Ray D. Stites Tel. (402) 379-5000 Fax (402) 391-5100

New Brunswick Theological Seminary,* (Reformed Church in America), 17 Seminary Pl., New Brunswick, NJ 08901-1107. President Norman J. Kansfield Tel. (732) 247-5241 Fax (732) 249-5412
Email: prf@nbts.edu
Website: www.nbts.edu

New Orleans Baptist Theological Seminary,* (Southern Baptist Convention), 3939 Gentilly Blvd., New Orleans, LA 70126. Charles S. Kelley Tel. (504) 282-4455 Fax (504) 286-3623
Email: nobts@nobts.edu
Website: www.nobts.edu

N.Y. City Full Gospel Theological Seminary, (Full Gospel Assembly), 6902 11th Ave., Brooklyn, NY 11228. Frank A. Garofalo Tel. (908) 302-9553 Fax (908) 302-9553

New York Theological Seminary,* (Non-Denominational), 5 W. 29th St., 9th Fl., New York, NY 10001. M. William Howard Tel. (212) 532-4012 Fax (212) 684-0757
Website: www.nyts.edu

North American Baptist Seminary,* (North American Baptist Conference), 1525 S. Grange Ave., Sioux Falls, SD 57105. Charles M. Hiatt Tel. (605) 336-6588 Fax (605) 335-9090
Email: train@nabs.edu
Website: www.nabs.edu

North Central Bible College, (Assemblies of God), 910 Elliot Ave. S., Minneapolis, MN 55404. Gordon L. Anderson Tel. (612) 332-3491 Fax (612) 343-4778

North Park Theological Seminary,* (The Evangelical Covenant Church), 3225 W. Foster Ave., Chicago, IL 60625. John E.

283

Phelan, President and Dean Tel. (773) 244-6214 Fax (773) 244-6244
Email: jphelan@northpark.edu
Website: www.northpark.edu/cs

Northern Baptist Theological Seminary,* (American Baptist Churches in the U.S.A.), 660 E. Butterfield Rd., Lombard, IL 60148-5698. Ian M. Chapman Tel. (630) 620-2100 Fax (630) 620-2194
Email: chapman@seminary.edu
Website: www.seminary.edu

Northwest College, (Assemblies of God), 5520 108th Ave. N.E., P.O. Box 579, Kirkland, WA 98083-0579. Don H. Argue, Ed.D. Tel. (425) 822-8266 Fax (425) 827-0148
Email: mail@ncag.edu
Website: www.nwcollege.edu

Notre Dame Seminary,* (The Roman Catholic Church), 2901 S. Carrollton Ave., New Orleans, LA 70118-4391. Most Rev. Gregory M. Aymond, D.D. Tel. (504) 866-7426 Fax (504) 866-3119

Oak Hills Christian College, (Interdenominational), 1600 Oak Hills Rd. S.W., Bemidji, MN 56601. Dr. Thomas J. Bower Tel. (218) 751-8670 Fax (218) 751-8825

Oblate College,* (The Roman Catholic Church), 391 Michigan Ave. N.E., Washington, DC 20017. Harry Winter Tel. (202) 529-6544 Fax (202) 636-9444

Oblate School of Theology,* (The Roman Catholic Church), 285 Oblate Dr., San Antonio, TX 78216-6693. J. William Morell Tel. (210) 341-1366 Fax (210) 341-4519

Oral Roberts University School of Theology and Missions,* (Interdenominational), 7777 S. Lewis Ave., Tulsa, OK 74171. Jerry Horner Tel. (918) 495-6096 Fax (918) 495-6259
Email: jhorner@oru.edu
Website: www.oru.edu

Ozark Christian College, (Christian Churches and Churches of Christ), 1111 N. Main St., Joplin, MO 64801. President Dr. Kenneth D. Idleman Tel. (417) 624-2518 Fax (417) 624-0090
Email: pres@occ.edu

Pacific Christian College, (Christian Churches and Churches of Christ), 2500 E. Nutwood Ave., Fullerton, CA 92831. President E. LeRoy Lawson Tel. (714) 879-3901 Fax (714) 526-0231
Email: rlawson@pacificc.edu

Pacific Lutheran Theological Seminary,* (Evangelical Lutheran Church in America), 2770 Marin Ave., Berkeley, CA 94708. President Timothy F. Lull Tel. (510) 524-5264 Fax (510) 524-2408
Email: president@plts.edu
Website: www.plts.edu

Pacific School of Religion,* (United Church of Christ), 1798 Scenic Ave., Berkeley, CA 94709. William McKinney Tel. (510) 848-0528 Fax (510) 845-8948
Email: comm@psr.edu
Website: www.psr.edu

Payne Theological Seminary,* (African Methodist Episcopal Church), P.O. Box 474, 1230 Wilberforce-Clifton Rd., Wilberforce, OH 45384-0474. Obery M. Hendricks, Jr., Ph.D. Tel. (937) 376-2946 Fax (937) 376-3330
Email: dbalsbau@payne.edu
Website: www.payne-seminary.org

Pepperdine University, (Churches of Christ), Religion Division, Malibu, CA 90263. Rick R. Marrs, Chair of Religion Division; David Davenport, President of University Tel. (310) 456-4352 Fax (310) 317-7271
Email: rmarrs@pepperdine.edu
Website: www.pepperdine.edu/seaver/religion/main.html

Perkins School of Theology (Southern Methodist University),* (The United Methodist Church), Kirby Hall, Dallas, TX 75275-0133. Robin W. Lovin Tel. (214) 768-2138 Fax (214) 768-1042
Email: theoadms@smu.edu
Website: www.smu.edu/~theology

Philadelphia College of Bible, (Nondenominational), 200 Manor Ave., Langhorne, PA 19047-2990. W. Sherrill Babb Tel. (215) 752-5800 Fax (215) 702-4341
Email: president@pcb.edu

Philadelphia Theological Seminary, (Reformed Episcopal Church), 7372 Henry Ave., Philadelphia, PA 19128-1401. Wayne A. Headman Tel. (215) 483-2480 Fax (215) 483-2484
Email: info@ptsorec.edu
Website: www.ptsofrec.edu

Phillips Theological Seminary,* (Christian Church- Disciples of Christ), 4242 S. Sheridan Rd., Tulsa, OK 74145. William Tabbernee Tel. (918) 610-8303 Fax (918) 610-8404
Email: ptspres@fullnet.net
Website: www.ptsem.org

Piedmont Baptist College, (Baptist-Independent), 716 Franklin St., Winston-Salem, NC 27101. Howard L. Wilburn Tel. (336) 725-8344 Fax (336) 725-5522
Email: admissions@pbc.edu
Website: www.pbc.edu

Pittsburgh Theological Seminary,* (Presbyterian Church- U.S.A.), 616 N. Highland Ave., Pittsburgh, PA 15206. Carnegie Samuel Calian Tel. (412) 362-5610 Fax (412) 363-3260

Point Loma Nazarene College, (Church of the Nazarene), 3900 Lomaland Dr., San Diego,

CA 92106. Tel. (619) 849-2200 Fax (619) 849-7007
Website: www.ptloma.edu

Pontifical College Josephinum,* (The Roman Catholic Church), 7625 N. High St., Columbus, OH 43235. Brian R. Moore, Acting President Tel. (614) 885-5585 Fax (614) 885-2307
Website: www.pcj.edu

Pope John XXIII National Seminary,* (The Roman Catholic Church), 558 South Ave., Weston, MA 02193. Francis D. Kelly Tel. (617) 899-5500 Fax (617) 899-9057

Practical Bible College, (Independent Baptist), Box 601, Bible School Park, NY 13737. Dale E. Linebaugh Tel. (607) 729-1581 Fax (607) 729-2962
Email: pbc@lakenet.org
Website: www.lakenet.org/~pbc

Princeton Theological Seminary,* (Presbyterian Church- U.S.A.), P.O. Box 821, Princeton, NJ 08542-0803. Thomas W. Gillespie Tel. (609) 921-8300 Fax (609) 924-2973
Email: comm-pub@ptsem.edu
Website: www.ptsem.edu

Protestant Episcopal Theological Seminary in Virginia,* (Episcopal Church), 3737 Seminary Rd., Alexandria, VA 22304. Martha J. Horne, Dean Tel. (703) 370-6600 Fax (703) 751-0214
Email: mhorne@vts.edu
Website: www.vts.edu

Puget Sound Christian College, (Christian Churches and Churches of Christ), 410 Fourth Ave. N., Edmonds, WA 98020-3171. R. Allan Dunbar Tel. (425) 775-8686 Fax (425) 775-8688
Email: psccpres@ricochet.net
Website: www.pscc.edu

Rabbi Isaac Elchanan Theological Seminary, (Jewish), 2540 Amsterdam Ave., New York, NY 10033. Dr. Norman Lamm Tel. (212) 960-5344 Fax (212) 960-0061
Website: www.yu.edu/riets/

Reconstructionist Rabbinical College, (Jewish), Church Rd. and Greenwood Ave., Wyncote, PA 19095. David A. Teutsch Tel. (215) 576-0800 Fax (215) 576-6143
Email: rrcinfo@rrc.edu

Reformed Bible College, (Interdenominational), 3333 East Beltline N.E., Grand Rapids, MI 49525. Nicholas Kroeze Tel. (616) 222-3000 Fax (616) 222-3045
Email: administration@reformed.edu
Website: www.reformed.edu

Reformed Presbyterian Theological Seminary,* (Reformed Presbyterian Church of North America), 7418 Penn Ave., Pittsburgh, PA 15208-2594. Jerry F. O'Neill Tel. (412) 731-8690 Fax (412) 731-4834
Email: rpseminary@aol.com
Website: www.rpts.edu

Reformed Theological Seminary,* (Non-denominational), 5422 Clinton Blvd., Jackson, MS 39209-3099. Luder G. Whitlock Tel. (601) 923-1600 Fax (601) 923-1654
Email: rts.jackson@rts.edu
Website: www.rts.edu

Regent University School of Divinity,* (Interdenominational), 1000 Regent University Dr., Virginia Beach, VA 23464-9801. Terry Lindvall Tel. (757) 579-4010 Fax (757) 579-4037
Email: uinssyn@regent.edu
Website: www.regent.edu

Roanoke Bible College, (Christian Churches and Churches of Christ), 714 N. Poindexter St, Elizabeth City, NC 27909-4054. William A. Griffin Tel. (252) 334-2090 or (252) 334-2070 Fax (252) 334-2071
Email: wag@roanokebible.edu
Website: www.roanokebible.edu

Sacred Heart Major Seminary,* (The Roman Catholic Church), 2701 Chicago Blvd., Detroit, MI 48206. Allen H. Vigneron Tel. (313) 883-8500 Fax (313) 868-6440

Sacred Heart School of Theology,* (The Roman Catholic Church), P.O. Box 429, Hales Corners, WI 53130-0429. James D. Brackin, S.C.J. Tel. (414) 425-8300 Fax (414) 529-6999
Email: shst@msn.com

Saint Bernard's Institute,* (The Roman Catholic Church), 1100 S. Goodman St., Rochester, NY 14620. Patricia A. Schoelles Tel. (716) 271-3657 Fax (716) 271-2045
Email: pschoelles@sbi.edu

St. Charles Borromeo Seminary,* (The Roman Catholic Church), 100 East Wynnewood Rd., Wynnewood, PA 19096-3001. Rev. Msgr. Michael F. Burbidge, Rector Tel. (610) 667-3394 Fax (610) 667-7635

St. Francis Seminary,* (The Roman Catholic Church), 3257 S. Lake Dr., St. Francis, WI 53235. Very Rev. Andrew L. Nelson Tel. (414) 747-6400 Fax (414) 747-6442
Email: anelson1@sfs.edu
Website: www.sfs.edu

St. John's Seminary,* (The Roman Catholic Church), 127 Lake St., Brighton, MA 02135. Timothy Moran Tel. (617) 254-2610 Fax (617) 787-2336

St. John's Seminary College,* (The Roman Catholic Church), 5118 Seminary Rd., Camarillo, CA 93012-2599. Edward Wm. Clark Tel. (805) 482-2755 Fax (805) 987-5097

St. John's University, School of Theology Seminary,* (The Roman Catholic Church), Box 7288, Collegeville, MN 56321-7288. William J. Cahoy, Dean Tel. (320) 363-2100 Fax (320) 363-3145
Website: www.csbsju.sot

St. Joseph's Seminary,* (The Roman Catholic Church), 201 Seminary Ave., (Dunwoodie) Yonkers, NY 10704. Edwin F. O'Brien Tel. (914) 968-6200 Fax (914) 968-7912

St. Louis Christian College, (Christian Churches and Churches of Christ), 1360 Grandview Dr., Florissant, MO 63033. Kenneth L. Beck Tel. (314) 837-6777 Fax (314) 837-8291

St. Mary Seminary and Graduate School of Theology,* (The Roman Catholic Church), 28700 Euclid Ave., Wickliffe, OH 44092. Donald B. Cozzens Tel. (216) 943-7600 Fax (216) 943-7577

St. Mary's Seminary, (The Roman Catholic Church), 9845 Memorial Dr., Houston, TX 77024-3498. Chester L. Borski Tel. (713) 686-4345 Fax (713) 681-7550

St. Mary's Seminary and University,* (The Roman Catholic Church), 5400 Roland Ave., Baltimore, MD 21210. Robert F. Leavitt Tel. (410) 323-3200 Fax (410) 323-3554

St. Meinrad School of Theology,* (The Roman Catholic Church), St. Meinrad, IN 47577. Mark O'Keefe Tel. (812) 357-6611 Fax (812) 357-6964

St. Patrick's Seminary,* (The Roman Catholic Church), 320 Middlefield Rd., Menlo Park, CA 94025. Gerald D. Coleman Tel. (415) 325-5621 Fax (415) 322-0997

Saint Paul School of Theology,* (The United Methodist Church), 5123 Truman Rd., Kansas City, MO 64127-2499. Lovett H. Weems, Jr. Tel. (816) 483-9600 Fax (816) 483-9605
Email: spst@spst.edu
Website: www.spst.edu

St. Paul Seminary School of Divinity,* (The Roman Catholic Church), 2260 Summit Ave., St. Paul, MN 55105. Phillip J. Rask Tel. (612) 962-5050 Fax (612) 962-5790

St. Tikhon's Orthodox Theological Seminary, (The Orthodox Church in America), Box 130, St. Tikhon's Rd., South Canaan, PA 18459-0121. Archbishop Herman Tel. (570) 937-4411 Fax (570) 937-3100
Email: stots@stots.edu (Admin.)
stotsfac@stots.edu (Faculty)
library@stots.edu (Library)
Website: www. stots.edu AND www.oca.org/OCA/pim/oca-stostots.html

St. Vincent de Paul Regional Seminary,* (The Roman Catholic Church), 10701 S. Military Trail, Boynton Beach, FL 33436-4899. Pablo A. Navarro Tel. (561) 732-4424 Fax (561) 737-2205

St. Vincent Seminary,* (The Roman Catholic Church), 300 Fraser Purchase Rd., Latrobe, PA 15650-2690. Very Rev. Thomas Acklin, O.S.B. Tel. (724) 537-4592 Fax (724) 532-5052

St. Vladimir's Orthodox Theological Seminary,* (The Orthodox Church in America), 575 Scarsdale Rd., Crestwood, NY 10707-1699. His Beatitude Metropolitan Theodosius Tel. (914) 961-8313 Fax (914) 961-4507
Email: info@svots.edu
Website: www.svots.edu

San Francisco Theological Seminary,* (Presbyterian Church- U.S.A.), 2 Kensington Rd., San Anselmo, CA 94960. Donald W. McCullough Tel. (415) 258-6500 Fax (415) 258-1608
Email: sftsinfo@sfts.edu
Website: www.sfts.edu

San Jose Christian College, (Christian Churches and Churches of Christ), 790 S. 12th St., P.O. Box 1090, San Jose, CA 95108. Bryce L. Jessup Tel. (408) 293-9058 Fax (408) 293-7352

Savonarola Theological Seminary, (Polish National Catholic Church of America), 1031 Cedar Ave., Scranton, PA 18505. John F. Swantek Tel. (570) 343-0100 Fax

Seabury-Western Theological Seminary,* (Episcopal Church), 2122 Sheridan Rd., Evanston, IL 60201-2976. James B. Lemler Tel. (847) 328-9300 Fax (847) 328-9624
Email: swts@nwu.edu
Website: www.swts.nwu.edu

Seattle University School of Theology and Ministry,* (The Roman Catholic Church and 10 Mainline Protestant Denominations and Associations), 900 Broadway, Seattle, WA 98122. Dean Loretta Jancoski Tel. (206) 296-5330 Fax (206) 296-5329
Email: jancoski@seattleu.edu
Website: www.seattleu.edu

Seminario Evangelico de Puerto Rico,* (Interdenominational), 776 Ponce de LeÛn Ave., San Juan, PR 00925. Samuel Pag·n Tel. (787) 763-6700 Fax (787) 751-0847
Email: drspagan@icepr.com / jvaldes@tld.net
Website: netministries.org/see/charmin/CM 01399

Seminary of the East (Conservative Baptist), (Conservative Baptist Association of America), 1605 N. Limekiln Pike, Dresher, PA 19025. Philip J. Baur Tel. (215) 641-4801 Fax (215) 641-4804

Seminary of the Immaculate Conception,* (The Roman Catholic Church), 440 West Neck

Rd., Huntington, NY 11743. Vincent F. Fullam Tel. (516) 423-0483 Fax (516) 423-2346

Seventh-day Adventist Theological Seminary,* (Seventh-day Adventist Church), Andrews University, Berrien Springs, MI 49104-1500. Werner Vyhmeister Tel. (616) 471-3537 Fax (616) 471-6202 Email: seminary@andrews.edu Website: www.andrews.edu/sem

Seventh Day Baptist School of Ministry, (Seventh Day Baptist General Conference), 3120 Kennedy Rd., P.O. Box 1678, Janesville, WI 53547. Gabriel Bevjani Tel. (608) 752-5055 Fax (608) 752-7711 Email: sdbgen@inwave.com

Shaw Divinity School, (Baptist), P.O. Box 2090, Raleigh, NC 27602. Talbert O. Shaw Tel. (919) 832-1701 Fax (919) 832-6082

Simpson College, (The Christian and Missionary Alliance), 2211 College View Dr., Redding, CA 96003. James M. Grant Tel. (916) 224-5600 Fax (916) 224-5608

Southeastern Baptist College, (Baptist Missionary Association of America), 4229 Highway 15N, Laurel, MS 39440. Jentry W. Bond Tel. (601) 426-6346 Fax (601) 426-6346

Southeastern Baptist Theological Seminary,* (Southern Baptist Convention), 150-A North White Street, P.O. Box 1889, Wake Forest, NC 27588-1889. President Paige Patterson Tel. (919) 556-3101 Fax (919) 556-0998 Website: www.sebts.edu

Southeastern Bible College, (Interdenominational), 3001 Highway 280 E., Birmingham, AL 35243. John D. Talley Tel. (205) 969-0880 Fax (205) 970-9207 Email: 102064.406@compuserve.com Website: www.sebc.edu

Southeastern College of the Assemblies of God, (Assemblies of God), 1000 Longfellow Blvd., Lakeland, FL 33801. James L. Hennesy Tel. (941) 667-5000 Fax (941) 667-5200

Southern Baptist Theological Seminary,* (Southern Baptist Convention), 2825 Lexington Rd., Louisville, KY 40280. R. Albert Mohler, Jr. Tel. (502) 897-4121 Fax (502) 899-1770 Email: mohler@sbts.edu Website: www.sbts.edu

Southern Christian University, (Churches of Christ), 1200 Taylor Rd., Montgomery, AL 36117-3553. President Dr. Rex A. Turner, Jr. Tel. (334) 277-2277 Fax (334) 271-0002 Email: scuniversity@mindspring.com Website: www.southernchristian.edu

Southern Wesleyan University, (The Wesleyan Church), 907 Wesleyan Dr., P.O. Box 1020,

Central, SC 29630-1020. President David J. Spittal Tel. (864) 639-2453 Fax (864) 639-0826 Email: dspittal@swu.edu Website: www.swu.edu

Southwestern Assemblies of God University, (Assemblies of God), 1200 Sycamore St., Waxahachie, TX 75165. Delmer R. Guynes Tel. (972) 937-4010 Fax (972) 923-0488

Southwestern Baptist Theological Seminary,* (Southern Baptist Convention), P.O. Box 22000, Fort Worth, TX 76122. Kenneth S. Hemphill Tel. (817) 923-1921 Fax (817) 923-0610 Website: www.swbts.edu

Southwestern College, (Conservative Baptist Association of America), 2625 E. Cactus Rd., Phoenix, AZ 85032. Brent D. Garrison Tel. (602) 992-6101 Fax (602) 404-2159

SS. Cyril and Methodius Seminary,* (The Roman Catholic Church), 3535 Indian Trail, Orchard Lake, MI 48324. Francis B. Koper Tel. (248) 683-0311 Fax (248) 683-0402 Email: 103244.3555@compuserve.com OR deansoff@sscms.edu Website: www.metronet.lib.mi.us/aml.html (Library www.sscms.edu/deansoff (Seminary

Starr King School for the Ministry,* (Unitarian Universalist Association), 2441 LeConte Ave., Berkeley, CA 94709. Rebecca Parker Tel. (510) 845-6232 Fax (510) 845-6273

Swedenborg School of Religion, (The Swedenborgian Church), 48 Sargent St., Newton, MA 02458. Dr. Mary Kay Klein Tel. (617) 244-0504 Fax (617) 558-0357 Email: maryk59988@aol.com

Talbot School of Theology,* (Nondenominational), 13800 Biola Ave., La Mirada, CA 90639-0001. Dennis H. Dirks Tel. (562) 903-4816 Fax (562) 903-4759 Email: biola.edu/biola/talbot/ Website: www.talbot.edu

Temple Baptist Seminary, (Independent Baptist), 1815 Union Ave., Chattanooga, TN 37404. Barkev Trachian Tel. (423) 493-4221 Fax (423) 493-4471

Theological School of the Protestant Reformed Churches, (Protestant Reformed Churches in America), 4949 Ivanrest Ave., Grandville, MI 49418. Robert D. Decker Tel. (616) 531-1490 Fax (616) 531-3033 Email: decker@prca.org

Toccoa Falls College, (The Christian and Missionary Alliance), P.O. Box 800777, Toccoa Falls, GA 30598. Paul L. Alford Tel. (706) 886-6831 Fax (706) 282-6005 Email: president@toccoafalls.edu Website: www.toccoafalls.edu

Trevecca Nazarene University, (Church of the Nazarene), 333 Murfreesboro Rd., Nashville, TN 37210. Millard Reed Tel. (615) 248-1200 Fax (615) 248-7728
Website: www.trevecca.edu

Trinity Bible College, (Assemblies of God), 50 S. 6th Ave., Ellendale, ND 58436. Howard Young Tel. (701) 349-3621 Fax (701) 349-5443

Trinity College of Florida, (Nondenominational), 2430 Trinity Oaks Blvd., New Port Richey, FL 34655. Paul L. Alford Tel. (727) 376-6911 Fax (727) 376-0781
Email: trinity@gte.net
Website: www.trinitycollege.edu

Trinity Episcopal School for Ministry,* (Episcopal Church), 311 Eleventh St., Ambridge, PA 15003. The Very Rev. Peter C. Moore, Dean and President Tel. (412) 266-3838 Fax (412) 266-4617
Email: tinalockett@tesm.edu
Website: www.episcopalian.org

Trinity International University,* (The Evangelical Free Church of America), 2065 Half Day Rd., Deerfield, IL 60015. Gregory L. Waybright Tel. (847) 945-8800 Fax (847) 317-8090
Email: tedsadm@tiu.edu
Website: www.tiu.edu

Trinity Lutheran College, (Interdenominational/Lutheran), 4221 - 228th Ave. S.E., Issaquah, WA 98029-9299. John M. Stamm Tel. (425) 392-0400 Fax (425) 392-0404
Email: admissn@lbi.edu
Website: www.lbi.edu

Trinity Lutheran Seminary,* (Evangelical Lutheran Church in America), 2199 E. Main St., Columbus, OH 43209-2334. Dennis A. Anderson Tel. (614) 235-4136 Fax (614) 238-0263
Email: webmaster@trinity.capital.edu
Website: www.trinity.capital.edu

Union Theological Seminary,* (Interdenominational), 3041 Broadway, New York, NY 10027. Holland L. Hendrix Tel. (212) 662-7100 Fax (212) 280-1416

Union Theological Seminary and Presbyterian School of Christian Education (Union-PSCE),* (Presbyterian Church- U.S.A.), 3401 Brook Rd., Richmond, VA 23227. Louis B. Weeks Tel. (804) 355-0671 Fax (804) 355-3919
Website: www.utsva.edu

United Theological Seminary,* (The United Methodist Church), 1810 Harvard Blvd., Dayton, OH 45406-4599. Tel. (937) 278-5817 Fax (937) 278-1218
Email: utsadmis@united.edu
Website: www.united.edu

United Theological Seminary of the Twin Cities,* (United Church of Christ), 3000 Fifth St. N.W., New Brighton, MN 55112. Wilson Yates Tel. (651) 633-4311 Fax (651) 633-4315
Email: general@unitedseminary-mn.org
Website: www.unitedseminary-mn.org

University of Chicago (Divinity School).* (Interdenominational), 1025 E. 58th St., Chicago, IL 60637. W. Clark Gilpin Tel. (773) 702-8221 Fax (773) 702-6048
Website: www2.uchicago.edu/divinity

University of Dubuque Theological Seminary,* (Presbyterian Church- U.S.A.), 2000 University Ave., Dubuque, IA 52001. Jeffrey Bullock Tel. (319) 589-3223 Fax (319) 589-3682

University of Notre Dame, Dept. of Theology,* (The Roman Catholic Church), Notre Dame, IN 46556. John C. Cavadini, Department Chair Tel. (219) 631-7811 Fax (219) 631-4268

University of St. Thomas School of Theology, (The Roman Catholic Church), 9845 Memorial Dr., Houston, TX 77024. Louis T. Brusatti Tel. (713) 686-4345 Fax (713) 683-8673

University of the South School of Theology,* (Episcopal Church), 335 Tennessee Ave., Sewanee, TN 37383-0001. Guy Fitch Lytle, Dean Tel. (931) 598-1288 Fax (931) 598-1412
Email: glytle@seraph1.sewanee.edu
Website: www.sewanee.edu

Valley Forge Christian College, (Assemblies of God), 1401 Charlestown Rd., Phoenixville, PA 19460. Earl Baldwin Tel. (610) 935-0450 Fax (610) 935-9353

Vanderbilt University Divinity School,* (Interdenominational), Nashville, TN 37240. Joseph C. Hough, Jr. Tel. (615) 322-2776 Fax (615) 343-9957
Email: HoughJC@CTRVax.Vanderbilt.edu
Website: www.vanderbilt.edu

Vennard College, (Interdenominational), Box 29, University Park, IA 52595. W. Edward Rickman Tel. (515) 673-8391 Fax (515) 673-8365
Email: wennard@vennard.edu
Website: www.vennard.edu

Virginia Union University (School of Theology),* (American Baptist Churches in the USA, National Baptist Convention, USA, Inc., Progressive National Baptist Convention, Inc., Lott Carey), 1500 N. Lombardy St., Richmond, VA 23220. John W. Kinney, Dean Tel. (804) 257-5715 Fax (804) 342-3911

Walla Walla College (School of Theology), (Seventh-day Adventist Church), 204 S. College Ave., College Place, WA 99324-1198. Ernest Bursey, Dean Tel. (509) 527-2194 Fax (509) 527-2253
Email: burser@wwc.edu
Website: www.wwc.edu

Wartburg Theological Seminary,* (Evangelical Lutheran Church in America), 333 Wartburg Pl., P.O. Box 5004, Dubuque, LA 52004-5004. Roger Fjeld Tel. (319) 589-0200 Fax (319) 589-0333
Email: mailbox@wartburgseminary.edu
Website: Duane Larson

Washington Bible College/Capital Bible Seminary, (Nondenominational), 6511 Princess Garden Pkwy., Lanham, MD 20706. Homer Heater Tel. (301) 552-1400 Fax (301) 552-2775

Washington Theological Consortium, (Nondenominational), 487 Michigan Ave. N.E., Washington, DC 20017. John W. Crossin, Exec. Dir. Tel. (202) 832-2675 Fax (202) 526-0818
Email: wtconsort@aol.com
Website: www.washtheocon.org

Washington Theological Union,* (The Roman Catholic Church), 6896 Laurel St. N.W., Washington, DC 20012. Daniel McLellan, O.F.M. Tel. (202) 726-8800 Fax (202) 726-1716
Website: www.wtu.edu

Wesley Biblical Seminary,* (Interdenominational), P.O. Box 9938, Jackson, MS 39286-0938. Robert R. Lawrence Tel. (601) 957-1314 Fax (601) 957-1314

Wesley Theological Seminary,* (The United Methodist Church), 4500 Massachusetts Ave. N.W., Washington, DC 20016-5690. G. Douglass Lewis Tel. (800) 882-4987 Fax (202) 885-8600
Email: admiss@clark.net
Website: www.WesleySem.org

Western Evangelical Seminary,* (Interdenominational), 12753 S.W. 68th Ave., Portland, OR 97223. Ed Stevens Tel. (503) 538-8383 Fax (503) 598-4338

Western Seminary, (Conservative Baptist Association of America), 5511 S.E. Hawthorne Blvd., Portland, OR 97215. Ronald E. Hawkins Tel. (503) 233-8561 Fax (503) 239-4216

Western Theological Seminary,* (Reformed Church in America), 101 E. 13th St., Holland, MI 49423. Dennis N. Voskuil Tel. (616) 392-8555 Fax (616) 392-7717
Website: www.westernsem.org

Westminster Theological Seminary,* (Nondenominational), Chestnut Hill, P.O. Box 27009, Philadelphia, PA 19118. Samuel T. Logan Tel. (215)887-5511 Fax (215)887-3459
Email: slogan@wts.edu
Website: www.wts.edu

Westminster Theological Seminary in California,* (Nondenominational), 1725 Bear Valley Pkwy, Escondido, CA 92027-4128. W.

Robert Godfrey Tel. (858) 480-8474 Fax (858) 480-0252

Weston Jesuit School of Theology,* (Roman Catholic), 3 Phillips Pl., Cambridge, MA 02138. Robert Manning Tel. (617) 492-1960 Fax (617) 492-5833
Email: rmanning@wjst.edu

William Tyndale College, (Interdenominational), 35700 W. Twelve Mile Rd., Farmington Hills, MI 48331. James C. McHann Tel. (810) 553-7200 Fax (810) 553-5963

Winebrenner Theological Seminary,* (Churches of God General Conference), 701 E. Melrose Ave., P.O. Box 478, Findlay, OH 45839. David E. Draper Tel. (419) 422-4824 Fax (419) 422-3999
Email: wtseminary@aol.com
Website: www.winebrenner.edu

Wisconsin Lutheran Seminary, (Wisconsin Evangelical Lutheran Synod), 11831 N. Seminary Dr., 65W, Mequon, WI 53092. David J. Valleskey Tel. (414) 257-8800 Fax (414) 257-8810

Yale University Divinity School,* 409 Prospect St., New Haven, CT 06511. Richard J. Wood Tel. (203) 432-5303 Fax (203) 432-5356
Email: ydsadmsn@yale.edu
Website: www.yale.edu/divinity

10. Theological Seminaries and Bible Colleges in Canada

The following list includes theological seminaries and departments in colleges and universities in which ministerial training is provided. Many denominations have additional programs. Consult Directory 4, "Religious Bodies in Canada," for headquarters information for these denominations. The list has been developed from direct correspondence with the institutions. Inclusion in or exclusion from this list implies no judgment about the quality or accreditation of any institution. Those schools that are members (both accredited and affiliated) of the Association of Theological Schools are marked with a "*". Each of the listings include: the institution name, denominational sponsor when appropriate, location, the president or dean, telephone and fax numbers when known, and email and website addresses when available.

Acadia Divinity College,* (United Baptist Convention of the Atlantic Provinces) Acadia University , Wolfville, NS B0P 1X0. Lee M. McDonald, Principal. Tel. (902)542-2285 Fax (902)542-7527
Email: adcinfo@acadiau.ca
Website: http://ace.acadiau.ca/divcol

Alberta Bible College, (Christian Churches and Churches of Christ in Canada) 635 Northmount Dr. N.W., Calgary, AB T2K 3J6. Ronald A. Fraser. Tel. (403)282-2994 Fax (403)282-3084
Email: abbible@cadvision.com
Website: www.abc-ca.org

Associated Canandian Theological Schools of Trinity Western University,* (Baptist General Conference of Canada, Evangelical Free Church of Canada, The Fellowship of Evangelical Baptist Churches in Canada, Christian and Missionary Alliance, Canadian Conference of Mennonite Brethren Churches) 7600 Glover Rd., Langley, BC V2Y 1Y1. Guy S. Saffold, Coordinator. Tel. (604)513-2044 Fax (604)513-2045
Email: acts@twu.ca
Website: www.acts.twu.ca

Atlantic Baptist University, (United Baptist Convention of the Atlantic Provinces) Box 6004, Moncton, NB E1C 9L7. W. Ralph Richardson. Tel. (506)858-8970 Fax (506)858-9694

Atlantic School of Theology,* (Interdenominational) 640 Francklyn St., Halifax, NS B3H 3B5. Gordon Mac Dermid. Tel. (902)423-6801 Fax (902)492-4048

Baptist Leadership Training School, (Canadian Baptist Ministries) 4330 16th St. S.W., Calgary, AB T2T 4H9. Hugh Fraser. Tel. (403)243-3770 Fax (403)287-1930
Email: blts@imag.net
Website: www.yet.ca

Bethany Bible College-Canada, (The Wesleyan Church) 26 Western St., Sussex, NB E4E 1E6. President Dr. David S. Medders. Tel. (506)432-4400 Fax (506)432-4425

Bethany Bible Institute, (Canadian Conference of Mennonite Brethren Churches) Box 160, Hepburn, SK S0K 1Z0. Rick Schellenberg. Tel. (306)947-2175 Fax (306)947-4229
Email: bethany@sk.sympatico.ca
Website: www.bethany.sk.ca

Briercrest Bible College, (Transdenominational) Enrollment Services, Briercrest family of schools 510 College Dr., Caronport, SK S0H 0S0. Dr. Paul Magnus. Tel. (800)667-5199 Fax (306)756-3366
Email: enrollment@briercrest.ca
Website: www.briercrest.ca

Briercrest Biblical Seminary,* (Interdenominational) Enrollment Services, Briercrest Family of Schools 510 College Dr., Caronport, SK S0H 0S0. Tel. (800)667-5199 Fax (306)756-3366
Website: www.briercrest.ca

Canadian Bible College, (Christian and Missionary Alliance in Canada) 4400-4th Ave., Regina, SK S4T 0H8. Dr. George Durance. Tel. (306)545-1515 Fax (306)545-0210
Email: gdurance@cbccts.sk.ca
Website: www.cbccts.sk.ca

Canadian Lutheran Bible Institute, (Lutheran) 4837 52A St., Camrose, AB T4V 1W5. Norman C. Miller. Tel. (780)672-4454 Fax (780)672-4455
Email: clbi@clbi.edu

Canadian Nazarene College, (Church of the Nazarene Canada) 610, 833 4th Ave. SW, Calgary, AB T2P 3T5. Riley Coulter. Tel. (403)571-2550 Fax (403)571-2556
Email: cncoff@cnaz.ab.ca
Website: www.cnaz.ab.ca

Canadian Theological Seminary,* (Christian and Missionary Alliance in Canada) 4400-4th Ave., Regina, SK S4T 0H8. Dr. George Durance. Tel. (306)545-1515 Fax (306)545-0210
Email: gdurance@cbccts.sk.ca
Website: www.cbccts.sk.ca

Central Pentecostal College, University of Saskatchewan, (The Pentecostal Assemblies of Canada) 1303 Jackson Ave., Saskatoon, SK S7H 2M9. D. Munk. Tel. (306)374-6655 Fax (306)373-6968

Centre for Christian Studies, (The Anglican Church of Canada, The United Church of Canada) 60 Maryland, Winnipeg, MB R3G 1K7. Tel. (204)783-4490 Fax (204)786-3012 Email: centre@escape.ca

Church Army College of Evangelism, (The Anglican Church of Canada) 397 Brunswick Ave., Toronto, ON M5R 2Z2. Roy E. Dickson. Tel. (416)924-9279 Fax (416)924-2931

College Biblique Québec, (The Pentecostal Assemblies of Canada) 740 Lebourgneuf, Ste. 100, Ancienne Lorette, QC G2J 1E2. William Raccah. Tel. (418)622-7552 Fax (418)622-1470

Collége Dominicain de Philosophie et de Théologie, (The Roman Catholic Church in Canada) 96 Avenue Empress, Ottawa, ON K1R 7G3. Michel Gourgues. Tel. (613)233-5696 Fax (613)233-6064

College of Emmanuel and St. Chad, (The Anglican Church of Canada) 1337 College Dr., Saskatoon, SK S7N 0W6. William Niels Christensen. Tel. (306)975-3753 Fax (306)934-2683 Email: christen@duke.usask.ca

Columbia Bible College, (Mennonite) 2940 Clearbrook Rd., Abbotsford, BC V2T 2Z8. Walter Unger. Tel. (604)853-3358 Fax (604)853-3063 Email: info@columbiabc.edu Website: www.columbiabc.edu

Concord College, (Mennonite Brethren Churches) 169 Riverton Ave., Winnipeg, MB R2L 2E5. Harry Olfert. Tel. (204)669-6583 Fax (204)663-2468

Concordia Lutheran Seminary,* (Lutheran Church-Canada) 7040 Ada Blvd., Edmonton, AB T5B 4E3. L. Dean Hempelmann. Tel. (780)474-1468 Fax (780)479-3067 Email: clsadmin@connect.ab.ca

Concordia Lutheran Theological Seminary,* (Lutheran Church-Canada) 470 Glenridge Ave., St. Catharines, ON L2T 4C3. Jonathan Grothe. Tel. (905)688-2362 Fax (905)688-9744

Covenant Bible College, (The Evangelical Covenant Church of Canada) Campuses: CANADA: 630 Westchester Rd., Strathmore, AB T1P 1H8 Tel. (403)934-6200 Fax (403)934-6220 COLORADO: 675 Southwood Ln., Windsor, CO 80550 Tel./Fax (970)686-6977 Email: CANADA: covbibco@cadvision.com E-mail: COLORADO: 103354.2431@compuserve.com Website: CANADA: www.covenantbiblecollege.ab.ca

Eastern Pentecostal Bible College, (The Pentecostal Assemblies of Canada) 780 Argyle St., Peterborough, ON K9H 5T2. Carl F. Verge. Tel. (705)748-9111 Fax (705)748-3931

Edmonton Baptist Seminary,* (North American Baptist Conference) 11525-23 Ave., Edmonton, AB T6J 4T3. Dr. Marvin Dewey. Tel. (780)431-5200 Fax (780)436-9416 Email: mdewey@nabcebs.ab.ca Website: www.nabcebs.ab.ca

Emmanuel Bible College, (The Evangelical Missionary Church of Canada) 100 Fergus Ave., Kitchener, ON N2A 2H2. Thomas E. Dow. Tel. (519)894-8900 Fax (519)894-5331 Email: dmin@ebcollege.on.ca Website: www.ebcollege.on.ca

Emmanuel College,* (The United Church of Canada) 75 Queens Park Crescent, Toronto, ON M5S 1K7. Roger C. Hutchinson. Tel. (416)585-4539 Fax (416)585-4516 Email: ec.office@utoronto.ca Website: http://vicu.utoronto.ca

Faculté De Théologie Évangélique, (Union d'Eglises Baptistes Françaises au Canada) 2285 Avenue Papineau, Montréal, QC H2K 4J5. Amar Djaballah. Tel. (514)526-2003 Fax (514)526-6887

Faith Alive Bible College, (Nondenominational) 637 University Dr., Saskatoon, SK S7N 0H8. David Pierce. Tel. (306)652-2230 Fax (306)665-1125

Full Gospel Bible Institute, (Apostolic Church of Pentecost of Canada Inc.) Box 579, Eston, SK S0L 1A0. Rev. Lauren E. Miller. Tel. (306)962-3621 Fax (306)962-3810

Gardner College, A Centre for Christian Studies, (Church of God-Anderson, Indiana) 4704 55th St., Camrose, AB T4V 2B6. John Alan Howard. Tel. (780)672-0171 Fax (780)672-6888 Email: gardnerc@cable-lynx.net Website: http://cable-lynx/~gardnerc

Grand Seminaire de Montréal,* (The Roman Catholic Church in Canada) 2065 Sherbrook Ouest, Montréal, QC H3H 1G6. Louis-Paul Gauvreau. Tel. (514)935-1169 Fax (514)935-5497 Email: Information Generale: infor@gsdm.qc.ca OR Bibliotheque: biblio@gsdm.qc.ca Website: www.gsdm.qc.ca

Great Lakes Bible College, (Churches of Christ in Canada) 62 Hickory St. W., Waterloo, ON N2L 3J4. Dr. Geoffrey Ellis, Principal. Tel. (905)885-6330 Fax (905)563-0818 Email: info@glcc.vaxxine.com

Heritage Baptist College/Heritage Theological Seminary, (The Fellowship of Evangelical Baptist Churches in Canada) 175 Holiday Inn

Dr., Cambridge, ON N3C 3T2. Marvin Brubacher. Tel. (519)651-2869 Fax (519)651-2870
Email: admin@heritage-theo.edu
Website: www.heritage-theo.edu

Huron College,* (The Anglican Church of Canada) 1349 Western Rd., London, ON N6G 1H3. Dr. David Bevan, Principal. Tel. (519)438-7224 Fax (519)438-3938

Institut Biblique Beree, (The Pentecostal Assemblies of Canada) 1711 Henri-Bourassa Est, Montréal, QC H2C 1J5. André L. Gagnon. Tel. (514)385-4238 Fax (514)385-4238

Institut Biblique Laval, (Canadian Conference of Mennonite Brethren Churches) 1775, boul Édouard-Laurin, Ville Saint-Laurent, QC H4L 2B9. Eric Wingender. Tel. (514)331-0878 Fax (514)331-0879
Email: iblinstitute@proxyma.net

Institute for Christian Studies, (Nondenominational) 229 College St., Suite 200, Toronto, ON M5T 1R4. Harry Fernhout. Tel. (416)979-2331 or 1 (888)326-5347 Fax (416)979-2332
Email: email@icscanada.edu
Website: www.icscanada.edu

International Bible College, (Church of God-Cleveland, Tennessee) 401 Trinity La., Moose Jaw, SK S6H 0E3. Alex Allan. Tel. (306)692-4041 Fax (306)692-7968

Joint Board of Theological Colleges,* (Interdenominational) 3473 University St., Montréal, QC H3A 2A8. Dr. John Simons. Tel. (514)849-8511 Fax (514)849-4113
Email: dio@colba.net
Website: www.mcgill.ca/religion/jbtc.htm

Key-Way-Tin Bible Institute, (Nondenominational) Box 540, Lac La Biche, AB T0A 2C0. Dir. Dave Petkau. Tel. (780)623-4565 Fax (780)623-1788

Knox College,* (Presbyterian Church of Canada) 59 St. George St., Toronto, ON M5S 2E6. Arthur Van Seters. Tel. (416)978-4500 Fax (416)971-2133
Email: knox.college@utoronto.ca
Website: www.utoronto.ca/knox

Living Faith Bible College, (Fellowship of Christian Assemblies- Canada) Box 100, Caroline, AB T0M 0M0. Cliff A. Stalwick. Tel. (403)722-2225 Fax (403)722-2459
Email: office@lfbc.net
Website: www.lfbc.net

Lutheran Theological Seminary,* (Evangelical Lutheran Church in Canada) 114 Seminary Crescent, Saskatoon, SK S7N 0X3. Faith Rohrbough. Tel. (306)966-7850 Fax (306)966-7852
Email: rohrb@duke.usask.ca
Website: www.stu.saskatoon.sk.ca

Maritime Christian College, (Christian Churches and Churches of Christ in Canada) 503 University Ave., Charlottetown, PE C1A 7Z4. Merle W. Zimmerman. Tel. (902)628-8887 Fax (902)892-3959
Email: registrar@maritimechristiancollege.pe.ca
Website: www.maritimechristiancollege.pe.ca

McGill University Faculty of Religious Studies,* (Interdenominational) 3520 University St., Montréal, QC H3A 2A7. Donna R. Runnalls. Tel. (514)398-4121 Fax (514)398-6665

McMaster Divinity College,* (Baptist) McMaster Divinity College , Hamilton, ON L8S 4K1. William H. Brackney. Tel. (905)525-9140 Ext 24401 Fax (905)577-4782
Email: divinity@mcmaster.ca
Website: www.mcmaster.ca/divinity

Millar College of the Bible, (Interdenominational) Box 25, Pambrun, SK S0N 1W0. A. Brian Atmore. Tel. (306)582-2033 Fax (306) 582-2027

Montreal Diocesan Theological College,* (The Anglican Church of Canada) 3473 University St., Montreal, QC H3A 2A8. The Rev. Dr. Jon Simons, Principal. Tel. (514)849-3004 Fax (514)849-4113
Email: diocoll@netrover.com
Website: www.montreal.anglican.org/mdtc

Mount Carmel Bible School, (Christian Brethren—also known as Plymouth Brethren) 4725 106 Ave., Edmonton, AB T6A 1E7. Gordon King. Tel. (780)465-3015 Toll-free 1(800) 561-6443 Fax (780)466-2485
Email: carmel@worldgate.com

National Native Bible College, (Elim Fellowship of Evangelical Churches and Ministers) Box 478, Deseronto, ON K0K 1X0. Carl Brant, Board Chair. Tel. (613)396-2311 Fax (613)396-2314

Newman Theological College,* (The Roman Catholic Church in Canada) 15611 St. Albert Trail, Edmonton, AB T6V 1H3. Kevin J. Carr. Tel. (780)447-2993 Fax (780)447-2685
Email: admin@newman.edu
Website: www.newman.edu

Nipawin Bible Institute, (Interdenominational) Box 1986, Nipawin, SK S0E 1E0. Mark Leppington. Tel. (306)862-5095 Fax (306) 862-3651
Email: nbi@sk.sympatico.ca

Northwest Baptist Theological College and Seminary,* (The Fellowship of Evangelical Baptist Churches in Canada) P.O. Box 790, Langley, BC V3A 8B8. Larry D. McCullough. Tel. (604)888-3310 Fax (604)888-3354
Email: College: enrolment@nbtc.bc.ca OR Seminary-NBS: acts@twu.ca
Website: www.nbtc.ba.ca

Northwest Bible College, (The Pentecostal Assemblies of Canada) 11617-106 Ave., Edmonton, AB T5H 0S1. G. Johnson. Tel. (780)452-0808 Fax (780)452-5803 Email: info@northwest.ab.ca Website: www.northwest.ab.ca

Ontario Christian Seminary, (Christian Churches and Churches of Christ in Canada) P.O. Box 324, Stn. D 260 High Park Ave., Toronto, ON M6P 3J9. James R. Cormode. Tel. (416)769-7115 Fax (416)769-7047

Pacific Life Bible College, (Foursquare) 15100 66 A Ave., Surrey, BC V3S 2A6. Rob Buzzq. Tel. (604)597-9082 Fax (604)597-9090 Email: paclife@pacificlife.edu

Parole de Vie Bethel/Word of Life Bethel, (Nondenominational) 1175 Chemin Woodward Hill, RR1, Lennoxville, QC J1M 2A2. Ken Beach. Tel. (819)823-8435 Fax (819)823-2468 Email: kenb@canada.wol.org

Peace River Bible Institute, (Interdenomi-national) Box 99, Sexsmith, AB T0H 3C0. Reuben Kvill. Tel. (780)568-3962 Fax (780)568-4431 Email: prbi@telusplanet.net Website: www.prbi.edu

Prairie Graduate School, (Interdenominational) 2540 S Ave. NW, Calgary, AB T2N 0T5. Rick Down. Tel. (403)777-0150 Fax (403)270-2336

The Presbyterian College, Montreal,* (Presby-terian Church in Canada) 3495 University St., Montreal, QC H3A 2A8. John Vissers, Principal. Tel. (514)288-5256 Fax (514)288-8072

Providence College and Theological Seminary,* (Interdenominational) General Delivery, Otterburne, MB R0A 1G0. Larry J. McKinney. Tel. (204)433-7488 Fax (204)433-7158 Email: info@providence.mb.ca Website: www.providence.mb.ca

Queens College,* (The Anglican Church of Canada) 210 Prince Phillip Dr., St. Johns, NF A1B 3R6. Boyd Morgan. Tel. (709)753-0116 Fax (709)753-1214

Queen's Theological College,* (The United Church of Canada) Queen's Theological College , Kingston, ON K7L 3N6. Hallett E. Llewellyn. Tel. (613)545-2110 Fax (613)545-6879 Email: theology@post.queensu.ca Website: http://info.queensu.ca/theology/qtc home.html

Reformed Episcopal Theological College, (Reformed Episcopal Church of Canada) 320 Armstrong St., Box 2532, New Liskeard, ON P0J 1P0. Rt. Rev. Michael Fedechko. Tel. (705)647-4565 Fax (705)647-4565 Fax E-mail: fed@nt.net Email: fed@nt.net Website: www.recorg.us

Regent College,* (Interdenominational) 5800 University Blvd., Vancouver, BC V6T 2E4. Walter C. Wright. Tel. (800)663-8664 Fax (604)224-3097 Email: regentcollege@compuserve.com Website: www.regent-college.edu

Regis College,* (The Roman Catholic Church in Canada) 15 St. Mary St., Toronto, ON M4Y 2R5. John Allan Loftus, S.J. Tel. (416)922-5474 Fax (416)922-2898 Email: regis.registrar@utoronto.ca Website: www.utoronto.ca/regis

Rocky Mountain College: Centre for Biblical Studies, (The Evangelical Missionary Church of Canada) 4039 Brentwood Rd. NW, Calgary, AB T2L 1L1. Gordon Dirks. Tel. (403)284-5100 Fax (403)220-9567 Email: admin@rockyme.edu Website: www.rockyme.edu

St. Andrew's Theological College,* (The United Church of Canada) 1121 College Dr., Saskatoon, SK S7N 0W3. Dr. Christopher Lind, President. Tel. (306)966-8970 Fax (306)966-8981 Website: www.stu.saskatoon.sk.ca

St. Augustine's Seminary of Toronto,* (The Roman Catholic Church in Canada) 2661 Kingston Rd., Scarborough, ON M1M 1M3. John A. Boissonneau. Tel. (416)261-7207 Fax (416)261-2529 Website: www. canxsys.com/staugust.htm

St. John's College, Univ. of Manitoba, Faculty of Theology, (The Anglican Church of Canada) 92 Dysart Rd., Winnipeg, MB R3T 2M5. B. Hudson McLean. Tel. (204)474-6852 Fax (204)261-1215

Saint Paul University, Faculty of Theology, (The Roman Catholic Church) 223 Main St., Ottawa, ON K1S 1C4. David B. Perrin. Tel. (613)236-1393 Fax (613)751-4016

St. Peter's Seminary,* (The Roman Catholic Church in Canada) 1040 Waterloo St., London, ON N6A 3Y1. Thomas C. Collins. Tel. (519)432-1824 Fax (519)432-0964

St. Stephen's College, Grad. & Continuing Theological Educucation,* (The United Church of Canada) 8810 112th St., Edmonton, AB T6G 2J6. Christopher V. Levan. Tel. (780)439-7311 Fax (780)433-8875

Salvation Army College for Officer Training, (The Salvation Army in Canada) 2130 Bayview Ave., North York, ON M4N 3K6. Wayne N. Pritchett (Principal). Tel. (416)481-6131 Fax (416)481-6810; (416)481-2895 (Library)

The Salvation Army William and Catherine Booth Bible College, (The Salvation Army in Canada) 447 Webb Pl., Winnipeg, MB R3B

2P2. Lloyd Hetherington. Tel. (204)947-6701 Fax (204)942-3856
Email: wcbc@cc.umanitoba.ca

Steinbach Bible College, (Mennonite) Box 1420, Steinbach, MB R0A 2A0. Stan Plett. Tel. (204)326-6451 Fax (204)326-6908
Email: pr@sbcollege.mb.ca
Website: www.sbcollege.mb.ca

Theological College of the Canadian Reformed Churches, (Canadian and American Reformed Churches) 110 West 27th St., Hamilton, ON L9C 5A1. N. H. Gootjes. Tel. (416)575-3688 Fax (416)575-0799

Toronto Baptist Seminary and Bible College, (Association of Regular Baptist Churches-Canada) 130 Gerrard St., E., Toronto, ON M5A 3T4. Andrew M. Fountain. Tel. (416)925-3263 Fax (416)925-8305
Email: tbs@tbs.edu
Website: www.tbs.edu

Toronto School of Theology,* (Interdenominational) 47 Queens Park Crescent E., Toronto, ON M5S 2C3. W. David Neelands, Dir. Tel. (416)978-4039 Fax (416)978-7821
Email: registrar.tst@utoronto.ca
Website: www.utoronto.ca/tst

Trinity College, Faculty of Divinity,* (The Anglican Church of Canada) 6 Hoskin Ave., Toronto, ON M5S 1H8. D. Wiebe, Dean. Tel. (416)978-2133 Fax (416)978-4949
Email: divinity@trinity.utoronto.ca
Website: www.trinity.utoronto.ca/divinity

Tyndale College and Seminary,* (Transdenominational) 25 Ballyconnor Ct., Toronto, ON M2M 4B3. Dr. Brian C. Stiller. Tel. (416)226-6380 Fax (416)226-6746
Email: info@tyndale-canada.edu
Website: www.tyndale-canada.edu

United Theological College/Le Séminaire Uni,* (The United Church of Canada) 3521 rue Université, Montréal, QC H3A 2A9. Rev. Philip Joudrey. Tel. (514)849-2042 Fax (514)849-8634
Email: infoutc@colba.net
Website: www.colba.net/~utc./

Université Laval, Faculé de théologie et de sciences religieuses, (The Roman Catholic Church in Canada) Cité Universitaire, Ste-Foy, QC G1K 7P4. Marc Pelchat. Tel. (418)656-2131 Fax (418)656-3273
Email: ftsr@ftsr.ulaval.ca
Website: www.ulaval.ca

Université de Montréal, Faculté de théologie, (The Roman Catholic Church in Canada) C. P. 6128 Succ. Centre Ville, Montréal, QC H3C 3J7. Jean-Marc Charron. Tel. (514)343-7160 Fax (514)343-5738
Email: theologie@ere.umontreal.ca
Website: www.theo.umontreal.ca

Université de Sherbrooke, Faculté de theologié, (The Roman Catholic Church in Canada) 2500 boul. Université, Sherbrooke, QC J1K 2R1. Jean-François Malherbe. Tel. (819)821-7600 Fax (819)821-7677

University of St. Michael's College, Faculty of Theology,* (The Roman Catholic Church in Canada) 81 St. Mary St., Toronto, ON M5S 1J4. Dean Brian F. Hogan. Tel. (416)926-7140 Fax (416)926-7294
Website: www.utoronto.ca/stmikes/index.html

The University of Winnipeg, Faculty of Theology,* (Multi-denominational and the United Church of Canada) 515 Portage Ave., Winnipeg, MB R3B 2E9. Ray Whitehead, Dean. Tel. (204)786-9390 Fax (204)772-2584
Email: theology@uwinnipeg.ca
Website: www.uwinnipeg.ca/academic/theology

Vancouver School of Theology,* (Interdenominational) 6000 Iona Dr., Vancouver, BC V6T 1L4. W. J. Phillips. Tel. (604)822-9031 Fax (604)822-9212
Email: dbartlet@vst.edu
Website: www.vst.edu

Waterloo Lutheran Seminary,* (Evangelical Lutheran Church in Canada) 75 University Ave. W., Waterloo, ON N2L 3C5. Richard C. Crossman. Tel. (519)884-1970 Fax (519)725-2434
Website: www.wlu.ca/~wwwsem/

Western Christian College, (Churches of Christ in Canada) Box 5000, 220 Whitmore Ave. W., Dauphin, MB R7N 2V5. John McMillan. Tel. (204)638-8801 Fax (204)638-7054

Western Pentecostal Bible College, (The Pentecostal Assemblies of Canada) Box 1700, Abbotsford, BC V2S 7E7. James G. Richards. Tel. (604)853-7491 Fax (604)853-8951
Email: wpbcr@uniserve.com

Winkler Bible Institute, (Canadian Conference of Mennonite Brethren Churches) 121 7 St. S., Winkler, MB R6W 2N4. Paul Kroeker. Tel. (204)325-4242 Fax (204)325-9028

Wycliffe College,* (The Anglican Church of Canada) 5 Hoskin Ave., Toronto, ON M5S 1H7. Rev. Dr. George R. Sumner, Jr. Tel. (416)946-3521 Fax (416)946-3545
Website: www.chass.utoronto.ca/wycliffe

11. Religious Periodicals
in the United States

This list focuses on publications of the organizations listed in Directory 3, "Religious Bodies in the United States," however there are also some independent publications listed. The list does not include all publications prepared by religious bodies, and not all the publications listed here are necessarily the official publication of a particular church. Regional publications and newsletters are not included. A more extensive list of religious periodicals published in the United States can be found in *Gale Directory of Publications and Broadcast Media*, (Gale Research, Inc., P.O. Box 33477, Detroit MI 48232-5477).

Each entry in this directory contains: the title of the periodical; frequency of publication; religious affiliation; editor's name, address, telephone and fax number; and e-mail and website addresses when available. The frequency of publication, which appears in parenthesis after the name of the publication, is represented by a "w" for weekly; "m" for monthly; "q" for quarterly.

21st Century Christian, (m) Churches of Christ, M. Norvel Young and Prentice A. Meador, Jr., Box 40304 Nashville, TN 37204. Tel. (800)331-5991 Fax (615)385-5915

The A.M.E. Christian Recorder, (bi-w) African Methodist Episcopal Church, Ricky Spain, 500 8th Ave., S. Suite 213 Nashville, TN 37203. Tel. (615)256-8548 Fax (615)244-1833

A.M.E. Review, (q) African Methodist Episcopal Church, Paulette Coleman, PhD., 500 Eighth Ave., S., Ste.211 Nashville, TN 37203-4181. Tel. (615)256-7020 Fax (615)256-7092 Email: AMERVW@aol.com

Action, (10/yr) Churches of Christ, Tex Williams, Box 9346 Austin, TX 78766. Tel. (512)345-8191 Fax (512)345-6634 Email: wbschool@bga.com

Adra Today, (q) Seventh-day Adventist Church, Beth Schaefer, 12501 Old Columbia Pike Silver Spring, MD 20904-6600. Tel. (301)680-6355 Fax (301)680-6370 Email: 74617.2105@compuserve.com Website: http://www.adra.org

Adult Lessons Quarterly, (q) Nondenominational, Darcy Quigley, J. Milton Society for the Blind 475 Riverside Dr., Rm. 455 New York, NY 10115-0122. Tel. (212)870-3335 Fax (212)870-3229 Website: http://www.jmsblind.org

The Adult Quarterly, (q) Associate Reformed Presbyterian Church (General Synod), Mr. W. H. F. Kuykendall PhD., P.O. Box 575 Due West, SC 29639. Tel. (864)232-8297

Advent Christian News, (m) Advent Christian Church, Rev. Keith D. Wheaton, P.O. Box 23152 Charlotte, NC 28227. Tel. (704)545-6161 Fax (704)573-0712 Email: Mayerpub@aol.com

The Advent Christian Witness, (m) Advent Christian Church, Rev. Keith D. Wheaton,

P.O. Box 23152 Charlotte, NC 28227. Tel. (704)545-6161 Fax (704)573-0712 Email: Mayerpub@aol.com

Adventist Review, (w) Seventh-day Adventist Church, W. G. Johnsson, 12501 Old Columbia Pike Silver Spring, MD 20904-6600. Tel. (301)680-6560 Fax (301)680-6638 Email: 74617,15.compuserve.com Website: www.adventistreview.com

The Advocate, (10/yr) Episcopal, Kay Collier-Slone, Ph.D., PO Box 610 Lexington, KY 40588-0610. Tel. (606)252-6527 Fax (606) 231-9077 Email: diolex@aol.com

Again Magazine, (q) The Antiochian Orthodox Christian Archdiocese of North, R. Thomas Zell, P.O. Box 76 Ben Lomond, CA 95005-0076. Tel. (408)336-5118 Fax (408)336-8882 Email: shouston@got.net Website: http://www.conciliarpress.co

Agenda, (10/yr) Church of the Brethren, Howard Royer and Nevin Dulabaum, 1451 Dundee Ave. Elgin, IL 60120-1676. Tel. (847)742-5100

Alive Now, (6/yr) The United Methodist Church, George Graham, P.O. Box 189 Nashville, TN 37202. Tel. (615)340-7218 Email: alivenow@upperroom.org Website: www.upperroom.org/alivenow/

The Allegheny Wesleyan Methodist, (m) Allegheny Wesleyan Methodist Connection (Original Allegheny Conference), Michael Marshall, P.O. Box 357 Salem, OH 44460. Tel. (330)337-9376 Fax (330)337-9700 Email: awmc@juno.com

Alliance Life, (bi-w) The Christian and Missionary Alliance, P.O. Box 35000 Colorado Springs, CO 80935. Tel. (719)599-5999 Fax (719)593-8692 Email: alife@concentric.net

American Baptist In Mission, (6/yr) American Baptist Churches in the USA, Richard W.

Schramm, P.O. Box 851 Valley Forge, PA 19482-0851. Tel. (610)768-2077 Fax (610) 768-2320
Email: richard.schramm@abc-usa.org
Website: http://www.abc-usa.org

American Baptist Quarterly, (q) American Baptist Churches in the USA, William R. Millar, P.O. Box 851 Valley Forge, PA 19482-0851. Tel. (610)768-2269 Fax (610)768-2266
Email: naomi.reynolds@abc-usa.org
Website: www.abc-usa/abhs

American Bible Society Record, (6/yr) Nondenominational, Peter Feuerherd, 1865 Broadway New York, NY 10023-7505. Tel. (212)408-1419 Fax (212)408-1456
Email: absrecord@americanbible.org
Website: www.americanbible.org

El Aposento Alto, (6/yr) The United Methodist Church, Carmen Gaud, P.O. Box 189 Nashville, TN 37202. Tel. (615)340-7253 Fax (615)340-7267
Email: ElAposentoAlto@upperroom.org
Website: www.upperroom.org

The Armenian Church, (m) Diocese of the Armenian Church of America, Michael A. Zeytoonian, 630 Second Avenue New York, NY 10016. Tel. (212)686-0710 Fax (212)779-3558

The Associate Reformed Presbyterian, (m) Associate Reformed Presbyterian Church (General Synod), Mr. Ben Johnston, One Cleveland St. Greenville, SC 29601. Tel. (864)232-8297 Fax (864)271-3729
Email: arpmaged@arpsynod.org
Website: http://www.arpsynod.org

At Ease, (bi-m) Assemblies of God, Charles W. Marvin, 1445 Boonville Ave. Springfield, MO 65802. Tel. (417)862-2781 Fax (417)863-7276
Email: chaplaincy@ag.org
Website: http://chaplaincy.ag.org

Attack, A Magazine for Christian Men, (q) National Association for Free Will Baptists, James E. Vallance, P.O. Box 5002 Antioch, TN 37011-5002. Tel. (615)731-4950 Fax (615) 731-0771

The Banner of Truth, (m) Netherlands Reformed Congregations, J. den Hoed, 824 18th Ave. S. Rock Valley, IA 51247. Tel. (712)476-2442

The Banner, (26/year) Christian Reformed Church in North America, John A. Suk, 2850 Kalamazoo Ave., S.E. Grand Rapids, MI 49560. Tel. (616)224-0732 Fax (616)224-0834
Email: editorial@thebanner.org

The Baptist Bible Tribune, (m) Baptist Bible Fellowship International, Mike Randall, P.O. Box 309 HSJ Springfield, MO 65801. Tel. (417)831-3996 Fax (417)831-1470
Email: BBFpubs@dialnet.net
Website: http://www.tribune.org

Baptist Bulletin, (m) General Association of Regular Baptist Churches, David M. Gower, 1300 N. Meacham Rd. Schaumburg, IL 60173-4806. Tel. (847)843-1600 Fax (847)843-3757
Email: baptistbulletin@garbc.org
Website: www.garbc.org

Baptist History and Heritage, (3/yr) Southern Baptist Historical Society, Merrill M. Hawkins, Jr., P.O. Box 71919 Jefferson City, TN 37760. Tel. (423)471-3246 Fax (423)471-3502
Email: hawkins@cacc.cn.edu

Baptist Leader, (q) American Baptist Churches in the USA, Ingrid Dvirnak, Managing Editor, P.O. Box 851 Valley Forge, PA 19842-0851. Tel. (610)768-2143 Fax (610)768-2056
Email: baptist.leader@abc-usa.org

Baptist Peacemaker, (q) Nondenominational, Ken Sehested, P.O. Box 280 Lake Junaluska, NC 28745. Tel. (704)456-1881 Fax (704)456-1883

Baptist Peacemaker, (q) Baptist, 4800 Wedgewood Dr. Charlotte, NC 28210. Tel. (704)521-6051 Fax (704)521-6053
Email: bpfna@bpfna.org
Website: www.bpfna.org

Baptist Progress, (q) Progresive National Baptist Convention, Inc., Archie Logan, 601 50th St. NE Washington, DC 20019. Tel. (202)396-0558 Fax (202)398-4998

Baptist Witness, (m) Primitive Baptists, Lasserre Bradley, Jr., Box 17037 Cincinnati, OH 45217. Tel. (513)821-7289 Fax (513)821-7303

The Bible Advocate, (10/yr) The Church of God (Seventh Day), Denver, Colo., Calvin Burrell, PO Box 33677 Denver, CO 80233. Tel. (303)452-7973 Fax (303)452-0657
Email: cofgsd@denver.net
Website: www.baonline.org

The Brethren Evangelist, (m) Brethren Church (Ashland, Ohio), Rev. Richard C. Winfield, 524 College Ave. Ashland, OH 44805. Tel. (419)289-1708 Fax (419)281-0450
Email: Brethren@bright.net

Brethren Journal, (10/yr) Unity of Brethren, Rev. Milton Maly, 6703 FM 2502 Brenham, TX 77833-9803. Tel. (409)830-8762

The Bridegroom's Messenger, (bi-m) The International Pentecostal Church of Christ, Janice Boyce, 121 W. Hunters Trail Elizabeth City, NC 27909. Tel. (919)338-3003 Fax (919)338-3003

Builder, (m) Mennonite Church, David R. Hiebert, 616 Walnut Ave. Scottdale, PA 15683. Tel. (724)887-3363 Fax (707)897-3788
Email: Hiebert%mph@mcimail.com
Website: www.mph.org/builder/

The Burning Bush, (q) The Metropolitan Church Association, Inc. (Wesleyan), Rev. E. L. Adams,

The Metropolitan Church Assoc. 323 Broad St. Lake Geneva, WI 53147. Tel. (414)248-6786

The Calvary Messenger, (m) Beachy Amish Mennonite Churches, David Sommers, Rt. 2, Box 187-A Abbeville, SC 29620. Tel. (814)662-2483 Fax

Campus Life, (9/yr) Nondenominational, Christopher Lutes, 465 Gunderson Dr. Carol Stream, IL 60188. Tel. (630)260-6200 Fax (630)260-0114
Email: cledit@aol.com
Website: www.campuslife.net

Capsule, (m) General Association of General Baptists, Jack Eberhardt, 100 Stinson Dr. Poplar Bluff, MO 63901. Tel. (573)785-7746 Fax (573)785-0564

Caring, (6/yr) Assemblies of God, Owen Wilkie, Gospel Publishing House 1445 Boonville Ave. Springfield, MO 65802. Tel. (417)862-2781 Fax (417)862-4832
Email: benevolences@ag.org

Cathedral Age, (q) Interdenominational, Craig W. Stapert, Mass & Wisconsin Ave. NW Washington, DC 20016-5098. Tel. (202)537-5681 Fax (202)364-6600
Email: cathedral_age@cathedral.org
Website: www.cathedral.org/cathedral

Catholic Chronicle, (bi-w) The Roman Catholic Church, Patricia Lynn Morrison, 2130 Madison Avenue PO Box 1866 Toledo, OH 43603-1866. Tel. (419)243-4178 Fax (419)243-4235

Catholic Digest, (m) The Roman Catholic Church, Richard Reece, 2115 Summit Avenue St. Paul, MN 55105-1081. Tel. (612)962-6725 Fax (612)962-6755
Email: Cdigest@stthomas.edu
Website: http://www.CatholicDigest.or

Catholic Herald, (w) The Roman Catholic Church, Ethel M. Gintoft, 3501 S. Lake Dr. St. Francis, WI 53235-0913. Tel. (414)769-3468
Email: chn@execpc.com
Website: www.execpc.com/~chn

Catholic Light, (bi-w) The Roman Catholic Church, Jerome M. Zufelt, 300 Wyoming Ave. Scranton, PA 18503. Tel. (570)346-8915 Fax (570)346-8917
Email: jzufeltcatholiclight@worldnet.att.net

The Catholic New World, (w) The Roman Catholic Church, Thomas H. Sheridan, 1144 W. Jackson Blvd. Chicago, IL 60607. Tel. (312)243-1300 Fax (312)243-1526
Email: Neworld201@aol.com
Website: catholicnewworld.com

The Catholic Peace Voice, (q) The Roman Catholic Church, Dave Robinson, 532 W. 8th Street Erie, PA 16502. Tel. (814)453-4955 Fax (814)452-4784

The Catholic Review, (w) The Roman Catholic Church, Daniel L. Medinger, P.O. Box 777 Baltimore, MD 21203. Tel. (410)625-8477 Fax (410)332-1069
Email: dmedinger@aol.com

Catholic Standard and Times, (w) The Roman Catholic Church, Rev Paul S. Quinter, 222 N. 17th St. Philadelphia, PA 19103. Tel. (215)587-3660 Fax (215)587-3979

The Catholic Transcript, (w) The Roman Catholic Church, Christopher M. Tiano, 785 Asylum Ave. Hartford, CT 06105-2886. Tel. (203)527-1175 Fax (203)947-6397

Catholic Universe Bulletin, (bi-w) The Roman Catholic Church, Dennis Sadowski, 1027 Superior Ave., N.E. Cleveland, OH 44114-2556. Tel. (216)696-6525 Fax (216)696-6519

Catholic Worker, (7/yr) The Roman Catholic Church, Brian Harte, 36 E. First St. New York, NY 10003. Tel. (212)777-9617

Cela Biedrs, (10/yr) The Latvian Evangelical Lutheran Church in America, Velta Pelcis, 5808 W. Carmen Ave. Milwaukee, WI 53218-2051. Tel. (414)463-6613

Celebration: An Ecumenical Worship Resource, (m) Interdenominational, Patrick Marrin, P.O. Box 419493 Kansas City, MO 64141-6493. Tel. (816)531-0538 Fax (816)968-2280
Email: patmarrin@aol.com
Website: www.natcath.org

The Challenge, (q) The Bible Church of Christ, Inc., A.M. Jones, 1358 Morris Ave. Bronx, NY 10456. Tel. (718)588-2284 Fax (718)992-5597

Charisma, (m) Nondenominational, J. Lee Grady, 600 Rinehart Rd. Lake Mary, FL 32746. Tel. (407)333-0600 Fax (407)333-7133
Email: grady@strang.com
Website: http://www.charismamag.com

Childlife, (q) Nondenominational, Terry Madison, PO Box 9716 Federal Way, WA 98063-9716. Tel. (206)815-2300 Fax (206)815-3445
Email: tmadison@aol.com

Children's Friend, (q) Seventh-day Adventist Church, Jerry Stevens, P.O. Box 6097 Lincoln, NE 68506. Tel. (402)488-0981 Fax (402)488-7582
Email: CRSnet@compuserve.com
Website: www.ChristianRecord.org

Christadelphian Advocate, (m) Christadelphians, Edward W. Farrar, 4 Mountain Park Ave. Hamilton, ON L9A 1A2. Tel. (905)383-1817 Fax (905)383-2705

Christadelphian Tidings, (m) Christadelphians, Donald H. Styles, 42076 Hartford Dr. Canton, MI 48187. Tel. (313)844-2426 Fax (313)844-8304

297

Christadelphian Watchman, (m) Christadelphians, George Booker, 2500 Berwyn Cir. Austin, TX 78745. Tel. (512)447-8882

The Christian Baptist, (m) Primitive Baptists, Elder S. T. Tolley, P.O. Box 68 Atwood, TN 38220. Tel. (901)662-7417
Email: cbl@aeneas.net

Christian Bible Teacher, (m) Churches of Christ, J. J. Turner, Box 1060 Abilene, TX 79604. Tel. (915)677-6262 Fax (915)677-1511

The Christian Century, (37/yr) Nondenominational, John Buchanan, 104 South Michigan Ave. Suite 700 Chicago, IL 60603. Tel. (312)263-7510 Fax (312)263-7540

The Christian Chronicle, (m) Churches of Christ, Bailey McBride, Box 11000 Oklahoma City, OK 73136-1100. Tel. (405)425-5070 Fax (405)425-5076

The Christian Community, (8/yr) International Council of Community Churches, Dr. J. Ralph Shotwell, 21116 Washington Pkwy. Frankfort, IL 60423. Tel. (815)464-5690 Fax (815)464-5692

Christian Education Counselor, (bi-m) Assemblies of God, Sylvia Lee, Sunday School Promotion and Training, 1445 Boonville Ave. Springfield, MO 65802-1894. Tel. (417)862-2781 Fax (417)862-0503
Email: salee@publish.ag.org
Website: www.we-build-people.org/cec

The Christian Endeavor World, (q) Nondenominational, David G. Jackson, P.O. Box 820 3575 Valley Rd. Liberty Corner, NJ 07938-0820. Tel. (908)604-9440 Fax (908)604-6075

The Christian Index, (m) Christian Methodist Episcopal Church, Rev. Lawrence L Reddick III, P.O. Box 665 Memphis, TN 38101-0665. Tel. (901)345-1173

Christian Leader, (m) U.S. Conference of Mennonite Brethren Churches, Don Ratzlaff, Box V Hillsboro, KS 67063. Tel. (316)947-5543 Fax (316)947-3266

Christian Living, (8/yr) Mennonite Church, Levi Miller, 616 Walnut Ave. Scottdale, PA 15683. Tel. (724)887-8500 Fax (724)887-3111
Email: cl@mph.org
Website: www.mph.org/cl/

The Christian Ministry, (6/yr) Nondenominational, John Buchanan, Publisher, 104 S. Michigan Ave. Suite 700 Chicago, IL 60603. Tel. (312)345-1914 Fax (312-345-8090
Email: ministry@christiancentury.org

Christian Monthly, (m) Apostolic Lutheran Church of America, Linda Mattson, Christian Monthly P.O. Box 220 Yamhill, OR 97148. Tel. (503)662-5909

Email: christianM@Apostolic-Lutheran.org
Website: www.Apostolic-Lutheran.org

Christian Outlook, (m) Pentecostal Assemblies of the World, Inc., Johnna E. Hampton, 3939 Meadows Dr. Indianapolis, IN 46205. Tel. (317)547-9541 Fax (317)543-0512

The Christian Reader, (bi-m) Nondenominational, Bonne Steffer, 465 Gunderson Dr. Carol Stream, IL 60188. Tel. (630)260-6200 Fax (630)260-0114

Christian Record, (q) Seventh-day Adventist Church, Jerry Stevens, P.O. Box 6097 Lincoln, NE 68506. Tel. (402)488-0981 Fax (402)488-7582
Email: CRSnet@compuserve.com
Website: www.ChristianRecord.org

The Christian Science Journal, (m) Church of Christ, Scientist, William E. Moody, One Norway St. Boston, MA 02115. Tel. (617)450-2000 Fax (617)450-2707
Email: moodyw@csps.com
Website: www.csjournal.com

The Christian Science Monitor, (d&w) Church of Christ, Scientist, David T. Cook, One Norway St. Boston, MA 02115. Tel. (617)450-2000 Fax (617)450-7575
Website: http://www.csmonitor.com

Christian Science Quarterly Weekly Bible Lessons, (q) Church of Christ, Scientist, Carol Humphry, Circulation Marketing Manager, One Norway St., C-40 Boston, MA 02115. Tel. (617)450-2000 Fax (617)450-7575
Email: service@csps.com
Website: www.biblelesson.com

Christian Science Sentinel, (w) Church of Christ, Scientist, William E. Moody, One Norway St. Boston, MA 02115-3112. Tel. (617)450-2000 Fax (617)450-2707
Email: moodyw@csps.com
Website: www.cssentinel.com

Christian Social Action, (bi-monthly) The United Methodist Church, Rev. Erik Alsgaard, 100 Maryland Ave. NE Washington, DC 20002. Tel. (202)488-5621 Fax (202)488-1617
Email: 1ranck@igc.org
Website: http://www.igc.apc.org/umoun

Christian Standard, (w) Christian Churches and Churches of Christ, Sam E. Stone, 8121 Hamilton Ave. Cincinnati, OH 45231. Tel. (513)931-4050 Fax (513)931-0950

Christian Woman, (bi-m) Churches of Christ, Sandra Humphrey, Box 150 Nashville, TN 37202. Tel. (615)254-8781 Fax (615)254-7411

Christianity & The Arts, (q) Nondenominational, Marci Whitney-Schenck, P.O. Box 118088 Chicago, IL 60611. Tel. (312)642-8606 Fax (312)266-7719
Email: chrnarts@aol.com

The Church Advocate, (q) Churches of God, General Conference, Mac Cordell, P.O. Box 926 700 E. Melrose Ave. Findlay, OH 45839. Tel. (419)424-1961 Fax (419)424-3433 Email: communications@cggc.org Website: www.cggc.org

Church of God Evangel, (m) Church of God (Cleveland, Tenn.), Bill George, P.O. Box 2250 Cleveland, TN 37320. Tel. (423)478-7592 Fax (423)478-7616 Email: bill_george@pathwaypress.org Website: www.pathwapress.org

Church of God Missions, (bi-m) Church of God (Anderson, Ind.), J. David Reames, Box 2337 Anderson, IN 46018-2337. Tel. (765)648-2128 Fax (765)642-4279 Email: mbchogvp@aol.com

Church of God Progress Journal, (bi-m) Church of God General Conference (Oregon, Ill. & Morrow, David Krogh, Box 100,000 Morrow, GA 30260. Tel. (404)362-0052 Fax (404)362-9307 Email: info@abc-coggc.org Website: www.abc-coggc.org

The Church Herald, (11/yr) Reformed Church in America, Christina Van Eyl, 4500 60th St., SE Grand Rapids, MI 49512. Tel. (616)698-7071 Fax (616)698-6606 Email: evaneyl@rca.org

Church History: Studies in Christianity and Culture, (q) Scholarly, Elizabeth A. Clark, Grant Wacker, Hans J. Hillerbrand, and Richard P. Heitzenrater, The Divinity School, Duke University Box 90975 Durham, NC 27708-0975. Tel. (919)660-3470 Fax (919-660-3473 Email: church-history@duke.edu

The Church Messenger, (bi-m) James S. Dutko, 280 Clinton St. Binghamton, NY 13905

Church School Herald, (q) African Methodist Episcopal Zion Church, Ms. Mary A. Love, P.O. Box 32305 Charlotte, NC 28232-2305. Tel. (704)332-9873 Fax (704)333-1769

Church & Society Magazine, (bi-m) Presbyterian Church (U.S.A.), Kathy Lancaster, 100 Witherspoon St. Louisville, KY 40202-1396. Tel. (502)569-5810 Fax (502)569-8116 Email: KATHY.LANCASTER@pcusa.org Website: horeb.pcusa.org/churchsociety

Church and State, (m) Independent, Joseph L. Conn, 1816 Jefferson Pl. N.W. Washington, DC 20036. Tel. (202)466-2587

Church and State, (m) Independent journal of religion and politics, Joseph L. Conn, 1816 Jefferson Place NW Washington, DC 20036. Tel. (202)466-2587 Email: conn@aol.com Website: http://www.netplexgroup.com/

The Churchman's Human Quest, Non-denominational, Edna Ruth Johnson, 1074 23rd Ave. N. St. Petersburg, FL 33704. Tel. (813)894-0097

Churchwoman, (q) Interdenominational, Rev. Martha M. Cruz, Editor and Elizabeth Young, Managing Editor, 475 Riverside Dr. New York, NY 10115. Tel. (212)870-2347 Fax (212)870-2338 Email: mmcruz@churchwomen.org Website: www.churchwomen.org

Circuit Rider, (6/yr) The United Methodist Church, Jill S. Reddig, 201 Eighth Ave. S Nashville, TN 37202. Tel. (615)749-6334 Fax (615)749-6512 Email: 102521.1510@compuserve.com

Clarion Herald, (bi-w) The Roman Catholic Church, Peter P. Finney, Jr., P. O. Box 53247 1000 Howard Ave. Suite 400 New Orleans, LA 70153. Tel. (504)596-3035 Fax (504)596-3020

The Clergy Journal, (10/yr) Nondenomi-national, Sharilyn A. Figueroa, Managing Editor & Clyde J. Steckel, Executive Editor, 6160 Carmen Avenue E Inver Grove Heights, MN 55076-4422. Tel. (800)328-0200 Fax (651)457-4617 Email: fig@logostaff.com

Club Connection, (q) Assemblies of God, Kerry Clarensau, 1445 Boonville Ave. Springfield, MO 65802-1894. Tel. (417)862-2781 Fax (417)862-0503 Email: clubconnection@ag.org Website: www.ag.org/missionettes

Co-Laborer, (bi-m) National Association of Free Will Baptists, Suzanne Franks, Women Nationally Active for Chris P.O. Box 5002 Antioch, TN 37011-5002. Tel. (615)731-6812 Fax (615)731-0771 Email: colaborer@nafwb.org

Collegiate Quarterly, (q) Seventh-day Adventist Church, Gary B. Swanson, 12501 Old Columbia Pike Silver Spring, MD 20904. Tel. (301)680-6160 Fax (301)680-6155

Columbia, (m) The Roman Catholic Church, Tim S. Hickey, One Columbus Plaza New Haven, CT 06510. Tel. (203)772-2130 Fax (203)777-0114 Email: info@kufc.org Website: www.kufc.org

The Commission, (12/yr) International Mission Board, Southern Baptist Convention, Mary Jane Welch, Box 6767 Richmond, VA 23230-0767. Tel. (804)219-1327 Fax (804)219-1410 Email: commission@imb.org Website: www.imb.org

Common Lot, (4/yr) United Church of Christ, Martha J. Hunter, 700 Prospect Ave. Cleveland, OH 44115. Tel. (216)736-2150 Fax (216)736-2156

Commonweal, (bi-w) The Roman Catholic Church, Margaret O'Brien Steinfels, 475 Riverside Drive, Rm 405 New York, NY 10115. Tel. (212)662-4200 Fax (212)662-4183

Communique, (m) National Baptist Convention of America, Inc., Robert Jeffrey, 1320 Pierre Avenue Shreveport, LA 71103. Tel. (318)221-3701 Fax (318)222-7512

The Congregationalist, (5/yr) National Association Congregational Christian Churches, Joseph B. Polhemus, 1105 Briarwood Rd. Mansfield, OH 44907. Tel. (419)756-5526 Fax (419)524-2621
Email: jbpedit@aol.com
Website: www.congregationalist.org

Conqueror, (bi-m) United Pentecostal Church International, John F. Sills, 8855 Dunn Rd. Hazelwood, MO 63042. Tel. (314)837-7300 Fax (314)837-4503
Email: GYouth8855@aol.com

Contact, (m) National Association of Free Will Baptists, Jack Williams, P.O. Box 5002 Antioch, TN 37011-5002. Tel. (615)731-6812 Fax (615)731-0771

Context, (22/yr) Nondenominational, Martin Marty, 205 W. Monroe St. Chicago, IL 60606-5013. Tel. (312)236-7782 Fax (312)236-8207
Email: editors@uscatholic.org
Website: www.contextonline.org

Cornerstone Connections, (q) Seventh-day Adventist Church, Gary B. Swanson, 12501 Old Columbia Pike Silver Spring, MD 20904. Tel. (301)680-6160 Fax (301)680-6155

Courage in the Struggle for Justic and Peace, (q) United Church of Christ, Sandy Sorensen, 110 Maryland Ave., Ste. 207, NE Washington, DC 20002. Tel. (202)543-1517 Fax (202)543-5994

Covenant Companion, (m) Evangelical Covenant Church, Jane K. Swanson-Nystrom, 5101 N. Francisco Ave. Chicago, IL 60625. Tel. (773)784-3000 Fax (773)784-4366
Email: covcom@compuserve.com

Covenant Home Altar, (q) Evangelical Covenant Church, Donald L. Meyer, 5101 N. Francisco Ave. Chicago, IL 60625. Tel. (773)784-3000 Fax (773)784-4366
Email: covcom@compuserve.com

Covenant Quarterly, (q) Evangelical Covenant Church, Wayne C. Weld, 3225 W. Foster Ave. Chicago, IL 60625-4895. Tel. (773)244-6230 Fax (773)244-6244
Email: WeldDone@aol.com

The Covenanter Witness, (11/yr) Reformed Presbyterian Church of North America, Drew Gordon and Lynne Gordon, 7408 Penn Ave. Pittsburgh, PA 15208. Tel. (412)241-0436 Fax (412)731-8861

Email: cwmailbag@aol.com
Website: www.psalms40.com

Credinta—The Faith, (q) The Romanian Orthodox Church in America, V. Rev. Archim. Dr. Vasile Vasilac, 45-03 48th Ave. Woodside, Queens, NY 11377. Tel. (313)893-8390

Credo, (m) The Antiochian Orthodox Christian Archdiocese of North, Charles Dinkler, P.O. Box 84 Stanton, NJ 08885-0084. Tel. (908)236-7890

The Criterion, (w) The Roman Catholic Church, John F. Fink, P. O. Box 1717 1400 N. Meridian Indianapolis, IN 46206. Tel. (317)236-1570

Cross Walk, (w) Church of the Nazarene, Jim Hampton, Word Action Publishing 6401 The Paseo Kansas City, MO 64131. Tel. (816)333-7000 Fax (816)333-4315
Email: crosswalk@nazarene.org
Website: http://www.nazarene.org

The Cumberland Flag, (m) Cumberland Presbyterian Church in America, Rev. Robert Stanley Wood, 226 Church St. Huntsville, AL 35801. Tel. (205)536-7481 Fax (205)536-7482

The Cumberland Presbyterian, (15/yr) Cumberland Presbyterian Church in America, M. Jacqueline De Berry Warren, 1978 Union Ave. Memphis, TN 38104. Tel. (901)276-4572 Fax (901)272-3913

Currents in Theology and Mission, (6/yr) Evangelical Lutheran Church in America, Ralph W. Klein, 1100 E. 55th St. Chicago, IL 60615. Tel. (773)256-0695 Fax (773)256-0782
Email: currents@lstc.edu
Website: http://www.lstc.edu/about/cu

Decision, (11/yr) Nondenominational, Kersten Beckstrom (Interim), 1300 Harmon Pl. Minneapolis, MN 55403. Tel. (612)338-0500 Fax (612)335-1299
Email: decision@bgea.org
Website: www.decisionmag.org

The Disciple, (10/yr) Christian Church (Disciples of Christ), Patricia R. Case, Box 1986 Indianapolis, IN 46206-1986. Tel. (317)635-3100 Fax (317)635-3700
Email: thedisciple@disciples.org
Website: www.thedisciple.com

Discovery, (q) Nondenominational, Braiile Only, for Youth, Darcy Quigley, J. Milton Society for the Blind 475 Riverside Drive, Rm 455 New York, NY 10115-0122. Tel. (212)870-3335 Fax (212)870-3229
Website: http://www.jmsblind.org

Doors and Windows, (q) The Evangelical Congregational Church, Rev. Timothy Christman, 100 W. Park Ave Myerstown, PA 17067

Ecu-Link, (q) Interdenominational, Sarah Vilankulu, 475 Riverside Drive, Rm 850 New York, NY 10115-0050. Tel. (212)870-2227

Fax (212)870-2030
Email: sarah@ncccusa.org

Ecumenical Trends, (m) Nondenominational, Kevin McMorrow, SA, Greymoor Ecumenical & Interreligious Institute PO Box 300 Garrison, NY 10524. Tel. (914)424-3671 Fax (914)424-2163

Eleventh Hour Messenger, (bi-m) Wesleyan Holiness Association of Churches, John Brewer, R R 2 Box 9 Winchester, IN 47394. Tel. (317)584-3199

Elim Herald, (q) Elim Fellowship, Bernard J. Evans, 1703 Dalton Road P.O. Box 57A Lima, NY 14485. Tel. (716)582-2790 Fax (716)624-1229
Email: 75551.743@compuserve.com

EMC Today, (bi-m) Evangelical Mennonite Church, Donald W. Roth, 1420 Kerrway Ct. Fort Wayne, IN 46805. Tel. (219)423-3649 Fax (219)420-1905

Emphasis on Faith and Living, (bi-m) The Missionary Church, Rev. Robert Ransom, PO Box 9127 Ft. Wayne, IN 46899. Tel. (219)747-2027 Fax (219)747-5331
Email: RLRansom@aol.com

Enrichment: A Journal for Pentecostal Ministry, (q) Assemblies of God, Wayde I. Goodall, 1445 Boonville Ave. Springfield, MO 65802. Tel. (417)862-2781 Fax (417)862-0416
Email: Wgoodall@ag.org
Website: www.enrichmentjournal.ag.org

The Ensign, (m) The Church of Jesus Christ Latter-day Saints, Jay M. Todd, Managing Editor, 50 E North Temple Street, 24th Fl Salt Lake City, UT 84150. Tel. (801)240-2950 Fax (801)240-5997
Email: JonesME@ldschurch.org

Epiphany Journal, (q) Interdenominational, Nun Macaria, 1516 N. Delaware Indianapolis, IN 46202. Tel. (317)926-7468

Episcopal Life, (m) The Episcopal Church, Jerrold Hames, 815 Second Ave. New York, NY 10017-4503. Tel. (800)334-7626 Fax (212)949-8059
Email: jerry.hames@ecunet.org
Website: www.ecusa.anglican.org/episcopal-life

The Evangel, (6/yr) American Association of Lutheran Churches, The, Charles D. Eidum, 10800 Lyndale Ave. S., #210 Minneapolis, MN 55420-5614. Tel. (612)884-7784 Fax (612)884-7894
Email: ChuckAALC@aol.com
Website: www.taalc.com

The Evangel, (q) The Evangelical Church Alliance, Derick Miller, 205 W. Broadway Bradley, IL 60915. Tel. (815)937-0720 Fax (815)937-0001

Email: eca@keynet.net
Website: www.keynet.net/~eca

The Evangelical Advocate, (m) Churches of Christ in Christian Union, Ralph Hux, P.O. Box 30 Circleville, OH 43113. Tel. (614)474-8856 Fax (614)477-7766

Evangelical Beacon, (7/yr) The Evangelical Free Church of America, Ms. Carol Madison, 901 East 78th St. Minneapolis, MN 55420-1300. Tel. (612)854-1300 Fax (612)853-8488

Evangelical Challenge, (q) The Evangelical Church, John F. Sills, 7733 West River Road Minneapolis, MN 55444. Tel. (612)561-0886 Fax (612)561-0774

Evangelical Visitor, (6/year) Brethren in Christ Church, Ronald C. Ross, P.O. Box 166 Nappanee, IN 46550. Tel. (219)773-3164 Fax (219)773-5934

Evangelism USA, (m) International Pentecostal Holiness Church, Dr. Ronald W. Carpenter, Sr., P.O. Box 12609 Oklahoma City, OK 73157. Tel. (405)787-7110 Fax (405)789-3957
Email: JDL@iphc.org
Website: http://www.iphc.org/evusa/ev

The Evangelist, (w) The Roman Catholic Church, James Breig, 40 N. Main Ave. Albany, NY 12203. Tel. (518)453-6688 Fax (518)453-6793
Email: evannews@global2000.net
Website: www.evangelist.org

Explorations, (4/yr) Nondenominational, Irvin J. Borowsky, 321 Chestnut Street, 4th Floor Philadelphia, PA 19106-2779. Tel. (215)925-2800 Fax (215)925-3800

Extension, (m) The Roman Catholic Church, Bradley Collins, 150 S. Wacker Drive 20th Floor Chicago, IL 60606. Tel. (312)236-7240 Fax (312)236-5276
Email: magazine@catholic-extension.org
Website: www.catholic-extension.org

Faith & Fellowship, (m) Church of the Lutheran Brethren of America, David Rinden, P.O. Box 655 Fergus Falls, MN 56538. Tel. (218)736-7357 Fax (218)736-2200
Email: rinden@prtel.com
Website: www.clba.org

Faith-Life, (bi-m) Lutheran, Pastor Marcus Albrecht, 2107 N. Alexander St. Appleton, WI 54911. Tel. (920)733-1839 Fax (920)733-4834

Faith and Truth, (m) Pentecostal Fire-Baptized Holiness Church, Edgar Vollratlt, 593 Harris-Lord Rd. Commerce, GA 30529. Tel. (706)335-5796

Fellowship, (6/yr) Interfaith, Richard Deats, P.O. Box 271 Nyack, NY 10960-0271. Tel. (914)358-4601 Fax (914)358-1179
Email: fellowship@forusa.org
Website: http://www.nonviolence.org/~

301

The Fellowship Magazine, (6/yr) Assemblies of God International Fellowship (Independent, Rev. T. A. Lanes, 5284 Eastgate Mall San Diego, CA 92121. Tel. (858)677-9701 Fax (858)677-0038 Email: TheodoreaLanes@compuserve.com Website: www.agifellowship.org

Fellowship News, (m) Bible Fellowship Church, Carol Snyder, 2660 Allentown Road Quakertown, PA 18951

Fellowship Tidings, (q) Full Gospel Fellowship of Churches and Ministers Intern, Chester P. Jenkins, 1000 N. Beltline Road Irving, TX 75061. Tel. (214)339-1200 Email: FGFCMI@aol.com Website: www.fgfcmi.org

Firm Foundation, (m) Churches of Christ, H. A. Dobbs, P.O. Box 690192 Houston, TX 77269-0192. Tel. (713)469-3102 Fax (713)469-7115 Email: HAD@onramp.net

First Things: A Monthly Journal of Religion & Public Life, (m) Interdenominational, Richard J. Neuhaus, 156 Fifth Ave., Ste. 400 New York, NY 10010. Tel. (212)627-1985 Fax (212)627-2184 Website: http://www.firstthings.com

The Flaming Sword, (m) Bible Holiness Church, Susan Davolt, 10th St. & College Ave. Independence, KS 67301. Tel. (316)331-2580 Fax (316)331-2580

For the Poor, (bi-m) Primitive Baptists, W. H. Cayce, PO Box 38 Thornton, AR 71766. Tel. (501)352-3694

Foresee, (bi-m) Conservative Congregational Christian Conference, Walter F. Smith, 7582 Currell Blvd., #108 St. Paul, MN 55125. Tel. (651)739-1474 Fax (651)739-0750 Email: cccc4@juno.com Website: www.ccccusa.org

Forum Letter, (m) Independent, Intra-Lutheran, Pastor Russell E. Saltzman, P.O. Box 638 Stover, MO 65078-0368. Tel. (573)377-2819 Email: Saltzman@midmo.net

Forward, (q) United Pentecostal Church International, Rev. J. L. Hall, 8855 Dunn Rd. Hazelwood, MO 63042. Tel. (314)837-7300 Fax (314)837-4503

Forward/Northwestern Lutheran, (m) Wisconsin Evangelical Lutheran Synod, Gary Baumler, 2929 N. Mayfair Rd. Milwaukee, WI 53222. Tel. (414)256-3888 Fax (414)256-3899 Email: nl@sab.wels.net

Foursquare World Advance, (6/yr) International Church of the Foursquare Gospel, Rev. Ron Williams, PO Box 26902 1910 W. Sunset Blvd., Ste 2 Los Angeles, CA 90026-0176. Tel. (213)989-4220 Fax (213)989-4544 Email: COMM@foursquare.org

Free Methodist World Mission People, (4/yr) Free Methodist Church of North America, Paula Innes, Magazine Coordinator, P.O. Box 535002 Indianapolis, IN 46253-5002. Tel. (317)244-3660 Fax (317)241-1248 Email: fmcPeople@aol.com Website: www.fmcna.org/fmwm

Free Will Baptist Gem, (m) National Association of Free Will Baptists, Nathan Ruble, P.O. Box 991 Lebanon, MO 65536. Tel. (417)532-6537

The Free Will Baptist, (m) Original Free Will Baptist Church, Tracy A McCoy, P.O. Box 159 811 N. Lee Street Ayden, NC 28513. Tel. (919)746-6128 Fax (919)746-9248

Free Will Bible College Bulletin, (6/yr) National Association of Free Will Baptists, Bert Tippett, 3606 West End Ave. Nashville, TN 37205. Tel. (615)383-1340 Fax (615)269-6028 Email: bert@fwbbc.edu Website: www.fwbbc.edu

Friend Magazine, (m) The Church of Jesus Christ of Latter-day Saints, Vivian Paulsen, 50 E South Temple Street, 23rd Fl Salt Lake City, UT 84150. Tel. (801)240-2210 Fax (801)240-5997

Friends Bulletin, (10/yr) Religious Society of Friends, Anthony Manousos, 5238 Andalucia Court Whittier, CA 90601. Tel. (562-699-5670 Fax (562-692-2472 Email: friendsbul@aol.com Website: www.quaker.org/fb and www.quaker.org/western

Friends Journal, (m) Friends General Conference, Vinton Deming, 1501 Cherry Street Philadelphia, PA 19102-1497. Tel. (215)241-7277 Fax (215)568-1377 Email: FriendsJnl@aol.com

The Friends Voice, (4/yr) Evangelical Friends International - North America Regio, Becky Towne, 2748 E. Pikes Peak Ave Colorado Springs, CO 80909. Tel. (719)635-4011 Fax (719)636-2194 Email: mincomp@kktv.com Website: evangelical-friends.org

Front Line, Conservative Baptist Association of America, Al Russell, P.O. Box 66 Wheaton, IL 60189. Tel. (630)260-3800 Fax (630)653-5387 Email: chaplruss@aol.com

Full Gospel Ministries Outreach Report, (q) Full Gospel Assemblies International, Simeon Strauser, P.O. Box 1230 . Coatsville, PA 19320. Tel. (610)857-2357 Fax (610)857-3109

The Gem, (w) Churches of God, General Conference, Mac Cordell, P.O. Box 926 Findlay, OH 45839. Tel. (419)424-1961 Fax (419)424-3433 Email: communications@cggc.org Website: www.cggc.org

General Baptist Messenger, (m) General Association of General Baptists, Samuel S. Ramdial, 400 Stinson Dr. Poplar Bluff, MO 63901. Tel. (573)686-9051 Fax (573)686-5198

The Gleaner, (m) Baptist Missionary Association of America, F. Donald Collins, Po Box 193920 Little Rock, AR 72219-3920. Tel. (501)455-4977 Fax (501)455-3636 Email: BMAAM@aol.com

Global Partners, (q) Baptist Bible Fellowship International, Loran McAlister, P.O. Box 191 Springfield, MO 65801. Tel. (417)862-5001 Fax (417)865-0794

God's Field, (bi-w) Polish National Catholic Church of America, Rt. Rev. Anthony M. Rysz, 1002 Pittston Ave. Scranton, PA 18505. Tel. (570)346-9131 Fax (570)346-2188

Gospel Advocate, (m) Churches of Christ, F. Furman Kearley, Box 150 Nashville, TN 37202. Tel. (615)254-8781 Fax (615)254-7411 Email: GospelADV@aol.com

Gospel Herald, (w) Mennonite Church, J. Lorne Peachey, 616 Walnut Ave Scottdale, PA 15683. Tel. (412)887-8500 Fax (412)887-3111

The Gospel Herald, (m) Church of God, Mountain Assembly, Inc., Bob Vance, P.O. Box 157 Jellico, TN 37762. Tel. (423)784-8260 Fax (423)784-3258 Email: cgmahdq@jellico.com Website: www.cgmahdq.org

The Gospel Light, (q) The Bible Church of Christ, Inc., Carol Crenshaw, 1358 Morris Ave. Bronx, NY 10456. Tel. (718)588-2284 Fax (718)992-5597

The Gospel Messenger, (m) Congregational Holiness Church, Cullen L. Hicks, Congregational Holiness Church 3888 Fayetteville Highway Griffin, GA 30223. Tel. (770-228-4833 Fax (770-228-1177

The Gospel News (m) The Church of Jesus Christ (Bickertonites), Donald Ross, 201 Royalbrooke Dr. Venetia, PA 15367. Tel. (412)348-6828 Fax (412)348-0919

Gospel Tidings, (bi-m) Fellowship of Evangelical Bible Churches, Robert L. Frey, 5800 S. 14th St. Omaha, NE 68107. Tel. (402)731-4780 Fax (402)731-1173 Email: febcoma@aol.com Website: http://members.aol.com/febcoma

The Gospel Truth, (m) Church of the Living God, W.E. Crumes, 430 Forest Avenue Cincinnati, OH 45229. Tel. (513)569-5660 Fax (513)569-5661

Grow Magazine, (4/yr) Church of the Nazarene, Neil B. Wiseman, 6401 The Paseo Kansas City, MO 64131. Tel. (816)333-7000 Fax (816)361-5202

Guide, (w) Seventh-day Adventist Church, Randy Fishell, 55 W. Oak Ridge Dr. Hagerstown, MD 21740. Tel. (301)393-4038 Fax (301)393-4055 Email: guide@rhpa.org Website: www.guidemagazine.org

The Happy Harvester, (m) Church of God of Prophecy, Diane Pace, P.O. Box 2910 Cleveland, TN 37320-2910. Tel. (423)559-5435 Fax (423)559-5444 Email: JoDiPace@wingnet.net

HeartBeat, (m) The Evangelical Church, John F. Sills, 7733 West River Road Minneapolis, MN 55444. Tel. (612)561-8404 Fax (612)561-2899

Heartbeat, (bi-m) National Association of Free Will Baptists, Don Robirds, Foreign Missions Office P.O. Box 5002 Antioch, TN 37011-5002. Tel. (615)731-6812 Fax (615)731-5345 Email: Heartbeat@NAFWB.org

Helping Hand, (bi-m) International Pentecostal Holiness Church, Mrs. Doris Moore, P.O. Box 12609 Oklahoma City, OK 73157. Tel. (405)787-7110 Fax (405)789-3957

The Herald of Christian Science, (m) Church of Christ, Scientist, William E. Moody, One Norway St. Boston, MA 02115. Tel. (617)450-2000 Fax (617)450-2707 Email: moodyw@csps.com Website: www.csherald.com

Heritage, (q) Assemblies of God, Wayne E. Warner, 1445 Boonville Ave. Springfield, MO 65802. Tel. (417)862-1447 Fax (417)862-6203 Email: wwarner@ag.org

High Adventure, (q) Assemblies of God, Marshall Bruner, Gospel Publishing House 1445 Boonville Ave. Springfield, MO 65802-1894. Tel. (417)862-2781 Fax (417)862-0416

Higher Way, (bi-m) Apostolic Faith Mission of Portland, Oregon, Dwight L. Baltzell, 6615 S.E. 52nd Ave. Portland, OR 97206. Tel. (503)777-1741 Fax (503)777-1743 Email: 74407.556@compuserve.com

Holiness Digest, (q) Nondenominational, Marlin Hotle, 263 Buffalo Road Clinton, TN 37716. Tel. (423)457-5978 Fax (423)463-7280

Holiness Today, (m) Church of the Nazarene, R. Franklin Cook, 6401 The Paseo Kansas City, MO 64131. Tel. (816)333-7000 Fax (816)333-1748 Email: HolinessToday@nazarene.org Website: www.nazarene.org

The Holiness Union, (m) United Holy Church of America, Inc., Dr. Joseph T. Durham, 13102 Morningside La. Silver Spring, MD 20904. Tel. (301)989-9093 Fax (301)989-9020

Homelife, (6/yr) United Pentecostal Church International, Scott Graham, 8855 Dunn Rd.

303

Hazelwood, MO 63042. Tel. (314)837-7300
Fax (314)837-4503
Email: gyouth8855@ol.com
Website: http://ww.upci.org/youth

Homiletic and Pastoral Review, (m) The Roman Catholic Church, Kenneth Baker, 10 Audrey Pl. Fairfield, NJ 7004. Tel. (201)882-8700

Horizons, (7/yr) Presbyterian Church (U.S.A.), Marie T. Cross, Presbyterian Women 100 Witherspoon St. Louisville, KY 40202-1396. Tel. (502)569-5367 Fax (502)569-8085
Email: MarieC@ctr.pcusa.org
Website: www/pcusa.org/horizons

Horizons, (m) Christian Churches and Churches of Christ, Reggie Hundley, Box 13111 Knoxville, TN 37920-0111. Tel. (800)655-8524 Fax (423)577-9743
Email: mission_services@csi.com
Website: www.missionservices.org

Insight, (w) Seventh-day Adventist Church, Lori L. Peckham, 55 W. Oak Ridge Dr. Hagerstown, MD 21740. Tel. (301)393-4038 Fax (301)393-4055
Email: insight@rhpa.org
Website: www.insightmagazine.org

Insight, (q) Advent Christian Church, Dawn Rutan, P.O. Box 23152 Charlotte, NC 28227. Tel. (704)545-6161 Fax (704)573-0712
Email: ACPub@adventchristian.org
Website: www.adventchristian.org

Interlit, (6/yr) Nondenominational magazine on Christian publishing worldwide, Kim A. Pettit, 4050 Lee Vance View Drive Colorado Springs, CO 80918. Tel. (719)536-0100 Fax (719)536-3266
Email: ccmintl@ccmi.org
Website: www.ccmi.org

International Bulletin of Missionary Research, (q) Nondenominational, Jonathan J. Bonk, 490 Prospect St. New Haven, CT 06511. Tel. (203)624-6672 Fax (203)865-2857
Email: ibmr@OMSC.org
Website: http://www.omsc.org

Interpretation, (q) Presbyterian Church (U.S.A.), John T. Carroll and William P. Brown, 3401 Brook Rd. Richmond, VA 23227. Tel. (804)278-4296 Fax (804)278-4208
Email: mpeters@utsva.edu
Website: www.interpretation.org

el Interprete, (6/yr) The United Methodist Church, Garlinda Burton, Editorial Director, P.O. Box 320 Nashville, TN 37202-0320. Tel. (615)742-5115 Fax (615)742-5460
Email: elinterprete@umcom.umc.org

Interpreter, (8/yr) The United Methodist Church, M. Garlinda Burton, P.O. Box 320 810 Twelfth Ave. S. Nashville, TN 37202-0320. Tel. (615)742-5107 Fax (615)742-5460
Website: http://www.umc.org/interpret

IssacharFile, (m) International Pentecostal Holiness Church, Shirley Spencer, P.O. Box 12609 Oklahoma City, OK 73157. Tel. (405)787-7110 Fax (405)789-3957

John Milton Magazine, (q) Nondenominational, Large Print, Darcy Quigley, J. Milton Society for the Blind 475 Riverside Drive, Rm 455 New York, NY 10115-0122. Tel. (212)870-3335 Fax (212)870-3229
Website: http://www.jmsblind.org

John Three Sixteen, (q) Bible Holiness Church, Mary Cunningham, 10th St. & College Ave. Independence, KS 67301. Tel. (316)331-2580 Fax (316)331-2580

Journal of the American Academy of Religion, (q) Nondenominational, Glenn Yocum, Whittier College PO Box 634 Whittier, CA 90608-0634. Tel. (562)907-4200 Fax (562)907-4910
Email: gyocum@whittier.edu
Website: http://www.scholars.cc.emory

Journal of Adventist Education, (5/yr) Seventh-day Adventist Church, Beverly Rumble, 12501 Old Columbia Pike Silver Spring, MD 20904-6600. Tel. (301)680-5075 Fax (301)622-9627
Email: 74617.1231@compuserve.com

Journal of Christian Education, (q) African Methodist Episcopal Church, Kenneth H. Hill, 500 Eighth Ave., S. Nashville, TN 37203. Tel. (615)242-1420 Fax (615)726-1866
Email: ameced@edge.net
Website: www.ameced.com

Journal of Ecumenical Studies, (q) Inter-denominational, Leonard Swidler, Temple Univ. (022-38) 1114 West Berks St. Philadelphia, PA 19122-6090. Tel. (215)204-7714 Fax (215)204-4569
Email: dialogue@vm.temple.edu

The Journal of Pastoral Care, (q) Nondenominational, Orlo Strunk Jr., 1068 Harbor Dr., SW Calabash, NC 28467. Tel. (910)579-5084 Fax (910)579-5084
Email: OrloS@aol.com

Journal of Presbyterian History: Studies in Reformed History and Culture, (q) Presbyterian Church (U.S.A.), Charles H. Moorhead, 425 Lombard St. Philadelphia, PA 19147. Tel. (215)627-1852 Fax (215)627-0509

Journal From the Radical Reformation, (q) Church of God General Conference (Oregon, IL & Morrow, Kent Ross and Anthony Buzzard and Mark Mattison, Box 100,000 Morrow, GA 30260-7000. Tel. (404)362-0052 Fax (404)362-9307
Email: 102503.232@compuserve.com

Journal of Theology, (4/yr) Church of the Lutheran Confession, Prof. John Lau, Immanuel Lutheran College 501 Grover Rd. Eau Claire, WI 54701-7199. Tel. (715)832-9936 Fax (715)836-6634

Email: johnhlau@execpc.com
Website: www.primenet.com/~clcpub/clc/clc.html

The Joyful Noiseletter, (10/yr) Interdenominational, Cal Samra, P.O. Box 895 Portage, MI 49081-0895. Tel. (616)324-0990 Fax (616) 324-3984

Keeping in Touch, (m) Universal Fellowship of Metropolitan Community Churches, Ravi Verma, 8704 Santa Monica Blvd, 2nd Fl. West Hollywood, CA 90069-4548. Tel. (310)360-8640 Fax (310)360-8680
Email: UFMCCHQ@aol.com
Website: http://www.ufmcc.com

Kindred Minds, (q) Sovereign Grace Baptists, Larry Scouten, P.O. Box 10 Wellsburg, NY 14894. Tel. (607)734-6985

The Lantern, (bi-m) National Baptist Convention of America, Inc., Robert Jeffrey, 1320 Pierre Avenue Shreveport, LA 71103. Tel. (318)221-3701 Fax (318)222-7512

Leadership: A Practical Journal for Church Leaders, (q) Nondenominational, Marshall Shelley, 465 Gundersen Dr. Carol Stream, IL 60188. Tel. (630)260-6200 Fax (630)260-0114
Email: LeaderJ@aol.com
Website: www.Leadershipjournal.net

Liahona, (varies by edition) The Church of Jesus Christ of Latter-day Saints, Marvin K. Gardner, 50 East North Temple St. Salt Lake City, UT 84150. Tel. (801)240-2490 Fax (801)240-4225
Email: CUR-Liahone-IMag@idschurch.org

Liberty, (bi-m) Seventh-day Adventist Church, Clifford R. Goldstein, 12501 Old Columbia Pike Silver Spring, MD 20904. Tel. (301)680-6691 Fax (301)680-6695

Lifeglow, (q) Seventh-day Adventist Church, Gaylena Gibson, P.O. Box 6097 Lincoln, NE 68506. Tel. (402)488-0981 Fax (402)488-7582

Light and Life Magazine, (m) , Douglas M. Newton, P.O. Box 535002 Indianapolis, IN 46253-5002. Tel. (317)244-3660 Fax (317) 244-1247
Email: tlic@ix.netcom.com
Website: www.licatholic.org

Liguorian, (m) The Roman Catholic Church, Allen J. Weinert, C.SS.R., 1 Liguori Dr. Liguori, MO 63057. Tel. (636)464-2500 Fax (636)464-8449
Email: 104626.1547@compuserve.com
Website: http://www.liguori.org

Listen, (m) Seventh-day Adventist Church, Lincoln E. Steed, 55 W. Oak Ridge Dr. Haggerstown, MD 21740. Tel. (301)791-7000 Fax (301)790-9734

Living Orthodoxy, (bi-m) The Russian Orthodox Church Outside of Russia, Fr. Gregory Williams, 1180 Orthodox Way

Liberty, TN 37095. Tel. (615)536-5239 Fax (615)536-5945
Email: AGAPE@DEKALB.net
Website: www.roca.org/kronstadt

The Lookout, (w) Christian Churches and Churches of Christ, David Faust, 8121 Hamilton Ave. Cincinnati, OH 45231. Tel. (513)931-4050 Fax (513)931-0950

The Lutheran, (m) Evangelical Lutheran Church in America, Rev. David L. Miller, 8765 W. Higgins Rd. Chicago, IL 60631-4183. Tel. (773)380-2540 Fax (773)380-2751
Email: lutheran@elca.org
Website: www.thelutheran.org

The Lutheran Ambassador, (16/yr) The Association of Free Lutheran Congregations, Craig Johnson, 86286 Pine Grove Rd. Eugene, OR 97402. Tel. (541)687-8643 Fax (541)683-8496
Email: cjohnson@efn.org

The Lutheran Educator, (q) Wisconsin Evangelical Lutheran Synod, Prof. John R. Isch, Martin Luther College 1995 Luther Ct. New Ulm, MN 56073. Tel. (507)354-8221 Fax (507)354-8225
Email: lutheraneducator@mlc-wels.edu

Lutheran Forum, (q) Interdenominational Lutheran, Ronald B. Bagnall, 207 Hillcrest Ave. Trenton, NJ 8618. Tel. (856)696-0417

The Lutheran Layman, (m) The Lutheran Church—Missouri Synod, Gerald Persch-bacher, 2185 Hampton Ave. St. Louis, MO 63139-2904. Tel. (314)951-4100 Fax (314)951-4295

Lutheran Parent, (bi-m) Wisconsin Evangelical Lutheran Synod, Kenneth J. Kremer, 1250 N. 113th Street Milwaukee, WI 53226-3284. Tel. (414)475-6600 Fax (414)475-7684

Lutheran Parent's Wellspring, (bi-m) Wisconsin Evangelical Lutheran Synod, Kenneth J. Kremer, 1250 N. 113th Street Milwaukee, WI 53226-3284. Tel. (414)475-6600 Fax (414)475-7684

Lutheran Partners, (6/yr) Evangelical Lutheran Church in America, Carl E. Linder, 8765 W. Higgins Rd. Chicago, IL 60631-4101. Tel. (773)380-2875 Fax (773)380-2829
Email: lutheran_partners.parti@ecunet.org or lpartmag@elca.org
Website: http://www.elca.org/dm/lp

Lutheran Sentinel, (m) Evangelical Lutheran Synod, Theodore Gullixson, 1451 Pearl Pl. Escondido, CA 92027. Tel. (619)745-0583 Fax (619)743-4440

The Lutheran Spokesman, (m) Church of the Lutheran Confession, Rev. Paul Fleischer, 710 4th Ave., SW Sleepy Eye, MN 56085. Tel. (507)794-7793 Fax (507)794-5410
Email: pgflei@prairie.lakes.com

Lutheran Synod Quarterly, (q) Evangelical Lutheran Synod, G.R. Schmeling, Bethany Lutheran Theological Semi 6 Browns Ct. Mankato, MN 56001. Tel. (507)344-7855 Fax (507)344-7426
Email: elsynod@blc.edu

The Lutheran Witness, (m) The Lutheran Church—Missouri Synod, Rev. David Mahsman, 1333 S. Kirkwood Road St. Louis, MO 63122-7295. Tel. (314)965-9000 Fax (314)965-3396
Email: ic_mahsmadl@lcms.org

Lutheran Woman Today, (10/yr) Evangelical Lutheran Church in America, Nancy J. Stelling, 8765 W. Higgins Rd. Chicago, IL 60631-4101. Tel. (773)380-2732 Fax (773)380-2419
Email: lwt@elca.org
Website: www.elca.org/wo/lwthome.html

Lyceum Spotlight, (10/yr) National Spiritualist Association of Churches, Rev. Cosie Allen, 1418 Hall St. Grand Rapids, MI 49506. Tel. (616)241-2761 Fax (616)241-4703
Email: cosie@grgig.net

Magyar Egyhaz, (q) Hungarian Reformed Church in America, Stephen Szabo, 464 Forrest Ave. Paramus, NJ 7652. Tel. (201)262-2338 Fax (914)359-2313

Maranatha, (q) Advent Christian Church, Dawn Rutan, P.O. Box 23152 Charlotte, NC 28227. Tel. (704)545-6161 Fax (704)573-0712
Email: acpub@adventchristian.org
Website: www.adventchristian.org

Marriage Partnership, (q) Nondenominational, Ron R. Lee, 465 Gundersen Dr. Carol Stream, IL 60188. Tel. (630)260-6200 Fax (630)260-0114
Email: Mpedit@aol.com
Website: http://www.christianity.net/

Maryknoll, (11/yr) The Roman Catholic Church, Joseph R. Veneroso, Maryknoll Fathers and Brothers, Maryknoll Fathers and Brothers PO Box 308 Maryknoll, NY 10545-0308. Tel. (914)941-7590 Fax (914)945-0670
Email: maryknollmag@igc.apc.org

Mature Years, (q) The United Methodist Church, Marvin W. Cropsey, 201 Eighth Ave. S Nashville, TN 37202. Tel. (615)749-6292 Fax (615)749-6512
Email: mcropsey@umpublishing.org

Mennonite Historical Bulletin, (q) Mennonite Church, John E. Sharp, 1700 South Main St. Goshen, IN 46526. Tel. (219)535-7477 Fax (219)535-7756
Email: johnes@goshen.edu
Website: www.Goshen.edu/mcarchives

Mennonite Quarterly Review, (q) Mennonite Church, John D. Roth, 1700 S. Main St. Goshen, IN 46526. Tel. (219)535-7433 Fax (219)535-7438
Email: MQR@goshen.edu
Website: http://www.goshen.edu/mgr

The Mennonite, (48/yr) General Conference Mennonite Church and the Mennonite Church, J. Lorne Peachey, 722 Main St., P.O. Box 347 Newton, KS 67114-0347. Tel. (316)283-5100 Fax (316)283-0454
Email: TheMennonite@gcmc.org
Website: www.mph.org/themennonite

Message, (bi-m) Seventh-day Adventist Church, Dr. Ron C. Smith, 55 West Oak Ridge Dr. Hagerstown, MD 21740. Tel. (301)393-4099 Fax (301)393-4103
Email: message@rhpa.org
Website: MESSAGEMAGAZINE.org

Message of the Open Bible, (bi-m) Open Bible Standard Churches, Inc., Andrea Johnson, 2020 Bell Ave. Des Moines, IA 50315-1096. Tel. (515)288-6761 Fax (515)288-2510
Email: message@openbible.org

Messenger, (11/yr) Church of the Brethren, Fletcher Farrar, 1451 Dundee Ave. Elgin, IL 60120. Tel. (847)742-5100 Fax (847)742-1407
Email: wmcfadden_gb@brethren.org

Messenger of Truth, (bi-w) Church of God in Christ (Mennonite), Gladwin Koehn, P.O. Box 230 Moundridge, KS 67107. Tel. (316)345-2532 Fax (316)345-2582

The Messenger, Bible Church of Christ, Inc., Gwendolyn Harris, 1358 Morris Ave. Bronx, NY 10456. Tel. (718)588-2284 Fax (718)992-5597

The Messenger, (m) The (Original) Church of God, Inc., Wayne Jolley and William Dale, PO Box 3086 Chattanooga, TN 37404-0086. Tel. (800)827-9234

The Messenger, (m) Pentecostal Free Will Baptist Church, Inc., George Thomas, P.O. Box 1568 Dunn, NC 28335. Tel. (910)892-4161 Fax (910)892-6876

The Messenger, (m) The Swedenborgian Church, Patte LeVan, PO Box 985 Julian, CA 92036. Tel. (760)765-2915 Fax (760)765-0218
Email: messenger@jinet.com

Methodist History, (q) The United Methodist Church, Charles Yrigoyen Jr., P.O. Box 127 Madison, NJ 07940. Tel. (973)408-3189 Fax (973)408-3909
Email: cyrigoyen@gcah.org
Website: www.gcah.org

Mid-Stream: The Ecumenical Movement Today, (q) Christian Church (Disciples of Christ), Robert K. Welsh, P.O. Box 1986 Indianapolis, IN 46206-1986. Tel. (317)635-3100 Fax (317)635-3700
Email: ccdc_council_on_unity@ecunet.org

Ministry, (m) Seventh-day Adventist Church, Willmore D. Eva, 12501 Old Columbia Pike Silver Spring, MD 20904. Tel. (301)680-6510 Fax (301)680-6502 Email: 74532.2425@compuserve.com

Mission Grams, (bi-m) Free Will Baptists, National Association of, Ida Lewis, Home Missions Office P.O. Box 5002 Antioch, TN 37011-5002. Tel. (615)731-6812 Fax (615) 731-7655 Email: ida@nafwb.org

Mission Herald, (bi-m) National Baptist Convention, U.S.A., Inc., William J. Harvey, 701 S. 19th Street Philadelphia, PA 19146. Tel. (215)735-9853 Fax (215)735-1721

Mission, Adult, and Youth Children's Editions, (q) Seventh-day Adventist Church, Charlotte Ishkanian, 12501 Old Columbia Pike Silver Spring, MD 20904. Tel. (301)680-6167 Fax (301)680-6155 Email: 74532.2435@compuserve.com

The Missionary Magazine, (9/yr) Bertha O. Fordham, 800 Risley Ave. Pleasantville, NJ 08232-4250

The Missionary Messenger, (m) Christian Methodist Episcopal Church, Barbara E. Bouknight, PO Box 172 Flint, MI 48501-0172. Tel. (810)733-7076

The Missionary Messenger, (6/yr) Cumberland Presbyterian Church, Carol Penn, 1978 Union Ave. Memphis, TN 38104. Tel. (901)276-4572 Fax (901)276-4578 Email: messenger@cumberland.org

Missionary Seer, (m) African Methodist Episcopal Zion Church, Rev. Kermit J. DeGraffenreidt, 475 Riverside Dr., Rm. 1935 New York, NY 10115. Tel. (212)870-2952 Fax (212)870-2808

The Missionary Signal, (bi-m) Churches of God, General Conference, Kathy Rodabaugh, P.O. Box 926 Findlay, OH 45839. Tel. (419)424-1961 Fax (419)424-3433

MissionsUSA, (bi-m) Southern Baptist Convention, Wayne Grinstead, 4200 North Point Pkwy. Alphretta, GA 30202-4174. Tel. (770)410-6251 Fax (770)410-6006

Monday Morning, (21/yr) Presbyterian Church (U.S.A.), Houston Hodges, 100 Witherspoon St. Louisville, KY 40202. Tel. (502)569-5502 Fax (502)569-8073 Email: H2@pcusa.org

Moody Magazine, (6/yr) Nondenominational, Bruce Anderson, 820 N. LaSalle Blvd. Chicago, IL 60610. Tel. (312)329-2164 Fax (312)329-2149 Email: moodyltrs@moody.edu Website: http://www.moody.edu/moodyma

The Moravian, (10/yr) Moravian Church in America (Unitas Fratrum), Ms. Roxann Miller, 1021 Center St., P.O. Box 1245 Bethlehem, PA 18016. Tel. (610)867-0594 Fax (610)866-9223

The Mother Church, (m) Western Diocese of the Armenian Church of North America, Rev. Fr. Sipan Mekhsian, 3325 N. Glenoaks Blvd. Burbank, CA 91504. Tel. (818)558-7474 Fax (818)558-6333 Email: armenianchwd@earthlink.net

My Soul Sings: A Magazine of Inspirational/ Gospel Music, (q) Nondenomi-national, Donald E. Franklin, Editor-in-chief, P.O. Box 16181 St. Louis, MO 16181. Tel. (888)862-0179 Fax (888)862-0179 Website: www.mysoulsings.com

NAE Washington Insight, (m) Interdenominational, Rev. Richard Cizik, 450 E. Gundersen Dr. Carol Stream, IL 60188. Tel. (630)665-0500 Fax (630)665-8575 Email: oga@nae.net Website: www.nae.net

National Baptist Union Review, (m) Non-denominational, Willie Paul, 6717 Centennial Blvd. Nashville, TN 37209-1000. Tel. (615) 350-8000 Fax (615)350-9018

National Catholic Reporter, (44/yr) The Roman Catholic Church, Michael J. Farrell, P.O. Box 419281 Kansas City, MO 64141. Tel. (816)531-0538 Fax (816)968-2280 Email: editor@natcath.com Website: http://www.natcath.com/

The National Christian Reporter, (w) Non-denominational, John A. Lovelace, P.O. Box 222198 Dallas, TX 75222. Tel. (214)630-6495 Fax (214)630-0079 Email: 76113.662@compuserve.com

The National Spiritualist Summit, (m) National Spiritualist Association of Churches, Rev. Sandra Pfortmiller, 3521 W. Topeka Dr. Glendale, AZ 85308-2325. Tel. (623)581-6686 Fax (623)581-5544 Email: g252pfort@aol.com

New Church Life, (m) General Church of the New Jerusalem, Rev. Donald L. Rose, Box 277 Bryn Athyn, PA 19009. Tel. (215)947-6225 Fax (215)938-1871 Email: BRYNATHYNC@aol.com

The New Era, (m) The Church of Jesus Christ of Latter-day Saints, Richard Romney, 50 E. North Temple St. Salt Lake City, UT 84150. Tel. (801)240-2951 Fax (801)240-5997 Email: rmromney@chq.byu.edu

New Horizons in the Orthodox Presbyterian Church, (11/yr) The Orthodox Presbyterian Church, Thomas E. Tyson, 607 N. Easton Rd., Bldg. E P.O. Box P Willow Grove, PA 19090-0920. Tel. (215)830-0900 Fax (215)830-0350

Email: tomtyson@aol.com
Website: http://www.opc.org/

New Oxford Review, (11/yr) The Roman Catholic Church, Dale Vree, 1069 Kains Ave. Berkeley, CA 94706. Tel. (510)526-5374 Fax (510)526-3492

New World Outlook, (bi-m) Mission Magazine of the The United Methodist Church, Alma Graham, 475 Riverside Dr., Rm. 1476 New York, NY 10115. Tel. (212)870-3765 Fax (212)870-3940 Email: NOW@gbgm-umc.org Website: http://gbgm-umc.org/nwo/

The News, (m) The Anglican Orthodox Church, Mrs. Margaret D. Lane, Anglican Orthodox Church P.O. Box 128 Statesville, NC 28687. Tel. (704)873-8365 Fax (704)873-8948

Newscope, (w) The United Methodist Church, J. Richard Peck, P.O. Box 801 Nashville, TN 37202. Tel. (615)749-6007 Fax (615)749-6061 Email: rpeck@umpublishing.org

The North American Catholic, (m) North American Old Roman Catholic Church, Theodore J. Remalt, 4200 N. Kedvale Ave. Chicago, IL 60641. Tel. (312)685-0461 Fax (312)286-5783

The North American Challenge, (m) Home Missions Division of The United Pentecostal Church International, Joseph Fiorino, 8855 Dunn Rd. Hazelwood, MO 63042-2299. Tel. (314)837-7300 Fax (314)837-5632

NRB Magazine, (10/yr) Nondenominational, Christine Pryor, National Religious Broadcasters 7839 Ashton Ave Manassas, VA 20109-2883. Tel. (703)330-7000 Fax (703)330-6996 Email: cpryor@nrb.org Website: www.nrb.org

Nuestra Parroquia, (m) The Roman Catholic Church, Carmen Aguinaco, 205 W. Monroe St. Chicago, IL 60606-5013. Tel. (312)236-7782 Fax (312)236-8207 Email: USCath@aol.com

On Course, (q) Assemblies of God, Melinda Booze, 1445 Boonville Ave. Springfield, MO 65802-1894. Tel. (417)862-2781 Fax (417) 866-1146 Email: oncourse@ag.org

On the Line, (m) Mennonite Church, Mary C. Meyer, 616 Walnut Ave. Scottdale, PA 15683. Tel. (724)887-8500 Fax (724-887-3111 Email: otl@mph.org Website: www.mph.org/otl

One Church, (bi-m) Patriarchal Parishes of the Russian Orthodox Church in the U.S.A., Bishop Paul, 15 E. 97th St. New York, NY 10029. Tel. (212)831-6294 Fax (212)427-5003

Open Hands, (q) Interdenominational, Chris Glaser, 3801 N. Keeler Ave. Chicago, IL

60641-3007. Tel. (312)736-5526 Fax (312) 736-5475 Email: openhands@rcp.org Website: www.rcp.org/ophands.html

Orthodox America, (8/yr) The Russian Orthodox Church Outside of Russia, Mary Mansur, P.O. Box 383 Richfield Springs, NY 13439-0383. Tel. (978)448-5592 Fax Email: niko@bicnet.net Website: www.roca.org/oa

The Orthodox Church, (m) The Orthodox Church in America, Leonid Kishkovsky, P.O. Box 675 Syosset, NY 11791. Tel. (516)922-0550 Fax (516)922-0954 Email: info@oca.org

Orthodox Family, (q) The Russian Orthodox Church Outside of Russia, George Johnson and Deborah Johnson, P.O. Box 45 Beltsville, MD 20705. Tel. (301)890-3552 Email: 1lew@cais.com Website: http://www.roca.org/orthodox

Orthodox Life, (bi-m) The Russian Orthodox Church Outside of Russia, Fr. Luke, Holy Trinity Monastery P.O Box 36 Jordanville, NY 13361-0036. Tel. (315)858-0940 Fax (315) 858-0505 Email: 72204.1465@compuserve.com

The Orthodox Observer, (m) Greek Orthodox Archdiocese of America, Jim Golding, 8 E. 79th St. New York, NY 10021. Tel. (212)628-2590 Fax (212)570-4005

Orthodox Russia (English translation of Pravoslavnaya Rus), (24/yr) The Russian Orthodox Church Outside of Russia, Archbishop Laurus, Holy Trinity Monastery P.O. Box 36 Jordanville, NY 13361-0036. Tel. (315)858-0940 Fax (315)858-0505 Email: orthrus@telenet.net

Orthodox Voices, (4/yr) The Russian Orthodox Church Outside of Russia, Thomas Webb and Ellen Webb, P.O. Box 23644 Lexington, KY 40523. Tel. (606)271-3877

The Other Side, (bi-m) Interdenominational, Dee Dee Risher and Douglas Davidson, 300 W. Apsley St. Philadelphia, PA 19144-4221. Tel. (215)849-2178 Fax (215)849-3755 Email: editors@theotherside.org Website: www.theotherside.org

Our Daily Bread, (m) The Swedenborgian Church, Lee Woofenden, P.O. Box 396 Bridgewater, MA 02324. Tel. (508)946-1767 Fax (508)946-1757 Email: odb@swedenborg.org Website: www.swedenborg.org/odb/odb.html

Our Little Friend, (w) Seventh-day Adventist Church, Aileen Andres Sox, P.O. Box 5353 Nampa, ID 83653-5353. Tel. (208)465-2500 Fax (208)465-2531

Our Sunday Visitor, (w) The Roman Catholic Church, David Scott, 200 Noll Plaza Huntington, IN 46750. Tel. (219)356-8400 Fax (219)356-8472
Email: 76440.3571@compuserve.com

Outreach, (10/yr) Armenian Apostolic Church of America, Iris Papazian, 138 E. 39th St. New York, NY 10016. Tel. (212)689-7810 Fax (212)689-7168

Pastoral Life, (m) The Roman Catholic Church, Anthony Chenevey, Box 595 Canfield, OH 44406-0595. Tel. (330)533-5503 Fax (330) 553-1076

The Path of Orthodoxy (Serbian), (m) Serbian Orthodox Church in the U.S.A. and Canada, V. Rev. Nedeljko Lunich, 300 Striker Ave. Joliet, IL 60436. Tel. (815)741-1023 Fax (815)741-1023
Email: dinara2@aol.com

Pentecostal Evangel, (w) Assemblies of God, Hal Donaldson, Gospel Publishing House 1445 Boonville Ave. Springfield, MO 65802-1894. Tel. (417)862-2781 Fax (417)862-0416
Email: pevangel@ag.org
Website: pe.ag.org

Pentecostal Evangel, Missions World Edition, (m) Assemblies of God, Randy Hurst, Editor; John Maempa, General Editor, Gospel Publishing House 1445 Boonville Ave. Springfield, MO 65802. Tel. (417)862-2781 Fax (417)862-0085
Email: jmaempa@publish.ag.org

The Pentecostal Herald, (m) United Pentecostal Church International, Rev. J. L. Hall, 8855 Dunn Rd. Hazelwood, MO 63042. Tel. (314)837-7300 Fax (314)837-4503

Pentecostal Leader, (q) The International Pentecostal Church of Christ, Clyde M. Hughes, P.O. Box 439 London, OH 43140. Tel. (740)852-4722 Fax (740)852-0348
Email: hqipcc@aol.com

The Pentecostal Messenger, (m) Pentecostal Church of God (Joplin, MO), Aaron Wilson, P.O. Box 850 Joplin, MO 64802. Tel. (417)624-7050 Fax (417)624-7102
Email: aaronw@peg.org
Website: www.pcg.org

The People's Mouthpiece, (q) Apostolic Overcoming Holy Church of God, Inc., Juanita R. Arrigton, Ph.D., 1120 North 24th St. Birmingham, AL 35234. Tel. (205)324-2202

Perspectives, (10/yr) Reformed Church in America, Evelyn Diephouse, P.O. Box 470 Ada, MI 49301-0470. Tel. (616)241-2053 Fax (616)241-2064
Email: perspectives_@hotmail.com

Perspectives on Science and Christian Faith, (q) Nondenominational, Roman Miller, P.O.

Box 668 Ipswich, MA 01938. Tel. (508)356-5656 Fax (508)356-4375
Email: a5a@a5a3.org
Website: http://asa.calvin.edu

The Pillar Monthly, (12/yr) Donald J. Wolfram and Mark Tomlin, PO Box 9045 Zarephath, NJ 08890. Tel. (908)356-0561

The Pilot, (w) The Roman Catholic Church, Peter V. Conley, 141 Tremont St. Boston, MA 02111. Tel. (617)482-4316 Fax (617)482-5647
Email: pilotpub@concentric.net
Website: www.rcab.org

Pockets, (11/yr) The United Methodist Church, Janet R. Knight, P.O. Box 189 Nashville, TN 37202. Tel. (615)340-7333 Fax (615)340-7767
Email: pockets@upperroom.org
Website: www.upperroom.org/pockets

Polka, (q) Polish National Catholic Church of America, Cecelia Lallo, 1127 Frieda St. Dickson City, PA 18519-1304. Tel. (570)489-4364 Fax (570)346-2188

Pravoslavnaya Rus (Russian), (24/yr) The Russian Orthodox Church Outside of Russia, Archbishop Laurus, Holy Trinity Monastery P.O. Box 36 Jordanville, NY 13361-0036. Tel. (315)858-0940 Fax (315)858-0505
Email: orthrus@telenet.net

Pravoslavnaya Zhisn (Monthly Supplement to Pravoslavnaya Rus), (m) The Russian Orthodox Church Outside of Russia, Archbishop Laurus, Holy Trinity Monastery P.O. Box 36 Jordanville, NY 13361-0036. Tel. (315)858-0940 Fax (315)858-0505
Email: Orthrus@telenet.net

Praying, (bi-m) Spirituality for Everyday Living, Rich Heffern, P.O. Box 419335 115 E. Armour Blvd. Kansas City, MO 64141. Tel. (816)968-2258 Fax (816)968-2280

Preacher's Magazine, (bi-m) Church of the Nazarene, Randal Denney, 10814 E. Broadway Spokane, WA 99206. Tel. (509)226-3464 Fax (509)926-8740

The Preacher, (q) Baptist Bible Fellowship International, Mike Randall, P.O. Box 309 HSJ Springfield, MO 65801. Tel. (417)831-3996 Fax (417)831-1470

Presbyterian News Service "News Briefs", (w) Presbyterian Church (U.S.A.), Jerry L. VanMarter, 100 Witherspoon St. Rm. 5418 Louisville, KY 40202. Tel. (502)569-5493 Fax (502)569-8073
Email: jerryv@ctr.pcusa.org

Presbyterian Outlook, (w) Presbyterian Church (U.S.A.), Robert H. Bullock Jr., Box 85623 Richmond, VA 23261-5623. Tel. (804)359-8442 Fax (804)353-6369
Email: outlook.parti@pcusa.org
Website: www.pres.outlook.com

Presbyterians Today, (10/yr) Presbyterian Church (U.S.A.), Eva Stimson, 100 Witherspoon St. Louisville, KY 40202-1396. Tel. (502)569-5637 Fax (502)569-8632
Email: today@pcusa.org
Website: www.pcusa.org/pcusa/today

Primary Treasure, (w) Seventh-day Adventist Church, Aileen Andres Sox, P.O. Box 5353 Nampa, ID 83653-5353. Tel. (208)465-2500 Fax (208)465-2531

The Primitive Baptist, (bi-m) Primitive Baptists, W. H. Cayce, PO Box 38 Thornton, AR 71766. Tel. (501)352-3694

Priority, (m) The Missionary Church, Rev. Robert Ransom, P.O. Box 9127 Ft. Wayne, IN 46899. Tel. (219)747-2027 Fax (219)747-5331
Email: mcdenomusa@aol.com
Website: mcusa.org

Providence Visitor, (w) The Roman Catholic Church, Michael Brown, 184 Broad St. Providence, RI 02903. Tel. (401)272-1010 Fax (401)421-8418
Email: 102344.3235@compuserve.com

Purpose, (w) Mennonite Church, James E. Horsch, 616 Walnut Ave. Scottdale, PA 15683. Tel. (412)887-8500 Fax (412)887-3111
Email: horsch@mph.org
Website: http://www.mph.org

Pursuit, (q) The Evangelical Free Church of America, Carol Madison, 901 East 78th St. Minneapolis, MN 55420-1300. Tel. (612)853-1763 Fax (612)853-8488

Qala min M'Dinkha (Voice from the East), (q) Apostolic Catholic Assyrian Church of the East, North A, Shlemon Hesequial, Diocesan Offices 7201 N. Ashland Chicago, IL 60626. Tel. (773)465-4777 Fax (773)465-0776

Quaker Life, (10/yr) Friends United Meeting, Johan Maurer, 101 Quaker Hill Dr. Richmond, IN 47374-1980. Tel. (765)962-7573 Fax (765)966-1293
Email: QuakerLife@xc.org

Quarterly Review, (q) The United Methodist Church, Hendrik R. Pieterse, Box 871 Nashville, TN 37202. Tel. (615)340-7334 Fax (615)340-7048
Email: hpieterse@gbhem.org

Quarterly Review, A.M.E. Zion, (q) African Methodist Episcopal Zion Church, Rev. James D. Armstrong, P.O. Box 33247 Charlotte, NC 28231. Tel. (704)334-0728 Fax (704)333-1769

Reflections, (bi-m) United Pentecostal Church International, Melissa Anderson, 8855 Dunn Rd. Hazelwood, MO 63402. Tel. (918)370-2659 Fax (918)371-6320

Reformation Today, (bi-m) Sovereign Grace Baptists, Erroll Hulse, c/o Tom Lutz 3743

Nichol Ave. Anderson, IN 46011-3008. Tel. (317)644-0994 Fax (317)644-0994

Reformed Herald, (m) Reformed Church in the United States, David Dawn, 1000 Evergreen Way Rock Springs, WY 82901-4104. Tel. (307)362-5107

Reformed Worship, (q) Christian Reformed Chuch in North America, Emily R. Brink, 2850 Kalamazoo Ave. SE Grand Rapids, MI 49560-0001. Tel. (616)224-0785 Fax (616)224-0834
Email: info@reformedworship.org
Website: www.reformedworship.org

Rejoice!, (q) Mennonite Church, Rose Mary Stutzman, 616 Walnut Ave. Scottdale, PA 15683. Tel. (724)887-8500 Fax (724)887-3111
Email: rstutz@mph.org

Rejoice!, (q) Mennonite & Mennonite Brethren Church, Philip Wiebe, 1218 Franklin St. NW Salem, OR 97304. Tel. (503)585-4458 Fax (503)585-4458

Report From The Capital, (24/yr) Baptist Joint Committee, Larry Chesser, 200 Maryland Ave. NE Washington, DC 20002-5797. Tel. (202)544-4226 Fax (202)544-2094
Email: Larry-Chesser@bjcpa.org
Website: www.bjcpa.org

Reporter, (m) The Lutheran Church—Missouri Synod, David Mahsman, 1333 S. Kirkwood Rd. St. Louis, MO 63122-7295. Tel. (314)965-9000 Fax (314)965-3396
Email: REPORTER@lcms.org
Website: http://www.lcms.org

The Rescue Herald, (q) American Rescue Workers, Col. Robert N. Coles, 1209 Hamilton Blvd. Hagerstown, MD 21742. Tel. (301)797-0061 Fax (301)797-1480

Response, (m) The United Methodist Church, Dana Jones, 475 Riverside Dr., Room 1356 New York, NY 10115. Tel. (212)870-3755 Fax (212)870-3940

The Restitution Herald, (bi-m) Church of God General Conference (Oregon, Ill. & Morrow, Jeffery Fletcher, Box 100,000 Morrow, GA 30260-7000. Tel. (504)543-0290 Fax (404) 362-9307

Restoration Herald, (m) Christian Churches and Churches of Christ, H. Lee Mason, 5664 Cheviot Rd. Cincinnati, OH 45247-7071. Tel. (513)385-0461 Fax (513)385-0660

Restoration Quarterly, (q) Churches of Christ, James W. Thompson, Box 28227 Abilene, TX 79699-8227. Tel. (915)674-3781 Fax (915) 674-3776
Email: rq@bible.acu.edu
Website: www.rq.acu.edu

Review for Religious, (bi-m) The Roman Catholic Church, David L. Fleming, S.J., 3601

310

Lindell Blvd. St. Louis, MO 63108. Tel. (314)977-7363 Fax (314)977-7362
Email: foppema@slu.edu

Review of Religious Research, (4/yr) Non-denominational, Dr. Darren E. Sherkat & Dr. Christopher Ellison, Co-editors, Sociology Department University of Texas-Austin Austin, TX 78712. Tel. (512)471-1122 Fax (512)471-1748
Email: cellison@jeeves.la.utexas.edu

Rocky Mountain Christian, (m) Churches of Christ, Ron L. Carter, P.O. Box 26620 Colorado Springs, CO 80936. Tel. (719)598-4197 Fax (719)528-1549
Email: 76102.2461@compuserve.com

Sabbath Recorder, (m) Seventh Day Baptist General Conference, USA and Canada, Rev. Kevin J. Butler, 3120 Kennedy Rd. P.O. Box 1678 Janesville, WI 53547. Tel. (608)752-5055 Fax (608)752-7711
Email: sdbmedia@inwave.com
Website: www.seventhdaybaptist.org

Sabbath School Leadership, (m) Seventh-day Adventist Church, Faith Crumbly, Review and Herald Publishing Assoc. 55 W. Oak Ridge Dr. Hagerstown, MD 21740. Tel. (301)393-4095 Fax (301)393-4055
Email: mharris@rhpa.org
Website: www.rhpa.org

Saint Anthony Messenger, (m) The Roman Catholic Church, Jack Wintz, O.F.M., 1615 Republic St. Cincinnati, OH 45210. Tel. (513)241-5616 Fax (513)241-0399
Email: StAnthony@AmericanCatholic.org

Saint Willibrord Journal, (q) Christ Catholic Church, The Rev. Monsignor Charles E. Harrison, P.O. Box 271751 Houston, TX 77277-1751. Tel. (713)515-8206 Fax (713)622-5311

Saints Herald, (m) Reorganized Church of Jesus Christ of Latter Day Saints, James C. Cable, P.O. Box 1059 Independence, MO 64051. Tel. (816)833-1000 Fax (816)521-3043

SBC Life, (10/yr) Southern Baptist Convention, Bill Merrell, 901 Commerce St. Nashville, TN 37203. Tel. (615)244-2355 Fax (615)782-8684
Email: jrevell@sbc.net

The Schwenkfeldian, (q) The Schwenkfelder Church, Andrew C. Anders, 105 Seminary Street Pennsburg, PA 18073. Tel. (215)244-2355

SCROLL- Computer Resources for Church and Family, (6/yr) Nondenominational, Marshall N. Surratt, 304C Crossfield Drive P.O. Box 603 Versailles, KY 40383-0603. Tel. (606)873-0550 Fax (606)879-0121
Email: scroll@deerhaven.com
Website: http://wwww.deerhaven.com/

Searching Together, (q) Sovereign Grace Believers, Jon Zens, Box 548 St. Croix Falls, WI 54024. Tel. (615)465-6516 Fax (612)465-5101

Secret Chamber, (q) African Methodist Episcopal Church, George L. Champion, Sr., 5728 Major Blvd. Orlando, FL 82819. Tel. (407)352-8797 Fax (407)352-6097

The Secret Place, (q) American Baptist Churches in the USA, Kathleen Hayes, Senior Editor, P.O. Box 851 Valley Forge, PA 19482-0851. Tel. (610)768-2240 Fax (610)768-2441

Seeds for the Parish, (bi-m) Evangelical Lutheran Church in America, Kate Elliott, 8765 W. Higgins Rd. Chicago, IL 60631-4101. Tel. (773)380-2949 Fax (773)380-1465
Email: kelliott@elca.org

Sharing, (q) Interdenominational Anabaptist, Judy Martin Godshalk, P.O. Box 438 Goshen, IN 46527. Tel. (219)533-9511 Fax (219)533-5264

Shiloh's Messenger of Wisdom, (m) Israelite House of David, William Robertson, P.O. Box 1067 Benton Harbor, MI 49023

The Shining Light, (bi-m) Church of God (Anderson, Ind), Wilfred Jordan, Box 1235 Anderson, IN 46015. Tel. (317)644-1593

Signs of the Times, (m) Seventh-day Adventist Church, Marvin Moore, P.O. Box 5353 Nampa, ID 83653-5353. Tel. (208)465-2577 Fax (208)465-2531

The Silver Lining, (m) Apostolic Christian Churches of America, Bruce Leman, R.R. 2 Box 50 Roanoke, IL 61561-9625. Tel. (309)923-7777 Fax (309)923-7359

Social Questions Bulletin, (bi-m) The United Methodist Church, Rev. Kathryn J. Johnson, 212 East Capitol St., NE Washington, DC 20003. Tel. (202-546-8806 Fax (202-546-6811
Email: mfsa@olg.com
Website: www.olg.com/mfsa

Sojourners, (6/yr) Nondenominational, Jim Wallis, 2401 15th St. NW Washington, DC 20009. Tel. (202)328-8842 Fax (202)328-8757
Email: sojourners@sojourners.com
Website: http://www.sojourners.com

Solia - The Herald, (m) The Romanian Orthodox Episcopate of America, Rev. Deacon David Oancea, P.O. Box 185 Grass Lake, MI 49240-0185. Tel. (517)522-3656 Fax (517)522-5907
Email: roeasolia@aol.com
Website: www.roea.org

The Southern Methodist, (bi-m) Southern Methodist Church, Thomas M. Owens, Sr., P.O. Box 39 Orangeburg, SC 29116-0039. Tel. (803)534-9853 Fax (803)535-3881
Email: smchq@juno.com

Spectrum, (bi-m) Conservative Baptist Association of America (CBAmerica), Mariel Kindl and Ed Mitchell, P.O. Box 66 Wheaton, IL 60189. Tel. (630)260-3800 Fax (630)653-5387
Email: arlenef@cb.usa.com

Spirit, (q) Volunteers of America, Arthur Smith and Denis N. Baker, 1321 Louisiana Ave. New Orleans, LA 70115. Tel. (504)897-1731

Spirit, (m) Pentecostal Church of God (Joplin, MO), Aaron Wilson, P.O. Box 850 Joplin, MO 64802. Tel. (417-624-7050 Fax (417)624-7102
Email: aaronw@pcg.org
Website: www.pcg.org

The Spiritual Sword, (q) Churches of Christ, Alan E. Highers, 1511 Getwell Rd. Memphis, TN 38111. Tel. (901)743-0464 Fax (901)743-2197
Email: getwellcc@aol.com

The Standard Bearer, (21/yr) Protestant Reformed Churches in America, David J. Engelsma, 4949 Ivanrest Ave. Grandville, MI 49418. Tel. (616)531-1490 Fax (616)531-3033
Email: engelsma@prca.org

The Standard, m) Baptist General Conference, Gary D. Marsh, 2002 S. Arlington Heights Rd. Arlington Heights, IL 60005. Tel. (847)228-0200 Fax (847)228-5376
Email: GMBGCSTD@aol.com

Star of Zion, (bi-w) African Methodist Episcopal Zion Church, Dr. Morgan W. Tann, P.O. Box 31005 Charlotte, NC 28231. Tel. (704)377-4329 Fax (704)377-2809
Email: star0zion@juno.com

Stewardship USA, (q) Nondenominational, Raymond Barnett Knudsen II, 4818 Quarton Rd. Bloomfield Hills, MI 48302. Tel. (248)737-0895 Fax (248-737-0895

Story Friends, (m) Mennonite Church, Rose Mary Stutzman, 616 Walnut Ave. Scottdale, PA 15683. Tel. (724)887-8500 Fax (724)887-3111
Email: rstutz@mph.org
Website: www.mph.org

The Student, (m) Seventh-day Adventist Church, Jerry Stevens, P.O. Box 6097 Lincoln, NE 68506. Tel. (402)488-0981 Fax (402)488-7582
Email: CRSnet@compuserve.com
Website: www.ChristianRecord.org

Sunday, (q) Interdenominational, Jack P. Lowndes, 2930 Flowers Rd., S., #16 Atlanta, GA 30341-5532. Tel. (770)936-5376 Fax (770)452-6582

The Tablet, (w) The Roman Catholic Church, Ed Wilkinson, 653 Hicks St. Brooklyn, NY 11231. Tel. (718)858-3838 Fax (718)858-2112

Teacher Touch, (q) Nondenominational, Marlene LeFever, 4050 Lee Vance View Colorado Springs, CO 80918. Tel. (800)708-

5550 Fax (719)535-3202
Email: lefeverm@cookministries.org

Theology Digest, (q) The Roman Catholic Church, 3634 Lindell Blvd. St. Louis, MO 63108-3395. Tel. (314)977-3410 Fax (314) 977-247

Theology Today, (q) Nondenominational, Patrick D. Miller, P.O. Box 29 Princeton, NJ 08542. Tel. (609)-497-7714 Fax (609)-497-7870

These Days, (bi-m) Interdenominational, Kay Snodgrass, 100 Witherspoon St. Louisville, KY 40202-1396. Tel. (502)569-5080 Fax (502)569-5113
Website: http://www.pcusa.org/ppc/

The Tidings, (w) The Roman Catholic Church, Tod M. Tamberg, 3424 Wilshire Blvd. Los Angeles, CA 90010. Tel. (213)637-7360 Fax (213)637-6360
Website: http://www.the-tidings.com

Timbrel: The Publication of Mennonite Women, (6/yr) Mennonite Church and General Conference Mennonite Churc, Cathleen Hockman-Wert, 828 Washington St. Apt. 3B Huntingdon, PA 16652. Tel. (814-641-5259
Email: timbrel@vicon.net

Today's Christian Woman, (6/yr) Nondenominational, Ramona Cramer Tucker, 465 Gunderson Dr. Carol Stream, IL 60188. Tel. (630)260-6200 Fax (630)260-0114
Email: TCWedit@aol.com
Website: http://www.christianity.net/

Tomorrow Magazine, (q) American Baptist Churches in the USA, Sara E. Hopkins, 475 Riverside Dr., Room 1700 New York, NY 10115-0049. Tel. (800)986-6222 Fax (800)986-6782

The Tover of St. Cassian, (bi-annually) Apostolic Episcopal Church-Province of the East, Rt. Rev. Francis C. Spataro DD, Order of Corporate Reunion- US Council 80-46 234th Street Jamaica, NY 11427. Tel. (718)740-4134
Email: vilatte@aol.com
Website: http://netministries.org/see/churches/ch04671

Truth, (bi-m) Grace Gospel Fellowship, Roger G. Anderson and Sherry Macy, 2125 Martindale SW Grand Rapids, MI 49509. Tel. (616)247-1999 Fax (616)241-2542
Email: ggfpres@aol.com

Truth Magazine, (bi-w) Churches of Christ, Mike Willis, Box 9670 Bowling Green, KY 42102. Tel. (800)428-0121

U.S. Catholic, (m) The Roman Catholic Church, Rev. Mark J. Brummel, 205 W. Monroe St. Chicago, IL 60606. Tel. (312)236-7782 Fax (312)236-8207
Email: editors@uscatholic.org
Website: www.uscatholic.org

Ubique, (q) The Liberal Catholic Church—Province of the United Sta, Rt. Rev. Joseph Tisch, P.O. Box 1117 Melbourne, FL 32902. Tel. (407)254-0499

Ukrainian Orthodox Herald, Ukrainian Orthodox Church in America (Ecumenical Patria, Rev. Dr. Anthony Ugolnik, P.O. Box 774 Allentown, PA 18105

United Church News, (10/yr) United Church of Christ, W. Evan Golder, 700 Prospect Ave. Cleveland, OH 44115. Tel. (216)736-2218 Fax (216)736-2223
Email: goldere@ucc.org
Website: www.ucc.org

UMR Communications, Inc., Independent, Protestant orgainization which publishes: The United Methodist Reporter (w); The United Methodist Reporter (bi-w); The National Christian Reporter (w); Good Works Online (daily Internet); Reporter Interactive (daily Internet), Ronald P. Patterson, Editor; Cynthia B. Astle, News Director, P.O. Box 660275 Dallas, TX 75266-0275. Tel. (214-630-6495 Fax (214)630-0079
Email: united_methodist_reporter@compu serve.com
Website: www.umr.org

The Upper Room, (6/yr) The United Methodist Church, Janice Grana, P.O. Box 189 Nashville, TN 37202. Tel. (615)340-7200 Fax (615)340-7006

Upreach, (bi-m) Churches of Christ, Randy Becton, Box 2001 Abilene, TX 79604. Tel. (915)698-4370 Fax (915)691-5736
Email: herald@abilene.com
Website: http://www.abilene.com/heral

Vibrant Life, (bi-m) Seventh-day Adventist Church, Larry Becker, 55 W. Oak Ridge Dr. Hagerstown, MD 21740. Tel. (301)393-4019 Fax (301)393-4055
Email: vleditor@rhpa.org

Victory (Youth Magazine), (m) Church of God of Prophecy, Dewayne Hamby, P.O. Box 2910 Cleveland, TN 37320-2910. Tel. (423)559-5207 Fax (423)559-5202
Email: CGPYOUTH@aol.com
Website: http://www.cogop.org

The Vindicator, (m) Old German Baptist Brethren, Steve Bayer, 6952 N. Montgomery Co. Line Rd. Englewood, OH 45322-9748. Tel. (937)884-7531 Fax (937)884-7531

Vista, (bi-m) Christian Church of North America, General Council, Gregory Miheli, 1294 Rutledge Rd. Transfer, PA 16154. Tel. (412)962-3501 Fax (412)962-1766
Email: ccna@nauticom.net

Voice!, (q) General Association of General Baptists, Rev. Ron Byrd, 100 Stinson Dr.

Poplar Bluff, MO 63901. Tel. (573)785-7746 Fax (573)785-0564
Email: gbnm@pbmo.net
Website: www.generalbaptist.com

The Voice, (q) The Bible Church of Christ, Inc., Montrose Bushrod, 1358 Morris Ave. Bronx, NY 10456. Tel. (718)588-2284 Fax (718)992-5597

The Voice, (6/yr) Independent Fundamental Churches of America, Richard I. Gregory, P.O. Box 810 Grandville, MI 49468-0810. Tel. (616)531-1840 Fax (616)531-1814
Email: Voice@ifca.org

The War Cry, (bi-w) The Salvation Army, Marlene Chase, 615 Slaters Lane Alexandria, VA 22313. Tel. (703)684-5500 Fax (703)684-5539
Email: warcry@asa.salvationarmy.org
Website: http://publications.salvationarmy-susa.org

The Wave, (q) General Association of General Baptists, Sandra Trivitt, 100 Stinson Dr. Poplar Bluff, MO 63901. Tel. (573)785-7746 Fax (573)785-0564

Weavings: A Journal of the Christian Spiritual Life, (6/yr) The United Methodist Church, John S. Mogabgab, P.O. Box 189 Nashville, TN 37202. Tel. (615)340-7254 Fax (615)340-7267
Email: weavings@upperroom.org
Website: www.upperroom.org

The Wesleyan Advocate, (11/yr) The Wesleyan Church, Norman G. Wilson, P.O. Box 50434 Indianapolis, ID 46250-0434. Tel. (317)570-5204 Fax (317)570-5260

Wesleyan Woman, (q) The Wesleyan Church, Martha Blackburn, P.O. Box 50434 Indianapolis, IN 46250. Tel. (317)570-5164 Fax (317)570-5254
Email: wwi@wesleyan.org
Website: www.wesleyan.org

Wesleyan World, (q) The Wesleyan Church, Wayne Derr, P.O. Box 50434 Indianapolis, IN 46250. Tel. (317)570-5172 Fax (317)570-5256
Email: wwm@iquest.net

The White Wing Messenger, (bi-w) Church of God of Prophecy, Virginia E. Chatham, P.O. Box 3000 Cleveland, TN 37320-3000. Tel. (423)559-5413 Fax (423)559-5444
Email: jenny@wingnet.net
Website: www.cogop.org

Whole Truth, (m) The Church of God in Christ, Larry Britton, P.O. Box 2017 Memphis, TN 38101. Tel. (901)578-3841 Fax (901)57-6807

Wineskins, (bi-m) Churches of Christ, Mike Cope and Rubel Shelly, Box 129004 Nashville, TN 37212-9004. Tel. (615)373-

313

5004 Fax (615)373-5006
Email: wineskins@edge.net

The Winner, (9/yr) Nondenominational, Lincoln Sterd, The Health Connection P.O. Box 859 Hagerstown, MD 21741. Tel. (301)790-9735 Fax (301)790-9734

Wisconsin Lutheran Quarterly, (q) Wisconsin Evangelical Lutheran Synod, John F. Brug, 11831 N. Seminary Dr. Mequon, WI 53092. Tel. (414)227-8839 Fax (414)257-8810 Email: brugj@wls.wels.net

With: The Magazine for Radical Christian Youth, (8/yr) Interdenominational, Carol Duerksen, P.O. Box 347 Newton, KS 67114. Tel. (316)283-5100 Fax (316)283-0454 Email: deliag@gcmc.org

The Witness, (10/yr) Nondenominational, Jeanie Wylie-Kellermann and Julie A. Wortman, 7000 Michigan Ave. Detroit, MI 48210. Tel. (313)841-1967 Fax (313)841-1956 Email: the.witness@ecunet.org

The Woman's Pulpit, (q) Nondenominational, LaVonne Althouse, 5227 Castor Ave. Philadelphia, PA 19124-1742. Tel. (215)743-4528

Woman's Touch, (bi-m) Assemblies of God, Lillian Sparks, 1445 Boonville Ave. Springfield, MO 65802-1894. Tel. (417)862-2781 Fax (417)862-0503 Email: womanstouch@ag.org

Women's Missionary Magazine, (9/yr) African Methodist Episcopal Church, Mrs. Bettye J. Allen, 1901 E. 169th Pl. South Holland, IL 60473. Tel. (708)895-0703 Fax (708)895-0706

Word and Work, (11/yr) Churches of Christ, Alex V. Wilson, 2518 Portland Ave. Louisville, KY 40212. Tel. (502)897-2831

The Word, (10/yr) The Antiochian Orthodox Christian Archdiocese of North America, V. Rev. John Abdalah, 1777 Quigg Dr. Pittsburgh, PA 15241-2071. Tel. (412)681-2988 Fax (412)831-5554 Email: frjpa@aol.com Website: www.heinz.cmv.edu/~klo

The Worker, (q) Progressive National Baptist Convention, Inc., Mattie A Robinson, 601 50th St. NE Washington, DC 20019. Tel. (202)398-5343

World Harvest Today, (q) United Pentecostal Church International, J. S. Leaman, 8855 Dunn Rd. Hazelwood, MO 63042. Tel. (314)837-7300 Fax (314)837-2387

World Parish: International Organ of the World Methodist Council, (s-m) Interdenominational Methodist (Christian World Communion of Methodist and WMC-Related Churches), Joe Hale, P.O. Box 518 Lake Junaluska, NC 28745. Tel. (828)456-9432 Fax (828)456-9433 Email: wmc6@juno.com

World Vision, (bi-m) Open Bible Standard Churches, Inc., Paul V. Canfield, 2020 Bell Ave. Des Moines, IA 50315-1096. Tel. (515)288-6761 Fax (515)288-2510 Email: missions@openbible.org Website: www.openbible.org

World Vision Today, (bi-m) Nondenominational, P.O. Box 9716 Federal Way, WA 98063-9716. Tel. (206)815-2300 Fax (206)815-3445 Email: tmadison@aol.com

Worldorama, (m) Pentecostal Holiness Church, International, Donald Duncan, P.O. Box 12609 Oklahoma City, OK 73157. Tel. (405)787-7110 Fax (405)787-7729 Email: jds@iphc.org

Worship, (6/yr) The Roman Catholic Church, R. Kevin Seasoltz, St. John's Abbey Collegeville, MN 56321. Tel. (320)363-3883 Fax (612)363-3145 Email: kseasoltz@csbsju.edu Website: www.users.csbsju.edu/~worship

Worship Arts, (6/yr) Nondenominational, David A Wiltse, P.O. Box 6247 Grand Rapids, MI 49516-6247. Tel. (616)459-4503 Fax (616)459-1051 Email: graphics@iserv.net

Young & Alive, (q) Seventh-day Adventist Church, Gaylena Gibson, P.O. Box 6097 Lincoln, NE 68506. Tel. (402)488-0981 Fax (402)488-7582

Youth Ministry Accent, (q) Seventh-day Adventist Church, David S.F. Wong, 12501 Old Columbia Pike Silver Spring, MD 20904-6600. Tel. (301)680-6180 Fax (301)680-6155 Email: 74532.1426@compuserve.com

Zion's Advocate, (m) Church of Christ, Mike McGhee, 18907 E. 6th St. N. Independence, MO 64051. Tel. (816)796-6255

Zion's Herald, (m) United Zion Church, Ms. Kathy Long, 5095 School Creek Lane Annville, PA 17003. Tel. (717)867-1201

12. Religious Periodicals in Canada

The religious periodicals below constitute a basic core of important journals and periodicals circulated in Canada. The list does not include all publications prepared by religious bodies, and not all the publications listed here are necessarily the official publication of a particular church. Each entry gives: the title of the periodical; frequency of publication; religious affiliation; editor's name, address, telephone and fax number; and email and website addresses when available. The frequency of publication, which appears in parenthesis after the name of the publication, is represented by a "w" for weekly; "m" for monthly; "q" for quarterly.

Again, (q) The Antiochian Orthodox Christian Archdiocese of North America, R. Thomas Zell, Conciliar Press, P.O. Box 76, Ben Lomond, CA 95005-0076. Tel. (800)967-7377 Fax (831)336-8882
Email: conciliar@got.net
Website: www.conciliarpress.com

Anglican Journal, (10/yr) The Anglican Church of Canada, David Harris, 600 Jarvis St., Toronto, ON M4Y 2J6. Tel. (416)924-9199 Fax (416)921-4452
Email: editor@national.anglican.ca

Anglican, The, (10/yr) The Anglican Church of Canada, Stuart Mann, 135 Adelaide St. E., Toronto, ON M5C 1L8. Tel. (416)363-6021 Fax (416)363-7678

Armenian Evangelical Church, (q) Armenian Evangelical Church, Yessayi Sarmazian, 2600 14th Avenue, Markham, ON L3R 3X1. Tel. (905)305-8144 Fax (905)305-8125

Aujourd'hui Credo, (10/yr) The United Church of Canada, Comite de redaction, 1332 Victoria, Greenfield Park, QC J4V 1L8. Tel. (450)446-7733 Fax (450)466-2664
Email: copermit@sympatico.ca
Website: www.egliseunie.org

B.C. Fellowship Baptist, (q.) The Fellowship of Evangelical Baptist Churches in BC and Yukon, Bruce Christensen, Box 800, Langley, BC V3A 8C9. Tel. (604)888-3616 Fax (604)888-3601

Banner, The, (biweekly) Christian Reformed Church in North America, John A. Suk, 2850 Kalamazoo Ave. SE, Grand Rapids, MI 49560. Tel. (616)224-0732 Fax (616)224-0834
Email: editorial@thebanner.org
Website: www.thebanner.org

Baptist Horizon, The, (m) Canadian Convention of Southern Baptists, Nancy McGough, P.O. Box 300, Cochrane, AB T0L 0W0. Tel. (403)932-5688 Fax (403)932-4937
Email: office@ccsb.ca

BGC Canada News, (4/yr) Baptist General Conference of Canada, Abe Funk, 4306 97th St. NW, Edmonton, AB T6E 5R9. Tel. (780)438-9127 Fax (780)435-2478
Email: BGCC@datanet.ab.ca

Blackboard Bulletin, (10/yr) Old Order Amish Church, Delbert Farmwald, Old Order Amish Church, Rt. 4, Aylmer, ON N5H 2R3

Budget, The, (w) Old Order Amish Church, George R. Smith, P.O. Box 249, Sugarcreek, OH 44681. Tel. (330)852-4634 Fax (330)852-4421

Cahiers de Spiritualite Ignatienne, (q) The Roman Catholic Church in Canada, Rene Champagne, Centre de Spiritualite Manrse, 2370 Rue Nicolas-Pinel, Ste-Foy, QC G1V 4L6. Tel. (418)653-6353 Fax (418)653-1208

Canada Update, (q) The Church of God of Prophecy in Canada, Adrian L. Varlack, P. O. Box 457, Brampton, ON L6V 2L4. Tel. (905)843-2379 Fax (905)843-3990

Canadian Adventist Messenger, (12/yr) Seventh-day Adventist Church in Canada, Shelley Nolan, 1148 King St. E., Oshawa, ON L1H 1H8. Tel. (905)433-0011 Fax (905)433-0982
Email: snolan@sdacc.org
Website: www.sdacc.org

Canadian Baptist, The, (10/yr) Baptist Convention of Ontario and Quebec, Larry Matthews, 195 The West Mall, Ste.414, Etobicoke, ON M9C 5K1. Tel. (416)622-8600 Fax (416)622-0780
Email: thecb@baptist.ca

Canadian Disciple, (4/yr) Christian Church (Disciples of Christ) in Canada, Stanley Litke, 255 Midvalley Dr. SE, Calgary, AB T2X 1K8. Tel. (403)256-3280 Fax (403)254-6178
Email: litkes@cia.com

Canadian Friend, The, (bi-m) Canadian Yearly Meeting of the Religious Society of Friends, Anne Marie Zilliacus, 218 Third Ave., Ottawa, ON K1S 2K3. Tel. (613)567-8628 Fax (613)567-1078
Email: zilli@cyberus.ca

Canadian Lutheran, (9/yr) Evangelical Lutheran Church in Canada, Kenn Ward, 302-393 Portage Avenue, Winnipeg, MB R3B 3H6. Tel. (204)984-9150 Fax (204)984-9185
Email: kward@elcic.ca
Website: www.elcic.ca/clweb

315

Canadian Mennonite, (bi-w) Mennonite Church Canada, Ron Rempel, 312 Marsland Drive, Waterloo, ON N2J 3Z1. Tel. (519)884-3810 Fax (519)884-3331 Email: editor@canadianmennonite.org Website: www.canadianmennonite.org

Canadian Orthodox Messenger, (q) Orthodox Church in America (Canada Section), Sr. Theodora (Zion), P.O. Box 179, Spencerville, ON K0E 1X0. Tel. (613)925-5226 Fax (613)925-1521 Email: theodora@recorder.ca

Catalyst, The, (8/yr) Nondenominational, Cathy Majtenyi, Citizens for Public Justice, 229 College St. #311, Toronto, ON M5T 1R4. Tel. (416)979-2443 Fax (416)979-2458 Email: cpj@web.net Website: http://www.web.net/~cpj

Catholic Register, The, (w) The Roman Catholic Church in Canada, Joseph Sinasac, 1155 Yonge St., Ste. 401, Toronto, ON M4Y 1W2. Tel. (416)934-3410 Fax (416)934-3409 Email: joes@cathreg.on.ca

Catholic Times (Montreal), The, (10/yr) The Roman Catholic Church in Canada, Eric Durocher, 2005 St. Marc St., Montreal, QC H3H 2G8. Tel. (514)937-2301 Fax (514)937-3051

Channels, (q) Presbyterian Church in Canada, J. H. (Hans) Kouwenberg, 5800 University Blvd., Vancouver, BC V6T 2E4. Tel. (604)224-3245 Fax (604)224-3097

Chinese Herald, (q) Canadian Conference of Mennonite Brethren Churches, Keynes Kan, 2622 St. Johns St., Port Moody, BC V3H 2B6. Tel. (604)939-8281 Fax (604)939-8201

Christian Contender, The, (m) Mennonite Church (Canada), James Baer, Box 584, McBride, BC V0J 2E0. Tel. (604)569-3302 Fax (604)569-0020

Christian Courier, (w) Nondenominational, Bert Witvoet, 261 Martindale Rd., Unit 4, St. Catharines, ON L2W 1A1. Tel. (905)682-8311 Fax (905)682-8313

Church of God Beacon, (q) Church of God (Cleveland, Tenn.), Canute Blake, P.O. Box 2036, Brampton Commercial Service Center, Brampton, ON L6T 3T0. Tel. (905)793-2213 Fax (905)793-2213

Clarion: The Canadian Reformed Magazine, (bi-w) Canadian and American Reformed Churches, C. Van Dam, One Beghin Ave., Winnipeg, MB R2J 3X5. Tel. (204)663-9000 Fax (204)663-9202 Email: clarion@compuserve.com Website: premier.mb.ca/clarion.html

CLBI-Cross Roads, (bi-m) Lutheran, Felicitas Ackermann, 4837-52A St., Camrose, AB T4V

1W5. Tel. (780)672-4454 Fax (780)672-4455 Email: clbipbad@cable-lynx.net

College News & Updates, (6/yr) Church of God (Anderson, Ind.), John Alan Howard, 4704 - 55 St., Camrose, AB T4V 2B6. Tel. (780)672-0171 Fax (780)672-6888 Email: garnderc@cable-lynx.net Website: http://cable-lynx/~gardnerc

Communications Bi Monthly, (6/yr) Congregational Christian Churches in Canada, Don Bernard, 5 Townsville Ct., Brantford, ON N3S 7H8. Tel. (519)751-0421 Fax (519)751-0852 Email: ccccnews@bfree.on.ca

Communicator, The, (3/yr) The Roman Catholic Church in Canada, P. Giroux, P.O. Box 142, Tantallon, NS B0J 3J0. Tel. (902)826-7236 Fax (902)826-7236

Companion Magazine, (11/yr) The Roman Catholic Church in Canada, Friar Philip Kelly, OFM, Conventual Franciscan Centre, 695 Coxwell Ave., Suite 600, Toronto, ON M4C 5R6. Tel. (416)690-5611 Fax (416)690-3320 Email: companion@franciscan.on.ca Website: www.franciscan.on.ca

Connexions, (4/yr) Interdenominational, Ulli Diemer, P.O. Box 158, Stn. D, Toronto, ON M6P 3J8. Tel. (416)537-3949 Email: connex@sources.com Website: www.connexions.org

Covenant Messenger, The, (5/yr) The Evangelical Covenant Church of Canada, 2791 Pembina Hwy., Winnipeg, MB R3T 2H5. Tel. (204)269-3437 Fax (204)269-3584 Email: messengr@escape.ca

Crux, (q) Nondenominational, Donald Lewis, Regent College, 5800 University Blvd., Vancouver, BC V6T 2E4. Tel. (604)224-3245 Fax (604)224-3097

Diakonia-A Magazine of Office-Bearers, (4/yr) Canadian and American Reformed Churches, J. Visscher, Brookside Publishing, 3911 Mt. Lehman Rd., Abbotsford, BC V4X 2M9. Tel. (604)856-4127 Fax (604)856-6724

Diary, The, (m) Old Order Amish Church, Don Carpenter, P.O. Box 98, Gordonville, PA 17529. Tel. (717)768-7262 Fax (717)768-7261

Die Botschaft, (w) Old Order Amish Church, James Weaver, Brookshire Publishing, Inc., 200 Hazel St., Lancaster, PA 17603. Tel. (717)392-1321 Fax (717)392-2078

Discover the Bible, (w) The Roman Catholic Church in Canada, Guy Lajoie, P.O. Box 2400, London, ON N6A 4G3. Tel. (519)439-7211 Fax (519)439-0207

Ecumenism/Oecumenisme, (q) Interdenominational, 2065 Sherbrooke St. W, Montreal,

QC H3H 1G6. Tel. (514)937-9176 Fax (514)937-2684
Email: 76261.716@compuserve.com

Edge, The, (10/yr) The Salvation Army in Canada, Pamela Richardson, 2 Overlea Blvd., Toronto, ON M4H 1P4. Tel. (416)422-6114 Fax (416)422-6120
Email: edge@sallynet.org

Eesti Kirik, (q) The Estonian Evangelical Lutheran Church, Rev. U. Petersoo, 383 Jarvis St., Toronto, ON M5B 2C7. Tel. (416)925-5465 Fax (416)925-5688

EMMC Recorder, (m) Evangelical Mennonite Mission Conference, Jack Heppner, Box 52059 Niakwa P.O., Winnipeg, MB R2M 5P9. Tel. (204)253-7929 Fax (204)256-7384
Email: emmc@mb.sympatico.ca
Website: ww.sbcollege.mb.ca/emmcl

En Avant!, (24/yr) The Salvation Army in Canada, Betty Lessard, 2050 Rue Stanley, bureau 602, Montreal, QB H3A 3G3. Tel. (514)288-2848 Fax (514)849-7600

Ensign, The, (m) The Church of Jesus Christ of Latter-day Saints in Canada, Jay M. Todd, 50 E. North Temple St., 24th Floor, Salt Lake City, UT 84150. Tel. (801)240-2950 Fax (801)240-5997
Email: toddjm@ldschurch.org

Esprit, (q) Evangelical Lutheran Church in Canada (Evangleical Lutheran Women), Gayle Johannesson, 302-393 Portage Avenue, Winnipeg, MB R3B 3H6. Tel. (204)984-9160 Fax (204)984-9162
Email: esprit@elcic.ca

Evangel: The Good News of Jesus Christ, (4/yr) Canadian and American Reformed Churches, D. Moes, 21804 52nd Ave., Langley, BC V3A 4R1. Tel. (604)576-2124 Fax (604)576-2101
Email: visscher@eznet.ca

Evangelical Baptist, The, (5/yr) The Fellowship of Evangelical Baptist Churches in Canada, Terry D. Cuthbert, 679 Southgate Dr., Guelph, ON N1G 4S2. Tel. (519)821-4830 Fax (519)821-9829
Email: president@fellowship.ca
Website: www.fellowship.ca

Expression, (q) Canadian Conference of Mennonite Brethren Churches, Dorothy Siebert, 225 Riverton Ave., Winnipeg, MB R2L 0N1. Tel. (204)667-9576 Fax (204)669-6079
Email: fln@mbcom.com
Website: www.mbcom.com

Faith & Friends, (m) The Salvation Army in Canada, Sharon Stinka, 2 Overlea Blvd., Toronto, ON M4H 1P4. Tel. (416)422-6110 Fax (416)422-6120
Email: faithandfriends@sallynet.org

Faith and Fellowship, (m) Church of the Lutheran Brethren, David Rinden, P.O. Box 655, Fergus Falls, MN 56538. Tel. (218)736-7357 Fax (218)736-2200
Email: rinden@prtel.com

Faith Today, (bi-m) Evangelical Fellowship of Canada (a cooperative organization), Larry Matthews, M.I.P. Box 3745, Markham, ON L3R 0Y4. Tel. (905)479-5885 Fax (905)479-4742
Email: ft@efc-canada.com
Website: www.efc-canada.com

Family Life, (11/yr) Old Order Amish Church, Joseph Stoll and David Luthy, Old Order Amish Church, Rt. 4, Aylmer, ON N5H 2R3.

Fellowship Magazine, (4/yr) The United Church of Canada, Gail Reid, Box 237, Barrie, ON L4M 4T3. Tel. (705)737-0114 or (800)678-2607 Fax (705)726-7160
Email: felmag@planeteer.com
Website: http://wwwebcity.com/fellowshipmug

Free Methodist Herald, The, (bi-m) Free Methodist Church in Canada, Donna Elford, 3719-44 St. SW, Calgary, AB T3E 3S1. Tel. (403)246-6838 Fax (403)686-3787
Email: fmccan@inforamp.net

Glad Tidings, (6/yr) Presbyterian Church in Canada, L. June Stevenson, Women's Missionary Society, 50 Wynford Dr., North York, ON M3C 1J7. Tel. (800)619-7301 Fax (416)441-2825
Email: jstevens@presbyterian.ca

Global Village Voice, (q) The Roman Catholic Church in Canada, Jack J. Panozzo, 420-10 Saint Mary St., Toronto, ON M4Y 1P9. Tel. (416)922-1592 Fax (416)922-0957

Good Tidings, (10/yr) The Pentecostal Assemblies of Newfoundland and Labrador, Rev. A.Earl Batstone, 57 Thorburn Rd., P.O. Box 8895, Sta. A, St. John's, NF A1B 3T2. Tel. (709)753-6314 Fax (709)753-4945
Email: paon@paon.nf.ca

Gospel Contact, The, (4/yr) Church of God (Anderson, Ind.), Editorial Committee, 4717 56th St., Camrose, AB T4V 2C4. Tel. (780)672-0772 Fax (780)672-6888
Email: wcdncog@cable-lynx.net
Website: www.cable-lynx.net/~wcdncog

Gospel Herald, (m) Churches of Christ in Canada, Wayne Turner and Eugene C. Perry, 4904 King St., Beamsville, ON L0R 1B6. Tel. (905)563-7503 Fax (905)563-7503
Email: eperry9953@aol.com OR wayneturner@home.com
Website: www.winnipeg.freenet.mb.ca/~wturner

Gospel Standard, The, (m) Nondenominational, Perry F. Rockwood, Box 1660, Halifax, NS B3J 3A1. Tel. (902)423-5540

317

Gospel Tidings, (m) Independent Holiness Church, R. E. Votary, 1564 John Quinn Rd., Greely, ON K4P 1J9. Tel. (613)821-2237 Fax (613)821-4663
Email: rvotary@hotmail.com
Website: http://members.truepath.com/holiness

Grape Vine, The, (12/yr) Reformed Episcopal Church in Canada, Barbara Brennan, 626 Blanshard Street, Victoria, BC V8W 3G6. Tel. (250)383-8915 Fax (250)383-8916
Email: bbrennan@islandnet.com
Website: www.churchofourlord

Hallelujah!, (bi-m) The Bible Holiness Movement, Wesley H. Wakefield, Box 223, Postal Stn. A, Vancouver, BC V6C 2M3. Tel. (250)492-3376

Handmaiden, (q) The Antiochian Orthodox Christian Archdiocese of North America, Mary Armstrong and Virgina Nieuwsma, Conciliar Press, P.O. Box 76, Ben Lomond, CA 95005-0076. Tel. (800)967-7377 Fax (831)336-8882
Email: marketing@conciliarpress.com
Website: conciliarpress.com

Herold der Wahrheit, (m) Old Order Amish Church, Cephas Kauffman, 1829 110th St., Kalona, IA 52247

Horizons, (bi-m) The Salvation Army in Canada, Frederich Ash, 2 Overlea Blvd., Toronto, ON M4H 1P4. Tel. (416)425-6118 Fax (416)422-6120
Email: horizons@sallynet.org

IdeaBank, (q) Canadian Conference of Mennonite Brethren Churches, David Wiebe, Christian Ed. Office, 3-169 Riverton Ave., Winnipeg, MB R2L 2E5. Tel. (204)669-6575 Fax (204)654-1865
Email: ccm@mbconf.ca
Website: www.mbconf.ca

In Holy Array, (9/yr) Canadian and American Reformed Churches, N. Gunnink, Canadian Ref. Young Peoples' Societies, 17655-48 Ave., Surrey, BC V4P 1M5. Tel. (604)574-6227

InfoMission, (11/yr) Canadian Baptist Ministries, Donna Lee Pancorvo, 7185 Millcreek Dr., Mississauga, ON L5N 5R4. Tel. (905)821-3533 Fax (905)826-3441
Email: dlpancorvo@cbmin.org
Website: www.cbmin.org

Insight*Insound*In Touch, (6/yr- Insight; 6/yr- In Sound; 4/yr- In Touch) Interdenominational. Insight (large print newspaper); In Sound (audio magazine); In Touch (braille newspaper), Barry Brown, 40 St. Clair Ave. E., Ste. 202, Toronto, ON M4T 1M9. Tel. (416)960-3953 Fax (416)960-3570
Email: jmscan@netcom.ca

Intercom, (bi-m) The Fellowship of Evangelical Baptist Churches in Canada, Terry D.

Cuthbert, 679 Southgate Dr., Guelph, ON N1G 4S2. Tel. (519)821-4830 Fax (519)821-9829
Email: president@fellowship.ca
Website: www.fellowship.ca

ISKRA, (20/yr) Union of Spiritual Communities of Christ (Orthodox Doukhobors in Canada), Dmitri E. (Jim) Popoff, Box 760, Grand Forks, BC V0H 1H0. Tel. (604)442-8252 Fax (604)442-3433
Email: iskra@sunshinecable.com

Istocnik, (4/yr) Serbian Orthodox Church in the U.S.A. and Canada, Diocese of Canada, Very Rev. VasilijeTomic, 7470 McNiven Rd., RR 3, Campbellville, ON L0P 1B0. Tel. (905)878-0043 Fax (905)878-1909
Email: vladika@istocnik.com
Website: www.istocnik.com

L'Eglise Canadienne, (11/yr) The Roman Catholic Church in Canada, Madame Rolande Parrot, C.P. 990, Ville Mont-Royal, QC H3P 3M8. Tel. (514)278-3020 x. 228 Fax (514)278-3030
Email: cmilette@novalis-inc.com
Website: www.novalis.ca

Lien, Le, (11/yr) Canadian Conference of Mennonite Brethren Churches, Annie Brosseau, 1775 Edouard-Laurin, St. Laurent, QC H4L 2B9. Tel. (514)331-0878 Fax (514)331-0879
Email: LeLien@total.net

Liturgie, Foi et Culture (Bulletin Natl. de Liturgie), (4/yr) The Roman Catholic Church in Canada, Service des Editions de la CECC, Office national de liturgie, 3530 rue Adam, Montreal, QC H1W 1Y8. Tel. (514)522-4930 Fax (514)522-1557
Email: onl@videotron.ca
Website: www.cccb.ca

Mandate, (4/yr) The United Church of Canada, Rebekah Chevalier, Div. of Communication, 3250 Bloor St W., Ste. 300, Etobicoke, ON M8X 2Y4. Tel. (416)231-5931 Fax (416)232-6004
Email: rchevali@uccan.org

Mantle, The, (m) Independent Assemblies of God International (Canada), Philip Rassmussen, P.O. Box 2130, Laguna Hills, CA 92654-9901. Tel. (514)522-4930 Fax (514)522-1557

Marketplace, The: A Magazine for Christians in Business, (bi-m) Interdenominational Mennonite, Wally Kroeker, 302-280 Smith St., Winnipeg, MB R3C 1K2. Tel. (204)956-6430 Fax (204)942-4001
Website: www.meda.org

Mennonite Brethren Herald, (bi-w) Canadian Conference of Mennonite Brethren Churches, Jim Coggins, 3-169 Riverton Ave., Winnipeg,

MB R2L 2E5. Tel. (204)669-6575 Fax (204)654-1865
Email: mbherald@mbconf.ca
Website: www.mbherald.com

Mennonite Historian, (q) Canadian Conference of Mennonite Brethren Churches, Conference of Mennonites in Canada, Abe Dueck and Ken Reddig, Ctr. for Menn. Brethren Studies, 169 Riverton Ave., Winnipeg, MB R2L 2E5. Tel. (204)669-6575 Fax (204)654-1865
Email: adueck@mbconf.ca
Website: http://mbconf.ca/mbstudies/

Mennonitische Post, Die, (bi-m) Interdenominational Mennonite, Abe Warkentin, Box 1120, 383 Main St., Steinbach, MB R0A 2A0. Tel. (204)326-6790 Fax (204)326-6302

Mennonitische Rundschau, (m) Canadian Conference of Mennonite Brethren Churches, Brigitte Penner; Marianne Dulder, 3-169 Riverton Ave., Winnipeg, MB R2L 2E5. Tel. (204)669-6575 Fax (204)654-1865
Email: MR@mbconf.ca

Messenger (of the Sacred Heart), (m) The Roman Catholic Church in Canada, F. J. Power, Apostleship of Prayer, 661 Greenwood Ave., Toronto, ON M4J 4B3. Tel. (416)466-1195

Messenger of Truth, (bi-w) Church of God in Christ (Mennonite), Gladwin Koehn, P.O. Box 230, Moundridge, KS 67107. Tel. (316)345-2532 Fax (316)345-2582

Messenger, The, (bi-m) Church of God (Anderson, Ind.), C. Paul Kilburn, 65 Albacore Cres., Scarborough, ON M2H 2L2. Tel. (416)431-9800
Email: dc581@torfree.net

Messenger, The, (22/yr) The Evangelical Mennonite Conference, Terry Smith, Box 1268, Steinbach, MB R0A 2A0. Tel. (204)326-6401 Fax (204)326-1613
Email: emconf@mts.net

Messenger, The, (q) The Reformed Episcopal Church of Canada, Rt. Rev. Michael Fedechko, 320 Armstrong St., New Liskeard, ON P0J 1P0. Tel. (705)647-4565 Fax (705)647-5429
Email: fed@nt.net

Missions Today, (bi-m) Pontifical Mission Societies (English Canada), Patricia McKinnon, 3329 Danforth Ave., Scarborough, ON M1L 4T3. Tel. (416)699-7077 or 800-897-8865 Fax (416)699-9019
Email: missions@eda.net
Website: http://www.eda.net/~missions

Monitor, The, (m) The Roman Catholic Church in Canada, Larry Dohey, P.O. Box 986, St. John's, NF A1C 5M3. Tel. (709)739-6553 Fax (709)739-6458
Email: ldohey@seascape.com
Website: www.delweb.com/rcec/monitor.htm

Multiply, (4/yr) Presbyterian Church in America (Canadian Section), Fred Marsh, 1852 Century Pl., Ste. 205, Atlanta, GA 30345. Tel. (404)320-3330 Fax (404)982-9108

N.A.B. Today, (6/yr) North American Baptist Conference, Marilyn Schaer, 1 S. 210 Summit Ave., Oakbrook Terrace, IL 60181. Tel. (630)495-2000 Fax (630)495-3301
Email: NABtoday@aol.com
Website: NABConference.org

National Bulletin on Liturgy, (4/yr) The Roman Catholic Church in Canada, Margaret Bick, 90 Parent Ave., Ottawa, ON K1N 7B1. Tel. (613)241-9461 Fax (613)241-8117
Email: liturgy@cccb.ca
Website: www.cccb.ca

New Church Canadian, (q) General Church of the New Jerusalem, T. J. Kerr and Erica Wyncoll, 152 Collingwood St., Kingston, ON K7L 3X5. Tel. (613)544-6176 Fax (416)239-4935

New Freeman, The, (w) The Roman Catholic Church in Canada, Bill Donovan, One Bayard Dr., Saint John, NB E2L 3L5. Tel. (506)653-6806 Fax (506)653-6818

News of Québec, Christian Brethren (also known as Plymouth Brethren), Richard E. Strout, P.O. Box 1054, Sherbrooke, QC J1H 5L3. Tel. (819)820-1693 Fax (819)821-9287

Orthodox Way, (m) Greek Orthodox Metropolis of Toronto (Canada), Orthodox Way Committee, 86 Overlea Blvd., 4th Floor, Toronto, ON M4H 1C6. Tel. (416)429-5757 Fax (416)429-4588

Passport, (q) Interdenominational, Dwight Friesen, Briercrest Family of Schools, 510 College Dr., Caronport, SK S0H 0S0. Tel. (306)756-3200 Fax (306)756-3366
Website: www.briercrest.ca

Pentecostal Testimony, (m) The Pentecostal Assemblies of Canada, Richard P. Hiebert, 6745 Century Ave., Mississauga, ON L5N 6P7. Tel. (905)542-7400 Fax (905)542-7313
Email: testimony@PAOC.org

PMC: The Practice of Ministry in Canada, (4-5/yr) Interdenominational, Jim Taylor, 10162 Newene Rd., Winfield, BC V4V 1R2. Tel. (604)766-2778 Fax (604)766-2736
Email: jimt@silk.net
Website: http://www.interword.com/pmc

Pourastan, (bi-m) Armenian Holy Apostolic Church - Canadian Diocese, N. Ouzounian, 615 Stuart Ave., Outremont, QC H2V 3H2. Tel. (514)279-3066 Fax (514)276-9960
Email: ararat@videotron.ca
Website: www.sourpkrikor.org

Prairie Messenger, (w) The Roman Catholic Church in Canada, Andrew M. Britz, O.S.B., Box 190, Muenster, SK S0K 2Y0. Tel. (306)682-1772 Fax (306)682-5285
Email: pmessenger@sk.sympatico.ca

Presbyterian Message, The, (10/yr) Presbyterian Church in Canada, Janice Carter, Kouchibouguac, NB E0A 2A0. Tel. (506)876-4379
Email: mjcarter@nb.sympatico.ca

Presence, (8/yr) The Roman Catholic Church in Canada, Jean-Claude Breton, Peres Dominicains, 2715 chemin de la Cote St. Catherine, Montreal, QC H3T 1B6. Tel. (514)739-9797 Fax (514)739-1664

Pulse, The, (4/yr) Evangelical Free Church of Canada, Rick Penner, EFCC Box 56109, Valley Ctr. P.O., Langley, BC V3A 8B3. Tel. (604)888-8668 Fax (604)888-3108
Email: efcc@twu.ca

Quaker Concern, (q) Canadian Yearly Meeting of the Religious Society of Friends, Peter Chapman, 60 Lowther Ave., Toronto, ON M5R 1C7. Tel. (416)920-5213 Fax (416)920-5214
Email: cfsc@web.net
Website: www.web.net

Reformed Perspective: A Magazine for the Christian Family, (m) Canadian and American Reformed Churches, Jon Dykstra, 13820-106 A Avenue, Edmonton, AB T5N 1C9. Tel. (780)452-3978
Email: penguin@edmc.net

Relations, (10/yr) The Roman Catholic Church in Canada, Carolyn Sharp, 25 Jarry Ouest, Montreal, QC H2P 1S6. Tel. (514)387-2541 Fax (514)387-0206
Email: relations@cjf.qc.ca

RESCUE, (bi-m) International Union of Gospel Missions, Phillip Rydman, 1045 Swift, N. Kansas City, MO 64116. Tel. (816)471-8020 Fax (816)471-3718
Email: iugm@iugm.org
Website: www.iugm.org

Resource: The National Leadership Magazine, (5/yr) The Pentecostal Assemblies of Canada, Michael P. Horban, 6745 Century Ave., Mississauga, ON L5N 6P7. Tel. (905)542-7400 Fax (905)542-7313
Email: mhorban@paoc.org

Revival Fellowship News, (q) Interdenominational, Harold Lutzer, Canadian Revival Fellowship, Box 584, Regina, SK S4P 3A3. Tel. (306)522-3685 Fax (306)522-3686
Email: crf@dlewest.com
Website: www.revivalfellowship.com

Rupert's Land News, (10/yr) The Anglican Church of Canada, J. D. Caird/ M.A. Jackson, Anglican Centre, 935 Nesbitt Bay, Winnipeg, MB R3J 3R1. Tel. (204)453-6130 Fax (204)452-3915

Saints Herald, (m) Reorganized Church of Jesus Christ of Latter Day Saints, James Cable, The Herald Publishing House, P.O. Box 1770, Independence, MO 64055-0770. Tel. (816) 252-5010 Fax (816)252-3976
Email: comdiv@rlds.org
Website: http://www.rlds.org

Sally Ann, (10/yr) The Salvation Army in Canada, Shirley Pavey, 2 Overlea Blvd., Toronto, ON M4H 1P4. Tel. (416)422-6113 Fax (416)422-6120

Scarboro Missions, (9/yr) The Roman Catholic Church in Canada, G. Curry, S.F.M., 2685 Kingston Rd., Scarborough, ON M1M 1M4. Tel. (416)261-7135 Fax (416)261-0820
Email: sfmmag@web.net

Servant Magazine, (4/yr) Interdenominational, Phil Callaway, Prairie Bible Institute, Box 4000, Three Hills, AB T0M 2N0. Tel. (403)443-5511 Fax (403)443-5540
Website: http://www.pbi.ab.ca

Shantyman, The, (bi-m) Nondenominational, Arthur C. Dixon, 2476 Argentia Rd., Ste. 213, Mississauga, ON L5N 6M1. Tel. (905)821-6310 Fax (905)821-6311
Email: shanty@pathcom.com

Sister Triangle, (q) churches of Christ, Marge Roberts, P.O. 948, Dauphin, MB R7N 3J5. Tel. (204)638-8156 Fax (204)638-6640
Email: amrobert@mb.sympatico.ca

Solia - The Herald, (m) The Romanian Orthodox Episcopate of America (Jackson, MI), Rev. Deacon David Oancea, P.O. Box 185, Grass Lake, MI 49240-0185. Tel. (517)522-3656 Fax (517)522-5907
Email: ROEASOLIA@aol.com
Website: www.roea.org

SR: Studies in Religion: Sciences religieuses, (q) Nondenominational, Willi Braun, University of Alberta, 347 Arts Bldg, Edmonton, AB T6H 2E6. Tel. (780)492-2879
Email: willi.braun@ualberta.ca

St. Luke Magazine, (m) Christ Catholic Church International, Donald W. Mullan, 5165 Palmer Ave., Niagara Falls, ON L2E 6S8. Tel. (905)354-2329 Fax (905)354-9934
Email: dmullan@cgocable.net
Website: http://www3.sympatico.ca/dwmullan

The Canadian Lutheran, (10/yr) Lutheran Church—Canada, Ian Adnams, 3074 Portage Ave., Winnipeg, MB R3K 0Y2. Tel. (204)895-3433 Fax (204)897-4319
Email: lcc@mts.net
Website: www.lutheranchurch-canada.ca

The Presbyterian Record, (11/yr) Presbyterian Church in Canada, John Congram, 50 Wynford Dr., Toronto, ON M3C 1J7. Tel. (416)441-1111 Fax (416)441-2825
Email: pcrecord@presbyterian.ca
Website: www.presbycan.ca/record

Topic, (m) The Anglican Church of Canada, Lorie Chortyk, 580-401 W. Georgia St., Vancouver, BC V6B 5A1. Tel. (604)684-6306

Fax (604)684-7017
Email: loriec@synod.nw.anglican.ca

Trait d'Union, Le, (4-5/yr) Union d'Eglises Baptistes Francaises au Canada, Fritz Obas, 2285 Ave. Papineau, Montreal, QC H2K 4J5. Tel. (514)526-6643 Fax (514)526-9269

United Church Observer, (m) The United Church of Canada, Muriel Duncan, 478 Huron St., Toronto, ON M5R 2R3. Tel. (416)960-8500 Fax (416)960-8477
Email: general@ucobserver.org
Website: www.ucobserver.org

Vie Chretienne, La (French), (m) Presbyterian Church in Canada, Jean Porret, PO Box 272, Suzz. Rosemont, Montreal, QC H1X 3B8. Tel. (514)737-4168

Vie des Communautes religieuses, La, (5/yr) The Roman Catholic Church in Canada, Andre Bellefeuille, 251 St-Jean-Baptiste, Nicolet, QC J3T 1X9. Tel. (819)293-8736 Fax (819)293-2419

Vie Liturgique, (8/yr) The Roman Catholic Church in Canada, Novalis, 6255 Rue Hutchison, Bureau 103, Montreal, QC H2V 4C7. Tel. (800)668-3020 Fax (514)278-3030
Email: info@novalis-inc.com

VIP Communique, Foursquare Gospel Church of Canada, Timothy Peterson, 8459-160th St., Ste. 100, Surrey, BC V3S 3T9. Tel. (604)543-8414 Fax (604)543-8417

Visnyk: The Herald, (m) Ukrainian Orthodox Church of Canada, Ihor Kutash and Marusia Tarnawecka Zurek, 9 St. John's Ave., Winnipeg, MB R2W 1G8. Tel. (204)586-3093 Fax (204)582-5241

Voce Evangelica/Evangel Voice, (bi-m) The Italian Pentecostal Church of Canada, Rev. Daniel Costanza, 140 Woodbridge Ave., Suite 400, Woodbridge, ON L4L 4K9. Tel. (905)850-1578 Fax (905)850-1578
Email: bethel@idirect.com

War Cry, The, (m) The Salvation Army in Canada, Sharon Stinka, 2 Overlea Blvd., Toronto, ON M4H 1P4. Tel. (416)425-2111 Fax (416)422-6120
Email: warcry@sallynet.org
Website: http://sallynet.org

Word Alive, (q) Nondenominational, Dwayne Janke, Wycliffe Bible Translators of Canada, 4316 10 St., NE, Calgary, AB T2E 6K3. Tel. (403)250-5411 Fax (403)250-2623
Email: dwayne_janke@wycliffe.org
Website: http://www.wbtc.org

Word, The, (10/yr) The Antiochian Orthodox Christian Archdiocese of North America, John P. Abdallah, 1777 Quigg Dr., Pittsburgh, PA 15241-2071

World: Journal of Unitarian Universalist Association, (bi-m) Unitarian, Tom Stites, 25 Beacon St., Boston, MA 02108. Tel. (617)742-2100 Fax (617)367-3237
Email: worldmag@uua.org
Website: http://www.uua.org

Young Companion, (11/yr) Old Order Amish Church, Joseph Stoll and Christian Stoll, Old Order Amish Church, Rt. 4, Aylmer, ON N5H 2R3

Young Soldier, The, (24/yr) The Salvation Army in Canada, Sharon Stinka, 2 Overlea Blvd., Toronto, ON M4H 1P4. Tel. (416)422-6114 Fax (416)422-6120

13. Church Archives and Historical Records Collections

American and Canadian history is interwoven with the social and cultural experience of religious life and thought. Most repositories of primary research materials in North America will include some documentation on religion and church communities. This directory is not intended to replace standard bibliographic guides to those resources. The intent is to give a new researcher entry to major archival holdings of religious collections and to programs of national scope. The repositories listed herein will not only provide information on materials in their custody, but also reference to significant regional and local church archives as well as specialized collections, such as those of religious orders, educational and charitable organizations, and personal papers. In the interest of space, no attempt has been made to list the plethora of research libraries of North America. Standard directories that serve this purpose are available in most public libraries.

Repositories marked with an asterisk (*) are designated by their denomination as the official archives. The reference departments at these archives will assist researchers in locating primary material of geographic or subject focus.

UNITED STATES

Adventist

Aurora University, Charles B. Phillips Library, 347 S. Gladstone, Aurora, IL 60506, Volunteer Curator: Dr. David T. Arthur, Tel. (630) 844-5437, Fax (630) 844-3848, E-mail: jhuggins@aurora.edu, Website: www.aurora.edu

Features the Jenks Memorial Collection of Adventual Materials with archival materials on the Millerite/Early Adventist movement (1830-1860); also denominational archives relating to Advent Christian Church, Life and Advent Union, and, to a lesser extent, Evangelical Adventists and Age-to-Come Adventists.

Adventist Heritage Center, James White Library, Andrews University, Berrien Springs, MI 49104, Curator: Jim Ford, Tel. (616) 471-3274, Fax (616) 471-6166, E-mail: ahc@andrews.edu, Website: http://www.andrews.edu/library/collections/departments/ahc.html

Large collection of Seventh-day Adventist material.

Department of Archives and Special Collections/ Ellen G. White Estate Branch Office, Loma Linda University Library, Loma Linda, CA 92350, Chairman/Director: Elder Merlin D. Burt, Tel. (909) 824-4942, Fax (909) 824-4188

Photographs, sound and video recordings, personal papers, and library pertaining to the Seventh-day Adventist Church.

Ellen G. White Estate, Inc., 12501 Old Columbia Pike, Silver Spring, MD 20904, Archivist: Tim Poirier, Tel. (301) 680-6540, Fax (301) 680-6559, Website: http://www.whiteestate.org

Records include letters and manuscripts (1840s to 1915), pamphlets and publications and the White papers.

*General Conference of Seventh-day Adventists: Archives and Statistics, 12501 Old Columbia Pike, Silver Spring, MD 20904-6600, Director: Bert Haloviak, Tel. (301) 680-5022, Fax (301) 680-6090

Repository of the records created at the world administrative center of the Seventh-day Adventist Church, including the period from the 1860s to the present.

Assemblies of God

*Flower Pentecostal Heritage Center, 1445 Boonville Ave., Springfield, MO 65802, Director: Wayne Warner, Tel. (417) 862-1447x4400, Fax (417) 862-6203, E-mail: archives@ag.org

Official repository for materials related to the Assemblies of God, as well as materials related to the early Pentecostal movement in general.

Baptist

American Baptist-Samuel Colgate Historical Library, 1106 S Goodman St., Rochester, NY 14620-2532, Ex. Director: Deborah Bingham van Broekhoven, Tel. (716) 473-1740, Fax (716) 473-1740 [Call first], E-mail: abhs@crds.edu, Website: http://www.crds.edu/bhs/default.htm

Manuscript holdings include collections of Baptist ministers, missionaries, and scholars, and some records of Baptist churches, associations, and national and international bodies.

*American Baptists Archives Center, P.O. Box 851, Valley Forge, PA 19482-0851, Archivist: Betty Layton, Tel. (610) 768-2374, Fax (610) 768-2266

Repository for the non-current records of the national boards and administrative organizations of American Baptist churches in the USA. Collections include mission files, publications, correspondence, official minutes and annual reports.

Andover Newton Theological School, Franklin

Trask Library, 169 Herrick Rd., Newton Centre, MA 02459, Associate Director: Diana Yount, Tel. (617) 964-1100 x.251, Fax (617) 965-9756, E-mail: dyount@ants.edu, Website: http://www.ants.edu

The collections document Baptist, Congregational and United Church history, including personal papers relating to national denominational work and foreign missions, with emphasis on New England Church history.

Primitive Baptist Library of Carthage, Illinois, 416 Main St., Carthage, IL 62321, Director of Library: Elder Robert Webb, Tel. (217) 357-3723, Fax (217) 357-3723, E-mail: bwebb9@juno.com, Website: http://www.carthage.lib.il.us/community/churches/primbap/pbl.html

Collects the records of congregations and associations.

*Seventh-day Baptist Historical Society, 3120 Kennedy Rd., P.O. Box 1678, Janesville, WI 53547, Historian: Rev. Don A. Sanford, Tel. (608) 752-5055, Fax (608) 752-7711, E-mail: sdbhist@inwave.com, Website: http://www.seventhdaybaptist.org

Serves as a depository for records of Seventh-day Baptists, Sabbath and Sabbath-keeping Baptists since the mid-seventeenth century.

*Southern Baptists Historical Library & Archives, 901 Commerce St., Suite 400, Nashville, TN 37203-3630, Director and Archivist: Bill Sumners, Tel. (615) 244-0344, Fax (615) 782-4821, Website: http://www.sbhla.org

Central depository of the Southern Baptist Convention. Materials include official records of denominational agencies; personal papers of denominational leaders; records of related Baptist organizations; and annual proceedings of national and regional bodies.

Brethren in Christ

*Archives of the Brethren in Christ Church, Messiah College, Grantham, PA 17027-9990, Archivist: Dr. E. Morris Sider, Tel. (717) 691-6048, Fax (717) 691-6042

Records of general church boards and agencies, regional conferences, congregations and personal papers of church leaders.

Church of the Brethren

*Brethren Historical Library and Archives, 1451 Dundee Ave., Elgin IL 60120, Librarian/Archivist: Kenneth M. Shaffer, Jr., Tel. (847) 742-5100, Fax (847) 742-6103, E-mail: kshaffer_gb@brethren.org

Archival materials dating from the 19th Century relating to the cultural, socio-economic, theological, genealogical, and institutional history of the Church of the Brethren.

Churches of God, General Conference

*Winebrenner Theological Seminary, 701 East Melrose Ave., Findlay, OH 45804, Director of Library Services: Dr. Gene Crutsinger, Tel. (419) 422-4824, Fax (419) 422-3999, E-mail: wtslib@aol.com

Archival materials of the Churches of God, General Conference including local conference journals.

Churches of Christ

Center for Restoration Studies, Abilene Christian University, 1700 Judge Ely Blvd., P.O. Box 29208, Abilene, TX 79699-8177, Special Services Librarian: Erma Jean Loveland, Tel. (915) 674-2538, Fax (915) 674-2202, E-mail: loveland@nicanor.acu.edu, Website: http://www.acu.edu/academics/library

Archival materials connected with the Stone-Campbell Movement. The chief focus is on the Church of Christ in the twentieth century.

Emmanuel School of Religion Library, One Walker Drive, Johnson City, TN 37601-9438, Director: Thomas E. Stokes, Tel. (423) 926-1186, Fax (423) 926-6198, E-mail: library@esr.edu, Website: http://www.esr.edu

Materials related to the Stone-Campbell/Restoration Movement tradition. Collection includes items from the Christian Church and Churches of Christ, the a cappella Churches of Christ, and the Christian Church (Disciples of Christ).

Disciples of Christ

*Disciples of Christ Historical Society, 1101 19th Ave. South, Nashville, TN 37212, Director of Library and Archives: David McWhirter, Tel. (615) 327-1444, Fax (615) 327-1445, E-mail: dishistsoc@aol.com, Website: http://www.users.aol.com/dishistsoc.index.html

Collects documents of the Stone-Campbell Movement.

Christian Theological Seminary Library, 1000 W. 42nd St., P.O. Box 88267, Indianapolis, IN 46208, Asst. Librarian for Serials & Archives: Don Haynnes, Tel. (317) 931-2368, Email: don.haynnes@cts.edu, Website: http://www.cts.edu

Archival materials dealing with the Disciples of Christ and related movements.

Episcopal

*Archives of the Episcopal Church, P.O. Box 2247, Austin, TX 78768-2247, Archivist: Mark J. Duffy, Tel. (512) 472-6816, Fax (512) 480-0437, E-mail: Research@Episcopal Archives. org, Website: http://www.Episcopal Archives.org

Repository for the official records of the national Church, its corporate bodies and affiliated agencies, personal papers, and some diocesan archives. Contact the Archives for reference to diocesan and parochial church records.

General Theological Seminary, Saint Mark's Library, 175 Ninth Ave., New York, NY 10011, Director of Special Collections: Isaac Gewirtz, Tel. (212) 243-5150 x. 360, Fax (212) 924-6304, E-mail: gewirtz@gts.edu, Website: www.gts.edu/library.shtml
Manuscript collections of early Episcopal bishops and organizations.

Evangelical Congregation Church

*Archives of the Evangelical Congregational Church, Evangelical School of Theology, Rostad Library, 121 S. College St., Myerstown, PA 17067, Archivist: Terry M. Heisey, Tel. (717) 866-5775, Fax (717) 866-4667, E-mail: theisey@evangelical.edu, Website: http://www.evangelical.edu
Repository of records of the administrative units of the denomination, affiliated organizations, and closed churches. Also collected are records of local congregations and materials related to the United Evangelical Church and the Evangelical Association.

Evangelical and Reformed

*Evangelical and Reformed Historical Society, Lancaster Theological Seminary, 555 W. James St., Lancaster, PA 17603, Archivist: Richard R. Berg, Tel. (717) 290-8711, E-mail: erhs@lts.org
Manuscripts and transcriptions of early German Reformed Church, pastoral records and minutes of synods and classes, as well as records of the Evangelical and Reformed Church (1934-1957).

Friends

Friends' Historical Library of Swarthmore, Swarthmore College, 500 College Ave., Swarthmore, PA 19081-1399, Curator: Mary Ellen Chijioke, Tel. (610) 328-8496, E-mail: friends@swarthmore.edu, Website: http://www.swarthmore.edu/library/friends/
Official depository for the records of the Philadelphia, Baltimore, and New York Yearly Meetings. Comprehensive collection of originals and copies of other Quaker meeting archives.

The Quaker Collection, Haverford College, Haverford, PA 19041-1392, Quaker Bibliographer: Elizabeth Potts-Brown, Tel. (610) 896-1161, Fax (610) 896-1102, E-mail: ebrown@haverford.edu, Website: http://www.haverford.edu/library/sc
Repository for material relating to the Society of Friends, especially to that segment of the Society known from 1827 to the mid-20th century as "Orthodox."

Jewish

American Jewish Historical Society, Friedman Memorial Library, 2 Thornton Rd., Waltham, MA 02453, Director: Dr. Michael Feldberg, Tel. (781) 891-8110, Fax (781) 899-9208
Archival repository of the Jewish people in America, including significant religious contributions to American life.

Jacob Rader Marcus Center of the American Jewish Archives, 3101 Clifton Ave., Cincinnati, OH 45220, Chief Archivist: Kevin Proffitt, Tel. (513) 221-1875, Fax (513) 221-7812, E-mail: aja@cn.huc.edu, Website: http://www.huc.edu/aja
Materials documenting the Jewish experience in the Western Hemisphere with emphasis on the Reform movement. Included in the collection are congregational and organizational records, personal papers of rabbis and secular leaders, and genealogical materials.

Latter-day Saints

Family History Library, 35 North West Temple, Salt Lake City, UT 84150, Tel. (801) 240-2331, Fax (801) 240-5551, E-mail: fhl@ldschurch.org, Manager: Jimmy B. Parker
Primarily microfilmed vital, church, probate, land, census, and military records including local church registers.

*Historical Department, Archives Division, Church of Jesus Christ of the Latter-day Saints, 50 E. North Temple, Salt Lake City, UT 84150-3800, Archives Division Director: Steven R. Sorensen, Tel. (801) 240-2272, Fax (801) 240-1845
Repository of official records of church departments, missions, congregations, and associated organizations. Includes personal papers of church leaders and members.

Lutheran

*Archives of the Evangelical Lutheran Church in America, 321 Bonnie Lane, Elk Grove Village, IL 60007, Archivist: Elizabeth Wittman, Tel. (773) 380-2818, Fax (773) 380-2977, E-mail: archives@elca.org, Website: http://www.elca.org
Official repository for the churchwide offices of the denomination and its predecessors. For further information on synod and regional archives, contact the Chicago archives or check the ELCA World Wide Web site. For ELCA college and seminary archives, contact those institutions directly, or consult the ELCA Archives.

*Concordia Historical Institute, Dept. of Archives and History, Lutheran Church-Missouri Synod, 801 De Mun Ave., St. Louis, MO 63105-3199, Director: Rev. Daniel Preus, Tel. (314) 505-7900, Fax (314) 505-7901, E-

mail: chi@chi.lcms.org, Website: http://www.
chi.lcms.org

Official repository of The Lutheran Church-Missouri Synod. Collects synodical and congregational records, personal papers and records of Lutheran agencies.

Mennonite

*Archives of the Mennonite Church, 1700 South Main, Goshen, IN 46526, Archivist, Dennis Stoesz, Tel. (219) 535-7477, Fax (219) 535-7756, E-mail: johnes@goshen.edu, Website: http://www.goshen.edu/mcarchives

Repository of the official organizational records of the Mennonite Church and personal papers of leaders and members.

*Mennonite Library and Archives, Bethel College, 300 E. 27th St., North Newton, KS 67117, Archivist: John Thiesen, Tel. (316) 284-5304, Fax (316) 284-5286, E-mail: mla@bethelks.edu, Website: http://www.bethelks.edu

Official repository for the General Conference Mennonite Church and several other organizations related to the General Conference.

*Center for Mennonite-Brethren Studies, 1717 S. Chestnut, Fresno, CA 93702, Archivist: Kevin Enns-Rempel, Tel. (209) 453-2225, Fax (209) 453-2124, E-mail: kennsrem@fresno.edu, Website: http://www.fresno.edu/affiliation/cmbs

Official repository for the General Conference of Mennonite Brethren churches.

Methodist

B. L. Fisher Library, Asbury Theological Seminary, 204 N. Lexington Ave., Wilmore, KY 40390, Archivist and Special Collections Librarian: Bill Kostlevy, Tel. (606) 858-3581, Fax (606) 858-2350, E-mail: bill_kostlevy @ats.wilmore.ky.us

Documents the Holiness Movement and evangelical currents in the United Methodist Church. Holdings include records of related associations, camp meetings, personal papers, and periodicals.

*Heritage Hall at Livingstone College, 701 W. Monroe St., Salisbury, NC 28144, Director: Dr. Phyllis H. Galloway, Tel. (704) 638-5664

Records of the African Methodist Episcopal Zion Church.

*Office of the Historiographer of the African Methodist Episcopal Church, P.O. Box 301, Williamstown, MA 02167, Historiographer: Dr. Dennis C. Dickerson, Tel. (413) 597-2484, Fax (413) 597-3673, E-mail: dennis.c.dickerson@williams.edu

General and annual conference minutes; reports of various departments such as missions and publications; and congregational histories and other local materials. The materials are housed in the office of the historiographer and other designated locations.

*General Commission on Archives and History, The United Methodist Church, P. O. Box 127, 36 Madison Ave., Madison, NJ 07940, Archivist/Records Administrator: Dr. L. Dale Patterson, Tel. (973) 408-3189, Fax (973) 408-3909, E-mail: research@gcah.org, Website: http://www.gcah.org

Collects administrative and episcopal records, and personal papers of missionaries and leaders. Holds limited genealogical information on ordained ministers. Will direct researchers to local and regional collections of congregational records and information on United Methodism and its predecessors.

Center for Evangelical United Brethren Heritage, United Theological Seminary, 1810 Harvard Blvd., Dayton, OH 45406-4599, Director: Dr. James D. Nelson, Tel. (937) 278-5817x214, Fax (937) 275-5701, E-mail: jnelson@united.edu, Website: http://www.united.edu

Documents predecessor bodies of the United Methodist Church including Church of the United Brethren in Christ, Evangelical Association, United Evangelical Church, Evangelical United Brethren Church, Evangelical Congregational Church, and Evangelical Church of North America.

Moravian

Archives of the Moravian Church, Northern Province, 41 W. Locust St., Bethlehem, PA 18018, Archivist: Vernon H. Nelson, Tel. (610) 866-3255, Fax (610) 866-9210

Records of the Northern Province of the Moravian Church in America, including affiliated provinces in the Eastern West Indies, Nicaragua, Honduras, Labrador, and Alaska.

Moravian Archives, Southern Province, 4 East Bank St., Winston-Salem, NC 27101, Archivist: Dr. C. Daniel Crews, Tel. (336) 722-1742

Repository of the records of the Moravian Church, Southern Province, its congregations, and its members.

Nazarene

*Nazarene Archives, Church of the Nazarene, 6401 The Paseo, Kansas City, MO 64131, Archives Manager: Stan Ingersol, Tel. (816) 333-7000x2437, Fax (816) 361-4983, E-mail: singersol@nazarene.org, Website: http://www.nazarene.org/hoo/archives.html

Focus is on denominational archives, including those of leaders, agencies, and study commissions. The Archives also collect materials on districts, congregations, church-related colleges and seminaries around the world.

Pentecostal

David du Plessis Archives, Fuller Theological Seminary, 135 North Oakland, Pasadena, CA

91182, Archivist: Kate McGin, Tel. (626) 584-5311, Fax (626) 584-5644, E-mail: kmcgin@fuller.edu

Collects interdenominational Pentecostal records specializing in international leaders.

*International Pentecostal Holiness Church Archives and Research Center, P. O. Box 12609, Oklahoma City, OK 73157, Director: Dr. Harold D. Hunter, Tel. (405) 787-7110 x. 3132, Fax (405) 789-3957, E-mail: archives@iphc.org, Website: http://www.pctii.org/arc/archives.html

Official repository for records produced by the international headquarters, conferences, and influential leaders.

*Hal Bernard Dixon Jr. Pentecostal Research Center, 260 11th St. NE, Cleveland, TN 37311, Director: David G. Roebuck, Tel. (423) 614-8576, Fax (423) 614-8555, E-mail: dixon_research@leeuniversity.edu, Website: http://www.leeuniversity.edu/library/dixon/html

Official repository of the Pentecostal Church of God. Also collects other Pentecostal and Charismatic materials.

United Pentecostal Church International Historical Center, 8855 Dunn Rd., Hazelwood, MO 63042, Chair, Historical Committee: Rev. J. L. Hall, Tel. (314) 837-7300, Fax (314) 837-4503, E-mail: upcimain@aol.com

Collects a variety of Pentecostal archives, primarily the United Pentecostal (Oneness) Branch.

Polish National Catholic

*Polish National Catholic Church Commission on History and Archives, 1031 Cedar Ave., Scranton, PA 18505, Chair: Dr. Joseph Wieczerzak, Tel. (717) 343-0100

Documents pertaining to the Church's national office, parishes, Prime Bishop, leaders, and organizations.

Presbyterian

*Department of History and Records Management Services, Presbyterian Church (USA),

Headquarters Office, 425 Lombard St., Philadelphia, PA 19147-1516, Manager: Marjorie N. Sly, Tel. (215) 627-1852, Fax (215) 627-0509, E-mail: preshist@shrsys.hslc.org, Website: http://www.libertynet.org/pacscl/phs

Southern Regional Office, P. O. Box 849, Montreat, NC 28757, Deputy Director: Michelle A. Francis, Tel. (828) 669-7061, Fax (828) 669-5369, E-mail: pcusadoh@montreat.edu

Collects the official records of the Church's national offices and agencies, synods, presbyteries, and some local congregations. The Department also houses records of the Church's predecessor denominations and personal papers of prominent Presbyterians. The Southern Regional Office holds records of the predecessor Presbyterian Church in the US and congregational records.

*Historical Foundation of the Cumberland Presbyterian Church, 1978 Union Ave., Memphis, TN 38104, Archivist: Susan Knight Gore, Tel. (901) 276-8602, Fax (901) 272-3913, E-mail: skg@cumberland.org, Website: http://www.cumberland.org/hfcpc

Princeton Theological Seminary Libraries, Library Place and Mercer Street, P. O. Box 111, Princeton, NJ 08542-0803, Librarian for Archives and Special Collections: William O. Harris, Tel. (609) 497-7950, Fax (609) 497-1826

Documents the history of American Presbyterianism, including an extensive collection of congregational histories and missionary reports.

Reformed

*Reformed Church Archives, 21 Seminary Place, New Brunswick, NJ 08901-1159, Archivist: Russell Gasero, Tel. (732) 246-1779, Fax (732) 249-5412, E-mail: rgasero@aol.com, Website: http://www.rca.org

Official repository for denominational records including congregations, classes, synods, missions, and national offices.

Evangelical and Reformed Historical Society, Lancaster Theological Seminary, 555 W. James St., Lancaster, PA 17603, Archivist: Richard R. Berg, Tel. (717) 290-8711, E-mail: erhs@lts.org

Materials on the early German Reformed Church and pastoral records and minutes of synods and classes, as well as records of the Evangelical and Reformed Church (1934-1957).

*Heritage Hall, Calvin College, 3201 Burton St. S.E., Grand Rapids, MI 49546, Curator of Archives: Dr. Richard H. Harms, Tel. (616) 957-6313, Fax (616) 957-6470, E-mail: rharms@calvin.edu, Website: http://www.calvin.edu

Repository of the official records of the Christian Reformed Church in North America, including classes, congregations, and denominational agencies and committees.

Roman Catholic

U.S. Catholic Documentary Heritage Project. For holdings information on various dioceses and religious orders, consult:

Catholic University of America (Mullen Library), 5 Mullen, Washington, DC 20064, Archivist: Timothy Meagher, Tel. (202) 319-5065, Fax (202) 319-6554, E-mail: meagher@cua.edu

Marquette University, Department of Special Collections and Archives, 1415 W. Wisconsin

Ave., P. O. Box 3141, Milwaukee, WI 53201-3141, Department Head: Charles Elston, Tel. (414) 288-7256, Fax (414) 288-6709, E-mail: charles.elston@marquette.edu, Website: http://www.marquette.edu/library/collections/archives/index.html

Collection strengths are in the areas of Catholic social action, American missions and missionaries, and other work with Native Americans and African Americans.

University of Notre Dame Archives, 607 Hesburgh Library, Notre Dame, IN 46556, Curator of Manuscripts: William Kevin Cawley, Tel. (219) 631-6448, Fax (219) 631-7980, E-mail: archives.1@nd.edu, Website: http://www.nd.edu/~archives

Papers of bishops and prominent Catholics and records of Catholic organizations. Includes parish histories, but few parish records.

Salvation Army

*Salvation Army Archives and Research Center, 615 Slaters Lane, Alexandria, VA 22313, Archivist: Susan Mitchem, Tel. (703) 684-5500, Fax (703) 299-5552

Holds the documents of Salvation Army history, personalities, and events in the United States from 1880.

Swedenborgian

*Bryn Athyn College of the New Church, Swedenborg Library, 2815 Huntingdon Pike, P.O. Box 278-68, Bryn Athyn, PA 19009, Carroll C. Odhner, Tel. (215) 938-2547, Fax (215) 938-2637, E-mail: ccodhner@newchurch.edu

Unitarian Universalist

*Andover-Harvard Theological Library, Harvard Divinity School, 45 Francis Ave., Cambridge, MA 02138, Curator: Timothy Driscoll, Tel. (617) 496-5153, Fax (617) 496-4111, E-mail: timothy_driscoll@harvard.edu, Website: http://www.divweb.harvard.edu/library

Institutional archives of the Unitarian Universalist Association (including some congregational records) and the Unitarian Universalist Service Committee. The library also houses numerous personal manuscript collections of Unitarian ministers and church leaders.

Meadville/Lombard Theological School Library, 5701 S. Woodlawn Ave., Chicago, IL 60637, Library Director and Professor: Neil W. Gerdes, Tel. (773) 256-3000, Fax (773) 256-3008, E-mail: ngerdes@meadville.edu

Repository for materials relating to Unitarian Universalism in particular and liberal religion in general. Includes personal papers and church records from many UU churches in the Midwestern USA.

United Church of Christ

*United Church of Christ Archives, 700 Prospect Ave., Cleveland, OH 44115, Archivist: Ng. George Hing, Tel. (216) 736-3285, Fax (216) 736-2120, E-mail: hingg@ucc.org

Records created in the national setting of the Church since its founding in 1957, including the General Synod, Executive Council, officers, instrumentalities, and bodies created by and/or related to the General Synod.

Andover Newton Theological School, Franklin Trask Library, 159 Herrick Rd., Newton Centre, MA 02159, Associate Director for Special Collections: Diana Yount, Tel. (617) 964-1100x252, Fax (617) 965-9756, E-mail: dyount@ants.edu, Website: http://www.ants.edu

Collections document Baptists, Congregational, and UCC history. Some personal papers relating to national denominational work and foreign missionary activity; majority of collections relate to New England history.

Archives of the Evangelical Synod of North America, Eden Theological Seminary, Luhr Library, 475 E. Lockwood Ave., Webster Groves, MO 63119-3192, Archivist: Clifton W. Kerr, Tel. (314) 961-3627x348, E-mail: ckerr@eden.edu

Archival records include organization records, personal papers and immigration records.

Congregational Library, 14 Beacon St., Boston, MA 02108, Archivist: Virginia A. Hunt, Tel. (617) 523-0470, Fax (617) 523-0491, E-mail: vhunt@14beacon.org, Website: http://www.14beacon.org

Documentation on the Congregational, Congregational Christian, Christian, and United Church of Christ throughout the world, including local church records, associations, charitable organizations, and papers of clergy, missionaries and others.

Elon College Library, P. O. Box 187, Elon College, NC 27244, Archivist/Technical Services Librarian: Connie L. Keller, Tel. (336) 538-6545, Fax (336) 538-6547, E-mail: keller@numen.elon.edu

Collection of membership records and other archival material on the predecessor churches of the UCC: Christian Church and the Southern Conference of the Christian Church; also maintains records of churches that no longer exist.

Interdenominational

American Bible Society Library, 1865 Broadway, New York, NY 10023-9980, Director: Mary Jane Ballou, Tel. (212) 408-1495, Fax (212) 408-1526, E-mail: mballou@americanbible.org, Website: http://www.americanbible.org

Billy Graham Center Archives, Wheaton College, 500 College Ave., Wheaton, Il 60187-5593, Director of Archives: Robert Shuster,

Tel. (630) 752-5910, Fax (630) 752-5916, E-mail: bgcarc@wheaton.edu, Website: http://www.wheaton.edu/bgc/archives.archhpl.html

National Council of Churches of Christ Archives, Department of History and Records Management Services, Presbyterian Church (USA), 425 Lombard St., Philadelphia, PA 19147-1516, Manager: Marjorie N. Sly, Tel. (215) 627-1852, Fax (215) 627-0509, E-mail: preshist@shrsys.hslc.org, Website: http://www.libertynet.org/pacscl/phs/

Graduate Theological Union Archives, 2400 Ridge Road, Berkeley, CA 94709, Archivist: Lucinda Glenn Rand, Tel. (510) 649-2507, Fax (510) 649-2508, E-mail: LGlenn@gtu.edu, Website: http://www.gtu. du/library/archives.html

Holy Spirit Research Center, Oral Roberts University Library, P.O. Box 2187, 7777 S. Lewis, Tulsa OK 74171, Director: Jim Zigler, Tel. (918) 495-6898, Fax (918) 495-6033, E-mail: hsrc@oru.edu

Schomburg Center for Research in Black Culture, 515 Malcolm X Blvd., New York, NY 10037, Manuscripts, Archives, and Rare Books Division, Tel. (212) 491-2200, Fax (212) 491-6760, Website: http://www.nypl.org

Union Theological Seminary, Burke Library, 3041 Broadway, New York, NY 10027, Archivist and Head of Special Collections: Claire McCurdy, Tel. (212) 280-1502, Fax (212) 280-1456, E-mail: awt@uts.columbia.edu, Website: http://www.uts.columbia.edu

University of Chicago, The Joseph Regenstein Library, 1100 E 57th St., Chicago, IL 60537-1502, Curtis Bochanyin, Tel. (312) 702-8740, Email: boc7@midway.uchicago.edu, Website: www.lib.uchicago.edu/LibInfo/Libraries/Rege nstein/

Yale Divinity School Library, 409 Prospect St., New Haven, CT 06511, Research Services Librarian: Martha Smalley, Tel. (203) 432-6374, Fax (203) 432-3906, E-mail: divinity.library@yale.edu, Website: http://www.library. yale.edu/div/

Standard Guides to Church Archives

William Henry Allison, *Inventory of Unpublished Material for American Religious History in Protestant Church Archives and other Depositories*, (Washington, DC, Carnegie Institution of Washington, 1910) 254 pp.

John Graves Barrow, *A Bibliography of Bibliographies in Religion*, (Ann Arbor, Mich., 1955), pp. 185-198

Edmund L. Binsfield, "Church Archives in the United States and Canada: A Bibliography," in *American Archivist*, V.21, No. 3 (July 1958) pp. 311-332, 219 entries.

Nelson R. Burr, "Sources for the Study of American Church History in the Library of Congress," 1953. 13 pp. Reprinted from *Church History*, Vol. XXII, No. 3 (Sept. 1953).

Canadian Archival Resources on the Internet: University of Saskatchewan Archives, Web Site maintained by Cheryl Avery and Steve Billington at http://www.usask.ca/archives/menu.html

Mable Deutrick, "Supplement to Church Archives in the United States and Canada, a Bibliography," (Washington, DC, 1964).

Donald L. DeWitt, "Articles Describing Archives & Manuscript Collections in the United States: An Annotated Bibliography," in Bibliographies & Indexes in Library & Information Science, V.11 (1997) p.480.

Andrea Hinding, ed., *Women's History Sources: A guide to Archives and Manuscript Collections in the U.S.*, (New York, Bowker, 1979) 2 vols.

Kay Kirkham, *A Survey of American Church Records, for the Period Before The Civil War, East of the Mississippi River*, (Salt Lake City, 1959-60) 2 vols. Includes the depositories and bibliographies.

Peter G. Mode, *Source Book and Bibliographical Guide for American Church History*, (Menasha, Wisc., George Banta Publishing Co., 1921) 735 pp.

Martha Lund Smalley, "Archives and Manuscript Collections in Theological Libraries," in *The American Theological Library Association*, ed. By M. Graham, (1996), pp. 122-130.

Society of American Archivists, *American Archivist*, 1936/37 (continuing). Has articles on church records and depositories. Website: www.archivists.org

A.R. Suelflow, *A Preliminary Guide to Church Records Repositories*, (Society of American Archivists, Church Archives Committee, 1969) Lists more than 500 historical-archival depositories with denominational and religious history in America.

Evangeline Thomas, *Women's Religious History Sources: A Guide to Repositories in the United States*, (New York, Bowker, 1983).

U.S. National Historical Publications and Records Commission, *Directory of Archives and Manuscript Repositories in the United States*, (Washington, D.C., 1988).

United States, Library of Congress, Division of Manuscripts, *Manuscripts in Public and Private Collections in the United States*, (Washington, DC, 1924).

U.S. Library of Congress, Washington, DC: *The National Union Catalog of Manuscript Collections*, Serially published from 1959 to 1993 (1959-1993).Contains many entries for collections of church archives. Researchers may consult the cumulative paper indexes or use the NUCMC home page to access the RLIN database of archives and manuscripts collections at http://lcweb.loc.gov/coll/nucmc/nucmc.html

Jean M. White, *Address List of Church Archives and Libraries*, (Glendale, AZ, J.M. White, 1993).

CANADA

Anglican

*General Synod Archives, 600 Jarvis St. Toronto, ON M4Y 2J6, Archivist: Terry Thompson, Tel. (416) 924-9199 x 279, Fax (416) 968-7983, E-mail: archives@national. anglican.ca, Website: http://www.anglican.ca

Collects the permanent records of the General Synod, its committees and its employees. The Archives has a national scope and provides referral services on local Church records.

Baptist

*Atlantic Baptist Historical Collection of the Acadia University Archives, Vaughan Memorial Library, Wolfville, NS B0P 1X0, Archivist: Patricia Townsend, Tel. (902) 585-1412, E-mail: patricia.townsend@acadiau.ca

Collection of denominational newspapers, mission materials, Atlantic Baptist Church records and microfilm collections on the Protestant Reformation.

Canadian Baptist Archives, McMaster Divinity College, Hamilton, ON L8S 4K1, Director: Dr. Kenneth R. Morgan, Tel. (905) 525-9140, Fax (905) 577-4782, E-mail: morgankr@mcmaster.ca

Friends

Canadian Yearly Meeting Archives, Pickering College, 16945 Bayview Avenue, New Market, ON L3Y 4X2, Yearly Meeting Archivist: Jane Zavitz-Bond, Tel. (905) 895-1700, Fax (905) 895-9076

Holds the extant records for Quakers in Canada beginning with Adolphus in 1798 to the present, including the records of the Canadian Friends Service Committee.

Jewish

Canadian Jewish Congress National Archives, 1590 Avenue Docteur Penfield, Montreal, Que. H3G 1C5, Director of Archives: Janice Rosen, Tel. (514) 931-7531, Fax (514) 931-0548, E-mail: archives@cjc.ca, Website: http://www.cjc.ca/htm

Collects documentation on all aspects of social, political and cultural history of the Jewish presence in Quebec and Canada.

Lutheran

*Archives of the Evangelical Lutheran Church in Canada, 302-393 Portage Ave., Winnipeg, MB R3B 3H6, National Secretary/Archivist: Robert H. Granke, Tel. (204) 984-9150, Fax (204) 984-9185, E-mail: rhgranke@elcic.ca, Website: http://www.elcic.ca

Official repository for the ELCIC and its predecessor bodies, the Evangelical Lutheran Church of Canada and the Evangelical Lutheran Church of America-Canada Section. Lutheran Historical Institute, 7100 Ada Blvd., Edmonton, Alberta T5B 4E4, Archivist: Karen Baron, Tel. (403) 474-8156, Fax (403) 477-9829, E-mail: abclcc@connect.ab.ca

Mennonite

*Archives of the Conference of Mennonites in Canada, 600 Shaftesbury Blvd., Winnipeg, MB R3P 0M4, Director: Kenneth W. Reddig, Tel. (204) 888-6781, Fax (204) 831-5675, E-mail: kreddig@confmenno.ca, Website: http://www.mbnet.mb.ca/~mhc/

Institutional records and personal papers of leaders within the Mennonite Community. Holdings include the records of the Conference, various Church boards and agencies.

*Center for Mennonite Brethren Studies, 1-169 Riverton Ave., Winnipeg, MB R2L 2E5, Director: Dr. Abe Dueck, Tel. (204) 559-6575, Fax (204) 654-1865, E-mail: adueck@conmbconf.ca

Institutional records of the boards and agencies of the Mennonite Brethren Church in Canada with some holdings pertaining to other parts of North America. Also personal papers of leaders.

Pentecostal

*Pentecostal Assemblies of Canada, 6745 Century Ave., Mississauga, ON L5N 6P7, Director of Archives: Douglas Rudd, Tel. (905) 542-7400, Fax (905) 542-7313, E-mail: admin@paoc.org, website: www.paoc.org

Repository of archival records created by the Pentecostal Assemblies of Canada.

Presbyterian

*Presbyterian Church in Canada Archives and Records, 50 Wynford Drive, North York, ON M3C 1J7, Archivist/Records Administrator: Kim M. Arnold, Tel. (416) 441-1111x310, Fax (416) 441-2825, E-mail: karnold@presbyterian.ca, Website: http://www.presbyterian.ca

Records of the Presbyterian Church in Canada, its officials, ministers, congregations and organizations.

Roman Catholic

Research Center in Religious History in Canada, St. Paul University, 223 Main St., Ottawa, ON K1S 1C4, Tel. (613) 237-0580

Holds guides to many Canadian Catholic archives.

Salvation Army

George Scott Railton Heritage Centre, 2130 Bayview Ave., Toronto, ON M4N 3K6, Director: Major Paul Murray, Tel. (416) 481-4441, Fax (416) 481-6096, E-mail: fpmur-

329

ray@sallynet.org, Website: www.salvation
army.ca

Records include publications and comprehensive financial, personnel, social welfare
and immigration records.

United Church of Canada

*United Church of Canada Central Archives,
Victoria University, 73 Queens Park Crescent,
Toronto, ON M5S 1K7, Chief Archivist: Jean
Dryden, Tel. (416) 585-4563, E-mail:
uccvu.archives@utoronto.ca, Website: http://
vicu.utoronto.ca/archives/archives.htm

Records of the United Church and its
antecedent denominations and local and
regional records of the United Church in
Ontario. Call or view the web page for information on other regional archives.

Interdenominational

Canadian Council of Churches Archives, on
deposit in National Archives of Canada, 395
Wellington, Ottawa, ON K1A 0N3, Mr. Ian E.
Wilson, National Archivist of Canada, Tel.
General information : 613-995-5138, Research
Services Division: (613) 992-3884;
Genealogical assistance: (613) 996-7458, E-
mail: reference@archives.ca, Website: http:/
/www.archives.ca

National Archives of Canada, 395 Wellington,
Ottawa, ON K1A 0N3, Mr. Ian E. Wilson,
National Archivist of Canada, Tel. General
information : 613-995-5138, Research
Services Division: (613) 992-3884; Genealogical assistance: (613) 996-7458, E-mail:
reference@archives.ca, Website: http:// www.
archives.ca

Records of interdenominational and ecumenical organizations, missionary societies,
denominational churches, parish registers and
papers of prominent clergy.

III

STATISTICAL SECTION

Guide to Statistical Tables

Since there are no questions regarding religion in the United States Census, the *Yearbook of American & Canadian Churches* is as near an "official" record of denominational statistics as is available.

Because the data represent the most complete annual compilation of church statistics, there is a temptation to expect more than is reasonable. These tables provide the answers to very simple and straightforward questions. Officials in church bodies were asked: "How many members does your organization have?" "How many clergy?" and "How much money does your organization spend?" Each respondent interprets the questions according to the policies of the organization.

Caution should, therefore, be exercised when comparing statistics across denominational lines, comparing statistics from one year to another, and adding together statistics from different denominations.

Some particular methodological issue, and therefore cautions, in interpretation include the following considerations:

1. Definitions of membership, clergy, and other important characteristics differ from religious body to religious body. In this section, full or confirmed membership refers to those with full communicant status. Inclusive membership refers to those who are full communicants or confirmed members plus other members baptized, non-confirmed, or non-communicant. Each church determines the age at which a young person is considered a member. Churches also vary in their approaches to statistics. For some, very careful counts are made of members. Other groups only make estimates.

2. Each year the data are collected with the same questions. While most denominations have consistent reporting practices from one year to the next, any change in practices is not noted in the tables. Church mergers and splits can also influence the statistics when they are compared over a number of years.

Churches have different reporting schedules and some do not report on a regular basis. Only data that have been reported within the last ten years are included.

3. The two problems listed above make adding figures from different denominations problematic. However, an additional complication is that individuals who attend two different churches may be included more than once. For example, a person who attends the Church of God in Christ Wednesday evening and an AME service on Sunday morning will likely be included in both counts.

Table 1. Membership Statistics in Canada

Religious Body	Year Reporting	Number of Churches Reporting	Full Communicant or Confirmed Members	Inclusive Membership	Number of Pastors Serving Parishes	Total Number of Clergy	Number of Sunday or Sabbath Schools	Total Enrollment
The Anglican Church of Canada	1996	2,957	736,699	739,699	1,622	3,368	1,827	66,756
Antiochian Orthodox Christian Archdiocese of North America	1996	215	350,000	350,000	400	445	200	
Apostolic Christian Church (Nazarene)	1985	14		830	49	49		
The Apostolic Church in Canada	1992	14	1,200	1,600	14	19	14	350
Apostolic Church of Pentecost of Canada, Inc.	1998	153	24,000	24,000	310	447		
Armenian Holy Apostolic Church—Canadian Diocese	1998	13	85,000	85,000	8	48	10	700
Associated Gospel Churches	1998	135	9,991	9,991	135	259		
Association of Regular Baptist Churches (Canada)	1994	12			8	11		
Baptist Convention of Ontario and Quebec	1997	386	32,000	57,800	408	734		
Baptist General Conference of Canada	1988	85	6,838	6,838	135	137		4,144
Baptist Union of Western Canada	1994	161	20,006	20,006	181	273	137	7,961
The Bible Holiness Movement	1998	18	728	871	12	14	18	
Brethren in Christ Church, Canadian Conference	1998	40	3,387	3,387	19	43		1,673

Table 1. Membership Statistics in Canada *(continued)*

Religious Body	Year Reporting	Number of Churches Reporting	Full Communicant or Confirmed Members	Inclusive Membership	Number of Pastors Serving Parishes	Total Number of Clergy	Number of Sunday or Sabbath Schools	Total Enrollment
British Columbia Baptist Conference	1995	24	2,427	2,427	40	50	19	1,247
Canadian and American Reformed Churches	1998	48	7,963	14,949	42	60		
Canadian Baptist Ministries	1996	1,133	129,055	129,055				
Canadian Conference of Mennonite Brethren Churches	1998	208	31,477	31,824	308		208	20,729
Canadian Convention of Southern Baptists	1997	130	8,228	8,228	111	133	120	7,872
Canadian District of the Moravian Church in America, Northern Province	1998	9	1,285	1,795	6	10	9	504
Canadian Evangelical Christian Churches	1999	25		5,000	30	100		325
Canadian Yearly Meeting of the Religious Society of Friends	1995	22	1,125	1,893			30	
Central Canada Baptist Conference, The	1993	36			50	51		
Christian Brethren (also known as Plymouth Brethren)	1997	600		50,000		250	550	
Christian Church (Disciples of Christ) in Canada	1997	30	2,053	3,285	22	46	15	291
Christian and Missionary Alliance in Canada	1995	376	31,719	87,197	1,054	1,211	376	36,860

Table 1. Membership Statistics in Canada (continued)

Religious Body	Year Reporting	Number of Churches Reporting	Full Communicant or Confirmed Members	Inclusive Membership	Number of Pastors Serving Parishes	Total Number of Clergy	Number of Sunday or Sabbath Schools	Total Enrollment
Christian Reformed Church in North America	1998	236	48,675	81,127	205	301		
Church of God (Anderson, Ind.)	1998	47	3,777	3,777	64	97	43	1,994
Church of God (Cleveland, Tenn.)	1998	126	10,281	10,281	96	116	116	8,524
Church of God in Christ (Mennonite)	1998	46	4,033	4,033	156	156	46	
Church of God of Prophecy in Canada	1995	40	3,107	3,107	98	100	37	
Church of Jesus Christ of Latter-day Saints in Canada	1998	433	151,000	151,000			433	
Church of the Lutheran Brethren	1998	11	404	628	10	11	9	487
Church of the Nazarene Canada	1998	166	12,042	12,042	130	275	149	15,035
Churches of Christ in Canada	1997	140	8,000	8,000				
Conference of Mennonites in Canada	1995	223	35,995	35,995	281	464		
Congregational Christian Churches in Canada	1997	96	4,302	4,302		230		
Coptic Orthodox Church in Canada	1992	12			20			
The Estonian Evangelical Lutheran Church	1997	11	5,089	5,089	10	13	17	106
The Evangelical Covenant Church of Canada	1997	22	1,290	1,290	15	25	3	1,763

334

Table 1. Membership Statistics in Canada (continued)

Religious Body	Year Reporting	Number of Churches Reporting	Full Communicant or Confirmed Members	Inclusive Membership	Number of Pastors Serving Parishes	Total Number of Clergy	Number of Sunday or Sabbath Schools	Total Enrollment
Evangelical Free Church of Canada	1996	133	7,169	22,528				
Evangelical Lutheran Church in Canada	1995	650	141,921	198,751	455	855	443	22,773
The Evangelical Mennonite Conference of Canada	1996	53	6,508	6,508	89	105	50	4,254
Evanglical Mennonite Mission Conference	1997	44	4,633	4,633	75	201		
The Evangelical Missionary Church of of Canada	1993	145	9,923	12,217	172	367	125	7,475
The Fellowship of Evangelical Baptist Churches in Canada	1995	506	72,288					
Foursquare Gospel Church of Canada	1996	54	3,063	3,063	66	103		1,258
Free Methodist Church in Canada	1998	128	6,444	11,396	145	245		
Free Will Baptists	1998	10	347		3	4	8	
Greek Orthodox Metropolis of Toronto (Canada)	1997	76	350,000	350,000	58	71	76	
Independent Assemblies of God International (Canada)	1997	214			265	508		
Independent Holiness Church	1994	5		150	4	10	4	118

Table 1. Membership Statistics in Canada *(continued)*

Religious Body	Year Reporting	Number of Churches Reporting	Full Communicant or Confirmed Members	Inclusive Membership	Number of Pastors Serving Parishes	Total Number of Clergy	Number of Sunday or Sabbath Schools	Total Enrollment
Jehovah's Witness	1998	1,383	113,136	184,787				
The Latvian Evangelical Lutheran Church in America	1995	17	4,162	4,647	11	13	4	104
Lutheran Church—Canada	1994	329	58,316	79,844	251	373	291	13,259
Mennonite Church (Canada)	1996	117	8,172	8,172	177	291	173	21,827
Moravian Church in America, Canadian District	1997	9	1,272	1,770	6	11	9	612
North American Baptist Conference	1997	123	17,557	17,557	125	199	123	
The Old Catholic Church of Canada	1996	3	40	40	4	5		
Old Order Amish Church	1992	930						
Open Bible Faith Fellowship of Canada	1998	58		5,700	100	295	62	4,510
Orthodox Church in America (Canada Section)	1993	606	1,000,000	1,000,000	740		502	
Patriarchal Parishes of the Russian Orthodox Church in Canada	1997	23	800	1,500	3	4	3	34
The Pentecostal Assemblies of Canada	1995	1,100		218,782	1,758	1,758	753	65,928
Pentecostal Assemblies of Newfoundland	1997	140	14,715	29,361	189	301	121	10,272

Table 1. Membership Statistics in Canada (continued)

Religious Body	Year Reporting	Number of Churches Reporting	Full Communicant or Confirmed Members	Inclusive Membership	Number of Pastors Serving Parishes	Total Number of Clergy	Number of Sunday or Sabbath Schools	Total Enrollment
Presbyterian Church in America (Canadian Section)	1997	16	701	1,140	20	27		457
Presbyterian Church in Canada	1997	1,012	143,784	211,812		1,245		
Reformed Church in Canada	1998	44	4,167	6,613	34	82		
The Reformed Episcopal Church of Canada	1998	10	780	965	9	13	4	46
Reinland Mennonite Church	1995	6	877	1,816	10	13	5	347
Reorganized Church of Jesus Christ of Latter Day Saints	1995	75	11,264	11,264	1,020	1,020		
The Roman Catholic Church in Canada	1997	5,716	12,498,605	12,498,605		10,760		
The Romanian Orthodox Episcopate of America (Jackson, MI)	1997	19	900		13	14	12	
The Salvation Army in Canada	1998	376	27,920	80,180	638	1,959	346	
Serbian Orthodox Church in the U.S.A. and Canada, Diocese of Canada	1998	23	6,000	230,000	24	27	14	1,876
Seventh-day Adventist Church in Canada	1997	336	46,962	46,962	172	282	381	29,507
Swedenborgians	1994	3	347	1,085	6	6	3	185
Syrian Orthodox Church of Antioch	1995	5	2,500	3,500	3	4		

Table 1. Membership Statistics in Canada (continued)

Religious Body	Year Reporting	Number of Churches Reporting	Full Communicant or Confirmed Members	Inclusive Membership	Number of Pastors Serving Parishes	Total Number of Clergy	Number of Sunday or Sabbath Schools	Total Enrollment
Ukranian Orthodox Church of Canada	1988	258		120,000	75	91		
United Baptist Convention of the Atlantic Provinces	1998	553	62,784	62,784	281	496	312	
United Brethren Church in Canada	1992	9	835	835	5	12	9	447
The United Church of Canada	1998	3,795	683,784	1,620,837	2,009	4,102	3,072	83,219
United Pentecostal Church in Canada	1997	199				340		
Universal Fellowship of Metropolitan Community Churches	1992	12	50	1,500	8	9	1	36
The Wesleyan Church of Canada	1997	82	5,166	5,374	85	171	64	19,296
Wisconsin Evangelical Lutheran Synod	1995	16	958	1,361	16	16	16	350
TOTALS		**27,874**	**17,095,026**	**19,023,385**	**15,173**	**35,954**	**11,393**	**465,511**

Table 2. Membership Statistics in the United States

Religious Body	Year Reporting	Number of Churches Reporting	Full Communicant or Confirmed Members	Inclusive Membership	Number of Pastors Serving Parishes	Total Number of Clergy	Number of Sunday or Sabbath Schools	Total Enrollment
Advent Christian Church	1998	305	16,953	25,821	290	420	300	15,143
African Methodist Episcopal Church	1999	6,200	2,500,000	2,500,000		8,000	8,000	
African Methodist Episcopal Zion Church	1998	3,098	1,035,963	1,252,369	2,571	2,767	1,672	67,320
Albanian Orthodox Diocese of America	1996	2	1,995	1,995	1	2	2	121
Allegheny Wesleyan Methodist Connection (Original Allegheny Conference)	1998	117	1,812	1,961	86	189	117	5,893
The American Association of Lutheran Churches	1998	103	14,682	19,128	95	141	83	3,713
The American Baptist Association	1998	1,760		275,000	1,740	1,760		
American Baptist Churches in the USA	1998	3,800	1,507,400	1,507,400	4,145	7,846		
The American Carpatho-Russian Orthodox Greek Catholic Church	1998	80	13,327	13,327	85	103	76	
American Catholic Church	1997	100		25,000	80	100		
American Rescue Workers	1999	15	2,500	2,500	35	35	8	285
Antiochian Orthodox Christian Archdiocese of North America	1998	220	65,000	65,000	263	320	200	17,200
Apostolic Christian Church (Nazarene)	1993	63	3,723	3,723	217	234	55	

Table 2. Membership Statistics in the United States *(continued)*

Religious Body	Year Reporting	Number of Churches Reporting	Full Communicant or Confirmed Members	Inclusive Membership	Number of Pastors Serving Parishes	Total Number of Clergy	Number of Sunday or Sabbath Schools	Total Enrollment
Apostolic Christian Churches of America	1998	89	12,700	12,700	301	375	89	7,084
Apostolic Episcopal Church	1999	225	12,000	12,000	225	238	45	1,035
Apostolic Faith Mission Church of God	1998	19	8,210	10,550	32	37	22	4,026
Apostolic Faith Mission of Portland, Oregon	1994	54	4,500	4,500	60	85	54	
Apostolic Lutheran Church of America	1998	61				63		
Apostolic Orthodox Catholic Church	1999	20		1,250	20	26	15	
Apostolic Overcoming Holy Catholic Church of God, Inc.	1997	146	12,871	12,871	358	378	146	
Armenian Apostolic Church of America	1998	28	200,000	200,000	25	31	17	932
Armenian Apostolic Church, Diocese of America	1991	72	14,000	414,000	49	70		
Assemblies of God	1998	11,937	1,453,907	2,525,812	18,148	32,337	11,316	1,385,306
Associated Reformed Presbyterian Church (General Synod)	1997	238	34,344	40,060	194	325	206	17,078
The Association of Free Lutheran Congregations	1997	243	24,488	32,659	141	207	213	6,345
Baptist Bible Fellowship International	1997	4,500	1,200,000	1,200,000		7,500	4,500	
Baptist General Conference	1998	876	141,445	141,445				
Baptist Missionary Association of America	1999	1,334	234,732	234,732	1,525	3,055	1,300	88,921

Table 2. Membership Statistics in the United States *(continued)*

Religious Body	Year Reporting	Number of Churches Reporting	Full Communicant or Confirmed Members	Inclusive Membership	Number of Pastors Serving Parishes	Total Number of Clergy	Number of Sunday or Sabbath Schools	Total Enrollment
Beachy Amish Mennonite Churches	1997	114	7,853	7,853	381	381		
Berean Fundamental Church	1997	51		8,000				
The Bible Church of Christ, Inc.	1993	6	4,150	6,850	11	52	6	
Bible Fellowship Church	1998	56	7,169	7,169	58	112	56	5,896
Brethren Church (Ashland, Ohio)	1998	116	13,494	13,494	82	175	104	
Brethren in Christ Church	1998	210	19,577	19,577	108	311		12,840
Christ Catholic Church	1996	7	1,205	2,728	7	8	2	23
Christ Community Church (Evangelical-Protestant)	1998	2	860	1,714	3	6	1	507
Christian Brethren (also known as Plymouth Brethren)	1997	1,150		100,000		500	1,000	
Christian Church of North America, General Council	1998	99	6,930	6,930	99	159	99	
Christian Church (Disciples of Christ)	1997	3,818	568,921	879,436	3,419	7,266	3,576	198,457
Christian Churches and Churches of Christ	1988	5,579		1,071,616	5,525			
The Christian Congregation, Inc.	1998	1,438	117,039	117,039	1,436	1,438	1,294	40,243
Christian Methodist Episcopal Church	1983	2,340	718,922	718,922				
The Christian and Missionary Alliance	1998	1,964	163,994	345,664	1,629	2,535	1,805	161,931
Christian Reformed Church in North America	1998	733	137,181	199,290	655	1,148		

341

Table 2. Membership Statistics in the United States *(continued)*

Religious Body	Year Reporting	Number of Churches Reporting	Full Communicant or Confirmed Members	Inclusive Membership	Number of Pastors Serving Parishes	Total Number of Clergy	Number of Sunday or Sabbath Schools	Total Enrollment
Church of the Brethren	1997	1,095	141,400	141,400	827	1,945	858	43.577
The Church of Christ (Holiness) U.S.A.	1998	167	10,383	10,383	199	207	162	7,357
Church of Christ, Scientist	1998	2,200						
Church of God of Prophecy	1997	1,908	76,531	76,531	2,000	2,049	1,880	81,608
Church of God (Anderson, Ind.)	1998	2,353	234,311	234,311	3,034	5,468		115,946
Church of God (Cleveland, Tenn.)	1995	6,060	753,230	753,230	3,121	5,556	5,354	407,445
Church of God by Faith, Inc.	1991	145	6,819	8,235	155	170		
Church of God General Conference (Oregon, IL and Morrow, GA)	1998	90	3,824	4,971	67	83	81	2,551
The Church of God in Christ	1991	15,300	5,499,875	5,499,875	28,988	33,593		
Church of God in Christ, Mennonite	1998	102	11,846	11,846	418	420	103	
The Church of God (Seventh Day), Denver, Colorado	1997	175	7,000	10,000	94	123	175	
The Church of God, Mountain Assembly, Inc.	1994	118	6,140	6,140				
The Church of Illumination	1996	3	300	1,200	8	15	2	216
The Church of Jesus Christ of Latter-day Saints	1997	10,811	4,417,700	4,923,100	32,433	36,418	10,811	3,963,700
The Church of Jesus Christ (Bickertonites)	1989	63		2,707	183	262		

Table 2. Membership Statistics in the United States (continued)

Religious Body	Year Reporting	Number of Churches Reporting	Full Communicant or Confirmed Members	Inclusive Membership	Number of Pastors Serving Parishes	Total Number of Clergy	Number of Sunday or Sabbath Schools	Total Enrollment
Church of the Living God (Motto: Christian Workers for Fellowship)	1985	170		4,200	170			
Church of the Lutheran Brethren of America	1998	115	8,234	13,682	139	238	110	9,113
Church of the Lutheran Confession	1998	72	6,462	8,628	59	86	72	1,271
Church of the Nazarene	1998	5,101	623,028	627,054	4,598	9,998	4,822	798,141
Church of the United Brethren in Christ	1997	228	23,585	23,585	315	449	228	12,837
Churches of Christ	1999	15,000	1,500,000	1,500,000	14,500	16,350	12,500	1,600,000
Church Christ in Christian Union	1998	226	9,858	9,858	318	540	188	11,629
Churches of God, General Conference	1998	339	31,833	31,833	252	434	339	22,581
Congregational Holiness Church	1993	190		2,468			190	
Conservative Baptist Association of America	1998	1,200	200,000	200,000				
Conservative Congregational Christian Conference	1998	236	38,996	38,996	301	541	215	14,251
Conservative Lutheran Association	1997	6	962	1,438	9	22	5	185
Coptic Orthodox Church	1992	85	180,000	180,000	65	68	85	

Table 2. Membership Statistics in the United States *(continued)*

Religious Body	Year Reporting	Number of Churches Reporting	Full Communicant or Confirmed Members	Inclusive Membership	Number of Pastors Serving Parishes	Total Number of Clergy	Number of Sunday or Sabbath Schools	Total Enrollment
Cumberland Presbyterian Church	1998	774	87,198	87,198	634	835		37,221
Cumberland Presbyterian Church in America	1996	152	15,142	15,142	141	156	152	9,465
Elim Fellowship	1998	98			600	790		
Episcopal Church	1996	7,390	1,593,413	2,364,559	8,131	14,925	6,270	396,643
The Estonian Evangelical Lutheran Church	1997	21	3,508	3,508	10	12		
The Evangelical Church	1998	132	12,369	12,369	152	250	125	9,030
The Evangelical Congregational Church	1998	148	22,868	22,868	110	192	144	13,173
The Evangelical Covenant Church	1998	628	96,552	96,552	607	1,177	577	93,136
The Evangelical Free Church of America	1995	1,224	124,499	242,619	1,936	2,436		
Evangelical Friends International—North American Region	1995	92	8,666	8,666		185	90	7,226
Evangelical Lutheran Church in America	1998	10,862	3,840,136	5,178,225	9,646	17,589	8,913	948,735
Evangelical Lutheran Synod	1998	139	16,897	22,264	100	176	126	3,610
Evangelical Mennonite Church	1998	32	4,511	4,511	29	66	32	4,022

Table 2. Membership Statistics in the United States *(continued)*

Religious Body	Year Reporting	Number of Churches Reporting	Full Communicant or Confirmed Members	Inclusive Membership	Number of Pastors Serving Parishes	Total Number of Clergy	Number of Sunday or Sabbath Schools	Total Enrollment
Evangelical Methodist Church	1997	123	8,615	8,615	105	215	120	6,547
Evangelical Presbyterian Church	1998	187	57,181	61,347	262	443	172	35,758
Fellowship of Evangelical Bible Churches	1998	16	1,917	1,917	23	36	16	1,214
Fellowship of Fundamental Bible Churches	1999	22	1,125	1,125	29	46	22	1,036
Fellowship of Grace Brethren Churches	1997	260	30,371	30,371		564		
Free Methodist Church of North America	1998	990	62,176	73,236		1,898	878	94,859
Friends General Conference	1998	620	32,000	32,000	6	7	400	
Friends United Meeting	1997	501	41,614	41,614	242	360	409	
Full Gospel Assemblies International	1998	286	31,128	52,500	508		286	
Full Gospel Fellowship of Churches and Ministers International	1999	896	275,200	275,200	2,070	2,424	896	364,000
Fundamental Methodist Church, Inc.	1993	12	682	787	17	22	12	454
General Assembly of the Korean Presbyterian Church in America	1992	203	21,788	26,988	326	381		
General Association of General Baptists	1997	790	72,326	72,326	1,085	1,228	832	37,906

345

Table 2. Membership Statistics in the United States *(continued)*

Religious Body	Year Reporting	Number of Churches Reporting	Full Communicant or Confirmed Members	Inclusive Membership	Number of Pastors Serving Parishes	Total Number of Clergy	Number of Sunday or Sabbath Schools	Total Enrollment
General Association of Regular Baptist Churches	1998	1,415	101,854	101,854				
General Church of the New Jerusalem	1999	34	3,057	5,583	27	59		
General Conference of Mennonite Brethren Churches	1996	368	50,915	82,130	590			34,668
Grace Gospel Fellowship	1992	128		60,000	160	196	128	
Greek Orthodox Archdiocese of America	1998	523		1,954,500	596	806	500	
The Holy Eastern Orthodox Catholic and Apostolic Church in North America, Inc.	1998	19	4,300	4,300	10	12		
Hungarian Reformed Church in America	1998	27		6,000	27	30		
Hutterian Brethren	1997	428	36,000	42,800	500	575	50	8,900
Independent Fundamental Churches of America/IFCA International, Inc.	1999	659	61,655	61,655			659	57,768
International Church of the Foursquare Gospel	1998	1,851	238,065	238,065	4,900	7,300		
International Council of Community Churches	1998	150	250,000	250,000	182	263		
The International Pentecostal Church of Christ	1998	68	2,528	5,595	63	174	61	2,433
International Pentecostal Holiness Church	1998	1,716	176,846	176,846	1,507	1,936		94,645
Jehovah's Witnesses	1999	11,064	1,040,283	1,040,283				

Table 2. Membership Statistics in the United States (continued)

Religious Body	Year Reporting	Number of Churches Reporting	Full Communicant or Confirmed Members	Inclusive Membership	Number of Pastors Serving Parishes	Total Number of Clergy	Number of Sunday or Sabbath Schools	Total Enrollment
The Latvian Evangelical Lutheran Church in America	1998	72	14,000	15,550	50	72	18	
The Liberal Catholic Church—Province of the U.S.A.	1996	16	6,500	6,500	54	54		
The Lutheran Church—Missouri Synod	1998	6,218	1,952,020	2,594,404	5,227	8,316	5,688	572,868
Mar Thoma Syrian Church of India	1997	65	30,000	30,000	33	38	50	3,950
Mennonite Church	1998	926	92,161	92,161		2,688	907	
Mennonite Church, The General Conference	1998	313	36,600	36,600	214	444	313	26,153
The Missionary Church	1998	335	31,609	45,277	542	863	320	27,287
Moravian Church in America (Northern Province)	1998	94	20,764	26,641	89	177	91	6,537
National Association of Congregational Christian Churches	1998	416	66,626	66,626	534	690		
National Association of Free Will Baptists	1998	2,297	210,461	210,461	2,800	2,900	2,297	135,867
National Baptist Convention of America, Inc.	1987	2,500		3,500,000	8,000			
National Baptist Convention, USA, Inc.*								
National Missionary Baptist Convention of America	1992			2,500,000				

*Statistics for the National Baptist Convention U.S.A., Inc. are not available for 1998.

347

Table 2. Membership Statistics in the United States *(continued)*

Religious Body	Year Reporting	Number of Churches Reporting	Full Communicant or Confirmed Members	Inclusive Membership	Number of Pastors Serving Parishes	Total Number of Clergy	Number of Sunday or Sabbath Schools	Total Enrollment
National Organization of the New Apostolic Church of North America	1998	401	34,300	34,300	960	960	327	3,500
National Spiritualist Association of Churches	1997	130	3,530	3,530	99	134	44	
Netherlands Reformed Congregations	1998	23	4,270	8,930	8	11	20	
North American Baptist Conference	1997	268	43,850	43,850	276	422	268	
Old German Baptist Brethren	1998	57	5,966	5,966	253	253		
Old Order Amish Church	1993	898	80,820	80,820	3,592	3,617	55	
Open Bible Standard Churches, Inc.	1998	386				1,074		
The Orthodox Church in America	1998	625	1,000,000	1,000,000	700	785	476	
The Orthodox Presbyterian Church	1998	199	15,936	23,002		383	341	11,916
Patriarchal Parishes of the Russial Orthodox Church in the U.S.A.	1985	38		9,780	37	45		
Pentecostal Assemblies of the World, Inc.	1998	1,750	1,500,000	1,500,000	4,500	4,500		
Pentecostal Church of God	1998	1,237	50,200	104,300		1,802		
Pentecostal Fire-Baptized Holiness Church	1996	27	223	223		28	25	400

Table 2. Membership Statistics in the United States *(continued)*

Religious Body	Year Reporting	Number of Churches Members	Full Communicant or Confirmed	Inclusive Membership Parishes	Number of Pastors Serving	Total Number of Clergy	Number of Sunday or Sabbath Schools	Total Enrollment
The Pentecostal Free Will Baptist Church, Inc.	1998	150	28,000	28,000	175	280	160	
Polish National Catholic Church of America	1960	162						
Presbyterian Church (U.S.A.)	1998	11,260	2,587,674	3,574,959	9,390	20,940	9,240	1,048,669
Presbyterian Church in America	1997	1,340	224,154	279,549	1,642	2,665		116,720
Primitive Advent Christian Church	1993	10	345	345	11	11	10	292
Primitive Methodist Church in the U.S.A.	1998	78	4,780	6,746	70	108	78	3,374
Progressive National Baptist Convention, Inc.	1995	2,000	2,500,000	2,500,000				
Protestant Reformed Churches in America	1998	27	3,674	6,551	25	39	23	
Reformed Church in America	1998	902	179,085	295,651	915	1,784		
Reformed Church in the United States	1998	40	3,201	4,257	34	42	37	869
Reformed Episcopal Church	1998	125	6,400	6,400	150	185		
Reformed Mennonite Church	1993	10	331	346	20	20		
Reformed Presbyterian Church of North America	1997	86	4,363	6,105	70	137	78	3,373
Religious Society of Friends (Conservative)	1994	1,200		104,000				

Table 2. Membership Statistics in the United States (*continued*)

Religious Body	Year Reporting	Number of Churches Reporting	Full Communicant or Confirmed Members	Inclusive Membership	Number of Pastors Serving Parishes	Total Number of Clergy	Number of Sunday or Sabbath Schools	Total Enrollment
Reorganized Church of Jesus Christ of Latter Day Saints	1998	1,236	140,218	140,245	19,319	19,319		
The Roman Catholic Church	1998	19,584		62,018,436		47,199		
The Romanian Orthodox Episcopate of America	1996	37	65,000	65,000	37	81	30	1,800
The Russian Orthodox Church Outside of Russia	1994	177			319	319		
The Salvation Army	1998	1,388	124,721	471,416	2,920	5,248	1,388	102,601
The Schwenkfelder Church	1995	5	2,524	2,524	8	9	5	701
Separate Baptists in Christ	1992	100	8,000	8,000	95	140	100	
Serbian Orthodox Church in the U.S.A. and Canada	1986	68		67,000	60	82		
Seventh Day Baptist General Conference, USA and Canada	1995	80	4,800		46	74		
Seventh-day Adventist Church	1998	4,405	839,915	839,915	2,454	5,044	4,712	467,099
Southern Baptist Convention	1998	40,870	15,729,356	15,729,356	71,520	97,783	36,254	8,147,939
Southern Methodist Church	1997	122	7,992	7,992	112	151	118	6,075
Sovereign Grace Believers	1998	300	3,000	3,000	400	400	300	
The Swedenborgian Church	1998	37	1,558	2,113	25	45		

Table 2. Membership Statistics in the United States *(continued)*

Religious Body	Year Reporting	Number of Churches Reporting	Full Communicant or Confirmed Members	Inclusive Membership	Number of Pastors Serving Parishes	Total Number of Clergy	Number of Sunday or Sabbath Schools	Total Enrollment
Syrian Orthodox Church of Antioch	1997	21	32,500	32,500	14	20		
True Orthodox Church of Greece (Synod of Metropolitan Cyprian), American Exarchate	1993	9	1,095	1,095	18	19		
Ukranian Orthodox Church of America (Ecumenical Patriarachate)	1986	27		5,000	36	37		
United Christian Church	1998	11	328	328	6	11	9	523
United Church of Christ	1998	6,017	1,421,088	1,421,088	4,317	10,303		351,244
United House of Prayer	1998	135			270	500	135	
The United Methodist Church	1998	36,170	8,400,000	8,400,000			33,659	3,705,863
United Pentecostal Church International	1995	3,790			7,903			
United Zion Church	1998	13	883	883	13	23	11	818
Unity of the Brethren	1998	27	2,548	3,218	25	39	24	1,442
Universal Fellowship of Metropolitan Community Churches	1998	300		44,000	324	372		
The Wesleyan Church	1998	1,590	112,435	119,914	1,806	3,144	1,515	353,826
Wisconsin Evangelical Lutheran Synod	1997	1,240	315,355	411,295	1,222	1,648	1,197	45,667
Totals		**349,506**	**78,672,708**	**158,294,022**	**358,303**	**534,913**	**196,752**	**26,542,529**

Table 3. Membership Statistics for the National Council of the Churches of Christ in the U.S.A.

Religious Body	Year Reporting	Number of Churches Reporting	Inclusive Membership	Number of Pastors Serving Parishes
African Methodist Episcopal Church	1999	6,200	2,500,000	
African Methodist Episcopal Zion Church	1998	3,098	1,252,369	2,571
American Baptist Churches in the U.S.A.	1998	3,800	1,507,400	4,145
The Antiochian Orthodox Christian Archdiocese of North America	1998	220	65,000	263
Armenian Apostolic Church, Diocese of America	1991	72	414,000	49
Christian Church (Disciples of Christ)	1997	3,818	879,436	3,419
Christian Methodist Episcopal Church	1983	2,340	718,922	
Church of the Brethren	1997	1,095	141,400	827
Coptic Orthodox Church	1992	85	180,000	65
Episcopal Church	1996	7,390	2,364,559	8,131
Evangelical Lutheran Church in America	1998	10,862	5,178,225	9,646
Friends United Meeting^	1997	501	41,614	242
Greek Orthodox Archdiocese of America	1998	523	1,954,500	596
Hungarian Reformed Church in America	1998	27	6,000	27
International Council of Community Churches	1998	150	250,000	182
General Assembly of the Korean Presbyterian Church in America	1992	203	26,988	326
Mar Thoma Syrian Church of India	1997	65	30,000	33
Moravian Church in America (Northern Province)	1998	94	26,641	89
National Baptist Convention of America, Inc.	1987	2,500	3,500,000	8,000

Table 3. Membership Statistics for the National Council of the Churches of Christ in the U.S.A. (*continued*)

Religious Body	Year Reporting	Number of Churches Reporting	Inclusive Membership	Number of Pastors Serving Parishes
National Baptist Convention, USA, Inc.*	-	-	-	-
National Missionary Baptist Convention of America	1992		2,500,000	
The Orthodox Church in America	1998	625	1,000,000	700
Patriarchal Parishes of the Russian Orthodox Church in the U.S.A.	1985	38	9,780	37
Polish National Catholic Church of America	1960	162		
Presbyterian Church (U.S.A.)	1998	11,260	3,574,959	9,390
Progressive National Baptist Convention, Inc.	1995	2,000	2,500,000	
Reformed Church in America	1998	902	259,651	915
Serbian Orthodox Church in the U.S.A. and Canada	1986	68	67,000	601,998
The Swedenborgian Church	1998	37	2,113	25
Syrian Orthodox Church of Antioch	1997	21	32,500	14
Ukranian Orthodox Church of America (Ecumenical Patriarachate)	1986	27	5,000	36
United Church of Christ	1998	6,017	1,421,088	4,317
The United Methodist Church	1998	36,170	8,400,000	

*Statistics for the National Baptist Convention, U.S.A., Inc. are unavailable for 1998.

353

Table 4. Selected Statistics of Churcl

				TOTAL CONTRIBUTIONS		
Religious Body	**Year**	**Full or Confirmed Members**	**Inclusive Members**	**Total Contributions**	**Per Capita Full or Confirmed Members**	**Per Capi Inclusiv Member**
The Antiochian Orthodox Christian Archdiocese of North America	1996	350,000	350,000	$3,475,000	$9.93	$9.93
Armenian Holy Apostolic Church—Canadian Diocese	1998	85,000	85,000	$709,900	$8.35	$8.35
The Bible Holiness Movement	1998	728	871	$313,959	$431.26	$360.46
Brethren in Christ Church, Canadian Conference	1998	3,387	3,387	$5,283,709	$1,560.00	$1,560.0
Canadian District of the Moravian Church in America, Northern Province	1998	1,285	1,795	$1,279,871	$996.01	$713.02
Canadian Evangelical Christian Churches	1999	5,000	5,000	$163,500	$32.70	$32.70
Christian Church (Disciples of Christ) in Canada	1997	2,053	3,285	$1,353,560	$659.31	$412.04
Church of God (Anderson Ind.)	1998	3,777	3,777	$630,769	$167.00	$167.00
Church of God (Cleveland, Tenn.)	1998	10,281	10,281	$3,761,922	$365.91	$365.91
Church of the Nazarene in Canada	1998	12,042	12,042	$8,773,477	$728.57	$728.57
The Evangelical Covenant Church of Canada	1997	1,290	1,290	$7,690,321	$5,961.49	$5,961.4
Evangelical Lutheran Church in Canada	1995	141,921	198,751	$54,609,875	$384.79	$274.77
Foursquare Gospel Church of Canada	1996	3,063	3,063	$4,376,923	$1,428.97	$1,428.9
Free Methodist Church in Canada	1998	6,444	11,396	$3,177,707	$493.13	$278.84
The Latvian Evangelical Lutheran Church in America	1995	4,162	4,647	$1,201,332	$288.64	$258.52
Lutheran Church—Canada	1994	58,316	79,844	$26,046,000	$446.64	$326.21
Mennonite Church (Canada)	1996	8,172	8,172	$12,924,965	$1,581.62	$1,581.6
Moravian Church in America, Canadian District	1997	1,272	1,770	$1,142,954	$898.55	$645.74
North American Baptist Conference	1997	17,557	17,557	$24,308,553	$1,384.55	$1,384.5
Pentecostal Assemblies of Newfoundland	1997	14,715	29,361	$3,143,197	$213.60	$107.05
Presbyterian Church in America (Canadian Section)	1997	701	1,140	$1,708,607	$2,437.39	$1,498.7
The Presbyterian Church in Canada	1997	143,784	211,812	$85,326,113	$593.43	$402.84
Reformed Church in Canada	1998	4,167	6,613	$6,483,147	$1,555.83	$980.36
The Reformed Episcopal Church of Canada	1998	780	965	$190,240	$243.90	$197.14
Seventh-day Adventist in Canada	1997	46,962	46,962	$57,546,475	$1,225.38	$1,225.3
The United Church of Canada	1998	683,784	1,620,837	$297,652,430	$435.30	$183.64
The Wesleyan Church of Canada	1997	5,166	5,374	$10,193,278	$1,973.15	$1,896.7
Wisconsin Evangelical Lutheran Synod	1995	958	1,361	$830,695	$867.11	$610.36

Finances—Canadian Churches

CONGREGATIONAL FINANCES			BENEVOLENCES			
Total Congregational Contributions	Per Capita Full or Confirmed Members	Per Capita Inclusive Members	Total Benevolences	Per Capita Full or Confirmed Members	Per Capita Inclusive Members	Benevolences as a Percentage of Total Giving
$1,385,000	$3.96	$3.96	$2,090,000	$5.97	$5.97	60%
$300,000	$3.53	$3.53	$409,900	$4.82	$4.82	58%
$40,103	$55.09	$46.04	$273,856	$376.18	$314.42	87%
$4,597,458	$1,357.38	$1,357.38	$686,251	$202.61	$202.61	13%
$1,160,199	$902.88	$646.35	$119,672	$93.13	$66.67	9%
$150,000	$30.00	$30.00	$13,500	$13,500	$2.70	8%
$1,237,213	$602.64	$376.62	$116.347	$56.67	$35.42	9%
$265,698	$70.35	$70.35	$365,071	$96.66	$96.66	58%
$3,495,189	$339,97	$339.97	$266,733	$25.94	$25.94	7%
$7,095,713	$589.25	$589.25	$1,677,764	$139.33	$139.33	19%
$2,096,979	$1,625.57	$1,625.57	$5,593,342	$4,335.92	$4,335.92	73%
$47,826,658	$336.99	$240.64	$6,783,217	$47.80	$34.13	12%
$4,248,451	$1,387.02	$1,387.02	$128,472	$41.94	$41.94	3%
$925,703	$143.65	$81.23	$2,252,004	$349.47	$197.61	71%
$1,014,766	$243.82	$218.37	$186,566	$44.83	$40.15	16%
$21,405,000	$367.05	$268.09	$4,641,000	$79.58	$58.13	18%
$9,310,612	$1,139.33	$1,139.33	$3,614,353	$442.28	$442.28	28%
$1,011,578	$795.27	$571.51	$131,376	$103.28	$74.22	11%
$18,715,211	$1,065.97	$1,065.97	$5,593,342	$318.58	$318.58	23%
$1,835,046	$124.71	$62.50	$1,308,151	$88.90	$44.55	42%
$1,486,362	$2,120.35	$1,303.83	$222,245	$317.04	$194.95	13%
$73,507,501	$511.24	$347.04	$11,818,612	$82.20	$55.80	14%
$5,319,371	$1,276.55	$804.38	$1,163,776	$279.28	$175.98	18%
$180,000	$230.77	$186.53	$10,240	$13.13	$10.61	5%
$18,473,256	$393.37	$393.37	$39,073,219	$832.02	$832.02	68%
$255,470,903	$373.61	$157.62	$42,181.527	$61.69	$26.02	14%
$8,755,161	$1,694.77	$1,629.17	$1,438,117	$278.38	$267.61	14%
$741,206	$773.70	$544.60	$89,490	$93.41	$65.75	11

Table 5. Selected Statistics of Church

Religious Body	Year	Full or Confirmed Members	Inclusive Members	TOTAL CONTRIBUTIONS		
				Total Contributions	Per Capita Full or Confirmed Members	Per Capita Inclusive Members
African Methodist Episcopal Zion Church	1998	1,035,963	1,252,369	$76,997,130	$74.32	$61.48
Albanian Orthodox Diocese of America	1996	1,995	1,995	$171,900	$86.17	$86.17
Allegheny Wesleyan Methodist Connection (Original Allegheny Conference)	1998	1,812	1,961	$4,663,002	$2,573.40	$2,377.87
American Baptist Churches in the U.S.A.	1998	1,507,400	1,507,400	363,567,052	270.97	270.97
Apostolic Faith Mission Church of God	1998	8,210	10,550	$907,000	$110.48	$85.97
Associate Reformed Presbyterian Church (General Synod)	1997	34,344	40,060	$31,848,213	$927.33	$795.01
Baptist Missionary Association of America	1998	234,732	234,732	$70,087,434	$298.58	$298.58
Bible Fellowship Church	1998	7,169	7,169	$12,220,021	$1,704.56	$1,704.56
Brethren in Christ Church	1998	19,577	19,577	$29,391,501	$1,501.33	$1,501.33
Christ Community Church (Evangelical-Protestant)	1998	860	1,714	$990,389	$1,151.62	$577.82
Christian Church (Disciples of Christ)	1997	568,921	879,436	$424,473,173	$746.10	$482.67
Christian Church of North America, General Council	1996	31,558	31,558	$20,783,896	$658.59	$658.59
The Christian and Missionary Alliance	1998	163,994	345,664	$321,652,426	$1,961.37	$930.53
Church of the Brethren	1997	141,400	141,400	$77,644,344	$549.11	$549.11
The Church of Christ (Holiness) U.S.A.	1998	10,383	10,383	$8,200,657	$789.82	$789.82
Church of God (Anderson, Ind.)	1997	229,302	229,302	$223,492,670	$974.67	$974.67
Church of God General Conference (Oregon, IL and Morrow, GA.)	1998	3,824	4,971	$3,776,756	$987.65	$759.76
Church of the Lutheran Brethren of America	1998	8,234	13,682	$11,579,314	$1,406.28	$846.32
Church of the Lutheran Confession	1998	6,462	8,628	$4,687,679	$725.42	$543.31
Church of the Nazarene	1998	623,028	627,054	$565,702,637	$907.99	$902.16
Church of the United Brethren in Christ	1997	23,585	23,585	$27,184,899	$1,152.64	$1,152.64
Churches of Christ	1997	1,400,000	1,800,000	$1,445,000,000	$1,032.14	$802.78
Churches of God, General Conference	1998	31,833	31,833	$22,192,659	$697.16	$697.16
Conservative Congregational Christian Conference	1998	38,996	38,996	$34,170,855	$876.27	$876.27
Cumberland Presbyterian Church	1998	87,198	87,198	$41,720,463	$478.46	$478.46
Cumberland Presbyterian Church in America	1996	15,142	15,142	$40,408,524	$2,668.64	$2,668.64

356

Finances—United States Churches

	CONGREGATIONAL FINANCES			BENEVOLENCES		
Total Congregation Contributions	Per Capita Full or Confirmed Members	Per Capita Inclusive Members	Total Benevolences	Per Capita Full or Confirmed Members	Per Capita Inclusive Members	Benevolences as a Percentage
$74,280,000	$71.70	$59.31	$2,717,130	$2.62	$2.17	4%
$164,600	$82.51	$82.51	$7,300	$3.66	$3.66	4%
$3,566,733	$1,968.40	$1,818.83	$1,096,269	$605.01	$559.04	24%
$321,397,430	$233.73	$233.73	$42,169,622	$37.24	$37.24	14%
$440,000	$53.59	$41.71	$467,000	$56.88	$44.27	51%
$25,241,384	$734.96	$630.09	$6,606,829	$192.37	$164.92	21%
$57,481,427	$244.88	$244.88	$12,606,007	$53.70	$53.70	18%
$9,752,170	$1,360.33	$1,360.33	$2,467,851	$344.24	$344.24	20%
$24,116,889	$1,231.90	$1,231.90	$5,274,612	$269.43	$269.43	18%
$794,934	$924.34	$463.79	$195,455	$227.27	$114.03	20%
$381,463,761	$670.50	$433.76	$43,009,412	$75.60	$48.91	10%
$17,136,919	$543.03	$543.03	$3,646,977	$115.56	$115.56	18%
$281,581,464	$1,717.02	$814.61	$40,070,962	$244.34	$115.92	12%
$60,923,817	$430.86	$430.86	$16,720,527	$118.25	$118.25	22%
$7,806,279	$751.83	$751.83	$394,378	$37.98	$37.98	5%
$194,438,623	$847.96	$847.96	$29,054,047	$126.71	$126.71	13%
$3,087,000	$807.27	$621.00	$689,756	$180.38	$138.76	18%
$9,687,807	$1,176.56	$708.07	$1,891,507	$229.72	$138.25	16%
$4,036,699	$624.68	$467.86	$650,980	$100.74	$75.45	14%
$460,776,715	$739.58	$734.83	$104,925,922	$168.41	$167.33	19%
$23,770,417	$1,007.86	$1,007.86	$3,414,482	$144.77	$144.77	13%
$1,414,000,000	$1,010.00	$785.56	$31,000,000	$22.14	$17.22	2%
$18,047,012	$566.93	$566.93	$4,145,647	$130.23	$130.23	19%
$28,976,122	$743.05	$743.05	$5,194,733	$133.21	$133.21	15%
$35,826,690	$410.87	$410.87	$5,893,773	$67.59	$67.59	14%
$34,921,064	$2,306.24	$2,306.24	$5,487,460	$362.40	$362.40	14%

STATISTICAL SECTION

Table 5. Selected Statistics of Churc

Religious Body	Year	Full or Confirmed Members	Inclusive Members	TOTAL CONTRIBUTIONS		
				Total Contributions	Per Capita Full or Confirmed Members	Per Cap Inclusi Membe
Episcopal Church	1997	1,717,069	2,364,559	$1,832,000,448	$1,066.93	$774.7
The Evangelical Church	1998	12,369	12,369	$14,556,445	$1,176.85	$1,176.8
The Evangelical Congregational Church	1998	22,868	22,868	$19,555,649	$855.15	$855.1
The Evangelical Covenant Church	1998	96,552	96,552	$160,958,308	$1,667.06	$1,667.0
Evangelical Lutheran Church in America	1998	3,840,136	5,178,225	$2,031,769,190	529.09	$392.3
Evangelical Lutheran Synod	1998	16,897	22,264	$10,483,512	$620.44	$470.8
Evangelical Mennonite Church	1999	4,511	4,511	$9,450,718	$2,095.04	$2,095.0
Fellowship of Evangelical Bible Churches	1998	1,917	1,917	$2,438,983	$1,272.29	$1,272.2
Free Methodist Church of North America	1998	62,176	73,236	$95,105,529	$1,529.62	$1,298.6
General Association of General Baptists	1997	72,326	72,326	$29,874,795	$413.06	$413.0
General Conference of Mennonite Brethren Churches	1996	50,915	82,130	$65,851,481	$1,293.36	$801.8
The Holy Eastern Orthodox Catholic and Apostolic Church in North America, Inc.	1998	4,300	4,300	$113,775	$26.46	$26.46
The International Pentecostal Church of Christ	1998	2,528	5,595	$5,866,882	$2,320.76	$1,048.5
The Latvian Evangelical Lutheran Church in America	1998	14,000	15,550	$4,260,000	$304.29	$273.9
The Lutheran Church— Missouri Synod	1998	1,952,020	2,594,404	$1,096,649,455	$561.80	$422.7
Mennonite Church	1998	92,161	92,161	$101,725,481	$1,103.78	$1,103.7
Mennonite Church, The General Conference	1998	36,600	36,600	$31,409,846	$858.19	$858.1
The Missionary Church	1998	31,609	45,277	$59,942,901	$1,896.39	$1,323.9
Moravian Church in America (Northern Province)	1998	20,764	26,641	$14,214,413	$684.57	$533.5
National Association of Free Will Baptists	1998	210,461	210,461	$93,056,784	$442.16	$442.1
North American Baptist Conference	1997	43,850	43,850	$45,387,274	$1,035.06	$1,035.0
The Orthodox Presbyterian Church	1998	15,936	23,002	$26,800,625	$1,681.77	$1,165.1
Presbyterian Church (U.S.A.)	1998	2,587,674	3,574,959	$2,529,111,852	$977.37	$707.4
Presbyterian Church in America	1997	224,154	279,549	$374,861,599	$1,672.34	$1,340.9
Primitive Methodist Church in the U.S.A.	1998	4,780	6,746	$5,330,888	$1,115.25	$790.2
Reformed Church in America	1998	179,085	295,651	$223,280,807	$1,246.79	$755.2
Reformed Church in the United States	1998	3,201	4,257	$3,657,850	$1,142.72	$859.2

CONGREGATIONAL FINANCES			BENEVOLENCES			
Total Congregation Contributions	Per Capita Full or Confirmed Members	Per Capita Inclusive Members	Total Benevolences	Per Capita Full or Confirmed Members	Per Capita Inclusive Members	Benevolences as a Percentage
1,594,945,240	$928.88	$674.52	$237,055,208	$138.06	$100.25	13%
11,891,562	$961.40	$961.40	$2,664,883	$215.45	$215.45	18%
$15,956,209	$697.75	$697.75	$3,599,440	$157.40	$157.40	18%
$140,823,872	$1,458.53	$1,458.53	$20,134,436	$208.53	$208.53	13%
$1,822,915,831	$474.70	$352.03	$208,853,359	$54.39	$40.33	10%
$9,363,126	$554.13	$420.55	$1,120,386	$66.31	$50.32	11%
$7,528,256	$1,668.87	$1,668.87	$1,922,462	$426.17	$426.17	20%
$1,936,144	$1,009.99	$1,009.99	$502,839	$262.31	$262.31	21%
$82,254,922	$1,322.94	$1,123.15	$12,850,607	$206.68	$175.47	14%
$28,093,944	$388.43	$388.43	$1,780,851	$24.62	$24.62	6%
$50,832,814	$998.39	$618.93	$15,018,667	$294.98	$182.86	23%
$110,275	$25.65	$25.65	$3,500	$0.81	$0.81	3%
$2,976,296	$1,177.33	$531.96	$2,890,586	$1,143.43	$516.64	49%
$3,220,000	$230.00	$207.07	$1,040,000	$74.29	$66.88	24%
$975,113,229	$499.54	$375.85	$121,536,226	$62.26	$46.85	11%
$76,087,609	$825.59	$825.59	$25,637,872	$278.19	$278.19	25%
$26,013,052	$710.74	$710.74	$5,396,794	$147.45	$147.45	17%
$51,185,864	$1,619.34	$1,130.50	$8,757,037	$277.04	$193.41	15%
$13,082,671	$630.07	$491.07	$1,131,742	$54.51	$42.48	8%
$75,322,059	$357.89	$357.89	$17,734,725	$84.27	$84.27	19%
$37,401,175	$852.93	$852.93	$7,986,099	$182.12	$182.12	18%
$22,362,292	$1,403.26	$972.19	$4,438,333	$278.51	$192.95	17%
$2,173,483,227	$839.94	$607.97	$355,628,625	$137.43	$99.48	14%
$304,848,405	$1,360.00	$1,090.50	$70,013,194	$312.34	$250.45	19%
$4,621,534	$966.85	$685.08	$709,354	$148.40	$105.15	13%
$189,390,759	$1,057.55	$640.59	$33,890,048	$189.24	$114.63	15%
$3,008,116	$939.74	$706.63	$649,734	$202.98	$152.63	18%

STATISTICAL SECTION

Table 5. Selected Statistics of Church

Religious Body	Year	Full or Confirmed Members	Inclusive Members	TOTAL CONTRIBUTIONS		
				Total Contributions	Per Capita Full or Confirmed Members	Per Capita Inclusive Members
Reformed Presbyterian Church of North America	1997	4,363	6,105	$6,446,899	$1,477.63	$1,056.00
Reorganized Church of Jesus Christ of Latter Day Saints	1997	140,218	140,245	$30,691,085	$218.88	$218.84
Seventh-day Adventist Church	1998	839,915	839,915	$857,906,605	$1,021.42	$1,021.42
Southern Baptist Convention	1998	15,729,356	15,729,356	$7,452,098,393	$473.77	$473.77
United Church of Christ	1998	1,421,088	1,421,088	$753,113,157	$529.96	$529.96
The United Methodist Church	1997	8,452,042	8,452,042	$3,990,329,491	$472.11	$472.11
Unity of the Brethren	1998	2,548	3,218	$165,184	$64.83	$51.33
The Wesleyan Church	1998	112,435	119,914	$184,066,585	$1,637.09	$1,534.99
Wisconsin Evangelical Lutheran Synod	1997	315,355	411,295	$216,578,830	$686.78	$526.58

Summary Statitistics

Nation	Number Reporting	Full or Confirmed Members	Inclusive Members	TOTAL CONTRIBUTIONS		
				Total Contributions	Per Capita Full or Confirmed Members	Per Capita Inclusive Members
United States	62	44,574,101	49,679,497	$26,242,626,313	$588.74	$528.24
Canada	28	1,616,767	2,726,353	$624,298,479	$386.14	$228.99

Finances—United States Churches (*continued*)

CONGREGATIONAL FINANCES			BENEVOLENCES			
Total Congregation Contributions	Per Capita Full or Confirmed Members	Per Capita Inclusive Members	Total Benevolences	Per Capita Full or Confirmed Members	Per Capita Inclusive Members	Benevolences as a Percentage
$5,792,856	$1,327.72	$948.87	$654,043	$149.91	$107.13	10%
$15,921,761	$113.55	$113.53	$14,769,324	$105.33	$105.31	48%
$269,679,595	$321.08	$321.08	$588,227,010	$700.34	$700.34	69%
$6,498,607,390	$413.15	$413.15	$953,491,003	$60.62	$60.62	13%
$678,251,694	$477.28	$477.28	$74,861,463	$52.68	$52.68	10%
$3,192,213,867	$377.69	$377.69	$798,115,624	$94.43	$94.43	20%
$51,465	$20.20	$15.99	$113,719	$44.63	$35.34	69%
$159,119,316	$1,415.21	$1,326.95	$24,947,269	$221.88	$208.04	14%
$164,256,655	$520.86	$399.36	$52,322,175	$165.92	$127.21	24%

of Church Finances

CONGREGATIONAL FINANCES			BENEVOLENCES			
Total Congregational Contributions	Per Capita Full or Confirmed Members	Per Capita Inclusive Members	Total Belevolences	Per Capita Full or Confirmed Members	Per Capita Inclusive Members	Benevolences as a Percentage of Total Contributions
$22,202,379,038	$498.10	$446.91	$4,040,247,275	$90.64	$81.33	15%
$492,050,337	$304.34	$180.48	$132,248,143	$81.80	$48.51	21%

Trends in Seminary Enrollment

Data Provided by The Association of Theological Schools (ATS) in the United States and Canada

Table 1: ATS total student enrollment figures include the number of individuals enrolled in degree programs as well as persons enrolled in non-degree programs of study. Growth in total enrollment is a function of both increased enrollment in the seminaries and the increased number of member schools in the Association. The number of students studying at ATS institutions has remained relatively stable. Over the past five years, for example, the total head count enrollment increased 5.8%, and the full-time equivalent (FTE) enrollment increased 2.7%.

Table 1 Number of Member Schools from 1988 to 1998

Year	Number of Schools	Total Enrollment	Canada Head Count	FTE	United States Head Count	FTE	By Membership Accredited	Non-Accredited
1988	207	55,746	3,995	2,679	51,751	34,827	51,863	4,063
1989	205	56,178	4,142	2,668	52,036	35,013	52,949	3,229
1990	211	59,003	4,053	2,636	54,950	37,590	54,052	4,951
1991	211	59,897	4,648	2,631	55,249	36,456	55,028	4,869
1992	220	63,484	4,897	2,999	58,587	39,554	57,784	5,700
1993	219	63,429	5,040	3,150	58,389	39,506	57,823	5,606
1994	226	65,089	5,241	3,212	59,848	40,293	60,490	4,599
1995	224	64,480	5,203	3,267	59,277	39,834	59,813	4,667
1996	233	65,637	5,568	3,304	60,069	40,111	60,527	5,110
1997	229	65,361	5,544	3,225	59,817	40,022	61,498	3,863
1998	237	68,875	5,847	3,683	63,028	40,994	64,412	4,463

Table 2: ATS computes enrollment both by the total number of individual students (Head Count) and the equivalent of full-time students (FTE). If all students were enrolled full-time, the Head Count number and the full-time equivalency number would be the same. The FTE is calculated by dividing the total number of credits required for the degree by the number of semesters prescribed for degree duration to determine the average academic load. The total of credit hours taken by all students in a given degree program in a semester is then divided by the average academic load. During the last five years, full time equivalent enrollment as a percentage of head count enrollment has decreased slightly, which indicates an increase in the number of part-time students.

Table 2 Head County and FTE for all Member Schools 1988 to 1997

Year	Head Count	% Change	FTE	% Change	FTE % of Head Count
1988	55,746	-0.04	37,506	-2.15	67.3%
1989	56,178	0.77	37,681	0.47	67.1%
1990	59,003	5.03	40,226	6.75	68.2%
1991	59,897	1.52	39,087	-2.83	65.3%
1992	63,484	5.99	42,553	8.87	67.0%
1993	63,429	0.09	42,656	0.24	67.2%
1994	65,089	2.62	43,505	1.99	66.8%
1995	64,480	-0.94	43,101	-0.93	66.8%
1996	65,637	1.79	43,415	0.73	66.1%
1997	65,361	-0.42	43,248	-0.38	66.2%
1998	68,875	5.38	44,678	3.31	64.9%

Table 3: ATS member schools offer a variety of degree programs, as reflected in Table 3, which displays enroll-ment by categories of degree programs. The Master of Divinity (M.Div.) degree is the normative degree to pre-pare persons for ordained ministry and for general pastoral and religious leadership responsibilities in congrega-tions. Enrollment in the M.Div. degree has increased 7.43% from 1994 to 1998. The largest increase (by percent-age) in student head count enrollment, over the same five-year period, has been in the Master of Arts in a variety of specialized ministry areas (27.26%) within the Basic Ministerial Leadership (Non-M.Div.) category. This is fol-lowed by an increase (in the same degree category) of 23.94% in the Master of Pastoral Studies degree program. Enrollment in Advanced Theological Research programs has increased over the past five years, largely due to ris-ing enrollment in Ph.D./Th.D. programs, up 13.59% since 1994, and an increase in the number of institutions within the Association that grant these advanced degrees.

Table 3 Total Enrollment By Degree Categories
Categories based on new accreditation standards—adopted in 1996)

Year	Basic Ministerial Leadership (M.Div.)	(Non-M.Div.)	General Theological Studies	Advanced Ministerial Leadership	Advanced Theological Research	Others
1987	26,977	5,025	5,175	6,590	4,062	7,516
1988	26,581	5,131	5,423	6,511	4,203	7,897
1989	25,954	5,080	5,485	7,004	4,186	8,469
1990	25,615	5,284	6,144	7,417	5,046	9,497
1991	25,710	5,805	6,105	7,598	5,044	9,635
1992	26,956	5,812	6,872	7,961	5,036	10,847
1993	27,264	6,536	7,131	8,302	5,157	9,039
1994	27,240	6,891	7,229	7,841	5,330	10,558
1995	27,497	6,964	7,211	8,233	5,302	9,273
1996	28,035	7,474	7,157	8,315	5,499	9,157
1997	28,283	7,463	7,048	8,195	5,391	8,981
1998	29,263	8,066	7,602	8,641	5,712	9,591

Table 4: In 1998, women constituted 33.6% of the total enrollment in all ATS schools. When ATS first began gathering enrollment data by gender in 1972, women represented 10.2% of enrollment. Only once in the past 25 years has the number of women students decreased from one year to the next, that being in 1993, with a 0.65% decrease. In 1998, women constituted 30% of the total enrollment in the Master of Divinity degree program.

Table 4 Women Student Head Count Enrollment 1988 to 1998

Year	Number of Students	% Annual Increase	% of Total Enrollment
1988	16,326	0.00	29.29%
1989	16,525	1.20	29.42%
1990	17,498	5.56	29.66%
1991	18,188	3.79	30.37%
1992	19,856	8.40	31.28%
1993	19,727	-0.65	31.10%
1994	20,564	4.07	31.59%
1995	20,795	1.12	32.25%
1996	21,523	3.50	32.76%
1997	21,652	0.60	33.10%
1998	23,176	7.04	33.65%

STATISTICAL SECTION

Table 5, 6, 7: Enrollment of North American racial/ethnic minority students in ATS schools has grown from 6.3% of total enrollment in 1977 to 19.88% in 1998. Over the past five years (1994 to 1998), the number of African American students increased by 14.5%; Hispanic students by 20.8%; and Pacific Asian American students by 28.6%. Tables 5, 6, and 7 show the number of African American, Hispanic and Pacific/Asian American students enrolled by year. The only race or ethnic group that experienced a decrease was the White enrollment, down 0.69% over five years. The percentage of racial/ethnic minority students in ATS schools continues to be smaller than the percentage of racial/ethnic minority persons in the North American population as a whole.

Table 5 African American Student Head Count Enrollment 1987–1998

Year	Number of Students	% Annual Increase	% of Total Enrollment
1987	3,341	0.00	6.04%
1988	3,660	8.72	6.57%
1989	3,925	6.75	6.99%
1990	4,265	7.97	7.23%
1991	4,658	8.44	7.78%
1992	5,558	16.19	8.75%
1993	5,223	-6.41	8.23%
1994	5,526	5.48	8.49%
1995	5,698	3.11	8.84%
1996	5,550	-2.60	8.45%
1997	5,802	4.54	8.87%
1998	6,328	9.07	9.19%

Table 6 Hispanic Student Head Count Enrollment 1987–1998

Year	Number of Students	% Annual Increase	% of Total Enrollment
1987	1,399	.000	2.53%
1988	1,415	1.13	2.54%
1989	1,485	4.71	2.64%
1990	1,912	22.33	3.24%
1991	1,626	-17.59	2.71%
1992	1,689	3.73	2.66%
1993	1,790	5.64	2.82%
1994	1,799	0.50	2.76%
1995	1,817	1.00	2.82%
1996	1,785	-1.76	2.72%
1997	1,915	7.28	2.93%
1998	2,175	13.58	3.16%

Table 7 Pacific/Asian American Student Head Count Enrollment 1987–1998

Year	Number of Students	% Annual Increase	% of Total Enrollment
1987	1,693	0.00	3.06%
1988	1,963	13.75	3.52%
1989	2,062	4.80	3.67%
1990	2,437	15.39	4.13%
1991	2,649	8.00	4.42%
1992	3,142	15.69	4.95%
1993	3,631	13.47	5.72%
1994	3,876	6.32	5.95%
1995	4,245	9.52	6.58%
1996	4,492	5.82	6.84%
1997	4,545	1.18	6.95%
1998	4,992	8.95	7.25%

IV

A CALENDAR FOR CHURCH USE

2000–2003

This Calendar presents for a four-year period the major days of religious observances for Christians, Jews, Baha'is, and Muslims; and, within the Christian community, major dates observed by Roman Catholic, Orthodox, Episcopal, and Lutheran churches. Within each of these communions many other days of observance, such as saints' days, exist, but only those regarded as major are listed. Dates of interest to many Protestant communions are also included.

Among the Orthodox dates, immovable observances are listed in accordance with the Gregorian calendar. Movable dates (those depending on the date of Easter) often will differ from Western days, since the date of Easter (Pascha) in the Orthodox communions does not always correlate with the date for Easter for the Western churches. For Orthodox churches that use the old Julian calendar, observances are held thirteen days later than listed here.

For Jews and Muslims, who follow differing lunar calendars, the dates of major observances are translated into Gregorian dates. Since the actual beginning of a new month in the Islamic calendar is determined by the appearance of the new moon, the corresponding dates given here on the Gregorian calendar may vary slightly. Following the lunar calendar, Muslim dates fall eleven days earlier each year on the Gregorian calendar, thus the month of Ramadan for 2000 actually begins in 1999.

(Note: "RC" stands for Roman Catholic, "O" for Orthodox, "E" for Episcopal, "L" for Lutheran, "ECU" for Ecumenical, "M" for Muslim).

Event	2000	2001	2002	2003
New Year's Day (RC-Solemnity of Mary: O-Circumcision of Jesus Christ; E-Feast of Holy Name; L-Name of Jesus)	Jan 01	Jan 01	Jan 01	Jan 01
Epiphany (RC)	Jan 02	Jan 07	Jan 06	Jan 05
Epiphany (Armenian Christmas)	Jan 06	Jan 06	Jan 06	Jan 06
Feast Day of St. John the Baptist (Armenian)	Jan 13	Jan 13	Jan 13	Jan 13
First Sunday After Epiphany (Feast of the Baptism of Our Lord)	Jan 09	Jan 07	Jan 13	Jan 12
Week of Prayer for Christian Unity (ECU)	Jan 18 to Jan 25	Jan 18 to Jan 25	Jan 18 to Jan 25	Jan 18 to Jan 25
Ecumenical Sunday (ECU)	Jan 23	Jan 21	Jan 20	Jan 19
Week of Prayer for Christian Unity, Canada (ECU)	Jan 24 to Jan 31	Jan 22 to Jan 29	Jan 21 to Jan 28	Jan 20 to Jan 27
First Day of the Month of Ramadan (M)	Nov 28	Nov 17	Nov 6	Oct 27
Presentation of Jesus in the Temple (O-The Meeting of Our Lord and Savior Jesus Christ)	Feb 02	Feb 02	Feb 02	Feb 02
Brotherhood Week (Interfaith)	Feb 20 to Feb 26	Feb 18 to Feb 24	Feb 17 to Feb 23	Feb 16 to Feb 22
Eid al- Fitr (M) (Festival of the End of Ramadan, celebrated on the first day of the month of Shawwal)	Jan. 08/ Dec 28*	Dec 17	Dec 06	Nov 26
Ash Wednesday (Western Churches)	Mar 08	Feb 28	Feb 13	Mar 5
Easter Lent Begins (Eastern Orthodox)	Mar 13	Feb 26	Mar 18	Mar 10
World Day of Prayer (ECU)	Mar 03	Mar 04	Mar 01	Mar 07
Fasting Season begins (Baha'i, 19 days)	Mar 02	Mar 02	Mar 02	Mar 02
Purim (Jewish)	Mar 21	Mar 09	Feb 26	Mar 18
Joseph, Husband of Mary (RC, E, L)	Mar 19	Mar 19	Mar 19	Mar 19

Event	2000	2001	2002	2003
Feast of Naw-Ruz (Baha'i New Year)	Mar 21	Mar 21	Mar 21	Mar 21
The Annunciation (O) (L-Apr 01; RC, E-Apr 08)	Mar 25	Mar 25	Mar 25	Mar 25
Holy Week (Western Churches)	Apr 16 to Apr 22	Apr 08 to Apr 15	Mar 24 to Mar 31	Apr 13 to Apr 20
First Day of the Month of Muharram (M) (Beginning of Muslim Liturgical Year)	Apr 06	Mar 26	Mar 15	Mar 05
Holy Thursday (Western Churches)	Apr 20	Apr 12	Mar 28	Apr 17
First Day of Passover (Jewish, 8 days)	Apr 20	Apr 98	Mar 28	Apr 17
Good Friday (Friday of the Passion of Our Lord (Western Churches)	Apr 21	Apr 13	Mar 29	Apr 18
Easter (Western Churches)	Apr 04	Apr 23	Apr 15	Mar 31
Palm Sunday (O)	Apr 23	Apr 08	Apr 28	Apr 20
Holy Week (O)	Apr 24	Apr 08	Apr 28	Apr 20
Holy Thursday (O)	Apr 27	Apr 12	May 02	Apr 24
Holy (Good) Friday, Burial of Jesus Christ (O)	Apr 28	Apr 13	May 03	Apr 25
Pascha (Orthodox Easter)	Apr 30	Apr 15	May 05	Apr 27
Feast of Ridvan (Baha'i) (Declaration of Baha'u'llah)	Apr 21 to May 02	Apr 21 to May 02	Apr 21 to May 02	Apr 21 to May 02
Eid al-Adha (M) (festival of Sacrifice at time of annual Pilgrimage to Mecca)	Mar 16	Mar 06	Feb 23	Feb 12
National Day of Prayer	May 04	May 03	May 02	May 01
May Fellowship Day (ECU)	May 05	May 04	May 03	May 02
Rural Life Sunday (ECU)	May 14	May 13	May 12	May 11
Ascension Thursday (Western Churches)	Jun 01	May 24	May 09	May 29
Ascension Day (O)	Jun 08	May 24	Jun 13	Jun 05
Declaration of the Bab (Baha'i)	May 23	May 23	May 23	May 23
First Day of Shavuout (Jewish, 2 days)	Jun 09	May 28	May 17	Jun 06
Pentecost (Whitsunday) (Western Churches)	Jun 11	Jun 03	May 19	Jun 08
Ascension of Baha'u'llah (Baha'i')	May 29	May 29	May 29	May 29
Visitation of the Blessed Virgin Mary (RC, E, L)	May 31	May 31	May 31	May 31
Pentecost (O)	Jun 18	Jun 03	Jun 23	Jun 15
Holy Trinity (RC, E, L)	Jun 18	Jun 10	May 26	Jun 15
Corpus Christi (RC)	Jun 25	Jun 17	Jun 02	Jun 22
Sacred Heart of Jesus (RC)	Jun 30	Jun 22	Jun 07	Jun 27
Nativity of St. John the Baptist (RC, E, L)	Jun 24	Jun 24	Jun 24	Jun 24
Saint Peter and Saint Paul, Apostles of Christ (O)	Jun 29	Jun 29	Jun 29	Jun 29
Feast Day of the Twelve Apostles of Christ (O)	Jun 30	Jun 30	Jun 30	Jun 30
Martyrdom of the Bab (Baha'i)	Jun 09	Jun 09	Jun 09	Jun 09
Mawlid an-Nabi (M) (Anniversary of Prophet Muhammed's Birthday)	Jun 15	Jun 04	May 24	May 14
Transfiguration of the Lord (RC, O, E)	Aug 06	Aug 06	Aug 06	Aug 06
Feast of the Blessed Virgin Mary (E) (RC-Assumption of Blessed Mary the Virgin; O-Falling Asleep (Domition) of the Blessed Virgin)	Aug 15	Aug 15	Aug 15	Aug 15
The Birth of the Blessed Virgin (RC, O)	Sep 08	Sep 08	Sep 08	Sep 08
Holy Cross Day (O' Adoration of the Holy Cross; RC-Triumph of the Cross)	Sep 14	Sep 14	Sep 14	Sep 14
First Day of Rosh Hashanah (Jewish, 2 days)	Sep 30	Sep 18	Sep 07	Sep 27
Yom Kippur (Jewish)	Oct 09	Sep 27	Sep 16	Oct 06
First Day of Sukkot (Jewish, 7 days)	Oct 14	Oct 02	Sep 21	Oct 11
World Communion Sunday (ECU)	Oct 01	Oct 07	Oct 06	Oct 05
Laity Sunday (ECU)	Oct 08	Oct 14	Oct 13	Oct 12
Thanksgiving Day (Canada)	Oct 09	Oct 08	Oct 14	Oct 13
Shemini Atzeret (Jewish)	Oct 21	Oct 09	Sep 28	Oct 18
Simhat Torah (Jewish)	Oct 22	Oct 10	Sep 29	Oct 19
Birth of the Bab (Baha'i)	Oct 20	Oct 20	Oct 20	Oct 20
Reformation Sunday (L)	Oct 29	Oct 28	Oct 27	Oct 26
Reformation Day (L)	Oct 31	Oct 31	Oct 31	Oct. 31
All Saints Day (RC, E, L)	Nov 01	Nov 01	Nov 01	Nov 01

Event	2000	2001	2002	2003
World Community Day (ECU)	Nov 03	Nov 02	Nov 01	Nov 07
Birth of Baha'u'llah (Baha'i)	Nov 12	Nov 12	Nov 12	Nov 12
Bible Sunday (ECU)	Nov 19	Nov 18	Nov 17	Nov 16
	to Nov 26	Nov 25	Nov 24	Nov 23
Presentation of the Blessed Virgin Mary in the Temple (also Presentation of the Theotokos) (O)	Nov 21	Nov 21	Nov 21	Nov 21
Last Sunday After Pentecost (RC, L-Feast of Christ the King)	Nov 19	Nov 25	Nov 24	Nov 23
Thanksgiving Sunday (U.S.)	Nov 19	Nov 18	Nov 24	Nov 23
The Day of the Covenant (Baha'i	Nov 26	Nov 26	Nov 26	Nov 26
Thanksgiving Day (U.S.)	Nov 23	Nov 22	Nov 28	Nov 27
Ascension of 'Abdu'l-Baha (Baha'i)	Nov 28	Nov 28	Nov 28	Nov 28
Feast Day of St. Andrew the Apostle (RC, O, E, L)	Nov 30	Nov 30	Nov 30	Nov 30
First Sunday of Advent	Dec 03	Dec 02	Dec 01	Nov 30
First Day of Hanukkah (Jewish, 8 days)	Dec 22	Dec 10	Nov 30	Dec 20
Immaculate Conception of the Blessed Virgin May (RC)	Dec 08	Dec 08	Dec 08	Dec 08
Fourth Sunday of Advent (Sunday before Christmas)	Dec 24	Dec 23	Dec 22	Dec 21
Christmas (Except Armenian)	Dec 25	Dec 25	Dec 25	Dec 25

The Calendar has been compiled from various sources, but with special assitance from Rev. Will Krieger, Editor of *The Ecumenical Daily Appointment Planner* in San Antonio, Texas. For more information about *The Ecumenical Daily Appointment Planner*, please call 1-800-325-9026.

V

INDEXES

Organizations

370

374

Individuals

377

INDEX

381

386

INDEX

389

390

INDEX

391

Lewis, W. Arthur 111
Lewis, William L. 102
Liebling, Mordechai............22
Liechty, Eric 132
Liew, Haleyon 233
Light, Rachel 237
Lightbody, C. Stuart..........181
Liimatta, Michael................36
Lile, Marcia 228
Lind, Christopher 293
Linder, Carl E.................305
Lindgren, A. Bruce 147
Lindholm, James 225
Lindner, Eileen W. 40, 41
Lindsay, Emery 90
Lindsay, R. Rex................154
Lindsey, D. L....................95
Lindsey, W. D. "Doc" 154
Lindvall, Terry 285
Linebaugh, Dale E. 285
Ling, Stanley T................162
Lingle, Mark...................222
Linscheid, David........131, 132
Linsey, Nathaniel L............87
Lintner, Jay......................40
Lintner, Jay E.................159
Lintzench, Steve...............226
Liolin, Arthur E. 67
Lipscomb, John B. 107
Litke, Stan.......................85
Litke, Stanley 315
Little, Dick 234
Little, Gloria 234
Little, Vanuel C................138
Littlejohn, Orin...............115
Litwiler, Thomas 69
Litwin, Paul 240
Liu, Felix......................282
Livingston, Michael E. 125
Llewellyn, Hallett E...........293
Lloyd, Roy T.....................40
Lloyd, Sharon E.................48
Lobb, Douglas L................134
Lobenstine, Clark..............224
Lockwood, Daniel R...........283
Lodmill, Richard E.............111
Loeppky, Mary Anne 184
Loewer, Jackie.................136
Loftus, John Allan.............293
Logan, Archie..................296
Logan, Samuel T................289
Logan, Willis H.................40
Logsdon, Gary B................244
Lohrmann, Marcus C. 112
Lollike, Inge Lise 51
Long, Don 125
Long, Helen 126
Long, Janet 231
Long, Kathy 314
Long, Lem, Jr....................66
Long, Ronald....................125
Looney, Bill.....................80
Looney, Richard C......164, 165

Looper, Kirk 152
Loori, John Daido 19
Lopez, Eddie 40
Lopez, Hector...................159
Lopoukhine, Nikita 191
Lopushinsky, Victor 191
Lorimer, Paul D. 181
Lotz, Denton.....................45
Lotz, Linda 43
Lougheed, Scot 56
Louttit, Henry, Jr. 106
Love, Aubra......................251
Love, Mary A..............65, 299
Love, Ralph E., Sr.............161
Lovejoy, Margaret.............235
Lovelace, John A. 307
Loveland, Erma Jean 323
Loveless, Alton 133
Lovin, Robin W.................284
Loving, James 138
Lovingood, Vivian 248
Lowe, Conrad......................69
Lowe, Marvin......................81
Lowen, A. Wayne...............279
Lowery, T. L..............92, 182
Lowndes, Jack P..........37, 312
Lucas, C. B......................143
Lucas, George 281
Lucas, J. P.......................94
Lucas, Sandy 234
Ludwig, John P., Jr...........158
Ludwig, Patricia...............240
Ludy, Lorene 118
Luebbert, Karen 235
Luetchens, Mel.................163
Luginbuhl, David........57, 196
Luhr, Gary W....................140
Luke, Fr.........................308
Lukowsky, Andrea 43
Lull, Timothy F. 284
Lundgren, Dean A..............109
Lundin, Jack 50
Lundquist, C. David...........165
Lundy, Sarah E...................93
Lunich, Nedeljko 309
Lutes, Christopher.............297
Luthy, David 190, 317
Lutz, Richard...................252
Lutzer, Harold 320
Luxa, Joseph....................227
Luxa, Marcey 227
Lyght, Ernest S.................163
Lyke, Lonnie 97
Lykins, Terry 126
Lyle, Kenneth R................154
Lynch, Damon, III.............242
Lynch, Robert N................148
Lynes, John W..................160
Lyngdal, Lloyd W..............111
Lytle, Guy Fitch...............288
Maahs, Charles H.......111, 112
Maas, Calvin W.................164
Maber, Philip...................61

Mac Dermid, Gordon 290
Macaria, Nun...................301
MacArthur, Earl N. 107
MacCarty, Skip 232
MacDonald, Margaret........235
MacDonald, Mark 105, 219
MacDonald, P. A. Sandy....272
MacFarlane, Diana............179
Macgo, Robert, Jr............141
Machen, James 125
Machin, Vilma M...............159
MacKenzie, Daryl.............178
MacKenzie, Margaret 62
MacKenzie, Robert 196
Mackey, Bill 154
MacKinnon, Melissa.........241
Macklin, Jerry 95
Maclean, Allen D..............240
MacNie, Peggy.................248
MacVicar, James 126
Macy, Sherry 312
Madenlian, Vatche.............76
Madison, Carol 301, 310
Madison, S. C..................161
Madison, Terry 297
Madushaw, Ednabelle 32
Maek, Paget......................73
Maempa, John 309
Magnus, Brian.................198
Magnus, Paul 57, 290
Magnus, Richard A., Jr. 111
Magrill, Richard 103
Mahlman, Margaret ...167, 168
Mahnke, Jon....................169
Mahony, Roger Cardinal ...149
Mahsman, David129, 306, 310
Maier, Donald H................111
Main, A. Donald 113, 247
Mains, Bill......................178
Majtenyi, Cathy................316
Maksoudian, Krikor.............76
Malave-Rivera, Osvaldo....160
Malayang, Jose A..............159
Malcolm, Barbara 222
Malcomson, Bill................252
Maldonado, Luis Fernando
    Hoyos 180
Malherbe, Jean-Francois....294
Malinovic, Mirko 197
Mallgren, J. David 69
Malliet, Jim 35
Mallon, Elias D. 35
Malone, Joan 43
Malone, Tom.............133, 279
Maly, Milton 167, 296
Manahan,
    Ronald E. 116, 117, 280
Manes, John 98
Mangassarian, Silva...........175
Mangeri, Carl 26
Maniscalco,
    Francis J.................147, 148
Mann, David 132

395

396

401

403

INDEX

Mosques and Islamic Centers: 1990 (Inside front cover)

Somewhere in the years surrounding the turn of the 21st century, Islam will have become the nation's second-largest religion, following only Christianity. The extent to which Islam has flourished on American soil is not yet deeply etched in America's self-consciousness. Here, a map may be worth ten thousand words. The map on the inside front cover depicts known mosques and centers as of 1990—a portent of more to come as the 21st century commences. The map's legend also suggests a notable diversity within American Islam.

Despite a long U.S. presence, an upsurge in Muslim growth came after 1965, with a change in immigration law. Since then, 25,000-35,000 Muslims have entered the United States annually, coming from more than sixty countries and settling predominantly in California's urban centers and in such others as Chicago, Detroit, Boston, New York City, and Washington D.C. While these centers are home to approximately half of all American Muslims, the Midwest (to the surprise of some) contains the nation's largest regional Muslim population. Indeed, America's oldest standing mosque is in Cedar Rapids, Iowa.

Maps, however, do not interpret themselves. For more context in the geography of religion, consult Edwin Scott Gaustad and Philip L. Barlow, *New Historical Atlas of Religion in America* (N.Y.: Oxford University Press, 2000), from which this map was, by permission, adapted.

Buddhists: c. 1990 (Inside back cover)

Between one and two million Americans formally practice Buddhism at the turn of the 21st century. It is difficult, however, to gauge the wider number of Americans who practice some form of Buddhist mediation or the number who selectively participate in some other Buddhist practices. Further, Buddhism continues to influence American popular culture in innumerable ways. Buddhist organizations are many, diverse, and often unconcerned with demographic realities. Besides the Buddhist Churches of America and the hundreds of independent meditation centers scattered across the nation, dozens of forms of ethnic Buddhism, representing all of the nations of east and southeast Asia, maintain temples. As many as 1,500 Buddhist centers may operate in the United States, though the map on the opposite page depicts the regional spread only of the smaller number documentable by the early 1990s. While many American Buddhists are ethnically non-Asian, Buddhist population density reflects patterns of Asian immigration initiated in the mid-19th century and deepened and amended since the mid-1960s. Concentrations are heaviest in Hawaii, along the mainland's west coast, and in New England (perhaps a consequence of Unitarianism's early openness to oriental thought). Buddhists temples appear in urban centers generally (especially in proximity to large universities). More than one-third of California's nearly two hundred centers, for example, cluster in Los Angeles, San Francisco, and Berkeley.

The accompanying map was adapted, by permission of Oxford University Press, from Edwin Scott Gaustad and Philip L. Barlow, *New Historical Atlas of Religion in America* (N.Y.: Oxford University Press, 2000). This source offers analysis, historical context, and hundreds of additional maps exploring the American presence of Hindus, Sikhs, Jains, Jews, Christians, and others of the world's religions.